18th International Conference on Spoken Language Translation (IWSLT 2021)

Bangkok, Thailand
5-6 August 2021

ISBN: 978-1-7138-3378-9

Printed from e-media with permission by:

Curran Associates, Inc.
57 Morehouse Lane
Red Hook, NY 12571

Some format issues inherent in the e-media version may also appear in this print version.

Association for Computational Linguistics
209 N. Eighth Street
Stroudsburg, Pennsylvania 18360

Phone: 1-570-476-8006
Fax: 1-570-476-0860

acl@aclweb.org

Additional copies of this publication are available from:

Curran Associates, Inc.
57 Morehouse Lane
Red Hook, NY 12571 USA
Phone: 845-758-0400
Fax: 845-758-2633
Email: curran@proceedings.com
Web: www.proceedings.com

IWSLT 2021

The 18th International Conference on Spoken Language Translation

Proceedings of the Conference

August 5 – 6, 2021
Bangkok, Thailand (online)

Preface

The International Conference on Spoken Language Translation (IWSLT) is the premiere annual scientific conference for the study, development and evaluation of spoken language translation technology. Launched in 2004 and spun out from the C-STAR speech translation consortium before it (1992-2003), IWSLT is the main venue for scientific exchange on all topics related to speech-to-text translation, speech-to- speech translation, simultaneous and consecutive translation, speech dubbing, cross-lingual communication including all multimodal, emotional, paralinguistic, and stylistic aspects and their applications in the field. The conference organizes evaluations around challenge areas, and presents scientific papers and system descriptions.

This year, IWSLT features four shared tasks: (i) Simultaneous Speech Translation; (ii) Offline Speech Translation; (iii) Multilingual Speech Translation; and (iv) Low-Resource Speech Translation. These topics represent open problems toward effective cross-lingual communication and we expect the community effort and discussion will greatly advance the state of the field. Each shared task was coordinated by a chair. The resulting evaluation campaigns attracted a total of 22 teams, from academy, research centers and industry. System submissions resulted in system papers that will be presented at the conference. Following our call for papers, this year 40 submissions were received. In a blind review process, 11 research papers were selected out of 19 for oral presentation (58%) in addition to 21 system papers. The program this year will also host 4 so-called ACL *findings* papers (not included in this proceedings), that expressed interest in being presented at IWSLT 2021. The program committee is excited about the quality of the accepted papers and expects lively discussion and exchange at the conference.

The conference chairs and organizers would like to express their gratitude to everyone who contributed and supported IWSLT. We thank the shared tasks chairs, organizers, and participants, the program chair and committee members, as well as all the authors that went the extra mile to submit system and research papers to IWSLT, and make this year's conference a most vibrants event. We also wish to express our sincere gratitude to ACL for hosting our conference and for arranging the logistics and infrastructure that allow us to hold IWSLT 2021 as a virtual online conference.

Welcome to IWSLT 2021 wherever you are joining from!

Marta R. Costa-jussà, Program Chair
Marcello Federico and Alex Waibel, Conference co-Chairs

Organizers:

Marcello Federico, Amazon, USA (Conference Chair)
Alex Waibel, CMU, USA (Conference Chair)
Marta R. Costa-jussà, UPC, Spain (Program Chair)
Jan Niehues, Maastricht U., Netherlands (Evaluation Chair)
Sebastian Stüker, KIT, Germany (Evaluation Chair)
Elizabeth Salesky, JHU, USA (Website Chair)

Shared Task Organizers:

Simultaneous Speech Translation
Juan Pino Facebook, USA, (Chair)
Katsuhito Sudoh, NAIST, Japan (Chair)
Satoshi Nakamura, NAIST, Japan
Ondřej Bojar, Charles University, Czech Republic
Xutai Ma, JHU/Facebook, USA
Maha Elbayad, Facebook, USA
Changhan Wang, Facebook, USA

Offline Speech Translation
Marco Turchi, FBK, Italy (Chair)
Sebastian Stüker, KIT, Germany
Jan Niehues, Maastricht University, Netherlands
Matteo Negri, FBK, Italy
Roldano Cattoni, FBK, Italy

Multilingual Speech Translation
Elizabeth Salesky, JHU, USA (Chair)
Jake Bremerman, UMD, USA
Jan Niehues, Maastricht University, Netherlands
Matt Post, JHU, USA
Matthew Wiesner, JHU, USA

Multilingual Speech Translation
Antonios Anastasopoulos, George Mason University, USA (Chair)
Grace Tang, Translators without Borders, Canada
Will Lewis, University of Washington, USA
Sylwia Tur, Appen, USA
Rosie Lazar, Appen, USA
Marcello Federico, Amazon, USA
Alex Waibel, CMU, USA

Program Committee:

Hirofumi Inaguma, Kyoto University, Japan
Surafel Melaku Lakew, Amazon AI, USA
Carlos Escolano, Universitat Politècnica de Catalunya, Spain
Jiatao Gu, Facebook AI Research, USA
Changhan Wang, Facebook AI Research, USA
Yun Tang, Facebook AI Research, USA
Akiko Eriguchi, Microsoft, USA
Xian Li, Facebook AI Research, USA
Qianqian Dong, Chinese Academy of Sciences, China
Yuchen Liu, Princeton, USA
Matthias Sperber, Apple, USA
Antonio Toral, U. Groningen, Netherlands
Thanh-le Ha, Karslruhe Institute of Technology, Germany
Krzystof Wolk, Polish-Japanese Academy of Information Technology, Poland
Gerard I. Gallego, Universitat Politècnica de Catalunya, Spain
Julian Salazar, Amazon AWS AI, USA
Chengyi Wang, Nankai University, China
Christian Hardmeier, Uppsala U., Sweden
David Vilar, Amazon, Germany
Elizabeth Salesky, JHU, USA
Evgeny Matusov, AppTek, Germany
Juan Pino, Facebook, USA
Katsuhito Sudoh, NAIST, Japan
Laurent Besacier, IMAG, France
Marco Turchi, FBK, Italy
Markus Freitag, Google, USA
Matteo Negri, FBK, Italy
Matthias Huck, LMU, Germany
Mattia di Gangi, AppTek, Germany
Cuong Hoang, Amazon AI, USA
Nguyen Bach, Alibaba, USA
Preslav Nakov, QCRI, Qatar
Yves Lepage, U. Waseda, Japan
Jiajun Zhang,Institute of Automation Chinese Academy of Sciences, China
Duygu Ataman, University of Zurich, Switzerland
Xutai Ma, Johns Hopkins University, USA
Melvin Johnson, Google, USA
Cuong Hoang, Amazon, USA
José Guilherme Camargo de Souza, Unbabel, Portugal

Table of Contents

Conference Program

Day 1

Evaluation Overview

FINDINGS OF THE IWSLT 2021 EVALUATION CAMPAIGN
Antonios Anastasopoulos, Ondřej Bojar, Jacob Bremerman, Roldano Cattoni, Maha Elbayad, Marcello Federico, Xutai Ma, Satoshi Nakamura, Matteo Negri, Jan Niehues, Juan Pino, Elizabeth Salesky, Sebastian Stüker, Katsuhito Sudoh, Marco Turchi, Alexander Waibel, Changhan Wang and Matthew Wiesner

Day 1-2

System Papers

The USTC-NELSLIP Systems for Simultaneous Speech Translation Task at IWSLT 2021
Dan Liu, Mengge Du, Xiaoxi Li, Yuchen Hu and Lirong Dai

NAIST English-to-Japanese Simultaneous Translation System for IWSLT 2021 Simultaneous Text-to-text Task
Ryo Fukuda, Yui Oka, Yasumasa Kano, Yuki Yano, Yuka Ko, Hirotaka Tokuyama, Kosuke Doi, Sakriani Sakti, Katsuhito Sudoh and Satoshi Nakamura

The University of Edinburgh's Submission to the IWSLT21 Simultaneous Translation Task
Sukanta Sen, Ulrich Germann and Barry Haddow

Without Further Ado: Direct and Simultaneous Speech Translation by AppTek in 2021
Parnia Bahar, Patrick Wilken, Mattia A. Di Gangi and Evgeny Matusov

The Volctrans Neural Speech Translation System for IWSLT 2021
Chengqi Zhao, zhicheng liu, Jian Tong, Tao Wang, Mingxuan Wang, Rong Ye, Qianqian Dong, Jun Cao and Lei Li

THE IWSLT 2021 BUT SPEECH TRANSLATION SYSTEMS
hari Krishna vydana, Martin Karafiat, Lukas Burget and Jan Černocký

Dealing with training and test segmentation mismatch: FBK@IWSLT2021
Sara Papi, Marco Gaido, Matteo Negri and Marco Turchi

The NiuTrans End-to-End Speech Translation System for IWSLT 2021 Offline Task
Chen Xu, Xiaoqian Liu, Xiaowen Liu, Tiger Wang, Canan Huang, Tong Xiao and Jingbo Zhu

Day 1-2 (continued)

Day 1-2 (continued)

Data Augmentation by Concatenation for Low-Resource Translation: A Mystery and a Solution
Toan Q. Nguyen, Kenton Murray and David Chiang

FINDINGS OF THE IWSLT 2021 EVALUATION CAMPAIGN

Antonios Anastasopoulos George Mason U.
Ondřej Bojar Charles University
Jacob Bremerman UMD
Roldano Cattoni FBK

Maha Elbayad Facebook
Marcello Federico Amazon AI
Xutai Ma JHU/Facebook
Satoshi Nakamura NAIST

Matteo Negri FBK
Jan Niehues Maastricht U.
Juan Pino Facebook
Elizabeth Salesky JHU

Sebastian Stüker KIT
Katsuhito Sudoh NAIST
Marco Turchi FBK
Alex Waibel CMU/KIT

Changhan Wang Facebook
Matthew Wiesner JHU

Abstract

The evaluation campaign of the International Conference on Spoken Language Translation (IWSLT 2021) featured this year four shared tasks: (i) Simultaneous speech translation, (ii) Offline speech translation, (iii) Multilingual speech translation, (iv) Low-resource speech translation. A total of 22 teams participated in at least one of the tasks. This paper describes each shared task, data and evaluation metrics, and reports results of the received submissions.

1 Introduction

The International Conference on Spoken Language Translation (IWSLT) is the premier annual scientific conference for all aspects of spoken language translation. For 18 years running (Akiba et al., 2004; Eck and Hori, 2005; Paul, 2006; Fordyce, 2007; Paul, 2008, 2009; Paul et al., 2010; Federico et al., 2011, 2012; Cettolo et al., 2013, 2014, 2015, 2016, 2017; Niehues et al., 2018, 2019; Ansari et al., 2020), the conference organizes and sponsors open evaluation campaigns around key challenges in simultaneous and consecutive translation, under real-time/low latency or offline conditions and under low-resource or multilingual constraints. System descriptions and results from participants' systems and scientific papers related to key algorithmic advances and best practice are published in proceedings and presented at the conference. IWSLT is also the venue of the SIGSLT, the Special Interest Group on Spoken Language Translation of ACL, ISCA and ELRA. With its long track record, IWSLT benchmarks and proceedings serve as reference for all researchers and practitioners working on speech translation and related fields.

This paper reports on the evaluation campaign organized by IWSLT 2021, which features four shared tasks:

- **Simultaneous speech translation**, addressing low latency translation of talks, from English to German and English to Japanese, either from a speech file into text, or from a ground-truth transcript into text;
- **Offline speech translation**, proposing speech translation of talks from English into German, using either cascade architectures or end-to-end models, able to directly translate source speech into target text;
- **Multilingual speech translation**, focusing

Proceedings of the 18th International Conference on Spoken Language Translation, pages 1–29
Bangkok, Thailand (Online), August 5–6, 2021. ©2021 Association for Computational Linguistics

Team	Organization
AppTek	AppTek, Germany (Bahar et al., 2021b)
BUT	Brno University of Technology, Czech Republic (Vydana et al., 2021)
ESPnet-ST	ESPnet-ST group, Johns Hopkins University, USA (Inaguma et al., 2021)
FBK	Fondazione Bruno Kessler, Italy (Papi et al., 2021)
FAIR	FAIR Speech Translation (Tang et al., 2021a)
HWN	Huawei Noah's Ark Lab, China (Zeng et al., 2021)
HW-TSC	Huawei Translation Services Center, China
IMS	University of Stuttgart, Germany (Denisov et al., 2021)
KIT	Karlsruhe Institute of Technology, Germany (Nguyen et al., 2021; Pham et al., 2021)
Li	Desheng Li
NAIST	Nara Institute of Science and Technology, Nara, Japan (Fukuda et al., 2021)
NiuTrans	NiuTrans Research, Shenyang, China (Xu et al., 2021b)
ON-TRAC	ON-TRAC Consortium, France (Le et al., 2021)
OPPO	Beijing OPPO Telecommunications Co., Ltd., China
UEdin	University of Edinburgh, UK (Zhang and Sennrich, 2021; Sen et al., 2021)
UM-DKE	Maastricht University, The Netherlands (Liu and Niehues, 2021)
UPC	Universitat Politècnica de Catalunya, Spain (Gállego et al., 2021)
USTC-NESLIP	USTC, iFlytek Research, China (Liu et al., 2021)
USYD-JD	University of Sydney, Peking University, JD Explore Academy (Ding et al., 2021)
VOLCTRANS	ByteDance AI Lab, China (Zhao et al., 2021)
VUS	Voithru, Upstage, Seoul National University, South Korea (Jo et al., 2021)
ZJU	Zhejiang University (Zhang, 2021)

Table 1: List of Participants

on the use of multiple languages to improve supervised and zero-shot speech translation between four Romance languages and English;

- **Low-resource speech translation**, focusing on resource-scarce settings for translating two Swahili varieties (Congolese and Coastal) into English and French.

The shared tasks were attended by 22 participants (see Table 1), including teams from both academic and industrial organizations. The following sections report on each shared task in detail, in particular: the goal and automatic metrics adopted for the challenge, the data used for training and testing data, the received submissions and the summary of results. Detailed results for each challenge are reported in a corresponding appendix.

2 Simultaneous Speech Translation

Simultaneous translation is the task of translating incrementally with partial text or speech input only. Such capability enables multilingual live communication and access to multilingual multimedia content in real-time. The goal of this challenge, organized for the second consecutive year, is to examine systems that translate text or audio in a source language into text in a target language from the perspective of both translation quality and latency.

2.1 Challenge

Participants were given three parallel tracks to enter and encouraged to enter all tracks:

- text-to-text: translating ground-truth transcripts in real time from English to German and English to Japanese.
- speech-to-text: translating speech into text in real time from English to German.

For the speech-to-text track, participants were encouraged to submit systems either based on cascaded or end-to-end approaches. In addition, the systems were run on a segmented and non-segmented version of the test set, i.e. processing one sound segment corresponding to an input sentence at a time, or processing the whole speech in one sound stream. Participants were required to upload their system as a Docker image so that it could be evaluated by the organizers in a controlled environment. We also provided an example implementation and a baseline system.[1]

2.2 Data and Metrics

For tracks related to English-German, participants were allowed to use the same training and development data as in the Offline Speech Translation track. More details are available in §3.2.

For the English-Japanese text-to-text track, participants could use the parallel data and monolingual data available for the English-Japanese WMT20 news task (Barrault et al., 2020). For development, participants could use the IWSLT 2017 development sets,[2] the IWSLT 2021 development set[3] and the simultaneous interpretation transcripts for the IWSLT 2021 development set.[4] The simultaneous interpretation was recorded as a part of NAIST Simultaneous Interpretation Corpus (Doi et al., 2021).

Systems were evaluated with respect to quality and latency. Quality was evaluated with the standard BLEU metric (Papineni et al., 2002a). Latency was evaluated with metrics developed for simultaneous machine translation, including average proportion (AP), average lagging (AL) and differentiable average lagging (DAL, Cherry and Foster 2019), and later extended to the task of simultaneous speech translation (Ma et al., 2020b).

The evaluation was run with the SIMULEVAL toolkit (Ma et al., 2020a). For the latency measurement of speech input systems, we contrasted computation-aware and non computation-aware latency metrics. The latency was calculated at the word level for English-German systems and at the character level for English-Japanese systems.

The systems were ranked by the translation quality (measured by BLEU) in different latency regimes, low, medium and high. Each regime was determined by a maximum latency threshold measured by AL on the Must-C English-German test set (tst-COMMON) for English-German or on the IWSLT21 dev set for English-Japanese. The thresholds were set to 3, 6 and 15 for the English-German text track, to 1000, 2000 and 4000 for the English-German speech track and to 8, 12 and 16 for English-Japanese text track, and were calibrated by the baseline system. Participants were asked to submit at least one system per latency regime and were encouraged to submit multiple systems for each regime in order to provide more data points for latency-quality trade-off analyses. The organizers confirmed the latency regime by running the systems on tst-COMMON and the IWSLT21 dev set.

2.3 Differences with the First Edition

English-to-Japanese Task This year, we added a new task of English-to-Japanese simultaneous translation. English-Japanese is a challenging language pair for simultaneous translation because of the large word order differences; a simultaneous machine translation model has to wait for the latter part of an English sentence in *Subject-Verb-Object* order to generate a Japanese sentence in *Subject-Object-Verb* order.

SimulEval We standardized the latency evaluation aspect of the task by leveraging the SIMULEVAL toolkit. In addition, speech input systems were run in a controlled environment (a p3.2xlarge AWS instance) in order to be able to fairly compare computation-aware AL.

Unsegmented input Based on feedback from the participants in the first edition of the task, for the speech track, systems were run on both segmented and unsegmented input. The latter setting required participants to implement a segmentation logic in their systems, which is closer to a real-world setting.

2.4 Submissions

The simultaneous task received submissions from 5 teams: 4 teams entered the English-German text track; 3 teams entered the English-Japanese text track and 2 teams entered the English-German speech track. Teams followed the suggestion to submit multiple systems per regime, which resulted in a total of 162 systems overall.

UEDIN (Sen et al., 2021) submitted systems to the text-to-text English-German track. In order to be able to reuse an offline system, UEDIN adapts the re-translation strategy to the simultaneous task. Re-translation is triggered based on a language model applied to the source input. In addition, a

[1] https://github.com/pytorch/fairseq/blob/master/examples/speech_to_text/docs/simulst_mustc_example.md

[2] https://wit3.fbk.eu/2017-01-c

[3] https://drive.google.com/drive/folders/1uSkOT-XqbICMohnvfXdEFffKLdaQX0X7

[4] https://drive.google.com/drive/folders/1bB1s9PKNoRoDFfc567J5zDMcYj_1FFEB

dynamic masking method is employed to stabilize the output translation.

VOLCTRANS (Zhao et al., 2021) submitted systems to the text-to-text English-German and English-Japanese tracks. The participants adopt the efficient wait-k strategy (Elbayad et al., 2020). They augment the training data using back-translation and knowledge distillation. During inference, a look ahead beam search strategy is investigated but the final submission uses greedy search.

USTC-NESLIP (Liu et al., 2021) submitted systems to all tracks, including both end-to-end and cascaded system for the speech tracks. The participants design a novel model architecture, Cross-Attention Augmented Transducer, that modifies RNN-T in order to support reordering between languages. They augment the training data using self-training, back-translation and by synthesizing the source side of the parallel corpora.

APPTEK (Bahar et al., 2021b) submitted systems to the English-German speech and text tracks, using a cascaded system for the speech track. Chunks that preserve monotonicity are extracted from a statistical word aligner. A classifier, part of the overall model, is trained on the boundaries in order to control the policy. To better control the latency quality tradeoff, consecutive chunks can be merged according to a probability.

NAIST (Fukuda et al., 2021) submitted systems to the text English-Japanese track. The participants employ the wait-k method and sequence-level knowledge distillation. Because Japanese does not have a strict word order, they randomly shuffle chunks on the target side to augment the training data. An alternative method, next constituent label prediction, was investigated but not submitted to the task.

2.5 Results

We discuss results for the text and speech tracks. More details are available in Appendix A.1.

2.5.1 Text Track

Results for the text track are summarized in the first two tables of Appendix A.1. Four teams (USTC-NESLIP, VOLCTRANS, APPTEK, UEDIN) submitted systems for English-German and three teams (USTC-NESLIP, VOLCTRANS, NAIST) for English-Japanese. In the table, only the models with the best BLEU score for a given latency regime are reported. In

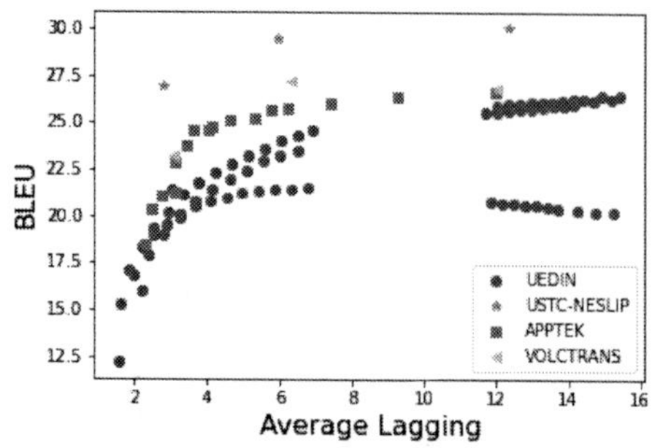

Figure 1: Latency-quality trade-off curves, measured by AL and BLEU, reported on the blind test set, for the systems submitted to the English-German text track.

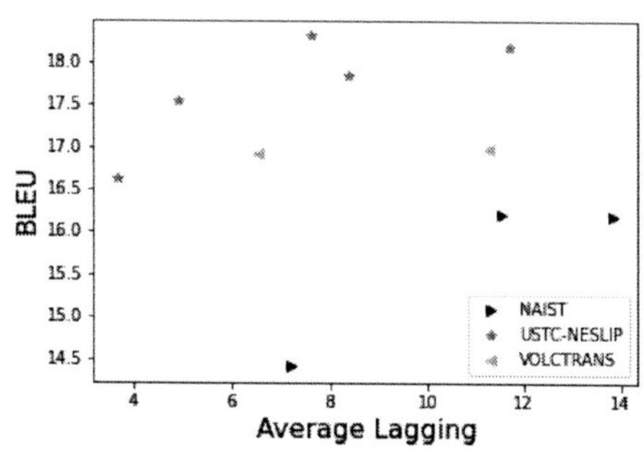

Figure 2: Latency-quality trade-off curves, measured by AL and BLEU, reported on the blind test set, for the systems submitted to the English-Japanese text track.

order to obtain a broader sense of latency-quality tradeoffs, we also plot all submitted systems for quality and latency.

English-German The ranking is consistent over all the regimes: 1. USTC-NESLIP 2. VOLCTRANS 3. APPTEK 4. UEDIN. We plot all the submitted English-German systems in Figure 1.

Japanese-English The ranking is consistent over all the regimes: 1. USTC-NESLIP 2. APPTEK 3. NAIST. We plot all the submitted English-Japanese systems in Figure 2.

2.5.2 Speech Track (English-German Only)

Results for the speech track are summarized in the third table of Appendix A.1. Two teams (USTC-NESLIP, APPTEK) submitted systems, with both segmented and unsegmented speech input. Latency regimes were defined for segmented input systems only. We plan to define latency

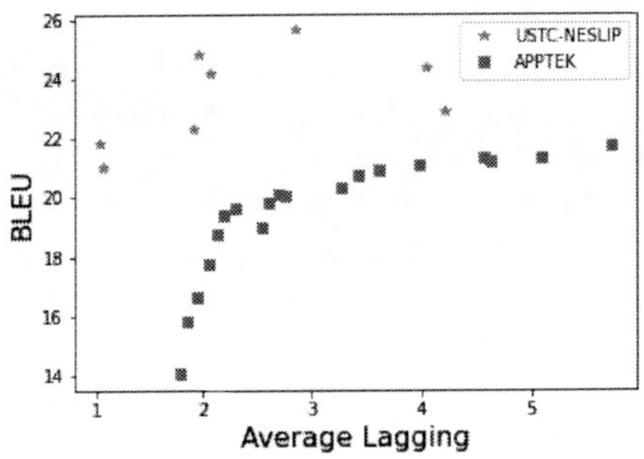

Figure 3: Latency-quality trade-off curves, measured by AL and BLEU, reported on the blind test set, for the systems submitted to the speech track with segmented input. AL is measured in seconds.

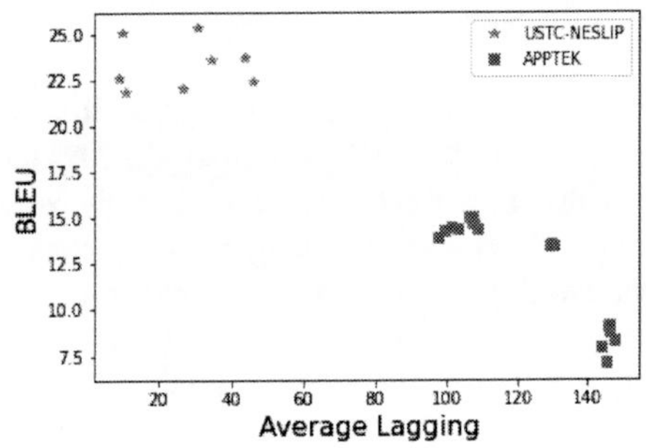

Figure 5: Latency-quality trade-off curves, measured by AL and BLEU, reported on the blind test set, for the systems submitted to the speech track with unsegmented input. AL is measured in seconds.

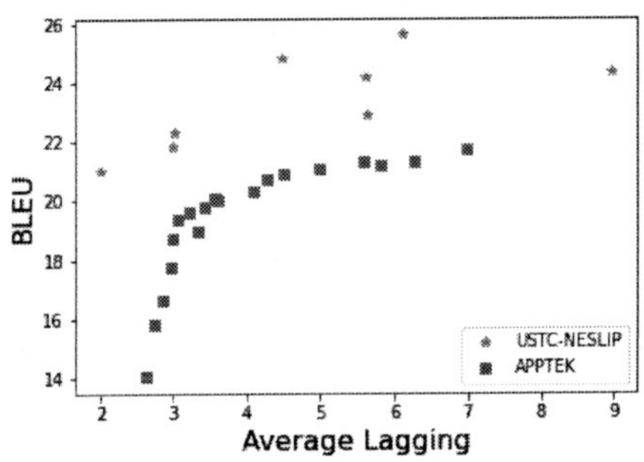

Figure 4: Latency-quality trade-off curves, measured by AL and BLEU, reported on the blind test set, for the systems submitted to the speech track with segmented input. AL is considering the computation time and measured in seconds.

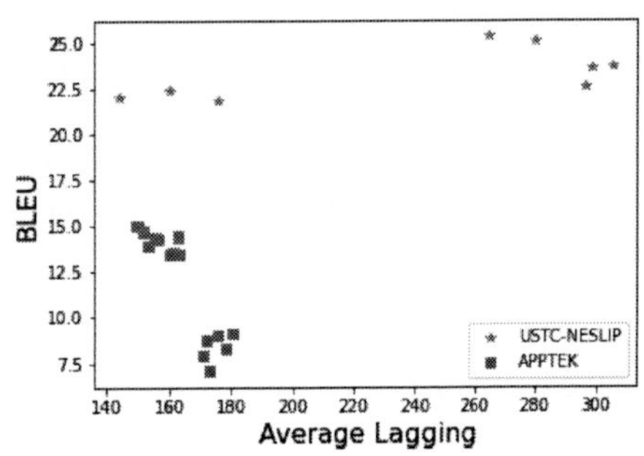

Figure 6: Latency-quality trade-off curves, measured by AL and BLEU, reported on the blind test set, for the systems submitted to the speech track with unsegmented input. AL is considering the computation time and measured in seconds.

regimes for unsegmented input in the next edition. The ranking is consistent over all the regimes in segmented systems and unsegmented systems: 1. USTC 2. AppTek We also report four latency-quality trade-off curves:

- Segmented input systems without considering computation time in Figure 3.
- Segmented input systems considering computation time in Figure 4.
- Unsegmented input systems without considering computation time in Figure 5.
- Unsegmented input systems considering computation time in Figure 6.

3 Offline Speech Translation

Offline speech translation, declined in various forms over the years, is one of the speech tasks with the longest tradition at the IWSLT campaign. Like in the last two evaluation rounds, this year[5] it focused on the translation of English audio data extracted from TED talks[6] into German.

3.1 Challenge

In recent years, offline speech translation (ST) has seen a rapid evolution, characterized by the steady advancement of *direct* end-to-end models (building on a single neural network that directly translates the input audio into target language text) that were able to significantly reduce the performance

[5] `http://iwslt.org/2021/offline`
[6] `http://www.ted.com`

gap with respect to the traditional *cascade* approach (integrating ASR and MT components in a pipelined architecture). In light of last year's IWSLT results (Ansari et al., 2020) and of the findings of recent works (Bentivogli et al., 2021) attesting that the gap between the two paradigms has substantially closed, also this year a key element of the evaluation was to set up a shared framework for their comparison. For this reason, and to reliably measure progress with respect to the past rounds, the general evaluation setting was kept unchanged. This stability mainly concerns two aspects: the allowed architectures and the test set provision.

On the architecture side, participation was allowed both with cascade and end-to-end (also known as direct) systems. In the latter case, valid submissions had to be obtained by models that: *i)* do not exploit intermediate symbolic representations (e.g., source language transcription or hypotheses fusion in the target language), and *ii)* rely on parameters that are all jointly trained on the end-to-end task.

On the test set provision side, also this year participants could opt for processing either a precomputed automatic segmentation of the test set or a version of the same test data segmented with their own approach. This option was maintained not only to ease participation (by removing one of the obstacles in audio processing) but also to gain further insights about the importance of a proper segmentation of the input speech. As highlighted in (Ansari et al., 2020), effective preprocessing to reduce the mismatch between the provided training material (often "clean" corpora split into sentence-like segments) and the supplied unsegmented test data is in fact a common trait of top-performing systems.

Multiple submissions were allowed, but participants had to explicitly indicate their "primary" (one at most) and "contrastive" runs, together with the corresponding type of system (cascade/end-to-end), training data condition (constrained/unconstrained), and test set segmentation (own/given).

3.2 Data and Metrics

Training and development data. Also this year, participants had the possibility to train their systems using several resources available for ST, ASR and MT. The major novelty on the data front is that a new TED-derived resource was added to the training corpora usually allowed to satisfy the "constrained" data condition. The new data come from the English-German section of the MuST-C V2 corpus[7] and include training, dev, and test (Test Common), in the same structure of the MuST-C V1 corpus (Cattoni et al., 2021) used last year. Since the 2021 test set was processed using the same pipeline applied to create MuST-C V2, the use of the new training resource was strongly recommended. The main differences with respect to MuST-C v1 are:

- More talks, which results in 20k more audio/text segments;
- Improved cleaning strategies able to better discard low-quality triplets (audio, transcript, translation), in particular when the text is not well-aligned with the audio and the audio is shorter than 50 millisecs;
- The talks were downloaded from the YouTube TED channel,[8] where higher quality audio/videos are available with respect to the TED website used for the previous version of MuST-C. The downloading was performed by means of youtube-dl,[9] the well-known open-source download manager, specifying the "-f bestaudio option". The audios were finally converted from two (stereo) to one (mono) channel and downsampled from 48 to 16 kHz, using FFmpeg.[10] Upon inspection of the spectrograms of the same talks in the two versions of MuST-C, it clearly emerges that the upper limit band in the audios used in MuST-C V1 is 5 kHz, while it is at 8 kHz in the latest version, coherently with the 16 kHz sample rate. This difference does not guarantee the fully compatibility between V1 and V2 of MuST-C.

Besides MuST-C V2, also this year the allowed training corpora include:

- MuST-C V1 (Di Gangi et al., 2019);
- CoVoST (Wang et al., 2020);

[7] `http://ict.fbk.eu/must-c/`
[8] `http://www.youtube.com/c/TED/videos`
[9] `http://youtube-dl.org/`
[10] `http://ffmpeg.org/`

- WIT[3] (Cettolo et al., 2012) ;
- Speech-Translation TED corpus[11];
- How2 (Sanabria et al., 2018)[12];
- LibriVoxDeEn (Beilharz and Sun, 2019)[13];
- Europarl-ST (Iranzo-Sánchez et al., 2020);
- TED LIUM v2 (Rousseau et al., 2014) and v3 (Hernandez et al., 2018);
- WMT 2019[14] and 2020[15];
- OpenSubtitles 2018 (Lison et al., 2018);
- Augmented LibriSpeech (Kocabiyikoglu et al., 2018)[16]
- Mozilla Common Voice[17] ;
- LibriSpeech ASR corpus (Panayotov et al., 2015).

The list of allowed development data includes the dev set from IWSLT 2010, as well as the test sets used for the 2010, 2013, 2014, 2015 and 2018 IWSLT campaigns. Using other training/development resources was allowed but, in this case, participants were asked to mark their submission as an "unconstrained" one.

Test data. This year's new test set was built from 17 TED talks that are not included yet in the public release of the corpus. Similar to last year, participants were presented with the option of processing either an unsegmented version (to be split with their preferred segmentation method) or an automatically segmented version of the audio data. For the segmented version, the resulting number of segments is 2,336 (corresponding to about 4h15m of translated speech from 17 talks). To measure technology progress with respect to last year's round, participants were asked to process also the undisclosed 2020 test set that, in the segmented version, consists of 2,263 segments (corresponding to about 4.1 hours of translated speech from 22 talks).

Metrics. Systems' performance was evaluated with respect to their capability to produce translations similar to the target-language references. Differently from previous rounds, where such similarity was measured in terms of multiple automatic metrics,[18] this year only the BLEU metric (computed with SacreBLEU (Post, 2018) with default settings) has been considered. Instead of multiple metrics, the attention focused on considering two different types of target-language references, namely:

- The original TED translations. Since these references come in the form of subtitles, they are subject to compression and omissions to adhere to the TED subtitling guidelines.[19] This makes them less literal compared to standard, unconstrained translations;
- Unconstrained translations. These references were created from scratch[20] by adhering to the usual translation guidelines. They are hence exact (more literal) translations, without paraphrasing and with proper punctuation.

Lang	Sentences	Words
EN	2,037	41,214
DE - Orig	2,037	33,925
DE - Uncon.	2,037	40,239

Table 2: Statistics of the official test set for the offline speech translation task (*tst2021*).

As shown in Table 2, the different approaches to generate the human translations lead to significantly different references. While the unconstrained translation has a similar length (counted in words) compared to the corresponding source sentence, the original is ~15% shorter in order to fulfil the additional constraints for subtitling.

Besides considering separate scores for the two types of references, results were also computed by considering both of them in a multi-reference setting. Similarly to last year, the submitted runs

[11] http://i13pc106.ira.uka.de/~mmueller/iwslt-corpus.zip

[12] only English - Portuguese

[13] only German - English

[14] http://www.statmt.org/wmt19/

[15] http://www.statmt.org/wmt20/

[16] only English - French

[17] http://voice.mozilla.org/en/datasets – English version en_1488h_2019-12-10

[18] These were: case-sensitive/insensitive BLEU (Papineni et al., 2002b), case-sensitive/insensitive TER (Snover et al., 2006), BEER (Stanojevic and Sima'an, 2014), and CharacTER (Wang et al., 2016)

[19] http://www.ted.com/participate/translate/subtitling-tips

[20] We would like to thank Facebook, and in particular Juan Pino, for providing us with this new set of references.

were ranked based on case-sensitive BLEU calculated on the test set by using automatic re-segmentation of the hypotheses based on the reference translations by mwerSegmenter.[21]

3.3 Submissions

We received submissions from 12 teams, which is a slight increase (+2) over last year's round. Also this year, participants come from the industry (the majority), the academia and other research institutions. In terms of ST paradigms, though quite evenly distributed, architectural choices show a slight preference for the cascade approach, which highlights a countertrend strategy with respect to the 2020 round, in which half of the participants opted for end-to-end submissions only. In detail:

- 5 teams (BUT, HW-TSC, LI, OPPO, VUS) participated only with cascade systems;
- 3 teams (FBK, NIUTRANS, UPC) participated only with end-to-end systems;
- 4 teams (APPTEK, VOLCTRANS, ESPNET-ST,KIT) participated with both cascade and end-to-end systems.

In total, 55 runs were evaluated: 24 obtained from cascade systems and 31 obtained from end-to-end systems. Concerning the segmentation of the test data (own/given), most of the primary submissions (7 out of 12) were obtained with "own" segmentation strategies aimed to improve the given automatic audio splits provided to participants like in last year's round of the task. As regards the data condition (constrained/unconstrained), all participants but two (BUT and UPC) opted for "constrained" submissions obtained by building their ST models only using the provided training resources.

In the following, we provide a bird's-eye description of each participant's approach.

APPTEK (Bahar et al., 2021b) participated with both cascade and end-to-end speech translation systems fed with "own" automatic segmentation of the test data. The primary cascade system is akin to the conventional cascade systems where source transcriptions are generated as an intermediate representation. ASR exploits an attention-based model (Bahdanau et al., 2015; Vaswani et al., 2017) trained following Zeyer et al. (2018), while the MT component is based on the big Transformer model model. Passing on the re-normalized ASR posteriors into the MT model, the model is trained in an end-to-end fashion (inspired by the posterior tight integrated model by Bahar et al. 2021a) using all ASR, MT, and ST available training data. The system uses an improved automatic segmentation based on voice activity detection (VAD) and endpoint detection (EP). The primary end-to-end system also processes the speech input with "own" automatic segmentation. It is based on an ensemble of 4 models combining an LSTM speech encoder and a big Transformer decoder, as well as a pure Transformer model for both the encoder and the decoder. The models are trained using CTC attention loss, spectrogram augmentation, pretraining, synthetic data using forward translation, and fine-tuned on the in-domain TED talks. Following Gaido et al. (2020a), the direct model is also fine-tuned on automatically segmented data to increase its robustness against sub-optimal non-homogeneous utterances.

BUT (Vydana et al., 2021) participated with a cascade system fed with the "given" automatic segmentation of the test data. The primary submission is obtained from a system exploiting joint training of the ASR and MT components, model ensembling and tight ASR-MT coupling. Both ASR and MT are pre-trained on pre-processed clean data and rely on Transformer-based components. Two different ASR models are respectively trained to generate normalized and punctuated text, the latter leading to better results. In the proposed joint training procedure, the context vectors from the final layer of the ASR-decoder are used as inputs by the MT module, and both models are jointly optimized using a multi-task loss. At inference time, beam search is used to obtain the ASR hypotheses, and the corresponding context vectors obtained from the ASR model are used by the MT model for generating translations. The MT model also uses a beam search to produce the hypothesis and the final ST hypothesis is obtained by a coupled search using the joint likelihood from ASR and MT.

ESPNET-ST (Inaguma et al., 2021) participated with both cascade and end-to-end speech translation systems, with primary focus on the direct approach. Both systems are fed with "own" automatic segmentation of the test data. The primary

[21] `http://www-i6.informatik.rwth-aachen.de/web/Software/mwerSegmenter.tar.gz`

cascade system exploits an ASR component based on Conformer (Gulati et al., 2020a) and an MT component built with Transformer-base trained without case information and punctuation marks. The primary end-to-end system is based on the Conformer encoder, a stacked multi-block architecture including a multi-head self-attention module, a convolution module, and a pair of position-wise feed-forward modules in the Macaron-Net style (Lu et al., 2019). The baseline conformer is improved by training with sequence-level knowledge distillation and by adopting a Multi-Decoder architecture (which equips dedicated decoders for speech recognition and translation tasks in a unified encoder-decoder model enabling search in both source and target language spaces during inference), model ensembling and improved VAD-based audio segmentation (a "bottom-up" variant of (Potapczyk and Przybysz, 2020; Gaido et al., 2021)).

FBK (Papi et al., 2021) participated with an end-to-end-system fed with "own" automatic segmentation of the test data. The primary submission is obtained from a Transformer-based architecture trained with a pipeline involving data augmentation (SpecAugment (Park et al., 2019) and MT-based synthetic data) and characterized by knowledge distillation and a two-step fine-tuning procedure. Both knowledge distillation and the first fine-tuning step (optimized by combining label smoothed cross entropy and the CTC scoring function described in Gaido et al. 2020b) are carried out on manually segmented real and synthetic data. The second fine-tuning step is carried out on a random segmentation of the MuST-C v2 En-De dataset, aimed to make the system robust to automatically segmented test audio data (Gaido et al., 2020a). For the same purpose, a custom hybrid segmentation procedure (Gaido et al., 2021) is applied to the test data before passing them to the system.

HW-TSC participated with a cascade system fed with "own" automatic segmentation of the test data. The ASR component is a Transformer-large model, which is trained on the combination of LibriSpeech, MUST-C v2 and COVOST, where transcriptions are pre-pended by a label indicating the source corpus to make them distinguishable. During inference, the model is forced to decode in the MUST-C alike style by setting the first token as the MUST-C tag. The MT model is a Transformer-large model trained on the WMT19 corpus and fine-tuned on IWSLT-2017 text translation corpus.

KIT (Nguyen et al., 2021) participated with both cascade and end-to-end speech translation systems fed with "own" automatic segmentation of the test data (obtained from the WerRTCVAD toolkit[22]). The primary cascade system exploits sequence-to-sequence ASR models trained with three architectures (LSTM, Transformer and Conformer). Before MT, a Transformer-based segmentation module is in charge to (monolingually) translate disfluent, broken, uncased ASR outputs into more fluent, written-style text with punctuation in order to match the data conditions of the translation system. This is done in a shifting window manner, in which decisions are drawn by means of a simple voting mechanism. For MT, the systems relies on an ensemble of Transformer-large models trained on both clean and noisy synthetic (TED-derived) data. The primary end-to-end system is an improved version of last year's Speech Relative Transformer architecture (Pham et al., 2020c). Its encoder self-attention layer uses Bidirectional relative attention (Pham et al., 2020a) to model the relative distance between one position and other positions in the sequence. Three models, trained with SpecAugment (Park et al., 2019) and different activation functions (GeLU, SiLU and ReLU), are eventually combined in an ensemble.

LI participated with a cascade system fed with the "given" automatic segmentation of the test data. Both the ASR (three models) and the MT components (two models) are based on fairseq (Ott et al., 2019)[23] and were trained on MuST-C data.

NIUTRANS (Xu et al., 2021b) participated with an end-to-end-system fed with "own" automatic segmentation of the test data. The primary submission relies on a deep Transformer model implemented in fairseq and improved by adding the CTC loss as auxiliary loss on the encoders. The system is also enhanced with Conformer (used to replace the Transformer blocks in the encoder), relative position encoding (to improve acoustic modeling and generalize better for unseen sequence lengths; Shaw et al., 2018), and stacked acoustic and textual encoding (to better encode the

[22] http://github.com/wiseman/py-webrtcvad

[23] http://github.com/pytorch/fairseq.git

speech features; Xu et al., 2021a). Data augmentation is also applied via spectrogram augmentation, speed perturbation and sequence-level knowledge distillation, as well as by generating new synthetic speech from MT data and by translating into German the English transcriptions of ASR and ST data. Finally, ensemble decoding is applied to integrate the predictions from several models trained with the different datasets.

OPPO participated with a cascade system fed with the "given" automatic segmentation of the test data. The primary submission is based on Transformer for both the ASR and MT components, which are trained on part of allowed training datasets (MUSTC, LibriSpeech, CoVost, and WMT20). Structured dropout is applied to increase the differences between different models, which are eventually combined via average ensembling.

UPC (Gállego et al., 2021) participated with an end-to-end-system fed with "own" automatic segmentation of the test data (inspired by (Potapczyk et al., 2019)). The primary submission combines a Wav2Vec 2.0 encoder and an mBART decoder, which are respectively pre-trained on the ASR and MT tasks. A length adaptor module, consisting of a stack of convolutional layers, alleviates the length discrepancy between the speech and text modalities. Model fine-tuning to the ST task was carried out following the LNA strategy proposed in (Li et al., 2021). In addition, based on the ST improvements reported in (Escolano et al., 2020), an Adapter module was added to extract richer representations from the output of the encoder (Bapna and Firat, 2019). Data augmentation is also performed via randomized on-the-fly perturbations obtained by adding an echo effect and by modifying tempo and pitch, as well as by applying masking to the output of the Wav2Vec 2.0 feature extraction module. Different approaches were explored to combine the fine-tuning of the pre-trained models and the training of the intermediate modules. The best performance was obtained with a two-stage strategy, where: 1) the Wav2Vec and mBART models are frozen and the intermediate modules are forced to learn how to couple them; 2) model fine-tuning follows the LNA strategy, starting from the solid initial point obtained in the previous step.

VOLCTRANS (Zhao et al., 2021) participated with both cascade and end-to-end speech translation systems fed with the "given" automatic segmentation of the test data. The primary cascade system exploits a Transformer-based ASR trained, using spectrogram augmentation, on both clean and filtered noisy data. MT processing relies on Transformer-based models trained with data augmentation (via back-translation, knowledge distillation and ASR output adaptation) and combined with model ensemble techniques. The primary end-to-end system is trained by exploiting knowledge distillation (leveraging ASR datasets and four MT models) for data augmentation. The encoder and the decoder are pre-trained in a progressive multi-task learning framework, also exploiting a fbank2vec network to learn contextualized audio representations from log Mel-filterbank features.

VUS (Jo et al., 2021) participated with a cascade system fed with the "given" automatic segmentation of the test data. For the ASR component, a pretrained wav2vec 2.0 model (Baevski et al., 2020) was used for the embeddings, and the training was conducted with a Transformer augmented on the output layer of the wav2vec module. Following Potapczyk and Przybysz (2020), data pre-processing was made to remove training samples (laughters, applauses and erroneous scripts) that can lower the ASR performance. ASR output post-processing was also carried out to obtain an accurate sentence-level output, such as setting the sentence boundary between the fragment texts and re-aggregating some wrongly merged sentences. The MT component, also based on Transformer, was trained on a pre-processed version (language identification and length-based filtering and written-to-spoken text conversion through lowercasing, punctuation removal and abbreviations' expansion similar to Bahar et al., 2020) of the WMT 20 en-de news task dataset.

3.4 Results

Detailed results for the offline ST task are provided in Appendix A.2. Specifically, two separate tables respectively show the BLEU scores of participants' primary submissions computed on this year's *tst2021* and last year's *tst2020* test sets. In each table, three BLEU scores are reported, namely:

- `BLEU_NewRef` – computed on the new (exact, literal) translations described in Section

3.2;

- BLEU_TEDRef – computed on the original (subtitle-like) TED translations;
- BLEU_MultiRef – computed using both references in a multi-reference setting.

Systems are ranked according to their BLEU_NewRef score. Background colours are used to differentiate between cascade (white background) and end-to-end architectures (gray background). Additionally, the segmentation strategy (Own vs Given) and the training data condition (Constrained vs Unconstrained) characterising each primary submission are shown in separate columns.

Official results. In terms of this year's BLEU_NewRef primary metric, the top-ranked system achieved a BLEU score of 24.6, which is slightly below the one obtained by last year's winning system (25.3). Also the average (19.8) and median scores (21.7) are inferior compared to last year's round of the evaluation (average: 20.15; median: 21.81). These results, however, are not comparable since they are computed on a different test set (built from different TED talks), which also comprises reference translations that are not the original ones. The evaluation of this year's systems on *tst2020*, which is discussed below, is hence more informative if we want to get an idea about the actual evolution of ST technology.

Computing BLEU on the original TED translations (BLEU_TEDRef) results in overall scores that are significantly lower (top submission: 20.3; average: 16.6; median: 18.2). This large drop indicates the difficulty for all systems to generate translations that are similar to the subtitle-like ones characterising the recent TED talks included in this year's test set.

Unsurprisingly, the BLEU_MultiRef results are considerably higher due to the positive effect of combining more references (top submission: 34.0; average: 27.7; median: 30.5). However, it is worth remarking that, in this multi-reference setting, 12 primary submissions out of 16 reached a BLEU score above 30.0.

Cascade vs end-to-end. A major finding from last year (Ansari et al., 2020) was about the complete reduction of the performance gap between cascade and end-to-end systems. In the same direction, the analysis proposed in (Bentivogli et al., 2021) has recently shown through manual analyses and post-editing-based evaluations that the two paradigms are now substantially on par. In apparent contradiction, this year's results depict a different situation: the two top ranked submissions in the official ranking (based on BLEU_NewRef) are in fact produced with cascade systems (respectively scoring 24.6 and 23.4 BLEU). The first end-to-end submission (obtained under the same segmentation and training data conditions) is two BLEU points below (22.6) the top-ranked system. However, it is interesting to note that the type of reference translations used for evaluation makes a big difference in terms of final results. While all systems perform significantly worse when BLEU is computed against the original TED translations, some low-ranked submissions would climb the rankings if BLEU_TEDRef were used as primary metric. Although this year's winner would remain the same, the 12th and 13th submission would jump respectively to the 3rd and 2nd position. Notably, with a ranking based on BLEU_TEDRef, 7 of the top 10 positions would be occupied by the end-to-end submissions.[24]

All in all, in terms of performance distance between the two paradigms, our findings support those of (Bentivogli et al., 2021) about relying on automatic scores computed against independent references. Across metrics, test sets and language directions, they are less coherent than those computed on human post-edits. Different from last year, in this round the clear winner according to all possible rankings is a cascade system. However, its distance from the other end-to-end systems varies considerably depending on the type of reference translations used (down to 0.7 BLEU points in the ranking based on BLEU_TEDRef). In light of this variability, manual analyses and post-editing-based evaluations like the ones presented in (Bentivogli et al., 2021), would help to precisely assess if the observed BLEU score differences (marginal with BLEU_TEDRef) actually make one approach preferable to the other by final users.

[24] System's ranking based on BLEU_NewRef would end up similarly, with 6 end-to-end submissions in the top 10 positions (the top 2 still being the same cascade systems dominating the official ranking).

The importance of input segmentation. Another important finding from last year's evaluation concerned the importance of properly segmenting the input speech at test time, so to feed the systems with inputs that are closer to the sentence-like segments present in the clean corpora on which they are trained. Also this year, the top five primary runs submitted are all obtained by systems operating with "own" segmentation strategies, which prove to be helpful independently of the underlying paradigm. This is confirmed by the fact that the three lowest BLEU scores are achieved by participants opting for the "given" segmentation. Similar trends emerge with all possible rankings (`BLEU_NewRef`, `BLEU_TEDRef`, and `BLEU_MultiRef`). The importance of a proper segmentation of the input speech is even more evident if we look at the results computed on the *tst2020* test set, where the top seven runs are obtained with custom segmentation and the worst 5 with the given one. These findings are in line with last year's observations and motivate further efforts on improving this critical pre-processing step.

Progress wrt 2020. Overall results computed on *tst2020* are higher compared to those obtained on *tst2021*. However, being the two test sets different as discussed above, the scores are not directly comparable to draw reliable conclusions about the ST technology evolution (which might wrongly be considered as an involution by merely comparing raw BLEU scores on the two benchmarks). Rather, more can be said if we only focus on how this year's systems behave on *tst2020*. The improvement is evident both if we look at the average performance (increasing by more than 1 BLEU point from 20.15 to 21.17) and if we concentrate on the best systems. Specifically, with "own" test data segmentation methods, three teams achieved BLEU scores that are higher (up to 0.7 points) than the one obtained by the 2020 winner under this condition (25.3). With the "given" automatic audio splits, two teams improved (up to 1.8 points) the highest score obtained last year under this condition (22.49). Interestingly, similar to last year, the best system is an end-to-end one. The performance distance with respect to the best cascade result on *tst2020* is even larger (0.6 BLEU points) compared to the one observed last year (0.24). On one side, these results confirm that, on last year's test data (and with BLEU scores computed on the original TED translations), the end-to-end paradigm has an edge on the cascade one. On the other side, they confirm the above observations about the variability of automatic evaluation outcomes, which are highly affected by the overall testing conditions.

Final remarks. By inspecting this year's results, we can draw two final observations that, with an eye at the future, provide us with possible indications for the next rounds of the IWSLT offline ST task. One is about the training data condition: additional training resources did not yield visible advantages. Unfortunately, having only two "unconstrained" submissions makes it hard to draw reliable conclusions on this aspect. However, one might wonder if differentiating between constrained and unconstrained submissions still makes sense if the general goal is to boost research on a rapidly evolving technology. *Is it a good source of interesting observations or has it become an irrelevant distinction?* Reasoning on this question might yield indications for future rounds of the task.

The other observation is about how performance is distributed with respect to the two ST paradigms: while the results of cascade systems are spread across the whole performance interval (3.6 – 24.6 for `BLEU_NewRef`), the scores obtained by end-to-end models are concentrated in a two-point interval (20.6 – 22.6). Such a close performance of direct models should stimulate reflection on the fact that either the architectural restrictions posed to define the "end-to-end" setting (i.e. bypass any intermediate symbolic representation), or other limitations of current technology, result in systems that are quite similar to each other. *Is it still reasonable, for the good of ST, limiting participant's freedom with arbitrary, pre-defined architectural constraints?* Setting less restrictive conditions to experiment with, thus opening to participation with alternative approaches (e.g. by avoiding explicit architectural constraints) is a possible direction to promote more innovation in future rounds of the evaluation campaign.

4 Multilingual Speech Translation

While multilingual translation is an established task, until recently, few parallel resources existed for speech translation and most remain only for translation from English speech. Multilingual models enable transfer from related tasks, which is particularly important for low-resource languages; however, parallel data between two otherwise high-resource languages can also often be rare, making multilingual and zero-shot translation important for many resource settings.

In addition to parallel speech and translations, many sources of data may be useful for speech translation: monolingual speech and transcripts, parallel text, and data from other languages or language pairs. While cascades of separately trained automatic speech recognition (ASR) and machine translation (MT) models can leverage all of these data sources, how to most effectively do so with end-to-end models remains an open and exciting research question.

Speech	Target Languages				
	en	es	fr	pt	it
es	Supervised	Supervised	Supervised	Supervised	Supervised
fr	Supervised	Supervised	Supervised	Supervised	—
pt	Supervised	Zero-shot	—	Supervised	—
it	Zero-shot	Zero-shot	—	—	Supervised

Table 3: **Multilingual task language pairs**. Languages are represented by their ISO 639-1 code. Speech, transcripts, and translations were provided for all **Supervised** tasks; for **Zero-shot** ST tasks, only speech and transcripts were provided during training, though target language text may be seen with other source languages. Participants were required to submit translations for all official translation directions.

4.1 Challenge

Motivated by the above, the multilingual speech translation task provided data for two conditions: supervised, and zero-shot. We provided speech and transcripts for four languages (Spanish, French, Portuguese, Italian) and translations in a subset of five languages (English, Spanish, French, Portuguese, Italian) as shown in Table 3. For zero-shot language pairs, data for ASR (speech and transcripts) was released for training, but not translations; the target languages could be observed in other language pairs in training. Both translation directions for one source language (Italian) and one of two translation directions for another (Portuguese) were chosen to be zero-shot to enable comparison between supervised and zero-shot conditions with the same source language, and to measure the impact of having no supervised ST data at all. Participants could use the provided resources in any way.

At evaluation time, we provided speech in the four source languages and asked participants to generate translations in both English and Spanish. Both constrained submissions (using the provided data only, e.g., no models pretrained on external data) and unconstrained submissions were encouraged and evaluated separately. Submitting translations for additional optional language pairs as well as generated transcripts (ASR) for evaluation was not mandatory but encouraged as a useful point of analysis.

4.2 Data and Metrics

For this task we use the Multilingual TEDx data (mTEDx) (Salesky et al., 2021). The data is derived from TEDx talks and translations. The mTEDx data is segmented and aligned at the sentence-level (using automatically generated segmentations and alignments). mTEDx is publicly available on OpenSLR.[25] The data released during the training period contained train, validation, and progress test sets. For the purposes of this task, ST data for three language pairs was withheld until after the evaluation period (Zero-shot in Table 3). Use of any of resources beyond Multilingual TEDx made a submission unconstrained. Any publicly available additional data or pretrained models were permitted for training unconstrained systems.

We evaluated translation output using BLEU as computed by SACREBLEU (Post, 2018) and WER for ASR output. We computed all scores using the provided utterance segmentations from Multilingual TEDx. WER was computed on lowercased text with punctuation removed.

4.3 Submissions

We received 15 submissions from 7 teams.

FAIR (Tang et al., 2021a) submitted unconstrained end-to-end models which leverage pretrained multilingual wav2vec 2.0 and mBART models, and finetune on the provided mTEDx MT and ST data as well as additional corpora. They compare different wav2vec 2.0 models trained on different multilingual corpora and either text (Baevski et al., 2020) or IPA targets (Wang et al., 2021), and mBART with BPE (Liu et al., 2020) or IPA representations (Tang et al., 2021b). They combine different joint and speech-only finetuning, and add an adaptor layer (Li et al., 2021) between the two pretrained models for adapta-

[25] http://openslr.org/100/

tion and downsampling. They ultimately ensemble three models for their final submission.

HWN (Zeng et al., 2021) used a unified Transformer architecture in which audio and text data can be featurized separately by a Conv-Transformer (Huang et al., 2020) and text embeddings, before being fused and used as input to a single encoder and decoder. They use curriculum learning by first training the unified model for the ASR and MT tasks, then continue training adding the ST task and finally fine-tuning using the ST task data only. They also use multiple data augmentation techniques and model ensembling.

KIT (Pham et al., 2021) trained deep Transformer models with relative attention for ASR and ST (Pham et al., 2019, 2020b) to create both cascaded and E2E models. They used additional techniques such as distillation, Macaron feed-forward layers, and the creation of synthetic data to significantly improve both models' performance. Their final submission is an ensemble of their cascade and E2E systems.

UM-DKE (Liu and Niehues, 2021) trained multilingual cascade and E2E models with a variety of techniques to improve performance. They start with a multilingual ASR model, which incorporates language embeddings, speed perturbation, and ensembling. They improve their multilingual MT by removing residual connections in the Transformer architecture, and further ensembling. Finally they train an E2E ST system which benefits from joint training with ASR, pseudo-labels for synthetic data to improve zero-shot pairs, and 'multi-view ensembling,' which ensembles probabilities based on three different speed perturbations.

ON-TRAC (Le et al., 2021) used a dual-decoder Transformer architecture (Le et al., 2020), which includes a single encoder for speech data and separate decoders (that interact with each other) for each of the ASR and ST tasks. They trained ASR and MT models to initialize the ST model and used SpecAugment augmentation. No synthetic data was created for zero-shot translation.

UEDIN (Zhang and Sennrich, 2021) trained multilingual Transformer models with adaptive feature selection (Zhang et al., 2020) to reduce data dimensionality by selecting the most informative speech features. They create pseudo-speech translation data which provides significant improvements on all language pairs, not only zero-shot. They additionally use sparsified linear attention, RMSNorm, scheduling language-specific modeling, and multi-task learning to improve their models, and ensemble models of multiple sizes for their final submission.

ZJU (Zhang, 2021) submitted an ensemble of cascaded ST models, using a Conformer (Gulati et al., 2020b) for ASR and a multilingual Transformer MT model. They use back-translation to create data for zero-shot pairs, add noised data to adapt their MT model to ASR output, and include masked training. They additionally compared end-to-end models with data augmentation and multi-task training.

4.4 Results

Results for the Multilingual Task are shown in Appendix A.3. We calculated task results using the average BLEU on all official ST language pairs: all primary submissions are shown in Table 5. The unconstrained submission from FAIR outperformed all other primary submissions on both supervised and zero-shot language pairs. The KIT submission was the strongest constrained system, aided in part by strong ASR pretraining: ASR results are shown in Table 8. All but one primary submission were ensembles of either multiple end-to-end systems, or end-to-end and cascaded models. We saw a mix of end-to-end and cascaded submissions across primary and constrastive submissions (Table 6); in general, the end-to-end models outperformed cascaded submissions, particularly under zero-shot conditions. We discuss different aspects of the task and submissions further below.

Constrained vs unconstrained. Use of additional data beyond mTEDx appeared to be a clear benefit on all ST pairs, as the FAIR system performed best on all language pairs. Interestingly, the performance difference between the best unconstrained and constrained systems across supervised and zero-shot tasks was similar. When we look at the constrastive submissions and ASR, however, the underlying reason appears not to be the additional data but rather how it is used. The FAIR baseline is initialized from the multilingual wav2vec2.0 model XLSR-53 and the mBART decoder, and is outperformed by many constrained systems. The other FAIR submissions used co-training with the text-to-text MT task and IPA representations for ASR and/or MT models for significant improvements.

Zero-shot performance. Overall we saw very encouraging performance on the zero-shot pairs, with very little degradation from the supervised language pairs for many systems. Three language pairs were zero-shot: pt-es, it-en, and it-es. While Portuguese speech was observed in another translation pair, Italian speech was only observed for ASR. The Italian pairs proved more challenging, but most systems nonetheless outperform the supervised end-to-end baselines in Salesky et al. (2021) through some combination of decoder pretraining, auto-encoding ASR data, or back-translation. Comparing supervised and zero-shot performance with the same source language (pt), we saw stronger performance on the zero-shot than supervised condition, likely indicative of the relatedness of the source and target languages, facilitating zero-shot translation. Though much more English target data has been seen (for constrained systems), pt-es and it-es are both more closely-related languages, and all but one system show better results on these two zero-shot language pairs than it-en. For teams which submitted both end-to-end and cascaded models, there were small but consistent improvements on zero-shot with end-to-end; this may suggest that E2E models more easily transfer from observed related languages and pairs, or perhaps that end-to-end models were more optimized. The systems with the greatest relative difference between supervised and zero-shot pairs were FAIR, HWN, and ON-TRAC. HWN had better performance for languages with more ASR data, and ON-TRAC struggled without e.g. auto-encoding text.

ASR performance impact. Interestingly, ASR performance was not necessarily indicative of ST performance; HWN and KIT ASR outperformed the FAIR ASR without additional training data or ensembling, with the exception of French where both systems struggled, particularly KIT. This was shown in ST performance; UEDIN outperformed KIT on language pairs where French was the source language, precisely where UEDIN had better ASR. All submitted ASR systems outperformed the end-to-end ASR in Salesky et al. (2021), in part through better optimization and use of multilingual models, and in particular use of the CTC objective. Their hybrid LF-MMI models remain generally stronger for Portuguese and French; not necessarily correlated with data size.

Ensembling. Most primary systems were ensembles of 2+ models, which provided improvements of up to 2 BLEU compared with the individual systems, some of which were submitted as constrastive (Table 6). We saw different ensembling techniques, using joint decoding or averaging model output probabilities. Ensembled models were alternatively models of different sizes (UEDIN), trained on different data (FAIR), different combinations of fine-tuning and knowledge distillation (HWN), system with back-translations and with ASR noise added (ZJU), speed perturbations of the same input (UM-DKE), or cascaded and end-to-end models (KIT).

Unofficial language pairs. The unofficial language pairs (Table 7) have the same source languages as the official language pairs, but different target languages. The test sets are parallel with the official blind evaluation sets. The relative performance between primary systems on these additional targets remains similar. Performance on more closely related languages (es-pt) was in fact generally higher, and language pairs with less-observed target languages (es-fr, es-it) were lower. The exception was FAIR, where average performance was almost exactly the same as on the official supervised pairs; the additional datasets used for pretraining likely erase some of these resource differences, supported by the differences between their constrastive submissions which use different pretraining sources.

End-to-End vs Cascade. Three groups submitted an end-to-end system and a cascaded system. In all three cases, the end-to-end system outperforms the cascaded approach. Since the tendency in the offline translation task (section 3) is different (there the cascaded approaches typically perform better than the end-to-end models), this opens up several interesting research questions that should be investigated further. There are several differences between the two tasks that could influence the ranking between the end-to-end and cascaded models: First of all, the amount of ASR and MT training data that is available in addition to end-to-end training data is different. In the offline task, there is significantly more data available for the auxiliary tasks (particularly MT), which may benefit cascaded models more. Secondly, the multilingual task uses provided automatic sentence segmentation which is consistent across train and test, while the offline task does not provide segmentation at test time, requiring teams to perform segmentation to translate, similar to online or simultaneous conditions, which cascaded models may be more robust to. And finally, the ability to facilitate multilingual and zero-shot speech translation might be different in end-to-end and cascaded models.

5 Low-Resource Speech Translation

The goal of the low-resource speech translation task is to investigate pathways for developing speech translation systems for currently underserved languages. The majority of the world's languages are predominantly oral, hence the need for speech-based language tools (translation included) is paramount for them to be of any use to the language community. At the same time, most of these languages are also under-resourced, with little to no data being available for speech transcription and translation.

While offline speech translation has a longstanding tradition at the IWSLT campaign and both monolingual and multilingual models offer impressive promises for downstream model deployment, the majority of recent advances in speech translation both require large amounts of data and are typically benchmarked on language pairs with such data abundance. However, for the vast majority of the world's languages there exist little speech-translation parallel data at the scale needed to train modern speech translation models. Instead, in a real-world situation one will have access to limited, disparate resources (e.g. word-level translations, speech recognition, small parallel text data, monolingual text, raw audio, etc). The low-resource track aims to fill this gap, by encouraging and facilitating research on speech-translation for data-scarce language pairs.

5.1 Challenge

As described above, the shared task focused on the problem of developing speech transcription and translation tools for under-resourced languages. This year's iteration in particular focused on speech translation tools that would match the real-world needs of humanitarian organizations.

There were no restrictions on the type of models (e.g. end-to-end vs. cascade) or additional data that were allowed, the goal for the participants being producing the best possible system under these challenging settings. In collaboration with the Translators without Border, we provided newly collected speech and transcripts in two languages, Coastal Swahili (ISO code: swh) and Congolese Swahili (ISO code: swc), as well as translations in English and French respectively. In addition, we provided pointers to other monolingual speech datasets in the source Swahili varieties, as well as textual parallel corpora between the source and target languages.

5.2 Data and Metrics

The Swahili Varieties Speech Translation Dataset For the purposes of the task we created and released a new speech translation dataset for the two Swahili varieties. The new dataset is publicly available.[26]

The training data were derived from the Gamayun minikits that the Translators without Borders had released for Congolese and Coastal Swahili text translation (Öktem et al., 2020), which included sentence-level translations between Coastal Swahili and English as well as Congolese Swahili and French.[27] We additionally collected read versions for 5,000 sentences from this dataset. For each variety the training set includes voices from 6 speakers (3 male and 3 female). The collection was carried out using mobile phones, as opposed to clean studio settings, to better match the real-world use-case scenarios the shared task envisions.

The development and test data are derived from the TICO-19 dataset (Anastasopoulos et al., 2020), which is a multi-parallel evaluation benchmark on the COVID-19 domain in more than 33 languages. The original English sentences were translated into Coastal Swahili and French, and the French translations were then translated into Congolese Swahili. All translations were performed by professional translators and an extensive quality assurance process was followed. For the purposes of the shared task we additionally collected read utterances in the two Swahili varieties for all 3k sentences. We follow the original dev and test splits. The dev set utterances encompass 2 speakers (1

[26] https://drive.google.com/file/d/1lhifoEY0Kzj6s1lW_taKoVW_mAvzzZ04/view?usp=sharing

[27] This dataset was previously used for developing text-based translation systems for humanitarian response (Öktem et al., 2021).

Language Pair	Train #utt.	Train #speakers	Dev #utt.	Dev #speakers	Test #utt.	Test #speakers
swh-eng	4599	6 (3M, 3F)	868	2 (1M, 1F)	1063	3 (2M, 1F)
swc-fra	5000	6 (3M, 3F)	868	2 (1M, 1F)	2124	6 (3M, 3F)

Table 4: Statistics of the newly-released Swahili varieties speech translation corpus.

male, 1 female) in each language, and the test set includes 3 (2M, 1F) and 6 (3M, 3F) speakers for swh and swc respectively.

Statistics on the whole dataset used for the shared task following cleaning and preprocessing are listed in Table 4. The final dataset is 4-way parallel; the English and French sides are translations of each other, creating opportunities for the evaluation of multilingual systems, as well as, in the future, speech-to-speech translation between the two Swahili varieties.

Additional Data Last, we reiterate that we allowed the use of any other available data, such as any data from the Offline and Multilingual Shared Tasks, any speech recognition corpora like the Swahili ALFFA dataset (Gelas et al., 2012) or the Mozilla Common Voice datasets (Ardila et al., 2020), as well as any text translation datasets like the Gamayun minikits (Öktem et al., 2020). We also allowed the use of pre-trained models like wav2vec (Schneider et al., 2019; Baevski et al., 2020) or mBART (Liu et al., 2020) (among others).

Metrics Systems' performance was evaluated with respect to their capability to produce translations similar to the target-language references. We used the BLEU metric computed with SacreBLEU, in a case-insensitive setting. In addition, we invited participants who produced speech transcriptions in the Swahili variety as a by-product of their system (e.g. if they use a ASR+MT cascade approach) to also submit them. These were evaluated using case-insensitive word error rate (WER). The choice of case-insensitivity is due to our focus on producing *usable* output that aids comprehension; we deem that the effect of proper casing is largely minor in such challenging settings.

5.3 Submissions

The shared task received 4 submissions (9 total runs across the {swh,swc}×{eng,fra} pairs) from 3 teams. All teams followed a cascade ASR→MT approach in their primary submission – this indicates that end-to-end learning is still very challenging in such data-scarce settings, and leaves a lot of room for further future exploration.[28]

In the following, we provide an overview of each submission.

USYD-JD (Ding et al., 2021) uses a pipeline approach, focusing in the MT component and its ability to handle ASR errors. The ASR component is trained on the Swahili Varieties dataset, the ALFFA corpus, and the IARPA Babel Swahili Language Pack using the default settings in Kaldi, also lowercasing all sentences and removing punctuation. The final ASR is post-corrected with the SlotRefine method (Wu et al., 2020). The MT component is a Transformer (Vaswani et al., 2017) that operates in a non-autoregressive manner, trained on almost all available OPUS swa-eng datasets, but additionally utilizing denoising pre-training and bidirectional self-training, tagged back-translation, transductive fine-tuning, output reranking and output post-processing. This NMT system is the only that explores extensive strategies for denoising and pre-training, reaching a

IMS (Denisov et al., 2021) uses a pipeline approach. The ASR component for the primary submission is a Conformer (Gulati et al., 2020b) in its ESPnet implementation, trained by fine-tuning a pretrained SPGISpeech model (O'Neill et al., 2021) on both Swahili varieties using the Swahili Varieties dataset, Gamayun samples, the ALFFA corpus, and the IARPA Babel Swahili Language Pack, also applying some preprocessing steps like converting all numbers to words and removing punctuation. The MT system is a Transformer (Vaswani et al., 2017) using multi-task learning by tagging the input (to distinguish clean text vs. ASR output). They also attempted an end-

[28] We note that the shared task received more than 20 initial registrations. We suspect that the limited amount of received submissions was exactly because of how challenging it can be to create a system that produces decent outputs in these extremely low-resource settings.

to-end ST system which however performed significantly worse.

ON-TRAC (Le et al., 2021) used a pipeline approach, using a hybrid HMM/TDNN automatic speech recognition system fed by wav2vec (Schneider et al., 2019) features, with its output then provided to a neural MT system. The ASR system was trained on the Swahili Varieties dataset, the ALFFA corpus, and the IARPA Babel Swahili Language Pack. The NMT system uses LSTMs with attention, with the swa-eng also using subwords, while the swc-fra system operates at the word level. The swa-eng MT system was trained on 2.2M sentence pairs, resulting from the filtering through langID of all data available on OPUS.[29] The swc-fra NMT system was trained on 1.1M parallel sentences.

5.4 Results

Out of the submitted systems, the USYD-JD submission that explored pre-training strategies was the clear winner of the eng-swa task achieving a BLEU score (case insensitive) of 25.3. Notably, they only focused on the MT component of the pipeline, making it robust to ASR errors and utilizing monolingual data effectively through denoising and pre-training. For the swc-fra pair, the IMS system was the best performing submission for the swc-fra pair with a BLEU score of 13.5. The evaluation of all submissions (including optional language pairs and ASR transcription accuracy) is provided in the Appendix.

The difference in accuracy between the two language pairs could potentially be attributed to the lack of data in Congolese Swahili (as most available datasets are in the Coastal variety). However, the pre-training approaches that the USYD-JD submission uses seem very promising towards building robust MT systems also for the Congolese variety. A clear path for future work towards even better ST systems could explore a pipeline of the improved ASR systems of the ON-TRAC or IMS submissions with the NMT system of the USYD-JD submission. The lack of end-to-end approaches in the submissions (and the evidence from the IMS contrastive submission) suggest that additional research is needed in order to achieve competitive results in such data-scarce settings with end-to-end models.

[29] https://opus.nlpl.eu/

References

Yasuhiro Akiba, Marcello Federico, Noriko Kando, Hiromi Nakaiwa, Michael Paul, and Jun'ichi Tsujii. 2004. Overview of the IWSLT04 Evaluation Campaign. In *Proceedings of the International Workshop on Spoken Language Translation*, pages 1–12, Kyoto, Japan.

Antonios Anastasopoulos, Alessandro Cattelan, Zi-Yi Dou, Marcello Federico, Christian Federmann, Dmitriy Genzel, Franscisco Guzmán, Junjie Hu, Macduff Hughes, Philipp Koehn, et al. 2020. Tico-19: the translation initiative for covid-19. In *Proceedings of the 1st Workshop on NLP for COVID-19 (Part 2) at EMNLP 2020*.

Ebrahim Ansari, Amittai Axelrod, Nguyen Bach, Ondrej Bojar, Roldano Cattoni, Fahim Dalvi, Nadir Durrani, Marcello Federico, Christian Federmann, Jiatao Gu, Fei Huang, Kevin Knight, Xutai Ma, Ajay Nagesh, Matteo Negri, Jan Niehues, Juan Pino, Elizabeth Salesky, Xing Shi, Sebastian Stüker, Marco Turchi, and Changhan Wang. 2020. Findings of the IWSLT 2020 Evaluation Campaign. In *Proceedings of the 17th International Conference on Spoken Language Translation (IWSLT 2020)*, Seattle, USA.

Rosana Ardila, Megan Branson, Kelly Davis, Michael Kohler, Josh Meyer, Michael Henretty, Reuben Morais, Lindsay Saunders, Francis Tyers, and Gregor Weber. 2020. Common voice: A massively-multilingual speech corpus. In *Proceedings of The 12th Language Resources and Evaluation Conference*, pages 4218–4222.

Alexei Baevski, Yuhao Zhou, Abdelrahman Mohamed, and Michael Auli. 2020. wav2vec 2.0: A framework for self-supervised learning of speech representations. In *Advances in Neural Information Processing Systems*, volume 33, pages 12449–12460. Curran Associates, Inc.

Parnia Bahar, Tobias Bieschke, Ralf Schluter, and Hermann Ney. 2021a. Tight integrated end-to-end training for cascaded speech translation. In *Proceedings of the IEEE Spoken Language Technology Workshop*, pages 950–957, Shenzhen, China.

Parnia Bahar, Patrick Wilken, Tamer Alkhouli, Andreas Guta, Pavel Golik, Evgeny Matusov, and Christian Herold. 2020. Start-Before-End and End-to-End: Neural Speech Translation by AppTek and RWTH Aachen University. In *Proceedings of the 17th International Conference on Spoken Language Translation (IWSLT)*.

Parnia Bahar, Patrick Wilken, Mattia di Gangi, and Evgeny Matusov. 2021b. Without Further Ado: Direct and Simultaneous Speech Translation by AppTek in 2021. In *Proceedings of the 18th International Conference on Spoken Language Translation (IWSLT)*.

Dzmitry Bahdanau, Kyung Hyun Cho, and Yoshua Bengio. 2015. Neural machine translation by jointly learning to align and translate. In *Proceedings of the 3rd International Conference on Learning Representations, ICLR 2015.*

Ankur Bapna and Orhan Firat. 2019. Simple, scalable adaptation for neural machine translation. In *Proceedings of the 2019 Conference on Empirical Methods in Natural Language Processing and the 9th International Joint Conference on Natural Language Processing (EMNLP-IJCNLP)*, pages 1538–1548, Hong Kong, China. Association for Computational Linguistics.

Loïc Barrault, Magdalena Biesialska, Ondřej Bojar, Marta R. Costa-jussà, Christian Federmann, Yvette Graham, Roman Grundkiewicz, Barry Haddow, Matthias Huck, Eric Joanis, Tom Kocmi, Philipp Koehn, Chi-kiu Lo, Nikola Ljubešić, Christof Monz, Makoto Morishita, Masaaki Nagata, Toshiaki Nakazawa, Santanu Pal, Matt Post, and Marcos Zampieri. 2020. Findings of the 2020 conference on machine translation (WMT20). In *Proceedings of the Fifth Conference on Machine Translation*, pages 1–55, Online. Association for Computational Linguistics.

Benjamin Beilharz and Xin Sun. 2019. LibriVoxDeEn - A Corpus for German-to-English Speech Translation and Speech Recognition.

Luisa Bentivogli, Mauro Cettolo, Marco Gaido, Alina Karakanta, Alberto Martinelli, and Marco Turchi Matteo Negri. 2021. Cascade versus Direct Speech Translation: Do the Differences Still Make a Difference? In *Proceedings of the 59th Annual Meeting of the Association for Computational Linguistics*, Bangkok, Thailand. Association for Computational Linguistics.

Roldano Cattoni, Mattia Antonino Di Gangi, Luisa Bentivogli, Matteo Negri, and Marco Turchi. 2021. Must-c: A multilingual corpus for end-to-end speech translation. *Computer Speech & Language*, 66:101155.

Mauro Cettolo, Marcello Federico, Luisa Bentivogli, Jan Niehues, Sebastian Stüker, K. Sudoh, K. Yoshino, and Christian Federmann. 2017. Overview of the IWSLT 2017 Evaluation Campaign. In *Proceedings of the 14th International Workshop on Spoken Language Translation (IWSLT 2017)*, pages 2–14, Tokyo, Japan.

Mauro Cettolo, Christian Girardi, and Marcello Federico. 2012. WIT^3: Web Inventory of Transcribed and Translated Talks. In *Proceedings of the Annual Conference of the European Association for Machine Translation (EAMT)*, Trento, Italy.

Mauro Cettolo, Jan Niehues, Sebastian Stüker, Luisa Bentivogli, Roldano Cattoni, and Marcello Federico. 2015. The IWSLT 2015 Evaluation Campaign. In *Proceedings of the 12th International Workshop on Spoken Language Translation (IWSLT 2015)*, Da Nang, Vietnam.

Mauro Cettolo, Jan Niehues, Sebastian Stüker, Luisa Bentivogli, and Marcello Federico. 2013. Report on the 10th IWSLT Evaluation Campaign. In *Proceedings of the Tenth International Workshop on Spoken Language Translation (IWSLT 2013)*, Heidelberg, Germany.

Mauro Cettolo, Jan Niehues, Sebastian Stüker, Luisa Bentivogli, and Marcello Federico. 2014. Report on the 11th IWSLT Evaluation Campaign, IWSLT 2014. In *Proceedings of the Eleventh International Workshop on Spoken Language Translation (IWSLT 2014)*, Lake Tahoe, USA.

Mauro Cettolo, Jan Niehues, Sebastian Stüker, Luisa Bentivogli, and Marcello Federico. 2016. The IWSLT 2016 Evaluation Campaign. In *Proceedings of the 13th International Workshop on Spoken Language Translation (IWSLT 2016)*, Seattle, USA.

Colin Cherry and George Foster. 2019. Thinking slow about latency evaluation for simultaneous machine translation. *arXiv preprint arXiv:1906.00048*.

Pavel Denisov, Manuel Mager, and Ngoc Thang Vu. 2021. IMS' Systems for the IWSLT 2021 Low-Resource Speech Translation Task. In *Proceedings of the 18th International Conference on Spoken Language Translation (IWSLT)*.

Mattia A. Di Gangi, Roldano Cattoni, Luisa Bentivogli, Matteo Negri, and Marco Turchi. 2019. MuST-C: a Multilingual Speech Translation Corpus. In *Proceedings of the 2019 Conference of the North American Chapter of the Association for Computational Linguistics: Human Language Technologies, Volume 1 (Long and Short Papers)*, pages 2012–2017, Minneapolis, Minnesota.

Liang Ding, Di Wu, and Dacheng Tao. 2021. The USYD-JD's Speech Translation System for IWSLT2021. In *Proceedings of the 18th International Conference on Spoken Language Translation (IWSLT)*.

Kosuke Doi, Katsuhito Sudoh, and Satoshi Nakamura. 2021. Large-Scale English-Japanese Simultaneous Interpretation Corpus: Construction and Analyses with Sentence-Aligned Data. In *Proceedings of the 18th International Conference on Spoken Language Translation (IWSLT)*.

Matthias Eck and Chiori Hori. 2005. Overview of the IWSLT 2005 evaluation campaign. In *Proceedings of the International Workshop on Spoken Language Translation*, pages 1–22, Pittsburgh, PA.

Maha Elbayad, Laurent Besacier, and Jakob Verbeek. 2020. Efficient Wait-k Models for Simultaneous Machine Translation. In *Proc. Interspeech 2020*, pages 1461–1465.

Carlos Escolano, Marta R. Costa-jussà, José A. R. Fonollosa, and Carlos Segura. 2020. Enabling zero-shot multilingual spoken language translation with language-specific encoders and decoders.

Marcello Federico, Luisa Bentivogli, Michael Paul, and Sebastian Stüker. 2011. Overview of the IWSLT 2011 Evaluation Campaign. In *Proceedings of the International Workshop on Spoken Language Translation*, pages 11–27, San Francisco, USA.

Marcello Federico, Mauro Cettolo, Luisa Bentivogli, Michael Paul, and Sebastian Stüker. 2012. Overview of the IWSLT 2012 Evaluation Campaign. In *Proceedings of the International Workshop on Spoken Language Translation*, pages 11–27, Hong Kong, HK.

Cameron Shaw Fordyce. 2007. Overview of the IWSLT 2007 evaluation campaign. In *Proceedings of the International Workshop on Spoken Language Translation*, pages 1–12, Trento, Italy.

Ryo Fukuda, Yui Oka, Yausumasa Kano, Yuki Yano, Yuka Ko, Hirotaka Tokuyama, Kosuke Doi, Sakriani Sakti, Katsuhito Sudoh, and Satoshi Nakamura. 2021. NAIST English-to-Japanese Simultaneous Translation System for IWSLT 2021 Simultaneous Text-to-text Task. In *Proceedings of the 18th International Conference on Spoken Language Translation (IWSLT)*.

Marco Gaido, Mattia Antonino Di Gangi, Matteo Negri, Mauro Cettolo, and Marco Turchi. 2020a. Contextualized translation of automatically segmented speech. In *Proceedings of Interspeech 2020, 21st Annual Conference of the International Speech Communication Association*, pages 1471—-1475, Shanghai, China.

Marco Gaido, Mattia Antonio Di Gangi, Matteo Negri, and Marco Turchi. 2020b. End-to-End Speech-Translation with Knowledge Distillation: FBK@IWSLT2020. In *Proceedings of the 17th International Conference on Spoken Language Translation (IWSLT)*.

Marco Gaido, Matteo Negri, Mauro Cettolo, and Marco Turchi. 2021. Beyond voice activity detection: Hybrid audio segmentation for direct speech translation.

Gerard I. Gállego, Ioannis Tsiamas, Carlos Escolano, and Marta R. Costa-jussà José A. R. Fonollosa. 2021. UPC's Speech Translation System for IWSLT 2021. In *Proceedings of the 18th International Conference on Spoken Language Translation (IWSLT)*.

Hadrien Gelas, Laurent Besacier, and Francois Pellegrino. 2012. Developments of Swahili resources for an automatic speech recognition system. In *SLTU - Workshop on Spoken Language Technologies for Under-Resourced Languages*, Cape-Town, Afrique Du Sud.

Anmol Gulati, James Qin, Chung-Cheng Chiu, Niki Parmar, Yu Zhang, Jiahui Yu, Wei Han, Shibo Wang, Zhengdong Zhang, Yonghui Wu, and Ruoming Pang. 2020a. Conformer: Convolution-augmented transformer for speech recognition. In *Proceedings of Interspeech 2020, 21st Annual Conference of the International Speech Communication Association*, pages 5036—-5040, Shanghai, China.

Anmol Gulati, James Qin, Chung-Cheng Chiu, Niki Parmar, Yu Zhang, Jiahui Yu, Wei Han, Shibo Wang, Zhengdong Zhang, Yonghui Wu, and Ruoming Pang. 2020b. Conformer: Convolution-augmented transformer for speech recognition. *Interspeech*, pages 5036–5040.

François Hernandez, Vincent Nguyen, Sahar Ghannay, Natalia A. Tomashenko, and Yannick Estève. 2018. TED-LIUM 3: twice as much data and corpus repartition for experiments on speaker adaptation. *CoRR*, abs/1805.04699.

Wenyong Huang, Wenchao Hu, Yu Ting Yeung, and Xiao Chen. 2020. Conv-transformer transducer: Low latency, low frame rate, streamable end-to-end speech recognition. *INTERSPEECH*.

Hirofumi Inaguma, Brian Yan, Siddharth Dalmia, Pengcheng Guo, Jiatong Shi, Kevin Duh, and Shinji Watanabe. 2021. ESPnet-ST IWSLT 2021 Offline Speech Translation System. In *Proceedings of the 18th International Conference on Spoken Language Translation (IWSLT)*.

Javier Iranzo-Sánchez, Joan Albert Silvestre-Cerdà, Javier Jorge, Nahuel Roselló, Adrià Giménez, Albert Sanchis, Jorge Civera, and Alfons Juan. 2020. Europarl-st: A multilingual corpus for speech translation of parliamentary debates. In *Proc. of 45th Intl. Conf. on Acoustics, Speech, and Signal Processing (ICASSP 2020)*, pages 8229–8233, Barcelona (Spain).

Yong Rae Jo, Young Ki Moon, Minji Jung, Jungyoon Choi, Jihyung Moon, and Won Ik Cho. 2021. VUS at IWSLT 2021: A Finetuned Pipeline for Offline Speech Translation. In *Proceedings of the 18th International Conference on Spoken Language Translation (IWSLT)*.

Ali Can Kocabiyikoglu, Laurent Besacier, and Olivier Kraif. 2018. Augmenting Librispeech with French Translations: A Multimodal Corpus for Direct Speech Translation Evaluation. In *Proceedings of LREC 2018*, Miyazaki, Japan.

Hang Le, Florentier Barbier, Ha Nguyen, Natalia Tomanshenko, Salima Mdhaffar, Souhir Gahbiche, Fethi Bougares, Benjamin Lecouteux, Didier Schwab, and Yannick Esteve. 2021. ON-TRAC's systems for the IWSLT 2021 low-resource speech translation and multilingual speech translation shared tasks. In *Proceedings of the 18th International Conference on Spoken Language Translation (IWSLT)*.

Hang Le, Juan Pino, Changhan Wang, Jiatao Gu, Didier Schwab, and Laurent Besacier. 2020. Dual-decoder transformer for joint automatic speech recognition and multilingual speech translation. In *COLING*, pages 3520–3533.

Xian Li, Changhan Wang, Yun Tang, Chau Tran, Yuqing Tang, Juan Pino, Alexei Baevski, Alexis Conneau, and Michael Auli. 2021. Multilingual speech translation with efficient finetuning of pretrained models.

Pierre Lison, Jörg Tiedemann, and Milen Kouylekov. 2018. OpenSubtitles2018: Statistical rescoring of sentence alignments in large, noisy parallel corpora. In *Proceedings of the Eleventh International Conference on Language Resources and Evaluation (LREC 2018)*, Miyazaki, Japan. European Language Resources Association (ELRA).

Dan Liu, Mengge Du, Xiaoxi Li, Yuchen Hu, and Lirong Dai. 2021. The USTC-NELSLIP Systems for Simultaneous Speech Translation Task at IWSLT 2021. In *Proceedings of the 18th International Conference on Spoken Language Translation (IWSLT)*.

Danni Liu and Jan Niehues. 2021. Maastricht University's Multilingual Speech Translation System for IWSLT 2021. In *Proceedings of the 18th International Conference on Spoken Language Translation (IWSLT)*.

Yinhan Liu, Jiatao Gu, Naman Goyal, Xian Li, Sergey Edunov, Marjan Ghazvininejad, Mike Lewis, and Luke Zettlemoyer. 2020. Multilingual denoising pre-training for neural machine translation. *Transactions of the Association for Computational Linguistics*, 8:726–742.

Yiping Lu, Zhuohan Li, Di He, Zhiqing Sun, Bin Dong, Tao Qin, Liwei Wang, and Tie-Yan Liu. 2019. Understanding and improving transformer from a multi-particle dynamic system point of view. *arXiv preprint arXiv:1906.02762*.

Xutai Ma, Mohammad Javad Dousti, Changhan Wang, Jiatao Gu, and Juan Pino. 2020a. SIMULEVAL: An evaluation toolkit for simultaneous translation. In *Proceedings of the 2020 Conference on Empirical Methods in Natural Language Processing: System Demonstrations*, pages 144–150, Online. Association for Computational Linguistics.

Xutai Ma, Juan Pino, and Philipp Koehn. 2020b. SimulMT to SimulST: Adapting simultaneous text translation to end-to-end simultaneous speech translation. In *Proceedings of the 1st Conference of the Asia-Pacific Chapter of the Association for Computational Linguistics and the 10th International Joint Conference on Natural Language Processing*, pages 582–587, Suzhou, China. Association for Computational Linguistics.

Tuan-Nam Nguyen, Thai-Son Nguyen, Christian Huber, Maximilian Awiszus, Ngoc-Quan Pham, Thanh-Le Ha, Felix Schneider, Sebastian Stuker, and Alexander Waibel. 2021. KIT's IWSLT 2021 Offline Speech Translation System. In *Proceedings of the 18th International Conference on Spoken Language Translation (IWSLT)*.

J. Niehues, R. Cattoni, S. Stüker, M. Negri, M. Turchi, T. Ha, E. Salesky, R. Sanabria, L. Barrault, L. Specia, and M. Federico. 2019. The IWSLT 2019 Evaluation Campaign. In *Proceedings of the 16th International Workshop on Spoken Language Translation (IWSLT 2019)*, Hong Kong, China.

Jan Niehues, Roldano Cattoni, Sebastian Stüker, Mauro Cettolo, Marco Turchi, and Marcello Federico. 2018. The IWSLT 2018 Evaluation Campaign. In *Proceedings of the 15th International Workshop on Spoken Language Translation (IWSLT 2018)*, pages 2–6, Bruges, Belgium.

Alp Öktem, Eric DeLuca, Rodrigue Bashizi, Eric Paquin, and Grace Tang. 2021. Congolese swahili machine translation for humanitarian response. arXiv:2103.10734.

Alp Öktem, Muhannad Albayk Jaam, Eric DeLuca, and Grace Tang. 2020. Gamayun-language technology for humanitarian response. In *2020 IEEE Global Humanitarian Technology Conference (GHTC)*, pages 1–4. IEEE.

Patrick K O'Neill, Vitaly Lavrukhin, Somshubra Majumdar, Vahid Noroozi, Yuekai Zhang, Oleksii Kuchaiev, Jagadeesh Balam, Yuliya Dovzhenko, Keenan Freyberg, Michael D Shulman, et al. 2021. Spgispeech: 5,000 hours of transcribed financial audio for fully formatted end-to-end speech recognition. arXiv:2104.02014.

Myle Ott, Sergey Edunov, Alexei Baevski, Angela Fan, Sam Gross, Nathan Ng, David Grangier, and Michael Auli. 2019. fairseq: A fast, extensible toolkit for sequence modeling. In *Proceedings of NAACL-HLT 2019: Demonstrations*.

Vassil Panayotov, Guoguo Chen, Daniel Povey, and Sanjeev Khudanpur. 2015. Librispeech: An asr corpus based on public domain audio books. *2015 IEEE International Conference on Acoustics, Speech and Signal Processing (ICASSP)*, pages 5206–5210.

Sara Papi, Marco Gaido, Matteo Negri, and Marco Turchi. 2021. Dealing with training and test segmentation mismatch: FBK@IWSLT2021. In *Proceedings of the 18th International Conference on Spoken Language Translation (IWSLT)*.

Kishore Papineni, Salim Roukos, Todd Ward, and Wei-Jing Zhu. 2002a. Bleu: a method for automatic evaluation of machine translation. In *Proceedings of the 40th annual meeting on association for computational linguistics*. Association for Computational Linguistics.

Kishore Papineni, Salim Roukos, Todd Ward, and Wei-Jing Zhu. 2002b. BLEU: a Method for Automatic Evaluation of Machine Translation. In *Proceedings of the 40th Annual Meeting of the Association for Computational Linguistics (ACL)*, pages 311–318, Philadelphia, USA.

Daniel S. Park, William Chan, Yu Zhang, Chung-Cheng Chiu, Barret Zoph, Ekin D. Cubuk, and Quoc V. Le. 2019. SpecAugment: A Simple Data Augmentation Method for Automatic Speech Recognition. *Interspeech 2019*.

Michael Paul. 2006. Overview of the IWSLT 2006 Evaluation Campaign. In *Proceedings of the International Workshop on Spoken Language Translation*, pages 1–15, Kyoto, Japan.

Michael Paul. 2008. Overview of the IWSLT 2008 Evaluation Campaign. In *Proceedings of the International Workshop on Spoken Language Translation*, pages 1–17, Waikiki, Hawaii.

Michael Paul. 2009. Overview of the IWSLT 2009 Evaluation Campaign. In *Proceedings of the International Workshop on Spoken Language Translation*, pages 1–18, Tokyo, Japan.

Michael Paul, Marcello Federico, and Sebastian Stüker. 2010. Overview of the IWSLT 2010 Evaluation Campaign. In *Proceedings of the International Workshop on Spoken Language Translation*, pages 3–27, Paris, France.

Ngoc-Quan Pham, Thanh-Le Ha, Tuan-Nam Nguyen, Thai-Son Nguyen, Elizabeth Salesky, Sebastian Stüker, Jan Niehues, and Alex Waibel. 2020a. Relative positional encoding for speech recognition and direct translation. In *INTERSPEECH*, pages 31–35. ISCA.

Ngoc-Quan Pham, Thanh-Le Ha, Tuan-Nam Nguyen, Thai-Son Nguyen, Elizabeth Salesky, Sebastian Stüker, Jan Niehues, and Alex Waibel. 2020b. Relative positional encoding for speech recognition and direct translation. In *INTERSPEECH*, pages 31–35. ISCA.

Ngoc-Quan Pham, Dan He, Tuan-Nam Nguyen, Thanh-Le Ha, Sebastian Stuker, and Alexander Waibel. 2021. Multilingual Speech Translation KIT @ IWSLT2021. In *Proceedings of the 18th International Conference on Spoken Language Translation (IWSLT)*.

Ngoc-Quan Pham, Thai-Son Nguyen, Jan Niehues, Markus Müller, Sebastian Stüker, and Alexander Waibel. 2019. Very deep self-attention networks for end-to-end speech recognition.

Ngoc-Quan Pham, Felix Schneider, Tuan-Nam Nguyen, Thanh-Le Ha, Thai-Son Nguyen, Maximilian Awiszus, Sebastian Stüker, and Alexander Waibel. 2020c. KIT's IWSLT 2020 SLT Translation System. In *Proceedings of the 17th International Conference on Spoken Language Translation (IWSLT)*.

Matt Post. 2018. A call for clarity in reporting BLEU scores. In *Proceedings of the Third Conference on Machine Translation: Research Papers*, pages 186–191, Belgium, Brussels. Association for Computational Linguistics.

Tomasz Potapczyk and Pawel Przybysz. 2020. SRPOL's System for the IWSLT 2020 End-to-End Speech Translation Task. In *Proceedings of the 17th International Conference on Spoken Language Translation (IWSLT)*.

Tomasz Potapczyk, Pawel Przybysz, Marcin Chochowski, and Artur; Szumaczuk. 2019. Samsung's System for the IWSLT 2019 End-to-End Speech Translation Task. In *Proceedings of 16th International Workshop on Spoken Language Translation (IWSLT)*, Hong Kong.

Anthony Rousseau, Paul Deléglise, and Yannick Esteve. 2014. Enhancing the ted-lium corpus with selected data for language modeling and more ted talks. In *LREC*.

Elizabeth Salesky, Matthew Wiesner, Jacob Bremerman, Roldano Cattoni, Matteo Negri, Marco Turchi, Douglas W. Oard, and Matt Post. 2021. Multilingual tedx corpus for speech recognition and translation.

Ramon Sanabria, Ozan Caglayan, Shruti Palaskar, Desmond Elliott, Loïc Barrault, Lucia Specia, and Florian Metze. 2018. How2: a large-scale dataset for multimodal language understanding. In *Proceedings of the Workshop on Visually Grounded Interaction and Language (ViGIL)*. NeurIPS.

Steffen Schneider, Alexei Baevski, Ronan Collobert, and Michael Auli. 2019. wav2vec: Unsupervised pre-training for speech recognition. In *INTERSPEECH*.

Sukanta Sen, Ulrich Germann, and Barry Haddow. 2021. The University of Edinburgh's Submission to the IWSLT21 Simultaneous Translation Task. In *Proceedings of the 18th International Conference on Spoken Language Translation (IWSLT)*.

Peter Shaw, Jakob Uszkoreit, and Ashish Vaswani. 2018. Self-attention with relative position representations. In *Proceedings of the 2018 Conference of the North American Chapter of the Association for Computational Linguistics: Human Language Technologies, Volume 2 (Short Papers)*, pages 464–468, New Orleans, Louisiana. Association for Computational Linguistics.

Matthew Snover, Bonnie Dorr, Richard Schwartz, Linnea Micciulla, and John Makhoul. 2006. A Study of Translation Edit Rate with Targeted Human Annotation. In *Proceedings of the The Seventh Conference of the Association for Machine Translation in the Americas (AMTA)*, pages 223–231, Cambridge, USA.

Milos Stanojevic and Khalil Sima'an. 2014. BEER: BEtter evaluation as ranking. In *Proceedings of the Ninth Workshop on Statistical Machine Translation*. Association for Computational Linguistics.

Yun Tang, Hongyu Gong, Xian Li, Changhan Wang, Juan Pino, Holger Schwenk, and Naman Goyal. 2021a. FST: the FAIR Speech Translation System for the IWSLT21 Multilingual Shared Task. In *Proceedings of the 18th International Conference on Spoken Language Translation (IWSLT)*.

Yun Tang, Juan Pino, Changhan Wang, Xutai Ma, and Dmitriy Genzel. 2021b. A general multi-task learning framework to leverage text data for speech to text tasks.

Ashish Vaswani, Noam Shazeer, Niki Parmar, Jakob Uszkoreit, Llion Jones, Aidan N Gomez, Łukasz Kaiser, and Illia Polosukhin. 2017. Attention is All You Need. In *Proceedings of NIPS 2017*.

Hari Krishna Vydana, Martin Karafiát, Lukáš Burget, and Honza Černocky. 2021. The IWSLT 2021 BUT Speech Translation Systems. In *Proceedings of the 18th International Conference on Spoken Language Translation (IWSLT)*.

Changhan Wang, Juan Pino, Anne Wu, and Jiatao Gu. 2020. Covost: A diverse multilingual speech-to-text translation corpus. In *Proceedings of The 12th Language Resources and Evaluation Conference*, pages 4197–4203.

Changhan Wang, Morgane Rivière, Ann Lee, Anne Wu, Chaitanya Talnikar, Daniel Haziza, Mary Williamson, Juan Pino, and Emmanuel Dupoux. 2021. Voxpopuli: A large-scale multilingual speech corpus for representation learning, semi-supervised learning and interpretation. *arXiv preprint arXiv:2101.00390*.

Weiyue Wang, Jan-Thorsten Peter, Hendrik Rosendahl, and Hermann Ney. 2016. CharacTer: Translation edit rate on character level. In *Proceedings of the First Conference on Machine Translation: Volume 2, Shared Task Papers*. Association for Computational Linguistics.

Di Wu, Liang Ding, Fan Lu, and Jian Xie. 2020. Slotrefine: A fast non-autoregressive model for joint intent detection and slot filling. In *Proceedings of the 2020 Conference on Empirical Methods in Natural Language Processing (EMNLP)*, pages 1932–1937.

Chen Xu, Bojie Hu, Yanyang Li, Yuhao Zhang, shen huang, Qi Ju, Tong Xiao, and Jingbo Zhu. 2021a. Stacked acoustic-and-textual encoding: Integrating the pre-trained models into speech translation encoders.

Chen Xu, Xiaoqian Liu, Xiaowen Liu, Laohu Wang, Canan Huang, Tong Xiao, and Jingbo Zhu. 2021b. The NiuTrans End-to-End Speech Translation System for IWSLT 2021 Offline Task. In *Proceedings of the 18th International Conference on Spoken Language Translation (IWSLT)*.

Xingshan Zeng, Liangyou Li, and Qun Liu. 2021. Multilingual Speech Translation with Unified Transformer: Huawei Noah's Ark Lab at IWSLT 2021. In *Proceedings of the 18th International Conference on Spoken Language Translation (IWSLT)*.

Albert Zeyer, Kazuki Irie, Ralf Schlüter, and Hermann Ney. 2018. Improved training of end-to-end attention models for speech recognition. In *Interspeech*, Hyderabad, India.

Biao Zhang and Rico Sennrich. 2021. Edinburgh's End-to-End Multilingual Speech Translation System for IWSLT 2021. In *Proceedings of the 18th International Conference on Spoken Language Translation (IWSLT)*.

Biao Zhang, Ivan Titov, Barry Haddow, and Rico Sennrich. 2020. Adaptive feature selection for end-to-end speech translation. In *Findings of EMNLP*, pages 2533–2544.

Linlin Zhang. 2021. ZJU's IWSLT 2021 Speech Translation System. In *Proceedings of the 18th International Conference on Spoken Language Translation (IWSLT)*.

Chengqi Zhao, Zhicheng Liu, Jian Tong, Tao Wang, Mingxuan Wang, Rong Ye, Qianqian Dong, Jun Cao, and Lei Li. 2021. The Volctrans Neural Speech Translation System for IWSLT 2021. In *Proceedings of the 18th International Conference on Spoken Language Translation (IWSLT)*.

Appendix A. Evaluation Results and Details

A.1. Simultaneous Speech Translation

· Summary of the results of the simultaneous speech translation **text track.**
· Results are reported on the blind test set and systems are grouped by latency regime (set on tst-COMMON v2 or IWSLT21 dev set)
· Raw system logs are also provided on the task web site.[30]

English-German	**tst-COMMON v2**				**Blind Test Set**			
	BLEU	AL	AP	DAL	BLEU	AL	AP	DAL
				Low Latency				
USTC-NESLIP	33.16	2.66	0.64	4.38	26.89	2.81	0.63	4.72
VOLCTRANS	28.76	2.86	0.69	4.22	23.24	3.08	0.68	4.25
APPTEK	30.03	2.94	0.68	4.40	22.84	3.12	0.66	4.66
UEDIN	25.06	2.33	0.63	3.69	22.30	4.22	0.71	5.54
				Medium Latency				
USTC-NESLIP	34.82	5.80	0.80	8.89	29.40	5.94	0.78	9.29
VOLCTRANS	32.88	5.80	0.83	9.05	27.22	6.30	0.81	9.24
APPTEK	31.73	5.89	0.80	9.57	25.70	6.22	0.78	10.40
UEDIN	30.58	5.89	0.80	7.20	24.56	6.92	0.81	8.20
				High Latency				
USTC-NESLIP	35.47	12.21	0.95	15.18	30.03	12.35	0.93	16.33
VOLCTRANS	33.23	11.03	0.93	11.40	26.82	12.03	0.92	12.39
APPTEK	33.16	11.19	0.92	14.44	26.62	12.00	0.91	16.05
UEDIN	33.10	14.69	0.98	15.17	26.50	15.41	0.96	16.04

English-Japanese	**IWSLT 21 DEV**				**Blind Test Set**			
	BLEU	AL	AP	DAL	BLEU	AL	AP	DAL
				Low Latency				
USTC-NESLIP	16.36	4.90	0.79	10.30	17.54	4.92	0.78	8.18
VOLCTRANS	15.80	6.34	0.89	13.57	16.91	6.54	0.89	11.26
NAIST	13.77	7.29	0.88	8.07	14.41	7.21	0.88	7.97
				Medium Latency				
USTC-NESLIP	17.53	8.42	0.92	11.81	18.30	7.61	0.90	10.59
VOLCTRANS	15.80	6.34	0.89	13.57	16.91	6.54	0.89	11.26
NAIST	15.22	11.48	0.97	11.98	16.20	11.54	0.97	11.98
				High Latency				
USTC-NESLIP	17.28	11.67	0.97	11.14	18.17	11.71	0.97	13.72
VOLCTRANS	15.85	11.19	0.97	0.97	16.97	11.27	0.97	11.90
NAIST	15.57	13.70	0.99	13.91	16.19	13.83	0.99	14.01

[30] https://iwslt.org/2021/simultaneous

· Summary of the results of the simultaneous speech translation (segmented and unsegmented) **speech track**
· Results are reported on the blind test set and systems are grouped by latency regime (set on tst-COMMON v2, only segmented input.)
· Raw logs are also provided on the task web site.

English-German	tst-COMMON v2						
	BLEU	AL	AP	DAL	AL(CA)	AP(CA)	DAL(CA)
Low Latency							
USTC-NESLIP	27.40	0.92	0.68	1.42	2.33	1.33	4.38
Medium Latency							
USTC-NESLIP	29.68	1.86	0.82	2.65	3.66	1.48	5.36
APPTEK	24.88	1.96	0.88	3.08	3.37	1.17	4.10
High Latency							
USTC-NESLIP	30.75	2.74	0.90	3.63	5.05	1.56	6.23
APPTEK	26.77	3.00	0.99	5.48	6.66	1.32	6.93

English-German	Blind Test Set						
	BLEU	AL	AP	DAL	AL(CA)	AP(CA)	DAL(CA)
Low Latency							
USTC-NESLIP	21.85	1.04	0.66	1.47	2.99	1.52	6.41
Medium Latency							
USTC-NESLIP	24.83	1.96	0.80	2.79	4.49	1.63	7.15
APPTEK	16.60	1.95	0.80	2.73	2.86	1.06	3.86
High Latency							
USTC-NESLIP	25.62	2.86	0.88	3.85	6.10	1.68	7.93
APPTEK	21.08	3.99	0.94	5.06	5.00	1.16	6.12
Unsegmented							
USTC-NESLIP	25.31	30.91	0.51	26.47	264.28	1.10	536.54
APPTEK	15.03	107.11	0.44	32.92	149.52	0.63	175.79

A.2. Offline Speech Translation

Speech Translation: TED English-German tst 2021

· Systems are ordered according to BLEU_NewRef: *BLEU* score computed on the NEW reference set (literal translations).
· *BLEU* scores are given as percent figures (%).
· End-to-end systems are indicated by gray background.
· The "segm." column indicates the segmentation strategy (Own vs **Given**).
· The "data condition" indicates the training data condition (Constrained vs **Unconstrained**).
· The † symbol indicates an end-to-end submission exploiting pre-trained models (not all parameters are jointly trained).

System	segm.	data condition	BLEU_NewRef	BLEU_TEDRef	BLEU_MultiRef
HW-TSC	Own	Constrained	24.6	20.3	34.0
KIT	Own	Constrained	23.4	19.0	32.0
APPTEK	Own	Constrained	22.6	18.3	31.0
KIT	Own	Constrained	22.0	18.1	30.3
APPTEK	Own	Constrained	21.9	18.1	30.4
VOLCTRANS	**Given**	Constrained	21.8	17.1	29.5
UPC†	Own	**Unconstrained**	21.8	18.3	30.6
VOLCTRANS	**Given**	Constrained	21.7	18.7	31.3
ESPNET-ST	Own	Constrained	21.7	18.2	30.6
FBK	Own	Constrained	21.6	18.4	30.6
OPPO	**Given**	Constrained	21.5	17.8	30.2
ESPNET-ST	Own	Constrained	21.2	19.3	31.4
NIUTRANS	Own	Constrained	20.6	19.6	30.3
VUS	**Given**	Constrained	15.3	12.4	20.9
BUT	**Given**	**Unconstrained**	11.7	9.8	16.1
LI	**Given**	Constrained	3.6	2.7	4.8

Speech Translation: TED English-German tst 2020

· Systems are ordered according to BLEU_TEDRef: *BLEU* score computed on the ORIGINAL reference set.
· *BLEU* scores are given as percent figures (%).
· End-to-end systems are indicated by gray background.
· The "segm." column indicates the segmentation strategy (Own vs **Given**).
· The "data condition" indicates the training data condition (Constrained vs **Unconstrained**).
· The † symbol indicates an end-to-end submission exploiting pre-trained models (not all parameters are jointly trained).

System	segm.	data condition	BLEU_TEDRef
ESPNET-ST	Own	Constrained	26.0
HW-TSC	Own	Constrained	25.4
KIT	Own	Constrained	25.4
ESPNET-ST	Own	Constrained	24.7
FBK	Own	Constrained	24.7
UPC†	Own	**Unconstrained**	24.6
APPTEK	Own	Constrained	24.5
VOLCTRANS	**Given**	Constrained	24.3
KIT	Own	Constrained	23.2
APPTEK	Own	Constrained	23.1
NIUTRANS	Own	Constrained	22.8
OPPO	**Given**	Constrained	22.6
VOLCTRANS	**Given**	Constrained	22.2
VUS	**Given**	Constrained	13.7
BUT	**Given**	**Unconstrained**	11.4
LI	**Given**	Constrained	0.2

A.3. Multilingual Speech Translation

· Submissions are ordered according to average ST performance across all official language pairs.
· ST systems are scored using the BLEU↑ metric as computed by SACREBLEU (Post, 2018).
· ASR systems are scored using WER↓ computed on lowercased text with punctuation removed.

Official Results:

	Condition			Supervised				Zero-shot			Avg
System	Constrained	E2E	Ensemble	es-en	fr-en	fr-es	pt-en	pt-es	it-en	it-es	
FAIR		✓	✓	42.2	38.7	36.5	31.0	38.2	29.4	37.3	36.2
KIT	✓		✓	39.3	27.1	29.2	30.7	37.3	26.5	32.4	31.8
UEDIN	✓	✓	✓	36.2	26.4	29.5	27.0	34.5	23.0	31.1	29.7
UM-DKE	✓	✓	✓	33.9	25.4	27.6	25.7	33.7	22.8	29.4	28.4
ZJU	✓		✓	34.5	25.2	27.4	25.7	31.6	20.8	27.3	27.5
HWN	✓	✓	✓	35.4	26.7	27.0	26.7	27.0	17.6	15.4	25.1
ON-TRAC	✓	✓		20.2	14.4	15.0	13.2	3.0	4.2	4.6	10.7

Table 5: **Multilingual ST:** Results of primary submissions on official language pairs in BLEU↑

All Submissions:

System		Condition			Supervised				Zero-shot			Avg
		Constrained	E2E	Ensemble	es-en	fr-en	fr-es	pt-en	pt-es	it-en	it-es	
FAIR	primary		✓	✓	42.2	38.7	36.5	31.0	38.2	29.4	37.3	36.2
FAIR	joint_U_W		✓		41.5	37.4	35.2	29.2	36.8	29.1	36.8	35.1
FAIR	joint_U		✓		40.4	36.4	34.4	29.0	38.2	28.4	34.6	33.9
FAIR	joint_X		✓		40.6	36.5	34.7	28.2	38.2	27.8	33.3	33.5
KIT	contrastive	✓	✓		38.9	28.5	29.7	30.2	37.1	25.8	33.0	31.9
KIT	primary	✓		✓	39.3	27.1	29.2	30.7	37.3	26.5	32.4	31.8
UEDIN	primary	✓	✓	✓	36.2	26.4	29.5	27.0	34.5	23.0	31.1	29.7
UEDIN	contrastive	✓	✓		35.0	25.5	28.8	26.2	33.3	22.4	30.1	28.8
UM-DKE	primary	✓	✓	✓	33.9	25.4	27.6	25.7	33.7	22.8	29.4	28.4
ZJU	primary	✓		✓	34.5	25.2	27.4	25.7	31.6	20.8	27.3	27.5
UEDIN	contrastive	✓			33.3	23.7	26.9	23.6	30.0	19.7	26.7	26.3
UM-DKE	contrastive	✓		✓	34.5	21.9	24.3	24.3	29.3	21.7	26.8	26.1
FAIR	baselines_R		✓		34.1	28.4	29.3	19.8	25.3	20.0	25.8	26.1
HWN	primary	✓	✓	✓	35.4	26.7	27.0	26.7	27.0	17.6	15.4	25.1
ON-TRAC	primary	✓	✓		20.2	14.4	15.0	13.2	3.0	4.2	4.6	10.7

Table 6: **Multilingual ST:** Results of all submissions (primary and contrastive) on official language pairs in BLEU↑

Additional Results (Unofficial Language Pairs and ASR):

	Condition			Supervised			
System	Const.	E2E	Ens.	es-fr	es-it	es-pt	fr-pt
FAIR		✓	✓	33.7	33.0	46.5	35.5
KIT	✓		✓	32.4	32.3	46.6	28.8
UEDIN	✓	✓	✓	30.3	32.9	44.5	30.1
HWN	✓	✓	✓	27.0	30.8	43.2	26.9
ON-TRAC	✓	✓		8.2	11.1	25.6	14.9

Table 7: **Multilingual ST:** Results of primary submissions on unofficial language pairs in BLEU↑ (optional)

	Condition			ASR				Avg
System	Const.	E2E	Ens.	es	fr	it	pt	
HWN	✓	✓		11.1	22.2	16.2	23.8	18.3
KIT	✓	✓		10.0	26.5	15.5	22.1	18.5
FAIR		✓	✓	11.2	18.7	19.6	27.4	19.2
UEDIN	✓	✓		12.0	23.4	18.7	25.9	20.0

Table 8: **ASR:** Results of primary submissions on ASR in WER↓ (optional), sorted by average WER

A.4. Low-Resource Speech Translation

Official Results:

System	swh-eng	swc-fra	swc-eng
IMS.primary	14.9	**13.5**	**7.7**
IMS.contrastive	6.7	2.7	3.9
ON-TRAC	12.9	9.1	–
USYD-JD	**25.3**	–	–

Table 9: **Low-Resource ST:** Results of all speech translation submissions (case-insensitive BLEU↑). The swc-eng and swa-fra pairs were optional.

System	Coastal Swahili (swh)	Congolese Swahili (swc)
ON-TRAC	31.2	36.8
USYD-JD	34.4	–

Table 10: **ASR:** Results of all (optional) speech transcriptions submissions (case-insensitive WER↓).

The USTC-NELSLIP Systems for Simultaneous Speech Translation Task at IWSLT 2021

Dan Liu[1,2], Mengge Du[2], Xiaoxi Li[2], Yuchen Hu[1], and Lirong Dai [1]

[1]University of Science and Technology of China, Hefei, China
[2]iFlytek Research, Hefei, China
{danliu, huyuchen}@mail.ustc.edu.cn
lrdai@ustc.edu.cn
{danliu, xxli16,mgdou}@iflytek.com

Abstract

This paper describes USTC-NELSLIP's submissions to the IWSLT2021 Simultaneous Speech Translation task. We proposed a novel simultaneous translation model, Cross Attention Augmented Transducer (CAAT), which extends conventional RNN-T to sequence-to-sequence tasks without monotonic constraints, e.g., simultaneous translation. Experiments on speech-to-text (S2T) and text-to-text (T2T) simultaneous translation tasks shows CAAT achieves better quality-latency trade-offs compared to *wait-k*, one of the previous state-of-the-art approaches. Based on CAAT architecture and data augmentation, we build S2T and T2T simultaneous translation systems in this evaluation campaign. Compared to last year's optimal systems, our S2T simultaneous translation system improves by an average of 11.3 BLEU for all latency regimes, and our T2T simultaneous translation system improves by an average of 4.6 BLEU.

1 Introduction

This paper describes the submission to IWSLT 2021 Simultaneous Speech Translation task by National Engineering Laboratory for Speech and Language Information Processing (NELSLIP), University of Science and Technology of China, China.

Recent work in text-to-text simultaneous translation tends to fall into two categories, fixed policy and flexible policy, represented by wait-k (Ma et al., 2019) and monotonic attention (Arivazhagan et al., 2019; Ma et al., 2020b) respectively. The drawback of fixed policy is that it may introduce over latency for some sentences and under latency for others. Meanwhile, flexible policy often leads to difficulties in model optimization.

Inspired by RNN-T (Graves, 2012), we aim to optimize the marginal distribution of all expanded paths in simultaneous translation. However, we found it's impossible to calculate the marginal probability based on conventional Attention Encoder-Decoder (Sennrich et al., 2016) architectures (Transformer (Vaswani et al., 2017) included), which is due to the deep coupling between source contexts and target history contexts. To solve this problem, we propose a novel architecture, Cross Attention augmented Transducer (CAAT), and a latency loss function to ensure CAAT model works with an appropriate latency. In simultaneous translation, policy is integrated into translation model and learned jointly for CAAT model.

In this work, we build simultaneous translation systems for both text-to-text (T2T) and speech-to-text S2T) task. We propose a novel architecture, Cross Attention Augmented Transducer (CAAT), which significantly outperforms wait-k (Ma et al., 2019) baseline in both text-to-text and speech-to-text simultaneous translation task. Besides, we adopt a variety of data augmentation methods, back-translation (Edunov et al., 2018), Self-training (Kim and Rush, 2016) and speech synthesis with Tacotron2 (Shen et al., 2018). Combining all of these and models ensembling, we achieved about 11.3 BLEU (in S2T task) and 4.6 BLEU (in T2T task) gains compared to the best performance last year.

2 Data

2.1 Statistics and Preprocessing

EN→DE Speech Corpora The speech datasets used in our experiments are shown in Table 1, where MuST-C, Europarl and CoVoST2 are speech translation specific (speech, transcription and translation included), and LibriSpeech, TED-LIUM3 are speech recognition specific (only speech and transcription). After augmented with speed and echo perturbation, we use Kaldi (Povey et al., 2011) to extract 80 dimensional log-mel filter bank features, computed with a $25ms$ window size and a

Proceedings of the 18th International Conference on Spoken Language Translation, pages 30–38
Bangkok, Thailand (Online), August 5–6, 2021.

$10ms$ window shift, and specAugment (Park et al., 2019) were performed during training phase.

Corpus	Segments	Duration(h)
MuST-C	250.9k	448
Europarl	69.5k	155
CoVoST2	854.4k	1090
LibriSpeech	281.2k	960
TED-LIUM3	268.2k	452

Table 1: Statistics of speech corpora.

Text Translation Corpora The bilingual parallel datasets for Englith to German(EN→DE) and English to Japanese (EN→JA) used are shown in Table 2, and the monolingual datasets in English, German and Japanese are shown in Table 3. And we found the Paracrawl dataset in EN→DE task is too big to our model training, we randomly select a subset of 14M sentences from it.

	Corpus	Sentences
EN→DE	MuST-C(v2)	229.7k
	Europarl	1828.5k
	Rapid-2019	1531.3k
	WIT3-TED	209.5k
	Commoncrawl	2399.1k
	WikiMatrix	6227.2k
	Wikititles	1382.6k
	Paracrawl	82638.2k
EN→JA	WIT3-TED	225.0k
	JESC	2797.4k
	kftt	440.3k
	WikiMatrix	3896.0k
	Wikititles	706.0k
	Paracrawl	10120.0k

Table 2: Statistics of text parallel datasets.

Language	Corpus	Sentences
EN	Europarl-v10	2295.0k
	News-crawl-2019	33600.8k
DE	Europarl-v10	2108.0k
	News-crawl-2020	53674.4k
JA	News-crawl-2019	3446.4k
	News-crawl-2020	10943.3k

Table 3: Statistics of monolingual datasets.

For EN→DE task, we directly use SentencePiece (Kudo and Richardson, 2018) to generate a unigram vocabulary of size 32,000 for source and target language jointly. And for EN→JA task, sentences in Japanese are firstly participled by MeCab (Kudo, 2006), and then a unigram vocabulary of size 32,000 is generated for source and target jointly similar to EN→DE task.

During data preprocessing, the bilingual datasets are firstly filtered by length less than 1024 and length ratio of target to source $0.25 < r < 4$. In the second step, with a baseline Transformer model trained with only bilingual data, we filtered the mismatched parallel pairs with log-likelihood from the baseline model, threshold is set to -4.0 for EN→DE task and -5.0 for EN→JA task. At last we keep 27.3 million sentence pairs for EN-DE task and 17.0 sentence pairs for EN→JA task.

2.2 Data Augmentation

For text-to-text machine translation, augmented data from monolingual corpora in source and target language are generated by self-training (He et al., 2019) and back translation (Edunov et al., 2018) respectively. Statistics of the augmented training data are shown in Table 4.

Data	EN→DE	EN→JA
Bilingual data	27.3M	17.0M
+back-translation	34.3M	22.0M
+self-training	41.3M	27.0M

Table 4: Augmented training data for text-to-text translation.

We further extend these two data augmentation methods to speech-to-text translation, detailed as:

1. Self-training: Maybe similar to sequence-level distillation (Kim and Rush, 2016; Ren et al., 2020; Liu et al., 2019). Transcriptions of all speech datasets (both speech recognition and speech translation specific) are sent to a text translation model to generate text $y^{'}$ in target language, the generated $y^{'}$ with its corresponding speech are directly added to speech translation dataset.

2. Speech Synthesis: We employ Tacotron2 (Shen et al., 2018) with slightly modified by introducing speaker representations to both encoder and decoder as our text-to-speech (TTS) model architecture, and trained on MuST-C(v2) speech corpora to generate filter-bank

speech representations. We randomly select 4M sentence pairs from EN→DE text translation corpora and generate audio feature by speech synthesis. The generated filter bank features and their corresponding target language text are used to expand our speech translation dataset.

The expanded training data are shown in Table 5. Besides, during the training period for all the speech translation tasks, we sample the speech data from the whole corpora with fixed ratio and the concrete ratio for different dataset is shown in Table 6.

Dataset	Segements	Duration(h)
Raw S2T dataset	1.17M	1693
+self-training	2.90M	4799
+Speech synthesis	7.22M	10424

Table 5: Expanded speech translation dataset with self-training and speech synthesis.

Dataset	Sample Ratio
MuST-C	2
Europarl	1
CoVoST2	1
LibriSpeech	1
TED-LIUM3	2
Speech synthesis	5

Table 6: Sample ratio for different datasets during training period.

3 Methods and Models

3.1 Cross Attention Augmented Transducer

Let $\mathbf{x}$ and $\mathbf{y}$ denote the source and target sequence, respectively. The policy of simultaneous translation is denoted as an action sequence $\mathbf{p} \in \{R, W\}^{|\mathbf{x}|+|\mathbf{y}|}$ where R denotes the READ action and W the WRITE action. Another representation of policy is extending target sequence $\mathbf{y}$ to length $|\mathbf{x}| + |\mathbf{y}|$ with blank symbol ϕ as $\hat{y} \in (\mathbf{v} \cup \{\phi\})^{|\mathbf{x}|+|\mathbf{y}|}$, where $\mathbf{v}$ is the vocabulary of the target language. The mapping from $\mathbf{y}$ to sets of all possible expansion $\hat{y}$ denotes as $H(\mathbf{x}, \mathbf{y})$.

Inspired by RNN-T (Graves, 2012), the loss function for simultaneous translation can be defined as the marginal conditional probability and expectation of latency metric through all possible expanded paths:

$$\begin{aligned} \mathcal{L}(x, y) &= \mathcal{L}_{nll}(x, y) + \mathcal{L}_{latency}(x, y) \\ &= -\log \sum_{\hat{y}} p(\hat{y}|x) + \mathbb{E}_{\hat{y}} l(\hat{y}) \\ &= -\log \sum_{\hat{y}} p(\hat{y}|x) + \sum_{\hat{y}} \Pr(\hat{y}|y, x) l(\hat{y}) \end{aligned} \quad (1)$$

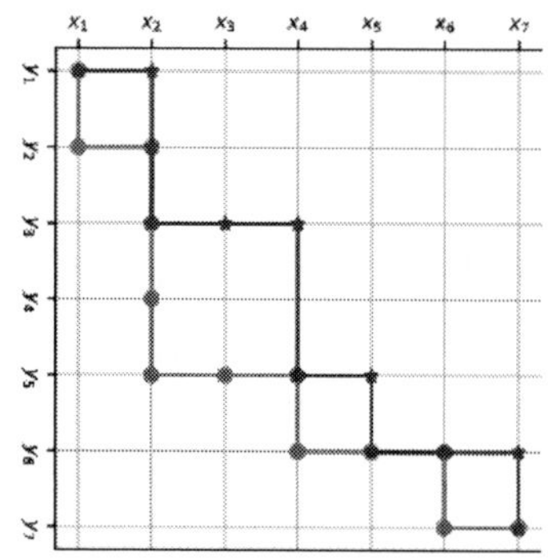

Figure 1: Expanded paths in simultaneous translation.

Where $\Pr(\hat{y}|y, x) = \frac{p(\hat{y}|x)}{\sum_{\hat{y}' \in H(x,y)} p(\hat{y}'|x)}$, and $\hat{y} \in H(x, y)$ is an expansion of target sequence $\mathbf{y}$, and $l(\hat{y}$ is the latency of expanded path $\hat{y}$.

However, RNN-T is trained and inferenced based on source-target monotonic constraint, which means it isn't suitable for translation task. And the calculation of marginal probability $\sum_{\hat{y} \in H(x,y)} \Pr(\hat{y}|x)$ is impossible for Attention Encoder-Decoder framework due to deep coupling of source and previous target representation. As shown in Figure 1, the decoder hidden states for the red path $\hat{y}^1$ and the blue path $\hat{y}^2$ is not equal at the intersection $s_2^1 \neq s_2^2$. To solve this, we separate the source attention mechanism from the target history representation, which is similar to joiner and predictor in RNN-T. The novel architecture can be viewed as a extension version of RNN-T with attention mechanism augmented joiner, and is named as Cross Attention Augmented Transducer (CAAT). Figure 2 is the implementation of RAAT based on Transformer.

Computation cost of joiner in CAAT is significantly more expensive than that of RNN-T. The complexity of joiner is $\mathcal{O}(|\mathbf{x}| \cdot |\mathbf{y}|)$ during training, which means $\mathcal{O}(|\mathbf{x}|)$ times higher than conventional Transformer. We solve this problem by making decisions with decision step size $d > 1$, and

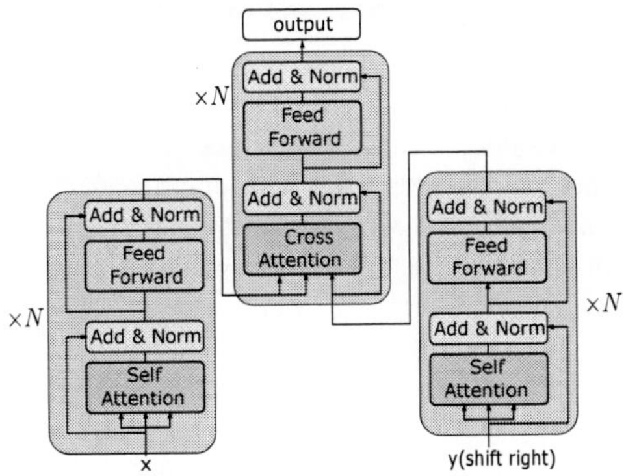

Figure 2: Architecture of CAAT based on Transformer.

reduce the complexity of joiner from $\mathcal{O}(|\mathbf{x}| \cdot |\mathbf{y}|)$ to $\frac{\mathcal{O}(|\mathbf{x}| \cdot |\mathbf{y}|)}{d}$. Besides, to further reduce video memory consumption, we split hidden states into small pieces before sent into joiner, and recombine it for back-propagation during training.

As the latency loss is defined as marginal expectation over all expanded paths $\hat{y}$, *mergeable* is also a requirement to the latency loss definition, which means latency loss through path $\hat{y}$ may be defined as $l(\hat{y}) = \sum_{k=1}^{|\mathbf{x}|+|\mathbf{y}|} l(\hat{y}_k)$ and $l(\hat{y}_k)$ is independent of $\hat{y}_{j' \neq j}$. However, both Average Lagging (Ma et al., 2019) and Differentiable Average Lagging (Arivazhagan et al., 2019) do not meet this requirement. We hence introduce a novel latency function based on wait-0 as oracle latency as follows:

$$
\begin{aligned}
d(i,j) &= \frac{1}{|\mathbf{y}|} \max\left(i - \frac{j \cdot |\mathbf{x}|}{|\mathbf{y}|}, 0\right) \\
l(\hat{y}_k) &= \begin{cases} 0 & \text{if } \hat{y}_k = \phi \\ d(i_k, j_k) & \text{else} \end{cases}
\end{aligned} \tag{2}
$$

Where $i_k = \sum_{k'=1}^{k} I(\hat{y}_{k'} = \phi)$ and $j_k = \sum_{k'=1}^{k} I(\hat{y}_{k'} \neq \phi)$ denote READ and WRITE actions number before $\hat{y}_k$. The latency for the whole expanded path $\hat{y}$ can be defined as

$$
l(\hat{y}) = \sum_{k=1}^{|\hat{\mathbf{y}}|} l(\hat{y}_k) \tag{3}
$$

Based on Eq. (3) the expectation of latency loss through all expanded paths may be defined as :

$$
\begin{aligned}
\mathcal{L}_{latency}(x,y) &= \mathbb{E}_{\hat{y} \in H(x,y)} l(\hat{y}) \\
&= \sum_{\hat{y}} \Pr(\hat{y}|y,x) l(\hat{y})
\end{aligned} \tag{4}
$$

Latency loss and its gradients can be calculated by the forward-backward algorithm, similar to Sequence Criterion Training in ASR (Povey, 2005).

At last, we add the cross entropy loss of offline translation model as an auxiliary loss to CAAT model training for two reasons. First we hope the CAAT model fall back to offline translation in the worst case; second, CAAT models is carried out in accordance with offline translation when source sentence ended. The final loss function for CAAT training is defined as follows:

$$
\begin{aligned}
\mathcal{L}(x,y) &= \mathcal{L}_{CAAT}(x,y) + \lambda_{latency} \mathcal{L}_{latency}(x,y) \\
&\quad + \lambda_{CE} \mathcal{L}_{CE}(x,y) \\
&= -\log \sum_{\hat{y}} p(\hat{y}|x) \\
&\quad + \lambda_{latency} \sum_{\hat{y}} \Pr(\hat{y}|y,x) d(\hat{y}) \\
&\quad - \lambda_{CE} \sum_{j} \log p(y_j|x, y_{<j})
\end{aligned} \tag{5}
$$

Where $\lambda_{latency}$ and λ_{CE} are scaling factors corresponding to the $\mathcal{L}_{latency}$ and $\mathcal{L}_{CE}$. And we set $\lambda_1 = \lambda_2 = 1.0$ if not specified.

3.2 Streaming Encoder

Unidirectional Transformer encoder (Arivazhagan et al., 2019; Ma et al., 2020b) is not effective for speech data processing, because of the closely related to right context for speech frame x_i. Block processing (Dong et al., 2019; Wu et al., 2020) is introduced for online ASR, but they lacks directly observing to infinite left context.

We process streaming encoder for speech data by block processing with right context and infinite left context. First, input representations $\mathbf{h}$ is divided into overlapped blocks with block step m and block size $m + r$. Each block consists of two parts, the main context $\mathbf{m}_n = [h_{m*n+1}, \cdots, h_{(m+1)*n}]$ and the right context $\mathbf{r}_n = [h_{(m+1)*n}, \cdots, h_{(m+1)*n+r}]$. The query, key and value of block $\mathbf{b}_n$ in self-attention can be described as follows:

$$
\mathbf{Q} = \mathbf{W}_q [\mathbf{m}_n, \mathbf{r}_n] \tag{6}
$$

$$
\mathbf{K} = \mathbf{W}_k [\mathbf{m}_1, \cdots, \mathbf{m}_n, \mathbf{r}_n] \tag{7}
$$

$$
\mathbf{V} = \mathbf{W}_v [\mathbf{m}_1, \cdots, \mathbf{m}_n, \mathbf{r}_n] \tag{8}
$$

By reorganizing input sequence and designed self-attention mask, training is effective by reusing conventional transformer encoder layers. And unidirectional transformer can be regarded as a special case of our method with $\{m = 1, r = 0\}$. Note that the look-ahead window size in our method is fixed, which ensures increasing transformer layers won't affect latency.

3.3 Text-to-Text Simultaneous Translation

We implemented both CAAT in Sec. 3.1 and wait-k (Ma et al., 2019) systems for text-to-text simultaneous translation, both of them are implemented based on fairseq (Ott et al., 2019).

All of wait-k experiments use the parameter settings based on big transformer (Vaswani et al., 2017) with unidirectional encoders, which corresponds to a 12-layer encoder and 6-layer decoder transformer with a embedding size of 1024, a feed forward network size of 4096, and 16 heads attention.

Hyper-parameters of our CAAT model architectures are shown in Table 7. CAAT training requires significantly more GPU memory than conventional Transformer (Vaswani et al., 2017), for the $\mathcal{O}\left(\frac{|x|\cdot|y|}{d}\right)$ complexity of joiner module. We mitigate this problem by reducing joiner hidden dimension for lower decision step size d.

3.4 Speech-to-Text Simultaneous Translation

3.4.1 End-to-End Systems

The main system of End-to-End Speech-to-Text simultaneous Translation is based on the aforementioned CAAT structure. For speech encoder, two 2D convolution blocks are introduced before the stacked 24 Transformer encoder layers. Each convolution block consists of a 3-by-3 convolution layer with 64 channels and stride size as 2, and a ReLU activation function. Input speech features are downsampled 4 times by convolution blocks and flattened to 1D sequence as input to transformer layers. Other hyper-parameters are shown in Table 7. The latency-quality trade-off may be adjusted by varying the decision step size d and the latency scaling factor $\lambda_{latency}$. We submitted systems with best performance in each latency region.

3.4.2 Cascaded Systems

The cascaded system consists of two modules, simultaneous automatic speech recognition (ASR) and simultaneous text-to-text Machine Translation (MT). Both simultaneous ASR and MT system are built with CAAT proposed in Sec. 3.1. And we found the cascaded systems outperforms end-to-end system in medium and high latency region.

3.5 Unsegmented Data Processing

To deal with unsegmented data, we segment the input text based on sentence ending marks for T2T track. For S2T task, input speech is simply segmented into utterances with duration of 20 seconds and each segmented piece is directly sent to our simultaneous translation systems to obtain the streaming results. We found an abnormally large average lagging (AL) on IWSLT tst2018 test set based on existed SimuEval toolkit(Ma et al., 2020a) and segment strategy, so relevant results are not presented here. A more reasonable latency criterion may be needed for unsegmented data in the future.

4 Experiments

4.1 Effectiveness of CAAT

To demonstrate the effectiveness of CAAT architecture, we compare it to wait-k with speculative beam search (SBS) (Ma et al., 2019; Zheng et al., 2019b), one of the previous state-of-the-art. The latency-quality trade-off curves on S2T and T2T tasks are shown in Figure 3 and Figure 4(a). We can find that CAAT significantly outperforms wait-k with SBS, especially in low latency section($AL < 1000ms$ for S2T track and $AL < 3$ for T2T track).

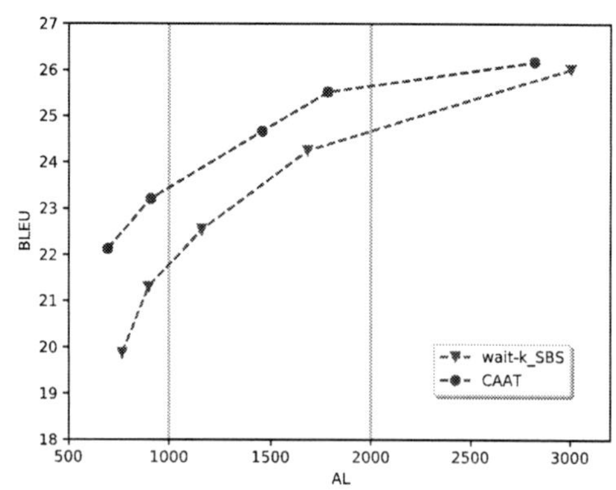

Figure 3: Comparison of CAAT and wait-k with SBS systems on EN→DE Speech-to-Text simultaneous translation.

4.2 Effectiveness of data augmentation

In order to testify the effectiveness of data augmentation, we compare the results of different data augmentation methods based on the offline and simultaneous speech translation task. As demonstrated in Table 8, adding new generated target sentences into the training corpora by using Self-training gives

	Parameters	S2T config	T2T config-A	T2T config-B
Encoder	layers	24	12	12
	attention heads	8	16	16
	FFN dimension	2048	4096	4096
	embedding size	512	1024	1024
Predictor	attention heads	8	16	16
	FFN dimension	2048	4096	4096
	embedding size	512	1024	1024
	output dimension	512	512	1024
Joiner	attention heads	8	8	16
	FFN dimension	1024	2048	4096
	embedding size	512	512	1024
/	decision step size	{16,64}	{4,10,16,32}	{10,32}
	latency scaling factor	{1.0,0.2}	{1.0,0.2}	0.2

Table 7: Parameters of CAAT in T2T and end-to-end S2T simultaneous translation. Noted that both predictor and joiner have 6 layers for T2T and S2T tasks, and the additional two parameters for end-to-end 2T simultaneous translation, which is the main context and right context described in Sec.3.2, are set $m = 32$ and $r = 16$.

Dataset	BLEU
Original speech corpora	21.24
+self-training	28.21
+Speech systhesis	29.72

Table 8: Performance of offline speech translation on MuST-C(v2) tst-COMMON with different datasets.

a boost of nearly 7 BLEU points and speech synthesis provides the other 1.5 BLEU points increase on MuST-C(v2) tst-COMMON. As illustrated in Figure 3, all the data augmentation methods are employed and provide nearly 3 BLEU points on average in the simultaneous task at different latency regimes. Note that our data augmentation methods alleviate the scarcity of parallel datasets in the End-to-End speech translation task and make a significant improvement.

4.3 Text-to-Text Simultaneous Translation

EN→DE Task The performances of text-to-text EN→DE task is shown in Figure 4(a). We can see that the performance of proposed CAAT is always better than that of wait-k with SBS and the best results from ON-TRAC in 2020 (Elbayad et al., 2020), especially in low latency regime, and the performance of CAAT with model ensemble is nearly equivalent to offline result. Moreover, it can be further noticed from Figure 4(a) that the model ensemble can also improve the BLUE score more or less under different latency regimes, and the increase is quite obvious in low latency regime. Compared with the best result in 2020, we finally get improvement by 6.8 and 3.4 BLEU in low and high latency regime respectively.

En→JA Task Results of Text-to-Text simultaneous translation (EN→JA) track are plotted in Figure 4(b), where the curve naming CAAT_bst is best performances in this track with or without model-ensembling method. Curves in this sub-figure show the similar conclusion to the former subsection, that the result of proposed CAAT significantly outperforms that of wait-k with SBS. While we can also find that the gap between CAAT and offline is more obvious (nearly 0.4 BLEU), this is mainly because parameters of joiner block for EN→JA track in high-latency regime is reduced a lot from that for EN→DE track, due to the unstable EN→JA training.

4.4 Speech-to-Text Simultaneous Translation

End-to-End System In this section, we discuss about our final results of End-to-End system based on CAAT. We tune the decision step size d and latency scaling factor $\lambda_{latency}$ to meet different latency regime requirements. For low, medium and high latency, the corresponding d and $\lambda_{latency}$ are set to (16,64,64) and (1.0,1.0,0.2) respectively. We show our final latency-quality trade-offs in Figure 5. Combined with our data augmentation methods and

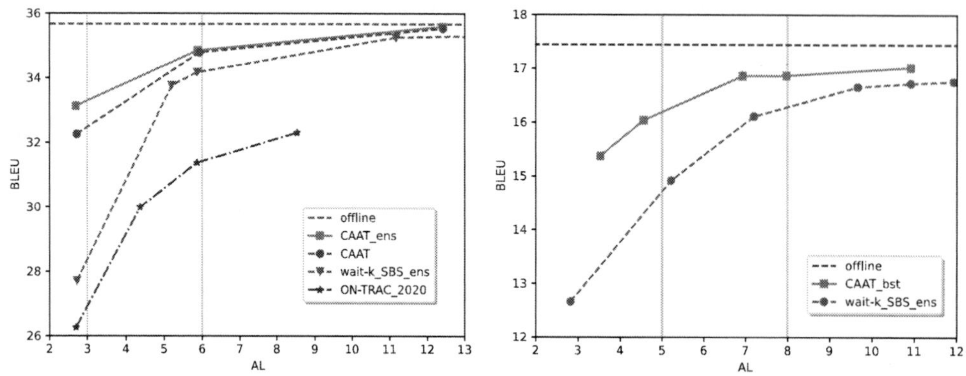

(a) tst-COMMON(v2) on EN→DE

(b) IWSLT dev2021 on EN→JA

Figure 4: Latency-quality trade-offs of Text-to-Text simultaneous translation.

new CAAT model structure, it can be seen that our single model system has already outperformed the best results of last year in all latency regimes and provides 9.8 BLEU scores increase on average. Ensembling different models can further boost the BLEU scores by roughly 0.5-1.5 points at different latency regimes.

Cascaded System Under the cascaded setting, we paired two well-trained ASR and MT systems, where the WER of ASR system's performance is 6.30 with 1720.20 AL, and the MT system is followed by the config-A in Table 7, whose results are 34.79 BLEU and 5.93 AL. We found the best medium and high-latency systems at decision step size pair (d_{asr}, d_{mt}) with $(6, 10)$ and $(12, 10)$ respectively. Performance of cascaded systems are shown in Figure 5. Note that under current configuration of ASR and MT systems, we can not provide valid results that satisfy the requirement of AL at low latency regime since cascaded system usually has a larger latency compared to End-to End system. During the online decoding of the cascaded system, only after specific tokens are recognized by the ASR system, the translation model can further translate them to obtain the final result. The decoded results from ASR model first has a delay compared to the actual contents of the audio, and the two-steps decoding further accumulates the delay, which contributes to the higher latency compared to the End-to-End system. However, it still can be seen that cascaded system has significant advantages over End-to-End system at medium and high latency regime and it still has a long way to go for End-to-End system in the simultaneous speech translation task.

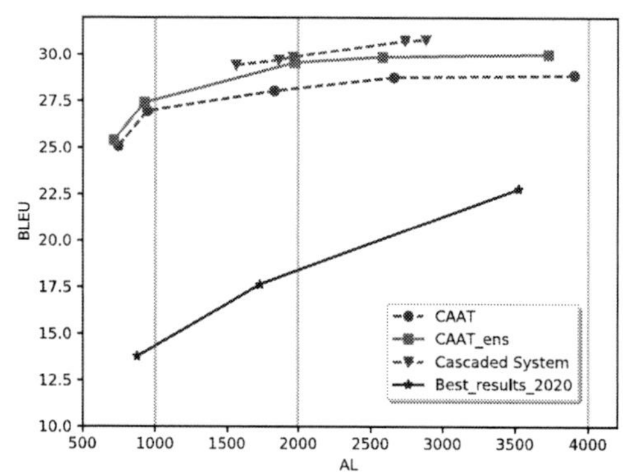

Figure 5: Latency-quality trade-offs of Speech-to-Text simultaneous translation on MuST-C(v2) tst-COMMON.

5 Related Work

Simultaneous Translation Recent work on simultaneous translation falls into two categories. The first category uses a fixed policy for the READ/WRITE actions and can thus be easily integrated into the training stage, as typified by *wait-k* approaches (Ma et al., 2019).The second category includes models with a flexible policy learned and/or adaptive to current context, e.g., by Reinforcement Learning (Gu et al., 2017), Supervise Learning (Zheng et al., 2019a) and so on. A special sub-category of flexible policy jointly optimizes policy and translation by monotonic attention customized to translation model, e.g., Monotonic Infinite Lookback (MILk) attention (Arivazhagan et al.,

2019) and Monotonic Multihead Attention (MMA) (Ma et al., 2020b). We propose a novel method to optimize policy and translation model jointly, which is motivated by RNN-T (Graves, 2012) in online ASR. Unlike RNN-T, the CAAT model removes the monotonic constraint, which is critical for considering reordering in machine translation tasks. The optimization of our latency loss is motivated by Sequence Discriminative Training in ASR (Povey, 2005).

Data Augmentation As described in Sec. 2, the size of training data for speech translation is significantly smaller than that of text-to-text machine translation, which is the main bottleneck to improve the performance of speech translation. Self-training, or sequnece-level knowledge distillation by text-to-text machine translation model, is the most effective way to utilize the huge ASR training data (Liu et al., 2019; Pino et al., 2020). On the other hand, synthesizing data by text-to-speech (TTS) has been demonstrated to be effective for low resource speech recognition task (Gokay and Yalcin, 2019; Ren et al., 2019). To the best of our knowledge, this is the first work to augment data by TTS for simultaneous speech-to-text translation tasks.

6 Conclusion

In this paper, we propose a novel simultaneous translation architecture, Cross Attention Augmented Transducer (CAAT), which significantly outperforms wait-k in both S2T and T2T simultaneous translation task. Based on CAAT architecture and data augmentation, we build simultaneous translation systems on text-to-text and speech-to-text simultaneous translation tasks. We also build a cascaded speech-to-text simultaneous translation system for comparison. Both T2T and S2T systems achieve significant improvements over last year's best-performing systems.

References

Naveen Arivazhagan, Colin Cherry, Wolfgang Macherey, Chung-Cheng Chiu, Semih Yavuz, Ruoming Pang, Wei Li, and Colin Raffel. 2019. Monotonic infinite lookback attention for simultaneous machine translation. In *Proceedings of the 57th Annual Meeting of the Association for Computational Linguistics*, pages 1313–1323, Florence, Italy. Association for Computational Linguistics.

Linhao Dong, Feng Wang, and Bo Xu. 2019. Self-attention aligner: A latency-control end-to-end model for ASR using self-attention network and chunk-hopping. In *IEEE International Conference on Acoustics, Speech and Signal Processing, ICASSP 2019, Brighton, United Kingdom, May 12-17, 2019*, pages 5656–5660. IEEE.

Sergey Edunov, Myle Ott, Michael Auli, and David Grangier. 2018. Understanding back-translation at scale. *arXiv preprint arXiv:1808.09381*.

Maha Elbayad, Ha Nguyen, Fethi Bougares, Natalia Tomashenko, Antoine Caubrière, Benjamin Lecouteux, Yannick Estève, and Laurent Besacier. 2020. On-trac consortium for end-to-end and simultaneous speech translation challenge tasks at iwslt 2020. *arXiv preprint arXiv:2005.11861*.

Ramazan Gokay and Hulya Yalcin. 2019. Improving low resource turkish speech recognition with data augmentation and tts. In *2019 16th International Multi-Conference on Systems, Signals & Devices (SSD)*, pages 357–360. IEEE.

Alex Graves. 2012. Sequence transduction with recurrent neural networks. *arXiv preprint arXiv:1211.3711*.

Jiatao Gu, Graham Neubig, Kyunghyun Cho, and Victor O.K. Li. 2017. Learning to translate in real-time with neural machine translation. In *Proceedings of the 15th Conference of the European Chapter of the Association for Computational Linguistics: Volume 1, Long Papers*, pages 1053–1062, Valencia, Spain. Association for Computational Linguistics.

Junxian He, Jiatao Gu, Jiajun Shen, and Marc'Aurelio Ranzato. 2019. Revisiting self-training for neural sequence generation. *arXiv preprint arXiv:1909.13788*.

Yoon Kim and Alexander M Rush. 2016. Sequence-level knowledge distillation. *arXiv preprint arXiv:1606.07947*.

Taku Kudo. 2006. Mecab: Yet another part-of-speech and morphological analyzer. *http://mecab.sourceforge.jp*.

Taku Kudo and John Richardson. 2018. SentencePiece: A simple and language independent subword tokenizer and detokenizer for neural text processing. In *Proceedings of the 2018 Conference on Empirical Methods in Natural Language Processing: System Demonstrations*, pages 66–71, Brussels, Belgium. Association for Computational Linguistics.

Yuchen Liu, Hao Xiong, Zhongjun He, Jiajun Zhang, Hua Wu, Haifeng Wang, and Chengqing Zong. 2019. End-to-end speech translation with knowledge distillation.

Mingbo Ma, Liang Huang, Hao Xiong, Renjie Zheng, Kaibo Liu, Baigong Zheng, Chuanqiang Zhang, Zhongjun He, Hairong Liu, Xing Li, Hua Wu, and

Haifeng Wang. 2019. STACL: Simultaneous translation with implicit anticipation and controllable latency using prefix-to-prefix framework. In *Proceedings of the 57th Annual Meeting of the Association for Computational Linguistics*, pages 3025–3036, Florence, Italy. Association for Computational Linguistics.

Xutai Ma, Mohammad Javad Dousti, Changhan Wang, Jiatao Gu, and Juan Pino. 2020a. SIMULEVAL: An evaluation toolkit for simultaneous translation. In *Proceedings of the 2020 Conference on Empirical Methods in Natural Language Processing: System Demonstrations*, pages 144–150, Online. Association for Computational Linguistics.

Xutai Ma, Juan Miguel Pino, James Cross, Liezl Puzon, and Jiatao Gu. 2020b. Monotonic multihead attention. In *8th International Conference on Learning Representations, ICLR 2020, Addis Ababa, Ethiopia, April 26-30, 2020*. OpenReview.net.

Myle Ott, Sergey Edunov, Alexei Baevski, Angela Fan, Sam Gross, Nathan Ng, David Grangier, and Michael Auli. 2019. fairseq: A fast, extensible toolkit for sequence modeling. In *Proceedings of the 2019 Conference of the North American Chapter of the Association for Computational Linguistics (Demonstrations)*, pages 48–53, Minneapolis, Minnesota. Association for Computational Linguistics.

Daniel S Park, William Chan, Yu Zhang, Chung-Cheng Chiu, Barret Zoph, Ekin D Cubuk, and Quoc V Le. 2019. Specaugment: A simple data augmentation method for automatic speech recognition. *arXiv preprint arXiv:1904.08779*.

Juan Pino, Qiantong Xu, Xutai Ma, Mohammad Javad Dousti, and Yun Tang. 2020. Self-training for end-to-end speech translation. *arXiv preprint arXiv:2006.02490*.

Daniel Povey. 2005. *Discriminative training for large vocabulary speech recognition*. Ph.D. thesis, University of Cambridge.

Daniel Povey, Arnab Ghoshal, Gilles Boulianne, Lukas Burget, Ondrej Glembek, Nagendra Goel, Mirko Hannemann, Petr Motlicek, Yanmin Qian, Petr Schwarz, et al. 2011. The kaldi speech recognition toolkit. In *IEEE 2011 workshop on automatic speech recognition and understanding*, CONF. IEEE Signal Processing Society.

Yi Ren, Jinglin Liu, Xu Tan, Chen Zhang, Tao Qin, Zhou Zhao, and Tie-Yan Liu. 2020. SimulSpeech: End-to-end simultaneous speech to text translation. In *Proceedings of the 58th Annual Meeting of the Association for Computational Linguistics*, pages 3787–3796, Online. Association for Computational Linguistics.

Yi Ren, Xu Tan, Tao Qin, Sheng Zhao, Zhou Zhao, and Tie-Yan Liu. 2019. Almost unsupervised text to speech and automatic speech recognition. In *International Conference on Machine Learning*, pages 5410–5419. PMLR.

Rico Sennrich, Barry Haddow, and Alexandra Birch. 2016. Neural machine translation of rare words with subword units. In *Proceedings of the 54th Annual Meeting of the Association for Computational Linguistics (Volume 1: Long Papers)*, pages 1715–1725, Berlin, Germany. Association for Computational Linguistics.

Jonathan Shen, Ruoming Pang, Ron J Weiss, Mike Schuster, Navdeep Jaitly, Zongheng Yang, Zhifeng Chen, Yu Zhang, Yuxuan Wang, Rj Skerrv-Ryan, et al. 2018. Natural tts synthesis by conditioning wavenet on mel spectrogram predictions. In *2018 IEEE International Conference on Acoustics, Speech and Signal Processing (ICASSP)*, pages 4779–4783. IEEE.

Ashish Vaswani, Noam Shazeer, Niki Parmar, Jakob Uszkoreit, Llion Jones, Aidan N. Gomez, Lukasz Kaiser, and Illia Polosukhin. 2017. Attention is all you need. In *Advances in Neural Information Processing Systems 30: Annual Conference on Neural Information Processing Systems 2017, December 4-9, 2017, Long Beach, CA, USA*, pages 5998–6008.

Chunyang Wu, Yongqiang Wang, Yangyang Shi, Ching-Feng Yeh, and Frank Zhang. 2020. Streaming transformer-based acoustic models using self-attention with augmented memory. *arXiv preprint arXiv:2005.08042*.

Baigong Zheng, Renjie Zheng, Mingbo Ma, and Liang Huang. 2019a. Simultaneous translation with flexible policy via restricted imitation learning. In *Proceedings of the 57th Annual Meeting of the Association for Computational Linguistics*, pages 5816–5822, Florence, Italy. Association for Computational Linguistics.

Renjie Zheng, Mingbo Ma, Baigong Zheng, and Liang Huang. 2019b. Speculative beam search for simultaneous translation. In *Proceedings of the 2019 Conference on Empirical Methods in Natural Language Processing and the 9th International Joint Conference on Natural Language Processing (EMNLP-IJCNLP)*, pages 1395–1402, Hong Kong, China. Association for Computational Linguistics.

NAIST English-to-Japanese Simultaneous Translation System for IWSLT 2021 Simultaneous Text-to-text Task

Ryo Fukuda, Yui Oka, Yausumasa Kano, Yuki Yano, Yuka Ko, Hirotaka Tokuyama, Kosuke Doi, Sakriani Sakti, Katsuhito Sudoh, Satoshi Nakamura
Nara Institute of Science and Technology, Nara, Japan
fukuda.ryo.fo3@is.naist.jp

Abstract

This paper describes NAIST's system for the English-to-Japanese Simultaneous Text-to-text Translation Task in IWSLT 2021 Evaluation Campaign. Our primary submission is based on *wait-k* neural machine translation with sequence-level knowledge distillation to encourage literal translation.

1 Introduction

Automatic simultaneous translation is an attractive research field that aims to translate an input before observing its end for real-time translation similar to human simultaneous interpretation. Starting from early attempts using rule-based machine translation (Matsubara and Inagaki, 1997; Ryu et al., 2006) and statistical methods using statistical machine translation (Bangalore et al., 2012; Fujita et al., 2013), recent studies successfully applied neural machine translation (NMT) into this task (Gu et al., 2017; Ma et al., 2019; Arivazhagan et al., 2019).

The simultaneous translation shared task in the IWSLT evaluation campaign started on 2020 with English-to-German (Ansari et al., 2020) speech-to-text and text-to-text tasks, and a new language pair of English-to-Japanese has been included on 2021 only in text-to-text task. English-to-Japanese is much more challenging than English-to-German due to the large language difference in addition to data scarsity.

We developed an automatic text-to-text simultaneous translation system for this shared task. We applied some extensions to a standard *wait-k* NMT in the training time: sequence-level knowledge distillation and target-side chunk shuffling. However, these techniques showed mixed results in different latency regimes on the IWSLT21 development set, so we configured the system differently for each latency regime. This paper describes the details of the system and the results on the development sets. We also describe our another attempt to include incremental constitutent label prediction that was not included in the primary system.

2 Simultaneous Neural Machine Translation with *wait-k*

Let $X = x_1, x_2, \ldots, x_{|X|}$ be an input sequence in a source language and $Y = y_1, y_2, \ldots, y_{|Y|}$ be an output sequence in a target language. Here, the input can be speech or text, but we assume the input is text because this paper discusses the text-to-text task. The task of simultaneous translation is to translate X to Y incrementally. In other words, each output prediction of Y is made upon partial input observations of X. Suppose an output prefix subsequence $Y_1^j = y_1, y_2, ..., y_j$ has already been predicted from prefix observations of the input $X_1^i = x_1, x_2, ..., x_i$. When we predict the next output subsequence $Y_{j+1}^{j'} = y_{j+1}, ..., y_{j'}$ after further partial observations $X_{i+1}^{i'} = x_{i+1}, ..., x_{i'}$, the prediction is made based on the following formula:

$$Y_{j+1}^{j'} = \operatorname*{argmax}_{\hat{Y}} P(\hat{Y}|X_1^i, X_{i+1}^{i'}, Y_1^j) \quad (1)$$

where $\hat{Y}$ is a possible prediction of the subsequence. In a usual *consecutive* machine translation, we can use the whole input sequence X anytime in the prediction of Y. The limitation of available input information is a key challenge of simultaneous translation.

Wait-k delays the decoding process in k input tokens (Ma et al., 2019). The *wait-k* model translates a token sequence of the source language X into that of the target language Y as follows.

$$\begin{aligned} H_i &= \mathit{Encoder}(x_1, \ldots, x_{i+k-1}), \\ \hat{y}_i &= \mathit{Decoder}(H_i, \hat{y}_1, \ldots, \hat{y}_{i-1}). \end{aligned} \quad (2)$$

The decoder has to predict an output token based on the attention over an observed portion of the input

Proceedings of the 18th International Conference on Spoken Language Translation, pages 39–45
Bangkok, Thailand (Online), August 5–6, 2021.

tokens. k is a hyperparameter for the fixed delay in this model; setting k larger causes longer delays, while smaller k would result in worse output predictions due to the poor context information.

3 Knowledge Distillation

Knowledge Distillation (KD) (Hinton et al., 2015) is a method that uses the distilled knowledge learned by a stronger teacher model in the learning of a weaker student model. When teacher distribution is $q(y|x; \theta_T)$, we minimize the cross-entropy with the teacher's probability distribution instead of reference data, as follows:

$$\mathcal{L}_{KD}(\theta; \theta_T) = -\sum_{k=1}^{|\mathcal{V}|} q(y = k|x; \theta_T) \times \log p(y = k|x; \theta) \quad (3)$$

where θ_T parameterizes the teacher distribution.

Sequence-level Knowledge Distillation (SKD), which gives the student model the output of the teacher model as knowledge, propagates a wide range of knowledge to the student model and trains it to mimic its knowledge (Kim and Rush, 2016). The teacher distribution $q(Y|X)$ is approximated by its mode $q(Y|X) \approx \mathbb{1}\{Y = \operatorname{argmax}_{X \in T} q(Y|X)\}$, and the loss objectives as follows:

$$\mathcal{L}_{SKD} = -\mathbb{E}_{x \sim data} \sum_{Y \in T} q(Y|X) \log p(Y|X)$$
$$\approx -\mathbb{E}_{X \sim data, \hat{Y} = \operatorname{argmax}_{Y \in T} q(Y|X)} [\log p(y = \hat{Y}|X)] \quad (4)$$

where $p(Y|X)$ is the sequence-level distribution, and $Y \in T$ is the space of possible target sentences. SKD can be implemented simply by training the student model using $(X, \hat{Y})$, where $\hat{Y}$ is derived from the teacher model outputs for the source language portion of the training corpus.

We use SKD for reduction of colloquial expressions in the spoken language corpus. Such colloquial expressions are highly dependent on languages and difficult to translate by NMT, which usually generates literal translations. Here, we firstly train a teacher, Transformer-based *offline* NMT model using the training corpus and use it to obtain pseudo-reference translations in the target language. Then, we train a student, Transformer-based *simultaneous* NMT model using the pseudo-parallel corpus with the original source language sentences and the corresponding translation results by the teacher model. The pseudo-references should consist of more literal and NMT-friendly translations, therefore the training of the student model becomes easier than that using the original parallel corpus. Since we have to train simultaneous translation using less context information than an offline translation model, the SKD would be helpful. This is motivated by the recent success of non-autoregressive NMT using SKD (Gu et al., 2018).

4 Target-side chunk shuffling

Chunk shuffling is a kind of data augmentation that reorders Japanese chunks (called *bunsetsu*). Our motivation for this one is to encourage monotonic IMT utilizing a characteristic of Japanese as an agglutinative language, in which the order of *bunsetsu* chunks is not so strict. When we have a target language sequence $T = t_1, \ldots, t_{|T|}$ in the training set, we apply greedy left-to-right chunking to it; T is divided as a chunk sequence $\bar{T} = \mathcal{C}_1, \ldots, \mathcal{C}_Q$, in which each chunk consists of k (i.e., delay hyperparameter in *wait-k*) tokens $\mathcal{C}_q = t_{q_1}, \ldots, t_{q_k}$. Note that the last chunk $\mathcal{C}_Q$ may be shorter than k according to the length of T. Then, we choose to shuffle or keep the chunks in $\bar{T}$ with a probability p_r, defined as a hyperparameter. We tried only the random shuffling with the fixed chunk size of k in this time; More linguistically-motivated chunk reordering would be worth trying as future work.

5 Primary system

5.1 Implementation

Our system implementation was based on the official baseline[1] using fairseq (Ott et al., 2019) and SimulEval (Ma et al., 2020).

5.2 Setup

Data All of the models were based on Transformer, trained using 17.9 million English-Japanese parallel sentences from WMT20 news task and fine-tuned using 223 thousand parallel sentences from IWSLT 2017. During fine-tuning, we examined the effectiveness of knowledge distillation and chunk shuffling with several hyperparameter settings and reported the results by the models that resulted in the higher BLEU on IWSLT 2021 development set. The text was preprocessed by Byte Pair Encoding (BPE) (Sennrich et al., 2016)

[1] `https://github.com/pytorch/fairseq/blob/master/examples/simultaneous_translation/docs/enja-waitk.md`

System	BLEU	AL
offline	16.8	-
Baseline		
wait-10	11.8	7.27
wait-20	14.69	11.47
wait-30^{high}	15.57	13.7
Proposed		
wait-10 + CShuf^{low}	13.77	7.29
wait-10 + SKD	13.5	7.28
wait-20 + SKD^{medium}	15.22	11.48
wait-30 + SKD	15.21	13.71

Table 1: In-house results of our systems on IWSLT 2021 En-Ja development set. Superscripts ^{low}, ^{medium} and ^{high} represent the systems submitted for low-, medium-, and high-latency regimes, respectively.

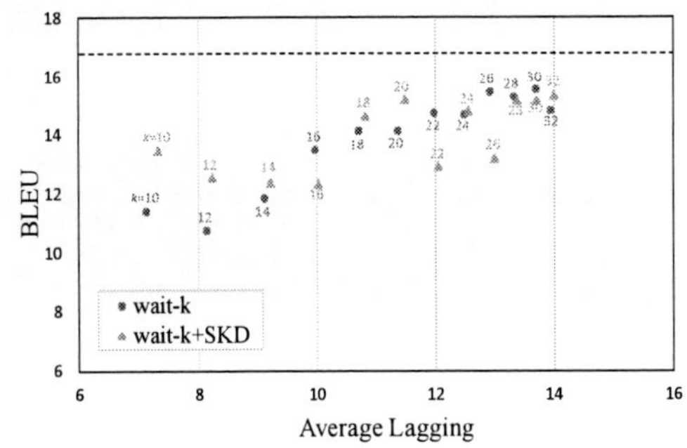

Figure 1: Translation quality against latency for *wait-k* and SKD-based *wait-k* on IWSLT 2021 En-Ja development set. The broken line shows the score of the offline model.

for subword segmentation. The vocabulary was shared over English and Japanese, and its size was 16,000.

Model The hyperparameters of the model almost followed the Transformer Base settings (Vaswani et al., 2017). The encoder and decoder were composed of 6 layers. We set the word embedding dimensions, hidden state dimensions, feed-forward dimensions to 512, 512, and 2,048, respectively. We performed the sub-layer's dropout with a probability of 0.1. The number of attention heads was eight for both the encoder and decoder. The model was optimized using Adam with an initial learning rate of 0.0007, $\beta_1 = 0.9$, and $\beta_2 = 0.98$, following Vaswani et al. (2017).

Evaluation To evaluate the performance, we calculated BLEU and Average lagging (AL) (Ma et al., 2019) with SimulEval on IWSLT 2021 development set.

5.3 Results on the development set

Table 1 shows the excerpt of system results for the full-sentence topline (offline), *wait-k* baselines (wait-k), and our extensions: SKD (+ SKD) and chunk shuffling (+ CShuf).

We tried some different latency hyperparameter values $k = \{10, 12, 14, \ldots, 32\}$ for comparison. Figure 1 plots our BLEU-AL results for *wait-k* and *wait-k*+SKD. It shows that the use of SKD gave some improvements in low-latency settings with $k = \{10, 12, 14\}$, however, the results with larger k were mixed. These results support our assumption on the difficulty of the translation into colloquial expressions discussed in Section 3.

System	p_r	BLEU	len_{hyp}	len_{ref}
Baseline	0	11.80	34,376	27,891
+ CShuf	0.01	10.57	38,257	27,891
	0.02	**13.77**	29,369	27,891
	0.03	9.87	42,296	27,891

Table 2: Target-side chunk shuffling result in $p_r = \{0, 0.01, 0.02, 0.03\}$

We also tried chunk shuffling with different hyperparameter values[2] $p_r = \{0, 0.01, 0.02, 0.03\}$. Table 2 shows the result using the target-side chunk shuffling. Here, the chunk shuffling results are only shown for *wait-10*. The use of larger latency hyperparameter k did not show remarkable differences from the baseline. Chunk shuffling with $p_r = 0.02$ resulted in the best BLEU and outperformed the baseline, but the other values $0.01, 0.03$ did not work. These differences should be due to the output length shown in len_{hyp} column in Table 2; the output length became much shorter than the baseline using the chunk shuffling with $p_r = 0.02$. In contrast, $p_r = 0.01$ and $p_r = 0.03$ increased the output length.

Table 3 shows translation examples by the baseline and chunk-shuffling ($p_r = 0.02$). Here, the baseline translation results do not have end-of-sentence expressions like です (*desu*), ます (*masu*), ですよね (*desuyone*). These differences were not straightforward with the chunk shuffling, but a certain value of $p_r = 0.02$ worked in our experiment.

The results above suggest that the target-side

[2]Higher values of p_r resulted in much worse results and are not included in this paper.

En-input	I see other companies that say, "I'll win the next innovation cycle, whatever it takes."
Baseline	他 の 会社 が 「 次 の イノベーション サイクル に <unk> 」 と 言う の は どんな もの で あれ
CShuf	他 の 会社 が 「 次 の イノベーション サイクル に 勝てる 」 と 言う の を 見 ます
Ja-ref	私 の 経験 で も 沢山 の 企業 が 同じ よう に 「 何 が なんでも 次 の イノベーション サイクル を 制覇 する 」 と 言い 続け て ます
En-input	She's a musical instrument maker, and she does a lot of wood carving for a living.
Baseline	彼女 は 楽器 の 製造 者 で 木彫り を し て 生き て いる 間 に
CShuf	彼女 は 楽器 の 製作 者 で 木彫り を し て い ます
Ja-ref	彼女 は 楽器 の 制作 技師 です 木 を 削る こと で 生計 を 立て て い ます
En-input	Humans are very good at considering what might go wrong if we try something new, say, ask for a raise.
Baseline	人間 は 何 が うまく いけ ば 何 が うまく いけ ば 何 が うまく いけ ば 何 が うまく いけ ば 何 が うまく いけ ば 何 が うまく いけ ば 何 が うまく いけ ば 何 が うまく いけ ば 何 が うまく いけ ば 何 が うまく いけ ば 何 が うまく いけ ば 何 が うまく いけ ば 何 が うまく いけ ば 何 が 起き て も 何 が 起き て も 何 が 起き て も 何 が 起き て も 何 が 起き て も 何 が 起き て も 何 が 起き て
CShuf	人間 は 何 が 間違っ て いる の か を 考える の が 得意 です 新しい こと を 試し て み て も いい です よ ね
Ja-ref	昇給 を 求める という よう な 何 か 新しい こと を 試みよ う という とき 人 は どう まずい こと に なり 得る か 考える こと に 長け て い ます

Table 3: Translation examples by *wait-k* baseline and *wait-k* with chunk shuffling ($p_r = 0.02$).

System	BLEU	AL
wait-10 + CShuf^{low}	14.41	7.21
wait-20 + SKD^{medium}	16.20	11.54
wait-30^{high}	16.19	13.83

Table 4: Official results of our submissions on IWSLT 2021 En-Ja test set.

train	**dev**	**eval**
2,762,408	27,903	21,941

Table 5: Number of NCLP instances.

chunk shuffling may work as a perturbation, and we need further investigation.

5.4 Official results on the test set

Table 4 shows BLEU and AL results on the test set. The system with the medium latency regime (wait-20 + SKD) worked relatively well; it achived a comparable BLEU result with wait-30. However, the results were worse than those of the other teams by around two points in BLEU in all the latency regimes.

6 Another attempt: Incremental Next Constituent Label Prediction

We tried another technique described below in the shared task, but it was not included in our primary submission because it did not outperform the baseline. Here, we also describe this for further investigation in future.

For simultaneous machine translation, deciding how long to wait for input before translation is important. Predicting what kind of phrase comes next is a part of useful information in determining the timing. In this study, we tried incremental Next Constituent Label Prediction (NCLP).

In SMT-based simultaneous translation, Oda et al. (2015) proposed a method to predict unseen syntactic constituents to determine when to start translation for partially-observed input, using a multi-label classifier based on linear SVMs (Fan et al., 2008). Motivated by this study, we used a neural network-based classifier using BERT (Devlin et al., 2019) for NCLP. The problem of NCLP is defined as the label prediction of a syntactic constituent coming next to a given word subsequence in the pre-order tree traversal. In this work, we used 1-lookahead prediction, so the problem was relaxed into the prediction of a label of a syntactic constituent given its preceding words and the first word composing it. A predicted constituent label was inserted at the corresponding position in the input word sequence, immediately after its preceding word. That doubled the length of input sequences. For subword-based NMT, we applied BPE only onto words in the input sequences and put dummy labels after subwords other than end-of-word ones, to order the input in an alternating way.

We used Huggingface transformers (Wolf et al., 2020) for our implementation of NCLP with `bert-base-uncased`. We used Penn Treebank 3 (Marcus et al., 1993) for the NCLP training and development sets, and NAIST-NTT TED Talk Treebank (Neubig et al., 2014) for the NCLP evaluation set. Table 5 shows the number of training, development, and evaluation instances extracted from the datasets. Note that we can extract many instances from a single parse tree.

Table 6 shows the results of the 5 most frequent labels in the NCLP training data. NP and VP are

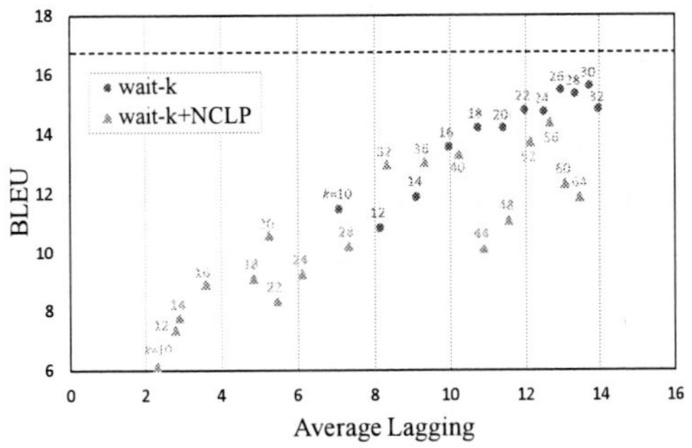

Figure 2: Translation quality against latency for *wait-k* and NCLP-based *wait-k* on IWSLT21 En-Ja dev set. The broken line shows the score of the offline model.

Label	Precision	Recall	F1
NP	0.90	0.94	0.92
VP	0.89	0.97	0.93
NN	0.95	0.97	0.96
,	0.98	1.00	0.99
PP	0.85	0.93	0.89

Table 6: NCLP results on the evaluation set.

important clues of the sentence structure, and their F1 scores were over 90% on the NCLP evaluation data.

However, the results by *wait-k* using NCLP results as its input did not outperform the baseline *wait-k*, as shown in Figure 2. We can observe NCLP-based *wait-k* gave smaller ALs with the same latency hyperparameter k. One possible problem of current NCLP-based *wait-k* is that the length of an input length is doubled by the additional constitutent labels. Since we ran wait-k-based simultaneous NMT for such an augmented input sequence, the decoder using NCLP-augmented input has roughly half of the information compared to the decoder using original input if we use the same k. This forces the decoder to perform very aggressive anticipation with limited information from an input prefix.

Table 7 shows the translation input and output examples of baseline and NCLP. Input sentences include constituents labels. The first example shows that NCLP could translate "publication" before a verb "work" following the Japanese sentence order. Second example shows NCLP output is constructed naturally in terms of grammar, while the baseline has repetitive and unnatural phrases. We observed NCLP sentences are tend to be shorter and more natural than baseline like these examples. However, many sentences are not informative and missing details compared to the baseline. We'll investigate a more effective way to use NCLP in our future work.

7 Conclusion

In this paper, we described our English-to-Japanese text-to-text simultaneous translation system. We extended the baseline *wait-k* with the knowledge distillation to encourage literal translation and target-side chunk shuffling to relax the output order in Japanese. They achieved some improvements on IWSLT 2021 development set in certain latency regimes.

Acknowledgments

Part of this work was supported by JSPS KAKENHI Grant Number JP17H06101.

References

Ebrahim Ansari, Amittai Axelrod, Nguyen Bach, Ondřej Bojar, Roldano Cattoni, Fahim Dalvi, Nadir Durrani, Marcello Federico, Christian Federmann, Jiatao Gu, Fei Huang, Kevin Knight, Xutai Ma, Ajay Nagesh, Matteo Negri, Jan Niehues, Juan Pino, Elizabeth Salesky, Xing Shi, Sebastian Stüker, Marco Turchi, Alexander Waibel, and Changhan Wang. 2020. FINDINGS OF THE IWSLT 2020 EVALUATION CAMPAIGN. In *Proceedings of the 17th International Conference on Spoken Language Translation*, pages 1–34, Online. Association for Computational Linguistics.

Naveen Arivazhagan, Colin Cherry, Wolfgang Macherey, Chung-Cheng Chiu, Semih Yavuz, Ruoming Pang, Wei Li, and Colin Raffel. 2019. Monotonic infinite lookback attention for simultaneous machine translation. In *Proceedings of the 57th Annual Meeting of the Association for Computational Linguistics*, pages 1313–1323, Florence, Italy. Association for Computational Linguistics.

Srinivas Bangalore, Vivek Kumar Rangarajan Sridhar, Prakash Kolan, Ladan Golipour, and Aura Jimenez. 2012. Real-time incremental speech-to-speech translation of dialogs. In *Proceedings of the 2012 Conference of the North American Chapter of the Association for Computational Linguistics: Human Language Technologies*, pages 437–445, Montréal, Canada. Association for Computational Linguistics.

Jacob Devlin, Ming-Wei Chang, Kenton Lee, and Kristina Toutanova. 2019. BERT: Pre-training of deep bidirectional transformers for language understanding. In *Proceedings of the 2019 Conference*

En-input	I won't work with you until your publication, or your organization, is more inclusive of all kinds of difference."
En-input (with label)	I VP won NP 't NNP work PP with NP you SBAR until NP your NN public@@ @@@ ation , , CC or NP your NN organization , , VP is ADJP more JJ in@@ @@@ clusive PP of NP all NNS kinds PP of NP difference . . : "
Baseline	出版までは一緒に働かないし組織もすべての種類の違いを包括している」
NCLP	私はあなたと仕事をしません出版されるまでは
Ja-ref	「あなたの出版物や組織が多様性を受け入れるまではご一緒に仕事はできません」と言うこともできます
En-input	Those of us who are underrepresented and invited to participate in such projects, can also decline to be included until more of us are invited through the glass ceiling, and we are tokens no more.
En-input (with label)	Those PP of NP us SBAR who SQ are VP under@@ @@@ represented CC and VP invited PP to VP participate PP in NP such NNS projects , , VP can ADVP also VP decline PP to VP be VP included PP until NP more PP of NP us VP are VP invited PRT through NP the NN glass NN ceiling , , CC and S we VP are NP tok@@ @@@ ens ADVP no RBR more . .
Baseline	私たちはこのようなプロジェクトに参加している人たちは私たちがこのようなプロジェクトに参加している人たちはガラスの天井を通して招待されるまではその人たちはその人たちの中に含まれることを拒否することができますそして私たちはもうトークンを持っていません
NCLP	私たちの代表であり、招待されている人たちは、このようなプロジェクトに参加することもできます。
Ja-ref	過@@小評価されている私たちのような者が招待されたプロジェクトへの参加を断@@ることもできます更に多くの者がガラスの天井をぬ@@け名ばかりの女性参@@画ではなくなるまでは

Table 7: Translation examples by *wait-k* baseline and *wait-k* with NCLP.

of the North American Chapter of the Association for Computational Linguistics: Human Language Technologies, Volume 1 (Long and Short Papers), pages 4171–4186, Minneapolis, Minnesota. Association for Computational Linguistics.

Rong-En Fan, Kai-Wei Chang, Cho-Jui Hsieh, Xiang-Rui Wang, and Chih-Jen Lin. 2008. *LIBLINEAR: A library for large linear classification.* The Journal of Machine Learning Research.

Tomoki Fujita, Graham Neubig, Sakriani Sakti, Tomoki Toda, and Satoshi Nakamura. 2013. Simple, Lexicalized Choice of Translation Timing for Simultaneous Speech Translation. In *Proceedings of the 14th Annual Conference of the International Speech Communication Association (INTERSPEECH-2013)*, pages 3487–3491.

Jiatao Gu, James Bradbury, Caiming Xiong, Victor O.K. Li, and Richard Socher. 2018. Non-Autoregressive Neural Machine Translation. In *6th International Conference on Learning Representations (ICLR 2018)*.

Jiatao Gu, Graham Neubig, Kyunghyun Cho, and Victor O.K. Li. 2017. Learning to translate in real-time with neural machine translation. In *Proceedings of the 15th Conference of the European Chapter of the Association for Computational Linguistics: Volume 1, Long Papers*, pages 1053–1062, Valencia, Spain. Association for Computational Linguistics.

Geoffrey Hinton, Oriol Vinyals, and Jeffrey Dean. 2015. Distilling the knowledge in a neural network. In *NIPS Deep Learning and Representation Learning Workshop*.

Yoon Kim and Alexander M. Rush. 2016. Sequence-level knowledge distillation. In *Proceedings of the 2016 Conference on Empirical Methods in Natural Language Processing*, pages 1317–1327, Austin, Texas. Association for Computational Linguistics.

Mingbo Ma, Liang Huang, Hao Xiong, Renjie Zheng, Kaibo Liu, Baigong Zheng, Chuanqiang Zhang, Zhongjun He, Hairong Liu, Xing Li, Hua Wu, and Haifeng Wang. 2019. STACL: Simultaneous translation with implicit anticipation and controllable latency using prefix-to-prefix framework. In *Proceedings of the 57th Annual Meeting of the Association for Computational Linguistics*, pages 3025–3036, Florence, Italy. Association for Computational Linguistics.

Xutai Ma, Mohammad Javad Dousti, Changhan Wang, Jiatao Gu, and Juan Pino. 2020. SIMULEVAL: An evaluation toolkit for simultaneous translation. In *Proceedings of the 2020 Conference on Empirical Methods in Natural Language Processing: System Demonstrations*, pages 144–150, Online. Association for Computational Linguistics.

Mitchell P. Marcus, Beatrice Santorini, and Mary Ann Marcinkiewicz. 1993. Building a large annotated corpus of English: The Penn Treebank. *Computational Linguistics*, 19(2):313–330.

Shigeki Matsubara and Yasuyoshi Inagaki. 1997. Incremental Transfer in English-Japanese Machine Translation. *IEICE Transactions on Information and Systems*, E80-D(11):1122–1130.

Graham Neubig, Katsuhito Sudoh, Yusuke Oda, Kevin Duh, Hajime Tsukada, and Masaaki Nagata. 2014. The NAIST-NTT TED talk treebank. In *Proceedings of the 11th International Workshop on Spoken Language Translation (IWSLT)*, Lake Tahoe, USA.

Yusuke Oda, Graham Neubig, Sakriani Sakti, Tomoki Toda, and Satoshi Nakamura. 2015. Syntax-based simultaneous translation through prediction of unseen syntactic constituents. In *Proceedings of the 53rd Annual Meeting of the Association for Computational Linguistics and the 7th International Joint Conference on Natural Language Processing (Volume 1: Long Papers)*, pages 198–207, Beijing, China. Association for Computational Linguistics.

Myle Ott, Sergey Edunov, Alexei Baevski, Angela Fan, Sam Gross, Nathan Ng, David Grangier, and Michael Auli. 2019. fairseq: A fast, extensible toolkit for sequence modeling. In *Proceedings of the 2019 Conference of the North American Chapter of the Association for Computational Linguistics (Demonstrations)*, pages 48–53, Minneapolis, Minnesota. Association for Computational Linguistics.

Koichiro Ryu, Shigeki Matsubara, and Yasuyoshi Inagaki. 2006. Simultaneous English-Japanese spoken language translation based on incremental dependency parsing and transfer. In *Proceedings of the COLING/ACL 2006 Main Conference Poster Sessions*, pages 683–690, Sydney, Australia. Association for Computational Linguistics.

Rico Sennrich, Barry Haddow, and Alexandra Birch. 2016. Neural machine translation of rare words with subword units. In *Proceedings of the 54th Annual Meeting of the Association for Computational Linguistics (Volume 1: Long Papers)*, pages 1715–1725, Berlin, Germany. Association for Computational Linguistics.

Ashish Vaswani, Noam Shazeer, Niki Parmar, Jakob Uszkoreit, Llion Jones, Aidan N Gomez, Łukasz Kaiser, and Illia Polosukhin. 2017. Attention is all you need. In *Advances in neural information processing systems*, pages 5998–6008.

Thomas Wolf, Lysandre Debut, Victor Sanh, Julien Chaumond, Clement Delangue, Anthony Moi, Pierric Cistac, Tim Rault, Remi Louf, Morgan Funtowicz, Joe Davison, Sam Shleifer, Patrick von Platen, Clara Ma, Yacine Jernite, Julien Plu, Canwen Xu, Teven Le Scao, Sylvain Gugger, Mariama Drame, Quentin Lhoest, and Alexander Rush. 2020. Transformers: State-of-the-art natural language processing. In *Proceedings of the 2020 Conference on Empirical Methods in Natural Language Processing: System Demonstrations*, pages 38–45, Online. Association for Computational Linguistics.

The University of Edinburgh's Submission to the IWSLT21 Simultaneous Translation Task

Sukanta Sen, Ulrich Germann and Barry Haddow
University of Edinburgh
{ssen, ugermann, bhaddow}@inf.ed.ac.uk

Abstract

We describe our submission to the IWSLT 2021 shared task[1] on simultaneous text-to-text English-German translation. Our system is based on the re-translation approach where the agent re-translates the whole source prefix each time it receives a new source token. This approach has the advantage of being able to use a standard neural machine translation (NMT) inference engine with beam search, however, there is a risk that incompatibility between successive re-translations will degrade the output. To improve the quality of the translations, we experiment with various approaches: we use a fixed size wait at the beginning of the sentence, we use a language model score to detect translatable units, and we apply dynamic masking to determine when the translation is unstable. We find that a combination of dynamic masking and language model score obtains the best latency-quality trade-off.

1 Introduction

In spoken language translation (SLT), there is often a need to produce translations *simultaneously*, without waiting for the speaker to finish. For example, we may be targeting live events such as conferences or meetings where excessive latency will disrupt the user experience. In order to achieve low latency SLT, however, translation systems must be able to cope well with incomplete utterances, and we find that we need to trade off latency for translation quality. In research on simultaneous SLT, we would like to understand how to produce the best possible trade-off between these two measures. In the IWSLT 2021 shared task on simultaneous translation, the aim was to build and evaluate simultaneous SLT systems at three different latency regimes (low, medium and high), as measured using the Average Lagging (AL; Ma et al. (2019)).

There are two main approaches to simultaneous translation: streaming (Cho and Esipova, 2016; Ma et al., 2019) where the system appends the output to a growing hypothesis as new inputs are available, and re-translation (Niehues et al., 2016, 2018; Arivazhagan et al., 2020a,b), where, as the name suggests, the system re-translates the whole prefix on every update to a completely new output. Re-translation approach has the advantage that we can use an unmodified, general purpose, optimised MT engine with beam-search, but we have to address the problem of *flicker*. That is to say, the translation of a prefix may be changed by the translation of an extended prefix. Recent work by Arivazhagan et al. (2020a) has shown that, if measures are taken to mitigate flicker, then re-translation produces results comparable to streaming approach. Since the shared task does not permit any revision of a committed hypothesis (i.e. flicker is not allowed) we focus on adapting the re-translation approach for our submission without introducing any flicker into a growing hypothesis.

2 Overview of Our Submission

We participated in the English→German text-to-text simultaneous task. Since we re-translate the incomplete input (know as a prefix) each time it is updated, our system will try to modify the translations produced from earlier prefixes. But as the task is evaluated using SimulEval (Ma et al., 2020) which does not permit the modification of committed output (also known as flickering), we use a simple approach to generate incremental output at each re-translation step.

Concretely, we apply a method inspired by the wait-k streaming approach (Ma et al., 2019) in our re-translation system in the following manner. In the task, a simultaneous SLT system is implemented as an agent which must choose between

[1] https://iwslt.org/2021/

Proceedings of the 18th International Conference on Spoken Language Translation, pages 46–51
Bangkok, Thailand (Online), August 5–6, 2021. ©2021 Association for Computational Linguistics

READ (read more input) and WRITE (append to the current translation hypothesis) operations. Our overall approach is shown in Algorithm 1. The agent first performs k consecutive READ operations and then alternatively READs and WRITEs until the full input sentence is read. Once the input is consumed, the agent keeps performing WRITE operations until it reaches the end of the translated sentence. The WRITE operation involves re-translating the prefix S and finding the next output word w from output prefix T. If the output prefix T has a length longer than the committed hypothesis H, it picks the $(i+1)$th word of T, else sends READ signal to the agent, i being the length of the current hypothesis.

Algorithm 1 Our Re-translation Approach

Require: NMT system ϕ, k

1: Initialize: $S \leftarrow \{\}, H \leftarrow \{\}, w \leftarrow \varepsilon$
2: **while** w is not $\langle \text{eos} \rangle$ **do**
3:   **if** $|S| - |H| < k$ and not finished reading **then**
4:     READ next input s
5:     $S \leftarrow S \cup \{s\}$
6:   **else**
7:     $T \leftarrow \phi(S)$
8:     **if** $|T| > |H|$ **then**
9:       $w \leftarrow T[|H| + 1]$
10:     **else**
11:       $w \leftarrow \varepsilon$
12:     **end if**
13:     **if** w is not ε or finished reading **then**
14:       $H \leftarrow H \cup \{w\}$
15:       WRITE w
16:     **end if**
17:   **end if**
18: **end while**

However, there is a potential problem with this approach. In each WRITE step, the output word w is selected from the $(|H| + 1)$th position of output prefix T. Thus if any correction is made by a re-translation in the initial $|H|$ words, the WRITE operation won't be able to recover the mistake. In other words, our approach is able to suppress the flicker caused by re-translation, but could end up gluing together incompatible fragments of the hypothesis. This problem can be worse when the output prefix T flickers too much. To improve translation quality, we employ two approaches which aim at detecting meaningful units (MU) and allowing extra READs when inside an MU. An MU is a chunk of words that has a definite translation and can be translated independently without having to wait for more input words (Zhang et al., 2020).

Our first method of detecting MUs relies on the language model (LM) score. The agent keeps track of the language model (LM) score of the previous token and compares it with the score of the current token. If the LM score is higher than the previous token, it keeps reading more tokens and does a re-translation only when this condition is not met. Here the LM score is the log probability of the current token given the context. Though LM score doesn't guarantee to find meaningful unit every time but this simple approach shows it is better than the baseline approach in terms of BLEU score.

Our second method of stabilising the re-translation approach is based on the idea of dynamic masking (Yao and Haddow, 2020). The dynamic mask approach finds the stable part of the target prefix by comparing the translation of the current prefix, with the translation of an extension of the current prefix. The longest common prefix (LCP) of the two translations is taken as the stable part. Figure 1 shows how dynamic masking works in general. Yao and Haddow (2020) showed that using dynamic mask could give a better flicker-latency trade-off than using a fixed mask, without affecting the translation quality of full sentences.

For our IWSLT submission, we generate the extended prefixes for dynamic mask simply by appending *UNK* (i.e the unknown word symbol) to the prefix. In Figure 2, we show an example of how dynamic mask stabilises the translation, by masking the least stable part of the MT output. This translation-with-dynamic-mask provides a drop-in replacement for the MT system $\phi()$ in line 7 of Algorithm 1, except when the agent has read the full input sentence, when we do not need to apply any mask.

3 Experimental Details

We use only the officially allowed IWSLT 2021 data sets. The training data include high quality English-German parallel data from WMT 2020 (Barrault et al., 2020), English-German data from MuST-C.v2 (Di Gangi et al., 2019), the TED corpus (Cettolo et al., 2012) and OpenSubtitle (Lison and Tiedemann, 2016). For development, we use the concatenation of IWSLT test sets from 2014 and 2015. We test on IWSLT 2018 test set and tst-

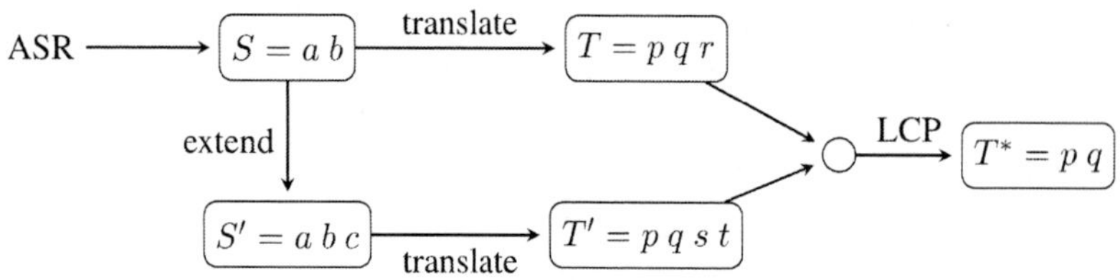

Figure 1: Dynamic Masking. The string $a\ b$ is provided as input to the agent (in a full SLT system it would come from ASR). The MT system then produces translations of the string and its extension, compares them, and outputs the longest common prefix (LCP)

	Source	Translation	MT Output
prefix	Back in New York,	Zurück in New York,	
extension	Back in New York, UNK	Damals in New York, in	
prefix	Back in New York, I	Damals in New York have ich	
extension	Back in New York, I UNK	Damals in New York war I	Damals in New York

Figure 2: An example of dynamic mask applied during translation. For the first prefix, the translation of the prefix and its extension disagree, so no output is produced (i.e. all output is masked). For the second prefix, the translation is more stable.

COMMON from MuST-C.v2. As the there is a significant overlap between MuST-C.v2 and tst-20{14,15,18}, we remove the overlaps from the MuST-C.v2 training data before training.

For preprocessing we rely only on Sentence-Piece tokenization (Kudo and Richardson, 2018); no other preprocessing tools are applied. We use a shared vocabulary size of 32k. Standard NMT models perform well when translation is done on a full sentence but as our approach is based on re-translation, we use training data that is a 1:1 mix of full sentences and prefix pairs (Niehues et al., 2018; Arivazhagan et al., 2020a). This ensures that our model can translate both full sentences and prefixes. To create prefix pairs, we first randomly choose a position in the source sentence and then take the proportionate length of the target sentence. Along with that we also add modified prefix pairs in which the source side has a shorter target prefix appended with the source prefix. The purpose of these modified prefix pairs was to investigate an alternative type of stabilisation, where the previous target prefix is fed into the translation of the current source prefix, but in early testing this method did not work well, so we did not pursue it further. The validation data is also pre-processed similarly to the training set. Note that this preprocessed validation set is used at training for early stopping and not for reporting the validation scores in the Table 2.

For training, we use the Marian toolkit (Junczys-Dowmunt et al., 2018) with the 'base' transformer architecture (Vaswani et al., 2017). First, we train a model using the aforementioned pre-processed training data and then fine-tune the model using MuST-C.v2 training data which is more of a domain specific data for simultaneous translation task. To train the language model for stabilisation, we use KenLM (Heafield, 2011) to train a 6-gram language model on the source-side training data. We have shown the number of sentences in each corpus in Table 1.

Corpus	Sentence pairs
Europarl	1.79 M
Rapid	1.45 M
News Commentary	0.35 M
OpenSubtitle	22.51 M
TED corpus	206 K
MuST-C.v2	248 K

Table 1: Corpora used in training the systems

4 Result and Analysis

We evaluate the model's performance on the full sentence translation before doing actual simultaneous translation. For this evaluation we use Sacre-BLEU (Post, 2018) on the MuST-C.v2 and TED 2018 test sets. The results on full sentence is shown in the Table 2. We see there is a significant improve-

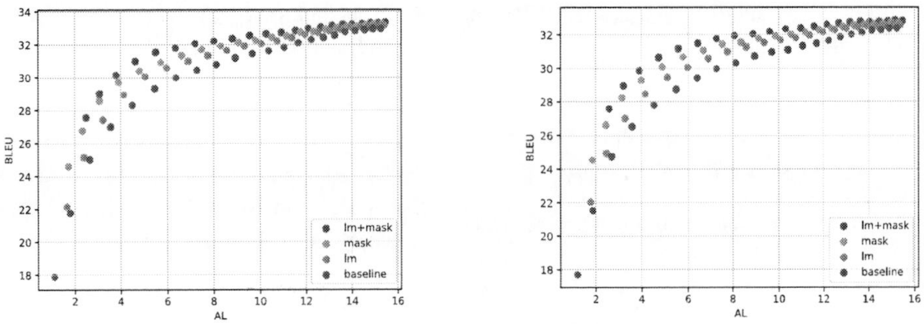

(a) Beam size = 12, Normalization = 1.0 (b) Beam size = 12, Normalization = 0.6

Figure 3: BLEU vs AL plots for English-German with different beam sizes and length normalization.

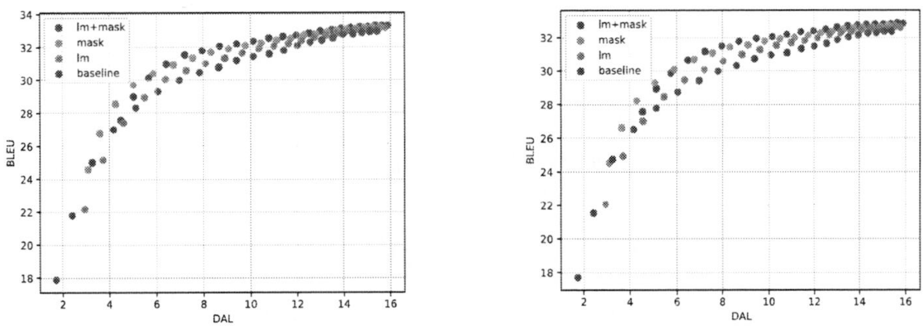

(a) Beam size = 12, Normalization = 1.0 (b) Beam size = 12, Normalization = 0.6

Figure 4: BLEU vs DAL plots for English-German with different beam sizes and length normalization.

ment after fine-tuning. For full sentence (or prefix in case of re-translation) translation we set beam size 12 and length normalization 1.0 in Marian.

	Validation	Test	
	TED 2014,15	TED 2018	MuST-C.v2
Baseline	30.8	27.5	32.7
Fine-tuned	31.9	29.4	33.6

Decoder settings: Beam size = 12; Normalization = 1.0

Table 2: BLEU scores on full sentence translation, computed with SacreBLEU.[a]

[a] BLEU+case.mixed+numrefs.1+smooth.exp+tok.13a+version.1.5.1

For evaluating the simultaneous translation, we use SimulEval (Ma et al., 2020) which calculates SacreBLEU for quality and Average Lagging (AL) (Ma et al., 2019), differential AL (DAL) (Cherry and Foster, 2019), and average proportion (AP) (Cho and Esipova, 2016) for latency. The official evaluation uses a blind test set, however, for submission purpose, we evaluate it on the MuST.v2 test set (tst-COMMON) set. We have following settings for re-translation:

Type	k	AL	BLEU	Approach
Full Sentence	-	-	33.60	-
High	20	14.73	33.09	lm
High	21	14.94	33.2	mask
High	20	14.8	**33.3**	lm+mask
Medium	6	5.98	30.58	lm
Medium	6	5.72	30.92	mask
Medium	5	5.49	**31.55**	lm+mask
Low	2	2.38	25.16	lm
Low	2	2.32	26.77	mask
Low	1	2.48	**27.57**	lm+mask

Table 3: AL vs BLEU scores for three regimes (Low, Medium, High) on MuST-C.v2 test set using beam size 12 and normalization 1.0. Best scores are in bold.

- *baseline*: The agent waits for initial k tokens and then alternates between READ and WRITE (using re-translation). This is similar to the wait-k approach by Ma et al. (2019).
- *lm*: After the initial k tokens, the agent uses the language model to determine the "mean-

ingful unit" boundaries, and only WRITEs when at a boundary.

- *mask*: This is similar to the baseline, except that the agent applies dynamic masking to produce a more stable translation.

- *lm+mask*: Combination of *lm* and *mask*. Thus in this approach, the agent first uses the *lm* score to decide whether to translate, and then uses dynamic mask to obtain a more stable translation.

The official evaluation has three regimes of latency: low (AL$\leq$ 3), medium (AL$\leq$ 6) and high (AL$\leq$ 15). In Table 3, we show the AL and BLEU scores for the three regimes with different approaches. We find that LM score and Dynamic masking combined achieve the best AL-BLEU trade-off.

To gain a fuller comparison of approaches, we calculate AL vs. BLEU and DAL vs. BLEU for a range of k values, and different stabilisation approaches and plot them as shown in Figures 3 and 4. Whilst for any given k, the *lm+mask* approach has higher AL (because it adds WAIT operations), we can see from the trajectory of the plot in Figure 3 that the *lm+mask* approach has the best AL-BLEU trade-off. While training the models, we set the length normalization to 0.6 which is used for scoring the development set for the purpose of early-stopping. However, we find that a normalization 1.0 performs slightly better than normalization 0.6 when doing re-translation. We show the plots for both normalization values in figures 3 and 4.

When the AL is 15, for many sentences it is a full sentence translation and thus all the approaches have similar BLEU scores. We also notice many sentences have negative AL scores. As the corpus AL scores is the average of the sentence level AL scores, negative scores can reduce the actual AL score. To address this shortcoming of AL, Cherry and Foster (2019), propose *Differentiable Average Lagging* (DAL) as an alternative. In Figure 4, we show the DAL vs BLEU scores. In Figure 4, we also observe that the proposed LM and masking improve the baseline by a significant margin in DAL-BLEU trade-off.

5 Conclusion

In this paper, we describe our submission to the IWSLT 2021 shared task on simultaneous text-to-text German-English translation. We work with a re-translation approach, enabling use to use an unmodified MT inference engine, together with an adaptation of wait k to trade off quality and latency. Additionally we proposed two techniques (dynamic masking and LM score) to improve translation quality by reducing the potential for flicker. We find that the combination of the proposed approaches achieves the best AL-BLEU trade-off.

Acknowledgments

This work was performed using resources provided by the Cambridge Service for Data Driven Discovery (CSD3) operated by the University of Cambridge Research Computing Service (http://www.csd3.cam.ac.uk/), provided by Dell EMC and Intel using Tier-2 funding from the Engineering and Physical Sciences Research Council (capital grant EP/P020259/1), and DiRAC funding from the Science and Technology Facilities Council (`www.dirac.ac.uk`).

This work has received funding from the European Union's Horizon 2020 Research and Innovation Programme under Grant Agreements No 825460 (Elitr) and No 825627 (European Language Grid).

References

Naveen Arivazhagan, Colin Cherry, Wolfgang Macherey, and George Foster. 2020a. Re-translation versus streaming for simultaneous translation. In *Proceedings of the 17th International Conference on Spoken Language Translation*, pages 220–227, Online. Association for Computational Linguistics.

Naveen Arivazhagan, Colin Cherry, Isabelle Te, Wolfgang Macherey, Pallavi Baljekar, and George Foster. 2020b. Re-translation strategies for long form, simultaneous, spoken language translation. In *ICASSP 2020-2020 IEEE International Conference on Acoustics, Speech and Signal Processing (ICASSP)*, pages 7919–7923. IEEE.

Loïc Barrault, Magdalena Biesialska, Ondřej Bojar, Marta R. Costa-jussà, Christian Federmann, Yvette Graham, Roman Grundkiewicz, Barry Haddow, Matthias Huck, Eric Joanis, Tom Kocmi, Philipp Koehn, Chi-kiu Lo, Nikola Ljubešić, Christof Monz, Makoto Morishita, Masaaki Nagata, Toshiaki Nakazawa, Santanu Pal, Matt Post, and Marcos Zampieri. 2020. Findings of the 2020 conference on machine translation (WMT20). In *Proceedings of the Fifth Conference on Machine Translation*, pages 1–55, Online. Association for Computational Linguistics.

Mauro Cettolo, Christian Girardi, and Marcello Federico. 2012. Wit3: Web inventory of transcribed and translated talks. In *Conference of european association for machine translation*, pages 261–268.

Colin Cherry and George Foster. 2019. Thinking slow about latency evaluation for simultaneous machine translation. *arXiv preprint arXiv:1906.00048*.

Kyunghyun Cho and Masha Esipova. 2016. Can neural machine translation do simultaneous translation? *arXiv preprint arXiv:1606.02012*.

Mattia A Di Gangi, Roldano Cattoni, Luisa Bentivogli, Matteo Negri, and Marco Turchi. 2019. Must-c: a multilingual speech translation corpus. In *2019 Conference of the North American Chapter of the Association for Computational Linguistics: Human Language Technologies*, pages 2012–2017. Association for Computational Linguistics.

Kenneth Heafield. 2011. Kenlm: Faster and smaller language model queries. In *Proceedings of the sixth workshop on statistical machine translation*, pages 187–197.

Marcin Junczys-Dowmunt, Roman Grundkiewicz, Tomasz Dwojak, Hieu Hoang, Kenneth Heafield, Tom Neckermann, Frank Seide, Ulrich Germann, Alham Fikri Aji, Nikolay Bogoychev, André F. T. Martins, and Alexandra Birch. 2018. Marian: Fast neural machine translation in C++. In *Proceedings of ACL 2018, System Demonstrations*, pages 116–121, Melbourne, Australia. Association for Computational Linguistics.

Taku Kudo and John Richardson. 2018. SentencePiece: A simple and language independent subword tokenizer and detokenizer for neural text processing. In *Proceedings of the 2018 Conference on Empirical Methods in Natural Language Processing: System Demonstrations*, pages 66–71, Brussels, Belgium. Association for Computational Linguistics.

Pierre Lison and Jörg Tiedemann. 2016. OpenSubtitles2016: Extracting large parallel corpora from movie and TV subtitles. In *Proceedings of the Tenth International Conference on Language Resources and Evaluation (LREC'16)*, pages 923–929, Portorož, Slovenia. European Language Resources Association (ELRA).

Mingbo Ma, Liang Huang, Hao Xiong, Renjie Zheng, Kaibo Liu, Baigong Zheng, Chuanqiang Zhang, Zhongjun He, Hairong Liu, Xing Li, Hua Wu, and Haifeng Wang. 2019. STACL: Simultaneous translation with implicit anticipation and controllable latency using prefix-to-prefix framework. In *Proceedings of the 57th Annual Meeting of the Association for Computational Linguistics*, pages 3025–3036, Florence, Italy. Association for Computational Linguistics.

Xutai Ma, Mohammad Javad Dousti, Changhan Wang, Jiatao Gu, and Juan Pino. 2020. Simuleval: An evaluation toolkit for simultaneous translation. In *Proceedings of the EMNLP*.

Jan Niehues, Thai Son Nguyen, Eunah Cho, Thanh-Le Ha, Kevin Kilgour, Markus Müller, Matthias Sperber, Sebastian Stüker, and Alex Waibel. 2016. Dynamic transcription for low-latency speech translation. In *Interspeech*, pages 2513–2517.

Jan Niehues, Ngoc-Quan Pham, Thanh-Le Ha, Matthias Sperber, and Alex Waibel. 2018. Low-latency neural speech translation. *arXiv preprint arXiv:1808.00491*.

Matt Post. 2018. A call for clarity in reporting BLEU scores. In *Proceedings of the Third Conference on Machine Translation: Research Papers*, pages 186–191, Brussels, Belgium. Association for Computational Linguistics.

Ashish Vaswani, Noam Shazeer, Niki Parmar, Jakob Uszkoreit, Llion Jones, Aidan N Gomez, Łukasz Kaiser, and Illia Polosukhin. 2017. Attention is all you need. In *Advances in Neural Information Processing Systems*, pages 5998–6008.

Yuekun Yao and Barry Haddow. 2020. Dynamic masking for improved stability in online spoken language translation. In *Proceedings of the 14th Conference of the Association for Machine Translation in the Americas (Volume 1: Research Track)*, pages 123–136, Virtual. Association for Machine Translation in the Americas.

Ruiqing Zhang, Chuanqiang Zhang, Zhongjun He, Hua Wu, and Haifeng Wang. 2020. Learning adaptive segmentation policy for simultaneous translation. In *Proceedings of the 2020 Conference on Empirical Methods in Natural Language Processing (EMNLP)*, pages 2280–2289, Online. Association for Computational Linguistics.

Without Further Ado: Direct and Simultaneous Speech Translation by AppTek in 2021

Parnia Bahar*, Patrick Wilken*, Mattia di Gangi, Evgeny Matusov
Applications Technology (AppTek), Aachen, Germany
{pbahar,pwilken,mdigangi,ematusov}@apptek.com

Abstract

This paper describes the offline and simultaneous speech translation (ST) systems developed at AppTek for IWSLT 2021. Our offline ST submission includes the direct end-to-end system and the so-called posterior tight integrated model, which is akin to the cascade system but is trained in an end-to-end fashion, where all the cascaded modules are end-to-end models themselves. For simultaneous ST, we combine hybrid automatic speech recognition (ASR) with a machine translation (MT) approach whose translation policy decisions are learned from statistical word alignments. Compared to last year, we improve general quality and provide a wider range of quality/latency trade-offs, both due to a data augmentation method making the MT model robust to varying chunk sizes. Finally, we present a method for ASR output segmentation into sentences that introduces a minimal additional delay.

1 Introduction

In this paper, we describe the AppTek speech translation systems that participate in the offline and simultaneous tracks of the IWSLT 2021 evaluation campaign. This paper is organized as follows: In Section 2, we briefly address our data preparation. Section 3 describes our offline ST models followed by the experimental results in Section 3.6. For the offline end-to-end translation task, we train deep Transformer models that benefit from pretraining, data augmentation in the form of synthetic data and SpecAugment, as well as domain adaptation on TED talks. Motivated by Bahar et al. (2021), we also collapse the ASR and MT components into a *posterior model* which passes on the ASR posteriors as input to the MT model. This system is not considered a direct model since it is closer to the cascade system while being end-to-end trainable. Our simultaneous translation systems are covered in Section 4 with discussions on experimental results in Section 4.5. We resume the work on our streaming MT model developed for IWSLT 2020, which is based on splitting the stream of input words into chunks learned from statistical word alignment. Most notably, we can implement a flexible quality/latency trade-off by simulating different latencies at training time. We also meet this year's requirement to support unsegmented input by developing a neural sentence segmenter that splits the ASR output into suitable translation units, using a varying number of future words as context which minimizes the latency added by this component.

The experiments have been done using RASR (Wiesler et al., 2014), RETURNN (Zeyer et al., 2018a), and Sisyphus (Peter et al., 2018).

2 Data Preparation

2.1 Text Data

We participate in the constrained condition and divide the allowed bilingual training data into in-domain (the TED and MuST-C v2 corpora), clean (the NewsCommentary, Europarl, and WikiTitles corpora), and out-of-domain (the rest). The concatenation of MuST-C dev and IWSLT tst2014 is used as our dev set for all experiments. Our data preparation includes two main steps: data filtering and text conversion. We filter the out-of-domain data based on similarity to the in-domain data in the embedding space, reducing the size from 62.5M to 30.0M lines. For the details on data filtering, please refer to our last year's submission (Bahar et al., 2020).

For a tighter coupling between ASR and MT in the cascade system, we apply additional text normalization (TN) to the English side of the data. It lowercases the text, removes all punctuation

*equal contribution

Proceedings of the 18th International Conference on Spoken Language Translation, pages 52–63
Bangkok, Thailand (Online), August 5–6, 2021.

marks, expands abbreviations, and converts numbers, dates, and other digit-based entities into their spoken form. This year, our TN approach includes a language model to score multiple readings of digit-based entities and randomly samples one of the top-scoring readings. We refer to it as *ASR-like* preprocessing. The target text preserves the casing and punctuation such that the MT model is able to implicitly handle the mapping.

2.2 Speech Data

We use almost all allowed ASR data, including EuroParl, How2, MuST-C, TED-LIUM, LibriSpeech, Mozilla Common Voice, and IWSLT TED corpora in a total of approximately 2300 hours of speech. The MuST-C and IWSLT TED corpora are chosen to be the in-domain data. For the speech side of the data, 80-dimensional Mel-frequency cepstral coefficients (MFCC) features are extracted every 10ms. The English text is lower-cased, punctuation-free, and contains no transcriber tags.

3 Offline Speech Translation

3.1 Neural Machine Translation

Our MT model for the offline task is based on the *big* Transformer model (Vaswani et al., 2017). Both self-attentive encoder and decoder are composed of 6 stacked layers with 16 attention heads. The model size is 1024 with a ReLu layer equipped with 4096 nodes. The effective batch size has been increased by accumulating gradient with a factor of 8. Adam is used with an initial learning rate of 0.0003. The learning rate decays by a factor of 0.9 in case of 20 checkpoints of non-decreased dev set perplexity. Label smoothing (Pereyra et al., 2017) and dropout rates of 0.1 are used. SentencePiece (Kudo and Richardson, 2018) segmentation with a vocabulary size of 30K is applied to both the source and target sentences. We use a translation factor to predict the casing of the target words (Wilken and Matusov, 2019).

3.2 Automatic Speech Recognition

We have trained attention-based models (Bahdanau et al., 2015; Vaswani et al., 2017) for the offline task mainly following (Zeyer et al., 2019). To enable pre-training of the ST speech encoder with different architectures, we have trained two attention-based models. The first model is based on the 6-layer bidirectional long short-term memory (BiLSTM) (Hochreiter and Schmidhuber, 1997) in the encoder and 1-layer LSTM in the decoder with 1024 nodes each. Another model is based on the Transformer architecture with 12 layers of self-attentive encoder and decoder. The model size is chosen to be 512, while the feed-forward dimension is set to 2048. Both models employ layer-wise network construction (Zeyer et al., 2018b, 2019), SpecAugment (Park et al., 2019; Bahar et al., 2019) and the connectionist temporal classification (CTC) loss (Kim et al., 2017) during training. We further fine-tune the models on the in-domain data plus TED-LIUM. As shown in Table 1, the models obtain low word error rates without using an external language model (LM). These attention-based models also outperform the hybrid LSTM/HMM model used in our simultaneous speech translation task.

#	Model	TED tst2015	MuST-C tst-HE	MuST-C tst-COMMON
1	LSTM	6.9	7.5	9.7
2	Transformer	5.2	5.5	7.3

Table 1: ASR word error rate results in [%].

3.3 Speech Translation

The ST models are trained using all the speech translation English→German corpora i.e. IWSLT TED, MuST-C, EuroParl ST, and CoVoST. After removing the off-limits talks from the training data, we end up with 740k segments. 5k and 32k byte-pair-encoding (BPE) (Sennrich et al., 2016) is applied to the English and German texts, respectively. We have done the data processing as described in Section 2. We also fine-tune on the in-domain data, using a lower learning rate of 8×10^{-5}.

3.3.1 End-to-End Direct Model

Following our experiments from last year, the direct ST model uses a combination of an LSTM speech encoder and a big Transformer decoder. The speech LSTM encoder has 6 BiLSTM layers with 1024 nodes each. We refer to this model as *LSTM-enc Transformer-dec*. The model is initialized by the encoder of LSTM-based ASR (line 1 in Table 1) and the decoder of the MT Transformer model.

We also experiment with the pure Transformer model both in the encoder and decoder. The Transformer-based ST models follow the network configuration used for speech recognition in Section 3.2. In order to shrink the input speech sequence, we add 2 layers of BiLSTM interleaved with max-pooling on top of the feature vectors in the encoder with a total length reduction of 6.

Layer-wise construction is done including the decoder: we start with two layers in the encoder and decoder and double the number of layers after every 5 sub-epochs (approx. 7k batches). During this, we linearly increase the hidden dimensions from 256 to 512 nodes and disable dropout, afterwards it is set to 10%. Based on our initial observation, the layer-wise construction helps convergence, in particular for such deep architectures. The CTC loss is also applied on top of the speech encoder during training. The Transformer-based model uses 10 steps of warm-up with an initial learning rate of 8×10^{-4}. We set the minimum learning rate to be 50 times smaller than this initial value. We also apply SpecAugment without time warping to the input frame sequence to reduce overfitting.

3.3.2 Posterior Tight Integration

The *posterior* model is inspired by Bahar et al. (2021) where the cascade components, i.e. the end-to-end ASR and MT models, are collapsed into a single end-to-end trainable model. The idea is to benefit from all types of available data, i.e. the ASR, MT, and direct ST corpora, and optimize all parameters jointly. To this end, we concatenate the trained Transformer-based ASR and MT models, but instead of passing the one-hot vectors for the source words to the MT model, we pass on the word posteriors as a soft decision. We sharpen the source word distribution by an exponent γ and then renormalize the probabilities.

A value of $\gamma = 1$ produces the posterior distribution itself, while larger values produce a more peaked distribution (almost one-hot representation). To convey more uncertainty, we use $\gamma = 1.0$ in training and $\gamma = 1.5$ in decoding to pick the most plausible token. We further continue training of the end-to-end model using the direct ST parallel data as a fine-tuning step. The constraint is that the ASR output and the MT input must have the same vocabulary. Therefore, we need to train a new MT model with the appropriate English vocabulary with 5K subwords. The ASR model is trained with SpecAugment, the Adam optimizer with an initial learning rate of 1×10^{-4}, and gradient accumulation of 20 steps. We also apply 10 steps of learning warm-up. We employ beam search with a size of 12 to generate the best recognized word sequence and then pass it to MT with the corresponding word posterior vectors.

3.4 Synthetic Data

To provide more parallel audio-translation pairs, we translate the English side of the ASR data (Jia et al., 2019) with our MT model. From our initial observations, we exclude those corpora for which we have the ground-truth target reference and only add those with the missing German side. Therefore, combining the real ST data with the synthetic data generated from the How2, TED-LIUM, LibriSpeech corpora, and the English→French part of MuST-C (Gaido et al., 2020b), we obtain about 1.7M parallel utterances corresponding to 33M English and 37M German words, respectively.

3.5 Speech Segmentation

To comply with the offline evaluation conditions for a direct speech translation system with unsegmented input, we cannot rely on ASR source transcripts for sentence segmentation. Thus, we train a segmenter aiming to generate homogeneous utterances based on voice activity detection (VAD) and endpoint detection (EP). The segmenter is a frame-level acoustic model that applies a 5-layer feed-forward network and predicts 3530 class labels, including one silence and 3529 speech phonemes. It compares the average silence score of 10 successive frames with the average of the best phoneme score from each of those frames to classify silence segments. We wait for a minimum of 20 consecutive silence frames between two speech segments, whereas the minimal number of continuous speech frames to form a speech segment is 100.

Besides improving audio segmentation, following the idea by Gaido et al. (2020a), we fine-tune the direct model on automatically segmented data to increase its robustness against sub-optimal non-homogeneous utterances. To resegment the German reference translations, we first use the baseline direct model to generate the German MT output for the automatically determined English segments. Then, we align this MT output with the reference translations and resegment the latter using a variant of the edit distance algorithm implemented in the mwerSegmenter tool (Matusov et al., 2005).

3.6 Offline Speech Translation Results

The offline speech translation systems results in terms of BLEU (Papineni et al., 2002) and TER (Snover et al., 2006) are presented in Table 2. The first group of results shows the text translation using the ASR-like processing. By comparing lines 1 and 3, we see an improvement in our MT develop-

#	System	TED tst2015 BLEU	TED tst2015 TER	MuST-C tst-HE BLEU	MuST-C tst-HE TER	MuST-C tst-COMMON BLEU	MuST-C tst-COMMON TER
Text MT (ASR-like source processing)							
1	AppTek 2020 submission	32.7	57.3	31.0	59.4	32.7	55.0
2	Transformer	32.4	57.8	30.8	60.0	33.1	54.5
3	+ fine-tuning	33.8	56.5	32.0	58.6	34.5	53.1
Cascaded ASR → MT							
4	AppTek 2020 submission (single)	30.9	61.0	29.3	61.7	30.0	58.0
5	AppTek 2020 submission (ensemble)	31.0	61.2	29.5	61.8	30.8	57.3
6	Transformer	31.4	59.3	30.1	60.7	31.4	56.9
7	**Posterior ASR → MT**	31.3	59.8	29.2	60.7	31.8	56.3
Direct ST							
8	AppTek 2020 submission (single)	26.4	64.7	24.7	66.9	29.4	58.6
9	LSTM-enc Transformer-dec	28.8	62.7	28.5	61.9	31.4	56.9
10	+ fine-tuning	28.3	64.8	27.8	62.8	33.1	55.6
11	+ resegmentation	28.0	63.3	27.3	62.8	31.1	57.1
12	Transformer	29.7	62.5	28.6	62.1	30.7	57.3
13	+ fine-tuning	29.5	62.7	28.6	62.4	31.0	57.1
Ensemble							
14	AppTek 2020 submission	28.0	63.2	27.4	63.3	30.4	57.8
15	lines 10(2x), 13(2x)	30.4	61.7	29.6	60.2	33.8	54.5

Table 2: Offline speech translation results measured in BLEU [%] and TER [%].

ment over time. As intended, fine-tuning using the in-domain data brings a significant gain. The MT model in line 3 and the Transformer-based ASR model from Table 1 make up the cascade system that outperforms our last year's submission, which ranked first on tst2020 using given segmentation. However, note that this year's cascade system is a single-shot try without careful model choice and fine-tuning. This result indicates fast progress of the speech translation task. As discussed in Section 3.3.2, passing ASR posteriors into the MT model, we further fine-tune the cascade model on the direct ST data. Therefore, the posterior model guarantees better or equal performance compared to the cascade system. Line 7 shows its competitiveness.

Regarding direct ST, we observe that the pure Transformer model (line 12) performs on par with the model with the LSTM-based encoder (line 9). Our main goal has been to employ different model choices to potentially capture different knowledge. These models already use synthetic data. The direct model with the LSTM encoder uses pretraining of components, while all pretraining experiments on the Transformer model degrade the translation quality. The reason might be partly attributed to the fact that we use a deep encoder (12 layers with size 512) and a large decoder (6 layers with model size 1024) with 3 to 6 layers of adaptors in between. The training deals with a more complex error propagation, causing a sub-optimal solution for the entire optimization problem. Again, fine-tuning helps both models in terms of the translation quality, in particular on tst-COMMON. Using the resegmeted MuST-C training data (line 11) leads to degradation; however, we have observed that this model generates less noise and fewer repeated phrases.

Finally, we ensemble 4 models (two checkpoints each from lines 10 and 13) constituting our primary submission for the 2021 IWSLT evaluation. In comparison to the 2020 submission, improvements of more than 2% in BLEU can be observed for both single and ensemble models.

4 Simultaneous Speech Translation

For the IWSLT 2021 simultaneous speech translation English→German tracks, we continue exploring our last year's alignment-based approach (Wilken et al., 2020), which uses a cascade of a streaming ASR system and an MT model.

4.1 Simultaneous MT Model

This section gives a short summary of (Wilken et al., 2020). Our simultaneous MT method is based on the observation that latency in translation is mainly caused by word order differences between the source and target language. For example, an interpreter might have to wait for a verb at the end of a source sentence if it appears earlier in the target language. We therefore extract such word reordering information from statistical word alignments (generated using the Eflomal tool (Östling and Tiedemann, 2016)) by splitting sentence pairs into bilingual chunks such that word reordering happens only within chunk boundaries.

For the MT model, we use the LSTM-based attention model (Bahdanau et al., 2015). We make the following changes to support streaming decoding: **1.** We only use a forward encoder.[1] **2.** We add a binary softmax on top of the encoder trained to predict source chunk boundaries as extracted from the word alignment. Importantly, we add a delay D to the boundaries such that a detection at position j corresponds to a chunk boundary after position $j-D$. The future context available this way greatly increases the prediction accuracy. **3.** We add another softmax on top of the decoder to predict the target-side chunk boundaries. They are needed as a stopping criterion in beam search. **4.** We mask the attention energies such that when generating the k-th target chunk only the source words encoding in the chunks 1 to k can be accessed.

Inference happens by reading source words until a chunk boundary is predicted. Then the decoder is run using beam search until all hypotheses have predicted chunk end. During this, all source positions of the current sentence read so far are considered by the attention mechanism. Finally, the first best hypothesis is output and the process starts over.

4.2 Random Dropping of Chunk Boundaries

One evident limitation of our IWSLT 2020 systems (Bahar et al., 2020; Wilken et al., 2020) has been that we could not provide a range of different quality-latency trade-offs. This is because basing translation policy on hard word alignments leads to a fixed "operation point" whose average lagging is solely determined by the amount of differences in word order between the source and target language.

To overcome this, we make the observation that two subsequent chunks can be merged without violating the monotonicity constraint. This corresponds to skipping a chunk boundary at inference time and waiting for further context, at the cost of higher latency. The number of skipped chunk boundaries can be controlled by adjusting the threshold probability t_b which is used to make the source chunk boundary decision. In (Wilken et al., 2020), we have found that a threshold t_b different than 0.5 hurts MT performance because the decoder strongly adapts to the chunks seen in training, such that longer merged chunks are not translated well.

To solve this issue, we simulate higher detection thresholds t_b at training time by dropping each chunk boundary in the data randomly with a probability of p_{drop}. In fact, we create several duplicates of the training data applying different values of p_{drop} and shuffle them. This way the model learns to translate (merged) chunks with a wide variety of lengths, in the extreme case of $p_{\text{drop}} = 1$ even full sentences. This goes in the direction of general data augmentation by extracting prefix-pairs as done by Dalvi et al. (2018); Niehues et al. (2018). Importantly, we still train the source chunk prediction softmax on *all* boundaries to not distort the estimated probabilities.

4.3 Streaming ASR

As the ASR component, we use the same hybrid LSTM/HMM model (Bourlard and Wellekens, 1989) as in last year's submission (Bahar et al., 2020). The acoustic model consists of four BiLSTM layers with 512 units and is trained with the cross-entropy loss on triphone states. A count-based n-gram look-ahead language model is used. The streaming recognizer implements a version of chunked processing (Chen and Huo, 2016; Zeyer et al., 2016), where the acoustic model processes the input audio in fixed-length overlapping windows. The initial state of the backward LSTM is initialized for each window, while – as opposed to last year's system – the forward LSTM state is propagated among different windows. This state carry-over improves general recognition quality and allows us to use smaller window sizes W_{ASR} to achieve lower latencies.

4.4 Sentence Segmentation

This year's simultaneous MT track also requires supporting unsegmented input. To split the unsegmented source word stream into suitable translation units, we employ two different methods for the text and speech input condition.

[1] Although we experiment with a BiLSTM encoder in streaming, we are unable to achieve an improved performance.

4.4.1 Text Input

For the text-to-text translation task, the input contains punctuation marks that can be used for reliable sentence segmentation. We heuristically insert sentence ends whenever the following conditions are fulfilled:

1. the current token ends in sentence final punctuation (`. ? ! ;`), or punctuation plus quote (`." ?" !" ;"`), yet is not contained in a closed list of abbreviations (`Mrs. Dr. etc.`, ...);
2. the first character of the next word is not lowercased.

Those heuristics are sufficient to recover the original sentence boundaries of the MuST-C dev set with a precision of 96% and a recall of 82%, where most of the remaining differences can be attributed to lines with multiple sentences in the original segmentation. The described method uses one future word as context and therefore does not introduce additional delay into the system compared to awaiting a sentence end token. We enable this kind of sentence splitting also in the case of segmented input as we find that splitting lines with multiple sentences slightly increases translation performance.

4.4.2 Speech Input

For the speech-to-text translation task, sentence segmentation is a much harder problem. Our streaming ASR system does not require segmentation of the input; however, its output is lower-cased and punctuation-free text.

In the literature, the problem of segmenting ASR output into sentences has been approached using count-based language models (Stolcke and Shriberg, 1996), conditional random fields (Liu et al., 2005), and other classical models. Recently, recurrent neural networks have been applied, either in the form of language models (Wang et al., 2016) or sequence labeling (Iranzo-Sánchez et al., 2020). These methods either are meant for offline segmentation or require a fixed context of future words, thus increasing the overall latency of the system.

Wang et al. (2019) predict sentence boundaries with a various number of future words as context within the same model, allowing for dynamic segmentation decisions at inference time depending on the necessary context. We adopt the proposed model, which is a 3-layer LSTM with a hidden size of 512, generating softmax distributions over the labels $y^{(k)}$, $k \in \{0, \ldots, m\}$, where m is the maximum context length. For each timestep t, $y_t^{(k)}$ represents a sentence boundary at position $t - k$, i.e. k words in the past. $y^{(0)}$ represents the case of no boundary. To generate training examples, each sentence is extended with the first m words of the next sentence, and those words are labelled with $y^{(1)}$ to $y^{(m)}$.

However, we make a crucial change on how the model is applied: instead of outputting words only after a sentence end decision[2], we output words as soon as the model is confident that they still belong to the current sentence. For this purpose, we reinterpret the threshold vector $\theta^{(k)}$ such that $p(y_t^{(k)}) > \theta^{(k)}$ detects a *possible* instead of a definite sentence boundary at position $t - k$. The idea is that as long as no incoming word is considered a possible sentence end, all words can be passed on to MT *without any delay*. Only if $p(y^{(1)}) > \theta^{(1)}$, the current word is buffered, and we wait for the second word of context to make a more informed decision. If for $k = 2$ the boundary is still possible, a third word is read, and so on. A final sentence end decision is only made at the maximum context length ($k = m$). In this case, a sentence end token is emitted and the inference is restarted using the buffered words. If during the process $p(y^{(k)}) < \theta^{(k)}$ for any k, the word buffer is flushed, except for words still needed for pending decisions at later positions. Note that false negative decisions are not corrected later using more context because the corresponding words in the output stream have already been read and possibly translated by the MT system.

4.5 Simultaneous MT Experiments

4.5.1 MT Model Training

We use the data described in Section 2.1 to train the simultaneous MT models. For the text input condition, no ASR-like preprocessing is applied as the input is natural text. SentencePiece vocabularies of size 30K are used for source and target. We create copies of the training data with dropped chunk boundaries (Section 4.2) with probabilities of $p_{\text{drop}} = 0.0, 0.2, 0.5$ and 1.0. 6 encoder and 2 decoder layers with a hidden size of 1000 are used, the word embedding size is 620. The chunk boundary delay is set to $D = 2$. Dropout and label smoothing is used as for the offline MT model. Adam optimizer is used with an initial learning rate of 0.001, decreased by factor 0.9 after 10 subepochs of non-decreasing dev set perplexity. Train-

[2] This is only appropriate in their scenario of an offline MT system as the next step in the pipeline.

ing takes 150 and 138 sub-epochs of 1M lines each for text and speech input, respectively.

4.5.2 Latency/Quality Trade-Off Parameters

As described in Section 4.2, we can vary the boundary prediction threshold probability t_b to set different latency/quality trade-offs at inference time. In our experiments, we observe that the longer a chunk gets the less confident the model is in predicting its boundary, leading in some cases to very large chunks and thus high latency. To counteract this effect, we introduce another meta-variable Δt_b which defines a decrement of the threshold per source subword in the chunk, making the current threshold t'_b at a given chunk length l: $t'_b = t_b - \Delta t_b \cdot (l-1)$. This usually leads to chunks of reasonable length, while also setting a theoretical limit of $l \leq \lceil t_b/\Delta t_b \rceil + 1$.

For the speech input condition, we vary the ASR window size W_{ASR} of the acoustic model in the ASR system between 250ms, 500ms and 1000ms.

Finally, we apply length normalization by dividing the model scores by I^α, I being the chunk translation length in subwords, and tune α to values ≤ 1 for low latency trade-offs as we notice the MT model tends to overtranslate in this range.

4.5.3 Fine-tuning

We fine-tune all simultaneous MT models on in-domain data described in Section 2. We also add a copy of MuST-C where the transcriptions produced by our hybrid ASR system are used as source to make MT somewhat robust against ASR errors.

Furthermore, we create **low latency** systems by fine-tuning as above, but changing the chunk boundary prediction delay D from 2 to 1. This way the latency of the MT component is pushed to a minimum; however, at the cost of reduced translation quality caused by unreliable chunking decisions with a context of only one future word.

4.5.4 Sentence Segmenter

We train the sentence segmenter for unsegmented audio input (Section 4.4.2) on the English source side of the MT training data to which we apply ASR-like preprocessing and subword splitting. Note that the sentence splitting of the MT data itself is not perfect, and a better data selection might have improved results.

We set the maximum length of the future context to $m = 3$ as the baseline results in Wang et al. (2019) indicate no major improvement for longer contexts. Adam is used with a learning rate

W_{ASR} (ms)	**dev**	**tst-HE**	**tst-COMMON**
250	11.7	11.1	12.4
500	10.7	10.3	10.8
1000	10.4	9.7	10.4

Table 3: WER [%] of streaming hybrid ASR on MuST-C test sets for various window sizes W_{ASR}

of 0.001, reduced by factor 0.8 after 3 epochs of non-improved dev set perplexity. Training takes 27 sub-epochs of 690K sentences each. For inference, we set the threshold vector to $\theta = (0.05, 0.1, 0.5)$ by analysing the amount of false negatives depending on $\theta^{(k)}$ for $k = 1, 2$ and by determining a good recall/precision trade-off for $k = 3$. The resulting segmenter has a recall of 61.4% and a precision of 64.1% on the original tst-COMMON sentence boundaries. Words are buffered for only 0.4 positions on average.

4.5.5 Simultaneous MT Results

The simultaneous MT systems are evaluated with the SimulEval tool (Ma et al., 2020). The BLEU and Average Lagging (AL) (Ma et al., 2019) metrics are used to score the different latency/quality trade-offs. Beam size 12 is used in all cases.

Figure 1 shows the results for the text input condition for MuST-C tst-HE and tst-COMMON. The filled data points correspond to the main text-input MT model. The points without fill show the results after low-latency fine-tuning with $D = 1$. The different trade-offs are achieved by varying the boundary threshold t_b from 0.3 to 0.9 using various decrements Δt_b. The full list of trade-off parameters is given in the appendix, Table 6. With the low-latency system an AL value of 2 words is achieved; however, at the cost of low BLEU scores of 22.2 and 25.1 on tst-HE and tst-COMMON, respectively. A reasonable operation point could for example be at an AL of 4, where BLEU scores of around 29.8 and 31.6 are achieved. For higher latency values, translation quality increases less rapidly, peaking at 31.0 and 33.1 BLEU for the two test sets. On tst-COMMON, a bump in the graph can be observed between 4 and 6 AL. This correlates with a problem of too short translations of up to 3% less words than the reference in this range. Below 4 AL, we are able to tune the hypothesis lengths via the length normalization exponent α. But above 4 AL, the optimal α is already 1, and setting $\alpha > 1$ does not yield improvements.

Figure 2 shows the results for the speech input condition. The trade-offs are achieved using sim-

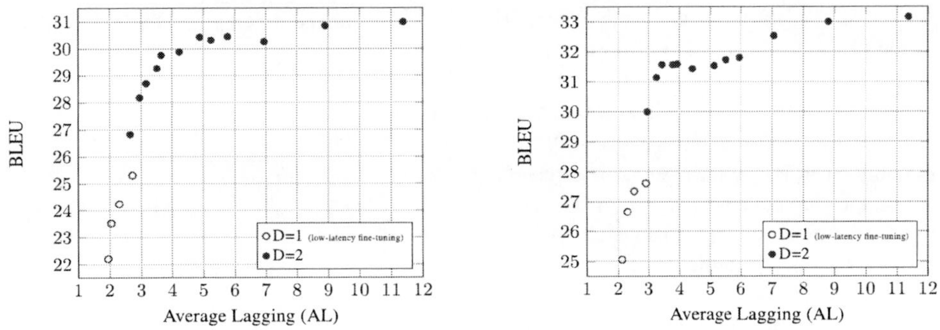

(a) tst-HE

(b) tst-COMMON

Figure 1: Results for English→German text-to-text simultaneous translation

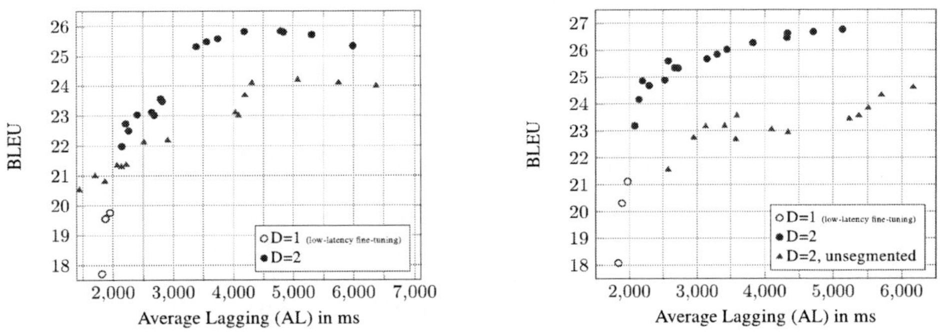

(a) tst-HE

(b) tst-COMMON

Figure 2: Results for English→German speech-to-text simultaneous translation

ilar parameters as for the text input (Table 7 in the appendix shows the full list). Additionally, we vary the ASR window size: for the 7 data points with lowest latency $W_{\text{ASR}} = 250\text{ms}$ is used, for the highest 3 $W_{\text{ASR}} = 1000\text{ms}$. The remaining points use a value of 500ms. The word error rates for different W_{ASR} are shown in Table 3. On tst-COMMON, the general shape of the curve is similar to text input. The lowest obtained AL is 1.8s. For high latencies, BLEU saturates at 26.8. On tst-HE, quality improves less rapidly with increased latency and even decreases slightly for AL values > 5s. This indicates that the trade-off parameters, which have been tuned on dev, do not translate perfectly to other test sets in all cases. When comparing text and speech input results for high latency values, we conclude that recognition errors in the ASR system lead to a drop in translation quality by about 5-6% absolute in terms of BLEU.

Figure 2 also shows results for unsegmented input[3]. Since no official scoring conditions have been defined, we therefore create partly unsegmented test sets ourselves by concatenating every 10 subsequent sentences of the test sets. The AL scores are taken as-is from SimulEval, the BLEU scores were computed using the mwerSegmenter tool. (Scoring the segmented results with mwerSegmenter leads to unaltered scores.) In general, the missing segmentation seems to lead to a drop of 2-3% BLEU. For tst-HE, unsegmented input leads to better results in the low latency range which is unrealistic and indicates that the AL values computed for single and multiple sentences are not comparable. In future work, we will analyze the scoring of the unsegmented case further and use trade-off parameters which are tuned for this case.

[3]For tst-COMMON we skip the 3 points with highest latency for better visibility of the other points.

5 Final Results

In comparison to last year's submission (Bahar et al., 2020), the result of offline speech translation models have improved. The official results on the tst2020 and tst2021 test sets are shown in Table 4, as evaluated by the IWSLT 2021 organizers. This year, there are two references along with the BLEU score using both of them together. *Ref1* is the original one from the TED website, while *Ref2* has been created to simulate shorter translations as used in subtitles.

Our end-to-end direct (an ensemble of 4 models), cascade (a single model) and posterior (a single model) systems correspond to the lines 15, 6 and 7 of Table 2, respectively. We observe that the provided reference segmentation negatively affects the ST quality regardless of the systems themselves. In contrast, the segmentation obtained by our segmentation model provides segments which apparently are more sentence-like including less noise and thus can be better translated. We note that our end-to-end direct primary and contrastive systems have the identical model parameters with an ensemble of 4 models while they utilize different speech segmentations. In the direct contrastive system, we apply our last year's segmentation which seems to be slightly better than that of this year. Similar to the MuST-C tst-COMMON set in Table 2, the direct model outperforms the cascaded-wise systems on tst2020 whereas it is behind on tst2021 with automatic segmentation. On the condition with reference segmentation, the difference between our cascade and direct models is lower where both systems almost preform the same. More results can be found in (Anastasopoulos et al., 2021).

System	TED tst2020	TED tst2021 Ref1	Ref2	both
reference segmentation				
direct (submission 2020)	20.5	-	-	-
direct	22.2	20.2	17.1	28.7
cascade	21.4	20.7	17.1	28.6
posterior	20.6	20.1	16.8	28.3
automatic segmentation				
direct (submission 2020)	23.5	-	-	-
direct primary	24.5	22.6	18.3	31.0
direct contrastive	25.1	22.8	18.9	32.0
cascade	24.0	23.3	19.2	32.1
posterior†	23.1	21.9	18.1	30.4

Table 4: AppTek IWSLT 2021 submission for offline speech translation measured by BLEU [%]. †: our cascade primary system at the time of submission.

Table 5 shows the official results for our simultaneous speech translation submission. The classification into different latency regimes is done by the organizers based on results on tst-COMMON. Due to dropping chunk boundaries in training, this year we are able to provide systems in all latency regimes, except for the speech track where a low-latency system (AL $<$ 1s) is not possible to achieve with our cascade approach where the individual components already have a relatively high minimal latency.

latency regime	BLEU [%]	AL
text-to-text		
low	22.8	3.1
mid	25.7	6.2
high	26.6	12.0
speech-to-text		
mid	16.6	2.0s
high	21.0	4.0s

Table 5: AppTek IWSLT 2021 official simultaneous speech translation results on the **blind** text and speech input test sets.

6 Conclusion

This work summarizes the results of AppTek's participation in the IWSLT 2021 evaluation campaign for the offline and simultaneous speech translation tasks. Compared to AppTek's systems at IWSLT 2020, the cascade and direct systems present an improvement of 0.9% and 2.6% in BLEU and TER, respectively, averaging over 3 test sets. This shows that we further decreased the gap in MT quality between the cascade and direct models. We have also explored the posterior model, which enables generating translations along with transcripts. This is particularly important for applications when both sequences have to be displayed to users.

For the simultaneous translation systems, this year we are able to provide configurations in a wide latency range, starting at AL values of 2 words and 1.8s for text and speech input, respectively. For speech input, a maximal translation quality of 25.8 BLEU is achieved on tst-HE, 3% BLEU improvement compared to the previous system at a similar latency. By using future context of variable length we are able to do reliable sentence segmentation of ASR output designed to introduce minimal additional delay to the system.

References

Antonios Anastasopoulos, Ondřej Bojar, Jacob Bremerman, Roldano Cattoni, Maha Elbayad, Marcello Federico, Xutai Ma, Satoshi Nakamura, Matteo Negri, Jan Niehues, Juan Pino, Elizabeth Salesky, Sebastian Stüker, Katsuhito Sudoh, Marco Turchi, Alex Waibel, Changhan Wang, and Matthew Wiesner. 2021. Findings of the IWSLT 2021 Evaluation Campaign. In *Proceedings of the 18th International Conference on Spoken Language Translation (IWSLT 2021)*, Online.

Parnia Bahar, Tobias Bieschke, Ralf Schlüter, and Hermann Ney. 2021. Tight integrated end-to-end training for cascaded speech translation. In *IEEE Spoken Language Technology Workshop*, pages 950–957, Shenzhen, China.

Parnia Bahar, Patrick Wilken, Tamer Alkhouli, Andreas Guta, Pavel Golik, Evgeny Matusov, and Christian Herold. 2020. Start-before-end and end-to-end: Neural speech translation by apptek and rwth aachen university. In *Proceedings of the 17th International Conference on Spoken Language Translation*, pages 44–54.

Parnia Bahar, Albert Zeyer, Ralf Schlüter, and Hermann Ney. 2019. On using specaugment for end-to-end speech translation. In *International Workshop on Spoken Language Translation (IWSLT)*.

Dzmitry Bahdanau, Kyunghyun Cho, and Yoshua Bengio. 2015. Neural machine translation by jointly learning to align and translate. In *Proceedings of the International Conference on Learning Representations (ICLR)*.

Hervé Bourlard and Christian J. Wellekens. 1989. Links between Markov models and multilayer perceptrons. In D.S. Touretzky, editor, *Advances in Neural Information Processing Systems I*, pages 502–510. Morgan Kaufmann, San Mateo, CA, USA.

Kai Chen and Qiang Huo. 2016. Traininpg deep bidirectional LSTM acoustic model for LVCSR by a context-sensitive-chunk BPTT approach. *IEEE/ACM Transactions on Audio, Speech, and Language Processing*, 24(7):1185–1193.

Fahim Dalvi, Nadir Durrani, Hassan Sajjad, and Stephan Vogel. 2018. Incremental decoding and training methods for simultaneous translation in neural machine translation. *arXiv preprint arXiv:1806.03661*.

Marco Gaido, Mattia Antonino Di Gangi, Matteo Negri, Mauro Cettolo, and Marco Turchi. 2020a. Contextualized translation of automatically segmented speech. In *Interspeech 2020, 21st Annual Conference of the International Speech Communication Association, Virtual Event, Shanghai, China, 25-29 October 2020*, pages 1471–1475. ISCA.

Marco Gaido, Mattia Antonino Di Gangi, Matteo Negri, and Marco Turchi. 2020b. End-to-end speech-translation with knowledge distillation: Fbk@iwslt2020. In *Proceedings of the 17th International Conference on Spoken Language Translation, IWSLT 2020, Online, July 9 - 10, 2020*, pages 80–88. Association for Computational Linguistics.

Sepp Hochreiter and Jürgen Schmidhuber. 1997. Long short-term memory. *Neural Computation*, 9(8):1735–1780.

Javier Iranzo-Sánchez, Adrià Giménez Pastor, Joan Albert Silvestre-Cerdà, Pau Baquero-Arnal, Jorge Civera Saiz, and Alfons Juan. 2020. Direct segmentation models for streaming speech translation. In *Proceedings of the 2020 Conference on Empirical Methods in Natural Language Processing (EMNLP)*, pages 2599–2611.

Ye Jia, Melvin Johnson, Wolfgang Macherey, Ron J. Weiss, Yuan Cao, Chung-Cheng Chiu, Naveen Ari, Stella Laurenzo, and Yonghui Wu. 2019. Leveraging weakly supervised data to improve end-to-end speech-to-text translation. In *IEEE International Conference on Acoustics, Speech and Signal Processing, ICASSP 2019, Brighton, United Kingdom, May 12-17, 2019*, pages 7180–7184. IEEE.

Suyoun Kim, Takaaki Hori, and Shinji Watanabe. 2017. Joint ctc-attention based end-to-end speech recognition using multi-task learning. In *Proc. Int. Conf. on Acoustics, Speech, and Signal Processing*, pages 4835–4839, New Orleans, LA, USA.

Taku Kudo and John Richardson. 2018. Sentencepiece: A simple and language independent subword tokenizer and detokenizer for neural text processing. In *Proceedings of the 2018 Conference on Empirical Methods in Natural Language Processing: System Demonstrations*, pages 66–71.

Yang Liu, Andreas Stolcke, Elizabeth Shriberg, and Mary Harper. 2005. Using conditional random fields for sentence boundary detection in speech. In *Proceedings of the 43rd Annual Meeting of the Association for Computational Linguistics (ACL'05)*, pages 451–458.

Mingbo Ma, Liang Huang, Hao Xiong, Renjie Zheng, Kaibo Liu, Baigong Zheng, Chuanqiang Zhang, Zhongjun He, Hairong Liu, Xing Li, Hua Wu, and Haifeng Wang. 2019. STACL: Simultaneous translation with implicit anticipation and controllable latency using prefix-to-prefix framework. In *Proceedings of the 57th Annual Meeting of the Association for Computational Linguistics*, pages 3025–3036, Florence, Italy. Association for Computational Linguistics.

Xutai Ma, Mohammad Javad Dousti, Changhan Wang, Jiatao Gu, and Juan Pino. 2020. Simuleval: An evaluation toolkit for simultaneous translation. *arXiv preprint arXiv:2007.16193*.

Evgeny Matusov, Gregor Leusch, Oliver Bender, and Hermann Ney. 2005. Evaluating machine translation output with automatic sentence segmentation. In *International Workshop on Spoken Language Translation*, pages 148–154, Pittsburgh, PA, USA.

Jan Niehues, Ngoc-Quan Pham, Thanh-Le Ha, Matthias Sperber, and Alex Waibel. 2018. Low-latency neural speech translation. *arXiv preprint arXiv:1808.00491*.

Robert Östling and Jörg Tiedemann. 2016. Efficient word alignment with Markov Chain Monte Carlo. *Prague Bulletin ofMathematical Linguistics*, 106:125–146.

Kishore Papineni, Salim Roukos, Todd Ward, and Wei-Jing Zhu. 2002. BLEU: a Method for Automatic Evaluation of Machine Translation. In *Proceedings of the 41st Annual Meeting of the Association for Computational Linguistics*, pages 311–318, Philadelphia, Pennsylvania, USA.

Daniel S Park, William Chan, Yu Zhang, Chung-Cheng Chiu, Barret Zoph, Ekin D Cubuk, and Quoc V Le. 2019. SpecAugment: A simple data augmentation method for automatic speech recognition.

Gabriel Pereyra, George Tucker, Jan Chorowski, Lukasz Kaiser, and Geoffrey E. Hinton. 2017. Regularizing neural networks by penalizing confident output distributions. *CoRR*, abs/1701.06548.

Jan-Thorsten Peter, Eugen Beck, and Hermann Ney. 2018. Sisyphus, a workflow manager designed for machine translation and automatic speech recognition. In *Conference on Empirical Methods in Natural Language Processing*, Brussels, Belgium.

Rico Sennrich, Barry Haddow, and Alexandra Birch. 2016. Neural machine translation of rare words with subword units. In *Proceedings of the 54th Annual Meeting of the Association for Computational Linguistics, ACL 2016, August 7-12, 2016, Berlin, Germany, Volume 1: Long Papers*.

Matthew Snover, Bonnie Dorr, Richard Schwartz, Linnea Micciulla, and John Makhoul. 2006. A Study of Translation Edit Rate with Targeted Human Annotation. In *Proceedings of the 7th Conference of the Association for Machine Translation in the Americas*, pages 223–231, Cambridge, Massachusetts, USA.

Andreas Stolcke and Elizabeth Shriberg. 1996. Automatic linguistic segmentation of conversational speech. In *Proceeding of Fourth International Conference on Spoken Language Processing. ICSLP'96*, volume 2, pages 1005–1008. IEEE.

Ashish Vaswani, Noam Shazeer, Niki Parmar, Jakob Uszkoreit, Llion Jones, Aidan N Gomez, Łukasz Kaiser, and Illia Polosukhin. 2017. Attention is all you need. In *Advances in Neural Information Processing Systems*, pages 5998–6008.

Xiaolin Wang, Andrew Finch, Masao Utiyama, and Eiichiro Sumita. 2016. An efficient and effective online sentence segmenter for simultaneous interpretation. In *Proceedings of the 3rd Workshop on Asian Translation (WAT2016)*, pages 139–148.

Xiaolin Wang, Masao Utiyama, and Eiichiro Sumita. 2019. Online sentence segmentation for simultaneous interpretation using multi-shifted recurrent neural network. In *Proceedings of Machine Translation Summit XVII Volume 1: Research Track*, pages 1–11.

Simon Wiesler, Alexander Richard, Pavel Golik, Ralf Schlüter, and Hermann Ney. 2014. RASR/NN: The RWTH neural network toolkit for speech recognition. In *IEEE International Conference on Acoustics, Speech, and Signal Processing*, pages 3313–3317, Florence, Italy.

Patrick Wilken, Tamer Alkhouli, Evgeny Matusov, and Pavel Golik. 2020. Neural simultaneous speech translation using alignment-based chunking. In *International Workshop on Spoken Language Translation*.

Patrick Wilken and Evgeny Matusov. 2019. Novel applications of factored neural machine translation. *arXiv preprint arXiv:1910.03912*.

Albert Zeyer, Tamer Alkhouli, and Hermann Ney. 2018a. RETURNN as a generic flexible neural toolkit with application to translation and speech recognition. In *Proceedings of ACL 2018, Melbourne, Australia, July 15-20, 2018, System Demonstrations*, pages 128–133.

Albert Zeyer, Parnia Bahar, Kazuki Irie, Ralf Schlüter, and Hermann Ney. 2019. A comparison of transformer and lstm encoder decoder models for asr. In *IEEE Automatic Speech Recognition and Understanding Workshop*, pages 8–15, Sentosa, Singapore.

Albert Zeyer, Kazuki Irie, Ralf Schlüter, and Hermann Ney. 2018b. Improved training of end-to-end attention models for speech recognition. In *19th Annual Conf. Interspeech, Hyderabad, India, 2-6 Sep.*, pages 7–11.

Albert Zeyer, Ralf Schlüter, and Hermann Ney. 2016. Towards online-recognition with deep bidirectional LSTM acoustic models. In *Interspeech*, pages 3424–3428, San Francisco, CA, USA.

A Appendix

trade-off id	D	t_b	Δt_b	α
1'	1	0.3	0.006	0.3
2'	1	0.4	0.008	0.6
3'	1	0.5	0.012	0.8
4'	1	0.6	0.012	1.0
1	2	0.3	0.006	0.3
2	2	0.4	0.008	0.4
3	2	0.5	0.012	0.6
4	2	0.6	0.012	0.8
5	2	0.6	0.008	0.8
6	2	0.7	0.012	1.0
7	2	0.9	0.032	1.0
8	2	0.9	0.027	1.0
9	2	0.9	0.023	1.0
10	2	0.9	0.017	1.0
11	2	0.9	0.012	1.0
12	2	0.9	0.008	1.0

Table 6: Trade-off parameters for submitted **text input** simultaneous MT systems, sorted from low to high latency. $D = 1$ refers to low latency fine-tuning described in Section 4.5.3. Other parameters are explained in Section 4.5.2.

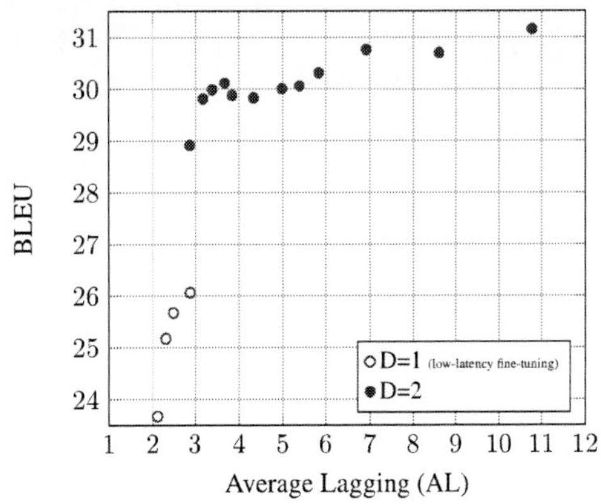

Figure 3: Results for English→German text-to-text simultaneous translation on MuST-C dev

trade-off id	D	W_{ASR} (ms)	t_b	Δt_b	α
1'	1	250	0.3	0.006	0.3
2'	1	250	0.4	0.008	0.6
3'	1	250	0.5	0.012	0.8
1	2	250	0.3	0.006	0.3
2	2	250	0.4	0.008	0.6
3	2	250	0.5	0.012	0.8
4	2	250	0.6	0.012	1.0
5	2	500	0.4	0.008	0.6
6	2	500	0.5	0.012	0.8
7	2	500	0.6	0.012	1.0
8	2	500	0.6	0.008	1.0
9	2	500	0.9	0.032	1.0
10	2	500	0.9	0.027	1.0
11	2	500	0.9	0.023	1.0
12	2	500	0.9	0.017	1.0
13	2	500	0.9	0.012	1.0
14	2	1000	0.9	0.017	1.0
15	2	1000	0.9	0.012	1.0
16	2	1000	0.9	0.008	1.0

Table 7: Trade-off parameters for submitted **speech input** simultaneous MT systems, sorted from low to high latency. $D = 1$ refers to low latency fine-tuning described in Section 4.5.3. Other parameters are explained in Section 4.5.2.

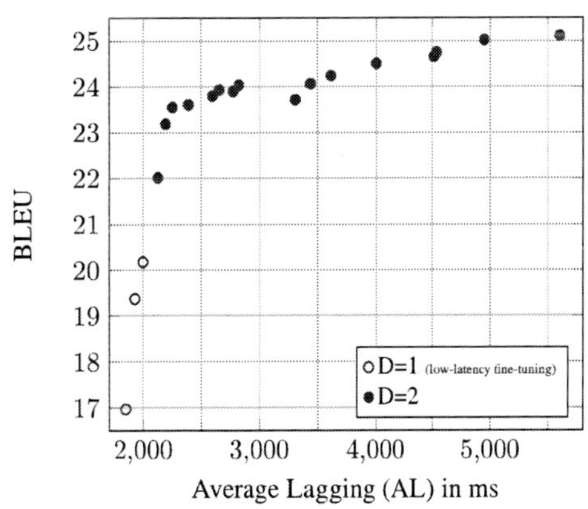

Figure 4: Results for English→German speech-to-text simultaneous translation on MuST-C dev

The Volctrans Neural Speech Translation System for IWSLT 2021

Chengqi Zhao Zhicheng Liu Jian Tong Tao Wang Mingxuan Wang
Rong Ye Qianqian Dong Jun Cao Lei Li
ByteDance AI Lab
{zhaochengqi.d, liuzhicheng.lzc, tongjian, wangtao.960826
wangmingxuan.89, yerong, dongqianqian
caojun.sh, lileilab}@bytedance.com

Abstract

This paper describes the systems submitted to IWSLT 2021 by the Volctrans team. We participate in the offline speech translation and text-to-text simultaneous translation tracks. For offline speech translation, our best end-to-end model achieves 7.9 BLEU improvements over the benchmark on the MuST-C test set and is even approaching the results of a strong cascade solution. For text-to-text simultaneous translation, we explore the best practice to optimize the `wait-k` model. As a result, our final submitted systems exceed the benchmark at around 7 BLEU on the same latency regime. We release our code and model to facilitate both future research works and industrial applications[1].

1 Introduction

This paper describes the neural speech translation systems submitted to IWSLT 2021 by the Volctrans team (also known as the team from ByteDance AI Lab), including cascade and end-to-end speech translation (ST) systems for the offline ST track and a simultaneous neural machine translation (NMT) system. We aim at finding the best practice for these two tracks.

For offline ST, the cascaded system often outperforms the fully end-to-end approach. Recent studies on the fully end-to-end approaches obtain promising results and attract a lot of interest. Last year's results have shown that an end-to-end model achieves an even better performance (Ansari et al., 2020) compared with the cascaded competitors. However, they introduce pre-training (Bansal et al., 2019; Stoian et al., 2020; Wang et al., 2020; Alinejad and Sarkar, 2020) and data augmentation techniques (Jia et al., 2019; Pino et al., 2020) to end-to-end models, while the cascaded is not that strong enough. Hence, in this paper, we would like to optimize the speech translation model in two aspects. First, we are devoted to building a strong cascade competitor and learns the best practice from WMT evaluation campaigns (Li et al., 2019; Wu et al., 2020), such as back translation (Sennrich et al., 2016a) and ensemble. Second, we explore various self-supervised learning methods and introduce as much semi-supervised data as possible towards finding the best practice of training end-to-end ST models. In our settings, ASR data, MT data, and monolingual text data are all considered in a progressively training framework. The results are very promising, and the final performance on the MuST-C test set surpasses the end-to-end baseline by 7.9 BLUE scores, while it is still lagging behind our cascade model by 1.5 BLUE scores. It is not surprising since some well-optimized methods for MT can not be easily used on ST, such as back translation. However, our experience shows that the external data can effectively close the gap between end-to-end models and cascade models.

In parallel, we also participate in the simultaneous NMT track, which translates in real-time. Our system is based on an efficient `wait-k` model (Elbayad et al., 2020). We investigate large-scale knowledge distillation (Kim and Rush, 2016; Freitag et al., 2017) and back translation methods. Specially, we develop a `multi-path` training strategy, which enables a unified model serving different `wait-k` paths. Our target is to obtain the best translation quality at different latency levels.

The remaining part of the paper proceeds as follows. Section 2 and section 3 describe our cascade and end-to-end systems respectively. Section 4 presents the implementation of simultaneous NMT models. Each section starts from the training sources and how we synthesize large-scale data. And then, we give details about the model structure and techniques for training and inference. We con-

[1]Code and models are available at `https://github.com/bytedance/neurst/tree/master/examples/iwslt21`

Proceedings of the 18th International Conference on Spoken Language Translation, pages 64–74
Bangkok, Thailand (Online), August 5–6, 2021. ©2021 Association for Computational Linguistics

Dataset	#samples	#hours
MuST-C	250,942	450
LibriSpeech	281,241	961
Common Voice	562,517	899
iwslt-corpus	157,909	231
TED-LIUM 3	111,600	165

Table 1: The statistics of audio datasets to train the ASR model. The *iwslt-corpus* and TED-LIUM 3 are filtered by an ASR model trained on MuST-C, LibriSpeech and Common Voice.

duct experiments using only the provided datasets by IWSLT 2021, and results are shown in Section 5.

2 Cascaded Speech Translation

2.1 Automatic Speech Recognition

The ASR model is transformer-like and trained on paired speech and transcript data

Datasets and Preprocessing We divide the allowed ASR datasets into two parts: clean and noisy and consider MuST-C[2], LibriSpeech (Panayotov et al., 2015), and Mozilla Common Voice as the clean datasets, and use them for training an ASR system to filter the noisy part, i.e., *iwslt-corpus*[3] and TED-LIUM 3 (Hernandez et al., 2018). We remove the training samples where the word error rate (WER) score between the ASR output and English transcript exceeds 75%. The statistics of the ASR datasets are shown in Table 1.

For model training, we extract 80-channel log Mel-filterbank coefficients with windows of 25ms and steps of 10ms on the audio input. The transcripts are lowercased and we remove all punctuation marks. Then, we apply Moses tokenizer[4] and byte pair encoding (BPE) (Sennrich et al., 2016b)[5] to the transcripts with 8,000 merge operations.

End-to-End ASR Model We refer to the recent progress of transformer-based ASR (Dong et al., 2018; Karita et al., 2019) and implement the speech transformer model, as illustrated in Figure 1 a). The feature extractor consists of two-layer CNN with 256 channels, 3×3 kernel, and stride size

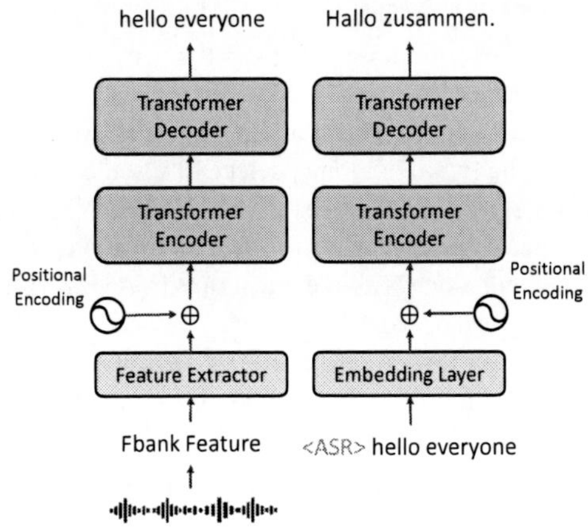

a) speech to text b) text to text

Figure 1: Overview of the cascaded speech translation model.

2, each of which is followed by a layer normalization and ReLU activation. The major architecture is the same as the transformer model, including 12 layers for the encoder and 6 layers for the decoder. The model width is 768, and the hidden size of the feed-forward layer is 3,072. The attention head is set to 12 for both self-attention and cross-attention. To train the model, we use Adam optimizer (Kingma and Ba, 2015) and set the warmup steps to 25,000. Empirically, we scale up the learning rate by 5.0 to accelerate the convergence. The ASR model is trained on 8 NVIDIA Tesla V100 GPUs with 320,000 frames per batch. And we truncate the audio frames to 3,000 and remove training samples whose transcript length exceeds 120 for GPU memory efficiency. To further improve the performance, we apply SpecAugment technique (Park et al., 2019) with frequency masking ($mF = 2, F = 27$) and time masking ($mT = 2, T = 70, p = 0.2$).

2.2 Neural Machine Translation

All MT models are based on transformer (Vaswani et al., 2017). We employ data augmentation and model ensemble techniques to improve the final performance.

Datasets and Preprocessing We utilize English-German (EN-DE) parallel sentences from WMT

[2]In this paper, MuST-C denotes the newly released English-German ST dataset (v2) by IWSLT 2021.

[3]The training corpus for IWSLT evaluation campaign over the last years.

[4]https://github.com/moses-smt/mosesdecoder/blob/master/scripts/tokenizer/tokenizer.perl

[5]https://github.com/rsennrich/subword-nmt

2020[6], OpenSubtitles 2018[7], MuST-C and *iwslt-corpus* for training. We filter the parallel corpora following the rules listed in Li et al. (2019), with a much stricter constrain on word alignment. Additionally, we randomly select 10% sentences separately from both sides of the original WMT and OpenSubtitles corpus for data augmentation (see below), along with the transcripts in ASR datasets described in sec 2.1.

As for text preprocessing, we apply Moses tokenizer and BPE with 32,000 merge operations on each side.

Tagged Back-Translation Back-translation (Sennrich et al., 2016a) is an effective way to improve the translation quality by leveraging a large amount of monolingual data and has been widely used in WMT evaluation campaigns. In our setting, we add a "<BT>" tag to the source side of back-translated data to prevent overfitting on the synthetic data, which is also known as tagged back-translation (Caswell et al., 2019; Marie et al., 2020).

Knowledge Distillation Sequence-level knowledge distillation (Kim and Rush, 2016; Freitag et al., 2017) is another useful technique to improve performance. In this way, we enlarge the training data by translating English sentences to German using a good teacher model.

ASR Output Adaptation Traditionally, the output of ASR systems is lowercased with no punctuation marks, while the MT systems receive natural texts. In our system, we attempt to make the MT systems robust to these irregular texts. A simple way to do so is to apply the same rules on the source side of the MT training set. However, empirical study shows it causes performance degradation. Inspired by the tagged back-translation method, we enhance the regular MT models with transcripts from both ASR systems and the ASR datasets, as illustrated in Figure 1 b). An extra tag "<ASR>" indicates the irregular input. Note that the basic idea to bridge the gap between the ASR output and the MT input involves additional sub-systems, like case and punctuation restoration. In our cascade system, we prefer to use fewer sub-systems, and the detailed comparison would be our future work.

Data Combination and Sampling Strategy We train transformer models with different combinations of data sets because increasing the model's diversity can benefit the model ensemble. The detailed setups are listed in Table 2. We over-sample the in-domain datasets (i.e., MuST-C/*iwslt-corpus*-related portions) to improve the in-domain performance. Specifically, to control the ratio of samples from different data sources, we sample a fixed number of sentences being proportional to $(\frac{N_s}{\sum_s N_s})^{\frac{1}{T}}$, where N_s is the number of sentences from data source s, and sampling temperature T is set to 5. Note that the MT#1 is trained on lowercased source texts without punctuation marks, while MT#2-5 use the tagged transcripts.

Model Setups We follow the transformer big setting, except that

- we deepen the encoder layers to 16.
- the dropout rate is set 0.15.
- the model width is changed to 768, the hidden size of the feed-forward layer is 3,072, and the attention head is 12 for MT#5 only.

We use Adam optimizer with the same schedule algorithm as Vaswani et al. (2017). All models are trained with a global batch size of 65,536.

2.3 Inference

We average the latest 10 checkpoints of a single training process for all the above experiments. And during inference, the "<ASR>" tag is added to the front of the ASR output. The beamwidth is set to 10 for both ASR and MT tasks.

3 End-to-End Speech Translation

Recent studies show that the fully end-to-end solution achieves promising performance when compared with the cascaded models (Ansari et al., 2020). This section will introduce how we build our end-to-end models for the offline ST task.

3.1 Training Data

The end-to-end model is trained on paired speech and translation data. We collect MuST-C and *iwslt-corpus* (after filtering described in section 2), with a total of only 681 hours transcribed and translated speech. To address the data scarcity problem, we explore the knowledge distillation technique to augment the data by leveraging ASR datasets and MT models, also known as pseudo labeling. In detail, we distill from four MT models: MT#1,

[6] `http://www.statmt.org/wmt20/translation-task.html`, including Common Crawl, Europarl v10, News Commentary v15, and ParaCrawl v5.1

[7] `https://opus.nlpl.eu/OpenSubtitles2018.php`

Dataset	Size	MT#1	MT#2		MT#3	MT#4	MT#5
			pretrain	fine-tune			
WMT 2020	13.7M	P	P	/	P	/	P
OpenSubtitles 2018	10.7M	P	P	/	P	P	/
MuST-C	0.25M	P	P/BT/SR	P/BT/SR	P/SR/KD	P/BT/SR	P/BT/SR
iwslt-corpus	0.16M	/	P/BT/SR	P/BT/SR	P/SR/KD	P/SR	P/BT/SR
TED-LIUM 3 (EN)	0.11M	/	/	/	KD	/	/
Common Voice (EN)	0.56M	/	/	/	KD	/	/
extra monolingual (EN/DE)	6.77M	/	/	BT	KD	BT	BT

Table 2: The statistics of MT datasets after data filtering and the detailed combination modes of datasets for difference MT models (MT#1-5). The MT#1 setting is used for training both DE→EN and EN→DE directions. "P" denotes the parallel corpus. "BT" is the back-translated data using MT#1 (DE→EN). "SR" indicates the irregular data from both ASR datasets and the ASR model. "KD" is the synthetic data generated by MT#2.

Dataset	#samples	#hours
MuST-C	1,198,056	2,186
iwslt-corpus	746,714	1,112
LibriSpeech	1,117,394	3,833
Common Voice	2,212,581	3,546
TED-LIUM 3	384,389	577

Table 3: The size of audio datasets with data augmentation to train the end-to-end ST model.

MT#2, an ensemble of MT#3-5, and MT#3-R2L which is trained with the same setting as MT#3 and generates the target translations in the right to left fashion. We filter the augmented samples with bad alignment scores as the same as data filtering in MT. The statistics of training data is shown in Table 3.

Moreover, two additional copies of the original and the augmented training data are created by modifying the speed to 110% and 90% of the initial rate, which makes a 3-fold training set.

3.2 Speech Transformer for End-to-End ST

As a baseline system, the model architecture and training configurations are the same as the end-to-end ASR in our cascade system, except for the learning rate, which is scaled up by 3.0 for ST. We initialize the feature extractor and encoder from the corresponding component of ASR.

We keep the cases and punctuation marks on the target side and apply Moses tokenizer and BPE to the translations with 32,000 merge operations.

3.3 Progressive Multi-task Learning

Inspired by the multi-task learning framework for ST and the progressive training strategy (Tang et al., 2020; Ye et al., 2021), we introduce PMTL-ST, a progressive multi-task learning framework for speech translation, which can leverage additional

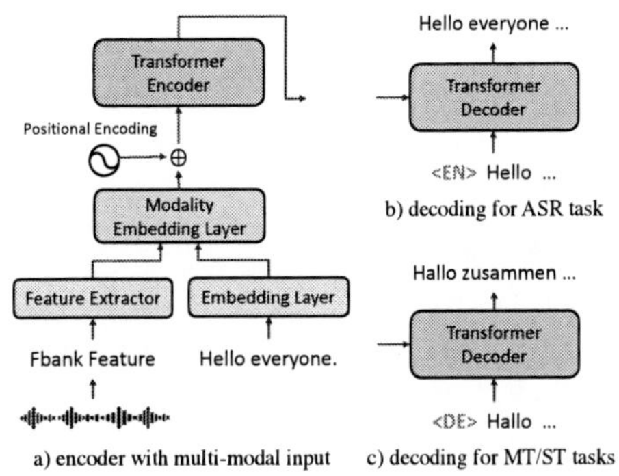

Figure 2: Overview of the end-to-end ST model with progressive multi-task learning. Note that the audio and text inputs are unnecessary to be aligned during training.

ASR and MT data for training. As illustrated in Figure 2 a), the encoder accepts both audio and text inputs. Then we add a modality embedding to the representation to indicate audio input or text before passing to the shared transformer encoder. For decoding, we involve "<EN>" and "<DE>" tokens to make the decoder compatible with ASR and translation (MT/ST) tasks, as shown in 2 b)/c).

For progressive training, we separately train an ASR model and an MT model via different branches in Figure 2. Then, we initialize the feature extractor and the audio modality embedding from the ASR model, and the rest of the model parameters are initialized by the MT model. The final model is trained jointly with ASR, MT, and ST.

All other training configurations, such as batch size and learning rate, are the same as the corresponding single task described before. Additionally, for the PMTL-ST models, we jointly learn the

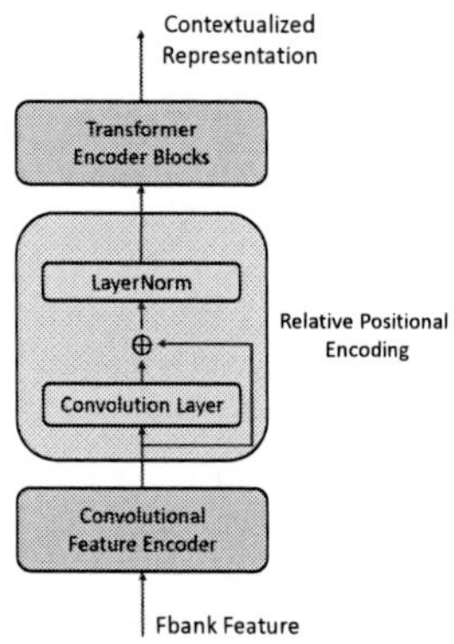

Figure 3: The proposed fbank2vec network for audio feature encoding.

sentencepiece[8] model with 16,000 tokens on the mixture of English and German texts.

3.4 Fbank2vec

Inspired by the recent progress of speech representation learning, like wav2vec 2.0 (Baevski et al., 2020), we introduce a fbank2vec network to learn contextualized audio representations from log Mel-filterbank features, as shown in Figure 3.

Convolutional Feature Encoder The encoder consists of two blocks containing a convolution followed by layer normalization and a GELU activation (Hendrycks and Gimpel, 2016). The convolution in each block has 512 channels with 3×3 kernel and stride size 2.

Relative Positional Encoding We use a group convolution layer to model the relative positional embeddings as Baevski et al. (2020) does. The kernel size is 128, and the number of groups is 16.

Contextualized Encoder The final contextualized audio representations are generated by several transformer encoder blocks. In our setting, we stack 6 layers of the post-norm transformer, and the inner activation function for the feed-forward layers is GELU. In turn, the number of shared encoder layers in Figure 2 is changed to 6.

We insert the fbank2vec network in the front of the feature extractor. The feature extractor further reduces the dimension of audio representations by one convolution layer with 5×5 kernel and stride size 2. The number of channels keeps the same as the dimension of fbank2vec output.

[8] https://github.com/google/sentencepiece

We experiment with two setups, fbank2vec-768 and fbank2vec-512. The fbank2vec-768 means that

- the dimension of fbank2vec output is 768;
- inner the contextualized encoder, the hidden size of feed-forward layers is 3,072, and the head of the self-attention layers is 12.

For the fbank2vec-512, the numbers are 512, 2,048, and 8, respectively. Note that the fbank2vec module is pretrained by an ASR task and the overall model follows the progressive multi-task learning framework, so the configurations of word embeddings, the shared encoder and decoder vary accordingly.

4 Simultaneous Translation

This section describes our submissions to the text-to-text simultaneous speech translation track for English to German (EN2DE) and English to Japanese (EN2JA). For versatility, we adopt identical methods for these two language pairs.

4.1 Training Data

The training data for EN→DE is from MuST-C, OpenSubtitles 2018, and WMT 2020 datasets. And for EN→JA, we use the parallel and monolingual data from the WMT 2020 news task.

Data Preprocessing We follow the data filtering process proposed in WMT works (Li et al., 2019; Wu et al., 2020), including language detection, length ratio filtering, dictionary alignment, and so on. For pre-processing, we first apply MeCab[9] tokenizer to the Japanese sentences. Then, words are segmented into subword units using sentencepiece toolkit for both language pairs. We jointly learn on the source and target side with a vocabulary of 10,000 tokens.

Data Augmentation Similar to section 2.2, we utilize tagged back-translation (BT) and knowledge distillation (KD) strategies to improve the performance of simultaneous NMT. We experiment with both LightConv (Wu et al., 2018) and transformer models. The model with the best BLEU score on the development set is chosen for data augmentation. The statistics of all training data and model settings are presented in Table 4 and Table 5 respectively.

[9] https://github.com/taku910/mecab

Dataset	Size	MT#0	MT#1	MT#2	MT#3	MT#4	MT#5
EN → DE							
WMT 2020(EN → DE)	41.14M	P	P	P	P	P/FT	FT
OpenSubtitles 2018	13.84M	P	P	P	P	P/BT/FT	FT/BT
MuST-C	0.23M	P	P/BT	P/BT	P/BT	P/BT/FT	FT/BT
monolingual(EN/DE)	10.25M	P	BT	BT	BT	BT	BT
EN → JA							
WMT 2020(EN → JA)	18.19M	P	P/BT	P/BT	P/BT	P/BT/FT	BT/FT

Table 4: The statistics of MT datasets and the combination modes of datasets for simultaneous NMT models. "P" indicates the parallel corpus. "BT" means the back-translated data generated by MT#0. "FT" is the forward-translated data generated by MT#1-3.

#	Model Arch	Enc	Dec	Emb
0	Transformer	6	6	1024
1	Transformer	6	6	1024
2	Transformer	50	6	1024
3	LightConv	6	6	1024
4	Transformer	16	3	768
5	Transformer	16	3	768

Table 5: The model setups. "Enc", "Dec" denote the number of encoder and decoder layers. "Emb" means the embedding size and the hidden size.

4.2 Efficient `wait-k` Model

Our simultaneous NMT systems are based on transformer `wait-k` models, which first read k source tokens and then alternate between reading and writing (translating). Formally, when decoding the sentence $\mathbf{x}$, the number of visible source tokens is constrained within $\min(k + t - 1, |\mathbf{x}|)$ at decoding step t, where k is the hyper-parameter controlling the latency. Furthermore, to avoid recomputing the hidden states of the encoder each time a token is read, we implement incremental unidirectional encoders (Elbayad et al., 2020). And `multi-path` training is also applied to leverage more possible `wait-k` paths which refers that hyper-parameter $k \in [3, 9]$ is random selected at each batch during training.

Models are trained with a batch size of 32,000 tokens on Tesla V100 GPUs. We average the last 6 checkpoints once the model converges.

4.3 Inference

We explore the look-ahead beam search strategy for inference. Specifically, we apply beam search to generate $M(M > 1)$ tokens at each decoding step and pick the first token in the one with the highest log-probability out of multiple decoding paths. The look-ahead beam search achieves consistent performance improvement when k_{eval} is small while its performance improvement is insignificant with a large k_{eval}. This search method is excluded from our final submissions due to its higher latency, and we choose the greedy search instead.

Additionally, we split the source sentences into sub-sentences once the end-of-sentence punctuation is recognized. Though it may result in a slight performance drop due to the lack of context, we can obtain a much lower latency.

For the final submissions, we use ensemble models. We train several models with different k_{train} values and disjoint subsets of training data for data diversity. Each model produces different latency-quality trade-offs.

5 Experimental Results

We conduct all our experiments using NeurST (Zhao et al., 2020) and report results for the submitted speech translation tasks in this section. It is worth noting that all transcripts and translations in the test sets are removed from the training data.

When evaluating the offline ST models, tags such as applause and laughing are removed from both hypothesis and reference. We use word error rate (WER) to evaluate the ASR model and report case-sensitive detokenized BLEU[10] for MT. No other data segmentation techniques are applied to the dev/test sets. Results on MuST-C *dev* and *tst-COMMON*, as well as *dev(v1)* and *tst-COMMON(v1)* from MuST-C v1 (Gangi et al., 2019) are listed together, which serve as strong baselines for comparison purpose in the end-to-end speech translation field.

When evaluating the simultaneous translation, we use the official SimulEval (Ma et al., 2020) toolkit and report case-sensitive detokenized BLEU (Post, 2018) and Average Lagging (Ma et al., 2019)

[10]`https://github.com/jniehues-kit/sacrebleu`

#	System	*dev*	*tst-COM*	*dev(v1)*	*tst-COM(v1)*	Training data composition
Pure MT						
1	MT (w/o punc. & lc)	32.0	34.1	32.2	34.0	MT (see Table 2)
2	MT (w/ punc. & tc)	33.8	36.2	33.7	35.9	
3	ensemble MT (w/o punc. & lc)	33.8	35.2	33.8	35.3	
4	ensemble MT (w/ punc. & tc)	34.7	36.7	34.6	36.2	
Cascaded ASR → MT						
5	AppTek/RWTH (Bahar et al., 2020)	-	-	-	29.7	/
6	ASR → MT	29.9	32.1	28.4	31.3	ASR+MT
7	ASR → ensemble MT	**31.7**	**33.3**	**30.1**	**32.3**	/
End-to-End ST						
8	direct ST baseline	23.9	23.9	-	-	MuST-C ONLY
9	direct ST	28.9	29.9	27.9	29.5	ST+ST Augm. by MT#1&2
10	direct ST++	29.6	**30.4**	**28.3**	**29.7**	ST All
11	direct ST++*	**30.0**	30.2	28.2	29.6	ST All
12	XSTNet-768 (Ye et al., 2021)	30.4	**31.1**	-	**30.3**	ASR+MT+ST All
13	direct ST + fbank2vec-512	28.7	29.1	26.7	27.6	ST All
14	PMTL-ST + fbank2vec-768	29.6	29.6	26.9	28.1	ASR+MT+ST All
15	PMTL-ST + fbank2vec-768 ++	30.8	**31.1**	**28.8**	30.1	ASR+MT+ST All+speed pertub
16	PMTL-ST + fbank2vec-768 ++*	**30.9**	**31.1**	**28.8**	30.1	ASR+MT+ST All+speed pertub
17	ensemble (9, 10, 11)	30.4	31.2	29.0	30.6	/
18	ensemble (15, 16)	31.0	31.1	28.8	30.1	/
19	ensemble (14, 15, 16)	31.4	31.5	29.3	30.6	/
20	ensemble (13, 14, 15, 16)	**31.6**	**31.8**	**29.5**	**30.8**	/

Table 6: The overall results of the offline speech translation. The MT model used in the cascade approach is MT#2 and the ensemble MT model is formed by MT#2-MT#5. The direct ST++* is the same as direct ST++ with different random seed for in-domain data over-sampling. The PMTL-ST + fbank2vec-768 ++* is continuously trained from PMTL-ST + fbank2vec-768 ++. *tst-COM* is the abbreviation for *tst-COMMON*.

Testset	WER
dev	5.2
tst-COMMON	5.7
dev(v1)	10.6
tst-COMMON(v1)	7.4

Table 7: The WER of the ASR system for the offline ST.

on MuST-C *tst-COMMON* (EN2DE) and IWSLT21 dev set (EN2JA).

5.1 Offline Speech Translation

The overall performance of the offline ST and the ASR component used in the cascade system are listed in Table 6 and Table 7 respectively.

In Table 6, line 1-4 show the performance of our pure MT systems, which translate the lowercased ground truth transcripts with no punctuation marks, and the natural texts. As seen, there may be no essential improvements with the "<ASR>" tag on the irregular input (up to 2 BLEU gap on the single model), and it suggests that text restoration has the potential to narrow the gap. Line 6-7 present the results of translating the ASR output, and we see our cascaded approach surpasses last year's best cascade system (line 5) by 2.6 BLEU. However, there is still a significant loss of up to 3 BLEU scores than line 1/3 due to ASR errors.

The results of our end-to-end solutions are presented in line 8-20, where line 8 is a benchmark model (Zhao et al., 2020) trained on the MuST-C dataset only. With the growth of model capacity (256d→768d) and data augmentation, we obtain 6 BLEU improvement on the *tst-COMMON* over the benchmark (line 8). Then, increasing the size of augmented data gains slight improvement, as comparing line 9 to line 10/11 (+0.3∼0.5 BLEU scores). Line 13-16 show the results of our proposed fbank2vec. As shown in line 15, we achieve 31.1 BLEU on *tst-COMMON*, the best single model with fbank2vec, progressive multi-task learning, and speed perturbation. We obtain 31.8 BLEU (line 20) for the final ensemble model, which surpasses the end-to-end benchmark by 7.9 BLEU scores and is approaching the cascade system with a nearly 1.5 BLEU gap.

Lastly, our primary cascade system is line 7, and the primary end-to-end system is line 20 for submission, which achieves higher performance via model ensemble.

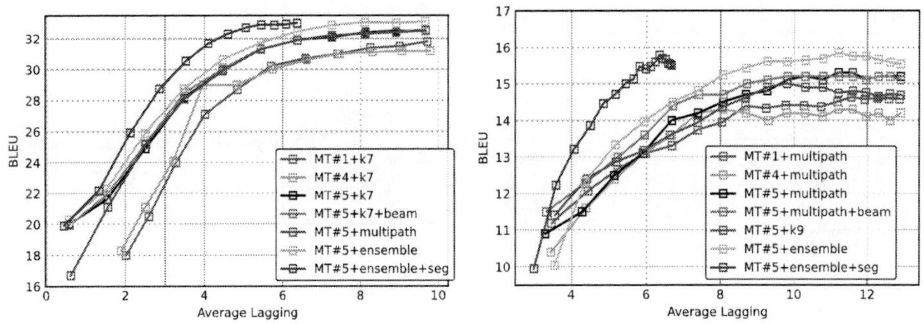

(a) EN→DE (b) EN→JA

Figure 4: Latency-quality trade-offs of the simultaneous NMT. $k7/9$ means $k_{\text{train}} = 7/9$. MT#X indicate the aforementioned training datasets and model settings in Table 4 and 5. `beam` refers to our look-ahead beam search strategy. `seg` means that the sentences are pre-splited during inference. `multipath` means that k is random selected during training.

		Low	Medium	High
EN → DE	Ensemble	25.86	31.73	33.21
	+seg	28.75	32.87	32.97
EN → JA	Ensemble	14.81	15.85	15.85
	+seg	15.79	15.79	15.79

Table 8: Performance of our final submissions models on MuST-C *tst-COMMON* for English-German and IWSLT21 dev set for English-Japanese.

5.2 Simultaneous Translation

We evaluate the simultaneous NMT systems with different combinations of strategies and present our results in Figure 4. Then we report the performance on different latency regimes in Table 8.

As shown in Figure 4, we can obtain remarkable BLEU improvements by training with only the knowledge distilled data (black) comparing to the filtered parallel data (green) and back-translated data (magenta), on average 1.0 BLEU improvement on EN→DE and 0.5 on EN→JA. The possible reasons may be: 1) Noise in origin data is migrated, like non-parallel sentence pairs. 2) Complex sentences with diverging word order are excluded, and the machine-translated texts, i.e., translationese, sometimes have simpler expressions.

We can see that the proposed look-ahead beam search (red) is competitive when k_{eval} is relatively small but is comparable with the greedy search when k_{eval} is large. So overall considering translation latency, we use the greedy search for our final submissions. As for `multi-path` training, we see it achieves limited BLEU improvement in our experiments.

# - System	tst2020	tst2021 ref2	tst2021 ref1	tst2021 both
7 - Cascade (ensemble)	22.2	21.8	17.1	29.5
6 - Cascade (single)	21.0	20.3	16.4	27.7
20 - Direct (ensemble)	24.3	21.7	18.7	31.3
16 - Direct (single)	23.5	21.6	18.2	30.6
17 - Direct (ensemble)	22.4	21.1	17.5	29.2
10 - Direct (single)	21.6	20.4	17.0	28.1

Table 9: BLEU of the IWSLT 2021 submissions for offline speech translation task. The rows in bold are our primary systems. The `ref1` of tst2021 is originally from the TED website, while the `ref2` is newly created for this year's campaign.

For our final submission of EN→DE, we use the ensemble model, which consists of three transformer models trained on different dataset combinations, with $k_{\text{train}} = 7$. For EN→JA, the submitted model is formed by two transformer models, with $k_{\text{train}} = \infty$ (trained on full sentences) and `multi-path` training respectively. As presented in Figure 4, the model ensemble technique leads to at least 0.5 BLEU improvement on average (yellow). Additionally, with the sentence segmentation (bleu), the average lagging is significantly reduced. As a result, our final submitted systems exceed the baseline system at around 7 BLEU on the same latency regime.

6 Final Results

Table 9 lists the final results of the IWSLT 2021 offline ST track. Surprisingly, we find that our end-to-end models significantly surpass the cascade systems, which is different from our conclusions on

System	BLEU	AL	AP	DAL
EN → DE				
MT(Low Latency)	23.24	3.08	0.68	4.25
MT(Mid Latency)	27.22	6.30	0.81	9.24
MT(High Latency)	26.82	12.03	0.92	12.39
EN → JA				
MT(Low Latency)	16.91	6.54	0.89	11.26
MT(Mid Latency)	16.91	6.54	0.89	11.26
MT(High Latency)	16.97	11.27	0.97	11.90

Table 10: Performance of the IWSLT 2021 submissions for simultaneous NMT on the blind test set.

the MuST-C test sets. We think this may be caused by the reference of tst2021. Since the `ref1` of tst2021 is the original one from the TED website, the translations could be much shorter for subtitling, and our end-to-end models may fit well on it.

Table 10 shows the official evaluation for our simultaneous NMT systems.

7 Conclusion

This paper summarizes the results of the shared tasks in the IWSLT 2021 produced by the Volctrans team. We investigate the performance of the end-to-end solutions with data augmentation and progressively training framework for the offline ST task. Our end-to-end approach surpasses the last year's best cascaded system by 1 BLEU, but it is still lagging behind our cascade model by 1.5 BLEU scores on MuST-C test sets. However, our end-to-end solutions achieve promising performance on tst2020 and tst2021. Afterwards, we develop the efficient `wait-k` model with `multi-path` training, and large-scale knowledge distillation and back translation methods. The final submitted systems exceed the baseline systems at 7 BLEU on the same regime. We see the data augmentation technique plays the most important role in these tasks. In the future, we would like to explore a more extensive data condition on both modality and quantity. We hope our practice could facilitate batch research works and industrial applications.

References

Ashkan Alinejad and Anoop Sarkar. 2020. Effectively pretraining a speech translation decoder with machine translation data. In *Proceedings of the 2020 Conference on Empirical Methods in Natural Language Processing (EMNLP)*, pages 8014–8020.

Ebrahim Ansari, Amittai Axelrod, Nguyen Bach, Ondrej Bojar, Roldano Cattoni, Fahim Dalvi, Nadir Durrani, Marcello Federico, Christian Federmann, Jiatao Gu, Fei Huang, Kevin Knight, Xutai Ma, Ajay Nagesh, Matteo Negri, Jan Niehues, Juan Pino, Elizabeth Salesky, Xing Shi, Sebastian Stüker, Marco Turchi, Alexander H. Waibel, and Changhan Wang. 2020. FINDINGS OF THE IWSLT 2020 EVALUATION CAMPAIGN. In *Proceedings of the 17th International Conference on Spoken Language Translation, IWSLT 2020*, pages 1–34.

Alexei Baevski, Yuhao Zhou, Abdelrahman Mohamed, and Michael Auli. 2020. wav2vec 2.0: A framework for self-supervised learning of speech representations. In *NeurIPS*.

Parnia Bahar, Patrick Wilken, Tamer Alkhouli, Andreas Guta, Pavel Golik, Evgeny Matusov, and Christian Herold. 2020. Start-before-end and end-to-end: Neural speech translation by apptek and RWTH aachen university. In *IWSLT*, pages 44–54. Association for Computational Linguistics.

Sameer Bansal, Herman Kamper, Karen Livescu, Adam Lopez, and Sharon Goldwater. 2019. Pre-training on high-resource speech recognition improves low-resource speech-to-text translation. In *NAACL-HLT (1)*, pages 58–68. Association for Computational Linguistics.

Isaac Caswell, Ciprian Chelba, and David Grangier. 2019. Tagged back-translation. In *Proceedings of the Fourth Conference on Machine Translation, WMT 2019*.

Linhao Dong, Shuang Xu, and Bo Xu. 2018. Speech-transformer: A no-recurrence sequence-to-sequence model for speech recognition. In *2018 IEEE International Conference on Acoustics, Speech and Signal Processing, ICASSP 2018*, pages 5884–5888.

Maha Elbayad, Laurent Besacier, and Jakob Verbeek. 2020. Efficient wait-k models for simultaneous machine translation. In *INTERSPEECH*, pages 1461–1465. ISCA.

Markus Freitag, Yaser Al-Onaizan, and Baskaran Sankaran. 2017. Ensemble distillation for neural machine translation. *CoRR*, abs/1702.01802.

Mattia Antonino Di Gangi, Roldano Cattoni, Luisa Bentivogli, Matteo Negri, and Marco Turchi. 2019. Must-c: a multilingual speech translation corpus. In *Proceedings of the 2019 Conference of the North American Chapter of the Association for Computational Linguistics: Human Language Technologies (NAACL-HLT 2019)*, pages 2012–2017.

Dan Hendrycks and Kevin Gimpel. 2016. Bridging nonlinearities and stochastic regularizers with gaussian error linear units. *CoRR*, abs/1606.08415.

François Hernandez, Vincent Nguyen, Sahar Ghannay, Natalia A. Tomashenko, and Yannick Estève. 2018. TED-LIUM 3: Twice as much data and corpus repartition for experiments on speaker adaptation. In

Speech and Computer - 20th International Conference, SPECOM 2018, Proceedings, Lecture Notes in Computer Science.

Ye Jia, Melvin Johnson, Wolfgang Macherey, Ron J. Weiss, Yuan Cao, Chung-Cheng Chiu, Naveen Ari, Stella Laurenzo, and Yonghui Wu. 2019. Leveraging weakly supervised data to improve end-to-end speech-to-text translation. In *ICASSP*, pages 7180–7184. IEEE.

Shigeki Karita, Xiaofei Wang, Shinji Watanabe, Takenori Yoshimura, Wangyou Zhang, Nanxin Chen, Tomoki Hayashi, Takaaki Hori, Hirofumi Inaguma, Ziyan Jiang, Masao Someki, Nelson Enrique Yalta Soplin, and Ryuichi Yamamoto. 2019. A comparative study on transformer vs RNN in speech applications. In *IEEE Automatic Speech Recognition and Understanding Workshop, ASRU 2019*, pages 449–456.

Yoon Kim and Alexander M. Rush. 2016. Sequence-level knowledge distillation. In *Proceedings of the 2016 Conference on Empirical Methods in Natural Language Processing, EMNLP 2016*.

Diederik P. Kingma and Jimmy Ba. 2015. Adam: A method for stochastic optimization. In *3rd International Conference on Learning Representations, ICLR 2015*.

Bei Li, Yinqiao Li, Chen Xu, Ye Lin, Jiqiang Liu, Hui Liu, Ziyang Wang, Yuhao Zhang, Nuo Xu, Zeyang Wang, Kai Feng, Hexuan Chen, Tengbo Liu, Yanyang Li, Qiang Wang, Tong Xiao, and Jingbo Zhu. 2019. The NiuTrans machine translation systems for WMT19. In *Proceedings of the Fourth Conference on Machine Translation*.

Mingbo Ma, Liang Huang, Hao Xiong, Renjie Zheng, Kaibo Liu, Baigong Zheng, Chuanqiang Zhang, Zhongjun He, Hairong Liu, Xing Li, Hua Wu, and Haifeng Wang. 2019. STACL: simultaneous translation with implicit anticipation and controllable latency using prefix-to-prefix framework. In *ACL (1)*, pages 3025–3036. Association for Computational Linguistics.

Xutai Ma, Mohammad Javad Dousti, Changhan Wang, Jiatao Gu, and Juan Pino. 2020. Simuleval: An evaluation toolkit for simultaneous translation. In *Proceedings of the 2020 Conference on Empirical Methods in Natural Language Processing: System Demonstrations*, pages 144–150.

Benjamin Marie, Raphael Rubino, and Atsushi Fujita. 2020. Tagged back-translation revisited: Why does it really work? In *Proceedings of the 58th Annual Meeting of the Association for Computational Linguistics, ACL 2020*.

Vassil Panayotov, Guoguo Chen, Daniel Povey, and Sanjeev Khudanpur. 2015. Librispeech: An ASR corpus based on public domain audio books. In *2015 IEEE International Conference on Acoustics, Speech and Signal Processing (ICASSP 2015)*, pages 5206–5210.

Daniel S. Park, William Chan, Yu Zhang, Chung-Cheng Chiu, Barret Zoph, Ekin D. Cubuk, and Quoc V. Le. 2019. Specaugment: A simple data augmentation method for automatic speech recognition. In *Interspeech 2019, 20th Annual Conference of the International Speech Communication Association, Graz, Austria, 15-19 September 2019*, pages 2613–2617.

Juan Pino, Qiantong Xu, Xutai Ma, Mohammad Javad Dousti, and Yun Tang. 2020. Self-training for end-to-end speech translation. In *Proc. Interspeech 2020*, pages 1476–1480.

Matt Post. 2018. A call for clarity in reporting BLEU scores. In *Proceedings of the Third Conference on Machine Translation: Research Papers*, pages 186–191, Belgium, Brussels. Association for Computational Linguistics.

Rico Sennrich, Barry Haddow, and Alexandra Birch. 2016a. Improving neural machine translation models with monolingual data. In *Proceedings of the 54th Annual Meeting of the Association for Computational Linguistics, ACL 2016*.

Rico Sennrich, Barry Haddow, and Alexandra Birch. 2016b. Neural machine translation of rare words with subword units. In *Proceedings of the 54th Annual Meeting of the Association for Computational Linguistics, ACL 2016, Berlin, Germany, Volume 1: Long Papers*.

Mihaela C. Stoian, Sameer Bansal, and Sharon Goldwater. 2020. Analyzing ASR pretraining for low-resource speech-to-text translation. In *ICASSP*, pages 7909–7913. IEEE.

Yun Tang, Juan Pino, Changhan Wang, Xutai Ma, and Dmitriy Genzel. 2020. A general multi-task learning framework to leverage text data for speech to text tasks. *CoRR*, abs/2010.11338.

Ashish Vaswani, Noam Shazeer, Niki Parmar, Jakob Uszkoreit, Llion Jones, Aidan N. Gomez, Lukasz Kaiser, and Illia Polosukhin. 2017. Attention is all you need. In *Advances in Neural Information Processing Systems 30: Annual Conference on Neural Information Processing Systems 2017*, pages 5998–6008.

Chengyi Wang, Yu Wu, Shujie Liu, Ming Zhou, and Zhenglu Yang. 2020. Curriculum pre-training for end-to-end speech translation. In *Proceedings of the 58th Annual Meeting of the Association for Computational Linguistics*, pages 3728–3738.

Felix Wu, Angela Fan, Alexei Baevski, Yann Dauphin, and Michael Auli. 2018. Pay less attention with lightweight and dynamic convolutions. In *International Conference on Learning Representations*.

Liwei Wu, Xiao Pan, Zehui Lin, Yaoming Zhu, Mingxuan Wang, and Lei Li. 2020. The volctrans machine translation system for WMT20. In *WMT@EMNLP*, pages 305–312. Association for Computational Linguistics.

Rong Ye, Mingxuan Wang, and Lei Li. 2021. End-to-end speech translation via cross-modal progressive training. *CoRR*, abs/2104.10380.

Chengqi Zhao, Mingxuan Wang, and Lei Li. 2020. Neurst: Neural speech translation toolkit. *CoRR*, abs/2012.10018.

The IWSLT 2021 BUT Speech Translation Systems

Hari Krishna Vydana, Martin Karafiát, Lukáš Burget, "Honza" Černocký
Brno University of Technology, Faculty of Information Technology, Speech@FIT, Czechia
harivydana@gmail.com

Abstract

The paper describes BUT's English to German offline speech translation (ST) systems developed for IWSLT2021. They are based on jointly trained Automatic Speech Recognition-Machine Translation models. Their performances is evaluated on MustC-Common test set. In this work, we study their efficiency from the perspective of having a large amount of separate ASR training data and MT training data, and a smaller amount of speech-translation training data. Large amounts of ASR and MT training data are utilized for pre-training the ASR and MT models. Speech-translation data is used to jointly optimize ASR-MT models by defining an end-to-end differentiable path from speech to translations. For this purpose, we use the internal continuous representations from the ASR-decoder as the input to MT module. We show that speech translation can be further improved by training the ASR-decoder jointly with the MT-module using large amount of text-only MT training data. We also show significant improvements by training an ASR module capable of generating punctuated text, rather than leaving the punctuation task to the MT module.

1 Introduction

Speech Translation (ST) systems are intended to generate text in target language from the audio in source language. The conventional ST systems are cascade ones, including (in the most popular form) three blocks i.e., an ASR, punctuation/segmentation module and an MT model (Ngoc-Quan Pham, 2019; Pham et al., 2020b; Jan et al., 2019; Ansari et al., 2020). Both Automatic Speech Recognition system (ASR) and Machine Translation (MT) models are independently trained, and the MT model processes the ASR output text (ASR hypotheses) to generate translations. In a cascade system, the advancements in ASR and MT can be directly extended to ST. These models can also leverage on the availability of large ASR and MT data-sets, and some of the state-of-the art ST systems are still cascade ones.

Recently, End-to-End ST systems have become widely popular. An End-to-End ST can directly generate text in target language from the audio in source language. These models are simpler in structure and they are more suitable for operating in streaming fashion. Most End-to-End speech translation systems are variants of encoder-decoder architecture with attention models (Bahdanau et al., 2015; Di Gangi et al., 2019; Zhao et al., 2020). This category includes the popular Transformer models, which have been adapted for training End-to-End ST in (Di Gangi et al., 2019). In (Inaguma et al., 2020), a better performance of ST was achieved by initializing the encoder and decoder modules from pre-trainied ASR and MT systems, respectively. Very-deep transformer models have been trained with stochastic depth for training End-to-End ST models in (Pham et al., 2019). The use of relative positional embeddings has also improved the performance of transformer (Pham et al., 2020a).

One major drawback or end-to-end ST is the data availability, i.e., paired speech-to-translation data is scarce compared to ASR or MT data. Data augmentations and use of synthetic data have been explored in (Bahar et al., 2019, 2020) to mitigate the issue. Unlike End-to-End ST systems, the data for training cascade systems is easily available and less costly.

A brief survey of existing approaches and their principal limitations are discussed in (Sperber and Paulik, 2020). Despite multiple advantages, the cascade systems suffer from a major drawback: propagating erroneous early decisions into MT models, which then cause degradation in the trans-

Proceedings of the 18th International Conference on Spoken Language Translation, pages 75–83
Bangkok, Thailand (Online), August 5–6, 2021. ©2021 Association for Computational Linguistics

lation performance. To mitigate this degradation, rather than passing a single ASR output sequence to MT model, other forms such as lattices, n-best hypotheses and continuous representations have been explored in (Anastasopoulos and Chiang, 2018; Zhang et al., 2019; Sperber et al., 2019; Vydana et al., 2021; Dong et al., 2020).

In this work, we use our jointly trained Automatic Speech Recognition-Machine Translation (Joint-ASR-MT) model previously described in (Vydana et al., 2021). Joint-ASR-MT model is a cascade system, but it has a differentiable path between ASR and MT modules. To create such differentible path, the continuous hidden representations (corresponding to each output token) from the ASR decoder are passed to the MT-Model. The hidden continuous tokens corresponding to each output token are the attention-weighted value vectors in the last layer of the transformer decoder. We refer to these continuous representations as"context vectors" as proposed in (Sperber et al., 2019).

Existing large separate ASR training data and MT training data can be used to pre-train these modules; then, the pre-trained modules are jointly optimized using a small amount of speech translation data. The joint optimization mitigates the degradation in performance due to erroneous early decisions.

In this paper, we generate German translation from English speech, and we focus on two main contributions: (1) We train different MT models that can translate normalized text or punctuated text. It is known that MT-models translating punctuated text provide superior performance, therefore, we propose to train an ASR system that can generate the punctuated text. We confirm that such ASR system provides superior performance in ASR-MT pipeline. (2) We use the internal continuous representations from the ASR-decoder as the input to MT module. In section 6, we show that speech translation can be further improved by adapting ASR-decoder to the MT module. This is achieved by training the ASR-decoder jointly with the MT-module using a large amount of text-only MT training data.

2 Datasets and Pre-processing

The Datasets used for training various models are described in Table. 1. ASR-Train-set and MT-Train-set are used for pre-training ASR and MT models respectively. The pre-trained models are fine-tuned using ASR-MT-Train-set. All models are evaluated using MustC-Common test set.

Table 1: Data used for training various models.

	Corpora	#Sentences	Audio	Source text	Target Text
MT -Train-set	ParaCrawl v3	31M	-	✓	✓
	OpenSubtitles 2018	12M	-	✓	✓
	Rapid 2019	1.5M	-	✓	✓
	Europarl v9	1.81M	-	✓	✓
	News Commentary	365K	-	✓	✓
	Common Crawl	2.4M	-	✓	✓
	Wikititles	1.3M	-	✓	✓
	WIT3	196K	-	✓	✓
	TED Talks	220K	-	✓	✓
ASR-MT -Train-set	Europarl-ST	32K	✓	✓	✓
	Must-C V2	230K	✓	✓	✓
	IWSLT2018	171K	✓	✓	✓
ASR -Train-set	Tedlium3	264K	✓	✓	-
	Librispeech	281K	✓	✓	-

2.1 Pre-processing and Feature Extraction

From audio data, 80-Dimensional Mel-Filter bank energies along with pitch features are extracted. The Moses toolkit is used for text tokenization and other standard text pre-processing. The umlauts from the German text are replaced by the special tokens. All the non ASCII characters are removed from the text data. The repetitions of the same sentences are removed from the corpora. We cleaned up the MT training data by identifying and manually removing the sentences where successive words were erroneously concatenated in to very long erroneous words. Sentence-piece models (Kudo and Richardson, 2018) are used for training BPE-tokenizers. 40M lines of text are used for training each BPE-tokenizer and all the tokenizers have a vocabulary of 20K units. Three separate tokenizers are trained using normalized English text, punctuated English text and punctuated German text. The output of MT module is always punctuated text, while input to MT (as well as ASR output) can be either normalized or punctuated text (see norm-MT and Punc-MT in sections 4).

2.2 Pruning Noisy ASR corpus

Some of the utterances in ASR-MT-Train-set (MustC, IWSLT and Europarl) sets are erroneous due to the shift in alignments between audio and text. Training an End-to-End ASR on this data directly did not lead to convergence. To remove erroneous transcripts, a hybrid TDNN-LFMMI ASR system based on KALDI (Povey et al., 2011, 2016) was trained and this ASR system was used to decode the ASR-MT-train set. The Word Error Rate (WER) for each sentence is computed and the sentences with more than 50% WER are deleted from the ASR-MT-Train-set (Potapczyk et al., 2019). Even with this cleaning, training the ASR systems only on ASR-MT-Train-set did not lead to convergence. Pre-training the ASR models on ASR-Train-set turned out to be crucial for convergence as described in section 3.

3 Automatic Speech Recognition (ASR)

ASR systems trained in this work are built on Transformer ASR models (Dong et al., 2018; Karita et al., 2019; Vydana et al., 2021; Vaswani et al., 2017). The ASR models have 12 encoder and 6 decoder layers with 4096 feed-forward units and 1024 attention dimension with 16 heads. Models are initially trained with ASR-Train-set and are later fine-tuned with ASR-MT-Train-set. A thresholding mechanism is used for pruning away the noisy end-of-sequence (EOS) tokens from beam search (Kahn et al., 2019). Models are trained with 30K warm-up updates and a check-point is saved after every 8K updates. The training is stopped with an early stopping criterion. 8-best check-points are averaged and the averaged weights are used for decoding the hypothesis. Vectorized beam search (Seki et al., 2019) was used for decoding the ASR hypotheses with a beam size of 10. Further in this paper, ASR models described in this section are referred to as Ext.ASR models (Externally trained ASR models).

Two different ASR systems were trained for generating normalized text (Norm-ASR) and punctuated text (Punc-ASR), and their performances are reported in Table 2. It can be observed that the WER of Punc-ASR appears to be higher than Norm-ASR. Punc-ASR is a obviously more difficult task than Norm-ASR — the punctuation tokens are considered as extra words and each error in those words contributes to the WER.

ASR-LM: A Transformer language model was trained on English text (Irie et al., 2019). The model has 6 layers, with 4096 feed-forward units and 1024 attention dimension with 8 heads. The model is initially pre-trained on Librispeech LM corpus and it is later fine-tuned on English text

Table 2: Performance of trained ASR systems reported on MustC-Common set. For Punc-ASR, the errors in punctuation tokens are considered, which makes it a more difficult task.

Model	WER
Norm-ASR	18.20
+LM	17.35
Punc-ASR	21.20

from MT-train-set and ASR-MT-train-set. An improvement in the performance is observed by shallow fusion of the ASR and language model (ASR-LM). Performances of these language models are presented in column 2 of Table. 5.

4 Machine Translation Systems(MT)

Transformer models (Vaswani et al., 2017) are also at the core of MT-systems. They have 6-encoder and 6-decoder layers with 4096 feed-forward units and 1024 attention dimensions and have 16 heads. The models are optimized with 30K warm-up updates and a check-point is saved every 8k updates. Training is stopped using an early stopping criterion. 8-best check-points are averaged and the averaged weights are used for decoding the hypotheses. The noisy EOS tokens are pruned out using (Kahn et al., 2019). Vectorized beam (Seki et al., 2019) search has been used for decoding the hypotheses with a beam size of 8. A large variance in the performance is observed w.r.t the decoding hyper-parameters such as maximum target sequence length and length-bonus. The maximum length of the target sequence is computed by multiplying the input sequence length with length-ratio: 1.2 was found as optimal on the development set. To control the length of the output sequence, the log-likelihood scores of the hypotheses are penalized by additive token insertion penalties. The optimal value for this penalty is tuned as a hyper-parameter on the development set. The hypothesis text is de-tokenized and BLEU score is evaluated using Moses Toolkit. All the BLEU scores reported in this paper are computed using the de-tokenized, punctuated German text using `multi-bleu-detok.perl`. The performances of the MT systems are reported in Table. 3. All BLEU scores reported in this paper are computed using punctuated text as reference.

In Table 3, Norm-MT, Punc-MT are MT models trained to predict punctuated German text. Norm-

Table 3: Performances of the MT systems reported on MustC-Common set.

Model	BLEU
Norm-MT	
+pretrain	27.18
+finetune	27.98
+MT-LM	28.12
Punc-MT	
+pretrain	31.02
+finetune	35.00
+MT-LM	35.04

MT uses the normalized English text as input while the Punc-MT uses the punctuated English text. Punc-MT model has performed better than Norm-MT. From Table 3, it can be observed that the punctuation tokens in the text are adding additional information for training the MT model. Fine-tuning the Punc-MT on in-domain text has improved the performance significantly. Further in this paper, MT models described in this section are referred to as Ext.MT models (Externally trained MT models).

MT-LM: A transformer language model has been trained on German text from MT-Train-set, ASR-MT-train-set. This LM is also used while decoding with the MT model (Irie et al., 2019). The architecture of the model is same as ASR-LM mentioned in section 3. A shallow fusion between the MT-model and the MT-LM Language model is performed. As shown in Table 3 and column 2 of Table 5, the additional language model (MT-LM) did not improve the performance significantly.

5 Jointly Trained ASR-MT Systems

The model has two modules: ASR and MT; their architecture is same as described in sections 3 and 4 respectively – see block diagram in Figure 1 and full description of the model in (Vydana et al., 2021). The context vectors from the final layer of the ASR-decoder are used as inputs to the MT module. Passing context vectors from ASR to MT models while training has also been explored in (Sperber et al., 2019). Both the models are jointly optimized using a multi-task cross-entropy (ASR cross-entropy and MT cross-entropy) – both losses are also shown in Figure 1. During the inference, beam search has been used to obtain the ASR hypotheses, and the corresponding context vectors obtained from the ASR model are used by

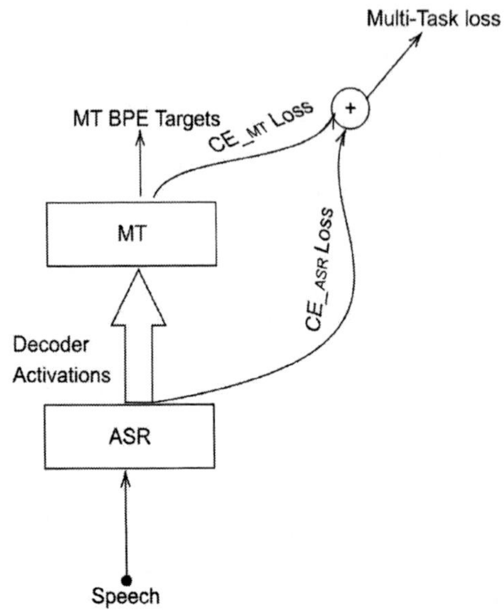

Figure 1: Joint-training of ASR-MT system using multi-task loss.

the MT model for generating translations. The MT model also uses a beam search, and the final ST hypotheses is obtained by a coupled search (Vydana et al., 2021) using the joint-likelihood from ASR and MT:

$$
\begin{aligned}
y* &= \arg\max_{y} \sum_{z \in \hat{Z}(x)} P(y|z)P(z|x) \\
&\equiv \arg\max_{y} \ \arg\max_{z \in \hat{Z}(x)} (\log(P(y|z)) \\
&\quad + \log(P(z|x))), \qquad (1)
\end{aligned}
$$

where x is the speech abnd z,y are the source and target sequences respectively. $\hat{Z}$ is the n-best source sequence and $y*$ is most likely decoded hypothesis. In this equation, $y*$ is always a discrete sequence, while z is a discrete sequence when we are using Ext.MT and a continuous one when using Joint-MT. Note that similar coupled search was used in (Tu et al., 2017), where the back translation likelihoods are used for re-scoring the hypothesis of the MT-system.

6 Adapting ASR decoder to the MT module

Joint-ASR-MT models are jointly optimized by having an end-to-end differentiable path from speech to translations. The internal continuous representations from the ASR-decoder are used as the input to MT module. Speech translation can be further improved by adapting ASR-decoder to the MT module. This is achieved by training the ASR-decoder jointly with the MT-module using large amount of text-only MT training data. The weights for the model are initialized from trained Joint-ASR-MT model. Speech translation data (ASR-MT-Train-set) is used to finetune Joint-ASR-MT model using a multi-task loss. Apart from that, the data from the MT-Train-set is used to jointly train the ASR-decoder and the MT-module of Joint-ASR-MT model. We alternately update the model using multi-task loss described in section 4 and the adaptation loss as described in this section.

A block diagram describing this training is presented in Figure 2. The input text sequence is given to the ASR-decoder and a sequence of zeros is considered as the encoder output sequence of the ASR model (i.e.,H_{ASR} in Figure 2). The context vectors computed from these two sequences are used for training the MT-module. Note that similar method has been adopted in (Potapczyk et al., 2019) for improving the performance of ASR system using only text data. This training further improves the performance as will be shown in section 7.

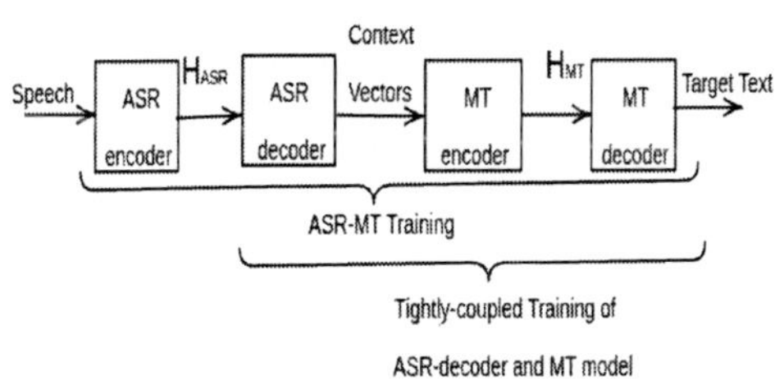

Figure 2: Adaptation of ASR-decoder to the MT-module in the Joint-ASR-MT model.

7 Speech Translation Results

Results for the various configurations of speech translation systems are given in Table 4. First, we focus on column A, where the Joint-ASR-MT models are trained using ASR-MT-Train-set (only speech translation data) with a multi-task loss as described in section 5. Note, however, that Ext.ASR and Ext.MT systems are trained on large amounts of data and finetuned to ASR-MT-Train-set as described in sections 3 and 4 respectively. For systems in column-A, normalized (unpunctuated) text is passed from ASR to MT model. Row 1 corresponds to the conventional cascade system, where the Ext.ASR systems generates the n-best hypotheses of discrete token sequences and an Ext.MT uses these token sequences for generating the translations as described in Eq. 1. We consider this system achieving BLEU 23.20 as a baseline.

Usually, transformer-ASR decoder uses the partial output hypothesis and extends it by a new token with every autoregressive decoding step. For the system in row 2, Ext.ASR generates the complete hypothesis and ASR module from Joint-ASR-MT is "asked" to extend it by one more token. As a byproduct "context vectors" (the continuous representations) are generated for the whole sequence — these are then passed to the MT-module in joint-ASR-MT model to generate translation. Compared to row 1 of column A, we see a degradation in performance (BLEU-20.19). This can be attributed to having only small amount of speech translation training data, which is not sufficient for robustly training the Joint-ASR-MT systems.

For the systems in row 3, Ext.ASR generates the ASR hypotheses which are used by Ext.MT similar to the system described in row 1; the hypotheses from Ext.ASR are used by Joint-MT similarly to the system described in row 2. To generate the translation, the hypotheses form both models are ensembled as follows: For each output token, a weighted average of Log-softmax outputs from the two MT models is computed. This weighted average is used in the beam-search to compute the n-best partial hypotheses. These partial hypotheses are further extended by both the models to generate the Log-softmax outputs for next tokens. We can see that this ensembling system achieves a BLEU score of 24.02 and outperforms the cascaded baseline.

The systems in rows 4-6 are essentially the same as the ones in rows 1-3, respectively, except that now, the ASR module from joint-ASR-MT system is directly used to produce the n-best ASR hypotheses and the corresponding context vectors. Rows 4-6 show the same trend as rows 1-3 with slightly improved performance; these improvements are mainly due to better performing ASR system: As described in Section 2.2, training ASR systems only on ASR-MT-Train-set (data from Mustc, IWSLT and Europarl with erroneous transcriptions) did not lead to convergence. How-

Table 4: Performances of Joint-ASR-MT systems under various ensemble combinations, the results are reported on MustC-Common test set.

		A		B		C		D	
		no-pretraining +Norm-ASR/MT		pre-training +Norm-ASR/MT		pre-training +Punc-ASR/MT		pretraining +Punc-ASR/MT+ tightly-coupled	
	[ASR]⇒[MT]	BLEU	WER	BLEU	WER	BLEU	WER	BLEU	WER
1.	[Ext-ASR]⇒[Ext-MT]	23.20	18.20	23.20	18.20	26.15	21.54	26.15	21.54
2.	[Ext-ASR]⇒[Joint-MT]	20.19	-	22.59	-	28.56	-	29.00	-
3.	[Ext-ASR]⇒[Joint-MT + Ext-MT]	24.02	-	24.13	-	29.07	-	29.44	-
4.	[Joint-ASR]⇒[Ext-MT]	23.86	16.14	23.86	13.01	29.70	15.71	30.24	15.63
5.	[Joint-ASR]⇒[Joint-MT]	20.75	-	23.97	-	31.23	-	32.68	-
6.	[Joint-ASR]⇒[Joint-MT + Ext-MT]	24.65	-	25.95	-	32.51	-	33.68	-
7.	[Ext-ASR + Joint-ASR]⇒[Ext-MT]	24.60	14.84	25.00	13.54	29.00	16.46	29.35	16.19
8.	[Ext-ASR + Joint-ASR]⇒[Joint-MT]	20.89	-	23.59	-	30.52	-	31.58	-
9.	[Ext-ASR + Joint-ASR]⇒[Joint-MT + Ext-MT]	25.11	-	25.65	-	31.86	-	32.67	-
10.	[Ext-ASR + Joint-ASR]⇒[Joint-MT + Ext-MT] +ens*	25.35	14.61	26.14	13.05	32.67	15.71	33.78	15.63

Table 5: Comparing the performance of Joint-ASR-MT systems while processing n-best hypotheses from the ASR.

	A		B		C		D	
	no-pretraining +Norm-ASR/MT		pre-training +Norm-ASR/MT		pre-training +Punc-ASR/MT		pretraining +Punc-ASR/MT+ tightly-coupled	
[ASR]⇒[MT]	BLEU	WER	BLEU	WER	BLEU	WER	BLEU	WER
[Ext-ASR + Joint-ASR]⇒[Joint-MT + Ext-MT] +ens*	25.35	14.61	26.14	13.05	32.67	15.71	33.78	15.63
+ASR-LM			26.90	12.80				
+MT-LM			27.16					
+2-best-input	-	-	27.24	-	32.69	-	33.82	-
+4-best-input	-	-	27.35	-	32.80	-	33.87	-
+6-best-input	-	-	27.35	-	32.85	-	33.86	-
+8-best-input	-	-	27.46	-	32.94	-	33.77	-
+10-best-input	-	-	27.51	-	32.87	-	33.79	-

ever, when the same data is used to train Joint-ASR-MT model for speech translation task, we observe that the ASR module in this model trained well. The reason for that is that the ASR-module is not directly trained on erroneous transcriptions, instead, it is trained to produce transcriptions that lead to good translations. This training can be seen as a form of light supervision which can mitigate the problem with the erroneous transcriptions. At the end, this system trained only on ASR-MT-Train-set achieves better ASR performance (WER 16.14%) compared to Ext.ASR (WER 18.20%), Which is pre-trained on ASR-Train-set (Approx 2000hrs) and fine-tuned on erroneous ASR-MT-Train-set. Similar trend will be observed with the systems in columns B, C and D.

The systems described in rows 7-9 are similar to those from rows 1-3, except that the ASR hypotheses are obtained by ensembling the Ext.ASR and ASR-module in Joint-ASR-MT model. The ensembling is performed in a similar way as described for the MT-system (row 2). All the ensemble systems in rows 3, 6, and 7-9 are ensembled giving equal weight to both the systems, except for row 10, where the ensemble weights are tuned on the development set. For all these systems, we can see that the ensembling consistently improves the performances.

The systems in column B are similar to the ones in Column A, but for the Joint-ASR-MT model, the weights of ASR and MT module are initialized from the Ext.ASR and Ext.MT. Only then, the Joint-ASR-MT model is fine-tuned using ASR-MT-Train-set. Comparing column-A and column-B, we can see that such pre-training has significantly improved the performance.

We also see that the MT system using continuous representations (Joint-MT) (row 5; BLEU 23.97) outperforms the system with the Ext.MT (row 4; BLEU-23.86) and similar trend can be seen in columns C and D. This is in contrast to the system in column A where we did not use enough data for training the Joint-ASR-MT model; now, with the pre-training, the joint-ASR-MT model is effectively trained on the same amount of data as the Ext.MT systems.

The systems in column C are similar to the ones in Column B, but the ASR and MT modules used here are Punc-ASR (ASR systems which can generate punctuated text) and Punc-MT (MT systems which can process punctuated text as input), respectively. We can see that the systems from column-C perform significantly and consistently better than the corresponding ones in column-B. This shows that it is more effective to train an ASR module to generate punctuated text rather than leaving the punctuation task to the MT module. Note that the ASR performances reported in columns C and D is computed including the punctuation symbols, which results in higher WERs.

Finally, the systems in column D are the same as the ones in column C except that we additionally use the ASR decoder adaptation scheme described in section 6. The consistent improvements observed in column D as compared to column C show the effectiveness of this adaptation scheme. They are able to make use of the large amount of text-only MT training data to train also the ASR decoder in order to tighten the coupling between ASR-decoder and MT-module. Apart from improving MT-module, this adaptation has also improved the performance of ASR-decoder on its own. This can be observed by comparing WER's of row 4 in columns C and D.

The results of passing the n-best hypotheses from ASR to MT models are presented in Table 5. Passing the n-best hypothesis from ASR to MT module has better performance, but not significantly. This result is not in line with out previous studies (Vydana et al., 2021), where we have seen significant gains from switching from 1-best to n-best.

8 Conclusion

In this work, we have explored joint-training of ASR-MT models for speech translation. Initializing these models from pre-trained ASR and MT models has helped in better optimization. The joint training has improved the performance of the ASR module significantly as the additional MT module has provided better (light) supervision in the context of erroneous ASR transcripts. Adding the punctuation information into the input text improves the performance of the MT-model greatly. In line with this observation, use of ASR system generating punctuated text also improves the MT performance significantly in a cascade pipeline. Use of the MT text only data to adapt the ASR decoder to the MT module in the joint-ASR-MT model further improves the performances of these systems. The systems trained in this work are offline models and their performances needs to be studied from the perspective of online or streaming models.

9 Acknowledgements

The work was supported by Czech National Science Foundation(GACR) project "NEUREM3" No. 19-26934X. Part of high-performance computation run on IT4I supercomputer and was supported by the Ministry of Education, Youth and Sports of the Czech Republic through e-INFRA CZ (ID:90140).

References

Antonios Anastasopoulos and David Chiang. 2018. Tied multitask learning for neural speech translation. *arXiv preprint arXiv:1802.06655*.

Ebrahim Ansari, Nguyen Bach, Ondřej Bojar, Roldano Cattoni, Fahim Dalvi, Nadir Durrani, Marcello Federico, Christian Federmann, Jiatao Gu, Fei Huang, et al. 2020. Findings of the iwslt 2020 evaluation campaign. In *Proceedings of the 17th International Conference on Spoken Language Translation*, pages 1–34.

Parnia Bahar, Patrick Wilken, Tamer Alkhouli, Andreas Guta, Pavel Golik, Evgeny Matusov, and Christian Herold. 2020. Start-before-end and end-to-end: Neural speech translation by AppTek and RWTH Aachen University. In *Proceedings of the 17th International Conference on Spoken Language Translation*, pages 44–54, Online. Association for Computational Linguistics.

Parnia Bahar, Albert Zeyer, Ralf Schlüter, and Hermann Ney. 2019. On using specaugment for end-to-end speech translation. *arXiv preprint arXiv:1911.08876*.

Dzmitry Bahdanau, Kyunghyun Cho, and Yoshua Bengio. 2015. Neural machine translation by jointly learning to align and translate. *arXiv preprint arXiv:1409.0473*.

Mattia A Di Gangi, Matteo Negri, and Marco Turchi. 2019. Adapting transformer to end-to-end spoken language translation. *Proc. INTERSPEECH*, pages 1133–1137.

Linhao Dong, Shuang Xu, and Bo Xu. 2018. Speech-transformer: a no-recurrence sequence-to-sequence model for speech recognition. In *Proc. IEEE Int. Conf. Acoust., Speech, Signal Processing*, pages 5884–5888. IEEE.

Qianqian Dong, Rong Ye, Mingxuan Wang, Hao Zhou, Shuang Xu, Bo Xu, and Lei Li. 2020. " listen, understand and translate": Triple supervision decouples end-to-end speech-to-text translation. *arXiv preprint arXiv:2009.09704*.

Hirofumi Inaguma, Shun Kiyono, Kevin Duh, Shigeki Karita, Nelson Enrique Yalta Soplin, Tomoki Hayashi, and Shinji Watanabe. 2020. Espnet-st: All-in-one speech translation toolkit.

Kazuki Irie, Albert Zeyer, Ralf Schlüter, and Hermann Ney. 2019. Language modeling with deep transformers. *arXiv preprint arXiv:1905.04226*.

Niehues Jan, Roldano Cattoni, Stuker Sebastian, Matteo Negri, Marco Turchi, Salesky Elizabeth, Sanabria Ramon, Barrault Loic, Specia Lucia, and Marcello Federico. 2019. The iwslt 2019 evaluation campaign. In *16th International Workshop on Spoken Language Translation 2019*.

Jacob Kahn, Ann Lee, and Awni Hannun. 2019. Self-training for end-to-end speech recognition. *arXiv preprint arXiv:1909.09116*.

Shigeki Karita, Nanxin Chen, Tomoki Hayashi, Takaaki Hori, Hirofumi Inaguma, Ziyan Jiang, Masao Someki, Nelson Enrique Yalta Soplin, Ryuichi Yamamoto, Xiaofei Wang, et al. 2019. A comparative study on transformer vs rnn in speech applications. *arXiv preprint arXiv:1909.06317*.

Taku Kudo and John Richardson. 2018. Sentencepiece: A simple and language independent subword tokenizer and detokenizer for neural text processing. *arXiv preprint arXiv:1808.06226*.

Thanh-Le Ha Juan Hussain Felix Schneider Jan Niehues Sebastian Stüker Alexander Waibel Ngoc-Quan Pham, Thai-Son Nguyen. 2019. The iwslt 2019 kit speech translation system. In *International Workshop on Spoken Language Translation (IWSLT)*. Hongkong.

Ngoc-Quan Pham, Thanh-Le Ha, Tuan-Nam Nguyen, Thai-Son Nguyen, Elizabeth Salesky, Sebastian Stueker, Jan Niehues, and Alexander Waibel. 2020a. Relative positional encoding for speech recognition and direct translation. *arXiv preprint arXiv:2005.09940*.

Ngoc-Quan Pham, Thai-Son Nguyen, Jan Niehues, Markus Muller, and Alex Waibel. 2019. Very deep self-attention networks for end-to-end speech recognition. *arXiv preprint arXiv:1904.13377*.

Ngoc-Quan Pham, Felix Schneider, Tuan-Nam Nguyen, Thanh-Le Ha, Thai Son Nguyen, Maximilian Awiszus, Sebastian Stüker, and Alex Waibel. 2020b. Kit's iwslt 2020 slt translation system. In *Proceedings of the 17th International Conference on Spoken Language Translation*, pages 55–61.

Tomasz Potapczyk, Pawel Przybysz, Marcin Chochowski, and Artur Szumaczuk. 2019. Samsung's system for the iwslt 2019 end-to-end speech translation task. In *Proc. of 16th International Workshop on Spoken Language Translation (IWSLT), Hong Kong*.

Daniel Povey, Arnab Ghoshal, Gilles Boulianne, Lukas Burget, Ondrej Glembek, Nagendra Goel, Mirko Hannemann, Petr Motlicek, Yanmin Qian, Petr Schwarz, et al. 2011. The kaldi speech recognition toolkit. CONF. IEEE Signal Processing Society.

Daniel Povey, Vijayaditya Peddinti, Daniel Galvez, Pegah Ghahremani, Vimal Manohar, Xingyu Na, Yiming Wang, and Sanjeev Khudanpur. 2016. Purely sequence-trained neural networks for asr based on lattice-free mmi. In *Proc. INTERSPEECH*, pages 2751–2755.

Hiroshi Seki, Takaaki Hori, Shinji Watanabe, Niko Moritz, and Jonathan Le Roux. 2019. Vectorized beam search for ctc-attention-based speech recognition. In *Proc. INTERSPEECH*, pages 3825–3829.

Matthias Sperber, Graham Neubig, Jan Niehues, and Alex Waibel. 2019. Attention-passing models for robust and data-efficient end-to-end speech translation. *Transactions of the Association for Computational Linguistics*, 7:313–325.

Matthias Sperber and Matthias Paulik. 2020. Speech translation and the end-to-end promise: Taking stock of where we are. *arXiv preprint arXiv:2004.06358*.

Zhaopeng Tu, Yang Liu, Lifeng Shang, Xiaohua Liu, and Hang Li. 2017. Neural machine translation with reconstruction. In *Proceedings of the AAAI Conference on Artificial Intelligence*, volume 31.

Ashish Vaswani, Noam Shazeer, Niki Parmar, Jakob Uszkoreit, Llion Jones, Aidan N Gomez, Łukasz Kaiser, and Illia Polosukhin. 2017. Attention is all you need. In *Proc. Advances in Neural Information Processing Systems*, pages 5998–6008.

Hari Krishna Vydana, Martin Karafi'at, Katerina Zmolikova, Luk'as Burget, and Honza Cernocky. 2021. Jointly trained transformers models for spoken language translation. In *Proc. IEEE Int. Conf. Acoust., Speech, Signal Processing*.

Pei Zhang, Boxing Chen, Niyu Ge, and Kai Fan. 2019. Lattice transformer for speech translation. *arXiv preprint arXiv:1906.05551*.

Chengqi Zhao, Mingxuan Wang, and Lei Li. 2020. Neurst: Neural speech translation toolkit. *arXiv preprint arXiv:2012.10018*.

Dealing with training and test segmentation mismatch: FBK@IWSLT2021

Sara Papi[1,2], **Marco Gaido**[1,2], **Matteo Negri**[1], **Marco Turchi**[1]
[1]Fondazione Bruno Kessler, Trento, Italy
[2]University of Trento, Italy
{spapi|mgaido|negri|turchi}@fbk.eu

Abstract

This paper describes FBK's system submission to the IWSLT 2021 Offline Speech Translation task. We participated with a direct model, which is a Transformer-based architecture trained to translate English speech audio data into German texts. The training pipeline is characterized by knowledge distillation and a two-step fine-tuning procedure. Both knowledge distillation and the first fine-tuning step are carried out on manually segmented real and synthetic data, the latter being generated with an MT system trained on the available corpora. Differently, the second fine-tuning step is carried out on a random segmentation of the MuST-C v2 En-De dataset. Its main goal is to reduce the performance drops occurring when a speech translation model trained on manually segmented data (i.e. an ideal, sentence-like segmentation) is evaluated on automatically segmented audio (i.e. actual, more realistic testing conditions). For the same purpose, a custom hybrid segmentation procedure that accounts for both audio content (pauses) and for the length of the produced segments is applied to the test data before passing them to the system. At inference time, we compared this procedure with a baseline segmentation method based on Voice Activity Detection (VAD). Our results indicate the effectiveness of the proposed hybrid approach, shown by a reduction of the gap with manual segmentation from 8.3 to 1.4 BLEU points.

1 Introduction

Speech translation (ST) is the task of translating a speech uttered in one language into its textual representation in a different language. Unlike *simultaneous* ST, where the audio is translated as soon as it is produced, in the *offline* setting the audio is entirely available and translated at once. In continuity with the last two rounds of the IWSLT evaluation campaign (Niehues et al., 2019; Ansari et al., 2020), the IWSLT2021 Offline Speech Translation task (Anastasopoulos et al., 2021) focused on the translation into German of English audio data extracted from TED talks. Participants could approach the task either with a cascade architecture or with a direct end-to-end system. The former represents the traditional pipeline approach (Stentiford and Steer, 1988; Waibel et al., 1991) comprising an automatic speech recognition (ASR) followed by a machine translation (MT) component. The latter (Bérard et al., 2016; Weiss et al., 2017) relies on a single neural network trained to translate the input audio into target language text bypassing any intermediate symbolic representation steps.

The two paradigms have advantages and disadvantages. Cascade architectures have historically guaranteed higher translation quality (Niehues et al., 2018, 2019) thanks to the large corpora available to train their ASR and MT sub-components. However, a well-known drawback of pipelined solutions is represented by error propagation: transcription errors are indeed hard (and sometimes impossible) to recover during the translation step. Direct models, although being penalized by the paucity of training data, have two theoretical competitive advantages, namely: *i)* the absence of error propagation as there are no intermediate processing steps, and *ii)* a less mediated access to the source utterance, which allows them to better exploit speech information (e.g. prosody) without loss of information.

The paucity of parallel (audio, translation) data for direct ST has been previously addressed in different ways, ranging from *model pre-training* to exploit knowledge transfer from ASR and/or MT (Bérard et al., 2018; Bansal et al., 2019; Alinejad and Sarkar, 2020), *knowledge distillation* (Liu et al., 2019; Gaido et al., 2021a), *data augmentation* (Jia et al., 2019; Bahar et al., 2019b; Nguyen et al., 2020), and *multi-task learning* (Weiss et al.,

Proceedings of the 18th International Conference on Spoken Language Translation, pages 84–91
Bangkok, Thailand (Online), August 5–6, 2021.

2017; Anastasopoulos and Chiang, 2018; Bahar et al., 2019a; Gaido et al., 2020b). Thanks to these studies, the gap between the strong cascade models and the new end-to-end ones has gradually reduced during the last few years. As highlighted by the IWSLT 2020 Offline Speech Translation challenge results (Ansari et al., 2020), the rapid evolution of the direct approach has eventually led it to performance scores that are similar to those of cascade architectures. In light of this positive trend, we decided to adopt only the direct approach (described in Section 3) for our participation in the 2021 round of the offline ST task.

Another interesting finding from last year's campaign concerns the sensitivity of ST models to different segmentations of the input audio. The 2020 winning system (Potapczyk and Przybysz, 2020) shows that, with a custom segmentation of the test data, the same model improved by 3.81 BLEU points the score achieved when using the basic segmentation provided by the task organizers. This noticeable difference is due to a well-known problem in MT, ST and in machine learning at large: any mismatch between training and test data (in terms of domain, text style or a variety of other aspects) can cause unpredictable, often large, performance drops at test time. In ST, this is a critical issue, inherent to the nature of the available resources: while systems are usually trained on corpora that are manually segmented at sentence level, test data come in the form of unsegmented continuous speech.

A possible solution to this problem is to automatically segment the test data with a Voice Activity Detection (VAD) tool (Sohn et al., 1999). This strategy tries to mimic the sentence-based segmentation observed in the training data using pauses as an indirect (hence known to be sub-optimal) cue for sentence boundaries. Custom segmentation strategies, which are allowed to IWSLT participants, typically go in this direction with the aim to reduce the data mismatch by working on evaluation data. An opposite way to look at the problem is to work on the training data. In this case, the goal is to "robustify" the ST model to noisy inputs (i.e. sub-optimal segmentations) at training time, by exposing it to perturbed data where sentence-like boundaries are not guaranteed. Our participation in the offline ST task exploits both solutions (see Section 4): at training time, by fine-tuning the model with a random segmentation of the available in-domain data; at test time, by feeding it with a custom hybrid segmentation of the evaluation data.

In a nutshell, our participation can be summarized as follows. After a preliminary model selection phase that was carried out in order to select the best architecture, we adopted a pipeline consisting of: *i)* ASR pre-training, *ii)* ST training with knowledge distillation with an MT teacher, and *iii)* two-step fine-tuning by varying the type and the amount of data between the two steps. The second fine-tuning step, which was carried out on artificially perturbed data to increase model robustness, represents the main aspect characterizing our participation to this year's round of the offline ST task together with our custom automatic segmentation of the test set (see Section 4). Our experimental results proved the effectiveness of our solutions: compared to a standard ST model and a baseline VAD-based method, on the MuST-C v2 English-German test set (Cattoni et al., 2021), the gap with optimal manual segmentation is reduced from 8.3 to 1.4 BLEU.

2 Training data

To build our models, we used most of the training data allowed for participation.[1] They include: MT corpora (English-German text pairs), ASR corpora (English audios and their corresponding transcripts) and ST corpora (English audios with corresponding English transcripts and German translations).

MT. Among all the available datasets, we selected those allowed for WMT 2019 (Barrault et al., 2019) and OpenSubtitles2018 (Lison and Tiedemann, 2016). Some pre-processing was required to isolate and remove different types of potentially harmful noise present in the data. These include non-unicode characters, both on the source and target side of the parallel sentence pairs, which would have led to an increased dictionary size hindering model training, and whole non-German target sentences (mostly in English). The cleaning of this two types of noise, which was respectively performed using a custom script and Modern MT (Bertoldi et al., 2017), resulted in the removal of roughly 25% of the data, with a final dataset of ~49 million sentence pairs.

ASR. ASR corpora, together with the ST ones described below, were collected for the ASR training. In detail, the allowed native ASR datasets are:

[1] https://iwslt.org/2021/offline

LibriSpeech (Panayotov et al., 2015), TEDLIUM v3 (Hernandez et al., 2018) and Mozilla Common Voice.[2] In all of them, English texts were lower-cased and punctuation was removed.

ST. The ST benchmarks we used are essentially three: *i)* Europarl-ST (obtained from European Parliament debates – Iranzo-Sánchez et al. 2020), *ii)* MuST-C v2 (built from TED talks – Cattoni et al. 2021), and *iii)* CoVoST 2 (containing the translations of a portion of the Mozilla Common Voice dataset – Wang et al. 2020a). To cope with the scarcity of ST data, we complemented these native ST corpora with synthetic data. To this aim, we used the MT system trained on the available MT data to translate into German the English transcripts of the aforementioned ASR datasets. The resulting texts were used as reference material during the ST model training. The combination of native and generated data resulted in a total of about 1.26 million samples. The transcription-translation pairs were tokenized using, respectively, source/target-language SentencePiece (Sennrich et al., 2016) unigram models trained on the MT corpora with a vocabulary size of 32k tokens. Similar to our last year's IWSLT submission (Gaido et al., 2020b), the entire dataset was used for training in a multi-domain fashion, where the two domains were *native* (original ST data) and *generated* (synthetic data).

Prior to the extraction of the speech features, the audio was pre-processed with the SpecAugment (Park et al., 2019) data augmentation technique, which masks consecutive portions of the input both in frequency and in time dimensions. From all the audio files, 80 log Mel-filter banks features were extracted using PyKaldi (Can et al., 2018), filtering out those samples containing more than 3,000 frames. Finally, we applied utterance level Cepstral Mean and Variance Normalization both during ASR pre-training and ST training phases. The configuration parameters used are the default ones as set in (Wang et al., 2020b).

3 Model and training

In order to select the best performing architecture, we trained several Transformer-based models (Vaswani et al., 2017), which consist of 12 encoder layers, 6 decoder layers, 8 attention heads, 512 features for the attention layers and 2,048 hidden units in the feed-forward layers. The ASR and ST models are based on a custom version of the model by (Wang et al., 2020b), which is a Transformer whose encoder has two initial 1D convolutional layers with *gelu* activation functions (Hendrycks and Gimpel, 2020). Also, the encoder self-attentions were biased using a logarithmic distance penalty in favor of the local context as per (Di Gangi et al., 2019). A Connectionist Temporal Classification (CTC) scoring function was applied as described in (Gaido et al., 2020b). This was done by adding a linear layer to either the 6th, 8th or 10th encoder layer to map the encoder states to the vocabulary size and compute the CTC loss. The choice of the final architecture, depending on where the CTC loss is applied, was made based on sacreBLEU score (Post, 2018) after training the models on MuST-C v1 En-De (Cattoni et al., 2021). ST results computed on the test set are reported on Table 1. As it can be seen from the table, two models obtained the highest, identical BLEU score (21.21): they both use logarithmic distance penalty but apply CTC loss to the 6th or the 8th encoder layer.

3.1 Training pipeline

In the following, we describe the pipeline used to build our ST models, as anticipated in Section 1. In details, the ASR model is trained and its encoder used as starting point for the ST model, which is first trained via knowledge distillation and then fine-tuned on native and synthetic data. Then, a second fine-tuning step is performed on a perturbed version of a subset of the native data, focused on reducing the model performance drop over different segmentations. For the initial ST training, we optimized KL divergence (Kullback and Leibler, 1951) and CTC losses. For the first fine-tuning step, we optimized label smoothed cross entropy (LSCE) or CTC+LSCE while, for the second fine-tuning step, the models were refined using LSCE only, with a lower learning rate in order not to override the knowledge acquired during the previous phases.

ASR pre-training. Due to the identical BLEU score obtained by applying the CTC loss to the 6th and 8th layer during the ST model selection phase, we opted for training the ASR system using both these architectures, and selected the final model by looking at the Word Error Rate (WER) achieved by averaging 7 checkpoints around the best one. As shown in Table 2, the best overall performing architecture is the one where the CTC is applied to

[2] https://commonvoice.mozilla.org/en/datasets

architecture	CTC encoder layer	distance penalty	**BLEU**
2d convolutional	6	no	19.04
1d convolutional	6	no	21.16
1d convolutional	6	log	21.21
1d convolutional	8	log	21.21
1d convolutional	10	log	21.08

Table 1: Results of 1d convolutional architectures trained computing CTC loss at different layers and with/without distance penalty. Also the result of a 2d convolutional architecture is reported where the structure is exactly the same except for the use of a different type of convolution.

model	dev	test
CTC on 6th encoder layer	8.67	12.19
CTC on 8th encoder layer	**7.52**	**10.70**

Table 2: Results of ASR pre-training in terms of WER. The dev and test sets used are, respectively, dev and tst-COMMON of MuST-C v1 En-De.

the 8th encoder layer. Accordingly, we used this architecture to perform all the successive training phases.

Training with knowledge distillation. Two ST models, one with 12 and one with 15 encoder layers, were trained by loading the pre-trained ASR encoder weights and applying word-level Knowledge Distillation (KD) as in (Kim and Rush, 2016). In KD, a *student* model is trained with the goal of learning how to produce the same output distribution as a *teacher* model, and this is obtained by computing the KL divergence between the two output distributions. In our setting, the student and the teacher are respectively the ST system and an MT system that we trained on the MT data described in Section 2. It consists in a plain Transformer model with 6 layers for both the encoder and the decoder, 16 attention heads, 1,024 features for the attention layers and 4,096 hidden units in the feed-forward layers. Evaluated on the MuST-C v2 En-De test set, it achieved a BLEU score of 33.3. For ST training with KD, we extracted only the top 8 tokens from the teacher distribution. According to (Tan et al., 2019), this choice results in a significant reduction of the memory required, with no loss in final performance. At the end of this phase, we decided to keep the model with 15 encoder layers as it performs better than the one with 12 encoder layers by 1 BLEU point.

Fine-tuning step #1: using native and synthetic data. Once the KD training phase was concluded, we performed a multi-domain fine-tuning where the ST model was jointly trained on native and synthetic data optimizing LSCE or its combination with the CTC loss.

4 Coping with training/test data mismatch

As mentioned in Section 1, the segmentation of audio files is a crucial aspect in ST. In fact, mismatches between the manual segmentation of the training data and the automatic one required when processing the unsegmented test set can produce significant performance drops. To mitigate this risk, we worked on two complementary fronts: at training and inference time. At training time, we tried to robustify our model by fine-tuning it on a randomly segmented subset of the training data. At inference time, we applied an automatic segmentation procedure to the test set in order to feed the model with input resembling, as much as possible, the gold manual segmentation. These two solutions, which characterize our final submission, are explained in the following.

Fine-tuning step #2: using randomly segmented data. For the second fine-tuning step, we re-segmented the MuST-C v2 En-De training set following the procedure described in (Gaido et al., 2020a). The method consists in choosing a random word in the transcript of each sample, and using it as sentence boundary instead of the linguistically-motivated (sentence-level) splits provided in the original data. The corresponding audio segments are then obtained by means of audio-text alignments performed with Gentle.[3] Similarly, the German translation of each re-segmented transcript is extracted with cross-lingual alignments generated by a fast_align (Dyer et al., 2013) model trained on all the MT data available for the task and on MuST-C v2. In case either of the alignments is

[3]https://github.com/lowerquality/gentle/

model	MuST-C2 manual	MuST-C2 VAD (WebRTC)		MuST-C2 hybrid		IWSLT2015 VAD (LIUM)		IWSLT2015 hybrid	
1-FT LSCE	27.6	20.8		24.8		16.1		21.9	
2-FT LSCE	-	23.4	(+2.6)	**26.4**	(+1.6)	20.7	(+4.6)	22.7	(+0.8)
1-FT LSCE+CTC	27.7	19.9		25.3		14.0		21.7	
2-FT LSCE+CTC	-	**23.7**	(+3.8)	26.3	(+1.0)	**20.9**	(+6.9)	**23.1**	(+1.4)

Table 3: Results of the best architectures deriving from KD training after one or two fine-tuning steps. 1-FT stands for one-step fine-tuning and 2-FT stands for two-step fine-tuning (see Section 3). MuST-C v2 results on manual segmentation have been not computed for the 2-step fine-tuned models as we were interested in the evaluation of the improvement on automatically segmented data.

not possible (because fast_align is not able to align enough words or Gentle does not recognize the position of the word in the audio), the sentence is discarded. The resulting material, which contains $\sim 5\%$ less segments than the original MuST-C release, was then used for our second (and final) fine-tuning step. As already stated, we used only the LSCE loss for this stage.

Automatic segmentation of the test data. At inference time, the test set was segmented with an hybrid approach that considers both the audio content and the length of the resulting segment (Gaido et al., 2021b). Specifically, every segment is ensured to be at least 17s and at most 20s long, but the exact splitting position is determined by the longest pause detected within this interval. Pauses are identified with the WebRTC VAD tool (Johnston and Burnett, 2012), using 20ms as *frame duration* and 2 as *aggressivity* level.

5 Experimental settings

Our implementation is built on top of fairseq Pytorch library (Ott et al., 2019). All our models were trained using the Adam optimizer (Kingma and Ba, 2015) with $\beta_1 = 0.9$, $\beta_2 = 0.98$. During training, the learning rate was set to increase linearly from 0 to 2e-3 for the first 10,000 warm-up steps and then to decay with an inverse square root policy. Differently, the learning rate was kept constant for model fine-tuning, with a value of 1e-3 for the first fine-tuning step and 1e-4 for the second one.

All the trainings were performed on 2 Tesla V100 GPUs with 32GB RAM. We set the maximum number of tokens to 10k per batch and 8 as update frequency. For generation, the maximum number of tokens was increased to 50k, using a single Tesla V100 GPU and by applying a standard 5-beam search strategy.

6 Results

For the evaluation of the fine-tuned models we considered three different test sets: MuST-C v2 En-De tst-COMMON, IWSLT 2015 and 2019 test sets (available on the Offline ST task Evaluation Campaign web page[4]). While for MuST-C v2 we originally had a manual segmentation of the audio files, for the IWSLT 2015 and 2019 test sets the organizers provided only automatic segmentations obtained by the LIUM VAD tool (Meignier and Merlin, 2010). Furthermore, we segmented MuST-C v2 tst-COMMON using the WebRTC VAD tool to have a comparable framework. Table 3 reports the results before and after the second fine-tuning step, which clearly show that performing the additional training on randomly segmented data highly improves the performance in the non-manual segmentation case, by up to 6 BLEU points. We also created an ensemble with the best two models reported in Table 3, whose KD training also used CTC loss. Results are not reported here since ensembling did not bring any improvement in terms of BLEU score compared to the two separate models. A possible motivation is that our two-step fine-tuning process is already sufficient to build a robust model, which is capable of generalizing without the need of combining two or more model outputs.

For our *primary* submission, we chose the two-step fine-tuned model that uses the LSCE+CTC losses for the first fine-tuning step (2-FT LSCE+CTC) since it achieved the highest BLEU on automatically segmented data. In order to measure the contribution of fine-tuning on randomly segmented data also on the official evaluation set, we selected the same model before the second fine-tuning step (1-FT LSCE+CTC) as our *contrastive* submission.

[4]https://iwslt.org/2021/offline

Our primary submission scored 30.6 BLEU on the tst2021 test set considering both references while our contrastive scored 29.3 BLEU, showing the effectiveness of our fine-tuning step. In addition, our primary submission scored 24.7 BLEU on the tst2020 test set.

7 Conclusions

We described FBK's participation in the IWSLT2021 Offline Speech Translation task (Anastasopoulos et al., 2021). Our work focused on a multi-step training pipeline involving data augmentation (SpecAugment and MT-based synthetic data), multi-domain transfer learning (KD training first and then fine-tuning on synthetic and native data) and ad-hoc fine-tuning on randomly segmented data. Based on the experimental results, our submission was characterized by the use of the CTC loss on transcripts during word-level knowledge distillation training, followed by a two-stage fine-tuning aimed to fill the gap between the performance of models when tested on manual and automatically segmented data. This huge gap was pointed out in our last year submission (Gaido et al., 2020b), where we highlighted that some strategies should have been adopted in order to mitigate the problem. This paper demonstrates that, following the above-mentioned pipeline, together with some data-driven techniques, we can obtain significant improvements in the performance of end-to-end ST systems. Research in this direction will help us to build models that are not only competitive with cascaded solutions, but also able to handle different segmentation strategies which are going to be more frequently used in the future.

References

Ashkan Alinejad and Anoop Sarkar. 2020. Effectively pretraining a speech translation decoder with Machine Translation data. In *Proceedings of the 2020 Conference on Empirical Methods in Natural Language Processing (EMNLP)*, pages 8014–8020, Online. Association for Computational Linguistics.

Antonios Anastasopoulos, Ondřej Bojar, Jacob Bremerman, Roldano Cattoni, Maha Elbayad and Marcello Federico, Xutai Ma, Satoshi Nakamura, Matteo Negri, Jan Niehues, Juan Pino, Elizabeth Salesky, Sebastian Stüker, Katsuhito Sudoh, Marco Turchi, Alex Waibel, Changhan Wang, and Matthew Wiesner. 2021. Findings of the IWSLT 2021 Evaluation Campaign. In *Proceedings of the 18th International Conference on Spoken Language Translation (IWSLT 2021)*, Online.

Antonios Anastasopoulos and David Chiang. 2018. Tied Multitask Learning for Neural Speech Translation. In *Proc. of the 2018 Conference of the North American Chapter of the Association for Computational Linguistics: Human Language Technologies*, pages 82–91, New Orleans, Louisiana.

Ebrahim Ansari, Amittai Axelrod, Nguyen Bach, Ondřej Bojar, Roldano Cattoni, Fahim Dalvi, Nadir Durrani, Marcello Federico, Christian Federmann, Jiatao Gu, Fei Huang, Kevin Knight, Xutai Ma, Ajay Nagesh, Matteo Negri, Jan Niehues, Juan Pino, Elizabeth Salesky, Xing Shi, Sebastian Stüker, Marco Turchi, Alexander Waibel, and Changhan Wang. 2020. FINDINGS OF THE IWSLT 2020 EVALUATION CAMPAIGN. In *Proceedings of the 17th International Conference on Spoken Language Translation*, pages 1–34, Online. Association for Computational Linguistics.

Parnia Bahar, Tobias Bieschke, and Hermann Ney. 2019a. A Comparative Study on End-to-End Speech to Text Translation. In *2019 IEEE Automatic Speech Recognition and Understanding Workshop (ASRU)*, pages 792–799.

Parnia Bahar, Albert Zeyer, Ralf Schlüter, and Hermann Ney. 2019b. On Using SpecAugment for End-to-End Speech Translation. In *Proc. of the International Workshop on Spoken Language Translation (IWSLT)*, Hong Kong, China.

Sameer Bansal, Herman Kamper, Karen Livescu, Adam Lopez, and Sharon Goldwater. 2019. Pretraining on High-resource Speech Recognition Improves Low-resource Speech-to-text Translation. In *Proc. of the 2019 Conference of the North American Chapter of the Association for Computational Linguistics: Human Language Technologies*, pages 58–68, Minneapolis, Minnesota.

Loïc Barrault, Ondřej Bojar, Marta R. Costa-jussà, Christian Federmann, Mark Fishel, Yvette Graham, Barry Haddow, Matthias Huck, Philipp Koehn, Shervin Malmasi, Christof Monz, Mathias Müller, Santanu Pal, Matt Post, and Marcos Zampieri. 2019. Findings of the 2019 conference on machine translation (WMT19). In *Proceedings of the Fourth Conference on Machine Translation (Volume 2: Shared Task Papers, Day 1)*, pages 1–61, Florence, Italy. Association for Computational Linguistics.

Alexandre Bérard, Laurent Besacier, Ali Can Kocabiyikoglu, and Olivier Pietquin. 2018. End-to-End Automatic Speech Translation of Audiobooks. In *Proc. of ICASSP 2018*, pages 6224–6228, Calgary, Alberta, Canada.

Nicola Bertoldi, Roldano Cattoni, Mauro Cettolo, Amin Farajian, Marcello Federico, Davide Caroselli, Luca Mastrostefano, Andrea Rossi, Marco Trombetti, Ulrich Germann, and David Madl. 2017. Mmt: New open source mt for the translation industry. In *The 20th Annual Conference of the European Association for Machine Translation (EAMT)*. 20th Annual Conference of the European Association for

Machine Translation, EAMT 2017 ; Conference date: 29-05-2017 Through 31-05-2017.

Alexandre Bérard, Olivier Pietquin, Christophe Servan, and Laurent Besacier. 2016. Listen and Translate: A Proof of Concept for End-to-End Speech-to-Text Translation. In *NIPS Workshop on end-to-end learning for speech and audio processing*, Barcelona, Spain.

Dogan Can, Victor R. Martinez, Pavlos Papadopoulos, and Shrikanth S. Narayanan. 2018. Pykaldi: A python wrapper for kaldi. In *Acoustics, Speech and Signal Processing (ICASSP), 2018 IEEE International Conference on*. IEEE.

Roldano Cattoni, Mattia A. Di Gangi, Luisa Bentivogli, Matteo Negri, and Marco Turchi. 2021. MuST-C: A multilingual corpus for end-to-end speech translation. *Computer Speech & Language*, 66:101155.

Mattia A. Di Gangi, Matteo Negri, and Marco Turchi. 2019. Adapting Transformer to End-to-End Spoken Language Translation. In *Proc. Interspeech 2019*, pages 1133–1137.

Chris Dyer, Victor Chahuneau, and Noah A. Smith. 2013. A Simple, Fast, and Effective Reparameterization of IBM Model 2. In *Proc. of the 2013 Conference of the North American Chapter of the Association for Computational Linguistics: Human Language Technologies (NAACL-HLT)*, pages 644–648, Atlanta, Georgia.

Marco Gaido, Mattia A. Di Gangi, Matteo Negri, Mauro Cettolo, and Marco Turchi. 2020a. Contextualized Translation of Automatically Segmented Speech. In *Proc. Interspeech 2020*, pages 1471–1475.

Marco Gaido, Mattia A. Di Gangi, Matteo Negri, and Marco Turchi. 2020b. End-to-end speech-translation with knowledge distillation: FBK@IWSLT2020. In *Proceedings of the 17th International Conference on Spoken Language Translation*, pages 80–88, Online. Association for Computational Linguistics.

Marco Gaido, Mattia A. Di Gangi, Matteo Negri, and Marco Turchi. 2021a. On Knowledge Distillation for Direct Speech Translation . In *Proceedings of CLiC-IT 2020*, Online.

Marco Gaido, Matteo Negri, Mauro Cettolo, and Marco Turchi. 2021b. Beyond voice activity detection: Hybrid audio segmentation for direct speech translation.

Dan Hendrycks and Kevin Gimpel. 2020. Gaussian Error Linear Units (GELUs).

François Hernandez, Vincent Nguyen, Sahar Ghannay, Natalia A. Tomashenko, and Yannick Estève. 2018. TED-LIUM 3: Twice as much data and corpus repartition for experiments on speaker adaptation. In *Speech and Computer - 20th International Conference, SPECOM 2018, Leipzig, Germany, September 18-22, 2018, Proceedings*, volume 11096 of *Lecture Notes in Computer Science*, pages 198–208. Springer.

Javier Iranzo-Sánchez, Joan Albert Silvestre-Cerdà, Javier Jorge, Nahuel Roselló, Adrià Giménez, Albert Sanchis, Jorge Civera, and Alfons Juan. 2020. Europarl-ST: A Multilingual Corpus for Speech Translation of Parliamentary Debates. In *ICASSP 2020 - 2020 IEEE International Conference on Acoustics, Speech and Signal Processing (ICASSP)*, pages 8229–8233.

Ye Jia, Melvin Johnson, Wolfgang Macherey, Ron J. Weiss, Yuan Cao, Chung-Cheng Chiu, Naveen Ari, Stella Laurenzo, and Yonghui Wu. 2019. Leveraging Weakly Supervised Data to Improve End-to-End Speech-to-Text Translation. In *Proc. of ICASSP 2019*, pages 7180–7184, Brighton, UK.

Alan B. Johnston and Daniel C. Burnett. 2012. *WebRTC: APIs and RTCWEB Protocols of the HTML5 Real-Time Web*. Digital Codex LLC, St. Louis, MO, USA.

Yoon Kim and Alexander M. Rush. 2016. Sequence-level knowledge distillation. In *Proceedings of the 2016 Conference on Empirical Methods in Natural Language Processing*, pages 1317–1327, Austin, Texas. Association for Computational Linguistics.

Diederik P. Kingma and Jimmy Ba. 2015. Adam: A method for stochastic optimization. In *3rd International Conference on Learning Representations, ICLR 2015, San Diego, CA, USA, May 7-9, 2015, Conference Track Proceedings*.

Solomon Kullback and Richard Arthur Leibler. 1951. On information and sufficiency. *Ann. Math. Statist.*, 22(1):79–86.

Pierre Lison and Jörg Tiedemann. 2016. OpenSubtitles2016: Extracting large parallel corpora from movie and TV subtitles. In *Proceedings of the Tenth International Conference on Language Resources and Evaluation (LREC'16)*, pages 923–929, Portorož, Slovenia. European Language Resources Association (ELRA).

Yuchen Liu, Hao Xiong, Jiajun Zhang, Zhongjun He, Hua Wu, Haifeng Wang, and Chengqing Zong. 2019. End-to-End Speech Translation with Knowledge Distillation. In *Proc. of Interspeech 2019*, pages 1128–1132.

Sylvain Meignier and Teva Merlin. 2010. LIUM SPKDIARIZATION: AN OPEN SOURCE TOOLKIT FOR DIARIZATION. In *CMU SPUD Workshop*, Dallas, United States.

Thai-Son Nguyen, Sebastian Stueker, Jan Niehues, and Alex Waibel. 2020. Improving Sequence-to-sequence Speech Recognition Training with On-the-fly Data Augmentation. In *Proc. of the 2020 Interna-*

tional Conference on Acoustics, Speech, and Signal Processing – IEEE-ICASSP-2020, Barcelona, Spain.

Jan Niehues, Roldano Cattoni, Sebastian Stüker, Mauro Cettolo, Marco Turchi, and Marcello Federico. 2018. The IWSLT 2018 Evaluation Campaign. In *Proceedings of the 15th International Workshop on Spoken Language Translation*, Bruges, Belgium.

Jan Niehues, Roldano Cattoni, Sebastian Stüker, Matteo Negri, Marco Turchi, Elizabeth Salesky, Ramon Sanabria, Loïc Barrault, Lucia Specia, Marcello Federico, and et al. 2019. The IWSLT 2019 Evaluation Campaign. In *Proceedings of the 16th International Workshop on Spoken Language Translation*.

Myle Ott, Sergey Edunov, Alexei Baevski, Angela Fan, Sam Gross, Nathan Ng, David Grangier, and Michael Auli. 2019. fairseq: A fast, extensible toolkit for sequence modeling. In *Proceedings of NAACL-HLT 2019: Demonstrations*.

Vassil Panayotov, Guoguo Chen, Daniel Povey, and Sanjeev Khudanpur. 2015. Librispeech: An asr corpus based on public domain audio books. In *2015 IEEE International Conference on Acoustics, Speech and Signal Processing (ICASSP)*, pages 5206–5210.

Daniel S. Park, William Chan, Yu Zhang, Chung-Cheng Chiu, Barret Zoph, Ekin D. Cubuk, and Quoc V. Le. 2019. SpecAugment: A Simple Data Augmentation Method for Automatic Speech Recognition. In *Proc. Interspeech 2019*, pages 2613–2617.

Matt Post. 2018. A call for clarity in reporting BLEU scores. In *Proceedings of the Third Conference on Machine Translation: Research Papers*, pages 186–191, Brussels, Belgium. Association for Computational Linguistics.

Tomasz Potapczyk and Pawel Przybysz. 2020. SR-POL's system for the IWSLT 2020 end-to-end speech translation task. In *Proc. of IWSLT*, Online.

Rico Sennrich, Barry Haddow, and Alexandra Birch. 2016. Neural machine translation of rare words with subword units. In *Proceedings of the 54th Annual Meeting of the Association for Computational Linguistics (Volume 1: Long Papers)*, pages 1715–1725, Berlin, Germany. Association for Computational Linguistics.

Jongseo Sohn, Nam Soo Kim, and Wonyong Sung. 1999. A statistical model-based voice activity detection. *IEEE Signal Processing Letters*, 6(1).

Frederick W. M. Stentiford and Martin G. Steer. 1988. Machine Translation of Speech. *British Telecom Technology Journal*, 6(2):116–122.

Xu Tan, Yi Ren, Di He, Tao Qin, and Tie-Yan Liu. 2019. Multilingual neural machine translation with knowledge distillation. In *International Conference on Learning Representations*.

Ashish Vaswani, Noam Shazeer, Niki Parmar, Jakob Uszkoreit, Llion Jones, Aidan N Gomez, Ł ukasz Kaiser, and Illia Polosukhin. 2017. Attention is all you need. In *Advances in Neural Information Processing Systems*, volume 30. Curran Associates, Inc.

Alex Waibel, Ajay N. Jain, Arthur E. McNair, Hiroaki Saito, Alexander G. Hauptmann, and Joe Tebelskis. 1991. JANUS: A Speech-to-Speech Translation System Using Connectionist and Symbolic Processing Strategies. In *Proceedings of the International Conference on Acoustics, Speech and Signal Processing, ICASSP 1991*, pages 793–796, Toronto, Canada.

Changhan Wang, Juan Pino, Anne Wu, and Jiatao Gu. 2020a. CoVoST: A diverse multilingual speech-to-text translation corpus. In *Proceedings of The 12th Language Resources and Evaluation Conference*, pages 4197–4203, Marseille, France. European Language Resources Association.

Changhan Wang, Yun Tang, Xutai Ma, Anne Wu, Dmytro Okhonko, and Juan Pino. 2020b. fairseq s2t: Fast speech-to-text modeling with fairseq. In *Proceedings of the 2020 Conference of the Asian Chapter of the Association for Computational Linguistics (AACL): System Demonstrations*.

Ron J. Weiss, Jan Chorowski, Navdeep Jaitly, Yonghui Wu, and Zhifeng Chen. 2017. Sequence-to-Sequence Models Can Directly Translate Foreign Speech. In *Proceedings of Interspeech 2017*, pages 2625–2629, Stockholm, Sweden.

The NiuTrans End-to-End Speech Translation System for IWSLT 2021 Offline Task

Chen Xu[1], Xiaoqian Liu[1], Xiaowen Liu[1], Laohu Wang[1], Canan Huang[1], Tong Xiao[1,2], Jingbo Zhu[1,2]
[1]NLP Lab, School of Computer Science and Engineering
Northeastern University, Shenyang, China
[2]NiuTrans Research, Shenyang, China
{xuchenneu,liuxiaoqianneu,liuxiaowenneu}@outlook.com,
{tigerneu,huangcananneu}@outlook.com,
{xiaotong,zhujingbo}@mail.neu.edu.cn

Abstract

This paper describes the submission of the NiuTrans end-to-end speech translation system for the IWSLT 2021 offline task, which translates from the English audio to German text directly without intermediate transcription. We use the Transformer-based model architecture and enhance it by Conformer, relative position encoding, and stacked acoustic and textual encoding. To augment the training data, the English transcriptions are translated to German translations. Finally, we employ ensemble decoding to integrate the predictions from several models trained with the different datasets. Combining these techniques, we achieve 33.84 BLEU points on the MuST-C En-De test set, which shows the enormous potential of the end-to-end model.

1 Introduction

Speech translation (ST) aims to learn models that can predict, given some speech in the source language, the translation into the target language. End-to-end (E2E) approaches have become popular recently for its ability to free designers from cascading different systems and shorten the pipeline of translation (Duong et al., 2016; Berard et al., 2016; Weiss et al., 2017). This paper describes the submission of the NiuTrans E2E ST system for the IWSLT 2021 (Anastasopoulos et al., 2021) offline task, which translates from the English audio to the German text translation directly without intermediate transcription.

Our baseline model is based on the DLCL Transformer (Vaswani et al., 2017; Wang et al., 2019) model with Connectionist Temporal Classification (CTC) (Graves et al., 2006) loss on the encoders (Bahar et al., 2019). We enhance it with the superior model architecture Conformer (Gulati et al., 2020), relative position encoding (RPE) (Shaw et al., 2018), and stacked acoustic and textual encoding (SATE) (Xu et al., 2021). To augment the training data, the English transcriptions of the automatic speech recognition (ASR) and speech translation corpora are translated to the German translation. Finally, we employ the ensemble decoding method to integrate the predictions from multiple models (Wang et al., 2018) trained with the different datasets.

This paper is structured as follows. The training data is summarized in Section 2, then we describe the model architecture in Section 3 and data augmentation in Section 4. We present the ensemble decoding method in Section 5. The experimental settings and final results are shown in Section 6.

2 Training Data

Our system is built under the constraint condition. The training data can be divided into three categories: ASR, MT, and ST corpora[1].

ASR corpora. ASR corpora are used to generate synthetic speech translation data. We only use the Common Voice (Ardila et al., 2020) and LibriSpeech (Panayotov et al., 2015) corpora. Furthermore, we filter the noisy training data in the Common Voice corpus by force decoding and keep 1 million utterances.

MT corpora. Machine translation (MT) corpora are used to translate the English transcription. We use the allowed English-German translation data from WMT 2020 (Barrault et al., 2020) and OpenSubtitles2018 (Lison and Tiedemann, 2016). We filter the training bilingual data followed Li et al. (2019), which includes length ratio, language detection, and so on.

[1]We only described the training data used in our system.

Proceedings of the 18th International Conference on Spoken Language Translation, pages 92–99
Bangkok, Thailand (Online), August 5–6, 2021.

ST corpora. The ST corpora we used include MuST-C (Gangi et al., 2019) English-German[2], CoVoST (Wang et al., 2020), Speech-Translation TED corpus[3], and Europarl-ST (Iranzo-Sánchez et al., 2020).

The statistics of the final training data are shown in Table 1. We augment the quantity of the ST training data by translating the English transcription (the details are unveiled in Section 4).

Task	Corpora	Size	Time
ASR	LibriSpeech	281241	960h
	Common Voice	1000000	1387h
	Total	1281241	2347h
MT	CommonCrawl	2014304	-
	Europarl	1802849	-
	ParaCrawl	31528317	-
	Wiki	5714363	-
	OpenSubtitles	14449099	-
	Total	55508932	-
ST	MuST-C	249462	435h
	CoVoST	289411	329h
	ST TED	170133	254h
	Europarl	69537	155h
	Total	778543	1173h

Table 1: Data statistics of the ASR, MT, and ST corpora.

3 Model Architecture

In this section, we describe the baseline model and the architecture improvements. Then, the experimental results are shown to demonstrate the effectiveness.

3.1 Baseline Model

Our system is based on deep Transformer (Vaswani et al., 2017) implemented on the fairseq toolkit (Ott et al., 2019). Furthermore, dynamic linear combination of layers (DLCL) (Wang et al., 2019) method is employed to train the deep model effectively (Li et al., 2020a,b).

To reduce the computational cost, the input speech features are processed by two convolutional layers, which have a stride of 2. This downsamples the sequence by a factor of 4 (Weiss et al., 2017). For strong systems, we use Connectionist Temporal Classification (CTC) (Graves et al., 2006) as the auxiliary loss on the encoders(Watanabe et al., 2017; Karita et al., 2019; Bahar et al., 2019). The weight of CTC objective α is set to 0.3 for all ASR and ST models. The model architecture is showed in Figure 1[4].

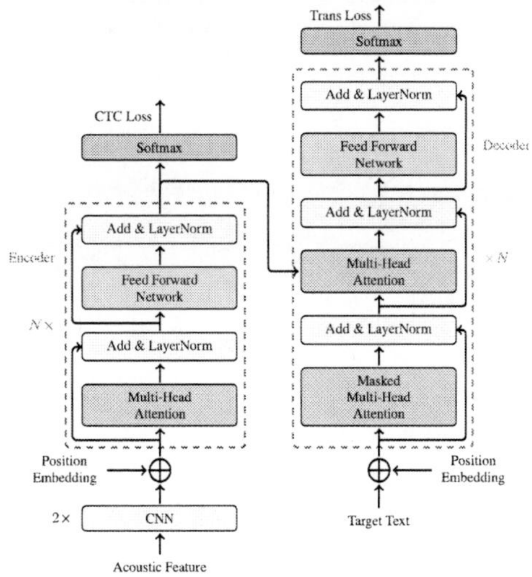

Figure 1: The baseline model architecture.

3.2 Conformer

Conformer (Gulati et al., 2020) models both local and global dependencies by combining the Convolutional Neural Network and Transformers. It has shown superiority and achieved promising results in ASR tasks.

We replace the Transformer blocks in the encoder by the conformer blocks, which include two macaron-like feed-forward networks, multi-head self attention modules, and convolution modules. Note that we use the RPE proposed in Shaw et al. (2018) rather than Transformer-XL (Dai et al., 2019).

3.3 Relative Position Encoding

Due to the non-sequential modeling of the original self attention modules, the vanilla Transformer employs the position embedding by a deterministic sinusoidal function to indicate the absolute position of each input element (Vaswani et al., 2017). However, this scheme is far from ideal for acoustic modeling (Pham et al., 2020).

[2]We use the latest MusST-C v2 dataset released by IWSLT 2021.

[3]http://i13pc106.ira.uka.de/~mmueller/ iwslt-corpus.zip

[4]https://github.com/NiuTrans/MTBook

Model	tst-COMMON
Baseline	23.98
+ Conformer	24.43
+ RPE	24.69
+ SATE	25.35

Table 2: Effects of the architecture improvements. We report SacreBLEU scores [%] on the MuST-C tst-COMMON set.

The latest work (Pham et al., 2020; Gulati et al., 2020) points out that the relative position encoding enables the model to generalize better for the unseen sequence lengths. It yields a significant improvement on the acoustic modeling tasks. We re-implement the relative position encoding scheme (Shaw et al., 2018). The maximum relative position is set to 100 for the encoder and 20 for the decoder. We use both absolute and relative positional representations simultaneously.

3.4 Stacked Acoustic and Textual Encoding

The previous work (Bahar et al., 2019) employs the CTC loss on the top layer of the encoder, which forces the encoders to learn soft alignments between speech and transcription. However, the CTC loss demonstrates strong preference for locally attentive models, which is inconsistent with the ST model (Xu et al., 2021).

In our systems, we use the stacked acoustic-and-textual encoding (SATE) (Xu et al., 2021) method to encode the speech features. It calculates the CTC loss based on the hidden states of the intermediate layer rather than the top layer. The layers below CTC also extract the acoustic representation like an ASR encoder, while the upper layers with no CTC encode the global representation for translation. An adaptor layer is introduced to bridge the acoustic and textual encoding.

3.5 Experimental Results

We use the architecture described in Section 3.1 as the baseline model. The encoder consists of 12 layers and the decoder consists of 6 layers. Each layer comprises 256 hidden units, 4 attention heads, and 2048 feed-forward size. The encoder of SATE includes an acoustic encoder of 8 layers and a textual encoder of 4 layers. The model is trained with MuST-C English-German dataset and we test the results on the tst-COMMON set based on the SacreBLEU. The other experimental details are shown in Section 6.

Data	Corpora	Size	Time
Synthetic	LibriSpeech	281241	960h
	Common Voice	1000000	1387h
	MuST-C	249462	435h
	ST TED	170133	254h
	Total	1700836	3036h
Real	Total	778543	1173h
Total		2479379	4209h

Table 3: All available ST corpora.

We report the experimental results after applying each architecture improvement in Table 2. Benefitting the power of the deep Transformer, our baseline model achieves 23.98 BLEU points. The Conformer and RPE methods strengthen the encoding and achieve an improvement of 0.45 and 0.26 BLEU points. SATE achieves a remarkable improvement by encoding the acoustic representation and textual representation respectively. We will explore better architecture designs in the future.

4 Data Augmentation

A large amount of the training data is necessary for a strong neural model. However, unlike the ASR and MT tasks, annotated speech-to-translation data is scarce, which prevents well-trained ST models. This is the main reason why cascaded systems are the dominant approach in the industrial scenarios. In this section, we describe our data augmentation method.

We train a deep DLCL Transformer (Wang et al., 2019) with the 25 encoder layers on all available MT data. To keep the domain consistency with the original ST data, we finetune the MT model on the MuST-C dataset. The model achieves the SacreBLEU of 35.89 of the MuST-C tst-COMMON test set. For the case-insensitive LibriSpeech dataset, we train a similar MT model except for lowercasing the source text without punctuation during training.

Then, we generate the German translation from English transcription in the LibriSpeech and Common Voice ASR datasets. Furthermore, sequence-level knowledge distillation (Kim and Rush, 2016) is applied to augment the training data. We generate the translation of the MuST-C and Speech-Translation TED ST datasets which are more related to the target domain.

Corrupting the acoustic feature is another data augmentation method, including SpecAugment, speed perturbation, and so on. SpecAugment (Park et al., 2019) is a simple data augmentation applied on the input acoustic features. The time masking and the frequency masking are applied in our systems. Speed perturbation transforms the audio by a speed rate, which changes the duration of the audio signal. Limited by the size of GPU resources, we do not use this method. Compared with the perturbed data, we think the synthetic samples improve the robustness more effectively. All available ST corpora are shown in Table 3.

5 Ensemble Decoding

Ensemble decoding is an effective method to improve performance by integrating the predictions from multiple models. It has been proved in the WMT competitions (Wang et al., 2018; Li et al., 2019). In our systems, we train multiple ST models with different training data for diverse ensemble decoding. The models are chosen based on the performance of the development set. This leads to a significant improvement over a single model.

6 Experiments

6.1 Preprocessing

We remove the utterances with more than 3000 frames or less than 5 frames. The 80-channel log-mel filterbank features are extracted from the audio file by torchaudio[5] library. We use the lower-cased transcriptions without punctuations for CTC loss computation. We learn SentencePiece[6] subword segmentation with a size of 10,000 based on a shared source and target vocabulary for all datasets.

6.2 Model Settings

All experiments are implemented based on the fairseq toolkit[7]. We use Adam optimizer and adopt the default learning schedule in fairseq. We apply dropout with a rate of 0.1 and label smoothing $\epsilon_{ls} = 0.1$ for regularization. We also set the activate function dropout to 0.1 and attention dropout to 0.1, which improves the regularization and overcomes the overfitting.

We use the best model architecture that combines all the improvements described in Section 3. The encoder includes an acoustic encoder of 12 conformer layers and a textual encoder of 6 transformer layers. The decoder consists of 6 Transformer layers. Each layer comprises 512 hidden units, 8 attention heads, and 2048 feed-forward size. Pre-norm is applied for training a deep model. The weight of CTC objective α for multitask learning is set to 0.3 for all models. All the models are trained for 50 epochs on one machine with 8 NVIDIA 2080Ti GPUs.

During inference, we average the model parameters on the final 10 checkpoints. We use beam search with a beam size of 5 for all models. The coefficient of length normalization is tuned on the development set. We report the case-sensitive SacreBLEU (Post, 2018) on the MuST-C tst-COMMON set, IWSLT tst2019 and tst2020 test set.

The organizers provide the segmentation of the test sets and allow the participants to use the own segmentation. We simply use the segmentation provided by the WerRTCVAD[8] toolkit.

6.3 Experimental Results

Firstly, We train the model on all training corpora, including real and synthetic speech-to-translation paired data. As shown in Table 4, we achieve a high BLEU on the tst-COMMON test set, but a low performance on the tst2019 test set compared with the previous work (Gaido et al., 2020). A possible reason is that the data distribution between IWSLT test sets and the synthetic data is different.

tst-COMMON	tst2019
32.65	14.16

Table 4: Performance of the model trained on all training corpora.

To verify this assumption, we pick some subsets from the available datasets for training, including MuST-C and ST TED from the real corpora and MuST-C and LibriSpeech from the synthetic corpora. We present the results in Table 5. Although the performance on the tst-COMMON test set drops by 0.8 BLEU points, the model achieves a reasonable performance on the tst2019 test set. Furthermore, we finetune the model on the MuST-C dataset with a small learning rate. This yields a slight improvement.

[5]https://github.com/pytorch/audio

[6]https://github.com/google/sentencepiece

[7]https://github.com/pytorch/fairseq

[8]https://github.com/wiseman/py-webrtcvad

Model	tst-COMMON	tst2019
Base	31.85	20.64
+ finetune	32.31	20.73

Table 5: Performance of the model trained with the subsets of all available corpora.

Test sets	Given	Own
tst-COMMON	33.84	-
tst2019	22.68	23.76
tst2020	21.8	22.8
tst2021†	19.0	19.6
tst2021‡	20.7	20.6
tst2021⋆	30.7	30.3

Table 6: Final results with ensemble decoding. We report the results with given and own segmentation. There are two references on the tst2021 test set: TED reference (†) and IWSLT reference (‡). The final results are based on both references (⋆) together.

We train multiple models with different training data for diverse ensemble decoding. We select a part of the synthetic corpora randomly, then mix them with the whole real training data. Finally, we use the ensemble decoding with 6 models for the final results and achieve a substantial improvement over a single model. As shown in Table 6, we achieve an excellent performance of 33.84 BLEU points on the MuST-C En-De tst-COMMON set.

The best end-to-end system of last year achieves 20.1 BLEU points on the tst2019 test set and 21.49 BLEU points on the tst2020 test set with the given segmentation. We achieve remarkable improvements of 2.58 and 0.31 BLEU points, which demonstrates the superiority of our systems.

There are two references available for tst2021 test set. The TED reference is the original one from the TED website. Since new regulations for the official regulation lead to translations that are much shorter, they created a second reference translation, called the IWSLT reference. The final results are based on both references. We achieve better performance with the own segmentation on the TED reference, which is consistent with the results on the previous test sets. However, the results with the own segmentation are worse on the IWSLT reference. A possible reason is that we do not optimize the segmentation tool for IWSLT test sets. We will explore better segmentation methods in the future.

7 Conclusion

This paper describes the submission of the NiuTrans E2E ST systems for the IWSLT 2021 offline task, which translates the English audio to German translation directly without intermediate transcription. We build our final submissions considering two mainstreams:

- Model architecture improvements for the speech translation task.
- Data augmentation by translating the English transcription to German translation.

We also find that the distribution of the training data has a great impact on the performance and alleviate it by ensemble decoding. Using the given segmentation, we achieve remarkable improvements over the best end-to-end system of last year.

8 Acknowledgement

This work was supported in part by the National Science Foundation of China (Nos. 61876035 and 61732005), the National Key R&D Program of China (No. 2019QY1801), and the Ministry of Science and Technology of the PRC (Nos. 2019YFF0303002 and 2020AAA0107900). The authors would like to thank anonymous reviewers for their comments.

References

Antonios Anastasopoulos, Ondřej Bojar, Jacob Bremerman, Roldano Cattoni, Maha Elbayad, Marcello Federico, Xutai Ma, Satoshi Nakamura, Matteo Negri, Jan Niehues, Juan Pino, Elizabeth Salesky, Sebastian Stüker, Katsuhito Sudoh, Marco Turchi, Alex Waibel, Changhan Wang, and Matthew Wiesner. 2021. Findings of the IWSLT 2021 Evaluation Campaign. In *Proceedings of the 18th International Conference on Spoken Language Translation (IWSLT 2021)*, Online.

Rosana Ardila, Megan Branson, Kelly Davis, Michael Kohler, Josh Meyer, Michael Henretty, Reuben Morais, Lindsay Saunders, Francis M. Tyers, and Gregor Weber. 2020. Common voice: A massively-multilingual speech corpus. In *Proceedings of The 12th Language Resources and Evaluation Conference, LREC 2020, Marseille, France, May 11-16, 2020*, pages 4218–4222. European Language Resources Association.

Parnia Bahar, Tobias Bieschke, and Hermann Ney. 2019. A comparative study on end-to-end speech to text translation. In *IEEE Automatic Speech Recognition and Understanding Workshop, ASRU 2019, Singapore, December 14-18, 2019*, pages 792–799. IEEE.

Loïc Barrault, Magdalena Biesialska, Ondrej Bojar, Marta R. Costa-jussà, Christian Federmann, Yvette Graham, Roman Grundkiewicz, Barry Haddow, Matthias Huck, Eric Joanis, Tom Kocmi, Philipp Koehn, Chi-kiu Lo, Nikola Ljubesic, Christof Monz, Makoto Morishita, Masaaki Nagata, Toshiaki Nakazawa, Santanu Pal, Matt Post, and Marcos Zampieri. 2020. Findings of the 2020 conference on machine translation (WMT20). In *Proceedings of the Fifth Conference on Machine Translation, WMT@EMNLP 2020, Online, November 19-20, 2020*, pages 1–55. Association for Computational Linguistics.

Alexandre Berard, Olivier Pietquin, Christophe Servan, and Laurent Besacier. 2016. Listen and translate: A proof of concept for end-to-end speech-to-text translation. *CoRR*, abs/1612.01744.

Zihang Dai, Zhilin Yang, Yiming Yang, Jaime G. Carbonell, Quoc Viet Le, and Ruslan Salakhutdinov. 2019. Transformer-xl: Attentive language models beyond a fixed-length context. In *Proceedings of the 57th Conference of the Association for Computational Linguistics, ACL 2019, Florence, Italy, July 28- August 2, 2019, Volume 1: Long Papers*, pages 2978–2988. Association for Computational Linguistics.

Long Duong, Antonios Anastasopoulos, David Chiang, Steven Bird, and Trevor Cohn. 2016. An attentional model for speech translation without transcription. In *NAACL HLT 2016, The 2016 Conference of the North American Chapter of the Association for Computational Linguistics: Human Language Technologies, San Diego California, USA, June 12-17, 2016*, pages 949–959. The Association for Computational Linguistics.

Marco Gaido, Mattia Antonino Di Gangi, Matteo Negri, and Marco Turchi. 2020. End-to-end speech-translation with knowledge distillation: Fbk@iwslt2020. In *Proceedings of the 17th International Conference on Spoken Language Translation, IWSLT 2020, Online, July 9 - 10, 2020*, pages 80–88. Association for Computational Linguistics.

Mattia Antonino Di Gangi, Roldano Cattoni, Luisa Bentivogli, Matteo Negri, and Marco Turchi. 2019. Must-c: a multilingual speech translation corpus. In *Proceedings of the 2019 Conference of the North American Chapter of the Association for Computational Linguistics: Human Language Technologies, NAACL-HLT 2019, Minneapolis, MN, USA, June 2-7, 2019, Volume 1 (Long and Short Papers)*, pages 2012–2017. Association for Computational Linguistics.

Alex Graves, Santiago Fernández, Faustino J. Gomez, and Jürgen Schmidhuber. 2006. Connectionist temporal classification: labelling unsegmented sequence data with recurrent neural networks. In *Machine Learning, Proceedings of the Twenty-Third International Conference (ICML 2006), Pittsburgh, Pennsylvania, USA, June 25-29, 2006*, volume 148 of *ACM International Conference Proceeding Series*, pages 369–376. ACM.

Anmol Gulati, James Qin, Chung-Cheng Chiu, Niki Parmar, Yu Zhang, Jiahui Yu, Wei Han, Shibo Wang, Zhengdong Zhang, Yonghui Wu, and Ruoming Pang. 2020. Conformer: Convolution-augmented transformer for speech recognition. In *Interspeech 2020, 21st Annual Conference of the International Speech Communication Association, Virtual Event, Shanghai, China, 25-29 October 2020*, pages 5036–5040. ISCA.

Javier Iranzo-Sánchez, Joan Albert Silvestre-Cerdà, Javier Jorge, Nahuel Roselló, Adrià Giménez, Albert Sanchís, Jorge Civera, and Alfons Juan. 2020. Europarl-st: A multilingual corpus for speech translation of parliamentary debates. In *2020 IEEE International Conference on Acoustics, Speech and Signal Processing, ICASSP 2020, Barcelona, Spain, May 4-8, 2020*, pages 8229–8233. IEEE.

Shigeki Karita, Nelson Enrique Yalta Soplin, Shinji Watanabe, Marc Delcroix, Atsunori Ogawa, and Tomohiro Nakatani. 2019. Improving transformer-based end-to-end speech recognition with connectionist temporal classification and language model integration. In *Interspeech*

2019, 20th Annual Conference of the International Speech Communication Association, Graz, Austria, 15-19 September 2019, pages 1408–1412. ISCA.

Yoon Kim and Alexander M. Rush. 2016. Sequence-level knowledge distillation. In *Proceedings of the 2016 Conference on Empirical Methods in Natural Language Processing, EMNLP 2016, Austin, Texas, USA, November 1-4, 2016*, pages 1317–1327. The Association for Computational Linguistics.

Bei Li, Yinqiao Li, Chen Xu, Ye Lin, Jiqiang Liu, Hui Liu, Ziyang Wang, Yuhao Zhang, Nuo Xu, Zeyang Wang, Kai Feng, Hexuan Chen, Tengbo Liu, Yanyang Li, Qiang Wang, Tong Xiao, and Jingbo Zhu. 2019. The niutrans machine translation systems for WMT19. In *Proceedings of the Fourth Conference on Machine Translation, WMT 2019, Florence, Italy, August 1-2, 2019 - Volume 2: Shared Task Papers, Day 1*, pages 257–266. Association for Computational Linguistics.

Bei Li, Ziyang Wang, Hui Liu, Quan Du, Tong Xiao, Chunliang Zhang, and Jingbo Zhu. 2020a. Learning light-weight translation models from deep transformer. *CoRR*, abs/2012.13866.

Bei Li, Ziyang Wang, Hui Liu, Yufan Jiang, Quan Du, Tong Xiao, Huizhen Wang, and Jingbo Zhu. 2020b. Shallow-to-deep training for neural machine translation. In *Proceedings of the 2020 Conference on Empirical Methods in Natural Language Processing, EMNLP 2020, Online, November 16-20, 2020*, pages 995–1005. Association for Computational Linguistics.

Pierre Lison and Jörg Tiedemann. 2016. Opensubtitles2016: Extracting large parallel corpora from movie and TV subtitles. In *Proceedings of the Tenth International Conference on Language Resources and Evaluation LREC 2016, Portorož, Slovenia, May 23-28, 2016*. European Language Resources Association (ELRA).

Myle Ott, Sergey Edunov, Alexei Baevski, Angela Fan, Sam Gross, Nathan Ng, David Grangier, and Michael Auli. 2019. fairseq: A fast, extensible toolkit for sequence modeling. In *Proceedings of the 2019 Conference of the North American Chapter of the Association for Computational Linguistics: Human Language Technologies, NAACL-HLT 2019, Minneapolis, MN, USA, June 2-7, 2019, Demonstrations*, pages 48–53. Association for Computational Linguistics.

Vassil Panayotov, Guoguo Chen, Daniel Povey, and Sanjeev Khudanpur. 2015. Librispeech: An ASR corpus based on public domain audio books. In *2015 IEEE International Conference on Acoustics, Speech and Signal Processing, ICASSP 2015, South Brisbane, Queensland, Australia, April 19-24, 2015*, pages 5206–5210. IEEE.

Daniel S. Park, William Chan, Yu Zhang, Chung-Cheng Chiu, Barret Zoph, Ekin D. Cubuk, and Quoc V. Le. 2019. Specaugment: A simple data augmentation method for automatic speech recognition. In *Interspeech 2019, 20th Annual Conference of the International Speech Communication Association, Graz, Austria, 15-19 September 2019*, pages 2613–2617. ISCA.

Ngoc-Quan Pham, Thanh-Le Ha, Tuan-Nam Nguyen, Thai-Son Nguyen, Elizabeth Salesky, Sebastian Stüker, Jan Niehues, and Alex Waibel. 2020. Relative positional encoding for speech recognition and direct translation. In *Interspeech 2020, 21st Annual Conference of the International Speech Communication Association, Virtual Event, Shanghai, China, 25-29 October 2020*, pages 31–35. ISCA.

Matt Post. 2018. A call for clarity in reporting BLEU scores. In *Proceedings of the Third Conference on Machine Translation: Research Papers, WMT 2018, Belgium, Brussels, October 31 - November 1, 2018*, pages 186–191. Association for Computational Linguistics.

Peter Shaw, Jakob Uszkoreit, and Ashish Vaswani. 2018. Self-attention with relative position representations. In *Proceedings of the 2018 Conference of the North American Chapter of the Association for Computational Linguistics: Human Language Technologies, NAACL-HLT, New Orleans, Louisiana, USA, June 1-6, 2018, Volume 2 (Short Papers)*, pages 464–468. Association for Computational Linguistics.

Ashish Vaswani, Noam Shazeer, Niki Parmar, Jakob Uszkoreit, Llion Jones, Aidan N. Gomez, Lukasz Kaiser, and Illia Polosukhin. 2017. Attention is all you need. In *Advances in Neural Information Processing Systems 30: Annual Conference on Neural Information Processing*

Systems 2017, December 4-9, 2017, Long Beach, CA, USA, pages 5998–6008.

Changhan Wang, Anne Wu, and Juan Pino. 2020. Covost 2: A massively multilingual speech-to-text translation corpus. *CoRR*, abs/2007.10310.

Qiang Wang, Bei Li, Jiqiang Liu, Bojian Jiang, Zheyang Zhang, Yinqiao Li, Ye Lin, Tong Xiao, and Jingbo Zhu. 2018. The niutrans machine translation system for WMT18. In *Proceedings of the Third Conference on Machine Translation: Shared Task Papers, WMT 2018, Belgium, Brussels, October 31 - November 1, 2018*, pages 528–534. Association for Computational Linguistics.

Qiang Wang, Bei Li, Tong Xiao, Jingbo Zhu, Changliang Li, Derek F. Wong, and Lidia S. Chao. 2019. Learning deep transformer models for machine translation. In *Proceedings of the 57th Conference of the Association for Computational Linguistics, ACL 2019, Florence, Italy, July 28- August 2, 2019, Volume 1: Long Papers*, pages 1810–1822. Association for Computational Linguistics.

Shinji Watanabe, Takaaki Hori, Suyoun Kim, John R. Hershey, and Tomoki Hayashi. 2017. Hybrid ctc/attention architecture for end-to-end speech recognition. *IEEE J. Sel. Top. Signal Process.*, 11(8):1240–1253.

Ron J. Weiss, Jan Chorowski, Navdeep Jaitly, Yonghui Wu, and Zhifeng Chen. 2017. Sequence-to-sequence models can directly translate foreign speech. In *Interspeech 2017, 18th Annual Conference of the International Speech Communication Association, Stockholm, Sweden, August 20-24, 2017*, pages 2625–2629. ISCA.

Chen Xu, Bojie Hu, Yanyang Li, Yuhao Zhang, Shen Huang, Qi Ju, Tong Xiao, and Jingbo Zhu. 2021. Stacked acoustic-and-textual encoding: Integrating the pre-trained models into speech translation encoders. *CoRR*, abs/2105.05752.

ESPnet-ST IWSLT 2021 Offline Speech Translation System

Hirofumi Inaguma[1*] **Brian Yan**[2*] **Siddharth Dalmia**[2] **Pengcheng Guo**[3]
Jiatong Shi[4] **Kevin Duh**[4] **Shinji Watanabe**[2,4]
[1]Kyoto University, Japan [2]Carnegie Mellon University, USA
[3]Northwestern Polytechnical University, China [4]Johns Hopkins University, USA
inaguma@sap.ist.i.kyoto-u.ac.jp
byan@cs.cmu.edu

Abstract

This paper describes the ESPnet-ST group's IWSLT 2021 submission in the offline speech translation track. This year we made various efforts on training data, architecture, and audio segmentation. On the data side, we investigated sequence-level knowledge distillation (SeqKD) for end-to-end (E2E) speech translation. Specifically, we used multi-referenced SeqKD from multiple teachers trained on different amounts of bitext. On the architecture side, we adopted the Conformer encoder and the Multi-Decoder architecture, which equips dedicated decoders for speech recognition and translation tasks in a unified encoder-decoder model and enables search in both source and target language spaces during inference. We also significantly improved audio segmentation by using the `pyannote.audio` toolkit and merging multiple short segments for long context modeling. Experimental evaluations showed that each of them contributed to large improvements in translation performance. Our best E2E system combined all the above techniques with model ensembling and achieved 31.4 BLEU on the 2-ref of tst2021 and 21.2 BLEU and 19.3 BLEU on the two single references of tst2021.

1 Introduction

This paper presents the ESPnet-ST group's English→German speech translation (ST) system submitted to the IWSLT 2021 offline speech translation track. ESPnet (Watanabe et al., 2018) has been widely used for many speech applications; automatic speech recognition (ASR), text-to-speech (Hayashi et al., 2020), speech translation (Inaguma et al., 2020), machine translation (MT), and speech separation/enhancement (Li et al., 2021). The purpose of this submission is not only to show the recent progress on ST researches, but also to encourage future research by building strong systems along with the open-sourced project.

This year we focused on (1) sequence-level knowledge distillation (SeqKD) (Kim and Rush, 2016), (2) Conformer encoder (Gulati et al., 2020), (3) Multi-Decoder architecture (Dalmia et al., 2021), (4) model ensembling, and (5) better segmentation with a neural network-based voice activity (VAD) system (Bredin et al., 2020) and a novel algorithm to merge multiple short segments for long context modeling. Our primary focus was E2E models, although we also compared them with cascade systems with our best effort. All experiments were conducted with the ESPnet-ST toolkit (Inaguma et al., 2020), and the recipe is publicly available at `https://github.com/espnet/espnet/tree/master/egs/iwslt21`.

2 Data preparation

In this section, we describe data preparation for each task. The corpus statistics are listed in Table 1. We removed the off-limit talks following previous evaluation campaigns[1]. To fit the GPU memory, we excluded utterances having more than 3000 speech frames or more than 400 characters. All sentences were tokenized with the `tokenizer.perl` script in the Moses toolkit (Koehn et al., 2007).

2.1 ASR

We used Must-C (Di Gangi et al., 2019), Must-C v2[2], ST-TED (Jan et al., 2018), Librispeech (Panayotov et al., 2015), and TEDLIUM2 (Rousseau et al., 2012) corpora. We used the cleaned version of ST-TED following (Inaguma et al., 2019). The speech

*Equal contribution

[1]`https://sites.google.com/view/iwslt-evaluation-2019/speech-translation/off-limit-ted-talks`

[2]`https://ict.fbk.eu/must-c-release-v2-0/`

Proceedings of the 18th International Conference on Spoken Language Translation, pages 100–109
Bangkok, Thailand (Online), August 5–6, 2021.

	#Hour	#Sentence
ASR		
Must-C	408 × 3	0.68M
Must-C v2	458 × 3	0.74M
ST-TED (cleaned)	200 × 3	0.40M
Librispeech	960	0.28M
TEDLIUM2	210 × 3	0.27M
E2E-ST		
Must-C	408 × 3	0.68M
Must-C v2	458 × 3	0.74M
ST-TED (cleaned)	200 × 3	0.40M
MT		
Must-C		0.68M
Must-C v2		0.74M
ST-TED (cleaned)		0.40M
Europarl		1.82M
Commoncrawl	-	2.39M
Paracrawl		34.37M
NewsCommentary		0.37M
WikiTitles		1.38M
RAPID		1.63M
WikiMatrix		1.57M

Table 1: Corpus statistics

Filtering method	#Sentence		
	WMT5M	WMT10M	WMT20M
In-domain LM	5.00M	10.00M	20.00M
+ langid	3.42M	7.90M	15.33M
+ length/character	3.15M	7.77M	15.01M

Table 2: MT bitext filtering

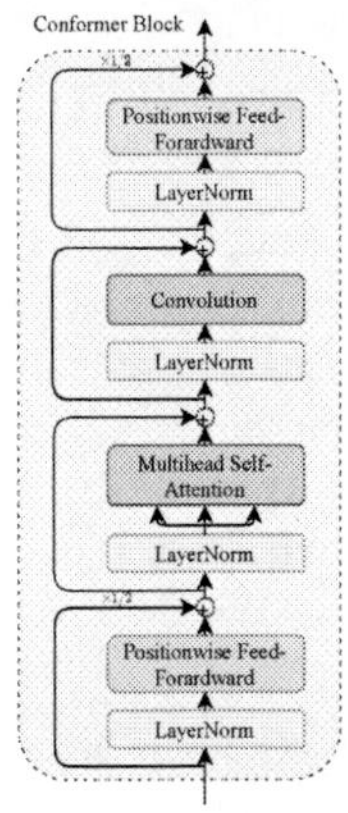

Figure 1: Block diagram of Conformer architecture

data was augmented by three-fold speed perturbation (Ko et al., 2015) with speed ratios of 0.9, 1.0, and 1.1 except for Librispeech. We removed case information and punctuation marks except for apostrophes from the transcripts. The 5k unit vocabulary was constructed based on the byte pair encoding (BPE) algorithm (Sennrich et al., 2016) with the `sentencepiece` toolkit[3] using the English transcripts only.

2.2 E2E-ST

We used Must-C, Must-C v2, and ST-TED only. The shared source and target vocabulary of BPE16k units was constructed using cased and punctuated transcripts and translations.

2.3 MT

We used available bitext for WMT20[4] in addition to the in-domain TED data used for E2E-ST systems. We first performed perplexity-based filtering with an in-domain n-gram language model (LM) (Moore and Lewis, 2010). We controlled the WMT data size by thresholding and obtained three data pools: 5M, 10M, and 20M sentences. Next, we removed non-printing characters and performed language identification with the `langid.py` toolkit (Lui and Baldwin, 2012)[5] and kept sentences whose language IDs were identified correctly on both English and German sides. We also removed sentences having more than 250 tokens in either language or a source-target length ratio of more than 1.5 with the `clean-corpus-n.perl` script in Moses. Finally, we removed sentences having CJK and other unrelated characters in either language with the built-in `regex` module in Python. The resulting data size is shown in Table 2. We found that our filtering strategy removed 22-37% of data. Note that the above filtering process was performed over the WMT data only. For each data size, the joint source and target vocabulary of BPE32k units was constructed using cased and punctuated sentences after the filtering. We did not use additional monolingual data.

3 System

3.1 Conformer encoder

Conformer encoder (Gulati et al., 2020) is a stacked multi-block architecture and has shown consistent improvement over a wide range of E2E speech processing applications (Guo et al., 2020). The architecture of each block is depicted in Figure 1. It includes a multi-head self-attention module, a convolution module, and a pair of position-wise feed-forward modules in the Macaron-Net style. While the self-attention module learns the long-

[3]https://github.com/google/sentencepiece

[4]Europarl, Commoncrawl, Paracrawl, NewsCommentary, WikiTitles, RAPID and WikiMatrix

[5]https://github.com/saffsd/langid.py

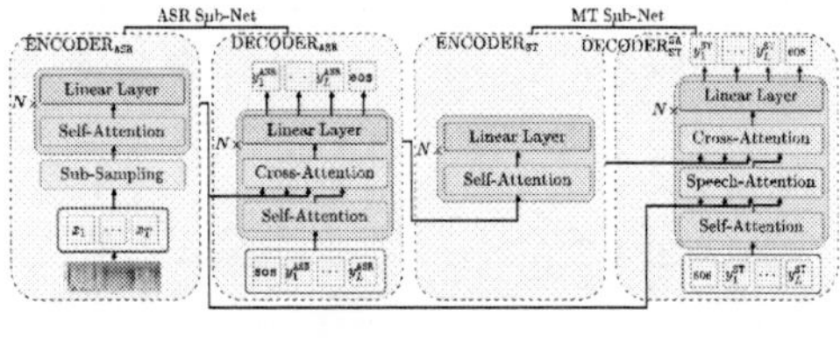

Figure 2: The Multi-Decoder (MD) architecture decomposes the overall ST task with ASR and MT subnets while maintaining E2E differentiability.

range global context, the convolution module aims to model the local feature patterns synchronously. Recent studies have shown improvements by introducing Conformer in the E2E-ST task (Guo et al., 2020; Inaguma et al., 2021b), which motivated us to adopt this architecture as our system.

3.2 SeqKD

Sequence-level knowledge distillation (SeqKD) (Kim and Rush, 2016) is an effective method to transfer knowledge in a teacher model to a student model via discrete symbols. Our recent studies (Inaguma et al., 2021a,b) showed a large improvement in ST performance with this technique. Unlike the previous studies, however, we used more training data than bitext in ST training data to train teacher MT models. We translated source transcripts in the ST training data by the teacher MT models with a beam width of 5 and then replaced the original ground-truth translation with the generated translation. We used cased and punctuated transcripts as inputs to the MT teachers. We also combined both the original and pseudo translations as data augmentation (*multi-referenced training*) (Gordon and Duh, 2019).

3.3 Multi-Decoder architecture

The Multi-Decoder is an E2E-ST model using Searchable Hidden Intermediates to decompose the overall ST task into ASR and MT subtasks (Dalmia et al., 2021). As shown in Figure 2, the Multi-Decoder consists of two encoder-decoder models, an ASR sub-net and a subsequent MT subnet, where the hidden representations of the ASR decoder are passed as inputs to the encoder of the MT sub-net. During inference, the best ASR decoder hidden representations are retrieved using beam search decoding at this intermediate stage.

Since this framework decomposes the overall ST task, it brings several advantages of cascaded approaches into the E2E setting. For instance, the Multi-Decoder allows for greater search capabilities and separation of speech and text encoding. However, one trade-off is a greater risk of error propagation from the ASR sub-net to the downstream MT sub-net. To alleviate this issue, we condition the decoder of the MT sub-net on the ASR encoder hidden representations in addition to the MT encoder hidden representations using multi-source cross-attention. This improved variant of the architecture is called the Multi-Decoder with Speech Attention.

3.4 Model ensembling

We use posterior probability combination to ensemble models trained with different data and architectures. During inference, we perform a posterior combination at each step of beam search decoding by first computing the softmax normalized posterior probabilities for each model in the ensemble and then taking the mean value. In this ensembling approach, a single unified beam search operates over the combined posteriors of the models to find the most likely decoded sequence.

3.5 Segmentation

How to segment audio during inference significantly impacts ST performances (Gaido et al., 2020; Pham et al., 2020; Potapczyk and Przybysz, 2020; Gaido et al., 2021). This is because the ST systems are usually trained with utterances segmented based on punctuation marks (Di Gangi et al., 2019) while the audio segmentation by voice activity detection (VAD) at test time does not access such meta information. Since VAD splits a long speech recording into chunks by silence regions, it would prevent models from extracting semantically coherent contextual information. Therefore, it is very important to seek a better segmentation strategy in order to minimize this gap in training and test conditions and evaluate models correctly. In fact, the last year's winner obtained huge improvements by using their own segmentation strategy.

Motivated by this fact, we investigated two VAD systems apart from the provided segmentation. Specifically, we used WebRTC[6] and pyannote.audio (Bredin et al., 2020)[7] toolkits. For We-

[6]https://github.com/wiseman/py-webrtcvad

[7]https://github.com/pyannote/pyannote-audio

Algorithm 1 Merge short segments after VAD for long context modeling

function MERGESEGMENT($\boldsymbol{x}, M_{\text{dur}}, M_{\text{int}}$)
  $Q \leftarrow VAD(\boldsymbol{x})$ ▷ $\{(s_1, e_1), \cdots, (s_M, e_M)\}$
  while True **do**
    $N_{\text{merge}} \leftarrow 0$
    $Q_{\text{next}} \leftarrow \{\}$ ▷ Queue
    $S, T \leftarrow s_1, e_1$ ▷ Start/End time
    for $(s_m, e_m) \in Q$ **do**
      if $e_m - S < M_{\text{dur}}$ and $s_m - E < M_{\text{int}}$ **then**
        $N_{\text{merge}} \leftarrow N_{\text{merge}} + 1$ ▷ Merge segments
      else
        $Q_{\text{next}}.enqueue((S, E))$
        $S \leftarrow s_m$ ▷ Reset
      end if
      $E \leftarrow e_m$
    end for
    $Q \leftarrow Q_{\text{next}}$
    if $N_{\text{merge}} = 0$ **then**
      break
    end if
  end while
  return Q
end function

bRTC, we set the frame duration, padding duration, and aggressive mode to 10ms, 150ms, and 3, respectively. For pyannote.audio, we used a publicly available model pre-trained on the DIHARD corpus (Ryant et al., 2019).

However, we observed that VAD systems are more likely to generate short segments because they do not take contextual information into account. Therefore, we propose a novel algorithm to merge multiple short segments into a single chunk to enable long context modeling by self-attention in both encoder and decoder modules. The proposed algorithm is shown in Algorithm 1. We first perform VAD and obtain multiple segments. Then, we check the segments in a greedy way from left to right and merge adjacent segments if (1) the total utterance duration is below a threshold M_{dur} [10ms] and (2) the time interval of the two segments is below a threshold M_{int} [10ms]. This process continues until no segment is merged in an iteration. Although recent studies proposed similar methods (Potapczyk and Przybysz, 2020; Gaido et al., 2021), our algorithm is a bottom-up approach while theirs are top-down.

4 Experimental setting

In this section, we describe the experimental setting for each task. The detailed configurations for each task are summarized in Table 3.

Configuration	ASR	E2E-ST		MT
		non-MD	MD	
Warmup step	25k	25k	25k	8k
Learning rate factor	10.0	2.5	12.5	1.0
Batch size	200 utt	128 utt	120 utt	65k tok
Epoch	30	30	30	40
Validation metric	Accuracy	BLEU	BLEU	BLEU
Model average	5	5	5	5
Beam width	10	4	16, 10	4

Table 3: Summary of training configuration

4.1 Feature extraction

We extracted 80-channel log-mel filterbank coefficients computed with 25-ms window size and shifted every 10-ms with 3-dimensional pitch features using the Kaldi toolkit (Povey et al., 2011). The features were normalized by the mean and the standard deviation calculated on the entire training set. We applied SpecAugment (Park et al., 2019) with mask parameters $(m_T, m_F, T, F) = (2, 2, 40, 30)$ and time-warping for both ASR and E2E-ST tasks.

4.2 ASR

We used both Transformer and Conformer architectures. The encoder had two CNN blocks followed by 12 Transformer/Conformer blocks following (Karita et al., 2019; Guo et al., 2020). Each CNN block consisted of a channel size of 256 and a kernel size of 3 with a stride of 2×2, which resulted in time reduction by a factor of 4. Both architectures had six Transformer blocks in the decoder. In both encoder and decoder blocks, the dimensions of the self-attention layer d_{model} and feed-forward network d_{ff} were set to 512 and 2048, respectively. The number of attention heads H was set to 8. The kernel size of depthwise separable convolution in Conformer blocks was set to 31. We optimized the model with the joint CTC/attention objective (Watanabe et al., 2017) with a CTC weight of 0.3. We also used CTC scores during decoding but did not use any external LM for simplicity. We adopted the best model configuration from the Librispeech ASR recipe in ESPnet.

4.3 MT

We used the Transformer-Base and -Big configurations in (Vaswani et al., 2017).

4.4 E2E-ST

We used the same Conformer architecture as ASR except for the vocabulary. We initialized the en-

Model	WER (↓)		
	Librispeech `test-other`	TEDLIUM2 `test`	Must-C `tst-COMMON`
Transformer	9.4	6.4	7.0
Conformer	**7.1**	**6.2**	**5.6**

Table 4: Word error rate (WER) of ASR systems

VAD	M_{dur}	M_{int}	WER (↓)				
			tst2010	tst2015	tst2018	tst2019	Avg.
Provided	–	–	18.2	32.1	23.5	20.8	23.65
	1500	200	14.4	29.3	18.4	15.5	19.40
	2000	200	12.7	27.7	16.4	11.5	17.08
	2500	200	14.5	29.9	15.1	12.2	17.93
WebRTC	–	–	35.3	35.1	44.0	22.7	34.28
	1500	200	19.4	26.7	27.7	13.8	21.90
	2000	200	19.8	27.7	27.1	11.9	21.63
	2500	200	22.9	29.5	27.1	11.6	22.78
pyannote	–	–	9.5	24.0	15.5	7.3	14.08
	1500	200	8.0	23.0	12.4	7.3	12.68
	1500	100	7.5	22.2	12.4	6.5	12.15
	2000	200	10.3	22.5	12.2	6.5	12.88
	2000	150	9.6	21.8	12.3	6.1	12.45
	2000	100	8.1	**21.5**	**12.0**	5.8	11.90
	2000	50	**7.3**	21.9	12.4	**5.9**	**11.88**

Table 5: Impact of audio segmentation for ASR

coder parameters with those of the Conformer ASR. On the decoder side, we initialized parameters like BERT (Devlin et al., 2019), where weight parameters were sampled from $\mathcal{N}(0, 0.02)$, biases were set to zero, and layer normalization parameters were set to $\beta = 0$, $\gamma = 1$. This technique led to better translation performance and faster convergence.

5 Results

5.1 ASR

5.1.1 Architecture

We compared Transformer and Conformer ASR architectures in Table 4. We observed that Conformer significantly outperformed Transformer. Therefore, we use the Conformer encoder in the following experiments.

5.1.2 Segmentation

Next, we investigated the VAD systems and the proposed segment merging algorithm for long context modeling in Table 5. We used the same decoding hyperparameters tuned on Must-C. We firstly observed that merging short segments was very effective probably because it alleviated frame classification errors in the VAD systems. Among three audio segmentation methods, we confirmed that pyannote.audio significantly reduced the WER while WebRTC had negative impacts compared to the provided segmentation. Specifically, we found that the `dihard` option in pyannote.audio worked very well while the rest options did not. The optimal maximum duration M_{dur} was around 2000 frames (i.e., 20 seconds). In the last experiments, we tuned the maximum interval M_{int} among $\{50, 100, 150, 200\}$ and found 50 and 100 (i.e., 0.5 and 1 second) was best on average. Compared to the provided segmentation, we obtained a 49.6% improvement on average.

5.2 MT

In this section, we show the results of our MT systems used for cascade systems and pseudo labeling in SeqKD. We report case-sensitive detokenized BLEU scores (Papineni et al., 2002) with the `multi-bleu-detok.perl` script in Moses. We carefully investigated the effective amount of WMT training data to improve the performance of the TED domain. The results are shown in Table 6. We confirmed that adding the WMT data improved the performance by more than 4 BLEU. Regarding the WMT data size, using up to 10M sentences was helpful, but 20M did not show clear improvements, probably because of the undersampling of the TED data. Oversampling as in multilingual NMT (Arivazhagan et al., 2019) could alleviate this problem, but this is beyond our scope.

After training with a mix of the WMT and TED data, we also tried to finetune the model with the TED data only, but this did not lead to clear improvement, especially for the IWSLT test sets. Increasing the model capacity was not helpful, although the conclusion might change by adding more training data and evaluating the model in other domains such as news. Because our primary focus to use MT systems was pseudo labeling for SeqKD, we decided to use the Base configuration to speed up decoding.

Finally, we checked the BLEU scores on the Must-C training data used for SeqKD. We observed that adding more WMT data decreased the BLEU score, from which we can conclude that using more WMT data gradually changed the MT output from the TED style. Therefore, we decided to use the models trained on `WMT5M` and `WMT10M` as teachers for SeqKD.

5.3 Speech translation

5.3.1 E2E-ST

SeqKD The results are shown in Table 7. We first observed the baseline Conformer model

Model	BLEU (↑)							
	Must-C		Must-C v2	tst2010	tst2015	tst2018	tst2019	Must-C
	`dev`	`tst-COMMON`	`tst-COMMON`					`Train`
Base (Must-C only)	–	30.02	29.86	27.28	24.92	21.13	20.37	
Base (`WMT5M`)	31.31	34.13	33.85	31.61	32.44	28.30	28.28	45.68
+ Big	27.32	29.11	28.85	27.61	28.44	24.42	23.92	–
Base (`WMT10M`)	**33.28**	**35.09**	34.80	**33.58**	33.26	29.24	28.87	38.31
+ In-domain finetune	30.67	**35.50**	**35.30**	30.79	31.43	25.35	26.10	–
Base (`WMT20M`)	33.15	35.06	**34.87**	33.26	**33.56**	**29.94**	**29.08**	33.60

Table 6: BLEU scores of text-based MT systems

ID	Model	BLEU (↑)							
		Must-C			Must-C v2	tst2010	tst2015	tst2018	tst2019
		`dev`	`tst-COMMON`	`tst-HE`	`tst-COMMON`				
-	Bidir SeqKD (E2E) (Inaguma et al., 2021b)	25.67	27.01	25.36	–	–	–	–	–
	Multi-Decoder (E2E) (Dalmia et al., 2021)	–	26.4	–	–	–	–	–	–
	RWTH (Cascade) (Bahar et al., 2021)	–	26.50	26.80	–	–	28.4	–	–
	KIT (E2E) (Pham et al., 2020)	–	30.60	–	–	24.27	21.82	–	–
	KIT (Cascade) (Pham et al., 2020)	–	–	–	–	26.68	24.95	–	–
	SRPOL (E2E) (Potapczyk and Przybysz, 2020)	–	–	–	–	29.44	24.6	–	23.96
`A1`	Baseline (`X`)	25.14	**35.63**	22.63	**36.07**	21.40	18.18	16.69	17.39
`A2`	+ SeqKD (`Y`)	26.31	29.29	26.33	29.50	23.34	21.24	21.09	22.25
`A3`	+ 2ref SeqKD (`X+Y`)	26.50	30.59	26.21	30.92	23.00	22.18	20.38	21.59
`A4`	+ 3ref SeqKD (`X+Y+Z`)	**27.66**	30.90	**27.44**	31.07	**24.97**	**22.66**	**22.20**	**23.41**
`B1`	MD + 2ref SeqKD	–	30.78	–	–	–	–	–	**23.78**
`C1`	Conformer ASR → Base MT (`WMT10M`)	27.01	29.42	26.13	29.75	**25.04**	**23.17**	**23.05**	23.19

Table 7: BLEU scores of ST systems. `X`: original, `Y`: `WMT5M`, `Z`: `WMT10M`. For unsegmented test sets, we used pyannote.audio with $M_{\text{dur}} = 2000$ and $M_{\text{int}} = 100$.

(`A1`) achieved 35.63 BLEU on the Must-C `tst-COMMON` set, and it is the new state-of-the-art record to the best of our knowledge. Surprisingly, it even outperformed text-based MT systems in Table 6. On the other hand, unlike our observations in (Inaguma et al., 2021a,b), SeqKD (`A2-4`) degraded the performance on the Must-C `tst-COMMON` set. However, the results on the Must-C `dev` and `tst-HE` sets showed completely different trends, where we observed better BLEU scores by SeqKD in proportion to the WMT data used for training the teachers. Therefore, after tuning audio segmentation, we also evaluated the models on the unsegmented IWSLT test sets. Here, we used the pyannote.audio based segmentation with $(M_{\text{dur}}, M_{\text{int}}) = (2000, 100)$ as described in §5.1.2. Then, we confirmed large improvements with SeqKD by 2-6 BLEU, and therefore we decided to determine the best model based on the IWSLT test sets. Multi-referenced training consistently improved the BLEU scores on the IWSLT sets. For example, `A4` outperformed `A1` by 6.02 BLEU on tst2019 although the tst2019 set was well-segmented (WER: 6.0%). Given these observations, we recommend evaluating ST models on multiple test sets for future research.

ID	Ensembled Models	tst2019
-	`B1`	21.06
`E1`	`B1, A4`	22.51
`E2`	`B1, A4, A1`	22.83
`E3`	`B1, A4, A1, A3`	23.36
`E4`	`B1, A4, A1, A3, A2`	**23.61**

Table 8: BLEU (↑) scores of ensembled E2E-ST systems on tst2019, using the provided segmentation with $M_{\text{dur}} = 2000$ and $M_{\text{int}} = 100$

Multi-Decoder architecture We combined the SeqKD and Multi-Decoder techniques in our `B1` system. `B1`, which used a conformer ASR encoder and `2ref` SeqKD, showed an improvement of 2.19 BLEU on tst2019 over `A3`, the encoder-decoder which also used `2ref` SeqKD. `B1` also achieved a slightly higher result on tst2019 compared to `A4` which used `3ref` SeqKD. These results suggest that the Multi-Decoder architecture is indeed compatible with SeqKD.

Model ensemble As shown in Table 8, ensembling our various ST systems using the posterior combination method described in §3.4 showed im-

VAD	M_{dur}	M_{int}	BLEU (↑)				
			tst2010	tst2015	tst2018	tst2019	Avg.
Provided†	–	–	–	–	–	20.1	–
Provided (E2E)	–	–	21.99	19.94	19.29	19.70	20.23
	1000	200	22.62	20.54	19.80	20.54	20.88
	1500	200	23.00	21.66	20.14	21.50	21.58
	2000	200	22.95	21.58	20.03	21.34	21.48
WebRTC (E2E)	–	–	13.13	12.97	11.07	13.32	12.62
	1000	200	20.95	20.66	17.09	20.87	19.89
	1500	200	21.00	20.99	17.67	21.05	20.18
	2000	200	20.25	21.81	17.08	20.71	19.96
pyannote (E2E)	–	–	22.26	16.84	17.78	19.98	19.22
	1500	200	25.00	22.22	21.97	22.67	22.97
	1500	100	**25.92**	**22.81**	**22.51**	22.88	**23.53**
	2000	200	24.10	21.98	21.00	22.71	22.45
	2000	150	24.25	22.26	21.41	22.99	22.73
	2000	100	24.97	22.66	22.20	**23.41**	23.31
	2000	50	24.50	20.67	22.14	22.89	22.55
pyannote (Cascade)	1500	200	25.06	22.65	23.01	22.51	23.31
	1500	100	**25.56**	22.85	23.03	22.82	23.57
	2000	200	24.41	22.76	22.15	22.08	22.85
	2000	150	24.50	23.03	**23.12**	23.11	23.44
	2000	100	25.04	**23.17**	23.05	**23.19**	**23.61**
	2000	50	24.33	20.79	**23.12**	23.11	22.84

Table 9: Impact of audio segmentation for ST. A4 was used for the E2E model. † (Potapczyk and Przybysz, 2020)

provements over the best single model, B1. We found that an ensemble of all of our models, A1−4 and B1, achieved the best result of 23.61 BLEU on tst2019 and outperformed B1 by 2.55 BLEU. Although A1 as a single system performs worse on tst2019 than the other single systems as shown in Table 7, including it in an ensemble with the two best single systems, B1 and A4, still yielded a slight gain of 0.32 BLEU (E2). Therefore, we can conclude that weak models are still beneficial for ensembling.

5.3.2 Segmentation

Similar to §5.1.2, we also investigated the impact of audio segmentation for E2E-ST models. To this end, we used the A4 model. Note that we used the same decoding hyperparameters tuned on Must-C. The results are shown in Table 9. We confirmed a similar trend to ASR. Although $(M_{\text{dur}}, M_{\text{int}}) = (1500, 100)$ showed the best performance on average, we decided to use $(M_{\text{dur}}, M_{\text{int}}) = (2000, 100)$ for submission considering the best performance on the latest IWSLT test, tst2019.

5.3.3 Cascade system

We also evaluated the cascade system with the Conformer ASR and the Transformer-Base MT trained on the WMT10M data (C1). The MT model was trained by feeding source sentences without case information and punctuation marks. The results in Table 9 showed that the BLEU scores correlated to the WER in Table ,5 and the performance was comparable with that of A4. Although there is some room for improving the performance of the cascade system further by using in-domain English LM, it is difficult to conclude which modeling (cascade or E2E) is effective because the cascade system had more model parameters in the ASR decoder and MT encoder. This means that the E2E model could also be enhanced by using a similar amount of parameters.

5.3.4 Final system

Our final system was the best ensemble system E4, using the pyannote.audio based segmentation with $(M_{\text{dur}}, M_{\text{int}}) = (2000, 200)^8$. This system, which was our primary submission, scored 24.14 BLEU on tst2019 as shown in Table 10. Compared to the result in Table 8, it improved by 0.53 BLEU thanks to better audio segmentation. It was also slightly higher than the IWSLT20 winner's submission by SPROL (Potapczyk and Przybysz, 2020).

We also present the results on tst2020 and tst2021 in Table 10. Our primary submission E4 outperformed the result of last year's winner system on tst2020.

6 Conclusion

In this paper, we have presented the ESPnet-ST group's offline systems on the IWSLT 2021 submission. We significantly improved the baseline Conformer performance with multi-referenced SeqKD, Multi-Decoder architecture, segment merging algorithm, and model ensembling. Our future work includes scaling training data and careful analysis of the performance gap in different test sets.

7 Acknowledgement

This work was partly supported by ASAPP and JHU HLTCOE. This work used the Extreme Science and Engineering Discovery Environment (XSEDE) (Towns et al., 2014), which is supported by National Science Foundation grant number ACI-1548562. Specifically, it used the Bridges system (Nystrom et al., 2015), which is supported by NSF award number ACI-1445606, at the Pittsburgh Supercomputing Center (PSC).

[8]Because of time limitation, we submitted the systems before completing tuning segmentation hyperparameters.

System	Segmentation	Segment merging	M_{int}	BLEU (↑)				
				tst2019	tst2020	tst2021		
						ref1	ref2	both
IWSLT'20 winner♣	given	–	–	20.1	21.5	–	–	–
	own	–	–	23.96	25.3	–	–	–
E4 (primary)	pyannote	✓	200	**24.14**	**25.6**	**19.3**	**21.2**	**31.4**
E4+*	pyannote	✓	200	24.41	25.5	**19.7**	20.6	30.8
E4+*	pyannote	✓	100	**24.87**	**26.0**	19.5	21.1	31.3
E4+*	given	✓	100	23.72	25.1	19.4	**21.4**	**31.5**
E4+*	given	✗	–	21.10	22.3	17.4	18.4	27.7
B1	pyannote	✓	100	23.78	25.0	18.9	20.9	31.1

Table 10: BLEU scores of submitted systems on tst2020 and tst2021. ♣ (Potapczyk and Przybysz, 2020). $M_{\text{dur}} = 2000$ was used for the segment merging algorithm. *Late submission (not official). E4+ denotes E4 trained for more steps.

References

Naveen Arivazhagan, Ankur Bapna, Orhan Firat, Dmitry Lepikhin, Melvin Johnson, Maxim Krikun, Mia Xu Chen, Yuan Cao, George Foster, Colin Cherry, et al. 2019. Massively multilingual neural machine translation in the wild: Findings and challenges. *arXiv preprint arXiv:1907.05019.*

Parnia Bahar, Tobias Bieschke, Ralf Schlüter, and Hermann Ney. 2021. Tight integrated end-to-end training for cascaded speech translation. In *Proceedings of SLT*, pages 950–957. IEEE.

Hervé Bredin, Ruiqing Yin, Juan Manuel Coria, Gregory Gelly, Pavel Korshunov, Marvin Lavechin, Diego Fustes, Hadrien Titeux, Wassim Bouaziz, and Marie-Philippe Gill. 2020. Pyannote.audio: neural building blocks for speaker diarization. In *Proceedings of ICASSP*, pages 7124–7128. IEEE.

Siddharth Dalmia, Brian Yan, Vikas Raunak, Florian Metze, and Shinji Watanabe. 2021. Searchable hidden intermediates for end-to-end models of decomposable sequence tasks. In *Proceedings of the 2021 Conference of the North American Chapter of the Association for Computational Linguistics: Human Language Technologies*, pages 1882–1896, Online. Association for Computational Linguistics.

Jacob Devlin, Ming-Wei Chang, Kenton Lee, and Kristina Toutanova. 2019. BERT: Pre-training of deep bidirectional transformers for language understanding. In *Proceedings of the 2019 Conference of the North American Chapter of the Association for Computational Linguistics: Human Language Technologies, Volume 1 (Long and Short Papers)*, pages 4171–4186, Minneapolis, Minnesota. Association for Computational Linguistics.

Mattia A. Di Gangi, Roldano Cattoni, Luisa Bentivogli, Matteo Negri, and Marco Turchi. 2019. MuST-C: a Multilingual Speech Translation Corpus. In *Proceedings of the 2019 Conference of the North American Chapter of the Association for Computational Linguistics: Human Language Technologies, Volume 1 (Long and Short Papers)*, pages 2012–2017, Minneapolis, Minnesota. Association for Computational Linguistics.

Marco Gaido, Mattia A. Di Gangi, Matteo Negri, Mauro Cettolo, and Marco Turchi. 2020. Contextualized translation of automatically segmented speech. In *Proceedings of Interspeech*, pages 1471–1475.

Marco Gaido, Matteo Negri, Mauro Cettolo, and Marco Turchi. 2021. Beyond voice activity detection: Hybrid audio segmentation for direct speech translation. *arXiv preprint arXiv:2104.11710.*

Mitchell A Gordon and Kevin Duh. 2019. Explaining sequence-level knowledge distillation as data-augmentation for neural machine translation. *arXiv preprint arXiv:1912.03334.*

Anmol Gulati, James Qin, Chung-Cheng Chiu, Niki Parmar, Yu Zhang, Jiahui Yu, Wei Han, Shibo Wang, Zhengdong Zhang, Yonghui Wu, and Ruoming Pang. 2020. Conformer: Convolution-augmented Transformer for speech recognition. In *Proceedings of Interspeech*, pages 5036–5040.

Pengcheng Guo, Florian Boyer, Xuankai Chang, Tomoki Hayashi, Yosuke Higuchi, Hirofumi Inaguma, Naoyuki Kamo, Chenda Li, Daniel Garcia-Romero, Jiatong Shi, et al. 2020. Recent developments on ESPnet toolkit boosted by Conformer. *arXiv preprint arXiv:2010.13956.*

Tomoki Hayashi, Ryuichi Yamamoto, Katsuki Inoue, Takenori Yoshimura, Shinji Watanabe, Tomoki Toda, Kazuya Takeda, Yu Zhang, and Xu Tan. 2020. Espnet-TTS: Unified, reproducible, and integratable open source end-to-end text-to-speech toolkit. In *Proceedings of ICASSP*, pages 7654–7658. IEEE.

Hirofumi Inaguma, Kevin Duh, Tatsuya Kawahara, and Shinji Watanabe. 2019. Multilingual end-to-end speech translation. In *Proceedings of ASRU*, pages 570–577.

Hirofumi Inaguma, Yosuke Higuchi, Kevin Duh, Tatsuya Kawahara, and Shinji Watanabe. 2021a. Orthros: Non-autoregressive end-to-end speech translation with dual-decoder. In *Proceedings of ICASSP*.

Hirofumi Inaguma, Tatsuya Kawahara, and Shinji Watanabe. 2021b. Source and target bidirectional knowledge distillation for end-to-end speech translation. *arXiv preprint arXiv:2104.06457*.

Hirofumi Inaguma, Shun Kiyono, Kevin Duh, Shigeki Karita, Nelson Yalta, Tomoki Hayashi, and Shinji Watanabe. 2020. ESPnet-ST: All-in-one speech translation toolkit. In *Proceedings of the 58th Annual Meeting of the Association for Computational Linguistics: System Demonstrations*, pages 302–311, Online. Association for Computational Linguistics.

Niehues Jan, Roldano Cattoni, Stüker Sebastian, Mauro Cettolo, Marco Turchi, and Marcello Federico. 2018. The iwslt 2018 evaluation campaign. In *Proceedings of IWSLT*, pages 2–6.

Shigeki Karita, Nanxin Chen, Tomoki Hayashi, Takaaki Hori, Hirofumi Inaguma, Ziyan Jiang, Masao Someki, Nelson Enrique Yalta Soplin, Ryuichi Yamamoto, Xiaofei Wang, et al. 2019. A comparative study on Transformer vs RNN in speech applications. In *Proceedings of ASRU*, pages 499–456.

Yoon Kim and Alexander M. Rush. 2016. Sequence-level knowledge distillation. In *Proceedings of the 2016 Conference on Empirical Methods in Natural Language Processing*, pages 1317–1327, Austin, Texas. Association for Computational Linguistics.

Tom Ko, Vijayaditya Peddinti, Daniel Povey, and Sanjeev Khudanpur. 2015. Audio augmentation for speech recognition. In *Proceedings of Interspeech*, pages 3586–3589.

Philipp Koehn, Hieu Hoang, Alexandra Birch, Chris Callison-Burch, Marcello Federico, Nicola Bertoldi, Brooke Cowan, Wade Shen, Christine Moran, Richard Zens, Chris Dyer, Ondřej Bojar, Alexandra Constantin, and Evan Herbst. 2007. Moses: Open source toolkit for statistical machine translation. In *Proceedings of the 45th Annual Meeting of the Association for Computational Linguistics Companion Volume Proceedings of the Demo and Poster Sessions*, pages 177–180, Prague, Czech Republic. Association for Computational Linguistics.

Chenda Li, Jing Shi, Wangyou Zhang, Aswin Shanmugam Subramanian, Xuankai Chang, Naoyuki Kamo, Moto Hira, Tomoki Hayashi, Christoph Boeddeker, Zhuo Chen, and Shinji Watanabe. 2021. ESPnet-SE: End-to-end speech enhancement and separation toolkit designed for ASR integration. In *Proceedings of SLT*, pages 785–792. IEEE.

Marco Lui and Timothy Baldwin. 2012. langid.py: An off-the-shelf language identification tool. In *Proceedings of the ACL 2012 System Demonstrations*, pages 25–30, Jeju Island, Korea. Association for Computational Linguistics.

Robert C. Moore and William Lewis. 2010. Intelligent selection of language model training data. In *Proceedings of the ACL 2010 Conference Short Papers*, pages 220–224, Uppsala, Sweden. Association for Computational Linguistics.

Nicholas A Nystrom, Michael J Levine, Ralph Z Roskies, and J Ray Scott. 2015. Bridges: a uniquely flexible hpc resource for new communities and data analytics. In *Proceedings of the 2015 XSEDE Conference: Scientific Advancements Enabled by Enhanced Cyberinfrastructure*, pages 1–8.

Vassil Panayotov, Guoguo Chen, Daniel Povey, and Sanjeev Khudanpur. 2015. Librispeech: an ASR corpus based on public domain audio books. In *Proceedings of ICASSP*, pages 5206–5210. IEEE.

Kishore Papineni, Salim Roukos, Todd Ward, and Wei-Jing Zhu. 2002. Bleu: a method for automatic evaluation of machine translation. In *Proceedings of the 40th Annual Meeting of the Association for Computational Linguistics*, pages 311–318, Philadelphia, Pennsylvania, USA. Association for Computational Linguistics.

Daniel S Park, William Chan, Yu Zhang, Chung-Cheng Chiu, Barret Zoph, Ekin D Cubuk, and Quoc V Le. 2019. SpecAugment: A simple data augmentation method for automatic speech recognition. In *Proceedings of Interspeech*, pages 2613–2617.

Ngoc-Quan Pham, Thanh-Le Ha, Tuan-Nam Nguyen, Thai-Son Nguyen, Elizabeth Salesky, Sebastian Stüker, Jan Niehues, and Alex Waibel. 2020. Relative positional encoding for speech recognition and direct translation. In *Proceedings of Interspeech*, pages 31–35.

Tomasz Potapczyk and Pawel Przybysz. 2020. SRPOL's system for the IWSLT 2020 end-to-end speech translation task. In *Proceedings of the 17th International Conference on Spoken Language Translation*, pages 89–94, Online. Association for Computational Linguistics.

Daniel Povey, Arnab Ghoshal, Gilles Boulianne, Lukas Burget, Ondrej Glembek, Nagendra Goel, Mirko Hannemann, Petr Motlicek, Yanmin Qian, Petr Schwarz, et al. 2011. The kaldi speech recognition toolkit. In *Proceedings of ASRU*.

Anthony Rousseau, Paul Deléglise, and Yannick Estève. 2012. TED-LIUM: An automatic speech recognition dedicated corpus. In *Proceedings of LREC*, pages 125–129.

Neville Ryant, Kenneth Church, Christopher Cieri, Alejandrina Cristia, Jun Du, Sriram Ganapathy, and Mark Liberman. 2019. The second DIHARD diarization challenge: Dataset, task, and baselines. In *Proceedings of Interspeech*, pages 978–982.

Rico Sennrich, Barry Haddow, and Alexandra Birch. 2016. Neural machine translation of rare words with subword units. In *Proceedings of the 54th Annual Meeting of the Association for Computational Linguistics (Volume 1: Long Papers)*, pages 1715–1725, Berlin, Germany. Association for Computational Linguistics.

John Towns, Timothy Cockerill, Maytal Dahan, Ian Foster, Kelly Gaither, Andrew Grimshaw, Victor Hazlewood, Scott Lathrop, Dave Lifka, Gregory D Peterson, et al. 2014. Xsede: Accelerating scientific discovery computing in science & engineering, 16 (5): 62–74, sep 2014. *URL https://doi.org/10.1109/mcse*, 128.

Ashish Vaswani, Noam Shazeer, Niki Parmar, Jakob Uszkoreit, Llion Jones, Aidan N Gomez, Łukasz Kaiser, and Illia Polosukhin. 2017. Attention is all you need. In *Proceedings of NeurIPS*, pages 5998–6008.

Shinji Watanabe, Takaaki Hori, Shigeki Karita, Tomoki Hayashi, Jiro Nishitoba, Yuya Unno, Nelson Enrique Yalta Soplin, Jahn Heymann, Matthew Wiesner, Nanxin Chen, Adithya Renduchintala, and Tsubasa Ochiai. 2018. ESPnet: End-to-end speech processing toolkit. In *Proceedings of Interspeech*, pages 2207–2211.

Shinji Watanabe, Takaaki Hori, Suyoun Kim, John R Hershey, and Tomoki Hayashi. 2017. Hybrid CTC/attention architecture for end-to-end speech recognition. *IEEE Journal of Selected Topics in Signal Processing*, 11(8):1240–1253.

End-to-End Speech Translation with Pre-trained Models and Adapters: UPC at IWSLT 2021

Gerard I. Gállego, Ioannis Tsiamas, Carlos Escolano,
José A. R. Fonollosa, Marta R. Costa-jussà
TALP Research Center, Universitat Politècnica de Catalunya, Barcelona
{gerard.ion.gallego,ioannis.tsiamas,carlos.escolano
jose.fonollosa,marta.ruiz}@upc.edu

Abstract

This paper describes the submission to the IWSLT 2021 offline speech translation task by the UPC Machine Translation group. The task consists of building a system capable of translating English audio recordings extracted from TED talks into German text. Submitted systems can be either cascade or end-to-end and use a custom or given segmentation. Our submission is an end-to-end speech translation system, which combines pre-trained models (Wav2Vec 2.0 and mBART) with coupling modules between the encoder and decoder, and uses an efficient fine-tuning technique, which trains only 20% of its total parameters. We show that adding an Adapter to the system and pre-training it, can increase the convergence speed and the final result, with which we achieve a BLEU score of 27.3 on the MuST-C test set. Our final model is an ensemble that obtains 28.22 BLEU score on the same set. Our submission also uses a custom segmentation algorithm that employs pre-trained Wav2Vec 2.0 for identifying periods of untranscribable text and can bring improvements of 2.5 to 3 BLEU score on the IWSLT 2019 test set, as compared to the result with the given segmentation.

1 Introduction

Typically, a speech translation (ST) system is composed of an automatic speech recognition (ASR) and a machine translation (MT) model, which is known as *cascade* system. However, in recent years, *end-to-end* models have gained popularity within the research community. These systems are encoder-decoder architectures capable of directly translating speech without intermediate symbolic representations. This approach solves classical shortcomings of *cascade* ST systems, e.g. the error propagation or the slow inference time (Weiss et al., 2017). Nevertheless, while there are plenty of data available to train ASR and MT systems, there are not as many datasets for ST, despite some recent efforts (Di Gangi et al., 2019a; Wang et al., 2020b). Moreover, this approach is inherently more difficult because the encoder has to perform both acoustic modeling and semantic encoding. For these reasons, end-to-end ST systems still struggle to achieve the performance of cascade ST models. Still, last year's IWSLT was the first time an end-to-end system had the best performance in the evaluation campaign (Potapczyk and Przybysz, 2020; Ansari et al., 2020). Hence, given the increasing interest in end-to-end ST systems, and the potential gains from advancing research on them, we decided to focus on developing such a system for this year's offline task.

When there are not enough data for a task, a common practice is to use pre-trained components, like BERT (Devlin et al., 2019) for various NLP tasks. In the ST field, the idea of pre-training the encoder for ASR was introduced by Berard et al. (2018) and has become a standard technique for developing modern end-to-end systems (Pino et al., 2019; Di Gangi et al., 2019b). By contrast, pre-training the decoder for MT does not lead to better performance (Bansal et al., 2019). Recently, Li et al. (2021) proposed a multilingual ST system that combines a pre-trained Wav2Vec 2.0 (Baevski et al., 2020) as the encoder and a pre-trained mBART decoder (Liu et al., 2020a). Furthermore, they proposed a minimalist fine-tuning strategy that trains only the 20% of the model parameters, while achieving similar performance to fine-tuning the whole model. From our perspective, this approach might become a turning point in the field, including bilingual scenarios like the IWSLT offline task. Hence, we decided to adopt this architecture[1] and fine-tuning strategy in our system (§2.1). In addi-

[1] Since the pre-trained modules were trained on external data, our submission is unconstrained.

Proceedings of the 18th International Conference on Spoken Language Translation, pages 110–119
Bangkok, Thailand (Online), August 5–6, 2021.

tion, we introduce an Adapter module to extract better representations from the encoder (§2.2), and we propose a two-step training strategy (§4.1) that brings improvements to the translation quality.

During training, we used data augmentation techniques to boost our system's performance. Specifically, we applied randomized on-the-fly augmentations by adding an echo effect and modifying tempo and pitch (§3.3). Since our system works directly on the audio waveform, we could not use SpecAugment (Park et al., 2019; Bahar et al., 2019). Instead, we applied masking to the output of the Wav2Vec 2.0 feature extraction module, thereby obtaining a similar effect.

The test data are provided with an automatic segmentation that does not ensure sentence-like segments. Considering the trend observed in 2019 and 2020 IWSLT offline task, where submission with own segmentation algorithms are strictly better than those with the given segmentation, we also decided to work with a custom segmentation algorithm. We base it on the approach of Potapczyk et al. (2019), but we replace the silence detection tool with an ASR system (§3.4). Our experiments on the IWSLT 2019 test set, show that our system works better when the data are segmented with our own segmentation algorithm (§4.3).

2 System description

We built an end-to-end ST system, mainly composed of pre-trained modules. We couple a Wav2Vec 2.0 encoder (Baevski et al., 2020) and an mBART decoder (Liu et al., 2020a), following the strategy proposed by Li et al. (2021). When combining these two models, there is a length discrepancy between the target sentence length and the encoder output. For this reason, it is necessary to use a module to shorten the encoder output, which we refer to as the Length Adaptor. Additionally, we introduce an Adapter module to reduce the gap between the different modalities of the pre-trained models (Bapna and Firat, 2019). A method that Escolano et al. (2020) proved to be beneficial for ST models.

2.1 Pre-trained modules

Our motivation is to get the most out of pre-trained components, which were obtained by self-supervision or supervised tasks. Concretely, we use a Wav2Vec 2.0 encoder and an mBART decoder, both trained initially by self-supervision and fine-tuned for ASR and multilingual MT, respectively.

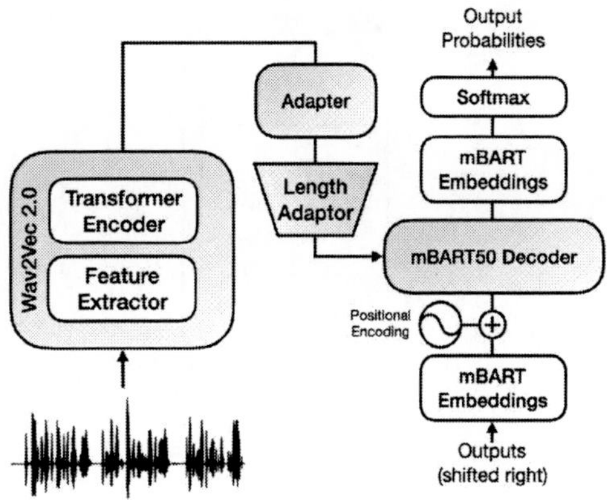

Figure 1: System overview. The original architecture proposed by Li et al. (2021) includes a pre-trained Wav2Vec 2.0 as the encoder, a pre-trained mBART decoder and a Length Adaptor. In this work, we add an Adapter module after the encoder.

Wav2Vec 2.0 is a speech encoder proposed by Baevski et al. (2020). This model is pre-trained by self-supervision, i.e. without explicit targets such as transcriptions. Its main contribution is that it achieves excellent performance in ASR after fine-tuning it with just a few minutes of transcribed speech. Moreover, it can process raw audio waveforms directly, unlike other systems which work with spectrogram-like representations (Di Gangi et al., 2019d).

This model is composed of two main blocks. Firstly, a feature extractor made of seven 1-D convolutional layers processes the raw audio waveform. The representation obtained from this step has a stride of 20ms between samples, and each one has a receptive field of 25ms. Secondly, a Transformer (Vaswani et al., 2017) encoder with 24 layers extracts contextualized representations. For the purpose of our system, we discard the rest of the components that are used during the self-supervised pre-training (e.g. the quantization modules).

The Wav2Vec 2.0 model that we employ is already fine-tuned on ASR. Specifically, we use the *Large* architecture, pre-trained with 53.2k hours of untranscribed speech from LibriVox (Kahn et al., 2020), fine-tuned on the 960h of transcribed speech from Librispeech (Panayotov et al., 2015), and on pseudo-labels (Xu et al., 2020).

mBART is a sequence-to-sequence denoising autoencoder, which reconstructs the input text sen-

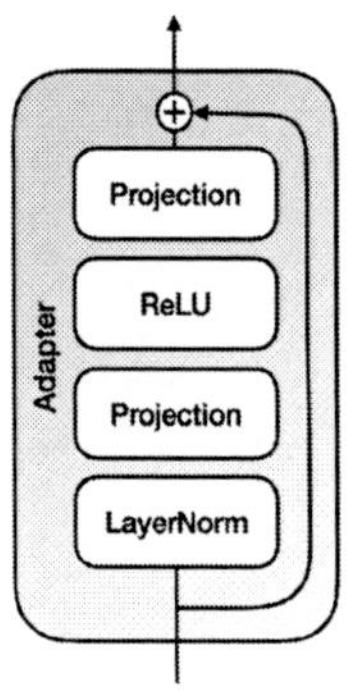

Figure 2: Adapter module

tence given a corrupted version of it (Liu et al., 2020a). It follows the same approach as BART (Lewis et al., 2020) but, instead of using just English monolingual data, it is trained with multiple languages. This strategy does not require any parallel corpora, so it can be used as a pre-training step and then fine-tuned for MT tasks.

Specifically, we use the 12-layer Transformer decoder of an mBART model, fine-tuned on multilingual MT, from English to 49 languages (Tang et al., 2020).

2.2 Coupling modules

In addition to the two main blocks that constitute our system, we implement another two other modules placed after the Wav2Vec 2.0 encoder (Figure 1). The objective of these modules is to overcome the multimodal gap by adapting the encoder output to the decoder. With them, we adapt the representations to the decoder's modality, and reduce its length.

The **Adapter** is a module that was introduced by Bapna and Firat (2019) to adapt pre-trained models to multiple tasks. The Adapter projects its input to a higher-dimensional space before reducing it to the original size. Moreover, it applies layer normalization at the input (Ba et al., 2016), a ReLU activation after the first projection and a residual connection (Figure 2).

In work done by Escolano et al. (2020), they proposed to use this module to adjust the representation from the speech encoder to the language-specific decoders. Hence, we have used this module with a similar purpose, since we also needed to combine different pre-trained components and modalities.

The **Length Adaptor** is a module that reduces the length discrepancy between the input and output sequences. It achieves an 8x down-sampling of the encoder representation by applying a stack of 3 convolutional layers with a kernel size of 3 and a stride of 2.

2.3 LNA Finetuning

We follow the LayerNorm and Attention (LNA) fine-tuning strategy proposed by Li et al. (2021). The main idea is that only some of the modules of Wav2Vec 2.0 and mBART need to be fine-tuned to build a system capable of ST. More specifically, these are the layer normalization, encoder self-attention and encoder-decoder attention, which account for the 20% of the total parameters. It was shown that this minimal fine-tuning not only creates a powerful ST system, but its performance also approximates what is obtained by fine-tuning all the parameters. Even more importantly, it allows fast and memory-efficient training, which enabled us to work with such a large architecture.

3 Data

Here we introduce the datasets used for our experiments and describe the filtering and data augmentation methods that were employed during training.

3.1 Datasets

For our experiments, we are using the English-to-German data from three ST datasets, namely the MuST-C v2 [2] (Di Gangi et al., 2019a), EuroparlST (Iranzo-Sánchez et al., 2020) and CoVoST 2 (Wang et al., 2020b) [3]. Our training set is a concatenation of the respective train splits of these datasets, while we discarded the train-noisy split of EuroparlST due to low quality. We only consider MuST-C to be in-domain, since its data come from TED talks, and thus EuroparlST and CoVoST are considered out-of-domain due to differences in setting, use of language and segment duration. Given this, our development data are comprised only of the development split of MuST-C, which allows us to concatenate the development splits of EuroparlST and CoVoST to our training data. Furthermore, we down-sample the CoVoST splits during each training epoch to shift the importance towards the MuST-C data. We do not down-sample EuroparlST

[2]The second version of MuST-C has not been officially released yet, but the En-De data is available in advance at https://ict.fbk.eu/must-c/.

[3]The EuroparlST and CoVoST 2 data are converted to 16khz, which is required for the input of the Wav2Vec 2.0 encoder.

Split	Available References	Aligned Segmentation
MuST-C-dev	✓	✓
MuST-C-test	✓	✓
IWSLT.tst2019	✓	
IWSLT.tst2020		
IWSLT.tst2021		

Table 1: Development and Test splits

Split	Original	Filtered	S.Ratio
MuST-C-train	450	415	1.0
EuroparlST-train	77	75	1.0
EuroparlST-dev	3	3	1.0
CoVoST-train	430	410	0.3
CoVoST-dev	26	24	0.3
Total	986	927	-

Table 2: Training splits with their original and filtered sizes measured in hours, and the sampling ratios for each split in every training epoch.

due to its already small size compared to MuST-C (Table 2). We use two different sets for evaluating the performance of our system, the test split of MuST-C and the IWSLT 2019 test set (Niehues et al., 2019). The latter one provides us with an opportunity to additionally test our segmentation algorithm, since the given segmentation and the reference translations are not perfectly aligned nor sentence-like. Finally we generate our predictions for the IWSLT test sets of 2020 (Ansari et al., 2020) and 2021 (Anastasopoulos et al., 2021), for which the reference translations have not been made available (Table 1). We do not use the rest of the IWSLT test sets, since they are already included in the 2nd version of MuST-C.

3.2 Data filtering

We remove examples where the duration of the source audio is more than 25 seconds (400,000 samples) to avoid out-of-memory errors during the training of the ST system. Apart from that, we use another two filtering stages to ensure that our training data are of high quality, for which we provide the details bellow. The size of the training data after all the filtering stages can be found in Table 2.

Text Filtering. We perform text filtering on the target German text of MuST-C to remove speaker names and non-textual events. Speaker names in MuST-C are used to differentiate between speakers, when multiple of them are interacting in a talk. They appear in the beginning of a sentence, as full names or capitalized initials, followed by a colon. We remove the text in the beginning of each sentence if it matches the described pattern. Non-textual events are enclosed in parentheses, with some common examples being "(Gelächter)" or "(Applaus)", which are the German translations of "laughter" and "applause". In such cases we keep the examples but we remove the events. The only exception are cases where there are actual utterances coming from a secondary speaker. For those cases, we strip the parentheses and the speaker names. For EuroparlST, large numbers use spaces as the thousands-separator, which we convert to commas, in order to match the number format of MuST-C and IWSLT data. No specific text filtering is done for CoVoST. Finally, we remove the examples that are empty after applying the text filtering.

ASR Filtering. For the final stage of filtering, we use an Automatic Speech Recognition (ASR) model to identify noisy examples. We employ a pre-trained Wav2Vec 2.0 (Baevski et al., 2020), from the HuggingFace Transformers library (Wolf et al., 2020) and perform inference on all our training examples. The pre-trained Wav2Vec 2.0 is quite effective in this task and achieves an average word-error-rate (WER) of 0.135. Consecutively we remove those examples where the predicted text has a WER greater than 0.5, as compared to its English reference text. At this stage of filtering we remove approximately 4% of our total training data. For ASR inference, all English target text was normalized, lower-cased, stripped from punctuation and numbers were converted to spelled-out words.

3.3 Data augmentation

Data augmentation has been shown to provide increased performance in both ASR (Park et al., 2019) and ST (Di Gangi et al., 2019c), by enriching and diversifying the training data. Thus, following Potapczyk et al. (2019), we perform data augmentation on the English source audio. We apply the "tempo" and "pitch" effects to force our system to adapt to speeches of different speeds, and the "echo" effect to simulate the echoing which is usually present in large rooms, where TED talks are taking place. Compared to Potapczyk et al. (2019), we replace the "speed" effect in favor of "pitch", since "speed" also modifies the "tempo", which is a separate effect. Data augmentation is

Parameter	Min value	Max value
tempo	0.85	1.3
pitch	-300	300
echo-delay	20	200
echo-decay	0.05	0.2

Table 3: Data Augmentation parameter ranges. Echo is controlled by two parameters. Tempo and echo-decay are coefficients, pitch is measured in semitones and echo-delay in milliseconds.

applied on-the-fly, during training, using WavAugment (Kharitonov et al., 2020), which is build on top of the SoX library [4]. Each example in the batch has a probability of $p_{aug} = 0.8$ to be augmented, in which case we apply all three effects to it. We sample uniformly the parameters of each effect from the ranges shown at Table 3.

3.4 Data Segmentation

Similarly to 2019 and 2020 (Niehues et al., 2019; Ansari et al., 2020), this year's evaluation data are segmented using an automatic tool (Meignier and Merlin, 2010), which does not ensure that segments are proper sentences nor that they are aligned with the translated text. This assigns extra importance to developing methods for proper segmentation of the audio data, which was confirmed in the previous year's evaluation campaign, where all top submissions used their own segmentation algorithm. For creating our own segmentation of the IWSLT 2020 and 2021 test sets, we modify the technique described in Potapczyk et al. (2019), where they use a silence detection tool [5] to progressively split each audio file into smaller segments. Their algorithm terminates when all segments do not exceed a maximum segment length (max_seg_len) threshold, which they tune to maximize the BLEU score on IWSLT 2015 test set (Cettolo et al., 2015). In our approach we replace the silence detection tool with a pre-trained Wav2Vec 2.0 model (Baevski et al., 2020) from the Huggingface Transformer library (Wolf et al., 2020), to identify periods of untranscribable English text. Since the IWSLT 2015 test set is included in MuST-C v2, we tune our algorithm on IWSLT 2019 test set. First, we perform inference with Wav2Vec 2.0 on the IWSLT 2019 test set, and obtain a token prediction for every 20ms for each audio file. Then we proceed to split each audio file on the largest untranscribable period, which is identified by the absence of English characters in it. The algorithm terminates when the max segment length condition is satisfied or no further splits are possible due to a minimum untranscribable period length, which we set to 0.2 seconds. We test $max\_seg\_len \in [5, 25]$, and for each value we produce a segmentation, generate translations using one of our ST systems [6], use the mwerSegmenter [7] software to align the generated translations with the reference translations, and finally obtain a BLEU score using SACREBLEU (Post, 2018). We find that the maximum BLEU score is obtained using $max\_seg\_len = 22$ seconds (Figure 3), which we use to segment the IWSLT 2020 and 2021 test sets for our submission.

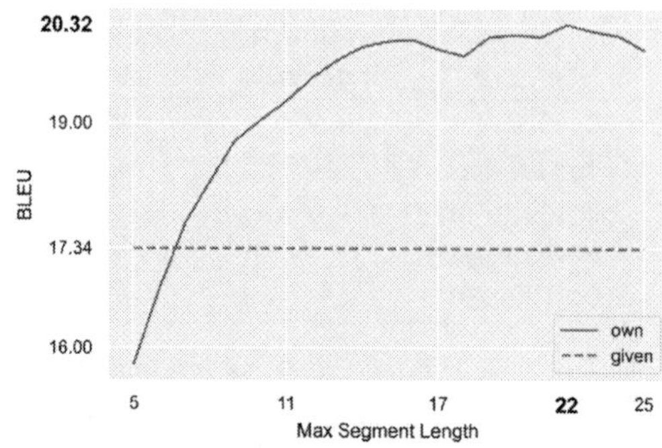

Figure 3: BLEU scores for our segmentation algorithm with different values of max_seg_len on IWSLT.tst2019. X-axis is in seconds. With red color is the BLEU score for the given segmentation.

4 Experiments

Here we describe our experiments, along with their implementation details and the results on MuST-C and the IWSLT 2019 test set.

4.1 Experimental Setup

LNA-ED The first experiment is to train our baseline model, which is an encoder-decoder model with a length adaptor module (§2.2) in between. As in Li et al. (2021), we initialize the encoder with a pre-trained Wav2Vec 2.0, the decoder with the decoder of a pre-trained mBART50 (§2.1) and we only train the parameters of the layer normalization in both encoder and decoder, the encoder self-attention in the encoder, the encoder cross-attention in the decoder, and Length Adaptor (§2.3).

[4]SoX - https://sox.sourceforge.net

[5]Audacity - https://www.audacityteam.org

[6]For the purpose of this experiment we used the best checkpoint from the LNA-ED-Adapt experiment (Table 4)

[7]https://github.com/jniehues-kit/SLT.KIT

LNA-ED-Adapt Following we experiment with adding an Adapter module (§2.2) prior to the Length Adaptor, while we train the same parameters as in LNA-ED. We expect that this module will adapt the encoder output to the decoder's modality, before down-sampling it with the convolutional layers of the Length Adaptor.

LNA-ED-Adapt-2step Our next experiment aims at initializing all the sub-modules from pretrained checkpoints. Thus, our first step is to train only the coupling modules of the LNA-ED-Adapt system, while everything else is frozen. Then, in the second step we proceed by training all the active parameters of LNA-ED-Adapt. We hypothesize that in the prior experiments the initially random weights of the coupling modules are slowing down the learning process and potentially also hurting the final performance of the system.

In-domain FT We experiment with fine-tuning our systems for some additional epochs only on the in-domain data of MuST-C. During this fine-tuning we also disable data augmentation.

Ckpt AVG We average checkpoints around the best, indicated by the highest BLEU score in the development split of MuST-C. This technique has been shown to provide more generalizable models, achieving higher scores in the hidden test sets (Gaido et al., 2020; Lakumarapu et al., 2020).

Ensemble For our final model, we ensemble our two best single models. To increase the diversity of the two single models and, consecutively, the performance of the ensemble, we choose one that is further fine-tuned on in-domain data and one that is not. We expect that, although there is a potential boost in the performance of a system by fine-tuning to in-domain data, there is the risk of catastrophic forgetting of the more general data properties of the combined and augmented corpus. Thus, we combine a model specialized to the in-domain data and one which is potentially more general.

4.2 Implementation details

For the encoder and decoder of our models, we are using the same architecture as the Wav2Vec 2.0 and mBART decoder (§2.1). More specifically the encoder has a 7-layer convolutional feature extractor and a 24-layer Transformer encoder, while the decoder has 12 layers. The feature extractor has 512 channels, while each Transformer layer has a dimensionality of 1024, feed-forward dimension of 4096, and 16 heads. For the Adapter, we use an inner dimensionality of 4096, which was shown to work better in Escolano et al. (2020) and for the Length Adaptor we set the kernel size to 3 and the stride to 2. The decoder uses a vocabulary of 250,000 tokens, and the embedding layer is shared between source and target.

We train all our models with the LNA method (§2.3), unless stated otherwise. The training data for each epoch are coming from the 5 splits show in Table 2, with their respective sampling ratios. We limit the length of the source examples to 400,000 samples (i.e. 25 seconds) and to 1024 tokens for the target. For each example, we apply data augmentation (§3.3) on the source speech and subsequently, normalize it to zero mean and unit variance. We construct mini-batches with a maximum of 440,000 samples, and use data parallelism on 4 GPUs and gradient accumulation with 16 steps, to increase the effective batch size by a factor of 64.

For optimization we use Adam (Kingma and Ba, 2017) with parameters $\beta_1 = 0.99$, $\beta_2 = 0.98$. We set the base learning rate to 10^{-4}, which is controlled during training by a tri-stage scheduler with the ratios for the warm-up, hold and decay phases being 0.15, 0.15, and 0.7 accordingly, and initial and final scales of 0.01. We clip gradients to a maximum norm of 20, and we apply a dropout of 0.1 before every non-frozen layer or sub-layer in our models. Following Liu et al. (2020b), the optimizer is minimizing the standard cross-entropy loss with a label smoothing of 0.2. All models are trained for 16 epochs (approximately 23,000 updates), apart from the pre-training step of the LNA-ED-Adapt-2step and the in-domain fine-tuning, which are carried out for 4 epochs.

We pick the checkpoint with the highest BLEU score on the development set of MuST-C, for which then we report the BLEU on the test set of MuST-C and the IWSLT 2019 test set. We ensemble the 2 best models according to the BLEU score on the test set of MuST-C. For generation, we are using a standard beam search with a size of 5. All our experiments are done in a machine with 4 Nvidia GeForce RTX 2080 Ti GPUs, using 16 floating-point precision, and are implemented in fairseq (Wang et al., 2020a). The training of each model took approximately 60 hours. The code for our experiments is available in a public repository[8].

[8]https://github.com/mt-upc/iwslt-2021

4.3 Results

The results of our experiments (§4.1) on the development and test sets of MuST-C can be found in Table 4. We also provide the BLEU score on the IWSLT 2019 test set, for both the given and our own segmentation, using a max segment length of 22 (§3.4). The addition of the Adapter module provides an increase of 0.76 BLEU in MuST-C test set, as compared to LNA-ED. We observe that training our system in two steps can bring further improvements to the quality of translations. The first step of training of the LNA-ED-Adapt-2step experiment, with only the coupling modules being active, achieves a BLEU score of 15.54 after 4 epochs of training. Subsequently, the 2nd step is initialized from a much better checkpoint, as compared to the previous experiments, and can converge faster, as we can observe in Figure 4, eventually achieving a BLEU score of 27.25.

Both the LNA-ED-Adapt and LNA-ED-Adapt-2step bring improvements to the base model, without a significant computational burden. The Adapter module has 8.4 million parameters, which accounts for an increase of only 5% in the total trainable parameters of the LNA method. In the first step of LNA-ED-Adapt-2step we are only training 9.1 million parameters for 4 epochs, a process that is completed rather fast compared to the training of the second step.

We achieve increased performance by fine-tuning the best checkpoint of LNA-ED-Adapt on the in-domain data of MuST-C for another 4 epochs. What stands out from this further fine-tuning is the large improvements in the IWSLT 2019 test set, providing us with our best score on the own segmentation from a single model. Due to time constraints, we carried out this fine-tuning only on LNA-ED-Adapt and not on LNA-ED-Adapt-2step. Finally, we average the checkpoints around the best for the in-domain fine-tuned LNA-ED-Adapt and the LNA-ED-Adapt-2step. Using them in an ensemble, we obtain a BLEU score of 28.22 on the test set of MuST-C, which is an improvement of 0.92 points from our best single model, while smaller improvements are observed in the IWSLT 2019 test set.

Regarding the translation quality on the IWSLT 2019 test set, we can observe that using our own segmentation algorithm, we can obtain large improvements, from 2.5 to 3 in BLEU score.

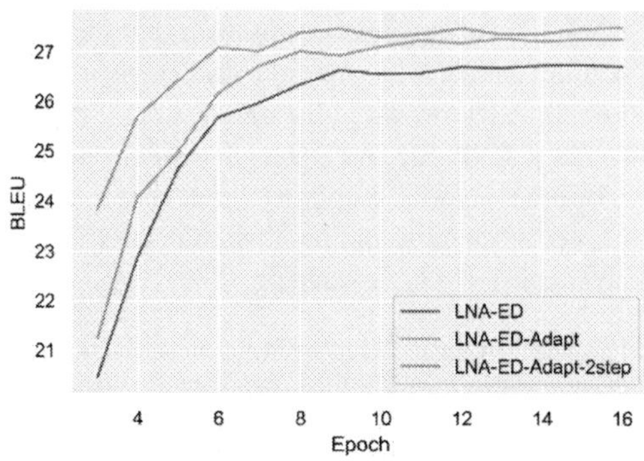

Figure 4: BLEU scores on MuST-C-dev during training

Model	MuST-C		IWSLT.tst2019	
	dev	test	given	own
LNA-ED	26.76	26.23	17.25	20.06
LNA-ED-Adapt	27.28	26.99	17.34	20.32
↪ In-domain FT	27.36	27.25	18.79	**21.29**
↪ ckpt AVG (a)	27.36	27.29	**18.97**	21.13
LNA-ED-Adapt-2step	27.49	27.25	17.56	20.37
↪ ckpt AVG (b)	**27.5**	**27.3**	17.51	20.38
Ensemble (a) & (b)	**28.5**	**28.22**	**19.05**	**21.43**

Table 4: BLEU scores on dev and test sets of MuST-C and on the IWSLT.tst2019 with given and own segmentation. With bold are the best scores by single models and with underlined bold are the best scores overall.

4.4 Submission results

Model	Segmentation	Reference			
		2020	2021†	2021‡	2021⋆
Ensemble	**Own**	**24.6**	**21.8**	**18.3**	**30.6**
Ensemble	Given	20.5	19.5	16.0	26.7
Single	Own	23.0	20.7	17.5	29.0
Single	Given	19.0	18.4	15.0	25.0

Table 5: Final results of our submission on the IWSLT 2020 and 2021 test sets, measured in BLEU, against the IWSLT (†) and TED (‡) references separately and both at once (⋆). With bold is our primary submission. The *Single* is our best single model from Table 4 (LNA-ED-Adapt-2step with ckpt AVG) and the *Ensemble* to the ensemble of our best single model and the LNA-ED-Adapt with In-domain FT and ckpt AVG.

There are two references available for this year's test set (Anastasopoulos et al., 2021), one corresponding to the official TED talks subtitles and another generated by the IWSLT organizers. Our primary submission is the ensemble of the two best models with our segmentation, which scores 18.3 BLEU against the TED references, 21.8 BLEU with the IWSLT references, and 30.6 BLEU with both together (Table 5). Meanwhile, when using the given segmentation, we get a decrease of 2.3 BLEU in both references, which is consistent to the results obtained in the IWSLT 2019 test set (Table 4). As a contrastive system, we also submitted the results obtained with our best single model, corresponding to the LNA-ED-Adapt-2step model with checkpoint averaging. This system scores approximately 1 BLEU less with respect to the ensemble, similarly to the results we get in the IWSLT 2019 test set (Table 4).

We also evaluated our systems on the IWSLT 2020 test set, for tracking year-to-year progress. Our best model obtains a BLEU score of 24.6 (Table 5) and, in general, the results follow the same trend as on the IWSLT 2021 test set. For comparison, our best model would have been place 3rd in last year's leaderboard (Ansari et al., 2020), 0.7 BLEU points behind the best system (Potapczyk and Przybysz, 2020).

5 Conclusions

We described the UPC Machine Translation group participation in the IWSLT 2021 offline ST task. We built our system by combining pre-trained components, using Wav2Vec 2.0 as an encoder and an mBART decoder. In order to fine-tune such a large model with approximately 770 million parameters, we followed the strategy proposed by Li et al. (2021), in which just a 20% of the parameters are trained. Originally, this method was proposed for multilingual ST, and it had not been applied to initialize a bilingual system yet. With this approach, we got a score of 26.23 BLEU in the MuST-C test set. Then, we introduced an Adapter module to reduce the gap between the different modalities of the pre-trained components, which brought an improvement of 0.76 BLEU. We also explored a two-step training where we initialized the coupling modules before fine-tuning the rest of the model, which resulted in an increase of 1.02 BLEU with respect to the original model. Furthermore, we applied other techniques like fine-tuning with in-domain data, checkpoint averaging and ensembling our two best models. Our final score in the MuST-C test set was 28.22 BLEU. Apart from using Wav2Vec 2.0 as the encoder of our ST system, we additionally leveraged it in our ASR-based data filtering and as part of our segmentation algorithm. Applying this custom segmentation we gained an increase of 2.5 to 3 BLEU score in the IWSLT 2019 test set, as compared to the result of with given segmentation.

As was shown in Li et al. (2021), and confirmed in this work for a bilingual scenario, large pre-trained models can be very effective in ST. We believe that future work should focus on exploring better methods to adapt these pre-trained models to new languages and tasks, with Adapter modules being promising candidates.

Acknowledgments

This work was supported by the project ADAVOICE, PID2019-107579RB-I00 / AEI / 10.13039/501100011033 and by the European Research Council (ERC) under the European Union's Horizon 2020 research and innovation programme (grant agreement No. 947657).

References

Antonios Anastasopoulos, Ondřej Bojar, Jacob Bremerman, Roldano Cattoni, Maha Elbayad, Marcello Federico, Xutai Ma, Satoshi Nakamura, Matteo Negri, Jan Niehues, Juan Pino, Elizabeth Salesky, Sebastian Stüker, Katsuhito Sudoh, Marco Turchi, Alex Waibel, Changhan Wang, and Matthew Wiesner. 2021. Findings of the IWSLT 2021 Evaluation Campaign. In *Proceedings of the 18th International Conference on Spoken Language Translation (IWSLT 2021)*, Online.

Ebrahim Ansari, Amittai Axelrod, Nguyen Bach, Ondrej Bojar, Roldano Cattoni, Fahim Dalvi, Nadir Durrani, Marcello Federico, Christian Federmann, Jiatao Gu, Fei Huang, Kevin Knight, Xutai Ma, Ajay Nagesh, Matteo Negri, Jan Niehues, Juan Pino, Elizabeth Salesky, Xing Shi, Sebastian Stüker, Marco Turchi, Alexander H. Waibel, and Changhan Wang. 2020. FINDINGS OF THE IWSLT 2020 EVALUATION CAMPAIGN. In *Proceedings of the 17th International Conference on Spoken Language Translation, IWSLT 2020, Online, July 9 - 10, 2020*, pages 1–34. Association for Computational Linguistics.

Jimmy Lei Ba, Jamie Ryan Kiros, and Geoffrey E Hinton. 2016. Layer normalization. *arXiv preprint arXiv:1607.06450*.

Alexei Baevski, Yuhao Zhou, Abdelrahman Mohamed, and Michael Auli. 2020. wav2vec 2.0: A framework for self-supervised learning of speech representations. In *Advances in Neural Information Processing Systems*, volume 33, pages 12449–12460. Curran Associates, Inc.

Parnia Bahar, Albert Zeyer, Ralf Schlüter, and Hermann Ney. 2019. On Using SpecAugment for End-to-End Speech Translation. In *Proceedings of the 16th International Workshop on Spoken Language Translation*, Hong Kong. Publisher: Zenodo.

Sameer Bansal, Herman Kamper, Karen Livescu, Adam Lopez, and Sharon Goldwater. 2019. Pre-training on high-resource speech recognition improves low-resource speech-to-text translation. In *Proceedings of the 2019 Conference of the North American Chapter of the Association for Computational Linguistics: Human Language Technologies*, pages 58–68, Minneapolis, Minnesota. Association for Computational Linguistics.

Ankur Bapna and Orhan Firat. 2019. Simple, scalable adaptation for neural machine translation. In *Proceedings of the 2019 Conference on Empirical Methods in Natural Language Processing and the 9th International Joint Conference on Natural Language Processing (EMNLP-IJCNLP)*, pages 1538–1548, Hong Kong, China. Association for Computational Linguistics.

Alexandre Berard, Laurent Besacier, Ali Can Kocabiyikoglu, and Olivier Pietquin. 2018. End-to-End Automatic Speech Translation of Audiobooks. In *2018 IEEE International Conference on Acoustics, Speech and Signal Processing (ICASSP)*, pages 6224–6228, Calgary, AB. IEEE.

M. Cettolo, J. Niehues, S. Stüker, L. Bentivogli, R. Cattoni, and Marcello Federico. 2015. The iwslt 2015 evaluation campaign. In *Proceedings of the 12th International Workshop on Spoken Language Translation*.

Jacob Devlin, Ming-Wei Chang, Kenton Lee, and Kristina Toutanova. 2019. BERT: Pre-training of deep bidirectional transformers for language understanding. In *Proceedings of the 2019 Conference of the North American Chapter of the Association for Computational Linguistics: Human Language Technologies, Volume 1 (Long and Short Papers)*, pages 4171–4186, Minneapolis, Minnesota. Association for Computational Linguistics.

Mattia A. Di Gangi, Roldano Cattoni, Luisa Bentivogli, Matteo Negri, and Marco Turchi. 2019a. MuST-C: a Multilingual Speech Translation Corpus. In *Proceedings of the 2019 Conference of the North American Chapter of the Association for Computational Linguistics: Human Language Technologies, Volume 1 (Long and Short Papers)*, pages 2012–2017, Minneapolis, Minnesota. Association for Computational Linguistics.

Mattia A. Di Gangi, Matteo Negri, Viet Nhat Nguyen, Amirhossein Tebbifakhr, and Marco Turchi. 2019b. Data Augmentation for End-to-End Speech Translation: FBK@IWSLT '19. In *Proceedings of the 16th International Workshop on Spoken Language Translation*, Hong Kong. Publisher: Zenodo.

Mattia A. Di Gangi, Matteo Negri, Viet Nhat Nguyen, Amirhossein Tebbifakhr, and Marco Turchi. 2019c. Data augmentation for end-to-end speech translation: Fbk@iwslt '19. In *Proceedings of the 16th International Workshop on Spoken Language Translation*. Zenodo.

Mattia A. Di Gangi, Matteo Negri, and Marco Turchi. 2019d. Adapting Transformer to End-to-End Spoken Language Translation. In *Interspeech 2019*, pages 1133–1137. ISCA.

Carlos Escolano, Marta R Costa-jussà, José AR Fonollosa, and Carlos Segura. 2020. Enabling zero-shot multilingual spoken language translation with language-specific encoders and decoders. *arXiv preprint arXiv:2011.01097*.

Marco Gaido, Mattia A. Di Gangi, Matteo Negri, and Marco Turchi. 2020. End-to-end speech-translation with knowledge distillation: FBK@IWSLT2020. In *Proceedings of the 17th International Conference on Spoken Language Translation*, pages 80–88, Online. Association for Computational Linguistics.

Javier Iranzo-Sánchez, Joan Albert Silvestre-Cerdà, Javier Jorge, Nahuel Roselló, Adrià Giménez, Albert Sanchis, Jorge Civera, and Alfons Juan. 2020. Europarl-st: A multilingual corpus for speech translation of parliamentary debates.

J. Kahn, M. Rivière, W. Zheng, E. Kharitonov, Q. Xu, P. E. Mazaré, J. Karadayi, V. Liptchinsky, R. Collobert, C. Fuegen, T. Likhomanenko, G. Synnaeve, A. Joulin, A. Mohamed, and E. Dupoux. 2020. Libri-light: A benchmark for asr with limited or no supervision. In *ICASSP 2020 - 2020 IEEE International Conference on Acoustics, Speech and Signal Processing (ICASSP)*, pages 7669–7673. `https://github.com/facebookresearch/libri-light`.

Eugene Kharitonov, Morgane Rivière, Gabriel Synnaeve, Lior Wolf, Pierre-Emmanuel Mazaré, Matthijs Douze, and Emmanuel Dupoux. 2020. Data augmenting contrastive learning of speech representations in the time domain. *arXiv preprint arXiv:2007.00991*.

Diederik P. Kingma and Jimmy Ba. 2017. Adam: A method for stochastic optimization.

Nikhil Kumar Lakumarapu, Beomseok Lee, Sathish Reddy Indurthi, Hou Jeung Han, Mohd Abbas Zaidi, and Sangha Kim. 2020. End-to-end offline speech translation system for IWSLT 2020 using modality agnostic meta-learning. In *Proceedings of the 17th International Conference on Spoken Language Translation*, pages 73–79, Online. Association for Computational Linguistics.

Mike Lewis, Yinhan Liu, Naman Goyal, Marjan Ghazvininejad, Abdelrahman Mohamed, Omer Levy, Veselin Stoyanov, and Luke Zettlemoyer. 2020. BART: Denoising sequence-to-sequence pre-training for natural language generation, translation, and comprehension. In *Proceedings of the 58th Annual Meeting of the Association for Computational Linguistics*, pages 7871–7880, Online. Association for Computational Linguistics.

Xian Li, Changhan Wang, Yun Tang, Chau Tran, Yuqing Tang, Juan Pino, Alexei Baevski, Alexis Conneau, and Michael Auli. 2021. Multilingual speech translation with efficient finetuning of pretrained models.

Yinhan Liu, Jiatao Gu, Naman Goyal, Xian Li, Sergey Edunov, Marjan Ghazvininejad, Mike Lewis, and Luke Zettlemoyer. 2020a. Multilingual denoising pre-training for neural machine translation. *Transactions of the Association for Computational Linguistics*, 8:726–742.

Yinhan Liu, Jiatao Gu, Naman Goyal, Xian Li, Sergey Edunov, Marjan Ghazvininejad, Mike Lewis, and Luke Zettlemoyer. 2020b. Multilingual denoising pre-training for neural machine translation.

Sylvain Meignier and Teva Merlin. 2010. Lium spkdiarization: an open source toolkit for diarization. In *CMU SPUD Workshop*.

J. Niehues, R. Cattoni, S. Stüker, M. Negri, M. Turchi, Elizabeth Salesky, Ramon Sanabria, Loïc Barrault, Lucia Specia, and Marcello Federico. 2019. The iwslt 2019 evaluation campaign. In *Proceedings of the 16th International Workshop on Spoken Language Translation*.

Vassil Panayotov, Guoguo Chen, Daniel Povey, and Sanjeev Khudanpur. 2015. Librispeech: An asr corpus based on public domain audio books. In *2015 IEEE International Conference on Acoustics, Speech and Signal Processing (ICASSP)*, pages 5206–5210.

Daniel S. Park, William Chan, Yu Zhang, Chung-Cheng Chiu, Barret Zoph, Ekin D. Cubuk, and Quoc V. Le. 2019. SpecAugment: A Simple Data Augmentation Method for Automatic Speech Recognition. In *Interspeech 2019*, pages 2613–2617. ISCA.

Juan Pino, Liezl Puzon, Jiatao Gu, Xutai Ma, Arya D. McCarthy, and Deepak Gopinath. 2019. Harnessing Indirect Training Data for End-to-End Automatic Speech Translation: Tricks of the Trade. In *Proceedings of the 16th International Workshop on Spoken Language Translation*, Hong Kong. Publisher: Zenodo.

Matt Post. 2018. A call for clarity in reporting BLEU scores. In *Proceedings of the Third Conference on Machine Translation: Research Papers*, pages 186–191, Brussels, Belgium. Association for Computational Linguistics.

Tomasz Potapczyk and Pawel Przybysz. 2020. SRPOL's system for the IWSLT 2020 end-to-end speech translation task. In *Proceedings of the 17th International Conference on Spoken Language Translation*, pages 89–94, Online. Association for Computational Linguistics.

Tomasz Potapczyk, Pawel Przybysz, Marcin Chochowski, and Artur Szumac. 2019. Samsung's system for the iwslt 2019 end-to-end speech translation task. In *Proceedings of the 16th International Workshop on Spoken Language Translation*. Zenodo.

Yuqing Tang, Chau Tran, Xian Li, Peng-Jen Chen, Naman Goyal, Vishrav Chaudhary, Jiatao Gu, and Angela Fan. 2020. Multilingual translation with extensible multilingual pretraining and finetuning. *arXiv preprint arXiv:2008.00401*.

Ashish Vaswani, Noam Shazeer, Niki Parmar, Jakob Uszkoreit, Llion Jones, Aidan N Gomez, Ł ukasz Kaiser, and Illia Polosukhin. 2017. Attention is all you need. In *Advances in Neural Information Processing Systems*, volume 30. Curran Associates, Inc.

Changhan Wang, Yun Tang, Xutai Ma, Anne Wu, Dmytro Okhonko, and Juan Pino. 2020a. Fairseq S2T: Fast speech-to-text modeling with fairseq. In *Proceedings of the 1st Conference of the Asia-Pacific Chapter of the Association for Computational Linguistics and the 10th International Joint Conference on Natural Language Processing: System Demonstrations*, pages 33–39, Suzhou, China. Association for Computational Linguistics.

Changhan Wang, Anne Wu, and Juan Pino. 2020b. Covost 2: A massively multilingual speech-to-text translation corpus.

Ron J. Weiss, Jan Chorowski, Navdeep Jaitly, Yonghui Wu, and Zhifeng Chen. 2017. Sequence-to-Sequence Models Can Directly Translate Foreign Speech. In *Interspeech 2017*, pages 2625–2629. ISCA.

Thomas Wolf, Lysandre Debut, Victor Sanh, Julien Chaumond, Clement Delangue, Anthony Moi, Pierric Cistac, Tim Rault, Remi Louf, Morgan Funtowicz, Joe Davison, Sam Shleifer, Patrick von Platen, Clara Ma, Yacine Jernite, Julien Plu, Canwen Xu, Teven Le Scao, Sylvain Gugger, Mariama Drame, Quentin Lhoest, and Alexander Rush. 2020. Transformers: State-of-the-art natural language processing. In *Proceedings of the 2020 Conference on Empirical Methods in Natural Language Processing: System Demonstrations*, pages 38–45, Online. Association for Computational Linguistics.

Qiantong Xu, Alexei Baevski, Tatiana Likhomanenko, Paden Tomasello, Alexis Conneau, Ronan Collobert, Gabriel Synnaeve, and Michael Auli. 2020. Self-training and pre-training are complementary for speech recognition. *arXiv preprint arXiv:2010.11430*.

VUS at IWSLT 2021: A Finetuned Pipeline for Offline Speech Translation

Yong Rae Jo
Voithru Inc.

Young Ki Moon
Voithru Inc.

Minji Jung
Voithru Inc.

Jungyoon Choi
Voithru Inc.

Jihyung Moon
Upstage

Won Ik Cho
Seoul National University

{yongrae.jo, minji.jung, jungyoon.choi}@voithru.com
ykmoon0814@gmail.com, jihyung.moon@upstage.ai
tsatsuki@snu.ac.kr

Abstract

In this technical report, we describe the *fine-tuned*[1] ASR-MT pipeline used for the IWSLT shared task. We remove less useful speech samples by checking WER with an ASR model, and further train a wav2vec and Transformers-based ASR module based on the filtered data. In addition, we cleanse the errata that can interfere with the machine translation process and use it for Transformer-based MT module training. Finally, in the actual inference phase, we use a sentence boundary detection model trained with constrained data to properly merge fragment ASR outputs into full sentences. The merged sentences are post-processed using part of speech. The final result is yielded by the trained MT module. The performance using the dev set displays BLEU 20.37, and this model records the performance of BLEU 20.9 with the test set.

1 Introduction

Offline speech translation is a task that infers the text of a target language by using speech as input. A pipeline system is used as a representative method, which converts source speech into the source text via automatic speech recognition and machine translates it. Recently, many speech corpora have been disclosed, and studies are being conducted on an end-to-end method, namely directly decoding speech input into the text of a target language (Bérard et al., 2016, 2018).

In this IWSLT shared offline task, we implement an English-German speech translation system in a pipeline format. The advantage of pipeline architecture is that it can explain whether the given speech translation is challenging in view of the acoustic domain or the translation perspective, considering the whole process of converting source speech to the target text. This makes it easier for us to discern difficult or erroneous parts in speech and text processing.

In general, a limitation of a pipeline system compared to an end-to-end system is that the quality of the final result is largely influenced by the intermediate text representation, which is usually obtained in an explicit format (Liu et al., 2020). Therefore, we primarily remove training samples that can lower the ASR performance, following the method used in Potapczyk and Przybysz (2020). Thereafter, based on the trained ASR module, the output of test speech samples is transformed into the text and fed to the machine translation system to produce a final output. In this process, we conduct post-processing to obtain an accurate sentence-level output, such as setting the sentence boundary between the fragment texts and re-aggregating some wrongly merged sentences.

The performance is checked mainly with BLEU score (Papineni et al., 2002). Through the system construction, we obtained a BLEU score of 20.9 in en-de speech translation. In detail, the performance of the ASR module reaches WER 28.3% based on 2015 test set, and the MT module records a BLEU score of 32.2 based on the WMT dataset (Barrault et al., 2020). In addition, we have observed that various pre- and post-processings lead to meaningful performance gains.

In this paper, we first skim the related works on speech translation, automatic speech recognition, and machine translation, focusing on the publicly available datasets. Then we describe how we obtained the ASR and MT module used for the campaign. Next, we demonstrate how we finally reach the translation for the dev and test set, along with some pre- and post-processing techniques. The results are provided with the analysis.

[1] We use 'fine-tuned' to describe that our approach is not fully end-to-end but incorporates a well-organized set of strategies to reach better performance. It does not denote the wav2vec-transformer ASR module either.

Proceedings of the 18th International Conference on Spoken Language Translation, pages 120–124
Bangkok, Thailand (Online), August 5–6, 2021. ©2021 Association for Computational Linguistics

2 Related Work

Various datasets exist for speech translation using English as the source language, being utilized in the training and evaluation in a wide range of studies. The representative one is MuST-C (Di Gangi et al., 2019), which provides English speech of TED talks, its transcript, and the translation to other Indo-European languages, including German, where we exploit en-de in this study. In addition, CoVoST enables multilingual speech translation based on Common Voice (CV) data (Wang et al., 2020), of which the Wikipedia articles are the source text. Europarl-ST (Koehn, 2005) also provides various translations, for the debates in European Parliament.

Data used for speech translation can also be used for automatic speech recognition and machine translation, but there are also corpora built for ASR and MT only, on a large scale. Librispeech (Panayotov et al., 2015), which is used for evaluation of ASR models, is the most famous example, and TedLium is also the case[2]. They consist of the speech of the source language (English) and Latin alphabet-based transcription. In contrast, since only text data is used in MT, the scale is much larger. Typically used sources are WMT datasets (Bojar et al., 2016, 2018; Barrault et al., 2020) and Open subtitles. [3] All of the above datasets can be usefully used in speech translation, so they have been actively utilized in the previous IWSLT campaigns (Niehues et al.).

3 Model

We chose the cascading scheme to leverage the high performance of ASR and MT modules. Thus, we exploit a large variety of corpora mentioned above to train each module.

3.1 Automatic Speech Recognition

We train the ASR module using Librispeech and MuST-C. The pretrained wav2vec 2.0 base model was used for embedding (Baevski et al., 2020), and the training was conducted with a Transformer (Vaswani et al., 2017) decoder part augmented on the output layer of the wav2vec module, with character as vocab. In this process, we performed two preprocessing for the source corpus.

- **Script normalization:** In the sentences containing laughter and applause tag, the expressions that might deter ASR performance were removed.

- **Filtering out erroneous scripts:** Following SRPOL's approach (Potapczyk and Przybysz, 2020), we performed the filtering of audio files based on bad WER. In this process, sentences showing WER below 75% were removed, assuming as if there were some flaws in the acoustic level or some errors in the script.

Using the cleansed corpus created through the above process, we conducted the training for 80,000 steps using 8 RTX 3090 devices. The optimization was done with adam, learning rate 1e-5, and dropout 0.1. As a result of utilizing the evaluation set 2015 test set, we obtained an ASR module that displays the WER of 28.3%.

3.2 Machine Translation

We trained the MT module using the WMT 20 en-de news task dataset and Transformer architecture.

For English, the script was normalized, and for German, the cased text was used. Vocabulary was constructed in consideration of both English and German, using subword tokenization (Sennrich et al., 2016). Some preprocessings were performed as follows:

- **Language identification:** We conduct language identification to remove the instances where the source and the target language do not match the language of interest (en, de). This refers to Lui and Baldwin (2011, 2012); Heafield et al. (2015).

- **Filter by length:** We filter out the sentences where the length of the source and the target sentence displays more than 50% of difference.

- **Written-to-spoken text conversion:** We first transform the source text into the format of speech transcript, namely lowercasing the text and removing all punctuation marks. Then we expand common abbreviations, especially for measurement units, by converting numbers, dates, and other entities expressed with digits into their spoken form. The overall scheme follows Bahar et al. (2020).

[2] `https://www.openslr.org/7/`
[3] `https://www.opensubtitles.org/`

Using the cleansed WMT script, we conducted the training for 300,000 steps, using 8 RTX 3090 devices. The optimization was done with adam, with FFN decoder 8,192 and dropout 0.1. With WMT20 dev set, we obtained an MT module that shows the BLEU of 32.3.

4 Inference

We infer the final output with the speech instances of the dev set using the trained ASR and MT modules. After the inference, we submit the inference of the test set using the model that yields the best results with the dev set.

In the inference process of the dev and test set, a proper sentence split is additionally required. For the dev and test set, we separated the utterances from silence using the given segmentation information. The segmented audio files were transcribed with the ASR module.

In the post-processing of the transcribed speech, we use the following strategies.

- **DeepSegment**: We merge the output of the ASR module using publicly available DeepSegment recipe[4] based on bidirectional long short term memory and conditional random field (BiLSTM-CRF) (Huang et al., 2015). At this time, the BiLSTM-CRF model is trained using 1 RTX TITAN. Here, no information other than the training corpus is used for the training, and the usage of NLTK in featurization does not violate the constrained condition.

- **Sentence concatenation**: We compensate for probable segmentation errors by using part-of-speech (POS) information. We selected POS tags that are rarely placed in sentence-first and sentence-final from 46 tags of NLTK POS tagger (Loper and Bird, 2002). In detail, we set two cases of `PROHIBIT_AS_FIRST` and `PROHIBIT_AS_FINAL` as follows:

  - `PROHIBIT_AS_FIRST`: ['MD', 'TO', 'RP', 'VB', 'VBN', 'VBD']

  - `PROHIBIT_AS_FINAL`: ['CC', 'DT', 'EX', 'MD', 'PDT', 'POS', 'WDT', 'WP', 'WP$', 'WRB']

  Whenever the segmented sentence regards either case, it is concatenated with the previous sentence or the following sentence. `PROHIBIT_AS_FINAL` was primarily applied.

The list of sentences obtained from the above process is translated by the trained MT module.

5 Experiment

Overall, our speech translation pipeline has the following procedure.

1. Voice segmentation
2. Automatic speech recognition
3. Sentence concatenation
4. Machine translation
5. Checking the performance

Voice segmentation was done separately in the whole pipeline. ASR was performed with 1 RTX 3090. DeepSegment and sentence concatenation were performed with 1 RTX TITAN. MT was performed with 1 RTX 3090. The performance of each trial was checked with the BLEU score.

We achieved the performance of BLEU 20.37 with the official dev set. We finally obtained the performance of BLEU 20.9 with the test set using given segmentation.

6 Conclusion

In this paper, we report the VUS ASR-MT pipeline system for en-de speech translation. The featured engineering schemes are wav2vec-based ASR module, Transformer-based MT, speech segmentation and post-processing, and various cleansing for the enhancement. We obtained similar performance with both dev and test set, the BLEU score of 20.37 and 20.9 respectively. Our model is explainable and partially improvable, given the transparent description of our pipeline system.

Acknowledgments

We thank anonymous reviewers for helpful feedbacks.

References

Alexei Baevski, Henry Zhou, Abdelrahman Mohamed, and Michael Auli. 2020. wav2vec 2.0: A framework for self-supervised learning of speech representations. *arXiv preprint arXiv:2006.11477*.

[4]`https://github.com/notAI-tech/deepsegment`

Parnia Bahar, Patrick Wilken, Tamer Alkhouli, Andreas Guta, Pavel Golik, Evgeny Matusov, and Christian Herold. 2020. Start-before-end and end-to-end: Neural speech translation by AppTek and RWTH Aachen University. In *Proceedings of the 17th International Conference on Spoken Language Translation*, pages 44–54, Online. Association for Computational Linguistics.

Loïc Barrault, Magdalena Biesialska, Ondřej Bojar, Marta R. Costa-jussà, Christian Federmann, Yvette Graham, Roman Grundkiewicz, Barry Haddow, Matthias Huck, Eric Joanis, Tom Kocmi, Philipp Koehn, Chi-kiu Lo, Nikola Ljubešić, Christof Monz, Makoto Morishita, Masaaki Nagata, Toshiaki Nakazawa, Santanu Pal, Matt Post, and Marcos Zampieri. 2020. Findings of the 2020 conference on machine translation (WMT20). In *Proceedings of the Fifth Conference on Machine Translation*, pages 1–55, Online. Association for Computational Linguistics.

Alexandre Bérard, Laurent Besacier, Ali Can Kocabiyikoglu, and Olivier Pietquin. 2018. End-to-end automatic speech translation of audiobooks. In *2018 IEEE International Conference on Acoustics, Speech and Signal Processing (ICASSP)*, pages 6224–6228. IEEE.

Alexandre Bérard, Olivier Pietquin, Christophe Servan, and Laurent Besacier. 2016. Listen and translate: A proof of concept for end-to-end speech-to-text translation. *arXiv preprint arXiv:1612.01744*.

Ondřej Bojar, Rajen Chatterjee, Christian Federmann, Yvette Graham, Barry Haddow, Matthias Huck, Antonio Jimeno Yepes, Philipp Koehn, Varvara Logacheva, Christof Monz, Matteo Negri, Aurélie Névéol, Mariana Neves, Martin Popel, Matt Post, Raphael Rubino, Carolina Scarton, Lucia Specia, Marco Turchi, Karin Verspoor, and Marcos Zampieri. 2016. Findings of the 2016 conference on machine translation. In *Proceedings of the First Conference on Machine Translation: Volume 2, Shared Task Papers*, pages 131–198, Berlin, Germany. Association for Computational Linguistics.

Ondřej Bojar, Christian Federmann, Mark Fishel, Yvette Graham, Barry Haddow, Philipp Koehn, and Christof Monz. 2018. Findings of the 2018 conference on machine translation (WMT18). In *Proceedings of the Third Conference on Machine Translation: Shared Task Papers*, pages 272–303, Belgium, Brussels. Association for Computational Linguistics.

Mattia A. Di Gangi, Roldano Cattoni, Luisa Bentivogli, Matteo Negri, and Marco Turchi. 2019. MuST-C: a Multilingual Speech Translation Corpus. In *Proceedings of the 2019 Conference of the North American Chapter of the Association for Computational Linguistics: Human Language Technologies, Volume 1 (Long and Short Papers)*, pages 2012–2017, Minneapolis, Minnesota. Association for Computational Linguistics.

Kenneth Heafield, Rohan Kshirsagar, and Santiago Barona. 2015. Language identification and modeling in specialized hardware. In *Proceedings of the 53rd Annual Meeting of the Association for Computational Linguistics and the 7th International Joint Conference on Natural Language Processing (Volume 2: Short Papers)*, pages 384–389, Beijing, China. Association for Computational Linguistics.

Zhiheng Huang, Wei Xu, and Kai Yu. 2015. Bidirectional lstm-crf models for sequence tagging. *arXiv preprint arXiv:1508.01991*.

Philipp Koehn. 2005. Europarl: A Parallel Corpus for Statistical Machine Translation. In *Conference Proceedings: the tenth Machine Translation Summit*, pages 79–86, Phuket, Thailand. AAMT, AAMT.

Yuchen Liu, Jiajun Zhang, Hao Xiong, Long Zhou, Zhongjun He, Hua Wu, Haifeng Wang, and Chengqing Zong. 2020. Synchronous speech recognition and speech-to-text translation with interactive decoding. In *Proceedings of the AAAI Conference on Artificial Intelligence*, volume 34, pages 8417–8424.

Edward Loper and Steven Bird. 2002. NLTK: the natural language toolkit. In *Proceedings of the ACL-02 Workshop on Effective tools and methodologies for teaching natural language processing and computational linguistics-Volume 1*, pages 63–70.

Marco Lui and Timothy Baldwin. 2011. Cross-domain feature selection for language identification. In *Proceedings of 5th International Joint Conference on Natural Language Processing*, pages 553–561, Chiang Mai, Thailand. Asian Federation of Natural Language Processing.

Marco Lui and Timothy Baldwin. 2012. langid.py: An off-the-shelf language identification tool. In *Proceedings of the ACL 2012 System Demonstrations*, pages 25–30, Jeju Island, Korea. Association for Computational Linguistics.

Jan Niehues, Roldano Cattoni, Sebastian Stuker, Mauro Cettolo, Marco Turchi, and Marcello Federico. The iwslt 2018 evaluation campaign. In *IWSLT 2018*.

Vassil Panayotov, Guoguo Chen, Daniel Povey, and Sanjeev Khudanpur. 2015. Librispeech: an asr corpus based on public domain audio books. In *2015 IEEE international conference on acoustics, speech and signal processing (ICASSP)*, pages 5206–5210. IEEE.

Kishore Papineni, Salim Roukos, Todd Ward, and Wei-Jing Zhu. 2002. BLEU: a method for automatic evaluation of machine translation. In *Proceedings of the 40th Annual Meeting of the Association for Computational Linguistics*, pages 311–318, Philadelphia, Pennsylvania, USA. Association for Computational Linguistics.

Tomasz Potapczyk and Pawel Przybysz. 2020. SR-POL's system for the IWSLT 2020 end-to-end speech translation task. In *Proceedings of the 17th International Conference on Spoken Language Translation*, pages 89–94, Online. Association for Computational Linguistics.

Rico Sennrich, Barry Haddow, and Alexandra Birch. 2016. Neural machine translation of rare words with subword units. In *Proceedings of the 54th Annual Meeting of the Association for Computational Linguistics (Volume 1: Long Papers)*, pages 1715–1725, Berlin, Germany. Association for Computational Linguistics.

Ashish Vaswani, Noam Shazeer, Niki Parmar, Jakob Uszkoreit, Llion Jones, Aidan N Gomez, Łukasz Kaiser, and Illia Polosukhin. 2017. Attention is all you need. In *Proceedings of the 31st International Conference on Neural Information Processing Systems*, pages 6000–6010.

Changhan Wang, Juan Pino, Anne Wu, and Jiatao Gu. 2020. CoVoST: A diverse multilingual speech-to-text translation corpus. In *Proceedings of the 12th Language Resources and Evaluation Conference*, pages 4197–4203, Marseille, France. European Language Resources Association.

KIT's IWSLT 2021 Offline Speech Translation System

Tuan-Nam Nguyen, Thai-Son Nguyen, Christian Huber, Maximilian Awiszus,
Ngoc-Quan Pham, Thanh-Le Ha, Felix Schneider, Sebastian Stüker, Alexander Waibel
Karlsruhe Institute of Technology
firstname.lastname@kit.edu

Abstract

This paper describes KIT'submission to the IWSLT 2021 Offline Speech Translation Task. We describe a system in both cascaded condition and end-to-end condition. In the cascaded condition, we investigated different end-to-end architectures for the speech recognition module. For the text segmentation module, we trained a small transformer-based model on high-quality monolingual data. For the translation module, our last year's neural machine translation model was reused. In the end-to-end condition, we improved our Speech Relative Transformer architecture to reach or even surpass the result of the cascade system.

1 Introduction

As in previous years, the cascade system's pipeline is constituted by an ASR module, a text segmentation module and a machine translation module. In this year's evaluation campaign, we investigated only sequence-to-sequence ASR models with three architectures. The segmentation module is basically a monolingual system which translates a disfluent, broken, uncased text (i.e. ASR outputs) into a more fluent, written-style text with punctuations in order to match the data conditions of the translation system. The machine translation module's architecture is the same as the previous year's. For the end-to-end system, we improved from our last year's Speech Relative Transformer architecture (Pham et al., 2020a). As a result, the end-to-end system can produce better results on certain test sets and approach the performance on some others compared to the cascade system this year, while the end-to-end system was the dominant approach last year.

The rest of the paper is organized as followed. Section 2 describes the data set used to train and test the system. It is then followed by Section 3 providing the description and experimental results of both the cascade and the end-to-end system. In the end, we conclude the paper with Section 4.

2 Data

Speech Corpora. For training and evaluation of our ASR models, we used Mozilla Common Voice v6.1 (Ardila et al., 2019), Europarl (Koehn, 2005), How2 (Sanabria et al., 2018), Librispeech (Panayotov et al., 2015), MuST-C v1 (Di Gangi et al., 2019), MuST-C v2 (Cattoni et al., 2021) and Tedlium v3 (Hernandez et al., 2018) dataset. The data split is presented in the following table 1.

Table 1: Summary of the English data-sets used for speech recognition

Corpus	Utterances	Speech data [h]
A: Training Data		
Mozilla Common Voice	1225k	1667
Europarl	33k	85
How2	217k	356
Librispeech	281k	963
MuST-C v1	230k	407
MuST-C v2	251k	482
Tedlium	268k	482
B: Test Data		
Tedlium	1155	2.6
Librispeech	2620	5.4

Text Corpora. We collected the text parallel training data as presented in Table 2.

3 Offline Speech Translation

We address the offline speech translation task by two main approaches, namely cascade and end-to-end. In the cascade condition, the ASR module (Section 3.1) receives audio inputs and generates raw transcripts, which will then pass through a Segmentation module (Section 3.2) to formulate well normalized inputs to our Machine Translation module (Section 3.3). The MT outputs are the final outputs of the cascade system. On the other hand,

Proceedings of the 18th International Conference on Spoken Language Translation, pages 125–130
Bangkok, Thailand (Online), August 5–6, 2021.

Table 2: Text Training Data

Dataset	Sentences
TED Talks (TED)	220K
Europarl (EPPS)	2.2MK
CommonCrawl	2.1M
Rapid	1.21M
ParaCrawl	25.1M
OpenSubtitles	12.6M
WikiTitle	423K
Back-translated News	26M

the end-to-end architecture is trained to directly translate English audio inputs into German text outputs (Section 3.4).

3.1 Speech Recognition

Data preparation and Segmentation tool After collecting all audios from all data sets mentioned in Section 2, we calculated 40 features of Mel-filterbank coefficients for ASR training. To generate labels for the sequence-to-sequence ASR models, we used the Sentence-Piece toolkit (Kudo and Richardson, 2018) to train 4000 different byte-pair-encoding (BPE). The WerRTCVAD toolkit (Wiseman, 2016) was used to segment the audio in the testing phase.

Model As in previous years (Pham et al., 2019a, 2020b), we used only sequence-to-sequence ASR models, which are based on three different network architectures: The long short-term memory (LSTM), the Transformer and the Conformer. LSTM-based models (Nguyen et al., 2020) consist of 6 bidirectional layers for the encoder and 2 unidirectional layers for the decoder, both encoder and decoder layers have 1536 units. The Transformer-based models presented in (Pham et al., 2019b) have 24 layers for the encoder and 8 layers for the decoder. The Conformer-based models (Gulati et al., 2020) comprise 16 layers for the encoder and 6 layers for the decoder. In both the Transformer-based and the Conformer-based models, the size of each layer is 512 and the size of the hidden state in the feed-forward sublayer is 2048. The speech data augmentation technique was used to reduce overfitting as described in (Nguyen et al., 2020). In order to train a deep network effectively, we also applied Stochastic Layers (Pham et al., 2019b) with a dropping layer rate of 0.5 on both Transformer-based and Conformer-based models.

3.2 Text Segmentation

The text segmentation in the cascaded pipeline serves as a normalization on the ASR output, which usually lacks punctuation marks, proper sentence boundaries and reliable casing. On the other hand, the machine translation system is often trained on well-written, high-quality bilingual data. Following the idea from (Sperber et al., 2018a), we build the segmentation as a monolingual translation system, which translates from lower-cased, without-punctuation texts into texts with case information and punctuation, prior to the machine translation module.

The monolingual translation for text segmentation is implemented using our neural speech translation framework `NMTGMinor`[1] (Pham et al., 2020a). It is a small transformer architecture, consisting of a 4-layer encoder and 4-layer decoder, in which each layer' size is 512, while the inner size of feed-forward network inside each layer is 2048. The encoder and decode are self-attention blocks, which have 4 parallel attention heads. The training data for that are the English part extracted from available multilingual corpora: EPPS, NC, Global Voices and TED talks. We trained the model for 10 epochs, then we fine-tuned it on the TED corpus for 30 epochs more with stronger drop-out rate. Furthermore, to simulate possible errors in the ASR outputs, a similar model is trained on artificial noisy data and the final model is the ensemble of the two models.

The trained model is then utilized to translate the ASR outputs in a shifting window manner and the decisions are drawn by a simple voting mechanism. For more details, please refer to (Sperber et al., 2018a).

3.3 Machine Translation

For the machine translation module, we re-use the English→German machine translation model from our last year' submission to IWSLT (Pham et al., 2020b). More than 40 millions sentence pairs being extracted from TED, EPPS, NC, CommonCrawl, ParaCrawl, Rapid and OpenSubtitles corpora were used for training the model. In addition, 26 millions sentence pairs are generated from the back-translation technique by a German→English translation system. A large transformer architecture was trained with Relative Attention. We adapted to the in-domain by fine-tuning on TED talk data with

[1] `https://github.com/quanpn90/NMTGMinor`

stricter regularizations. The same adapted model was trained on noised data synthesized from the same TED data. The final model is the ensemble of the two.

3.4 End-to-End Model

Corpora This year, the training data consists of the second version of the MUST-C corpus (Di Gangi et al., 2019), the Europarl corpus (Iranzo-Sánchez et al., 2020), the Speech Translation corpus and the CoVoST-2 (Wang et al., 2020) corpus provided by the organizer. The speech features are generated with the in-house Janus Recognition Toolkit. The ST dataset is handled with an additional filtering step using an English speech recognizer (trained with the its transcripts with the additional Tedlium-3 training data).

Following the success of generating synthetic audio utterances, the transcripts in the Tedlium-3 corpus are translated into German using the cascade built in the previous year's submission (Pham et al., 2020b). In brief, the translation process required us to preserve the audio-text alignment from the original data collection and segmentation process. As a results, we used the Transformer-based punctuation inserting system from IWSLT2018 (Sperber et al., 2018b) to reconstruct the punctuations for the transcripts followed by the translation process that preserves the same segmentation information. Compared to the human translation from the speech translation datasets, this translation is relative noisier and incomplete (due to the segmentations are not necessarily aligned with grammatically correct sentences).

The end result of the filtering and synthetic creation process is the complete translation set, as summarised in Table 3

Table 3: Training data for E2E translation models.

Data	Utterances	Total time
MuST-C	229K	408h
Europarl	32K	60h
Speech Translation	142K	160h
Tedlium-3	268K	415h
CoVoST	288K	424h

During training, the validation data is the Development set of the MuST-C corpus. The reason is that the SLT testsets often do not have the aligned audio and translation, while training end-to-end models often rely on perplexity for early stopping.

Modeling The main architecture is the deep Transformer (Vaswani et al., 2017) with stochastic layers (Pham et al., 2019b). The encoder self attention layer uses Bidirectional relative attention (Pham et al., 2020a) which models the relative distance between one position and other positions in the sequence. This modeling is bidirectional because the distance is distinguished for each direction from the perspective of one particular position. The main models use a "Big" configuration with 16 encoder layers and 6 decoder layers, and they are randomly dropped in training according to the linear schedule presented in the original work, where the top layer has the highest dropout rate $p = 0.5$. The model size of each layer is 1024 and the inner size is 4096. We experimented with different activation functions including GELU (Hendrycks and Gimpel, 2016), SiLU (Elfwing et al., 2018) and the gated variants similar to the gated linear units (Dauphin et al., 2017). Also, each transformer block (encoder and decoder) is equipped with another feed-forward neural network in the beginning (Lu et al., 2019). Our preliminary experiments showed that GeLU and SiLU provided a slightly better performance than ReLU, and our final model is the ensemble of the three configurations that are identical except the activation functions.

First, the encoders are pretrained using the data portions containing English texts to make training SLT stable. With the initialized encoder, the networks can be trained with an aggressive learning rate with 4096 warm-up steps. Label-smoothing and dropout rates are set at 0.1 and 0.3 respectively for all models. Furthermore, all speech inputs are augmented with spectral augmentation (Park et al., 2019; Bahar et al., 2019). All models are trained for 200000 steps, each consists of accumulated 360000 audio frames. Using the model setup like above, we managed to fit a batch size of around 16000 frames to 24 GB of GPU memory.

Speech segmentation As reflected from last year's experiments, audio segmentation plays an important role in the performance of the whole system, and the end-to-end model unfortunately does not have control of segmentation, as it is a prerequisite before training one. During evaluation, we relied on the WerRTCVAD toolkit (Wiseman, 2016) to cut the long audio files into segments of reasonable length, and the tool is also able to rule out silence and events that do not belong to human speech, such as noise and music.

Overall, we improved the submission from last year (Pham et al., 2020b) using stronger models together with a more accurate segmentation tool.

3.5 Experimental Results

3.5.1 Cascade Offline Speech Translation

Speech Recognition. We tested our ASR systems on two datasets, Tedlium and Libri test set. The ensemble of LSTM-based and Conformer-based sequence-to-sequence model provide the best results, which are 2.4 and 3.9 WERs respectively for two test set Table 4.

Table 4: WER on Libri and Tedlium sets

Data	Libri	Tedlium
Conformer-based	3.0	4.8
Transformer-based	3.2	4.9
LSTM-based	**2.6**	**3.9**
Ensemble	**2.4**	3.9

Machine Translation. We do not train any new machine translation module but re-use last year's model, thus, we do not conduct experiments and comparisons with different machine translation systems. We submitted one cascased model with our audio segmentation.

3.5.2 End-to-end Offline Speech Translation

Our models are tested on two different setups. On the one hand, we evaluated the model on the tst-COMMON (2nd version) of the MuST-C corpora. Due to the incompatibility between the models and the audio data that requires resegmentation, we rely on the dev and test sets of MuST-C to evaluate the ability to translate on "ideal" conditions. As mentioned above, our ensemble managed to reach 32.4 BLEU points on this test set[2].

On the other hand, we used the testsets from 2010 to 2015 to measure the progress from last year in the condition requiring audio segmentation. In this particular comparison as shown in Table 5, we showed that using a stronger model together with better voice detection not only improves the SLT results by up to 1.9 BLEU points (in *tst2014*) but also outperforms the strong cascade in 2 different sets: *tst2013* and *tst2014*, in which the difference could be even 1 BLEU point. There is still a performance gap in the last two tests, however, a strong E2E system can now trade blow with a strongly tuned cascade. The deciding factor, in our opinion, is audio segmentation because this is the sole advantage of the cascade which can recover from badly cut segments[3].

Table 5: ST: Translation performance in BLEU↑ on IWSLT testsets (re-segmentation required). Progressive results from this year and last year end-to-end (E2E) and cascades (CD) are provided.

Testset →	CD 2020	E2E 2020	E2E 2021
tst2010	**26.68**	24.27	25.28
tst2013	28.60	28.13	**29.62**
tst2014	25.64	25.46	**27.32**
tst2015	**24.95**	21.82	22.13

4 Conclusion

In this year's evaluation campaign, the end-to-end model proves to be a very promising approach since it can compete or even transcend the best cascade model in offline speech translation task. As a note for future work, we would like to investigate two-stage speech translation models (Sperber et al., 2019) using transformer architectures and compare them with our recent speech translation end-to-end models.

Acknowledgments

The work leading to these results has received funding from the European Union under grant agreement n°825460 and the Federal Ministry of Education and Research (Germany)/DLR Projektträger Bereich Gesundheit under grant agreement n° 01EF1803B.

References

Rosana Ardila, Megan Branson, Kelly Davis, Michael Henretty, Michael Kohler, Josh Meyer, Reuben Morais, Lindsay Saunders, Francis M Tyers, and Gregor Weber. 2019. Common voice: A massively-multilingual speech corpus. *arXiv preprint arXiv:1912.06670.*

Parnia Bahar, Albert Zeyer, Ralf Schlüter, and Hermann Ney. 2019. On using specaugment for end-to-end speech translation. *arXiv preprint arXiv:1911.08876.*

Roldano Cattoni, Mattia Antonino Di Gangi, Luisa Bentivogli, Matteo Negri, and Marco Turchi. 2021.

[2]Unfortunately the comparison to last year tst-COMMON (30.6 is not available due to version mismatch.

[3]Changing the VAD parameters does not affect the performance of the cascade significantly, while the E2E can be badly afffected

Must-c: A multilingual corpus for end-to-end speech translation. *Computer Speech & Language*, 66:101155.

Yann N Dauphin, Angela Fan, Michael Auli, and David Grangier. 2017. Language modeling with gated convolutional networks. In *International conference on machine learning*, pages 933–941. PMLR.

Mattia A. Di Gangi, Roldano Cattoni, Luisa Bentivogli, Matteo Negri, and Marco Turchi. 2019. MuST-C: a Multilingual Speech Translation Corpus. In *Proceedings of the Conference of the North American Chapter of the Association for Computational Linguistics (NAACL)*.

Stefan Elfwing, Eiji Uchibe, and Kenji Doya. 2018. Sigmoid-weighted linear units for neural network function approximation in reinforcement learning. *Neural Networks*, 107:3–11.

Anmol Gulati, James Qin, Chung-Cheng Chiu, Niki Parmar, Yu Zhang, Jiahui Yu, Wei Han, Shibo Wang, Zhengdong Zhang, Yonghui Wu, and Ruoming Pang. 2020. Conformer: Convolution-augmented transformer for speech recognitio. In *Proc. Interspeech 2020*.

Dan Hendrycks and Kevin Gimpel. 2016. Gaussian error linear units (gelus). *arXiv preprint arXiv:1606.08415*.

François Hernandez, Vincent Nguyen, Sahar Ghannay, Natalia Tomashenko, and Yannick Estève. 2018. Ted-lium 3: twice as much data and corpus repartition for experiments on speaker adaptation. In *International Conference on Speech and Computer*, pages 198–208. Springer.

Javier Iranzo-Sánchez, Joan Albert Silvestre-Cerdà, Javier Jorge, Nahuel Roselló, Adrià Giménez, Albert Sanchis, Jorge Civera, and Alfons Juan. 2020. Europarl-st: A multilingual corpus for speech translation of parliamentary debates. In *ICASSP 2020-2020 IEEE International Conference on Acoustics, Speech and Signal Processing (ICASSP)*, pages 8229–8233. IEEE.

Philipp Koehn. 2005. Europarl: A parallel corpus for statistical machine translation. In *MT summit*, volume 5, pages 79–86.

Taku Kudo and John Richardson. 2018. Sentencepiece: A simple and language independent subword tokenizer and detokenizer for neural text processing. In *Proceedings of the 2018 Conference on Empirical Methods in Natural Language Processing: System Demonstrations*, pages 66–71.

Yiping Lu, Zhuohan Li, Di He, Zhiqing Sun, Bin Dong, Tao Qin, Liwei Wang, and Tie-Yan Liu. 2019. Understanding and improving transformer from a multi-particle dynamic system point of view. *arXiv preprint arXiv:1906.02762*.

Thai-Son Nguyen, Sebastian Stueker, Jan Niehues, and Alex Waibel. 2020. Improving sequence-to-sequence speech recognition training with on-the-fly data augmentation. *arXiv preprint arXiv:1910.13296*.

Vassil Panayotov, Guoguo Chen, Daniel Povey, and Sanjeev Khudanpur. 2015. Librispeech: an asr corpus based on public domain audio books. In *2015 IEEE international conference on acoustics, speech and signal processing (ICASSP)*, pages 5206–5210. IEEE.

Daniel S Park, William Chan, Yu Zhang, Chung-Cheng Chiu, Barret Zoph, Ekin D Cubuk, and Quoc V Le. 2019. Specaugment: A simple data augmentation method for automatic speech recognition. *arXiv preprint arXiv:1904.08779*.

Ngoc-Quan Pham, Thanh-Le Ha, Tuan-Nam Nguyen, Thai-Son Nguyen, Elizabeth Salesky, Sebastian Stüker, Jan Niehues, and Alex Waibel. 2020a. Relative Positional Encoding for Speech Recognition and Direct Translation. In *Proc. Interspeech 2020*, pages 31–35.

Ngoc-Quan Pham, Thai-Son Nguyen, Thanh-Le Ha, Juan Hussain, Felix Schneider, Jan Niehues, Sebastian Stüker, and Alexander Waibel. 2019a. The iwslt 2019 kit speech translation system. In *Proceedings of the 16th International Workshop on Spoken Language Translation (IWSLT 2019)*.

Ngoc-Quan Pham, Thai-Son Nguyen, Jan Niehues, Markus Muller, and Alex Waibel. 2019b. Very deep self-attention networks for end-to-end speech recognition. *arXiv preprint arXiv:1904.13377*.

Ngoc-Quan Pham, Felix Schneider, Tuan-Nam Nguyen, Thanh-Le Ha, Thai-Son Nguyen, Maximilian Awiszus, Sebastian Stüker, and Alexander Waibel. 2020b. Kit's iwslt 2020 slt translation system. In *Proceedings of the 17th International Workshop on Spoken Language Translation (IWSLT 2020)*.

Ramon Sanabria, Ozan Caglayan, Shruti Palaskar, Desmond Elliott, Loïc Barrault, Lucia Specia, and Florian Metze. 2018. How2: a large-scale dataset for multimodal language understanding. *arXiv preprint arXiv:1811.00347*.

Matthias Sperber, Graham Neubig, Jan Niehues, and Alex Waibel. 2019. Attention-Passing Models for Robust and Data-Efficient End-to-End Speech Translation. In *Proc. ACL 2019*.

Matthias Sperber, Ngoc-Quan Pham, Thai-Son Nguyen, Jan Niehues, Markus Müller, Thanh-Le Ha, Sebastian Stüker, and Alex Waibel. 2018a. KIT's IWSLT 2018 SLT Translation System. In *15th International Workshop on Spoken Language Translation 2018*. IWSLT.

Matthias Sperber, Ngoc Quan Pham, Thai Son Nguyen, Jan Niehues, Markus Müller, Thanh-Le Ha, Sebastian Stüker, and Alex Waibel. 2018b. KIT's IWSLT 2018 SLT Translation System. In *"Proceedings of the 15th International Workshop on Spoken Language Translation (IWSLT 2018)"*, Brussels, Belgium.

Ashish Vaswani, Noam Shazeer, Niki Parmar, Jakob Uszkoreit, Llion Jones, Aidan N Gomez, Łukasz Kaiser, and Illia Polosukhin. 2017. Attention is all you need. In *Advances in Neural Information Processing Systems*, pages 5998–6008.

Changhan Wang, Anne Wu, and Juan Pino. 2020. Covost 2: A massively multilingual speech-to-text translation corpus.

John Wiseman. 2016. python-webrtcvad. `https://github.com/wiseman/py-webrtcvad`.

FST: the FAIR Speech Translation System for the IWSLT21 Multilingual Shared Task

Yun Tang* **Hongyu Gong*** **Xian Li** **Changhan Wang**
Juan Pino **Holger Schwenk** **Naman Goyal**
Facebook AI Research
{yuntang,hygong,xianl,changhan,juancarabina,schwenk,naman}@fb.com

Abstract

In this paper, we describe our end-to-end multilingual speech translation system submitted to the IWSLT 2021 evaluation campaign on the Multilingual Speech Translation shared task. Our system is built by leveraging transfer learning across modalities, tasks and languages. First, we leverage general-purpose multilingual modules pretrained with large amounts of unlabelled and labelled data. We further enable knowledge transfer from the text task to the speech task by training two tasks jointly. Finally, our multilingual model is finetuned on speech translation task-specific data to achieve the best translation results. Experimental results show our system outperforms the reported systems, including both end-to-end and cascaded based approaches, by a large margin. In some translation directions, our speech translation results evaluated on the public Multilingual TEDx test set are even comparable with the ones from a strong text-to-text translation system, which uses the oracle speech transcripts as input.

1 Introduction

Multilingual speech translation (Inaguma et al., 2019) enables translation from audio to text in multiple language directions with a single model. Similar to multilingual text translation, it is sample efficient as the model supports more languages. Furthermore, multilingual speech models can facilitate positive transfer across languages by learning a common representation space from speech inputs, typically either raw audio or filterbank features.

In this paper, we provide a description of our submission to the first multilingual speech translation task at IWSLT 2021. The task evaluates speech translations from Spanish (es), French (fr), Portuguese (pt) and Italian (it) into English (en) and Spanish (es). Among them, three translation directions (it-en, it-es and pt-es) are considered zero-shot with respect to the constrained track. In addition, participants are encouraged to submit transcriptions for the relevant languages.

Our team, FAIR Speech Translation (FST), participated in the unconstrained track, where we submitted one primary system and four contrastive systems. We are interested in exploring the effectiveness of building a general-purpose multilingual multi-modality model. We leverage large amounts of data, including unlabelled and labelled data from different modalities, to alleviate the data scarcity issue. We build the multilingual model to perform speech translation and speech recognition tasks for all evaluation directions. Our model leverages self-supervised pretraining on both the encoder and the decoder. The model is further improved by knowledge transferring from the text-to-text translation task to the speech-to-text translation task under the multitask learning framework. Finally, we finetune the model on parallel speech translation corpora as well as weakly aligned speech translation data through data mining to achieve the best result.

In section 2, we described data sources and our method for speech translation data mining. Models and training methods are then described in section 3. Finally, we present the results for the primary and contrastive systems in section 4.

2 Data

Provided by the IWSLT 2021 shared task, the multilingual TEDx dataset collected from TED talks provides speech translations in 13 directions (Salesky et al., 2021). We focus on the seven competition directions in the shared task: es-en, fr-en, pt-en, it-en, fr-es, pt-es and it-es.

*Yun Tang and Hongyu Gong have equal contribution to this work.

Proceedings of the 18th International Conference on Spoken Language Translation, pages 131–137
Bangkok, Thailand (Online), August 5–6, 2021. ©2021 Association for Computational Linguistics

Table 1: Audio Length in Hours of TEDx, CoVoST, EuroParl and Mined Data

	es-en	fr-en	it-en	pt-en	fr-es	pt-es	it-es
TEDx	163.7	119.9	-	134.2	85.5	-	-
CoVoST	113.0	264.1	10.3	44.1	-	-	-
EuroParl	20.7	31.0	35.5	14.6	20.0	9.5	20.6
Common Voice (mined data)	52.7	39.6	12.8	9.6	18.7	4.4	6.6
MLS (mined data)	23.9	64.7	2.3	-	42.7	1.3	3.4

2.1 Public data

Besides TEDx dataset provided by the shared task, we also include two other public datasets, CoVoST and EuroParl, which provides parallel audio-text samples in some of the test directions of TEDx.

- CoVoST (Wang et al., 2020). As a large scale dataset for multilingual speech translation, CoVoST contains translations from 11 languages to English. We use its data in 5 language directions [2].

- EuroParl (Iranzo-Sánchez et al., 2020). Collected from debates in European Parliment, EuroParl provides speech-to-text translations in 6 European languages. Its data in 11 language directions [3] is used in model training.

2.2 Mined data

We also mined additional speech-to-text data from unlabeled corpora. The audio corpora used in our experiments include Common Voice and Multilingual LibriSpeech (MLS).

- Common Voice (Ardila et al., 2020). It is a massive collection of multilingual audios and their transcriptions in 29 languages.

- MLS (Pratap et al., 2020). It is a speech corpus collected from audiobooks of LibriVox in 8 languages.

The text corpus used for mining is CCNet, which serves as the source of target translations (Wenzek et al., 2020). Collected from snapshots of CommonCrawl dataset, CCNet provides a large-scale and high-quality monolingual datasets.

Since the audio corpora provide transcripts for audios, we could align source audios with target translations by finding the alignments between source transcripts and target texts. LASER alignment is applied for the crosslingual text alignment (Artetxe and Schwenk, 2019). It generates sentence embeddings with a pre-trained multilingual text encoder (Schwenk and Douze, 2017), and use them to measure the semantic similarity between sentences.

Table 1 summarizes the statistics of the data used in our experiments. It reports the total length of audios in TEDx, CoVost and EuroParl datasets. Moreover, we include the statistics of mined speech from Common Voice and MLS. The mined data has an equivalent size to TEDx dataset in training directions. It also provides a good amount of speech data in zero-shot directions including it-en, pt-es and it-es.

2.3 Text Data

We use additional text data to train mBART model, which later is used to initialize our speech-to-text model. mBART model is first trained with monolingual text data from five languages[4] using self-supervised training. Then they are finetuned with parallel text data from seven evaluation directions as a multilingual text-to-text translation model. The monolingual text data comes from the CC100 dataset (Conneau et al., 2020b) and the parallel text data are downloaded from OPUS (Tiedemann, 2012). [5]

3 Methods

Our evaluation system is based on an encoder decoder model with the state-of-the-art Transformer architecture. The submitted model is developed

[2] {es, fr, it, pt, ru}-en

[3] es-{en, fr, it, pt}, fr-{en, es, pt}, it-{en, es}, pt-{en, es}, ru-en

[4] Five languages include en,es,fr,it and pt.

[5] The following datasets are used: CommonCrawl, OPUS-Books v1, CAPES v1, DGT v2019, ECB v1, ELRA-W0138 v1, ELRA-W0201 v1, ELRC 2682 v1, EMEA v3, EUbookshop v2, EuroPat v1, Europarl v8, GlobalVoices v2018q4, JRC-Acquis v3.0, JW300 v1b, Multi ParaCrawl v7.1, MultiUN v1, News-Commentary v14, QED v2.0a, SciELO v1, TED2013 v1.1, TED2020 v1, Tanzil v1, Tatoeba v2020-11-09, TildeMODEL v2018,UNPC v1.0, and UN v20090831, Wikipedia v1.0.

	→ en				→ es			
	es	fr	pt	it	fr	pt	it	Ave.
MT (M2M-100) (Salesky et al., 2021)	34.0	40.9	38.7	34.6	42.4	45.8	44.2	40.1
Cascaded System (Salesky et al., 2021)	21.5	25.3	22.3	21.9	26.9	26.3	28.4	24.7
Multilingual E2E (Salesky et al., 2021)	12.3	12.0	12.0	10.7	13.6	13.7	13.1	12.5
ST Baseline	27.8	32.4	26.6	20.6	35.0	28.7	28.3	28.5
XLSR-IPA	32.1	36.8	35.1	30.0	38.3	38.5	37.5	35.5
XLSR-SPM	33.2	37.8	35.0	29.3	39.5	36.7	35.3	35.3
VP100K-IPA	31.6	37.1	35.3	29.3	38.2	37.9	37.1	35.2
Ensemble (3 models)	34.0	38.7	37.2	30.9	39.7	40.4	38.6	37.1

Table 2: Main results on the public test set from the Multilingual TEDx Corpus (Salesky et al., 2021).

with a transfer learning approach (Li et al., 2020), including three ingredients: single-modality modules pretrained from self-supervised learning, multitask joint training, and task-specific fine-tuning. The pretrained modules make use of a large amount of unlabeled data, joint training focuses on transferring knowledge from a relatively simple text-to-text task to a speech-to-text task, and the model is fine-tuned on speech-to-text translation task to boost in-task performance.

3.1 Modality Dependent Pretraining

Our model leverages large amounts of unlabelled data from different modalities through two pretrained models: a wav2vec 2.0 (Baevski et al., 2020) and a multilingual BART (mBART) (Liu et al., 2020).

wav2vec 2.0 is a simple and powerful framework to learn high quality speech representation from unlabelled audio data. Given the raw input audio samples, the model learns both latent representations and context representations through a contrastive task to distinguish true latent from distractors. Two multilingual wav2vec 2.0 models are explored during our development. One ("XLSR-53") is trained on 56K-hour speech in 53 languages (Conneau et al., 2020a), and another ("VP-100K") is trained on 100K-hour speech in 23 languages (Wang et al., 2021). The pretrained wav2vec 2.0 models are used to initialize the speech encoder in the jointly trained model of the next stage.

As will be discussed in our experiments, the two encoders are strong in different language directions. We ensemble models with XLSR-53 encoder and VP-100K encoder respectively to achieve the best performance.

mBART is a sequence-to-sequence generative pretraining scheme, specifically a denoising autoencoder (DAE) to predict the original text from its noisy version such as random span masking and order permutation (Liu et al., 2020). The model is pretrained with monolingual data and finetuned with parallel data as described in subsection 2.3. The encoder and decoder in mBART model are used to initialize the encoder and decoder in the joint trained model of the second stage.

Previous study (Tang et al., 2021b) shows that it makes the knowledge transfer from the text-to-text task to speech-to-text task easier by representing the input text as its pronunciation form, i.e., the phoneme sequence. We also investigate representing the input text as its pronunciation forms rather than sentencepiece tokens during our development. We choose International Phonetic Alphabet (IPA) as input text representation since it can be shared across different languages. espeak[6] is used to convert the text word into IPA phonemes.

3.2 Multitask Joint Training

In the second stage, we choose to optimize the speech-to-text translation model along with a text-to-text translation model. Two encoders are used to process text input and speech input respectively. The speech encoder is with the large wav2vec 2.0 configuration. The feature extractor and the bottom 12 transformer layers in the context extractor are initialized with the corresponding parameters from the pretrained wav2vec 2.0 model in subsection 3.1. The top 12 transformer layers in the speech encoder are shared with the text encoder. They are initialized with the pretrained mBART encoder (Tang et al., 2021a). An adaptor (Li et al., 2020), which consists of 3 1-D convolution layers with stride 2 to achieve 8x down-sampling of speech encoder out-

[6]http://espeak.sourceforge.net/index.html

	BLEU							WER			
	→ en				→ es						
	es	fr	pt	it	fr	pt	it	es	fr	it	pt
ST Baseline	34.1	28.4	19.8	20.0	29.3	25.3	25.8	18.6	25.7	33.2	44.5
XLSR-IPA	40.4	36.4	29.0	28.4	34.4	34.4	34.6	13.0	21.8	21.8	29.9
Ensemble (3 models)	42.2	38.7	31.0	29.4	36.5	38.2	37.3	11.2	18.7	19.6	27.4

Table 3: Main results on the blind test set from the Multilingual TEDx Corpus.

	Data			→ en				→ es			Ave.
	ASR	Public	Mined	es	fr	pt	it	fr	pt	it	
M0	✗	✗	✗	22.3	26.7	21.7	5.9	28.2	23.6	8.4	19.5
M1	✓	✗	✗	24.2	29.1	26.3	18.1	31.7	28.9	27.3	26.5
M2	✓	✓	✗	25.2	30.8	26.9	19.2	32.5	29.4	28.1	27.4
M3 (ST Baseline)	✓	✓	✓	27.8	32.4	26.6	20.6	35.0	28.7	28.3	28.5

Table 4: Ablation studies of training data (Public: CoVoST and EuroParl, Mined: mined data from Common Voice, MLS and CCMatrix, ASR: ASR data in mTEDx). The results are BLEU scores on TEDx test set. The models considered here are built upon pretrained XLSR-53 encoder and mbart decoder, and they do not have joint training. The speeach translation data from mTEDx is used by all models.

puts, is placed between the last non-shared speech encoder layer and the first shared speech text encoder layer. The decoder is shared by two tasks and initialized with the pretrained mBART decoder.

Two techniques (Tang et al., 2021a): cross attentive regularization (CAR) and online knowledge distillation (online KD), are employed to enhance the knowledge transferring. Text input data comes from the corresponding transcripts in the speech translation dataset. Due to time limits, we don't use extra parallel text data to enhance the performance.

3.3 Speech only Finetuning

In the last stage, the model is fine-tuned in the speech-to-text translation task with speech input only. The text encoder is dropped and no text input data is used.

4 Experiments

4.1 Experimental Setting

Both wav2vec 2.0 model and mBART model are trained with the large configuration. There are 24 transformer layers in the wav2vec 2.0 model, and 12 transformer layers in both mBART encoder and decoder. We build the mBART model with a target vocabulary of 64,000 SentencePiece (Kudo and Richardson, 2018) tokens, which are shared among all 6 evaluation languages[7]. For the mBART model with IPA phoneme input, the vocabulary size is 516 which includes phoneme variants with "_" attached to denote the word leading phoneme.

A language id symbol "⟨LID⟩" is used as the initial token to predict the sentence. Speech recognition task is treated as the same as the speech translation task but with the source speech language id symbol.

The primary system results submitted are from an ensemble system with three models. All three models are trained with 3-stage optimization discussed in section 3 with different initialization models. The first one is initialized with "XLSR-53" wav2vec model and IPA mBART model ("XLSR-IPA"). Compared with the first model, the second model chooses sentence piece mBART model ("XLSR-SPM") while the third one is initialized with "VP-100K" wav2vec model ("VP100K-IPA") [8].

We use 8 V100 GPUs for each model during the jointly training and fine-tuning stages. It takes approximate five days to jointly train the models for 15 epochs and another two days for speech only fine tuning. The last 5 checkpoints are averaged for inference with beam size 5.

To provide a deep insight into the factors affect-

[7] In our evaluation, the new mBART model achieves comparable results as the public available mBART model, which is with 250k vocabulary, but with much smaller memory footprint.

[8] We will release the training and evaluation recipe under https://github.com/pytorch/fairseq/tree/master/examples/speech_text_joint_to_text

	Train		→ en				→ es			Ave.
	JT	FT	es	fr	pt	it	fr	pt	it	
M3	✗	✗	27.8	32.4	26.6	20.6	35.0	28.7	28.3	28.5
M4	✓	✗	32.3	36.6	33.8	28.4	38.3	35.9	35.7	34.4
M5	✓	✓	33.2	37.8	35.0	29.3	39.5	36.7	35.3	35.3

Table 5: Ablation studies of training approaches (JT: joint training of text and speech translation, FT: finetuning a trained model on TEDx data in speech translation). The results are BLEU scores reported on TEDx test set. The models considered here are built upon pretrained XLSR-SPM encoder and mbart decoder. They are trained with the combination of TEDx including the ASR portion, public data as well as mined data.

	Encoder	→ en				→ es			Ave.
		es	fr	pt	it	fr	pt	it	
M4	XLSR-SPM	32.3	36.6	33.8	28.4	38.3	35.9	35.7	34.4
M6	VP100K-SPM	30.5	35.6	33.7	28.5	36.9	36.9	36.2	34.0

Table 6: Ablation studies of different encoders. BLEU scores are reported on TEDx test set. Models are jointly trained on all data, but they are not further finetuned on speech translation.

ing translation performance, we conduct ablation studies on different model configurations.

4.2 Main Results

We summarize our main results at Table 2. The first row presents results from a large text-to-text translation system (M2M-100) using oracle speech transcripts (Salesky et al., 2021) as input. The second two rows list best results from the cascaded system and multilingual end to end system from literature (Salesky et al., 2021). The fourth row to eighth row are results from our systems. The fourth row presents our multilingual baseline, which is initialized with pretrained wav2vec 2.0 model ("XLSR-53") for encoder and mBART model ("SPM") for decoder. The model is fine-tuned with Multilingual TEDx data, public data and mined data listed in section 2. No joint training is applied. "XLSR-IPA", "XLSR-SPM" and "VP100K-IPA" from row 5 to 8 are results from the 3 best systems we built. Compared with the baseline in the third row, these three systems have an extra step to co-train with the text-to-text translation task.

It is clear that we create a very strong baseline (row 4) with the help from the large amounts of speech/text training data. In comparison to the previous reported cascaded system (row 2) or multilingual end-to-end system (row 3), the results are 3.8 and 16.0 BLEU scores higher on average.

Row 5 to 8 provide evaluation results from our 3 best single models built with single-modality based pre-training, multitask joint training and task-specific fine-tuning. They are built with different pre-training data or input text representations. Compared with the baseline in row 4, another 6.7 $\sim$ 7.0 BLEU improvement are observed. IPA phoneme based text representation gives slight gain compared with text units separated with SentencePiece model ("XLSR-IPA" v.s. "XLSR-SPM"), which is smaller than we expected. We hypothesis that it is due to the imperfect text to phoneme conversion for different languages. The difference due to different pre-training data is also small that there are only 0.3 BLEU in average when the speech pre-training is changed ("XLSR-IPA" v.s. "VP100K-IPA").

The ensemble of three models achieves the best performance with a 1.6 BLEU improvement over the best single model. It indicates those three models are complementary to each other, though they give similar BLEU scores in our test. The results are even close to the ones from the strong text-to-text translation system (M2M-100 in row 1), which takes speech transcript as translation input. Our primary system achieves the same BLEU score as the text-to-text translation system on translation direction "es-en" and the average BLEU score gap from 7 directions is 3.0.

The corresponding blind test results are reported in Table 3. Similar to our observation in Table 2, the model trained with the 3-stage approach significantly improves the translation accuracy compared with the baseline. The ensemble system outperforms other systems in all speech translation directions as well as the speech recognition tasks.

4.3 Analysis

Data. Table 4 compares models trained with different sets of data. Additional data is shown to improve the translation performance. In our multitask training, we combine the text-to-text and speech-to-text translation tasks together. We don't include ASR task as separated task, instead we treat ASR task as a special translation direction. It shows ASR data is helpful for speech translation, especially for translation directions with small amount of speech training data ("it-en" and "it-es"). On average, we observe a significant gain of 7.0 BLEU from the comparison between M0 and M1 .

When we continue adding public datasets including CoVost and EuroParl to the training set, M2 has an average improvement of 0.9 BLEU over M1. The mined data brings another 1.1 BLEU gain as we compare M3 and M2.

Training. Different training approaches are compared in Table 5. We observe significant gains brought by joint training of text and speech translation. Compared against M3, M4 with joint training demonstrates an improvement of 5.9 BLEU over 7 language directions. When the jointly trained model is further finetuned with speech translation data, an extra gain of 0.9 is achieved as we compare M5 against M4.

Encoder. We compare XLSR-53 and VP-100K encoder in Table 6. XLSR-53 is strong at encoding audios in Spanish and French, achieving BLEU gains of 1.8 and 1.0 in es-en and fr-en respectively. VP100k encoder outperforms XLSR-53 in pt-es and it-es directions with gains of 1.0 and 0.5 respectively. This can be explained by the fact that VP100K encoder is trained on more Portuguese and Italian Speech.

5 Conclusion

In this work, we described our multilingual end-to-end speech translation system submitted to IWSLT 2021. We leverage the large amount of training data from different domains and modalities to improve the speech translation performance. We adopt a progressive approach to build the model with three stages. Compared with our strong baseline, the proposed system achieves 8.6 BLEU score improvement, which also outperforms other reported systems, including both end-to-end and cascaded based, by a large margin.

References

Rosana Ardila, Megan Branson, Kelly Davis, Michael Kohler, Josh Meyer, Michael Henretty, Reuben Morais, Lindsay Saunders, Francis Tyers, and Gregor Weber. 2020. Common voice: A massively-multilingual speech corpus. In *Proceedings of The 12th Language Resources and Evaluation Conference*, pages 4218–4222.

Mikel Artetxe and Holger Schwenk. 2019. Margin-based parallel corpus mining with multilingual sentence embeddings. In *Proceedings of the 57th Annual Meeting of the Association for Computational Linguistics*, pages 3197–3203.

Alexei Baevski, Henry Zhou, Abdelrahman Mohamed, and Michael Auli. 2020. wav2vec 2.0: A framework for self-supervised learning of speech representations. In *NeurIPS*.

Alexis Conneau, Alexei Baevski, Ronan Collobert, Abdelrahman Mohamed, and Michael Auli. 2020a. Unsupervised cross-lingual representation learning for speech recognition. *arXiv preprint arXiv:2006.13979*.

Alexis Conneau, Kartikay Khandelwal, Naman Goyal, Vishrav Chaudhary, Guillaume Wenzek, Francisco Guzmán, E. Grave, Myle Ott, Luke Zettlemoyer, and Veselin Stoyanov. 2020b. Unsupervised cross-lingual representation learning at scale. In *ACL*.

Hirofumi Inaguma, Kevin Duh, Tatsuya Kawahara, and Shinji Watanabe. 2019. Multilingual end-to-end speech translation. In *2019 IEEE Automatic Speech Recognition and Understanding Workshop (ASRU)*, pages 570–577. IEEE.

Javier Iranzo-Sánchez, Joan Albert Silvestre-Cerdà, Javier Jorge, Nahuel Roselló, Adrià Giménez, Albert Sanchis, Jorge Civera, and Alfons Juan. 2020. Europarl-st: A multilingual corpus for speech translation of parliamentary debates. In *ICASSP 2020-2020 IEEE International Conference on Acoustics, Speech and Signal Processing (ICASSP)*, pages 8229–8233. IEEE.

T. Kudo and J. Richardson. 2018. Sentencepiece: A simple and language independent subword tokenizer and detokenizer for neural text processing. In *EMNLP*.

Xian Li, Changhan Wang, Yun Tang, C. Tran, Yuqing Tang, Juan Pino, Alexei Baevski, Alexis Conneau, and Michael Auli. 2020. Multilingual speech translation with efficient finetuning of pretrained models. *arXiv: Computation and Language*.

Yinhan Liu, Jiatao Gu, Naman Goyal, X. Li, Sergey Edunov, Marjan Ghazvininejad, M. Lewis, and Luke Zettlemoyer. 2020. Multilingual denoising pre-training for neural machine translation. *Transactions of the Association for Computational Linguistics*, 8:726–742.

Vineel Pratap, Qiantong Xu, Anuroop Sriram, Gabriel Synnaeve, and Ronan Collobert. 2020. Mls: A large-scale multilingual dataset for speech research. *Proc. Interspeech 2020*, pages 2757–2761.

Elizabeth Salesky, Matthew Wiesner, Jacob Bremerman, Roldano Cattoni, Matteo Negri, Marco Turchi, Douglas W. Oard, and Matt Post. 2021. Multilingual tedx corpus for speech recognition and translation.

Holger Schwenk and Matthijs Douze. 2017. Learning joint multilingual sentence representations with neural machine translation. In *Proceedings of the 2nd Workshop on Representation Learning for NLP*, pages 157–167.

Yun Tang, Juan Pino, Xian Li, Changhan Wang, and Dmitriy Genzel. 2021a. Improving speech translation by understanding and learning from the auxiliary text translation task. In *ACL*.

Yun Tang, Juan Pino, Changhan Wang, Xutai Ma, and Dmitriy Genzel. 2021b. A general multi-task learning framework to leverage text data for speech to text tasks. In *ICASSP*.

J. Tiedemann. 2012. Parallel data, tools and interfaces in opus. In *LREC*.

Changhan Wang, Juan Pino, Anne Wu, and Jiatao Gu. 2020. Covost: A diverse multilingual speech-to-text translation corpus. In *Proceedings of The 12th Language Resources and Evaluation Conference*, pages 4197–4203.

Changhan Wang, M. Rivière, A. Lee, Anne Wu, C. Talnikar, Daniel Haziza, Mary Williamson, J. Pino, and Emmanuel Dupoux. 2021. Voxpopuli: A large-scale multilingual speech corpus for representation learning, semi-supervised learning and interpretation. *ArXiv*, abs/2101.00390.

Guillaume Wenzek, Marie-Anne Lachaux, Alexis Conneau, Vishrav Chaudhary, Francisco Guzmán, Armand Joulin, and Édouard Grave. 2020. Ccnet: Extracting high quality monolingual datasets from web crawl data. In *Proceedings of The 12th Language Resources and Evaluation Conference*, pages 4003–4012.

Maastricht University's Multilingual Speech Translation System for IWSLT 2021

Danni Liu, Jan Niehues
Department of Data Science and Knowledge Engineering, Maastricht University
{danni.liu, jan.niehues}@maastrichtuniversity.nl

Abstract

This paper describes Maastricht University's participation in the IWSLT 2021 multilingual speech translation track. The task of this track is to build multilingual speech translation systems in supervised and zero-shot directions. Our primary system is an end-to-end model that performs both speech transcription and translation. We observe that the joint training for the two tasks is complementary especially when the speech translation data is scarce. On the source and target side, we use data augmentation and pseudo-labels respectively to improve the performance of our systems. We also introduce an ensembling technique that consistently improves the quality of transcriptions and translations. The experiments show that the end-to-end system is competitive with its cascaded counterpart especially in zero-shot conditions.

1 Introduction

In this paper, we describe our systems for the multilingual speech translation track of IWSLT 2021. Speech translation (Bérard et al., 2016; Weiss et al., 2017) is the task of converting speech utterances to their translation in other languages. While "end-to-end" modeling (Di Gangi et al., 2019; Sperber et al., 2019) of the speech translation pipeline has become the dominant approach, an open challenge remains in terms of data scarcity. As the amount of speech directly paired with translation is lower compared to speech transcription or text-to-text translation, it is especially crucial for models to be data-efficient. In this context, multilingual speech translation (Inaguma et al., 2019; Li et al., 2021) presents itself as a promising direction to alleviate data scarcity by leveraging commonalities across languages.

In this multilingual translation track, we submit: 1) an end-to-end system (§5.2) that directly translates from speech and 2) a cascaded system (§5.1) that consists of a multilingual speech transcription module (§3) followed by a multilingual text translation module (§4).

Our efforts to improve the speech translation system can be categorized as follows. When **training**, on the source side, we augment the speech data by speed perturbation. On the target side, we apply pseudo-labeling[1] by translating the ASR transcriptions. Furthermore, we train multilingual systems for both speech transcription and translation to alleviate the scarcity of training data. When **testing**, we use different ensembling techniques to increase the diversity of output distribution and improve output quality.

The main findings from our experiments are:

- Multilingual training and jointly training speech transcription and translation are beneficial when data scarcity limits the performance of mono- or bilingual systems.
- The gain in the overall speech-to-text systems also propagates to cascaded systems as a result of stronger ASR performance.
- Pseudo-labeling strongly improves speech translation quality, especially in directions that are originally zero-shot.

2 Setup

2.1 Corpus Statistics

Our systems are trained on the multilingual TEDx (mTEDx) speech recognition and translation corpus (Salesky et al., 2021). We do not use any data outside this corpus. Table 1 outlines some statistics about the training set of the mTEDx corpus.

2.2 Preprocessing

For the audio data, we downsample the original audio files from 48kHz to 16kHz and mix the two channels into one. We then extract 40-dimensional

[1] or forward-translation in analogy to back-translation

Proceedings of the 18th International Conference on Spoken Language Translation, pages 138–143
Bangkok, Thailand (Online), August 5–6, 2021.

Source	transcription (hour, # utts.)	Target (# utts.) en	es	fr	pt	it
es	178, 102k	36k		4k	21k	6k
fr	176, 116k	30k	20k		13k	–
pt	153, 90k	31k	–	–		–
it	101, 50k	–	–	–	–	

Table 1: Data amount of speech transcription and translation in the training set of mTEDx.

Mel Frequency Cepstral Coefficients (MFCC) with 3-dimensional pitch using Kaldi (Povey et al., 2011). We concatenate adjacent 4 audio frames, resulting in an input dimension of 172.

For the text data, we combine all transcriptions and translations from the training set and learn a joint byte pair encoding (BPE) (Sennrich et al., 2016b) of size 16k using SentencePiece (Kudo and Richardson, 2018). With this joint BPE, we can translate from tokenized ASR transcriptions in our cascaded system.

2.3 Training Details

We use the dev partition of mTEDx as validation set and average the model weights from last 5 best checkpoints. When decoding, we use a beam size of 8. The specific models for different tasks will be described in the corresponding sections.

3 Automatic Speech Recognition (ASR)

The ASR performance is summarized in Table 2. We report case-insensitive word error rates (WER) after removing all punctuation marks.

3.1 Model Description

Multilingual Baseline We start from a Transformer (Vaswani et al., 2017) with stochastic layer dropout (Pham et al., 2019a) rate of 0.5. We use 36 encoder layers and 12 decoders layers, following the original work (Pham et al., 2019a). The hidden dimension is 512 and the inner dimension 2048. We use dropout rate of 0.2 and label smoothing rate of 0.1.

The model is jointly trained on all four languages. As the data volume for each individual language is relatively low, after initially seeing poor performance of monolingual ASR models, we proceed with a multilingual system for all four languages, with the intention of better utilizing common acoustic features.

Language Embedding While the multilingual ASR system does not need to explicitly know the target language, we find it beneficial to provide the decoder more guidance by feeding in target language embeddings. Specifically, we achieve this by language embeddings concatenated with decoder input embeddings (Pham et al., 2019b). Meanwhile, the decoder begin token is replaced by the target language embedding. With this approach, we reduce the WER on average by 0.6% absolute (2.4% relative; model A2 in Table 2). More importantly, this approach allows us to easily extend the model to speech translation, where the number of target languages can be more than one.

Speed Perturbation We augment the training data by speed perturbation with factor 0.9 and 1.1 (Ko et al., 2015) using the corresponding Kaldi script[2]. After speed perturbation, we further observe a reduction of 2.4% absolute WER (9.3% relative; model A3 in Table 2). Here we did not use SpecAugument (Park et al., 2019), but would expect further gains from this approach.

Ensembling By ensembling two independently trained models on the output distributions, we further reduce WER by 1% absolute (4.4% relative; model A4 in Table 2).

Joint Training with Speech Translation We can directly apply the same ASR model to speech translation, as we control the output language by the target language embedding. As described later in §5.2, we train end-to-end systems using both ASR and ST data. The strongest system from ASR and ST training (model E5) achieves a large reduction of WER from 21.9% to 18.7% (14.7% relative) on average.

ID	Model	es	fr	it	pt
A1	Multilingual baseline	24.3	24.5	25.9	28.7
A2	A1 + language emb.	23.8	23.9	25.5	27.7
A3	A2 + speed perturb	21.0	22.1	23.1	25.3
A4	A3 + ensembling	20.4	21.0	22.0	24.1
E5	A3 + ST joint training	17.6	18.4	18.6	20.0

Table 2: ASR performance in WER$\downarrow$ (%) (lower-cased, no punctuation) of the multilingual ASR system on mTEDx test set.

3.2 Main Findings

As summarized in Table 2, we reduce the WER of our baseline multilingual Transformer from 25.8%

[2] `https://github.com/kaldi-asr/kaldi/blob/master/egs/wsj/s5/utils/data/perturb_data_dir_speed_3way.sh`

ID	Model	es-en	fr-en	fr-es	pt-en	pt-es*	it-en**	it-es*
M1	Transformer (6-6 encoder-decocder layers)	32.3	38.0	41.3	37.1	42.3	23.0	32.5
M2	M1 + residual drop	32.9	38.1	40.7	37.0	42.5	24.1	32.8
M3	Ensemble M1 and M2	33.4	39.4	41.8	37.9	43.3	24.8	34.0
M4	Ensemble M1×2 and M2×2	33.7	39.3	42.1	38.3	44.0	24.9	34.8

Table 3: Machine translation performance in BLEU↑[3] of the multilingual MT system on mTEDx test set by directly translating from ground-truth transcriptions. *: zero-shot directions for speech translation. **: zero-shot direction for text translation.

	en	es	fr	it	pt
en	-	36	30	0	30
es		-	24	6	21
fr			-	0	13
it				-	0
pt					-

Table 4: Overview of MT parallel training data amount (in 1k sentences) after including all directions with text-to-text translation data.

to 18.7% by a combination of techniques. Among these, the largest gain comes from joint training for speech translation. This highlights the benefit of multilingual training, especially when data scarcity limits the performance of monolingual end-to-end systems.

4 Machine Translation (MT)

When translating from speech, the MT module ingests ASR outputs. To assess the quality of the MT component alone, we first report the performance of directly translating from the ground truth transcriptions in Table 3. The results of cascading the ASR and MT systems are reported later in Table 5.

4.1 Data

For the MT component, we train our models on all translation directions from {en, es, fr, it, pt} with all text translation data in the training set, including both directions of transcription ↔ translation. In doing so, we cover more directions than tested in the evaluation campaign. A main advantage of this is additional training data on the target side. For instance, although the evaluation task does not involve translating from English, incorporating en→X directions provides around 30k sentences with each of {es, fr, pt} on the target side. Including these data largely expands the data amount when translating into the three target languages. The data amount for our MT training is outlined in Table 4. Note that while {pt→es, it→en, it→es} are zero-shot directions for speech translation, only it→en is zero-shot for MT.

[3]sacreBLEU: BLEU+case.mixed+numrefs.1+smooth .exp+tok.13a+version.1.4.12

4.2 Model Description

Multilingual Baseline We start with a Transformer-base with 6 encoder and decoder layers respectively (model M1 from Table 3). We use dropout rate of 0.2 and label smoothing rate of 0.1. The source and target embeddings are shared. The output language is controlled by the language embedding described in §3.1. As we observe no performance gain by increasing the number of encoder and decoder layers, we keep the Transformer-base setup.

Residual Drop We additionally use the Transformer with residual connections removed from the middle encoder layer (Liu et al., 2020) that was shown to improve zero-shot performance under English-centric scenarios. We see that the model (M2 from Table 3) outperforms the vanilla Transformer in the zero-shot direction (it-en) by 1.1 BLEU, while being on-par on other directions.

Ensembling We ensemble the two models above by averaging the output distributions (model M3 in Table 3). This brings a gain of 0.9 BLEU on average. By further incorporating another two independently trained vanilla model and residual-drop model (hence ensembling four models), we see a further gain of 0.4 BLEU (model M4 in Table 3). This MT system and will be used in the later cascaded speech translation system.

4.3 Main Findings

We build a multilingual translation model with results summarized in Table 3. We first confirm that the residual drop approach (Liu et al., 2020) improves zero-shot translation performance. Furthermore, ensembling different models brings gains up to 1.5 BLEU.

Type	ID	Model	es-en	fr-en	fr-es	pt-en	pt-es*	it-en*	it-es*	ASR (avg.)
Cascaded	C1	A4 + M2	25.6	30.1	32.2	28.1	31.4	19.1	26.0	-
	C2	A4 + M4	26.1	30.6	33.3	29.0	32.0	19.5	26.8	-
	C3	C2 + ASR multi-view ensemble	26.5	30.6	33.6	28.9	32.2	19.7	27.0	-
	C4	E5 + M4	27.3	31.6	34.2	31.0	34.6	20.5	27.8	-
End-to-end	E1	Transformer	17.0	20.1	21.2	17.5	11.7	5.8	6.6	-
	E2**	E1 + ASR joint training	18.0	20.8	24.7	20.1	19.0	8.2	10.2	25.3
	E3	E2 + pseudo labels (zero-shot dir.)	21.9	25.3	29.1	24.9	33.3	19.2	28.2	20.4
	E4	E2 + pseudo labels (all dir.)	25.0	30.0	33.3	28.5	34.4	20.4	28.8	19.5
	E5	E4 + multi-view ensemble (3 speeds)	25.2	30.1	33.3	28.7	34.5	20.5	29.1	18.7

Table 5: Speech translation performance in BLEU↑ on mTEDx test set. We mark the cascaded systems with "ASR-ID + MT-ID". For e2e systems trained to jointly perform ST and ASR, we additionally report average WER↓ over the 4 source languages {es, fr, it, pt}. *: zero-shot directions. **: Due to computation constraints, we terminated the training of model E2 early to combine with the other approaches.

5 Speech Translation (ST)

In Table 5, we report the performance of our cascaded (§5.1) and end-to-end (§5.2) speech translation systems.

5.1 Cascaded System

The performance of the cascaded systems is summarized in the upper section of the Table 5. We combine the stronger ASR system and MT system and derive cascaded models C1 and C2. Compared to the MT results in Table 3 that utilizes ground-truth transcriptions, we observe a clear drop in BLEU. This highlights the importance of high-quality transcriptions for the cascaded system.

Multi-View Ensemble (Transcription) Since at test time the ASR transcriptions are likely noisy, we propose an ensembling approach that incorporates multiple variants (or views) of ASR transcriptions. At test time, given an utterance, we transcribe it with different ASR models. The MT module then translates from these slightly different transcriptions and ensembles by averaging the output distribution. The results from this technique are shown in C3 in Table 3. With this ensembling technique, on average we see an improvement of 0.2 BLEU, with the all other modules unchanged from the previous model C2.

5.2 End-to-End System

For the end-to-end ST system, we use the provided ST training data augmented with three-way speed perturbation (Ko et al., 2015). We initialize the models with pre-trained encoder weights from our trained ASR system.

ASR Joint Training Since our decoder utilizes target language embeddings, we can conveniently incorporate ASR data for jointly training the ST system (Model E2 in Table 5). Upon seeing improvements over the setup without ASR data, we terminated the training of E2 and continued by combining with other approaches described next. Therefore if trained till convergence, the final performance of E2 would be better than reported here.

Pseudo-Labels Since the provided corpus contains no Italian ST data, the BLEU scores when translating from Italian are poor (8.2 and 10.2 for it-en and it-es from model E2 in Table 5). To have more training signals, we create pseudo-labels by translating the ASR transcription using our MT system. The model trained with the additional pseudo-labeled data (pt-es, it-en, it-es) is E3 in Table 5. As expected, incorporating pseudo-labels largely improves the performance on the three zero-shot directions (pt-es, it-en, it-es). It is worth noting that on these zero-shot directions the end-to-end system already surpassed the strongest cascaded system so far (C3), achieving 33.3, 19.2, 28.2 compared to 32.2, 19.7, 27.0 BLEU points.

Observing the strength of the pseudo-labeling, we take a step further and create pseudo-labels also for the supervised directions (model E4 in Table 5). This further improves the overall ST and ASR performance by +2.6 BLEU and −4.4% WER (relative) on average.

Multi-View Ensemble (Speech Speed) Similar to the motivation for the ensembling approach in §5.1, we utilize multiple views of the same input to create an ensemble. Since the input here is audio, we take the speed-perturbed variants with factors 0.9, 1.0, 1.1 (Ko et al., 2015) of the test utterances and ensemble the output distributions (model E5 of Table 5). This simple technique slightly yet

Type	ID	es-en	fr-en	fr-es	pt-en	pt-es*	it-en*	it-es*	avg.
Cascaded	C3	34.5	21.9	24.3	24.3	29.3	21.7	26.8	26.1
End-to-end	E5	33.9	25.4	27.6	25.7	33.7	22.8	29.4	28.4

Table 6: Speech translation performance in BLEU↑ on the blind test set. We mark the cascaded systems with "ASR-ID + MT-ID". *: zero-shot directions for speech translation.

consistently improves ST and ASR quality, gaining +0.2 BLEU and −4.1% WER (relative) on average. It is worth noting that the model has already been trained on speech data perturbed with the same speed factors. This suggests that we can further improve our model's prediction consistency for perturbed versions of the the same utterance, e.g. by consistency regularization (Sohn et al., 2020). Furthermore, although this ensembling approach leads to improvements in the current offline setting, we note that it could be difficult to apply under real-time constraints due to the computation load of generating 3 variants of speech utterances and applying ensembling on top of that.

Feeding Back to Cascaded System Till now, the series of improvements of the speech-to-text model also lead to better ASR performance. We therefore use the improved ASR transcriptions from model E5 as the MT input for the cascaded system. The resulting model is C4 in Table 5, which brings a gain of 1.2 BLEU for the cascaded system.

5.3 Main Findings

The results for cascaded and end-to-end ST systems are summarized in Table 5. First, using a unified end-to-end speech-to-text system for both ASR and ST improves the output quality for both tasks. This gain further propagates to the cascaded systems as a result of higher ASR quality. Second, confirming findings from the literature (Kahn et al., 2020; Pino et al., 2020), training with pseudo-labels is a strong method to improve end-to-end systems. Last but not least, by ensembling from different views of the same data, we can achieve further gains at inference time.

6 Results on Blind Test Set

We submitted systems C3 and E5 for evaluation on the blind test set. The results are summarized in Table 6. In line with the results on the public test set in Table 5, the end-to-end system outperforms the cascaded system on zero-shot directions. Different from on the public test set, the end-to-end system also shows large gains when translating from French speech. A potential reason is errors propagated from the French ASR transcriptions that led to weaker performance of the MT module in the cascaded system.

7 Conclusion

This paper summarizes our participation in the IWSLT 2021 multilingual speech translation track. We improved our end-to-end speech-to-text systems from different angles. On the source side, we augmented the input utterance. On the target side, we created pseudo-labels from ASR transcriptions. Furthermore, at test time we used different ensembling approaches to improve the performance of trained models. By experimenting under different data scenarios, we showed the benefit of multilingual training and the joint training speech transcription and translation.

We note a few directions to further improve our systems: First, we expect that utterances augmented by SpecAugment (Park et al., 2019) could improve the quality of the ASR and ST systems. Second, our MT module can be improved by synthetic data from back-translation (Sennrich et al., 2016a), especially for the zero-shot directions. Regarding upcoming work, since the source languages all belong to the same family, an interesting next step is to investigate how to better utilize the relatedness between these languages.

Acknowledgement

We thank the anonymous reviewers for their helpful feedback. This work is supported by a Facebook Sponsored Research Agreement.

References

Alexandre Bérard, Olivier Pietquin, Christophe Servan, and Laurent Besacier. 2016. Listen and Translate: A Proof of Concept for End-to-End Speech-to-Text Translation. In *NIPS Workshop on end-to-end learning for speech and audio processing*.

Mattia A. Di Gangi, Matteo Negri, and Marco Turchi. 2019. Adapting Transformer to End-to-End Spoken

Language Translation. In *Proc. Interspeech 2019*, pages 1133–1137.

Hirofumi Inaguma, Kevin Duh, Tatsuya Kawahara, and Shinji Watanabe. 2019. Multilingual end-to-end speech translation. In *Proc. ASRU 2019*.

Jacob Kahn, Ann Lee, and Awni Hannun. 2020. Self-training for end-to-end speech recognition. In *Proc. ICASSP 2020*, pages 7084–7088.

Tom Ko, Vijayaditya Peddinti, Daniel Povey, and Sanjeev Khudanpur. 2015. Audio augmentation for speech recognition. In *Proc. Interspeech 2015*, pages 3586–3589.

Taku Kudo and John Richardson. 2018. SentencePiece: A simple and language independent subword tokenizer and detokenizer for neural text processing. In *Proceedings of the 2018 Conference on Empirical Methods in Natural Language Processing: System Demonstrations*, pages 66–71, Brussels, Belgium. Association for Computational Linguistics.

Xian Li, Changhan Wang, Yun Tang, Chau Tran, Yuqing Tang, Juan Pino, Alexei Baevski, Alexis Conneau, and Michael Auli. 2021. Multilingual speech translation with efficient finetuning of pretrained models.

Danni Liu, Jan Niehues, James Cross, Francisco Guzmán, and Xian Li. 2020. Improving zero-shot translation by disentangling positional information. *CoRR*, abs/2012.15127.

Daniel S. Park, William Chan, Yu Zhang, Chung-Cheng Chiu, Barret Zoph, Ekin D. Cubuk, and Quoc V. Le. 2019. SpecAugment: A Simple Data Augmentation Method for Automatic Speech Recognition. In *Proc. Interspeech 2019*, pages 2613–2617.

Ngoc-Quan Pham, Thai-Son Nguyen, Jan Niehues, Markus Müller, and Alex Waibel. 2019a. Very Deep Self-Attention Networks for End-to-End Speech Recognition. In *Proc. Interspeech 2019*, pages 66–70.

Ngoc-Quan Pham, Jan Niehues, Thanh-Le Ha, and Alexander Waibel. 2019b. Improving zero-shot translation with language-independent constraints. In *Proceedings of the Fourth Conference on Machine Translation (Volume 1: Research Papers)*, pages 13–23, Florence, Italy. Association for Computational Linguistics.

Juan Pino, Qiantong Xu, Xutai Ma, Mohammad Javad Dousti, and Yun Tang. 2020. Self-Training for End-to-End Speech Translation. In *Proc. Interspeech 2020*, pages 1476–1480.

Daniel Povey, Arnab Ghoshal, Gilles Boulianne, Lukas Burget, Ondrej Glembek, Nagendra Goel, Mirko Hannemann, Petr Motlicek, Yanmin Qian, Petr Schwarz, et al. 2011. The kaldi speech recognition toolkit. In *Proc. ASRU 2011*.

Elizabeth Salesky, Matthew Wiesner, Jacob Bremerman, Roldano Cattoni, Matteo Negri, Marco Turchi, Douglas W. Oard, and Matt Post. 2021. The multilingual tedx corpus for speech recognition and translation. *CoRR*, abs/2102.01757.

Rico Sennrich, Barry Haddow, and Alexandra Birch. 2016a. Improving neural machine translation models with monolingual data. In *Proceedings of the 54th Annual Meeting of the Association for Computational Linguistics (Volume 1: Long Papers)*, pages 86–96, Berlin, Germany. Association for Computational Linguistics.

Rico Sennrich, Barry Haddow, and Alexandra Birch. 2016b. Neural machine translation of rare words with subword units. In *Proceedings of the 54th Annual Meeting of the Association for Computational Linguistics (Volume 1: Long Papers)*, pages 1715–1725, Berlin, Germany. Association for Computational Linguistics.

Kihyuk Sohn, David Berthelot, Nicholas Carlini, Zizhao Zhang, Han Zhang, Colin A Raffel, Ekin Dogus Cubuk, Alexey Kurakin, and Chun-Liang Li. 2020. Fixmatch: Simplifying semi-supervised learning with consistency and confidence. In *Advances in Neural Information Processing Systems*, volume 33, pages 596–608. Curran Associates, Inc.

Matthias Sperber, Graham Neubig, Jan Niehues, and Alex Waibel. 2019. Attention-passing models for robust and data-efficient end-to-end speech translation. *Transactions of the Association for Computational Linguistics*, 7:313–325.

Ashish Vaswani, Noam Shazeer, Niki Parmar, Jakob Uszkoreit, Llion Jones, Aidan N Gomez, Ł ukasz Kaiser, and Illia Polosukhin. 2017. Attention is all you need. In *Advances in Neural Information Processing Systems 30*, pages 5998–6008. Curran Associates, Inc.

Ron J. Weiss, Jan Chorowski, Navdeep Jaitly, Yonghui Wu, and Zhifeng Chen. 2017. Sequence-to-sequence models can directly translate foreign speech. In *Proc. Interspeech 2017*, pages 2625–2629.

ZJU's IWSLT 2021 Speech Translation System

Linlin Zhang
Zhejiang University
11921133@zju.edu.cn

Abstract

In this paper, we describe Zhejiang University's submission to the IWSLT2021 Multilingual Speech Translation Task. This task focuses on speech translation (ST) research across many non-English source languages. Participants can decide whether to work on constrained systems or unconstrained systems which can use external data. We create both cascaded and end-to-end speech translation constrained systems, using the provided data only. In the cascaded approach, we combine Conformer-based automatic speech recognition (ASR) with the Transformer-based neural machine translation (NMT). Our end-to-end direct speech translation systems use ASR pre-trained encoder and multi-task decoders. The submitted systems are ensembled by different cascaded models.

1 Introduction

In this paper, we introduce our submission to the IWSLT2021 Multilingual Speech Translation Task. This task focuses on speech translation (ST) research across many non-English source languages. Multilingual models enable transfer from related tasks, which is particularly important for low-resource languages; however, parallel data between two otherwise high-resource languages can often be rare, making multilingual translation and zero-shot translation important for many resource settings. The task provides data for two conditions (Salesky et al., 2021): supervised, and zero-shot, including speech and transcripts for four languages (Spanish, French, Portuguese, Italian) and translations in a subset of five languages (English, Spanish, French, Portuguese, Italian). At evaluation time, using the provided speech in the four source languages, participants submit the generated translations in both English and Spanish.

In the cascaded approach, we use a Conformer (Gulati et al., 2020) model for ASR for every language. For the MT component, we use a unified Transformer model for all language pairs. As previous works (Gangi et al., 2019; Bahar et al., 2020), we use both the clean and noisy speech transcripts, back translation data, and the mask noisy trick.

For the end-to-end direct speech translation, we also created a Transformer-based model. To obtain the best possible translation quality, we apply data augmentation on audio files, make a multitask decoding for incorporating the ASR task (Weiss et al., 2017).

We tried various experimental parameter settings and different architectures, and finally submitted an ensembled cascaded system.

2 Cascaded Speech Translation

As the task provides speech and transcripts for four languages (Spanish, French, Portuguese, Italian) and translations in a subset of five languages (English, Spanish, French, Portuguese, Italian). Zero-shot language pairs have ASR data released for training but not translations. Cascades of separately trained automatic speech recognition and machine translation (MT) models can leverage all of these data sources.

2.1 Automatic Speech Recognition

We only focus on sequence-to-sequence ASR models. We firstly used a Transformer-based (Vaswani et al., 2017) model on FAIRSEQ[1]. Our transformer-based models presented as Synnaeve et al. (2019) consist of 2 1-D convolutional subsampler layers and 12 transformer encoder layers, 6 transformer decoder layers. The input mel-filterbank features are 80 dimensions, and the audio files' sample frequency is 16K. As Transformer models

[1]This tool can be found via https://github.com/pytorch/fairseq

Proceedings of the 18th International Conference on Spoken Language Translation, pages 144–148
Bangkok, Thailand (Online), August 5–6, 2021.

WER	layers	es	fr	pt	it
Transformer	12	15.68	17.23	21.69	20.66
	16	15.91	17.90	19.65	19.74
Conformer	12	15.1	16.7	18.8	18.9

Table 1: The results of the Transformer and Conformer ASR models with different encoder layers.

option	range
tempo	$(0.85, 1.25)$
speed	$(0.95, 1.05)$

Table 2: Sox parameters value ranges used in processing of audio data.

are good at capturing content-based global interactions, while CNNs exploit local features effectively. Then, we used the convolution-augmented transformer ASR model, Conformer (Gulati et al., 2020). The architecture settings are as the Conformer-base model using ESPnet[2] which also uses a joint CTC/attention decoding (Hori et al., 2017). The Conformer model consists of 2-D convolutional subsampler layers and 12 encoder layers, 6 decoder layers. The input features combine 80-dimension mel-filterbank features and 3 pitch features.

We remove all text sequences longer than 200 tokens and all speech utterances longer than 3000 frames. The two models both use a variant of SpecAugment(Park et al., 2019) for data augmentation. The Conformer model also used the speed perturbation technique. The results of the Conformer automatic speech recognition models are shown on the Table 1.

2.2 Multilingual Machine Translation

We created text-to-text machine translation baselines using FAIRSEQ (Ott et al., 2019a). We followed the recommended Transformer hyperparameters as the IWSLT'17 multilingual task. This model uses a shared BPE vocabulary of 16k learned jointly across all languages. We appended language ID tags to the beginning of each sentence for both the encoder and decoder.

For the provided translation data, some language pairs are zero shot. For example, language pair Italian-to-Spanish has no training data, but Spanish-to-Italian is provided. So we use the Spanish-to-Italian corpus in reverse and supplement it as the Italian-to-Spanish training corpus. The corpus of French to Spanish is also used in reverse, add to the training set of Spanish to French. This reverse use also adds language pairs, such as English-to-Spanish. At the same time, back translation (BT) is also used to generate a pseudo-corpus.

There is a gap between the transcription generated by the ASR model and the ground-truth transcription. In practice, the ASR-generated transcripts can be seen as noisy data by Gangi et al. (2019). We add the ASR-generated transcripts noisy data to train the MT model, to increase the system's robustness (Sperber et al., 2017).

At the same time, we also adopted the mask trick used in BERT (Devlin et al., 2019). We randomly mask some words in the source language sentence and use the last layer of encoder output to predict the masked words. The probability p of the masked tokens is 0.1.

We have not applied an individual bilingual translation model for each language pair while using a unified translation model for all language pairs. Our experiments show that multilingual text translation is more conducive to solving the zero-sample problem.

3 End-to-End Direct Speech Translation

We used FAIRSEQ to train end-to-end Transformer-based models for ST, using 80-dimensional mel-filterbank features with global Cepstral Mean and Variance Normalization (CMVN), SpecAugment (Park et al., 2019), and 1-D convolutions downsampler with the pretrained Transformer-based ASR model. We remove all text sequences longer than 200 tokens and all speech utterances longer than 6000 frames.

In order to make full use of the speech translation data of all language pairs, we adopt a joint vocabulary of 10K for all language pairs. In the beginning, we used the ASR model trained with all 4 languages ASR corpus to pre-train the ST, but in the end, the ASR model trained with just 1 language was used to pre-train the ST and the latter result was better. Same as the multilingual machine translation model, we prepend the source language ID tag to the frame sequence after the down-sampling of 1-D CNN layers. At the same time, we also prepend the target language ID tag to

[2]This tool can be accessed via `https://github.com/espnet/espnet`

source	target				
	en	es	fr	pt	it
es	39k(69h)	107k(189h)	7k(11h)	24k(42h)	6k(11h)
fr	33k(50h)	24k(38h)	119k(189h)	16k(25h)	-
pt	34k(59h)	zero-shot	-	93k(164h)	-
it	zero-shot	zero-shot	-	-	53k(107h)

Table 3: The number of sentences and the segment of audios for the Multilingual TEDx dataset. Same source and target languages mean the ASR data.

	ES-EN	FR-EN	FR-ES	PT-EN	PT-ES	IT-EN	IT-ES	
end-to-end	19.20	21.76	22.46	20.45	18.21	4.45	5.47	
+multi-task	19.61	22.69	23.45	21.20	20.79	4.31	5.83	
cascaded+(BT data)	24.01	28.52	33.67	28.07	36.52	15.21	27.04	MT
	20.29	24.51	26.83	22.42	26.71	14.61	22.13	ST
cascaded+(ASR noisy data)	25.11	30.16	34.14	29.13	36.69	15.42	26.62	MT
	20.56	24.60	26.81	22.03	26.46	14.58	22.07	ST
ensemble+beam12	21.28	26.21	28.98	23.43	27.99	15.71	23.19	ST

Table 4: The speech translation results of the test sets in BLEU score of different end-to-end and cascaded models.

the target text token sequence.

We augmented the data by processing the audio files with two Sox's effects as Potapczyk and Przybysz (2020): tempo, speed. We sampled the parameters with uniform distribution within ranges presented in Table 2: For each audio file, we repeated the process 2 times. The effect of this operation is basically similar to speed perturbation. Because ESPnet already uses speed perturbation by default, we only apply Sox's effects on the FAIRSEQ models.

As in many previous works, we also introduced a second decoder with ASR task, making it a multi-task setup similar to Weiss et al. (2017). The ASR and ST tasks use a joint dictionary of size 10k as the baseline. The training loss can be calculated as follows:

$$\text{Loss} = \text{Loss}_{ST} + \alpha \, \text{Loss}_{ASR} \quad (1)$$

We tried setting the value of α to 0.7 and 0.5, and the result was better when it was set to 0.5. Thus, the ASR and ST decoder are trained jointly, and convolutional layers and encoder are shared. The experiments also proved that this kind of multi-task learning is useful.

All the models consist of 12 encoder layers and 6 decoder layers, including the multi-task model.

For the one encoder-one decoder baseline, we just pretrain the encoder. For the multi-task model, we use the pretrained ASR model to initialize the shared encoder and ASR decoder. We also tried to pretrain only the shared encoder of the multi-task model. Our experimental results show that pretraining the ASR decoder will not improve the final effect of speech translation, but it can reduce the loss of the ASR decoder and the convergence time of training. We also tried to increase the number of encoder layers from 12 to 16, and the translation performance almost did not improve, but the number of convergence epochs decreased.

4 Experiments

In this section, we report the results for cascaded and end-to-end direct speech translation models on various data and settings.

For the ASR task, we tried 2 different platforms, the results as Table 1. For the cascaded speech translation models, the ASR part is implied on the ESPnet (Watanabe et al., 2018), while the MT component is implied on the FAIRSEQ (Ott et al., 2019b). For the end-to-end direct speech translation models, including the pretrained ASR models, all models are built on the FAIRSEQ.

For the cascaded speech translation models, all MT models have used the mask tokens trick, the main difference is just the different adding data. For the end-to-end direct speech translation models, all the models including the pretrained ASR models are trained including the Sox's effects data. All the parameter settings are almost unchanged. The ASR model trained with just 1 language (Spanish) was used to pretrain the ST. We tried only using Spanish or French ASR to pretrain the ST model, compared with all 4 multilingual ASR. Using multilingual ASR initialization led to a decrease of nearly 2.9 BLEU on ES-EN testset with only ES ASR. Pretraining with one language ASR is better than with all four languages, which surprised us a bit. We originally felt that the performance of the richer corpus model should be better. Perhaps understanding this problem will help improve the effectiveness of the multilingual end-to-end model.

Our multilingual translation model and end-to-end multilingual speech translation model both adopt a unified model for all language pairs, and do not apply special processing to individual language pairs.

4.1 Settings

For the Transformer-based ASR models are trained using the Adam optimizer, dropout probability of 0.1, and label smoothing. The learning rate schedule is inverse sqrt, with a learning rate 0.001, warmup from 10000. The same architecture is used to pretrain our direct speech translation models. The Conformer-based ASR model is also trained using the Adam optimizer and label smoothing, while warmup from 25000. For all ASR models, we apply byte-pair-encoding (BPE) (Sennrich et al., 2016) with 4k merge operations for every language.

For all the end-to-end direct ST models, the training settings are the same as the Transformer-based ASR models. While the multilingual end-to-end ST models apply BPE with 10k merge operations. All the models are trained of the 320000 batch size.

4.2 Results

As shown in Table 4, our cascade models represent better scores than our end-to-end models, particularly for low-resource language pairs. End-to-end models are closing the performance gap for high-resource settings. The early models on the experimental phase set the beam search size as 5 for saving time, while the final submitted ensemble model has a beam search size of 12. Finally, we submitted an ensembled cascaded system, which ensembles all multilingual MT models. The submitted model's BLEU scores are 34.5 on ES-EN, 25.2 on FR-EN, 27.4 on FR-ES, 25.7 on PT-EN, 31.6 on PT-ES, 20.8 on IT-EN, 27.3 on IT-ES.

References

Parnia Bahar, Patrick Wilken, Tamer Alkhouli, Andreas Guta, Pavel Golik, Evgeny Matusov, and Christian Herold. 2020. Start-before-end and end-to-end: Neural speech translation by apptek and RWTH aachen university. In *Proceedings of the 17th International Conference on Spoken Language Translation, IWSLT 2020, Online, July 9 - 10, 2020*, pages 44–54. Association for Computational Linguistics.

Jacob Devlin, Ming-Wei Chang, Kenton Lee, and Kristina Toutanova. 2019. BERT: pre-training of deep bidirectional transformers for language understanding. In *Proceedings of the 2019 Conference of the North American Chapter of the Association for Computational Linguistics: Human Language Technologies, NAACL-HLT 2019, Minneapolis, MN, USA, June 2-7, 2019, Volume 1 (Long and Short Papers)*, pages 4171–4186. Association for Computational Linguistics.

Mattia Antonino Di Gangi, Robert Enyedi, Alessandra Brusadin, and Marcello Federico. 2019. Robust neural machine translation for clean and noisy speech transcripts. *CoRR*, abs/1910.10238.

Anmol Gulati, James Qin, Chung-Cheng Chiu, Niki Parmar, Yu Zhang, Jiahui Yu, Wei Han, Shibo Wang, Zhengdong Zhang, Yonghui Wu, and Ruoming Pang. 2020. Conformer: Convolution-augmented transformer for speech recognition. In *Interspeech 2020, 21st Annual Conference of the International Speech Communication Association, Virtual Event, Shanghai, China, 25-29 October 2020*, pages 5036–5040. ISCA.

Takaaki Hori, Shinji Watanabe, and John R. Hershey. 2017. Joint ctc/attention decoding for end-to-end speech recognition. In *Proceedings of the 55th Annual Meeting of the Association for Computational Linguistics, ACL 2017, Vancouver, Canada, July 30 - August 4, Volume 1: Long Papers*, pages 518–529. Association for Computational Linguistics.

Myle Ott, Sergey Edunov, Alexei Baevski, Angela Fan, Sam Gross, Nathan Ng, David Grangier, and Michael Auli. 2019a. fairseq: A fast, extensible toolkit for sequence modeling. In *Proceedings of the 2019 Conference of the North American Chapter of the Association for Computational Linguistics (Demonstrations)*, pages 48–53, Minneapolis, Minnesota. Association for Computational Linguistics.

Myle Ott, Sergey Edunov, Alexei Baevski, Angela Fan, Sam Gross, Nathan Ng, David Grangier, and Michael Auli. 2019b. fairseq: A fast, extensible toolkit for sequence modeling. In *Proceedings of the 2019 Conference of the North American Chapter of the Association for Computational Linguistics: Human Language Technologies, NAACL-HLT 2019, Minneapolis, MN, USA, June 2-7, 2019, Demonstrations*, pages 48–53. Association for Computational Linguistics.

Daniel S. Park, William Chan, Yu Zhang, Chung-Cheng Chiu, Barret Zoph, Ekin D. Cubuk, and Quoc V. Le. 2019. Specaugment: A simple data augmentation method for automatic speech recognition. In *Interspeech 2019, 20th Annual Conference of the International Speech Communication Association, Graz, Austria, 15-19 September 2019*, pages 2613–2617. ISCA.

Tomasz Potapczyk and Pawel Przybysz. 2020. Srpol's system for the IWSLT 2020 end-to-end speech translation task. In *Proceedings of the 17th International Conference on Spoken Language Translation, IWSLT 2020, Online, July 9 - 10, 2020*, pages 89–94. Association for Computational Linguistics.

Elizabeth Salesky, Matthew Wiesner, Jacob Bremerman, Roldano Cattoni, Matteo Negri, Marco Turchi, Douglas W. Oard, and Matt Post. 2021. The multilingual tedx corpus for speech recognition and translation. *CoRR*, abs/2102.01757.

Rico Sennrich, Barry Haddow, and Alexandra Birch. 2016. Neural machine translation of rare words with subword units. In *Proceedings of the 54th Annual Meeting of the Association for Computational Linguistics, ACL 2016, August 7-12, 2016, Berlin, Germany, Volume 1: Long Papers*. The Association for Computer Linguistics.

Matthias Sperber, Jan Niehues, and Alex Waibel. 2017. Toward robust neural machine translation for noisy input sequences. In *International Workshop on Spoken Language Translation (IWSLT)*.

Gabriel Synnaeve, Qiantong Xu, Jacob Kahn, Edouard Grave, Tatiana Likhomanenko, Vineel Pratap, Anuroop Sriram, Vitaliy Liptchinsky, and Ronan Collobert. 2019. End-to-end ASR: from supervised to semi-supervised learning with modern architectures. *CoRR*, abs/1911.08460.

Ashish Vaswani, Noam Shazeer, Niki Parmar, Jakob Uszkoreit, Llion Jones, Aidan N. Gomez, Lukasz Kaiser, and Illia Polosukhin. 2017. Attention is all you need. In *Advances in Neural Information Processing Systems 30: Annual Conference on Neural Information Processing Systems 2017, December 4-9, 2017, Long Beach, CA, USA*, pages 5998–6008.

Shinji Watanabe, Takaaki Hori, Shigeki Karita, Tomoki Hayashi, Jiro Nishitoba, Yuya Unno, Nelson Enrique Yalta Soplin, Jahn Heymann, Matthew Wiesner, Nanxin Chen, Adithya Renduchintala, and Tsubasa Ochiai. 2018. Espnet: End-to-end speech processing toolkit. In *Interspeech 2018, 19th Annual Conference of the International Speech Communication Association, Hyderabad, India, 2-6 September 2018*, pages 2207–2211. ISCA.

Ron J. Weiss, Jan Chorowski, Navdeep Jaitly, Yonghui Wu, and Zhifeng Chen. 2017. Sequence-to-sequence models can directly translate foreign speech. In *Interspeech 2017, 18th Annual Conference of the International Speech Communication Association, Stockholm, Sweden, August 20-24, 2017*, pages 2625–2629. ISCA.

Multilingual Speech Translation with Unified Transformer: Huawei Noah's Ark Lab at IWSLT 2021

Xingshan Zeng, Liangyou Li, Qun Liu
Huawei Noah's Ark Lab
{zeng.xingshan, liliangyou, qun.liu}@huawei.com

Abstract

This paper describes the system submitted to the IWSLT 2021 Multilingual Speech Translation (MultiST) task from Huawei Noah's Ark Lab. We use a unified transformer architecture for our MultiST model, so that the data from different modalities (i.e., speech and text) and different tasks (i.e., Speech Recognition, Machine Translation, and Speech Translation) can be exploited to enhance the model's ability. Specifically, speech and text inputs are firstly fed to different feature extractors to extract acoustic and textual features, respectively. Then, these features are processed by a shared encoder–decoder architecture. We apply several training techniques to improve the performance, including multi-task learning, task-level curriculum learning, data augmentation, etc. Our final system achieves significantly better results than bilingual baselines on supervised language pairs and yields reasonable results on zero-shot language pairs.

1 Introduction

Multilingual Speech Translation (MultiST) aims to develop a single system that can directly translate speech in different languages into text in many other languages. Due to data scarcity of Speech Translation (ST), multilingual and multimodal models are promising as they enable knowledge transferred from other languages and related tasks like Automatic Speech Recognition (ASR) or Neural Machine Translation (NMT). They also allow zero-shot translation in the settings of no direct parallel data. The IWSLT 2021 MultiST task is held for evaluating the performance under the circumstances. This paper describes our system for the task.

We build a unified model for both speech- and text-related tasks, so that the knowledge from different modalities (speech and text) and different tasks (in this work, the tasks include ST, ASR, and NMT) can be learned together to enhance ST. Specifically, our model consists of three parts – feature extractor, semantic encoder and decoder. For all the tasks, the semantic encoder and the decoder will be shared to learn unified representations. It follows the Transformer (Vaswani et al., 2017) encoder-decoder framework to learn modality-independent features and output text representations. We use the Conv-Transformer (Huang et al., 2020) as feature extractor for speech input, and the word embedding for text input. The extracted features are then fed to the semantic encoder regardless of the input modality.

However, it is difficult for such a unified model to directly digest knowledge from diverse tasks. Therefore, we apply task-level curriculum learning for our model. We presume the ST task is more difficult than the other two tasks (ASR and NMT), as it not only requires acoustic modeling to extract speech representations, but also needs alignment knowledge between different languages for translation. To this end, our training is divided into three steps – ASR and NMT pre-training, joint multi-task learning, and ST fine-tuning. What's more, to alleviate the data scarcity problem, we also apply CTC multi-task learning (Graves et al., 2006), data augmentation techniques including SpecAugment (Bahar et al., 2019) and Time Stretch (Nguyen et al., 2020), and knowledge distillation (Liu et al., 2019), etc.

We conduct experiments in the constrained setting, i.e., only the Multilingual TEDx (Salesky et al., 2021) dataset is used for training. It contains speech and transcripts from four languages (Spanish, French, Portuguese, and Italian), and some of them are translated into English and/or other languages of the four mentioned above. Several language pairs for ST are provided without parallel training corpus and evaluated as zero-shot transla-

Proceedings of the 18th International Conference on Spoken Language Translation, pages 149–153
Bangkok, Thailand (Online), August 5–6, 2021.

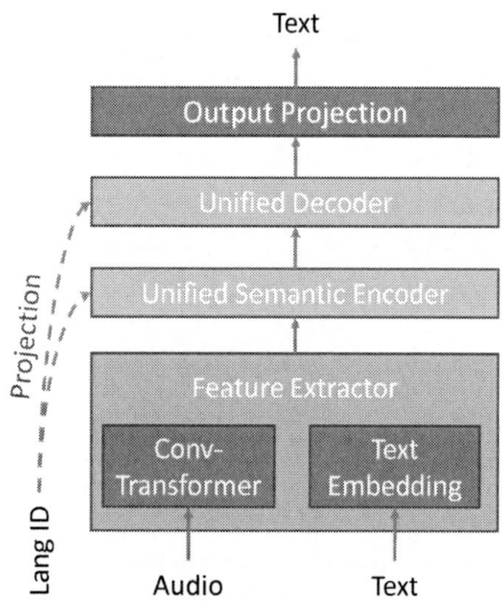

Figure 1: Overall structure of our unified model.

tion. The experimental results show that our unified model can achieve competitive results on both supervised settings and zero-shot settings.

2 Model Architecture

The architecture of our unified model, which is based on Transformer (Vaswani et al., 2017), is shown in Figure 1. The NMT part (both input and output is text) follows the basic Transformer setting, i.e. 6 layers for both the encoder and the decoder, each with 8 attention heads, 512 hidden dimensions, and 2048 hidden units in feed-forward layers. For the speech input, we replace the word embedding layer with the Conv-Transformer (Huang et al., 2020) encoder as acoustic modeling to extract audio features, and the rest are shared. The Conv-Transformer encoder gradually downsamples the speech input with interleaved convolution and Transformer layers. We downsample the speech input 8× times with three Conv-Transformer blocks, each contains three convolution layers (the stride number is 2 in the second convolution layer, and 1 in other layers) and two Transformer layers. The Conv-Transformer is set following Huang et al. (2020) and also consistent with the shared parts (in terms of hidden dimensions, etc). Then, the output is fed into the shared semantic encoder and decoder to produce text representations.

For language encoding, we apply language projection (Luo et al., 2021) to learn language-specific information. It replaces the language embedding in conventional multilingual models with a projection matrix before the positional embedding layer. With language IDs and input modality, our unified model can recognize the task that needs to be completed. For example, our model will perform ASR with speech input and the same language input and output IDs.

3 Techniques

Our model is trained in an end-to-end manner with all available data, including the ASR data (speech and transcript) and the ST data (speech, transcript and translation). From the ST data, we also extract the speech-transcript pairs as ASR data, and the transcript-translation pairs as NMT data. We apply task-level curriculum learning to train our model. At the same time, data augmentation, knowledge distillation, and model ensemble are used to further improve the performance. We describe the techniques in details in the rest of this section.

3.1 Task-Level Curriculum Learning

As a cross-modal and cross-lingual task, ST is more complicated than ASR or NMT. Therefore, we presume it is better for our unified model to learn in a smoother way. We divide the training procedure into three steps:

1. *ASR and NMT pre-training*: we use all the ASR and NMT data together to pre-train our unified model with a certain number of steps.

2. *Joint multi-task learning*: all the data including the ST data are used to jointly train the model in a multi-task manner.

3. *ST fine-tuning*: we fine-tune the model with only ST data to further improve the performance in specific language pairs[1].

For all the three steps, we use an additional CTC loss (Graves et al., 2006) on the output of the last layer of Conv-Transformer encoder to assist with the acoustic modeling. What's more, to make the model focus on the ST task, we assign less loss weights to ASR and NMT tasks (both 0.5, while 1.0 for ST) in step 2.

3.2 Data Augmentation

We use SpecAugment (Park et al., 2019; Bahar et al., 2019) and Time Stretch (Nguyen et al., 2020) to augment the speech data during training.

[1]Note that fine-tuning can only be applied in non zero-shot translation language pairs.

SpecAugment. SpecAugment is a data augmentation technique originally introduced for ASR, but proven to be effective in ST as well. It operates on the input filterbanks and consists of three kinds of operations, time warping, time masking, and frequency masking. We follow Bahar et al. (2019) and only apply time masking and frequency masking. It means that a number of consecutive portions of the speech input are masked in the time or the frequency dimensions. We always apply SpecAugment to both the ASR and ST tasks in the three training steps. We set the parameter for time masking T to 40 and that for frequency masking F to 4. The number of time and frequency masks applied m_T and m_F are 2 and 1, repsectively.

Time Stretch. Time stretching is a kind of augmentation method applied in extracted acoustic features like filterbanks to simulate conventional speed perturbation technique (Ko et al., 2015). Specifically, given a consecutive feature vectors of speech input, it stretches every window of w feature vectors by a factor of s obtained from an uniform distribution of range $[low, high]$. In this way, some frames are dropped (if $s > 1$) or repeated (if $s < 1$) to simulate audio speeding up or down. We only apply Time Stretch in the first two training steps, as we found it does not help much in fine-tuning. We set w to ∞, and $low = 0.8$, $high = 1.25$.

3.3 Knowledge Distillation

Teaching the ST model with a pre-trained NMT model using knowledge distillation has been shown effective (Liu et al., 2019). Hence we also use word-level knowledge distillation to help with training. Specifically, we minimize the KL divergence between the distribution produced by our model and that produced by the pre-trained NMT model. The tradeoff weight for the knowledge distillation part is set to 0.7 (i.e. 0.3 for cross entropy based on ground-truth targets). We use knowledge distillation only in the ST fine-tuning step.

3.4 Model Ensemble

Ensemble decoding is to average the word distribution output from diverse models at each decoding step. It is an very effective approach to improve the quality of NMT models. We select the top 2 or 3 models in terms of BLEU scores on development set for each language pair to perform ensemble decoding. The candidate models are trained with different hyper-parameters.

Source	Target Text				
	En	**Es**	**Fr**	**Pt**	**It**
Es	39k (69h)	107k (189h)	7k (11h)	24k (42h)	6k (11h)
Fr	33k (50h)	24k (38h)	119k (189h)	16k (25h)	–
Pt	34k (59h)	⋆	–	93k (164h)	–
It	⋆	⋆	–	–	53k (107h)

Table 1: The number of sentences and the duration of audios for the Multilingual TEDx dataset. Same source and target languages mean the ASR data. Noted with ⋆ are the language pairs for zero-shot translation.

4 Experiments and Results

4.1 Experimental Setup

We only participate in the constrained setting task. Therefore, only the data from the Multilingual TEDx (Salesky et al., 2021) is available. It contains speech and transcripts from four languages (Spanish, French, Portuguese, and Italian), and some of them are translated into other languages of the five (English and the four mentioned above). The data statistics are shown in Table 1.

We use 80-dimensional log-mel filterbanks as acoustic features, which are calculated with 25ms window size and 10ms step size and normalized by utterance-level Cepstral Mean and Variance Normalization (CMVN). For transcriptions and translations, SentencePiece[2] (Kudo and Richardson, 2018) is used to generate a joint subword vocabulary with the size of 10k. We share the weights for input and output embeddings, as well as the output projection in CTC module.

Our model is trained with 8 NVIDIA Tesla V100 GPUs, each with a batch size of 32. We use Adam optimizer (Kingma and Ba, 2015) during model training with learning rates selected in $\{2e^{-3}, 1e^{-3}, 8e^{-4}, 5e^{-4}, 3e^{-4}\}$ and warm-up steps selected in $\{2000, 6000, 10000\}$, followed by the inverse square root scheduler. Dropout rate is selected in $\{0.1, 0.2, 0.3\}$. We save checkpoints every epoch and average the last 10 checkpoints for evaluation with a beam size of 5. Our code is based on fairseq S2T[3] (Wang et al., 2020).

4.2 Results

This section shows the results of our unified model in Multilingual TEDx dataset. We display the results of our model for MultiST, as well as ASR and NMT, to show the efficacy of our unified model.

[2]https://github.com/google/sentencepiece

[3]https://github.com/pytorch/fairseq/tree/master/examples/speech_to_text

Model	Es-En	Es-Fr	Es-Pt	Es-It	Fr-En	Fr-Es	Fr-Pt	Pt-En	Pt-Es*	It-En*	It-Es*
Bilingual	16.60	0.70	16.16	0.50	17.49	13.74	1.26	16.83	–	–	–
+ASR data	19.17	9.55	29.59	14.19	24.56	25.13	23.38	21.95	–	–	–
Joint learn	23.97	21.76	33.52	22.04	27.65	30.08	30.62	26.36	24.50	14.99	12.34
Curriculum learn	25.13	22.72	35.54	24.51	29.75	31.88	31.91	28.07	26.14	15.82	14.98
+FT	25.01	22.72	35.04	24.12	29.91	31.87	31.81	27.83	–	–	–
+FT with KD	25.25	23.06	35.83	24.68	30.66	32.69	32.96	28.61	–	–	–
Ensemble	**26.47**	**23.94**	**36.59**	**25.25**	**31.60**	**33.86**	**34.07**	**29.02**	**27.12**	**16.14**	**16.82**

Table 2: BLEU scores of our unified model for Multilingual TEDx test sets. Those marked with * are the results for zero-shot translation. For each setting, we display the results with highest scores among different hyper-parameters. The ensemble results come from ensembling top 2 or 3 models based on the development sets.

MultiST. Table 2 shows the results of our model on MultiST. The first two rows display the results with only bilingual data. As can be seen, it is difficult for an end-to-end model to produce reasonable results with extremely low resources (less than 30 hours, including language pairs Es-Fr, Es-It and Fr-Pt as in Table 1). With sufficient additional ASR data, all language pairs are improved in a large scale, especially for those low-resource language-pairs (e.g. from 1.26 to 23.38 on Fr-Pt).

The rest rows are the results in multilingual settings, where we use all the available data. "Joint learn" means that we directly train the multilingual model from scratch. "Curriculum learn" displays the results after the first two training steps in Section 3.1, while "+FT" means adding the third fine-tuning step. "KD" refers to knowledge distillation. We can find that ASR and NMT pre-training helps the model learn better representations to perform translation. Then, fine-tuning with knowledge distillation further improve the results. This indicates the efficacy of our task-level curriculum learning for MultiST. However, we find that fine-tuning only with ground-truth targets would not improve the performance. This might be attributed to the limited ST training data, as all of them are less than 100 hours, which introduces difficulty to learn efficiently. By incorporating knowledge distillation, it enables our model to learn extra meaningful knowledge from NMT, so that it can further improve the results.

It can also be found that our unified model can perform reasonable zero-shot speech translation, as all the zero-shot language pairs achieve higher than 10 BLEU scores. Specifically, results for Pt-Es even achieve similar scores compared with other supervised language pairs. This is mostly because Portuguese and Spanish are similar languages so that it is easier for the model to transfer knowledge from other data.

Model	Es	Fr	Pt	It
Monolingual	19.93	22.49	24.86	22.94
Multilingual-ASR	13.75	16.79	17.67	16.22
Joint learn	15.69	17.46	19.85	19.12
Curriculum learn	14.99	16.97	18.06	18.42
+FT	**12.53**	**14.56**	**15.75**	**15.38**

Table 3: WER of our unified model for ASR test sets.

Model	Es-En	Es-Fr	Es-Pt	Es-It
Multilingual-NMT	30.41	22.35	41.99	25.62
Joint learn	31.11	**28.25**	**44.12**	**27.88**
Curriculum learn	30.82	27.87	43.36	27.46
+FT	**31.43**	27.81	43.53	27.46
Model	**Fr-En**	**Fr-Es**	**Fr-Pt**	**Pt-En**
Multilingual-NMT	35.44	36.89	37.46	33.83
Joint learn	**37.17**	**39.78**	**40.66**	**35.54**
Curriculum learn	36.15	38.83	39.38	34.40
+FT	36.42	38.99	39.43	34.78

Table 4: BLEU of our unified model for NMT test sets.

ASR and NMT. We also test our unified model on the ASR and NMT tasks. Table 3 and Table 4 display the results for ASR and NMT, respectively. "Multilingual-ASR (NMT)" is the model trained only with multilingual ASR (NMT) data. From the results, we can find that ASR also benefits from the task-level curriculum learning procedure. However, it only improves slightly compared to the model only with ASR data, probably because the speech in ST data is sampled from the ASR data (Salesky et al., 2021). It surprises us that NMT can also benefit from extra data from different modality (i.e. speech), although curriculum learning does not improve the performance (probably because we assign less loss weight to NMT task in step 2 as introduced in Section 3.1). This demonstrates the potential of leveraging data from different modalities to train a powerful unified model. Due to the time and data constraint, we leave the exploration into a more powerful unified model with multiple kinds of data as future work.

Submissions. We submit our results on ST evaluation sets with the ensemble model in Table 2, scoring BLEU scores 35.4 on Es-En, 27.0 on Es-Fr, 43.2 on Es-Pt, 30.8 on Es-It, 26.7 on Fr-En, 27.0 on Fr-Es, 26.9 on Fr-Pt, 26.7 on Pt-En, 27.0 on Pt-Es, 17.6 on It-En, and 15.4 on It-Es. We also submit our ASR results on evaluation sets with our fine-tuned model (i.e. "+FT" model in Table 3), scoring 11.1 WER on Es ASR, 22.2 on Fr ASR, 16.2 on It ASR, and 23.8 on Pt ASR.

5 Conclusions

We present our system submitted to IWSLT 2021 for multilingual speech translation task. In our system, we build a unified transformer-based model to learn the knowledge from different kinds of data. We introduce a task-level curriculum learning procedure to enable our unified model to be trained efficiently. Our results show the efficacy of our unified model to perform multilingual speech translation in both supervised settings and zero-shot settings. Moreover, the results demonstrate the potential of incorporating multilingual and even multi-modal data into one powerful unified model.

References

Parnia Bahar, Albert Zeyer, Ralf Schlüter, and Hermann Ney. 2019. On using specaugment for end-to-end speech translation. *CoRR*, abs/1911.08876.

Alex Graves, Santiago Fernández, Faustino J. Gomez, and Jürgen Schmidhuber. 2006. Connectionist temporal classification: labelling unsegmented sequence data with recurrent neural networks. In *Machine Learning, Proceedings of the Twenty-Third International Conference (ICML 2006)*, volume 148 of *ACM International Conference Proceeding Series*, pages 369–376. ACM.

Wenyong Huang, Wenchao Hu, Yu Ting Yeung, and Xiao Chen. 2020. Conv-transformer transducer: Low latency, low frame rate, streamable end-to-end speech recognition. In *Interspeech 2020, 21st Annual Conference of the International Speech Communication Association, Virtual Event, Shanghai, China, 25-29 October 2020*, pages 5001–5005. ISCA.

Diederik P. Kingma and Jimmy Ba. 2015. Adam: A method for stochastic optimization. In *3rd International Conference on Learning Representations, ICLR 2015, San Diego, CA, USA, May 7-9, 2015, Conference Track Proceedings*.

Tom Ko, Vijayaditya Peddinti, Daniel Povey, and Sanjeev Khudanpur. 2015. Audio augmentation for speech recognition. In *INTERSPEECH 2015, 16th Annual Conference of the International Speech Communication Association, Dresden, Germany, September 6-10, 2015*, pages 3586–3589. ISCA.

Taku Kudo and John Richardson. 2018. SentencePiece: A simple and language independent subword tokenizer and detokenizer for neural text processing. In *Proceedings of the 2018 Conference on Empirical Methods in Natural Language Processing: System Demonstrations*, pages 66–71, Brussels, Belgium. Association for Computational Linguistics.

Yuchen Liu, Hao Xiong, Jiajun Zhang, Zhongjun He, Hua Wu, Haifeng Wang, and Chengqing Zong. 2019. End-to-end speech translation with knowledge distillation. In *Interspeech 2019, 20th Annual Conference of the International Speech Communication Association, Graz, Austria, 15-19 September 2019*, pages 1128–1132. ISCA.

Shengjie Luo, Kaiyuan Gao, Shuxin Zheng, Guolin Ke, Di He, Liwei Wang, and Tie-Yan Liu. 2021. Revisiting language encoding in learning multilingual representations. *CoRR*, abs/2102.08357.

Thai-Son Nguyen, Sebastian Stüker, Jan Niehues, and Alex Waibel. 2020. Improving sequence-to-sequence speech recognition training with on-the-fly data augmentation. In *2020 IEEE International Conference on Acoustics, Speech and Signal Processing, ICASSP 2020, Barcelona, Spain, May 4-8, 2020*, pages 7689–7693. IEEE.

Daniel S. Park, William Chan, Yu Zhang, Chung-Cheng Chiu, Barret Zoph, Ekin D. Cubuk, and Quoc V. Le. 2019. Specaugment: A simple data augmentation method for automatic speech recognition. In *Interspeech 2019, 20th Annual Conference of the International Speech Communication Association, Graz, Austria, 15-19 September 2019*, pages 2613–2617. ISCA.

Elizabeth Salesky, Matthew Wiesner, Jacob Bremerman, Roldano Cattoni, Matteo Negri, Marco Turchi, Douglas W. Oard, and Matt Post. 2021. The multilingual tedx corpus for speech recognition and translation. *CoRR*, abs/2102.01757.

Ashish Vaswani, Noam Shazeer, Niki Parmar, Jakob Uszkoreit, Llion Jones, Aidan N. Gomez, Lukasz Kaiser, and Illia Polosukhin. 2017. Attention is all you need. In *Advances in Neural Information Processing Systems 30: Annual Conference on Neural Information Processing Systems 2017, December 4-9, 2017, Long Beach, CA, USA*, pages 5998–6008.

Changhan Wang, Yun Tang, Xutai Ma, Anne Wu, Dmytro Okhonko, and Juan Pino. 2020. Fairseq S2T: Fast speech-to-text modeling with fairseq. In *Proceedings of the 1st Conference of the Asia-Pacific Chapter of the Association for Computational Linguistics and the 10th International Joint Conference on Natural Language Processing: System Demonstrations*, pages 33–39, Suzhou, China. Association for Computational Linguistics.

Multilingual Speech Translation KIT @ IWSLT2021

Ngoc-Quan Pham, Dan He, Tuan-Nam Nguyen,
Thanh-Le Ha, Sebastian Stüker, Alexander Waibel
Karlsruhe Institute of Technology
ngoc.pham@kit.edu

Abstract

This paper contains the description for the submission of Karlsruhe Institute of Technology (KIT) for the multilingual TEDx translation task in the IWSLT 2021 evaluation campaign. Our main approach is to develop both cascade and end-to-end systems and eventually combine them together to achieve the best possible results for this extremely low-resource setting. The report also confirms certain consistent architectural improvement added to the Transformer architecture, for all tasks: translation, transcription and speech translation.

1 Introduction

The neural sequence-to-sequence models have revolutionalised both automatic speech recognition (ASR) and machine translation in many different aspects, from performance (Luong et al., 2015; Pham et al., 2019a) to various forms such as multimodal (Barrault et al., 2018) and multilingual (Kannan et al., 2019; Ha et al., 2016; Johnson et al., 2016). After multilingual text translation has been established, the recent focus is naturally shifted to multilingual speech translation especially with a series of public speech corpora with multiple translation being released (Iranzo-Sánchez et al., 2020; Wang et al., 2020; Salesky et al., 2021).

Recent evaluation campaigns in speech translation have seen a fierce competition between traditional cascade systems and end-to-end counterparts (Jan et al., 2018, 2019; Ansari et al., 2020). The competition without a doubt would continue in multilingual speech translation especially in a low-resource condition. However, the competition between two modeling schemes suggests that each of them possesses its own strengths and advantages. Notably the cascade models can easily benefit from the separated optimized architectures of each subtask and enjoy the larger available datasets, while the end-to-end models can theoretically avoid *error propagation*.

This manuscript describes the translation system for the multilingual TEDx task with the aim of combining the strong points of both approaches. We showed that optimizing the cascade models is necessary to bootstrap a powerful end-to-end model, while in the end combining their powers based on ensembling gives promising results.

2 Dataset overview

The Multilingual TEDx corpus (Salesky et al., 2021) provided us with the 5 languages Spanish (es), French (fr), Italian (it), Portuguese (pt) and English (en). While speech audio is available for the first 4 languages, text translation is available for all 20 language pairs, and the speech translation parallel data is largely more scarce than the other two. The data statistics is shown in Table 1 and 2.

Source → Target	**en**	**es**	**fr**	**it**	**pt**
es	36K	102K	3.6K	5.6K	21K
fr	30K	20K	116K	-	-
it	-	-	-	50K	-
pt	-	30K	-	-	90K

Table 1: Data statistics for speech recognition/translation in the number of utterances.

Source → Target	**en**	**es**	**fr**	**it**	**pt**
en	-	36.2K	30.5K	-	30.8K
es	36.2K	-	24.4K	5.6K	21.1K
fr	30.1K	24.4K	-	-	13.2K
it	-	5.6K	-	-	-
pt	30.8K	21.1K	13.2K	-	

Table 2: Data statistics for machine translation in the number of sentence pairs.

It is noticeable that the training data is severely lacking for speech translation when the number of sentences is only a fraction of the ASR or MT resources. As a result, our initial plan was to generate

Proceedings of the 18th International Conference on Spoken Language Translation, pages 154–159
Bangkok, Thailand (Online), August 5–6, 2021. ©2021 Association for Computational Linguistics

synthetic translations from the available transcripts, that can effectively increase the data size for training end-to-end SLT models.

3 General enhancement for Transformer Models

In this section, we describe the overall model descriptions that were applied in all three tasks.

Transformers (Vaswani et al., 2017) are constructed with blocks of transformation functions including self-attention and feed-forward neural networks.

Self-attention transforms a sequence of states using themselves as queries, keys and values, building up hierarchical representational powers since the output states are the weighted-sum of the input states that can be flexibly learned during training. Relative attention (Shaw et al., 2018) further improves the interaction between states by assigning learnable weights for each relative position. (Pham et al., 2020) incorporated this mechanism into speech models by extending the partially learnable relative positions in (Dai et al., 2019) to attend to all positions in the sequence bidirectionally.

Furthermore, the Transformer models are strengthened by using dual feed-forward (FFN) layers per block instead of one (Lu et al., 2019). As such, one feed-forward network block precedes the initial self-attention in either encoder and decoder. The outputs of both FFN layers are scaled by 0.5. Besides, it is possible to help training deep Transformer better by using RELU-inspired activation functions that do not suffer from dead neurons. GELU (Hendrycks and Gimpel, 2016) and SiLU (Elfwing et al., 2018) are combined with gated linear units (Dauphin et al., 2017), as used in our activation functions.

In most of our experiments and in the eventual submission, all of the above enhancements were incorporated. Ablation studies are unfortunately not fully possible because of the time constraint, but will be provided to depict the improvement of each addition.

4 Speech Recognition

Our speech recognition models are built based on both the LSTM and the Speech Deep Transformer (Pham et al., 2019a) enhanced with bidirectional relative attention (Pham et al., 2020). While LSTM models have been intensively experimented for the best results (Nguyen et al., 2019a; Park et al., 2019), Transformers have been recently adopted to this task with strong results (Pham et al., 2019a, 2020).

For the four languages in the Multilingual TEDx, we trained both multilingual Transformers and LSTM models on the combination of the datasets, using the factorization scheme. The LSTM has 6 encoder layers and 2 decoder layers with 1024 hidden units in each layer. The sole attention layer between encoder and decoder is an 8-head dot-product attention. On the other hand, we experimented the Transformers with the "Large" models having 16 encoder layers and 6 decoder layers with 1024 units in the hidden layers.

The models are trained with Adam and an inverse square-root learning rate schedules with 4096 warm-up steps following the same setting as (Vaswani et al., 2017) for up-to 120K steps or early-stopping on the development set. In order to facilitate training, layers are randomly dropped with the highest rate of 0.5 and linearly reducing from top to bottom (Pham et al., 2019a). Due to the relatively small size of the dataset, regularization is added with dropout probability 0.35 in all layers, and spec augmentation with dropped frequency range is $F = 16$ and the maximum dropped time $T = 64$ which is relatively aggressive.

Language	LSTM	bTF	eTF	Ensemble
es	16.9	16.4	15.25	14.37
fr	16.5	16.8	15.39	14.44
pt	18.3	19.5	17.1	16.79
it	19.5	16.4	17.24	15.47

Table 3: Comparison on Multilingual TEDx dataset (WER↓). Our baseline models include the baseline (b) and enhanced (e) Transformers (TF) and the LSTM.

Table 3 shows the experimental result of speech recognition, in which we can see that the Transformer with only Relative attention is as good as the LSTM, while using all enhancements allowed us to improve the result further. It is notable that those results are obtained using our own word error rate measuring method that does not remove punctuations, which are retained in ASR to be compatible with the subsequent MT models.

Removing the punctuations and using the evaluation scripts in the same repo with (Salesky et al., 2021) gave us 11.0, 13.88, 13.38 and 14.14 error rates for Spanish, Italian, French and Portuguese respectively, which are significantly lower than the

Hybrid LF-MMI provided.

5 Machine Translation

Our multilingual machine translation is built based on the universal multilingual framework (Ha et al., 2016; Johnson et al., 2016; Pham et al., 2019b), in which the vocabulary is shared between languages using a BPE size of 16000 merging units.

Thanks to the relatively small data size, the translation task was used to measure the incremental improvement of various features, including the relative attention and the Macaron feed-forward layers. Therefore, experiments were carried out using the base-setting of Transformer as the starting point. Dropout was increased to 0.35 together with word dropout (Gal and Ghahramani, 2016) at both encoder and decoder to help the models counter overfitting. The output language is controlled by the language embedding vectors added directly to the word embedding at every timestep (Ha et al., 2017; Pham et al., 2019b). The language pairs are randomly sampled based on the training size of each pair (no temperature was used). Training is done using the adaptive learning rate for Adam, with maximum learning rate at 0.7 achieved after 4096 warming-up steps, and is often early-stopped after 60000 training steps, each is approximately 48000 words.

Regularization is further improved via data diversification (Nguyen et al., 2019b). Carrying a similar idea of back-translation (Sennrich et al., 2016) that generates synthetic labels for untranslated monolingual data, the main idea of data diversification is to popularize the available training data with synthetic translation of both source sentences and target sentences.

According to the algorithm presented in (Nguyen et al., 2019b), the training process is divided into rounds in which the training data is incrementally added with synthetic data coming from the refining models themselves. Starting from the original training data in round 0, we use the best settings in round n to translate the source and target sentences in the training to the counterpart language and add the synthetic translation pairs to the current training data, proceeding to round $n + 1$. Each synthetic pair consists of one original sentence and one synthetic sentence. The idea is the combination of backtranslation, model distillation (Kim and Rush, 2016) and data augmentation (Wang et al., 2018) without any additional data.

Interestingly, thanks to the multilingual property, it is also possible to translate one sentence to a range of languages after each round, leading to different options and a massive amount of sentences to be added. However, it was empirically found out that the method did not scale after 1 round, and massively translating to all languages did not improve the training data. Therefore, after round 0, the best configuration which is an ensemble is used to generate synthetic parallel data for round 1 by just translating each sentence to the same language in the original dataset.

The translation result is seen in Table 4. We showed the progressive results as a result of adding each empirical feature, and measured the change in average over 14 language pairs. Even though the training data also contains language pairs that are not included for the SLT task, we found that adding those "reverse" language pairs is beneficial for the others.

In terms of improvement, it can be seen that even though in this extreme low-resource scenario, using more complicated architecture obtained better translations. A combination of relative attention, macaron FFN and 16 layers of depth allowed us to improve the baseline by 0.95 BLEU points, in which the relative attention seems to be the most useful. Ensembling multiple models is, as expected but costly to improve the results further.

Data diversification was very effective after the first round, by improving the average score by nearly 1 BLEU point. Italian-related language pairs enjoyed up to 2 BLEU points, due to the lowest amount of original sentences. This result somewhat went against the initial expectation, because by not changing the sampling method, the data ratio for those languages was even lower than in round 0.

We obtained the best configuration for text translation with ensembles on round 1. Proceeding to round 2 unfortunately did not produce any further improvement, which might be reasoned by the dominance of synthetic sentences in terms of quantity.

6 End-to-end Speech Translation

Naturally, end-to-end speech translation is developed at the last stage to benefit from the previous stages. The ASR models serve as providing the SLT with the pretrained encoder, while we used the MT model to fill the gaps, i.e translate all available ASR data. This allows us to increase the amount of training data for SLT significantly, especially for

Pair/Model	TF	+Rel	+MCR	+16L	+ESB	+DSF	+ESB	+DSF2
es-en	33.48	33.98	34.94	34.93	35.16	35.88	**36.14**	35.83
en-es	30.87	31.34	31.88	31.72	32.76	33.42	**33.97**	33.56
es-fr	40.65	41.40	41.19	41.26	42.06	42.87	**43.57**	43.12
fr-es	38.48	38.59	38.98	38.85	39.87	40.82	**41.09**	40.88
es-it	28.82	29.07	30.24	31.29	31.27	32.50	**33.80**	32.93
it-es	34.74	35.27	35.25	35.31	36.58	38.41	**39.01**	38.50
es-pt	43.04	43.40	43.65	43.53	44.30	44.96	**45.40**	45.03
pt-es	46.95	47.01	46.63	46.59	47.70	48.74	**48.95**	48.41
fr-en	38.29	38.62	39.64	39.53	40.32	41.09	**41.65**	40.93
en-fr	39.88	40.47	40.85	41.18	41.51	42.40	**43.17**	42.14
fr-pt	40.61	41.31	41.71	42.52	42.50	43.94	**44.25**	43.52
pt-fr	46.14	46.42	46.57	47.02	47.76	48.90	**49.66**	48.76
fr-pt	37.67	38.49	38.73	39.81	39.57	40.23	**40.55**	39.52
pt-fr	34.60	34.53	35.07	35.43	35.58	36.59	**37.05**	36.51
avg	38.16	38.56	38.95	39.21	39.78	40.76	41.3	40.68
		+0.4	+0.29	+0.26	+0.57	+0.98	+0.54	-0.62

Table 4: IWSLT 2021 machine translation progressive results. The features including Relative Attention (REL), Macaron FFN (MCR), 16 layer-deep (16L), ensembling (ESB) and diversification (DSF) are additive from left to right, starting from the base model. The last row shows the improvement compared to the previous increment.

languages such as Italian and French.

Architecture wise, we only used Transformers for SLT, that followed the same training procedure with ASR due to the fact that the encoders are transferred from the Transformer ASR models.

The results are shown in Table 5. Unfortunately the results without ASR pre-training are not available because training was unstable and likely to diverge in such harsh data condition. It is not unexpected that the end-to-end model (E2E) trained with only the initially limited amount of data falls behind the performance of the cascade models. With distillation from machine translation, the performance is largely boosted to be on par with the cascade. The 0.2 differential in average mostly comes from Portuguese-Spanish, Italian-English and Italian-Spanish.

Compared with pre-distillation, a lot of language-pairs enjoyed a significant improvement of up to 26 BLEU points, such as the sample Italian audio inputs, thanks to the distillation models changing zero-shot to supervised settings. The supervised language pair that was mostly improved is Spanish-French (12 BLEU points).

Finally, in this particular SLT setup, we found that it is useful to ensemble cascade and SLT models in a multi-modal manner. In the literature, it has been observed that each approach has its own strength. While the components of the cascade can be easily tuned individually because ASR and MT have lower mapping complexity than SLT, the end-to-end models can avoid error-propagation that plagues cascade systems. An ensemble suggests that we can combine the strengths of two approach, yet only available in certain experimental settings that leaves *audio segmentation* out of the scope. Here the ensemble is done by simply using the same bpe vocabulary for the MT and SLT models, and average the output probabilities of the MT and SLT models for every timestep. The result showed that this intuition can help improve the results further.

7 Final submission

Our final submissions include an ensemble of E2E and Cascade as primary, with the E2E model served as the contrastive. The official results are shown in Table 6.

In the final results, we can see that the ensemble quality depends on the ASR performance, which can be seen in test sets with Spanish audio and French audio. At the relatively low error rate, combining two approaches provides a significant boost to the translation quality. However, for French samples the deterioration of the cascade makes the combination worse than the sole end-to-end solu-

Model Pair	Cascade	E2E	+Syn	+ESB
es-en	30.44	25.58	30.27	**31.02**
es-fr	31.64	18.81	31.32	**32.25**
es-it	26.07	22.94	26.22	**26.21**
es-pt	39.33	34.73	39.53	**40.04**
fr-en	35.41	29.73	35.19	**36.06**
fr-es	37.71	30.13	38.48	**38.96**
fr-pt	38.21	30.98	37.97	**38.44**
pt-en	33.63	28.16	33.25	**34.15**
pt-es	37.53	25.55	38.41	**38.43**
it-en	24.28	5.37	24.92	**25.29**
it-es	32.29	7.20	33.67	**33.90**
avg	33.32	23.56	33.56	**34.06**

Table 5: End-to-end speech translation results on progressive testsets.

SLT Pair	Ensemble	E2E
es-en	39.3	38.9
es-fr	32.4	31.4
es-it	32.3	31.4
es-pt	46.6	46.7
fr-en	27.1	28.5
fr-es	29.2	29.7
fr-pt	28.8	28.7
pt-en	30.7	30.2
pt-es	37.3	37.1
it-en	26.5	25.8
it-es	32.4	33.0
ASR		
es	10.0	-
fr	26.5	-
it	15.5	-
pt	22.1	-

Table 6: Official IWSLT 2021 Speech recognition and translation results.

tion.

This experiment shows that error propagation is a serious problem and end-to-end SLT systems can be more robust than cascades with sufficient data and training efficiency improvement.

The evaluation also suggests us to investigate into zero-shot translation for multilingual SLT, which is extremely difficult because of the modality difference between the source and target sequences.

Acknowledgments

The work leading to these results has received funding from the European Union under grant agreement n°825460 and the Federal Ministry of Education and Research/DLR Projektträger Bereich Gesundheit (Germany) under grant agreement n° 01EF1803B.

References

Ebrahim Ansari, Nguyen Bach, Ondřej Bojar, Roldano Cattoni, Fahim Dalvi, Nadir Durrani, Marcello Federico, Christian Federmann, Jiatao Gu, Fei Huang, et al. 2020. Findings of the iwslt 2020 evaluation campaign. In *Proceedings of the 17th International Conference on Spoken Language Translation*, pages 1–34.

Loïc Barrault, Fethi Bougares, Lucia Specia, Chiraag Lala, Desmond Elliott, and Stella Frank. 2018. Findings of the third shared task on multimodal machine translation. In *THIRD CONFERENCE ON MACHINE TRANSLATION (WMT18)*, volume 2, pages 308–327.

Zihang Dai, Zhilin Yang, Yiming Yang, Jaime Carbonell, Quoc Le, and Ruslan Salakhutdinov. 2019. Transformer-XL: Attentive language models beyond a fixed-length context. In *Proceedings of the 57th Annual Meeting of the Association for Computational Linguistics (ACL)*.

Yann N Dauphin, Angela Fan, Michael Auli, and David Grangier. 2017. Language modeling with gated convolutional networks. In *International conference on machine learning*, pages 933–941. PMLR.

Stefan Elfwing, Eiji Uchibe, and Kenji Doya. 2018. Sigmoid-weighted linear units for neural network function approximation in reinforcement learning. *Neural Networks*, 107:3–11.

Yarin Gal and Zoubin Ghahramani. 2016. Bayesian convolutional neural networks with Bernoulli approximate variational inference. In *4th International Conference on Learning Representations (ICLR) workshop track*.

Thanh-Le Ha, Jan Niehues, and Alexander Waibel. 2016. Toward Multilingual Neural Machine Translation with Universal Encoder and Decoder. In *Proceedings of the 13th International Workshop on Spoken Language Translation (IWSLT 2016)*, Seattle, USA.

Thanh-Le Ha, Jan Niehues, and Alexander Waibel. 2017. Effective strategies in zero-shot neural machine translation. *arXiv preprint arXiv:1711.07893*.

Dan Hendrycks and Kevin Gimpel. 2016. Gaussian error linear units (gelus). *arXiv preprint arXiv:1606.08415*.

Javier Iranzo-Sánchez, Joan Albert Silvestre-Cerdà, Javier Jorge, Nahuel Roselló, Adrià Giménez, Albert Sanchis, Jorge Civera, and Alfons Juan. 2020. Europarl-st: A multilingual corpus for speech translation of parliamentary debates. In *ICASSP 2020-2020 IEEE International Conference on Acoustics, Speech and Signal Processing (ICASSP)*, pages 8229–8233. IEEE.

Niehues Jan, Roldano Cattoni, Stuker Sebastian, Matteo Negri, Marco Turchi, Salesky Elizabeth, Sanabria Ramon, Barrault Loic, Specia Lucia, and Marcello Federico. 2019. The iwslt 2019 evaluation campaign. In *16th International Workshop on Spoken Language Translation 2019*.

Niehues Jan, Roldano Cattoni, Stuker Sebastian, Marco Turchi, Mauro Cettolo, and Marcello Federico. 2018. The iwslt 2018 evaluation campaign. In *15th International Workshop on Spoken Language Translation 2018*.

M. Johnson, M. Schuster, Q. V. Le, M. Krikun, Y. Wu, Z. Chen, N. Thorat, F. B. Viegas, M. Wattenberg, G. Corrado, M. Hughes, and J. Dean. 2016. Google's multilingual neural machine translation system: Enabling zero-shot translation. *CoRR*, abs/1611.04558.

Anjuli Kannan, Arindrima Datta, Tara N Sainath, Eugene Weinstein, Bhuvana Ramabhadran, Yonghui Wu, Ankur Bapna, Zhifeng Chen, and Seungji Lee. 2019. Large-scale multilingual speech recognition with a streaming end-to-end model. *arXiv preprint arXiv:1909.05330*.

Yoon Kim and Alexander M Rush. 2016. Sequence-level knowledge distillation. *arXiv preprint arXiv:1606.07947*.

Yiping Lu, Zhuohan Li, Di He, Zhiqing Sun, Bin Dong, Tao Qin, Liwei Wang, and Tie-Yan Liu. 2019. Understanding and improving transformer from a multi-particle dynamic system point of view. *arXiv preprint arXiv:1906.02762*.

Minh-Thang Luong, Hieu Pham, and Christopher D Manning. 2015. Effective approaches to attention-based neural machine translation. *arXiv preprint arXiv:1508.04025*.

Thai-Son Nguyen, Sebastian Stueker, Jan Niehues, and Alex Waibel. 2019a. Improving sequence-to-sequence speech recognition training with on-the-fly data augmentation. *arXiv preprint arXiv:1910.13296*.

Xuan-Phi Nguyen, Shafiq Joty, Wu Kui, and Ai Ti Aw. 2019b. Data diversification: A simple strategy for neural machine translation. *arXiv preprint arXiv:1911.01986*.

Daniel S Park, William Chan, Yu Zhang, Chung-Cheng Chiu, Barret Zoph, Ekin D Cubuk, and Quoc V Le. 2019. Specaugment: A simple data augmentation method for automatic speech recognition. *arXiv preprint arXiv:1904.08779*.

Ngoc-Quan Pham, Thanh-Le Ha, Tuan-Nam Nguyen, Thai-Son Nguyen, Elizabeth Salesky, Sebastian Stüker, Jan Niehues, and Alex Waibel. 2020. Relative Positional Encoding for Speech Recognition and Direct Translation. In *Proc. Interspeech 2020*, pages 31–35.

Ngoc-Quan Pham, Thai-Son Nguyen, Thanh-Le Ha, Juan Hussain, Felix Schneider, Jan Niehues, Sebastian Stüker, and Alexander Waibel. 2019a. The iwslt 2019 kit speech translation system. In *Proceedings of the 16th International Workshop on Spoken Language Translation (IWSLT 2019)*.

Ngoc-Quan Pham, Jan Niehues, Thanh-Le Ha, and Alexander Waibel. 2019b. Improving zero-shot translation with language-independent constraints. In *Proceedings of the Fourth Conference on Machine Translation (Volume 1: Research Papers)*, pages 13–23, Florence, Italy. Association for Computational Linguistics.

Elizabeth Salesky, Matthew Wiesner, Jacob Bremerman, Roldano Cattoni, Matteo Negri, Marco Turchi, Douglas W Oard, and Matt Post. 2021. The multilingual tedx corpus for speech recognition and translation. *arXiv preprint arXiv:2102.01757*.

Rico Sennrich, Barry Haddow, and Alexandra Birch. 2016. Neural machine translation of rare words with subword units. *Proceedings of the 54th Annual Meeting of the Association for Computational Linguistics (Volume 1: Long Papers)*.

Peter Shaw, Jakob Uszkoreit, and Ashish Vaswani. 2018. Self-attention with relative position representations. In *Proceedings of the 2018 Conference of the North American Chapter of the Association for Computational Linguistics: Human Language Technologies, Volume 2 (Short Papers)*, pages 464–468, New Orleans, Louisiana. Association for Computational Linguistics.

Ashish Vaswani, Noam Shazeer, Niki Parmar, Jakob Uszkoreit, Llion Jones, Aidan N Gomez, Łukasz Kaiser, and Illia Polosukhin. 2017. Attention is all you need. In *Advances in Neural Information Processing Systems*, pages 5998–6008.

Changhan Wang, Anne Wu, and Juan Pino. 2020. Covost 2: A massively multilingual speech-to-text translation corpus.

Xinyi Wang, Hieu Pham, Zihang Dai, and Graham Neubig. 2018. SwitchOut: an efficient data augmentation algorithm for neural machine translation. In *Proceedings of the 2018 Conference on Empirical Methods in Natural Language Processing*, pages 856–861, Brussels, Belgium. Association for Computational Linguistics.

Edinburgh's End-to-End Multilingual Speech Translation System for IWSLT 2021

Biao Zhang[1] **Rico Sennrich**[2,1]

[1]School of Informatics, University of Edinburgh
[2]Department of Computational Linguistics, University of Zurich
B.Zhang@ed.ac.uk, sennrich@cl.uzh.ch

Abstract

This paper describes Edinburgh's submissions to the IWSLT2021 multilingual speech translation (ST) task. We aim at improving multilingual translation and zero-shot performance in the constrained setting (without using any extra training data) through methods that encourage transfer learning and larger capacity modeling with advanced neural components. We build our end-to-end multilingual ST model based on Transformer, integrating techniques including adaptive speech feature selection, language-specific modeling, multi-task learning, deep and big Transformer, sparsified linear attention and root mean square layer normalization. We adopt data augmentation using machine translation models for ST which converts the zero-shot problem into a zero-resource one. Experimental results show that these methods deliver substantial improvements, surpassing the official baseline by > 15 average BLEU and outperforming our cascading system by > 2 average BLEU. Our final submission achieves competitive performance (runner up).[1]

1 Introduction

Although end-to-end (E2E) speech translation (ST) has achieved great success in recent years, outperforming its cascading counterpart and delivering state-of-the-art performance on several benchmarks (Ansari et al., 2020; Zhang et al., 2020a; Zhao et al., 2020), it still suffers from the relatively low amounts of dedicated speech-to-translation parallel training data (Salesky et al., 2021). In text-based machine translation (MT), one solution to lack of training data is to jointly perform multilingual translation with the benefit of transferring knowledge across similar languages and to low-resource directions, and even enabling zero-shot translation, i.e. direct translation between language pairs unseen in training (Firat et al., 2016; Johnson et al., 2017). However, whether and how to obtain similar success in very low-resource (and practical) scenario for multilingual ST with E2E models remains an open question.

To address this question, we participated in the IWSLT2021 multilingual speech translation task, which focuses on low-resource ST language pairs in a multilingual setup. Apart from *supervised* evaluation, the task also offers *zero-shot* condition with a particular emphasis where only automatic speech recognition (ASR) training data is provided for some languages (without any direct ST parallel data). The task is organized in two settings: *constrained* setting and *unconstrained* setting. The former restricts participants to use the given multilingual TEDx data (Salesky et al., 2021) alone for experiment; while the latter allows for additional ASR/ST/MT/others training data. In this paper, we address the constrained one.

Our E2E multilingual ST model takes Transformer (Vaswani et al., 2017) as the backbone, and follows the adaptive feature selection (AFS) framework (Zhang et al., 2020a,b) as shown in Figure 1. AFS is capable of filtering out uninformative speech features contributing little to ASR, effectively reducing speech redundancy and improving ST performance (Zhang et al., 2020a). We adapt AFS to multilingual ST, and further incorporate several techniques that encourage transfer learning and larger capacity modeling, ranging from language-specific modeling, multi-task learning, deep and big Transformer, sparsified linear attention (ReLA) (Zhang et al., 2021b) to root mean square layer normalization (RMSNorm) (Zhang and Sennrich, 2019b). Inspired by Zhang et al. (2020c), we convert the zero-shot translation problem into a zero-resource one via data augmentation with multilingual MT models.

[1]Source code and pretrained models are available at https://github.com/bzhangGo/zero.

Proceedings of the 18th International Conference on Spoken Language Translation, pages 160–168
Bangkok, Thailand (Online), August 5–6, 2021.

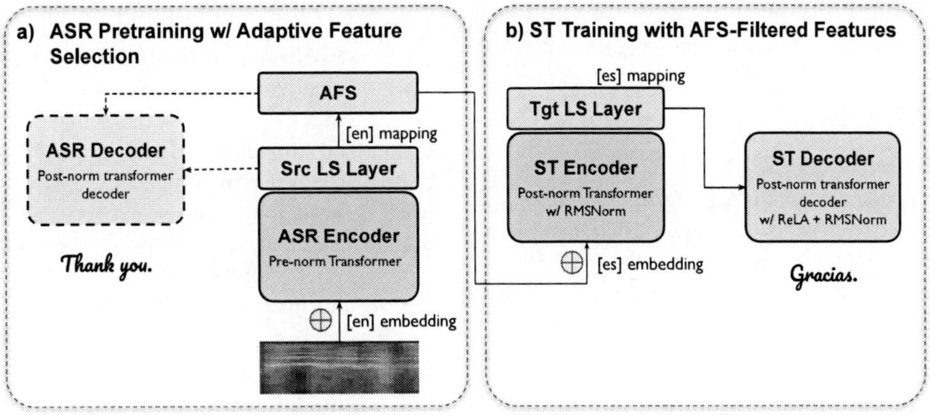

Figure 1: Overview of our multilingual ST model for an English-Spanish example. We first pretrain the ASR encoder paired with adaptive feature selection (AFS) to induce informative speech features (a), which are then carried over to the ST encoder-decoder model for translation (b). We adopt language embedding and language-specific (LS) linear mapping before and after ASR/ST encoder, respectively, to strengthen source/target (Src/Tgt) language modeling. The ASR decoder is discarded and the other ASR modules are frozen after the pretraining. Solid arrows illustrate the E2E translation procedure.

We integrate all these methods into one model for our submission. Our results reveal that:

- These methods are complementary in improving translation performance, where data augmentation and larger-capacity modeling contribute a lot.
- Low-resource E2E ST benefits greatly from multilingual modeling; our E2E multilingual ST performs very well in this task, outperforming its cascading counterpart by 2 average BLEU.

2 Methods

In this section, we elaborate crucial ingredients in our E2E multilingual ST, which individually have already been proven successful for ST or (multilingual) MT. We put them together to improve multilingual ST as shown in Figure 1. Note all encoder/decoder modules are based on Transformer (Vaswani et al., 2017).

2.1 Adaptive Feature Selection

Speech is lengthy and noisy compared to its text transcription. Also, information in an audio often distributes unevenly. All these increase the difficulty of extracting informative speech features. To solve this issue, researchers resort to methods compressing and grouping speech features (Salesky et al., 2019; Gaido et al., 2021). Particularly, Zhang et al. (2020a) propose adaptive feature selection (AFS) to sparsify speech encodings by pruning out those uninformative ones contributing little to ASR based on L_0DROP (Zhang et al., 2020b). Using AFS, Zhang et al. (2020a) observe significant performance improvements ($>$ 1 BLEU) with the removal of $\sim$84% speech features on bilingual ST.

Our model follows the AFS framework, which includes three steps: 1) pretraining the ASR encoder-decoder model; then 2) finetuning the ASR model with AFS; and 3) training ST model with the ASR encoder and the AFS module frozen.

2.2 Deep Transformer Modeling

Neural models often benefit from increased modeling capacity, and one way to achieve this is to deepen the models (He et al., 2015; Zhang et al., 2020d). However, simply increasing model depth for Transformer results in optimization failure, caused by gradient vanishing (Zhang et al., 2019a). To enable deep Transformer, Zhang et al. (2019a) propose depth-scaled initialization (DS-Init) that only requires changing parameter initialization without any architectural modification. DS-Init successfully helps to train up to 30-layer Transformer, substantially improving bilingual and also massively multilingual translation (Zhang et al., 2019a, 2020c). We adopt this strategy for all deep Transformer experiments.

Apart from DS-Init, researchers also find that changing the post-norm structure to its pre-norm alternative improves Transformer's robustness to deep modeling, albeit slightly reducing quality (Wang et al., 2019; Zhang et al., 2019a). We keep using post-norm Transformer for most modules but apply the pre-norm structure to the ASR encoder to stabilize the encoding of speeches from different languages.

2.3 Language-Specific Modeling

Analogous to multi-task learning, multilingual translation benefits from inter-task transfer learning but suffers from task interference. How to balance between shared modeling and language-specific (LS) modeling so as to maximize the transfer effect and avoid the interference remains challenging. A recent study suggests that scheduling language-specific modeling to top and/or bottom encoder/decoder sub-layers benefits translation the most (Zhang et al., 2021a), resonating with the findings of Zhang et al. (2020c). In particular, Zhang et al. (2020c) propose language-aware linear transformation, a language-specific linear mapping inserted in-between the encoder and the decoder which greatly improves massively multilingual translation.

We adopt such language-specific linear mapping and apply it to both ASR and ST encoders. We ground such modeling in the ASR and ST encoder to the source and target language, respectively. Following multilingual translation (Johnson et al., 2017; Gangi et al., 2019; Inaguma et al., 2019), we adopt language embedding (such as "*[en], [es]*") but add it to the inputs rather than appending an extra token.

2.4 Sparsified Linear Attention

Attention, as the key component in Transformer, takes the main responsibility to capture token-wise dependencies. However, not all tokens are semantically correlated, inspiring follow-up studies on sparsified attention that could explicitly zero-out some attention probabilities (Peters et al., 2019; Zhang et al., 2021b). Recently, Zhang et al. (2021b) propose rectified linear attention (ReLA) which directly induces sparse structures by enforcing ReLU activation on the attention logits. ReLA has achieved comparable performance on several MT tasks with the advantage of high computational efficiency against the sparsified softmax models (Peters et al., 2019).

Results on MT show that ReLA delivers better performance when applied to Transformer decoder (Zhang et al., 2021b). We follow this practice and apply it to the ST decoder. Our study also demonstrates that ReLA generalizes well to ST.

2.5 Root Mean Square Layer Normalization

Layer normalization (LayerNorm) stabilizes network activations and improves model performance (Ba et al., 2016), but raises non-negligible computational overheads reducing net efficiency, particularly to recurrent models (Zhang and Sennrich, 2019a). To overcome such overhead, Zhang and Sennrich (2019b) propose root mean square layer normalization (RMSNorm) which relies on root mean square statistic alone to regularize activations and is a drop-in replacement to LayerNorm. RMSNorm yields comparable performance to LayerNorm in a series of experiments (Zhang and Sennrich, 2019b) and show great scalability in large-scale pretraining (Narang et al., 2021).

We apply RMSNorm to the ST encoder and decoder, which benefits the training of deep and big Transformers.

2.6 Data Augmentation

Data augmentation (DA) is an effective strategy for low-resource tasks by increasing the training corpus with pseudo-labelled samples (Sennrich et al., 2016a; Zhang and Zong, 2016). Methods for generating such samples vary greatly, and we adopt the one following knowledge distillation (Kim and Rush, 2016). Note, prior to our study, knowledge distillation has already been successfully applied to ST tasks (Liu et al., 2019; Gaido et al., 2020). We regard the multilingual MT as the teacher since text-based translation is much easier than and almost upper-bounds the speech-based counterpart (Zhang et al., 2020a), and transfer its knowledge into our multilingual ST (student).

Concretely, we first train a multilingual MT model and then use it to translate each source transcript into all possible ST directions, including the zero-shot ones, based on beam search algorithm. We directly concatenate the generated pseudo speech-translation pairs with the original training corpus for multilingual ST training. This will convert the zero-shot translation problem into a zero-resource one for ST, which has been demonstrated effective in massively multilingual MT (Zhang et al., 2020c).

2.7 Multi-Task Learning

Multi-task learning aims at improving task performance by jointly modeling different tasks within one framework. Particularly, when tasks are of high correlation, they tend to benefit each other and de-

Speech	Target Languages				
	En	Es	Fr	Pt	It
Es	36K/102K	102K/-	3.6K/102K	21K/102K	5.6K/102K
Fr	30K/116K	21K/116K	116K/-	13K/116K	-/116K
Pt	31K/90K	-/90K	-/90K	90K/-	-/90K
It	-/50K	-/50K	-/50K	-/50K	50K/-

Table 1: Statistics for ST training data used for the IWSLT2021 multilingual ST task. "-": denotes no data available. "*a*/*b*": "*a*" denotes genuine data while "*b*" is for augmented data.

liver positive knowledge transfer. With datasets of different tasks combined, this also partially alleviates data scarcity.

We adopt multi-task learning by augmenting translation tasks with transcription tasks. We incorporate the ASR tasks for multilingual ST, and auto-encoding tasks (transcript-to-transcript in the same language) for multilingual MT.

3 Experimental Settings

In this section, we explain the used datasets, model architectures, optimization details and evaluation metrics in our experiments. All implementations are based on the *zero*[2] toolkit (Zhang et al., 2018).

Data We participate in the constrained setting, where only the provided data, i.e. Multilingual TEDx (Salesky et al., 2021), is permitted. Multilingual TEDx collects audios from TEDx talks in 8 source languages (Spanish/Es, French/Fr, Portuguese/Pt, Italian/It, Russian/Ru, Greek/El, Arabic/Ar, German/De) paired with their manual transcriptions, covering translations into 5 target languages (English/En, Es, Fr, Pt, It). It contains supervised training data for 13 ST directions, three of which (Pt-Es, It-En, It-Es) are masked-out for zero-shot evaluation. ASR training data is given for all 8 source languages. Overall, Multilingual TEDx is a small-scale dataset, whose ST training data size ranges from 5K utterances (It-Es) to at most 39K utterances (Es-En). Thus, studying and improving transfer across different languages is of great significance. The IWSLT2021 task requires participants to model translations from 4 source languages (Es, Fr, Pt, It), where the final evaluation only targets translations into En and Es. The statistics of ST (genuine and augmented) training data are shown in Table 1.

Regarding audio preprocessing, we use the given audio segmentation (train/dev/test) for experiments. We extract 40-dimensional log-Mel filterbanks with a step size of 10ms and window size of 25ms as the acoustic features, followed by feature expansion via second-order derivatives and mean-variance normalization. The final acoustic input is 360-dimensional, a concatenation of the features corresponding to three consecutive and non-overlapping frames. We tokenize and truecase all text data using Moses scripts (Koehn et al., 2007). We adopt subword processing (Sennrich et al., 2016b) with 8K merging operations (Sennrich and Zhang, 2019) on these texts to handle rare words. Note we use different subword models (but with the same vocabulary size) for ST, ASR and MT.

Architecture The architecture for ASR and ST is illustrated in Figure 1, while our MT model follows Zhang et al. (2020c). We apply AFS to ASR encoder outputs (after language-specific mapping) along both temporal and feature dimensions. By default, we adopt Transformer-base setting (Vaswani et al., 2017): we use 6 encoder/decoder layers and 8 attention heads with a model dimension of 512/2048. For deep Transformer, we equally increase the encoder and decoder depth, and adopt DS-Init for training. We also use Transformer-big for ST, where the number of attention heads and model dimension are doubled, increased to 16 and 1024/4096, respectively.

Optimization We train MT models with the maximum likelihood objective ($\mathcal{L}_{\text{MLE}}$). Apart from $\mathcal{L}_{\text{MLE}}$, we also incorporate the CTC loss (Graves et al., 2006) for ASR pretraining with a weight value of 0.3 following Zhang et al. (2020a). During AFS finetuning, the CTC loss is discarded and replaced with the L_0DROP sparsification loss (Zhang et al., 2020b) weighted by 0.5. We employ label smoothing of value 0.1 for $\mathcal{L}_{\text{MLE}}$.

We adopt Adam (β_1=0.9, β_2=0.98) for parameter tuning with a warmup step of 4K. We train all models (ASR, ST and MT) for 100K steps, and finetune AFS for 10K steps. We group instances of around 25K target subwords into one mini-batch. We apply dropout to attention weights and residual connections with a rate of 0.1 and 0.2, respectively. Dropout rate on residual connections is increased to 0.3 for ST big models to avoid overfitting, and to 0.5 for MT models inspired by low-resource MT (Sennrich and Zhang, 2019). Except dropout, we use *no* other regularization techniques. We use beam search for decoding, and set the beam size and length penalty to 4 and 0.6, separately. The

[2] https://github.com/bzhangGo/zero

Model	Es-En	Es-Pt	Es-Fr	Fr-En	Fr-Es	Fr-Pt	Pt-En	Pt-Es	It-En	It-Es	Avg
Bilingual Models*	25.5	39.3	2.0	28.3	30.5	19.0	27.9	29.9	18.9	1.0	22.23
Multilingual Models*	24.6	37.3	18.1	28.2	32.1	30.6	28.8	38.4	20.9	25.1	28.41
Our Multilingual MT											
+ 6 layers	28.7	42.1	29.3	33.6	38.3	36.7	33.2	42.9	20.3	32.7	33.78
+ 12 layers	31.8	44.7	31.7	36.4	40.9	39.9	35.6	44.0	23.0	34.9	36.29
+ 24 layers	32.8	44.9	32.4	37.3	41.8	40.7	36.8	43.2	23.2	35.3	**36.84**
Ablation Study											
+ 6 layers w/o LS layer	28.6	41.8	29.0	33.7	38.2	36.3	33.2	42.5	20.7	32.6	33.66
+ 6 layer + RoBT	28.1	40.3	28.6	34.1	38.3	33.6	33.6	42.7	21.1	32.9	33.33

Table 2: SacreBLEU↑ for MT on Multilingual TEDx testsets. *: results reported by Salesky et al. (2021). Note the results for Pt-Es, It-En and It-Es translation in our model are based on zero-shot evaluation. In spite of this unfairness, our model still substantially outperforms the supervised baseline (Salesky et al., 2021) by a large margin, +8.43 BLEU. *RoBT*: random online back-translation (Zhang et al., 2020c). Best average BLEU is highlighted in **bold**. Columns in red denote zero-shot evaluation.

Model	Es	Fr	Pt	It	Ru	El	Ar	De	Avg
Hybrid LF-MMI*	16.2	19.4	20.2	16.4	28.4	25.0	80.8	42.3	**31.09**
Transformer*	46.4	45.6	54.8	48.0	74.7	109.5	104.4	111.1	74.31
Our Multilingual ASR									
+ 6 layers	17.6	19.5	23.1	20.8	39.8	33.0	104.3	57.8	**39.49**
Ablation Study									
+ 6 layers w/o LS layer	18.0	19.5	23.2	21.6	40.8	35.2	97.8	62.6	39.84

Table 3: WER↓ for ASR on Multilingual TEDx testsets. *: results reported by Salesky et al. (2021). Best results are highlighted in **bold**.

model used for evaluation is averaged over the last 5 checkpoints.

Note, while the training data size varies across languages, we follow the original data distribution and adopt *no* specific sampling strategies for all multilingual experiments.

Evaluation We evaluate translation quality using tokenized case-sensitive (Sacre)BLEU (Papineni et al., 2002; Post, 2018), and report WER for ASR performance without punctuation on lowercased text. In ST experiments, we observe some repeated translations decreasing BLEU. We automatically post-process translations by removing repeated chunks of up to 10 words.

4 Results

4.1 Multilingual MT

Table 2 shows the results for text-based translation. Our best model, achieved with 24 layers, largely surpasses the official baseline (Salesky et al., 2021) by >8 average BLEU. With 6 layers, our model still largely surpasses this baseline by 5.37 average BLEU, suggesting the superiority of our model.

Increasing model depth greatly benefits multilingual MT (+2.51 average BLEU, 6 layers → 12 layers), even though the dataset is small. Note the benefit from increased depth diminishes as the depth goes larger (+0.55 average BLEU, 12 layers → 24 layers). We find that language-specific modeling slightly improves translation performance (+0.12 average BLEU). Such improvement seems uninteresting particularly compared to the significant gains on massively multilingual MT (Zhang et al., 2020c), but we ascribe this to the high language similarity in Multilingual TEDx and the relative small number of languages. We also confirm the effectiveness of random online back-translation (RoBT), which improves zero-shot translation via pseudo sentence pair augmentation (Zhang et al., 2020c). Table 2 shows that RoBT indeed benefits zero-shot translation, but sacrifices overall quality (-0.45 average BLEU).

Overall, our results reveal very positive transfer between these languages, and also great zero-shot translation performance. This is an encouraging finding for multilingual ST. We use our 24-layer model for data augmentation distillation in the following ST experiments.

Model	Es-En	Es-Pt	Es-Fr	Fr-En	Fr-Es	Fr-Pt	Pt-En	Pt-Es	It-En	It-Es	Avg
Multilingual Models*	12.3	17.4	6.1	12.0	13.6	13.2	12.0	13.7	10.7	13.1	12.41
Cascades with Multilingual MT*	21.5	26.5	23.4	25.3	26.9	23.3	22.3	26.3	21.9	28.4	24.58
Our Multilingual MT, w/ AFS, LS layer, DA, ReLA (decoder self-attention) and RMSNorm											
+ 6 layers	24.9	34.8	26.6	30.0	33.8	33.2	27.4	33.9	20.7	30.8	29.61
+ 12 layers	24.6	35.6	26.7	29.9	33.7	33.5	28.5	34.4	21.1	30.6	29.86
+ 6 layers + big model	26.1	36.2	27.5	31.0	34.9	34.3	28.7	35.1	21.6	31.5	**30.69**
Ablation Study											
+ 6 layers w/o AFS	25.2	35.1	26.4	29.9	33.2	32.7	28.4	33.7	20.3	29.6	29.45
+ 6 layers w/o AFS & DA	20.8	30.9	18.5	24.7	27.6	27.0	23.8	27.2	13.8	20.0	23.43
+ 6 layers w/o ReLA & RMSNorm	24.2	34.8	26.4	29.5	34.1	33.4	27.5	33.7	20.7	30.3	29.46
+ 6 layers + ReLA on cross-att.	24.8	35.3	27.1	30.2	34.3	33.8	27.6	34.1	20.5	30.5	**29.82**
Our Cascade Model w/ Multilingual ASR + 24-layer Multilingual MT											
	24.8	33.7	25.3	29.2	32.7	32.2	26.9	31.7	18.5	27.1	28.21
Final Submission: Ensemble of 4 base model, 1 12-layer model and 1 big model w/ length penalty of 0.9											
	26.6	36.6	27.9	31.8	35.6	35.4	29.7	35.8	22.0	32.0	**31.34**

Table 4: SacreBLEU↑ for ST on Multilingual TEDx testsets. *: results reported by Salesky et al. (2021). Note the results for Pt-Es, It-En and It-Es translation in our model are based on zero-shot evaluation. Our model substantially outperforms the official baseline (Salesky et al., 2021) by $>$ 10 average BLEU. *DA*: data augmentation. Best average BLEU is highlighted in **bold**.

4.2 Multilingual ASR

Table 3 shows the ASR performance. Following previous studies (Salesky et al., 2021; Zhang et al., 2020a), we experiment with the Transformer base setting. Our multilingual ASR model yields an average WER of 39.49, substantially outperforming the official baseline (Salesky et al., 2021) by 34.82 and narrowing the performance gap against the hybrid model to $\sim$ 8 WER. Note lower WER indicates better quality. We ascribe this large quality gain to the dedicated multilingual ASR model architecture, the better optimization, and particularly the incorporation of the CTC objective.

Removing the language-specific layer slightly hurts recognition performance (+0.35 average WER). It largely benefits ASR for Ar (-6.5 WER), but hurts that for De (+4.8 WER), showing the difficulty of multilingual modeling: it's hard to balance between different tasks (translation directions). We adopt the model with language-specific projection for AFS and ST.

Notice that we still include Ru, El, Ar and De for the ASR training, although they are not a part of the evaluation campaign. We regard this inclusion as some sort of model regularization: the extra training data could reduce overfitting and might enable potential cross-lingual transfer.

4.3 Multilingual ST

Table 4 summarizes the ST results. Our base model using 6 layers delivers an average BLEU of 29.61, largely outperforming the official baseline (Salesky et al., 2021) by $\sim$ 17 BLEU and also beating their cascading baseline. In a fair comparison where knowledge data augmentation is not used, our model still obtain an average BLEU of 23.43.

Increasing the ST model depth slightly improves quality (+0.25 average BLEU), while enlarging ST model yields a larger improvement, reaching 1.08. Although it's widely known that large neural model often suffers from overfitting in low-resource tasks, our results suggest that such model still gains quality with proper regularization (AFS, larger dropout, etc).

Our ablation study demonstrates the effectiveness of AFS, ReLA and RMSNorm, although the corresponding quality gains are marginal. In particular, we observe that applying ReLA to both self-attention and cross-attention in the ST decoder helps (Zhang et al., 2021b). AFS improves training efficiency, allowing larger batch size thus fewer gradient accumulation steps (Zhang et al., 2020a). Besides, data augmentation benefits multilingual ST very much, resulting in $\sim$ 6 average BLEU improvement, and the gain on zero-shot directions is even higher, + 7.54 BLEU. Thus, we mainly ascribe our success on zero-shot translation to the inclusion of pseudo parallel corpora – data matter! – which converts the zero-shot problem into a zero-resource one.

Our E2E model also largely outperforms the cascading system (+ 2.48 average BLEU). Notice that our cascading system is sub-optimal, since we

Model	Es-En	Es-Fr	Es-It	Es-Pt	Fr-En	Fr-Es	Fr-Pt	Pt-En	Pt-Es	It-En	It-Es	Avg
Ensemble of 6 E2E models: 4 base model, 1 12-layer model and 1 big model w/ length penalty of 0.9												
	36.2	30.3	32.9	44.5	26.4	29.5	30.1	27.0	34.5	23.0	31.1	**31.41**
Cascading model: base ASR model + 24-layer MT model												
	33.3	26.8	28.6	39.9	23.7	26.9	26.8	23.6	30.0	19.7	26.7	27.82
Single E2E Model: multilingual ST model + 6 layers, big Transformer												
	35.0	29.9	31.9	44.1	25.5	28.8	29.0	26.2	33.3	22.4	30.1	30.56

Table 5: SacreBLEU↑ for our submissions to the IWSLT2021 multilingual ST task.

didn't bias our MT model towards ASR outputs, and the mismatch between gold transcripts and ASR outputs often hurts cascading performance. Recent advances on avoiding such error propagation might deliver better cascading results (Cheng et al., 2018; Zhang et al., 2019b; Cheng et al., 2019; Sperber et al., 2019).

Our final submission is an ensemble of 6 E2E multilingual ST models, which reaches an average BLEU of 31.34. Apart from the ensemble, we also increase the decoding length penalty from 0.6 to 0.9, which performs slightly better.

5 Submission Results

The IWSLT2021 task prepares a held-out test set for the final evaluation. We submitted three systems: one cascading system, one E2E single model (w/ big ST Transformer) and one ensemble model. Results are shown in Table 5: our E2E multilingual ST model outperforms its cascading counterpart, and the ensemble model reaches the best performance. Our submission achieves runner-up results among all participants.

6 Conclusion and Future Work

We describe Edinburgh's end-to-end multilingual speech translation system for the IWSLT2021 multilingual speech translation task. We observe substantial performance improvement using larger-capacity modeling (deep or big modeling) and data augmentation. In spite of the scarcity of the training data, we show that E2E models benefit greatly from multilingual modeling and deliver promising results on zero-shot translation directions (even without data augmentation). Our E2E multilingual ST greatly surpasses its cascading counterpart.

Regarding future study, we argue that exploring the multilingual transfer behavior should be very practical and promising to ST. This work mainly studies transfer across similar languages. How the current model generalizes to distant languages is still an open question. Besides, a general trend for deep learning is to increase the model capacity via deep and/or big modeling. However, deep models for ST seem to be ineffective. Identifying the reason for this and proposing simple solutions would be of high interest.

Acknowledgements

We thank the reviewers for their insightful comments. This project has received funding from the European Union's Horizon 2020 Research and Innovation Programme under Grant Agreements 825460 (ELITR). Rico Sennrich acknowledges support of the Swiss National Science Foundation (MUTAMUR; no. 176727).

References

Ebrahim Ansari, Amittai Axelrod, Nguyen Bach, Ondřej Bojar, Roldano Cattoni, Fahim Dalvi, Nadir Durrani, Marcello Federico, Christian Federmann, Jiatao Gu, Fei Huang, Kevin Knight, Xutai Ma, Ajay Nagesh, Matteo Negri, Jan Niehues, Juan Pino, Elizabeth Salesky, Xing Shi, Sebastian Stüker, Marco Turchi, Alexander Waibel, and Changhan Wang. 2020. FINDINGS OF THE IWSLT 2020 EVALUATION CAMPAIGN. In *Proceedings of the 17th International Conference on Spoken Language Translation*, pages 1–34, Online. Association for Computational Linguistics.

Jimmy Ba, J. Kiros, and Geoffrey E. Hinton. 2016. Layer normalization. *ArXiv*, abs/1607.06450.

Qiao Cheng, Meiyuan Fang, Yaqian Han, Jin Huang, and Yitao Duan. 2019. Breaking the data barrier: Towards robust speech translation via adversarial stability training. *CoRR*, abs/1909.11430.

Yong Cheng, Zhaopeng Tu, Fandong Meng, Junjie Zhai, and Yang Liu. 2018. Towards robust neural machine translation. In *Proceedings of the 56th Annual Meeting of the Association for Computational Linguistics (Volume 1: Long Papers)*, pages 1756–1766, Melbourne, Australia. Association for Computational Linguistics.

Orhan Firat, Baskaran Sankaran, Yaser Al-onaizan, Fatos T. Yarman Vural, and Kyunghyun Cho. 2016. Zero-resource translation with multi-lingual neural machine translation. In *Proceedings of the 2016 Conference on Empirical Methods in Natural Language Processing*, pages 268–277, Austin, Texas. Association for Computational Linguistics.

Marco Gaido, Mauro Cettolo, Matteo Negri, and Marco Turchi. 2021. CTC-based compression for direct speech translation. In *Proceedings of the 16th Conference of the European Chapter of the Association for Computational Linguistics: Main Volume*, pages 690–696, Online. Association for Computational Linguistics.

Marco Gaido, Mattia A. Di Gangi, Matteo Negri, and Marco Turchi. 2020. End-to-end speech-translation with knowledge distillation: FBK@IWSLT2020. In *Proceedings of the 17th International Conference on Spoken Language Translation*, pages 80–88, Online. Association for Computational Linguistics.

Mattia Antonino Di Gangi, Matteo Negri, and Marco Turchi. 2019. One-to-many multilingual end-to-end speech translation. In *IEEE Automatic Speech Recognition and Understanding Workshop, ASRU 2019, Singapore, December 14-18, 2019*, pages 585–592. IEEE.

Alex Graves, Santiago Fernández, Faustino Gomez, and Jürgen Schmidhuber. 2006. Connectionist temporal classification: Labelling unsegmented sequence data with recurrent neural networks. In *Proceedings of the 23rd International Conference on Machine Learning*, ICML '06, page 369–376, New York, NY, USA. Association for Computing Machinery.

Kaiming He, Xiangyu Zhang, Shaoqing Ren, and Jian Sun. 2015. Deep residual learning for image recognition.

Hirofumi Inaguma, Kevin Duh, Tatsuya Kawahara, and Shinji Watanabe. 2019. Multilingual end-to-end speech translation. In *IEEE Automatic Speech Recognition and Understanding Workshop, ASRU 2019, Singapore, December 14-18, 2019*, pages 570–577. IEEE.

Melvin Johnson, Mike Schuster, Quoc V. Le, Maxim Krikun, Yonghui Wu, Zhifeng Chen, Nikhil Thorat, Fernanda Viégas, Martin Wattenberg, Greg Corrado, Macduff Hughes, and Jeffrey Dean. 2017. Google's multilingual neural machine translation system: Enabling zero-shot translation. *Transactions of the Association for Computational Linguistics*, 5:339–351.

Yoon Kim and Alexander M. Rush. 2016. Sequence-level knowledge distillation. In *Proceedings of the 2016 Conference on Empirical Methods in Natural Language Processing*, pages 1317–1327, Austin, Texas. Association for Computational Linguistics.

Philipp Koehn, Hieu Hoang, Alexandra Birch, Chris Callison-Burch, Marcello Federico, Nicola Bertoldi, Brooke Cowan, Wade Shen, Christine Moran, Richard Zens, Chris Dyer, Ondřej Bojar, Alexandra Constantin, and Evan Herbst. 2007. Moses: Open source toolkit for statistical machine translation. In *Proceedings of the 45th Annual Meeting of the Association for Computational Linguistics Companion Volume Proceedings of the Demo and Poster Sessions*, pages 177–180, Prague, Czech Republic. Association for Computational Linguistics.

Yuchen Liu, Hao Xiong, Jiajun Zhang, Zhongjun He, Hua Wu, Haifeng Wang, and Chengqing Zong. 2019. End-to-End Speech Translation with Knowledge Distillation. In *Proc. Interspeech 2019*, pages 1128–1132.

Sharan Narang, Hyung Won Chung, Yi Tay, William Fedus, Thibault Fevry, Michael Matena, Karishma Malkan, Noah Fiedel, Noam Shazeer, Zhenzhong Lan, Yanqi Zhou, Wei Li, Nan Ding, Jake Marcus, Adam Roberts, and Colin Raffel. 2021. Do transformer modifications transfer across implementations and applications?

Kishore Papineni, Salim Roukos, Todd Ward, and Wei-Jing Zhu. 2002. Bleu: a method for automatic evaluation of machine translation. In *Proceedings of the 40th Annual Meeting of the Association for Computational Linguistics*, pages 311–318, Philadelphia, Pennsylvania, USA. Association for Computational Linguistics.

Ben Peters, Vlad Niculae, and André F. T. Martins. 2019. Sparse sequence-to-sequence models. In *Proceedings of the 57th Annual Meeting of the Association for Computational Linguistics*, pages 1504–1519, Florence, Italy. Association for Computational Linguistics.

Matt Post. 2018. A call for clarity in reporting BLEU scores. In *Proceedings of the Third Conference on Machine Translation: Research Papers*, pages 186–191, Brussels, Belgium. Association for Computational Linguistics.

Elizabeth Salesky, Matthias Sperber, and Alan W Black. 2019. Exploring phoneme-level speech representations for end-to-end speech translation. In *Proceedings of the 57th Annual Meeting of the Association for Computational Linguistics*, pages 1835–1841, Florence, Italy. Association for Computational Linguistics.

Elizabeth Salesky, Matthew Wiesner, Jacob Bremerman, Roldano Cattoni, Matteo Negri, Marco Turchi, Douglas W. Oard, and Matt Post. 2021. The multilingual tedx corpus for speech recognition and translation.

Rico Sennrich, Barry Haddow, and Alexandra Birch. 2016a. Improving neural machine translation models with monolingual data. In *Proceedings of the 54th Annual Meeting of the Association for Computational Linguistics (Volume 1: Long Papers)*, pages

86–96, Berlin, Germany. Association for Computational Linguistics.

Rico Sennrich, Barry Haddow, and Alexandra Birch. 2016b. Neural machine translation of rare words with subword units. In *Proceedings of the 54th Annual Meeting of the Association for Computational Linguistics (Volume 1: Long Papers)*, pages 1715–1725, Berlin, Germany. Association for Computational Linguistics.

Rico Sennrich and Biao Zhang. 2019. Revisiting low-resource neural machine translation: A case study. In *Proceedings of the 57th Annual Meeting of the Association for Computational Linguistics*, pages 211–221, Florence, Italy. Association for Computational Linguistics.

Matthias Sperber, Graham Neubig, Ngoc-Quan Pham, and Alex Waibel. 2019. Self-attentional models for lattice inputs. In *Proceedings of the 57th Annual Meeting of the Association for Computational Linguistics*, pages 1185–1197, Florence, Italy. Association for Computational Linguistics.

Ashish Vaswani, Noam Shazeer, Niki Parmar, Jakob Uszkoreit, Llion Jones, Aidan N Gomez, Ł ukasz Kaiser, and Illia Polosukhin. 2017. Attention is all you need. In *Advances in Neural Information Processing Systems*, volume 30. Curran Associates, Inc.

Qiang Wang, Bei Li, Tong Xiao, Jingbo Zhu, Changliang Li, Derek F. Wong, and Lidia S. Chao. 2019. Learning deep transformer models for machine translation. In *Proceedings of the 57th Annual Meeting of the Association for Computational Linguistics*, pages 1810–1822, Florence, Italy. Association for Computational Linguistics.

Biao Zhang, Ankur Bapna, Rico Sennrich, and Orhan Firat. 2021a. Share or not? learning to schedule language-specific capacity for multilingual translation. In *International Conference on Learning Representations*.

Biao Zhang and Rico Sennrich. 2019a. A lightweight recurrent network for sequence modeling. In *Proceedings of the 57th Annual Meeting of the Association for Computational Linguistics*, pages 1538–1548, Florence, Italy. Association for Computational Linguistics.

Biao Zhang and Rico Sennrich. 2019b. Root mean square layer normalization. In *Advances in Neural Information Processing Systems*, volume 32. Curran Associates, Inc.

Biao Zhang, Ivan Titov, Barry Haddow, and Rico Sennrich. 2020a. Adaptive feature selection for end-to-end speech translation. In *Findings of the Association for Computational Linguistics: EMNLP 2020*, pages 2533–2544, Online. Association for Computational Linguistics.

Biao Zhang, Ivan Titov, and Rico Sennrich. 2019a. Improving deep transformer with depth-scaled initialization and merged attention. In *Proceedings of the 2019 Conference on Empirical Methods in Natural Language Processing and the 9th International Joint Conference on Natural Language Processing (EMNLP-IJCNLP)*, pages 898–909, Hong Kong, China. Association for Computational Linguistics.

Biao Zhang, Ivan Titov, and Rico Sennrich. 2020b. On sparsifying encoder outputs in sequence-to-sequence models.

Biao Zhang, Ivan Titov, and Rico Sennrich. 2021b. Sparse attention with linear units.

Biao Zhang, Philip Williams, Ivan Titov, and Rico Sennrich. 2020c. Improving massively multilingual neural machine translation and zero-shot translation. In *Proceedings of the 58th Annual Meeting of the Association for Computational Linguistics*, pages 1628–1639, Online. Association for Computational Linguistics.

Biao Zhang, Deyi Xiong, and Jinsong Su. 2020d. Neural machine translation with deep attention. *IEEE Transactions on Pattern Analysis and Machine Intelligence*, 42(1):154–163.

Biao Zhang, Deyi Xiong, jinsong su, Qian Lin, and Huiji Zhang. 2018. Simplifying neural machine translation with addition-subtraction twin-gated recurrent networks. In *Proceedings of the 2018 Conference on Empirical Methods in Natural Language Processing*, pages 4273–4283. Association for Computational Linguistics.

Jiajun Zhang and Chengqing Zong. 2016. Exploiting source-side monolingual data in neural machine translation. In *Proceedings of the 2016 Conference on Empirical Methods in Natural Language Processing*, pages 1535–1545, Austin, Texas. Association for Computational Linguistics.

Pei Zhang, Niyu Ge, Boxing Chen, and Kai Fan. 2019b. Lattice transformer for speech translation. In *Proceedings of the 57th Annual Meeting of the Association for Computational Linguistics*, pages 6475–6484, Florence, Italy. Association for Computational Linguistics.

Chengqi Zhao, Mingxuan Wang, and Lei Li. 2020. Neurst: Neural speech translation toolkit.

ON-TRAC' systems for the IWSLT 2021 low-resource speech translation and multilingual speech translation shared tasks

Hang Le[2], **Florentin Barbier**[4], **Ha Nguyen**[1,2], **Natalia Tomanshenko**[1], **Salima Mdhaffar**[1], **Souhir Gahbiche**[4], **Fethi Bougares**[3], **Benjamin Lecouteux**[2], **Didier Schwab**[2], **Yannick Estève**[1]
ON-TRAC consortium (LIA[1], LIG[2], LIUM[3], Airbus[4] - France)

Abstract

This paper describes the ON-TRAC Consortium translation systems developed for two challenge tracks featured in the Evaluation Campaign of IWSLT 2021, low-resource speech translation and multilingual speech translation. The ON-TRAC Consortium is composed of researchers from three French academic laboratories and an industrial partner: LIA (Avignon Université), LIG (Université Grenoble Alpes), LIUM (Le Mans Université), and researchers from Airbus. A pipeline approach was explored for the low-resource speech translation task, using a hybrid HMM/TDNN automatic speech recognition system fed by wav2vec features, coupled to an NMT system. For the multilingual speech translation task, we investigated the use of a dual-decoder Transformer that jointly transcribes and translates an input speech signal. This model was trained in order to translate from multiple source languages to multiple target ones.

1 Introduction

In the two last editions of the IWSLT evaluation campaigns, the ON-TRAC consortium focused on end-to-end offline speech translation and simultaneous speech translation (Nguyen et al., 2019; Elbayad et al., 2020). In 2021, we chose to focus on low-resource speech translation and multilingual speech translation by using two different kinds of approaches: a cascaded speech-to-text translation (combining source language automatic speech recognition (ASR) and source-to-target text translation) to process the low resource speech translation tasks, and a neural end-to-end model for the multilingual speech translation task. For the low resource task, we investigated the use of speech features extracted by a neural model pretrained by self supervision the wav2vec XLSR-53 model (Conneau et al., 2020) in order to process Swahili languages by a classical hybrid Markovian/neuronal ASR system. The ASR outputs were processed by neural machine text-to-text translation systems dedicated to the two targeted language pairs. For the multilingual speech translation task, we investigated the use of a dual-decoder Transformer that jointly transcribes and translates an input speech. This model was trained in order to translate from multiple source languages to multiple target ones.

The ON-TRAC Consortium is composed of researchers from three French academic laboratories and an industrial partner: LIA (Avignon Université), LIG (Université Grenoble Alpes), LIUM (Le Mans Université), and researchers from Airbus.

2 Low resource speech translation

The task of the low resource speech translation track was to build the speech transcription/translation system for transcribing and/or translating between the two language pairs:

- Coastal Swahili (swa) to English (eng)
- Congolese Swahili (swc) to French (fra)

2.1 ASR system

The same ASR models were used for both test datasets: Coastal Swahili (swa) and Congolese Swahili (swc).

2.1.1 Data

The training corpus for the ASR acoustic model (AM) comprises of several datasets:

- 5k instances for Congolese Swahili speech provided by the IWSLT-2021 organizers[1];
- a training subset of the ALFFA corpus (Gelas et al., 2012) (read speech and broadcast news);

[1]https://iwslt.org/2021/low-resource

Proceedings of the 18th International Conference on Spoken Language Translation, pages 169–174
Bangkok, Thailand (Online), August 5–6, 2021.

- a subset of the IARPA Babel Swahili Language Pack[2] (conversational and scripted telephone speech that spoken in the Nairobi dialect region of Kenya).

The total size of the training corpus is about 74 hours. In our preliminary experiments, we also tried to include a swa dataset (5k instances of Coastal Swahili), provided by the IWSLT-2021 organizers, into the training corpus, but this does not improve the ASR performance. Hence, for the submitted system and for the results reported in the paper, this corpus was not used.

2.1.2 Architecture

In this work, we investigated the impact of using self-supervised learning (Baevski et al., 2020) on the hybrid ASR HMM/DNN acoustic models, as well as on the pipeline ASR+MT system performance. Self-supervised learning (SSL) has shown to be effective for various speech-related tasks including ASR and MT (Schneider et al., 2019; Baevski et al., 2020; Evain et al., 2021; Nguyen et al., 2020) and could be especially beneficial for a low-resource scenario.

We trained several acoustic models (AM) with two different types of input features for comparison: (1) 40-dimensional high-resolution (*hires*) MFCC features; and (2) wav2vec 2.0 features (Baevski et al., 2020) extracted by the multilingual large model pretrained pretrained in 53 languages, XLSR-53-*large* (Conneau et al., 2020).

The phoneme set and transcriptions were the same as in the work (Gelas et al., 2012).

The AMs are state-of-the-art factorized time delay neural networks (TDNN-F) (Povey et al., 2018; Peddinti et al., 2015) and were trained using the Kaldi toolkit (Povey et al., 2011). The models have similar topology (except for the input features): 12 TDNN-F layers (1,024-dimensional, with projection dimension of 128) and a 2232-dimensional output layer. The AMs were trained using lattice-free maximum mutual information (LF-MMI) (Povey et al., 2016) and cross-entropy criteria. Speed and volume perturbations have been applied for data augmentation. 100-dimensional speaker i-vectors were appended to the input features.

We used a 3-gram LM with a 466K vocabulary provided in the ALLFA recipe (Gelas et al., 2012)[3].

[2]IARPA-babel202b-v1.0d, https://catalog.ldc.upenn.edu/LDC2017S05

[3]https://github.com/getalp/ALFFA_PUBLIC

2.2 Neural machine translation system

In order to translate the ASR outputs from source languages to target languages, two neural machine translation systems were built.

2.2.1 Data

For the swa-eng sentence pairs, training dataset for machine translation system includes:

- OPUS[4] english-swahili parallel data : CCAligned and MultiCCAligned (El-Kishky et al., 2020), WikiMatrix, Wikimedia, XLEnt and ParaCrawl.
- 5k parallel swa-eng dataset provided by IWSLT-2021.

The total size of the training dataset for swa-eng is about 3.2M sentence pairs. We applied language identification filtering LangID (Lui and Baldwin, 2012) keeping only swa-eng sentence pairs with correct English. Sentence pairs where the English side is detected as noisy are removed from the swa-eng training dataset. In total, we filter out about 30% of the original training set and obtains a dataset of 2.2M sentence pairs. As for swc-fra NMT system, training data includes parallel corpora made available by the organizers in addition to the available corpora for this language pair on OPUS website. Overall we used a training set of 1.1 M sentence pairs.

2.2.2 Architecture

We propose an NMT model using long short-term memory neural networks (LSTMs) (Hochreiter and Schmidhuber, 1997). NMT systems for swa-eng and for swc-fra were trained using the lstm_luong_wmt_en_de model template, a standard LSTM Encoder-Decoder architecture with Luong-style attention (Luong et al., 2015). Swa-eng system was built at the subword level using a joint BPE vocabulary of 32768 BPE unit, trained using source and target language. Swc-fra NMT model, on its side, was trained at the word level.

2.3 Results

The ASR results in terms of word error rate (WER) are reported in Table 1 on the development datasets for different types of acoustic features. We can see that using wav2vec features significantly decreases the WER and provides about 8% of relative WER reduction for both datasets. Table 2 shows

[4]https://opus.nlpl.eu

the official ASR results on the test datatests. For our submissions, we used wav2vec features only. These ASR results are the best ones among the ASR results submitted by the participants to this task.

Features	Dev swa	Dev swc
MFCC hires	19.90	29.57
wav2vec 2.0	18.34	27.29

Table 1: ASR performance (WER,%) for the development datasets of the low-resource task.

Features	Test swa	Test swc
wav2vec 2.0	31.25	36.75

Table 2: Official ASR performance (WER,%) for the test datasets of the low-resource task.

The MT results in terms of BLEU (Papineni et al., 2002) score are reported in Table 3. Notice that while the WER of the outputs of the ASR fed by wav2vec features is lower than the one fed by MFCC features, for the swc-fra language pair, the BLEU score of the translation from the MFCC-based ASR system is higher than the one got on the wav2vec-based ASR. By lack of time, we did not yet investigate the reason of this, but we will do as soon as possible.

Features	Dev swa-eng	Dev swc-fra
MFCC hires	13.39	9.60
wav2vec 2.0	14.19	9.45
reference text	18.36	14.07

Table 3: MT performance (BLEU) for the development datasets of the low-resource task.

3 Multilingual speech translation

Speech-to-text translation (ST) consists in translating a speech utterance in a source language to a text in another target language (*e.g.*, English audio to French text). In this section, we describe a *multilingual* ST system that can translate from multiple source languages to multiple target ones.

3.1 Data

The data provided for the multilingual ST task is a subset of the Multilingual TEDx corpus (Salesky

Features	Test swa-eng	Test swc-fra
wav2vec 2.0	12.9	9.1

Table 4: Official MT performance (BLEU) on the test datasets of the low-resource task for the submitted system.

et al., 2021), in which there are four source languages (Spanish (es), French (fr), Portuguese (pt), and Italian (it)) and five target languages (the aforementioned source languages plus English (en)). The sizes of the ASR talks range from 107 hours (it) to 189 hours (es). Translation data is part of the ASR talks for a given source language. Our experiments were performed in the *constrained* setting where only the provided data for the task is used.

3.2 Model architecture

Our system is based on the Dual-decoder Transformer (Le et al., 2020) which consists of an encoder and two decoders. This architecture jointly transcribes and translates an input speech. Each of the decoders is responsible for one task (ASR or ST) while interacting with each other. We refer the reader to the paper for further details.

We initially followed Le et al. (2020) and used 12 encoder layers, 6 decoder layers, and a hidden dimension of $d = 256$. However, this model produced poor results. We hypothesize that with this configuration, the model capacity is too large for the dataset described in the previous section. In the end, we ended up using only 6 encoder layers and 3 decoder layers (with the same $d = 256$). In addition, we also trained a Transformer model having the same encoder of 6 layers but with only one decoder as the baseline (hereafter called single-decoder model).

3.3 Implementation details

For text pre-processing, we normalize the punctuation and build the vocabulary on the concatenation of the transcript and translation text using SentencePiece (Kudo and Richardson, 2018) without pre-tokenization. We used 10k unigram vocabulary as it performed slightly better than a vocabulary of 8k tokens in our preliminary experiments. The speech features are 80-dimensional log Mel filterbank. Utterances having more than 3000 frames are removed for GPU efficiency. We used SpecAugment (Park et al., 2019) with Librispeech double (LD) policy for data augmentation.

	es-en	es-fr	es-pt	es-it	fr-en	fr-es	fr-pt	pt-en	pt-es	it-en	it-es
Training data (hours)	69	11	42	11	50	38	25	59	-	-	-
Results on the dev sets											
Single decoder	11.56	4.95	19.14	17.98	13.27	12.99	12.21	13.54	8.31	3.88	4.54
Single decoder*	12.75	5.32	21.95	16.82	11.27	12.15	11.01	12.37	10.25	2.24	2.50
Dual-decoder*	18.59	8.02	25.38	19.22	17.81	17.79	15.20	17.63	3.00	4.09	4.81
Official results on the hidden test sets											
Dual-decoder*	20.20	8.20	25.60	11.10	14.40	15.00	14.90	13.20	3.00	4.20	4.60

Table 5: **BLEU on the dev and hidden test sets.** * denotes the use of the transcripts in training.

For the target-forcing mechanism, we prepended a language-specific token to the target sequence (Inaguma et al., 2019; Le et al., 2020). In order to provide good initialization for our multilingual ST system, we separately trained a multilingual ASR system and a multilingual MT one on the allowed data. We then used the weights from the pre-trained ASR encoder, ASR decoder and MT decoder to initialize our ST encoder, ASR decoder, and ST decoder, respectively. We also used the obtained multilingual MT model to augment the training data by translating the transcripts to the target languages as well as translating the translations back to the source languages.

Our model was trained for 150 epochs using the Adam optimizer (Kingma and Ba, 2015) with the inverse square root scheduler. We averaged the last 10 checkpoints and used beam search with a beam size of 5 for decoding. The results reported are detokenized case-sensitive BLEU (Papineni et al., 2002). Our implementation is based on the FAIRSEQ S2T toolkit (Wang et al., 2020).

3.4 Results

Table 5 displays the results on the dev and hidden test sets. One can observe that the Dual-decoder Transformer outperforms the baselines of single decoder on all language pairs except for the pt-es direction where it is surpassed by the single-decoder models. The use of transcripts as additional languages (Gangi et al., 2019) in the single-decoder model improves the results for 4 out of 11 language pairs. Since we aim to obtain a single end-to-end multilingual ST system that can perform many-to-many translation, we selected the Dual-decoder Transformer for our final submission.

4 Conclusion

This paper described the ON-TRAC consortium submissions to the low-resource translation task and to the multilingual speech translation task. Our unique ASR system for both Swahili and Congolese Swahili languages uses XLSR-53 wav2vec features as speech representation input. It got the best results on both Swahili languages (respectively 31.25% and 36.75% of WER). The NMT systems used to translated these transcription into respectively to English and to French got BLEU scores of 12.9 (swa→eng) and 9.1 (swc→fr). The Dual-decoder Transformer we used in the multilingual speech translation got promising results. We did not try a specific strategy to handle language pairs without training data. The low results we got on such language pairs confirm that a specific treatment must be applied in these conditions.

Acknowledgments

This work was funded by the French Research Agency (ANR) through the ON-TRAC project under contract number ANR-18-CE23-0021.

References

Alexei Baevski, Henry Zhou, Abdelrahman Mohamed, and Michael Auli. 2020. wav2vec 2.0: A framework for self-supervised learning of speech representations. *arXiv preprint arXiv:2006.11477.*

Alexis Conneau, Alexei Baevski, Ronan Collobert, Abdelrahman Mohamed, and Michael Auli. 2020. Unsupervised cross-lingual representation learning for speech recognition. *arXiv preprint arXiv:2006.13979.*

Ahmed El-Kishky, Vishrav Chaudhary, Francisco Guzmán, and Philipp Koehn. 2020. CCAligned: A massive collection of cross-lingual web-document pairs. In *Proceedings of the 2020 Conference on*

Empirical Methods in Natural Language Processing (EMNLP 2020).

Maha Elbayad, Ha Nguyen, Fethi Bougares, Natalia Tomashenko, Antoine Caubrière, Benjamin Lecouteux, Yannick Estève, and Laurent Besacier. 2020. On-trac consortium for end-to-end and simultaneous speech translation challenge tasks at iwslt 2020. *arXiv preprint arXiv:2005.11861*.

Solene Evain, Ha Nguyen, Hang Le, Marcely Zanon Boito, Salima Mdhaffar, Sina Alisamir, Ziyi Tong, Natalia Tomashenko, Marco Dinarelli, Titouan Parcollet, et al. 2021. Lebenchmark: A reproducible framework for assessing self-supervised representation learning from speech. *arXiv preprint arXiv:2104.11462*.

Mattia Antonino Di Gangi, Matteo Negri, and Marco Turchi. 2019. One-to-many multilingual end-to-end speech translation. In *IEEE Automatic Speech Recognition and Understanding Workshop, ASRU 2019, Singapore, December 14-18, 2019*, pages 585–592. IEEE.

Hadrien Gelas, Laurent Besacier, and François Pellegrino. 2012. Developments of swahili resources for an automatic speech recognition system. In *Spoken Language Technologies for Under-Resourced Languages*.

Sepp Hochreiter and Jürgen Schmidhuber. 1997. Long short-term memory. *Neural Computation*, 9(8):1735–1780.

Hirofumi Inaguma, Kevin Duh, Tatsuya Kawahara, and Shinji Watanabe. 2019. Multilingual end-to-end speech translation. In *IEEE Automatic Speech Recognition and Understanding Workshop, ASRU 2019, Singapore, December 14-18, 2019*, pages 570–577. IEEE.

Diederik P. Kingma and Jimmy Ba. 2015. Adam: A method for stochastic optimization. In *3rd International Conference on Learning Representations, ICLR 2015, San Diego, CA, USA, May 7-9, 2015, Conference Track Proceedings*.

Taku Kudo and John Richardson. 2018. Sentencepiece: A simple and language independent subword tokenizer and detokenizer for neural text processing. In *Proceedings of the 2018 Conference on Empirical Methods in Natural Language Processing, EMNLP 2018: System Demonstrations, Brussels, Belgium, October 31 - November 4, 2018*, pages 66–71. Association for Computational Linguistics.

Hang Le, Juan Pino, Changhan Wang, Jiatao Gu, Didier Schwab, and Laurent Besacier. 2020. Dual-decoder transformer for joint automatic speech recognition and multilingual speech translation. In *Proceedings of the 28th International Conference on Computational Linguistics, COLING 2020, Barcelona, Spain (Online), December 8-13, 2020*, pages 3520–3533. International Committee on Computational Linguistics.

Marco Lui and Timothy Baldwin. 2012. langid.py: An off-the-shelf language identification tool. In *Proceedings of the ACL 2012 System Demonstrations*, pages 25–30, Jeju Island, Korea. Association for Computational Linguistics.

Thang Luong, Hieu Pham, and Christopher D. Manning. 2015. Effective approaches to attention-based neural machine translation. In *Proceedings of the 2015 Conference on Empirical Methods in Natural Language Processing*, pages 1412–1421, Lisbon, Portugal. Association for Computational Linguistics.

Ha Nguyen, Fethi Bougares, N. Tomashenko, Yannick Estève, and Laurent Besacier. 2020. Investigating Self-Supervised Pre-Training for End-to-End Speech Translation. In *Proc. Interspeech 2020*, pages 1466–1470.

Ha Nguyen, Natalia Tomashenko, Marcely Zanon Boito, Antoine Caubrière, Fethi Bougares, Mickael Rouvier, Laurent Besacier, and Yannick Estève. 2019. On-trac consortium end-to-end speech translation systems for the iwslt 2019 shared task. *arXiv preprint arXiv:1910.13689*.

Kishore Papineni, Salim Roukos, Todd Ward, and Wei-Jing Zhu. 2002. Bleu: a method for automatic evaluation of machine translation. In *Proceedings of the 40th Annual Meeting of the Association for Computational Linguistics*, pages 311–318, Philadelphia, Pennsylvania, USA. Association for Computational Linguistics.

Daniel S. Park, William Chan, Yu Zhang, Chung-Cheng Chiu, Barret Zoph, Ekin D. Cubuk, and Quoc V. Le. 2019. Specaugment: A simple data augmentation method for automatic speech recognition. In *Interspeech 2019, 20th Annual Conference of the International Speech Communication Association, Graz, Austria, 15-19 September 2019*, pages 2613–2617. ISCA.

Vijayaditya Peddinti, Daniel Povey, and Sanjeev Khudanpur. 2015. A time delay neural network architecture for efficient modeling of long temporal contexts. In *Sixteenth Annual Conference of the International Speech Communication Association*.

Daniel Povey, Gaofeng Cheng, Yiming Wang, Ke Li, Hainan Xu, Mahsa Yarmohammadi, and Sanjeev Khudanpur. 2018. Semi-orthogonal low-rank matrix factorization for deep neural networks. In *Interspeech*, pages 3743–3747.

Daniel Povey, Arnab Ghoshal, Gilles Boulianne, Lukas Burget, Ondrej Glembek, Nagendra Goel, Mirko Hannemann, Petr Motlicek, Yanmin Qian, Petr Schwarz, et al. 2011. The kaldi speech recognition toolkit. In *IEEE 2011 workshop on automatic speech recognition and understanding*, CONF. IEEE Signal Processing Society.

Daniel Povey, Vijayaditya Peddinti, Daniel Galvez, Pegah Ghahremani, Vimal Manohar, Xingyu Na, Yiming Wang, and Sanjeev Khudanpur. 2016. Purely sequence-trained neural networks for asr based on lattice-free mmi. In *Interspeech*, pages 2751–2755.

Elizabeth Salesky, Matthew Wiesner, Jacob Bremerman, Roldano Cattoni, Matteo Negri, Marco Turchi, Douglas W. Oard, and Matt Post. 2021. The multilingual tedx corpus for speech recognition and translation. *CoRR*, abs/2102.01757.

Steffen Schneider, Alexei Baevski, Ronan Collobert, and Michael Auli. 2019. wav2vec: Unsupervised pre-training for speech recognition. *arXiv preprint arXiv:1904.05862*.

Changhan Wang, Yun Tang, Xutai Ma, Anne Wu, Dmytro Okhonko, and Juan Pino. 2020. Fairseq S2T: fast speech-to-text modeling with fairseq. In *Proceedings of the 1st Conference of the Asia-Pacific Chapter of the Association for Computational Linguistics and the 10th International Joint Conference on Natural Language Processing: System Demonstrations, AACL/IJCNLP 2020, Suzhou, China, December 4-7, 2020*, pages 33–39. Association for Computational Linguistics.

IMS' Systems for the IWSLT 2021 Low-Resource Speech Translation Task

Pavel Denisov, Manuel Mager, Ngoc Thang Vu
Institute for Natural Language Processing, University of Stuttgart
{pavel.denisov,manuel.mager,thangvu}@ims.uni-stuttgart.de

Abstract

This paper describes the submission to the IWSLT 2021 Low-Resource Speech Translation Shared Task by IMS team. We utilize state-of-the-art models combined with several data augmentation, multi-task and transfer learning approaches for the automatic speech recognition (ASR) and machine translation (MT) steps of our cascaded system. Moreover, we also explore the feasibility of a full end-to-end speech translation (ST) model in the case of very constrained amount of ground truth labeled data. Our best system achieves the best performance among all submitted systems for Congolese Swahili to English and French with BLEU scores 7.7 and 13.7 respectively, and the second best result for Coastal Swahili to English with BLEU score 14.9.

1 Introduction

We participate in the low-resource speech translation task of IWSLT 2021. This task is organized for the first time, and it focuses on three speech translation directions this year: Coastal Swahili to English (`swa→eng`), Congolese Swahili to French (`swc→fra`) and Congolese Swahili to English (`swc→eng`). Working on under-represented and low-resource languages is of special relevance for the inclusion into technologies of big parts of the world population. The Masakhane initiative (Nekoto et al., 2020) has opened the doors for large scale participatory research on languages of the African continent, to which Swahili belongs to. Our Speech-to-Text translation systems aim to contribute to this global effort.

A common problem for these languages is the small amount of data. This is also true for the language pairs of the shared task: the provided data contains a small amount of translated speech samples for each pair, but the participants are allowed to use additional data and pre-trained models for the sub-tasks of ASR and MT. We utilize most of the suggested additional data resources to train and tune sequence-to-sequence ASR and MT components. Our primary submission is the cascaded system built of Conformer end-to-end ASR model and Transformer MT model. Our contrastive system is end-to-end ST system utilizing parameters transfer from the Encoder part of ASR model and the full MT model.

Both ASR and MT components of the cascaded system initially yield good results on their own, but the discrepancy between language formats (spoken vs. written) in ASR and MT corpora causes degradation by 47% in resulting scores. To adapt the MT system to the output of the ASR, we transform the Swahili source data to output similar to one of an ASR system. To further increase the performance of our MT system, we leverage both source formats (original Swahili text and simulated ASR output Swahili) into a multi-task framework. This approach improves our results by 17%, mostly for the English target language. Our system outperforms the next best system on `swc→fra` by 4.4 BLEU points, but got outperformed by 10.4 BLEU for `swa→eng`, being the second-best team. Our team was the only participating for `swc→eng` language pair with a score of 7.7 BLEU. The results of end-to-end system consistently appear to be about twice worse compared to the pipeline approach.

2 ASR

2.1 Data

Table 1 summarizes the datasets used to develop our ASR system. The training data comprises of the shared task training data, Gamayun Swahili speech samples[1] and the training subsets of ALFFA dataset (Gelas et al., 2012) and IARPA Babel Swahili Lan-

[1] https://gamayun.translatorswb.org/data/

Proceedings of the 18th International Conference on Spoken Language Translation, pages 175–181
Bangkok, Thailand (Online), August 5–6, 2021.

guage Pack (Andresen et al., 2017). The validation data comprises of 869 randomly sampled utterances from the shared task training data and the testing subset of ALFFA dataset. The testing data is the shared task's validation data. All audio is converted to 16 kHz sampling rate. Applied data augmentation methods are speed perturbation with the factors of 0.9, 1.0 and 1.1, as well as SpecAugment (Park et al., 2019). Transcriptions of the shared task data and Gamayun Swahili speech samples dataset are converted from written to spoken language similarly to Bahar et al. (2020), namely all numbers are converted to words[2], punctuation is removed and letters are converted to lower case. External LM is trained on the combination of transcriptions of the ASR training data and LM training data from ALFFA dataset. The validation data for the external LM contains only transcriptions of the ASR validation data.

Dataset	Training		Validation		Testing	
	Utt.	Hours	Utt.	Hours	Utt.	Hours
IWSLT'21 `swa`	4,162	5.3	434	0.5	868	3.7
IWSLT'21 `swc`	4,565	11.1	435	1.0	868	4.2
Gamayun	4,256	5.4	-	-	-	-
IARPA Babel	21,891	28.8	-	-	-	-
ALFFA	9,854	9.5	1,991	1.8	-	-
Total	44,728	60.3	2,860	3.4	1,736	7.9

Table 1: Datasets used for the ASR system.

2.2 Model

The ASR system is based on end-to-end Conformer ASR (Gulati et al., 2020) and its ESPnet implementation (Guo et al., 2020). Following the latest LibriSpeech recipe (Kamo, 2021), our model has 12 Conformer blocks in Encoder and 6 Transformer blocks in Decoder with 8 heads and attention dimension of 512. The input features are 80 dimensional log Mel filterbanks. The output units are 100 byte-pair-encoding (BPE) tokens (Sennrich et al., 2016). The warm-up learning rate strategy (Vaswani et al., 2017) is used, while the learning rate coefficient is set to 0.005 and the number of warm-up steps is set to 10000. The model is optimized to jointly minimize cross-entropy and connectionist temporal classification (CTC) (Graves et al., 2006) loss functions, both with the coefficient of 0.5. The training is performed for 35 epochs on 2 GPUs with the total batch size of 20M bins and gradient accumulation over each 2 steps. After that, 10 checkpoints with the best validation accuracy are averaged for the decoding. The decoding is performed using beam search with the beam size of 8 on the combination of Decoder attention and CTC prefix scores (Kim et al., 2017) also with the coefficients of 0.5 for both. In addition to that, external BPE token-level language model (LM) is used during the decoding in the final ASR system. The external LM has 16 Transformer blocks with 8 heads and attention dimension of 512. It is trained for 30 epochs on 4 GPUs with the total batch size of 5M bins, the learning rate coefficient 0.001 and 25000 warm-up steps. Single checkpoint having the best validation perplexity is used for the decoding.

2.3 Pre-trained models

In addition to training from scratch, we attempt to fine-tune several pre-trained speech models. These models include ESPnet2 Conformer ASR models from the LibriSpeech (Panayotov et al., 2015), SPGISpeech (O'Neill et al., 2021) and Russian Open STT[3] recipes, as well as wav2vec 2.0 (Baevski et al., 2020) based models XLSR-53 (Conneau et al., 2020) and VoxPopuli (Wang et al., 2021).

2.4 Results

Table 2 summarizes the explored ASR settings and the results on the shared task validation data. CTC weight 0.5 is selected in order to minimize the gap between ASR accuracy on the two Swahili languages. Evaluation of pre-trained English ASR models expectedly shows that SPGISpeech model results in better WER, likely because of the larger amount of training data or more diverse accent representation in this corpus compared to LibriSpeech. Surprisingly, pre-trained Russian Open STT model yields even better results than SPGISpeech model, even if the amount of the training data for them is quite similar (about 5000 hours). Since Swahili language is not closely related to English or Russian, we attribute better results of Russian Open STT model either to the larger amount of acoustic conditions and speaking styles in Russian Open STT corpus, or to more similar output vocabulary in the model: both Russian and Swahili models use 100 subword units, while English models use 5000 units. Validation accuracy of wav2vec 2.0 models does not look promising in our experiments

[2]Using `http://www.bantu-languages.com/en/tools/swahili_numbers.html`

[3]`https://github.com/snakers4/open_stt`

and we do not include their decoding results to the table. Freezing the first Encoder layer of Russian Open STT model during training on Swahili data gives us consistent improvement on both testing datasets, but freezing more layers does not appear to be beneficial. Interestingly enough, external LM also improves results on both Coastal and Congolese Swahili, however the best LM weights differ between languages, and we conclude to keep them separate in the final system.

#	System	swa	swc	Avg.
1.	CTC weight 0.3	25.9	26.5	26.2
2.	CTC weight 0.4	25.8	24.4	25.1
3.	CTC weight 0.5	25.2	25.0	**25.1**
4.	CTC weight 0.6	25.4	25.0	25.2
5.	CTC weight 0.7	26.4	24.9	25.7
6.	#3, pre-trained LibriSpeech	22.4	25.4	23.9
7.	#3, pre-trained SPGISpeech	20.8	22.9	21.9
8.	#3, pre-trained Russian Open STT	21.4	20.8	**21.1**
9.	#8, freeze Encoder layers #1–4	20.3	21.1	20.7
10.	#8, freeze Encoder layers #1–2	21.9	21.4	21.7
11.	#8, freeze Encoder layer #1	17.8	19.7	**18.8**
12.	#11, average 9 checkpoints	17.7	19.7	18.7
13.	#11, average 8 checkpoints	17.7	19.5	**18.6**
14.	#11, average 7 checkpoints	17.8	19.6	18.7
15.	#11, average 6 checkpoints	17.7	19.5	18.6
16.	#11, average 5 checkpoints	17.9	19.6	18.8
17.	#13, external LM weight 0.2	15.1	18.4	16.8
18.	#13, external LM weight 0.3	14.5	**18.3**	16.4
19.	#13, external LM weight 0.4	14.0	18.5	16.3
20.	#13, external LM weight 0.5	13.6	18.7	16.2
21.	#13, external LM weight 0.6	**13.5**	19.1	16.3
22.	#13, external LM weight 0.7	13.8	19.9	16.9

Table 2: ASR results (WER, %) on the shared task validation data. Bold numbers correspond to the selected configuration for the final system (the external LM weights are language-specific).

3 MT

3.1 Data

Table 3 summarizes the datasets used to train our MT systems. The training data comprises of the shared task training data, Gamayun kit[4] (English – Swahili and Congolese Swahili – French parallel text corpora) as well as multiple corpora from the OPUS collection (Tiedemann, 2012), namely: ELRC_2922 (Tiedemann, 2012), GNOME (Tiedemann, 2012), CCAligned and MultiCCAligned (El-Kishky et al., 2020), EUbookshop (Tiedemann, 2012), GlobalVoices (Tiedemann, 2012), JW300 for `sw` and `swc` source languages (Agić and Vulić, 2019), ParaCrawl and MultiParaCrawl[5], Tanzil (Tiedemann, 2012), TED2020 (Reimers and Gurevych, 2020), Ubuntu (Tiedemann, 2012), WikiMatrix (Schwenk et al., 2019) and wikimedia (Tiedemann, 2012). The validation data for each target language comprises of 434 randomly sampled utterances from the shared task training data. The testing data is the shared task validation data, that also has 434 sentences per target language.

Dataset	Words		Sentences	
	→eng	→fra	→eng	→fra
IWSLT'21	31,594	51,111	4,157	4,562
Gamayun	39,608	216,408	5,000	25,223
ELRC_2922	12,691	-	607	-
GNOME	170	170	40	40
CCAligned	18,038,994	-	2,044,993	-
MultiCCAligned	18,039,148	10,713,654	2,044,991	1,071,168
EUbookshop	228	223	17	16
GlobalVoices	576,222	347,671	32,307	19,455
JW300 sw	15,811,865	15,763,811	964,549	931,112
JW300 swc	9,108,342	9,094,008	575,154	558,602
ParaCrawl	3,207,700	-	132,517	-
MultiParaCrawl	-	996,664	-	50,954
Tanzil	1,734,247	117,975	138,253	10,258
TED2020	136,162	134,601	9,745	9,606
Ubuntu	2,655	189	986	53
WikiMatrix	923,898	271,673	51,387	19,909
wikimedia	66,704	1,431	771	13
Total	41,910,113	30,003,158	3,406,772	2,159,007

Table 3: Datasets used to train the MT systems and their sizes in numbers of words (source language) and sentences. Total numbers are lower due to the deduplication.

3.2 Model

For the text-to-text neural machine translation (NMT) system we use a Transformer big model (Vaswani et al., 2017) using the fairseq implementation (Ott et al., 2019). We train three versions of the translation model.

First we train a vanilla NMT (`vanillaNMT`) system using only the data from the parallel training dataset. For preprocessing we use the SentencePiece implementation (Kudo and Richardson, 2018) of BPEs (Sennrich et al., 2016). For our second experiment for the NMT system (`preprocNMT`), we apply the same written to spoken language conversion as used for the ASR transcriptions (section §2.1) to the source text S and obtain ASR-like text S_t. S_t is then segmented using a BPE model and used as input for our NMT model. The last approach was using a multi-task framework to train the system (`multiNMT`), where all parameters of the translation model were shared. The main task of this model is to translate ASR output S_t to the target language T (task `asrS`), while our auxiliary task is to translate regular source Swahili S to the target language T (task `textS`). We base or multi-task approach on the idea of mul-

[4] https://gamayun.translatorswb.org/data/

[5] https://www.paracrawl.eu/

Model	Input	swa→eng		swc→fra		swc→eng	
		BLEU	chrF	BLEU	chrF	BLEU	chrF
vanillaNMT	textS	25.72	53.47	17.70	44.80	10.55	38.07
	asrS	14.26	47.74	10.57	40.99	4.71	34.70
	ASR #20	13.21	46.11	10.67	40.53	4.67	33.94
	ASR #1	11.50	43.34	9.52	38.32	4.24	32.45
preprocNMT	textS	11.01	41.33	13.54	41.00	4.49	31.91
	asrS	16.00	45.86	14.09	42.05	7.10	34.35
	ASR #20	14.54	44.17	13.23	41.00	6.62	33.63
	ASR #1	12.45	40.95	11.21	38.08	5.47	31.63
multiNMT	textS	25.69	53.27	18.20	44.66	10.56	38.29
	asrS	20.07	50.31	14.69	43.07	8.73	36.72
	ASR #20	17.91	48.39	13.29	41.58	7.94	35.47
	ASR #1	15.81	45.31	11.97	39.09	7.03	33.78

Table 4: MT results on the shared task validation data. WER values on swa/swc validation data are 13.6/18.7% for ASR #20 and 25.9/26.5% for ASR #1.

tilingual NMT introduced by Johnson et al. (2017), using a special token at the beginning of each sentence belonging to a certain task, as we can see in the next example:

<asrS> sara je haujui tena thamani ya kikombe hiki → Tu ne connais donc pas, Sarah, la valeur de cette coupe ?
<textS> Sara, je! Haujui tena, thamani ya kikombe hiki? → Tu ne connais donc pas, Sarah, la valeur de cette coupe ?

Then, our multi-task training objective is to maximize the joint log-likelihood of the auxiliary task textS and the primary task asrS.

Hyperparameters For word segmentation we use BPEs (Sennrich et al., 2016) with separate dictionaries for the encoder and the encoder, using the SentencePiece implementation (Kudo and Richardson, 2018). Both vocabularies have a size of 8000 tokens. Our model has 6 layers, 4 attention heads and embedding size of 512 for the encoder and the decoder. To optimize our model we use Adam (Kingma and Ba, 2014) with a learning rate of 0.001. Training was performed on 40 epochs with early stopping and a warm-up phase of 4000 updates. We also use a dropout (Srivastava et al., 2014) of 0.4, and an attention dropout of 0.2. For decoding we use Beam Search, with a size of 5.

3.3 Results

Table 4 shows the results of our MT system in combination with different inputs. We trained three models using the techniques described in section §3.2 (vanillaNMT, preprocNMT, and multiNMT). Then we used the official validation set as input (textS), and also applied asrS preprocessing. We used both inputs to test the performance of all models with different inputs. As expected, the vanillaNMT systems performs well with textS input (i.e 25.72 BLEU for swa→eng), but drops when using asrS. This pattern was later confirmed when using real ASR output (ASR #20 and ASR #1). We noticed, that training our model with asrS, instead of using textS improves slightly the results (i.e 16.00 BLEU with preprocNMT compared with 14.26 on vanillaNMT for swa→eng). But when we use multiNMT the performance strongly increase to 20.07 for swa→eng. This pattern also can be seen when using real ASR output (ASR #20 and ASR #1), and across all language pairs. We hypothesize that the multi-task framework helps the model to be more robust to different input formats, and allows it to generalize more the language internals.

4 End-to-End ST

4.1 Data

End-to-end ST is fine-tuned on the same speech recordings, as ASR data, but with transcriptions in English or in French. English and French transcriptions are obtained either from the datasets released with the shared task, or by running our MT system on Swahili transcriptions. External LMs for English and French outputs are trained on 10M sentences of the corresponding language from the OSCAR corpus (Ortiz Suárez et al., 2020).

4.2 Model

The end-to-end ST system comprises of the Encoder part of our ASR system and the whole MT system with removed input token embedding layer. All layers are frozen during the fine-tuning except of the top four layers of ASR Encoder and bottom three layers of MT Encoder. SpecAugment and gradient accumulation are disabled during the fine-tuning. Compared to the ASR system, end-to-end ST system has larger dictionary, what leads to shorter output sequences and allows us to increase the batch size to 60M bins. The rest of hyperparameters are the same as in the ASR system. We evaluate ST model separately and also with external LM that is set up as described in the ASR section.

4.3 Results

It can be seen from Table 5 that the end-to-end ST systems do not yet match the cascaded systems in translation quality in low resource settings. External LMs, however, slightly improve the results for both target languages.

Setting	swa→eng		swc→fra		swc→eng	
	BLEU	chrF	BLEU	chrF	BLEU	chrF
No LM	7.81	30.83	2.94	22.98	3.59	23.50
LM weight 0.4	8.82	31.26	3.73	22.07	4.06	23.89
LM weight 0.6	9.11	31.45	3.58	20.57	4.17	23.62

Table 5: End-to-end ST results on the shared task validation data.

5 Final systems

Table 6 shows validation scores of our final systems, as well as their evaluation scores provided by the organizers of the shared task. Our primary (cascaded) system here uses increased beam sizes: 30 for the ASR, 10 for the English MT and 25 for the French MT. `swc/swa` WERs of the final ASR systems are 12.5/17.6% on the validation sets. We did not observe improvement from the increased beam size on the contrastive systems and leave it at 2. It should be noted that the contrastive system is evaluated on incomplete output[6] for the `swc→fra` pair because of the technical issue on our side. We observe a large gap between the validation and evaluation scores for Coastal Swahili source language, what might indicate some sort of bias towards the validation set in our ASR or MT, or both. It is unclear why it does not happen for Congolese Swahili source language, because we optimized all our systems for the best performance on the validation sets for both source languages.

System	Set	swa→eng	swc→fra	swc→eng
Primary (cascaded)	Val.	18.3	13.7	7.9
	Eval.	14.9	13.5	7.7
Contrastive (end-to-end)	Val.	9.1	3.7	4.0
	Eval.	6.7	2.7	3.9

Table 6: Results (BLEU) of the primary and contrastive systems on the validation and evaluation data of the shared task.

6 Conclusion

This paper described the IMS submission to the IWSLT 2021 Low-Resource Shared Task on Coastal and Congolese Swahili to English and French, explaining our intermediate ideas and results. Our system is ranked as the best for Congolese Swahili to French and English, and the second for Coastal Swahili to English. In spite of the simplicity of our cascade system, we show that the improving of ASR system with pre-trained models and afterward the tuning of MT system to optimize its fit to the ASR output achieves good results, even in challenging low resource settings. Additionally, we tried an end-to-end ST system with a lower performance. However, we learned that there is still room for improvement, and in future work we plan to investigate this research direction.

[6] 406 of 2124 hypothesis are empty.

7 Acknowledgements

The authors acknowledge support by the state of Baden-Württemberg through bwHPC. This product contains or makes use of IARPA data, IARPA Babel Swahili Language Pack, IARPA-babel202b-v.1.0d (LDC2017S05). Manuel Mager received financial support by DAAD Doctoral Research Grant for this work.

References

Željko Agić and Ivan Vulić. 2019. JW300: A Wide-Coverage Parallel Corpus for Low-Resource Languages. In *Proceedings of the 57th Annual Meeting of the Association for Computational Linguistics*, pages 3204–3210.

Jess Andresen, Aric Bills, Thomas Conners, Eyal Dubinski, Jonathan G. Fiscus, Mary Harper, Kirill Kozlov, Nicolas Malyska, Jennifer Melot, Michelle Morrison, Josh Phillips, Jessica Ray, Anton Rytting, Wade Shen, Ronnie Silber, Evelyne Tzoukermann, and Jamie Wong. 2017. IARPA Babel Swahili Language Pack IARPA-babel202b-v1.0d LDC2017S05.

Alexei Baevski, Yuhao Zhou, Abdelrahman Mohamed, and Michael Auli. 2020. wav2vec 2.0: A framework for Self-Supervised Learning of Speech Representations. *Advances in Neural Information Processing Systems*, 33.

Parnia Bahar, Patrick Wilken, Tamer Alkhouli, Andreas Guta, Pavel Golik, Evgeny Matusov, and Christian

Herold. 2020. Start-before-end and end-to-end: Neural speech translation by apptek and rwth aachen university. In *Proceedings of the 17th International Conference on Spoken Language Translation*, pages 44–54.

Alexis Conneau, Alexei Baevski, Ronan Collobert, Abdelrahman Mohamed, and Michael Auli. 2020. Unsupervised cross-lingual representation learning for speech recognition. *arXiv preprint arXiv:2006.13979*.

Ahmed El-Kishky, Vishrav Chaudhary, Francisco Guzmán, and Philipp Koehn. 2020. CCAligned: A massive collection of cross-lingual web-document pairs. In *Proceedings of the 2020 Conference on Empirical Methods in Natural Language Processing (EMNLP)*, pages 5960–5969.

Hadrien Gelas, Laurent Besacier, and François Pellegrino. 2012. Developments of Swahili resources for an automatic speech recognition system. In *SLTU - Workshop on Spoken Language Technologies for Under-Resourced Languages*, Cape-Town, Afrique Du Sud.

Alex Graves, Santiago Fernández, Faustino Gomez, and Jürgen Schmidhuber. 2006. Connectionist temporal classification: labelling unsegmented sequence data with recurrent neural networks. In *Proceedings of the 23rd international conference on Machine learning*, pages 369–376.

Anmol Gulati, James Qin, Chung-Cheng Chiu, Niki Parmar, Yu Zhang, Jiahui Yu, Wei Han, Shibo Wang, Zhengdong Zhang, Yonghui Wu, et al. 2020. Conformer: Convolution-augmented Transformer for Speech Recognition. *Proc. Interspeech 2020*, pages 5036–5040.

Pengcheng Guo, Florian Boyer, Xuankai Chang, Tomoki Hayashi, Yosuke Higuchi, Hirofumi Inaguma, Naoyuki Kamo, Chenda Li, Daniel Garcia-Romero, Jiatong Shi, et al. 2020. Recent Developments on ESPnet Toolkit Boosted by Conformer. *arXiv preprint arXiv:2010.13956*.

Melvin Johnson, Mike Schuster, Quoc V. Le, Maxim Krikun, Yonghui Wu, Zhifeng Chen, Nikhil Thorat, Fernanda Viégas, Martin Wattenberg, Greg Corrado, Macduff Hughes, and Jeffrey Dean. 2017. Google's multilingual neural machine translation system: Enabling zero-shot translation. *Transactions of the Association for Computational Linguistics*, 5:339–351.

Naoyuki Kamo. 2021. ESPnet2 LibriSpeech recipe.

Suyoun Kim, Takaaki Hori, and Shinji Watanabe. 2017. Joint CTC-attention based end-to-end speech recognition using multi-task learning. In *2017 IEEE international conference on acoustics, speech and signal processing (ICASSP)*, pages 4835–4839. IEEE.

Diederik P Kingma and Jimmy Ba. 2014. Adam: A method for stochastic optimization. *arXiv preprint arXiv:1412.6980*.

Taku Kudo and John Richardson. 2018. Sentencepiece: A simple and language independent subword tokenizer and detokenizer for neural text processing. In *Proceedings of the 2018 Conference on Empirical Methods in Natural Language Processing: System Demonstrations*, pages 66–71.

Wilhelmina Nekoto, Vukosi Marivate, Tshinondiwa Matsila, Timi Fasubaa, Taiwo Fagbohungbe, Solomon Oluwole Akinola, Shamsuddeen Muhammad, Salomon Kabongo Kabenamualu, Salomey Osei, Freshia Sackey, Rubungo Andre Niyongabo, Ricky Macharm, Perez Ogayo, Orevaoghene Ahia, Musie Meressa Berhe, Mofetoluwa Adeyemi, Masabata Mokgesi-Selinga, Lawrence Okegbemi, Laura Martinus, Kolawole Tajudeen, Kevin Degila, Kelechi Ogueji, Kathleen Siminyu, Julia Kreutzer, Jason Webster, Jamiil Toure Ali, Jade Abbott, Iroro Orife, Ignatius Ezeani, Idris Abdulkadir Dangana, Herman Kamper, Hady Elsahar, Goodness Duru, Ghollah Kioko, Murhabazi Espoir, Elan van Biljon, Daniel Whitenack, Christopher Onyefuluchi, Chris Chinenye Emezue, Bonaventure F. P. Dossou, Blessing Sibanda, Blessing Bassey, Ayodele Olabiyi, Arshath Ramkilowan, Alp Öktem, Adewale Akinfaderin, and Abdallah Bashir. 2020. Participatory research for low-resourced machine translation: A case study in African languages. In *Findings of the Association for Computational Linguistics: EMNLP 2020*, pages 2144–2160, Online. Association for Computational Linguistics.

Patrick K O'Neill, Vitaly Lavrukhin, Somshubra Majumdar, Vahid Noroozi, Yuekai Zhang, Oleksii Kuchaiev, Jagadeesh Balam, Yuliya Dovzhenko, Keenan Freyberg, Michael D Shulman, et al. 2021. SPGISpeech: 5,000 hours of transcribed financial audio for fully formatted end-to-end speech recognition. *arXiv preprint arXiv:2104.02014*.

Pedro Javier Ortiz Suárez, Laurent Romary, and Benoît Sagot. 2020. A monolingual approach to contextualized word embeddings for mid-resource languages. In *Proceedings of the 58th Annual Meeting of the Association for Computational Linguistics*, pages 1703–1714, Online. Association for Computational Linguistics.

Myle Ott, Sergey Edunov, Alexei Baevski, Angela Fan, Sam Gross, Nathan Ng, David Grangier, and Michael Auli. 2019. fairseq: A fast, extensible toolkit for sequence modeling. In *Proceedings of the 2019 Conference of the North American Chapter of the Association for Computational Linguistics (Demonstrations)*, pages 48–53, Minneapolis, Minnesota. Association for Computational Linguistics.

Vassil Panayotov, Guoguo Chen, Daniel Povey, and Sanjeev Khudanpur. 2015. LibriSpeech: an ASR corpus based on public domain audio books. In *2015 IEEE international conference on acoustics, speech and signal processing (ICASSP)*, pages 5206–5210. IEEE.

Daniel S Park, William Chan, Yu Zhang, Chung-Cheng Chiu, Barret Zoph, Ekin D Cubuk, and Quoc V Le. 2019. SpecAugment: A Simple Data Augmentation Method for Automatic Speech Recognition. *Proc. Interspeech 2019*, pages 2613–2617.

Nils Reimers and Iryna Gurevych. 2020. Making Monolingual Sentence Embeddings Multilingual Using Knowledge Distillation. In *Proceedings of the 2020 Conference on Empirical Methods in Natural Language Processing (EMNLP)*, pages 4512–4525.

Holger Schwenk, Vishrav Chaudhary, Shuo Sun, Hongyu Gong, and Francisco Guzmán. 2019. WikiMatrix: Mining 135M Parallel Sentences in 1620 Language Pairs from Wikipedia. *arXiv preprint arXiv:1907.05791*.

Rico Sennrich, Barry Haddow, and Alexandra Birch. 2016. Neural Machine Translation of Rare Words with Subword Units. In *Proceedings of the 54th Annual Meeting of the Association for Computational Linguistics (Volume 1: Long Papers)*, pages 1715–1725.

Nitish Srivastava, Geoffrey Hinton, Alex Krizhevsky, Ilya Sutskever, and Ruslan Salakhutdinov. 2014. Dropout: A simple way to prevent neural networks from overfitting. *Journal of Machine Learning Research*, 15(56):1929–1958.

Jörg Tiedemann. 2012. Parallel Data, Tools and Interfaces in OPUS. In *Proceedings of the Eighth International Conference on Language Resources and Evaluation (LREC'12)*, pages 2214–2218.

Ashish Vaswani, Noam Shazeer, Niki Parmar, Jakob Uszkoreit, Llion Jones, Aidan N Gomez, Łukasz Kaiser, and Illia Polosukhin. 2017. Attention is All you Need. *Advances in Neural Information Processing Systems*, 30:5998–6008.

Changhan Wang, Morgane Rivière, Ann Lee, Anne Wu, Chaitanya Talnikar, Daniel Haziza, Mary Williamson, Juan Pino, and Emmanuel Dupoux. 2021. VoxPopuli: A Large-Scale Multilingual Speech Corpus for Representation Learning, Semi-Supervised Learning and Interpretation. *arXiv preprint arXiv:2101.00390*.

The USYD-JD Speech Translation System for IWSLT2021

Liang Ding
The University of Sydney
ldin3097@sydney.edu.au

Di Wu*
Peking University
inbath@163.com

Dacheng Tao
JD Explore Academy, JD.com
dacheng.tao@gmail.com

Abstract

This paper describes the University of Sydney & JD's joint submission of the IWSLT 2021 low resource speech translation task. We participated in the Swahili→English direction and got the best scareBLEU (25.3) score among all the participants. Our constrained system is based on a pipeline framework, i.e. ASR and NMT. We trained our models with the officially provided ASR and MT datasets. The ASR system is based on the open-sourced tool Kaldi and this work mainly explores how to make the most of the NMT models. To reduce the punctuation errors generated by ASR model, we employ our previous work SlotRefine to train a punctuation correction model. To achieve better translation performance, we explored the most recent effective strategies, including back translation, knowledge distillation, multi-feature reranking and transductive finetuning. For model structure, we tried autoregressive and non-autoregressive models, respectively. In addition, we proposed two novel pre-train approaches, i.e. *de-noising training* and *bidirectional training* to fully exploit the data. Extensive experiments show that adding the above techniques consistently improves the BLEU scores, and the final submission system outperforms the baseline (Transformer ensemble model trained with the original parallel data) by approximately 10.8 BLEU score, achieving the SOTA performance.

1 Introduction

Recent years have seen a surge of interest in speech translation (ST, Ney 1999) task, that translates the source-side speech to the target-side text directly. The ST task contains two major components, Automatic Speech Recognition (ASR, Jelinek 1997) and Machine Translation (MT, Koehn 2009). In this year's IWSLT low-resource speech translation task, our USYD-JD translation team participated in the Swahili to English track. We break the speech translation task into "ASR→NMT" pipeline, and mainly focus on the NMT component.

For model frameworks, we tried autoregressive neural machine translation, including Transformer-BASE and -BIG (Vaswani et al., 2017), and non-autoregressive translation models (Gu et al., 2018). Also, we employ our previous work SlotRefine (Wu et al., 2020a) to tackle the case and punctuation problems after ASR. To make the most of the parallel and monolingual data, we proposed two pretrain strategies, i.e. BIDIRECTIONAL PRETRAINING §2.2 and DENOISING PRETRAINING §2.3, and employed two data augmentation strategies, i.e. BIDIRECTIONAL SELF-TRAINING §2.5 and TAGGED BACK TRANSLATION §2.7. Where the data used for tagged back translation are carefully selected with our proposed multi-feature in-domain selection approach in §2.6. For post finetune/ process, we employed TRANSDUCTIVE FINE-TUNE §2.8 and a simple postprocessing approach §2.10.

This paper is structured as follows: Section 2 describes the major approaches we used. We present the data descriptions in Section 3. The experiments settings and main results are shown in Section 4. Finnaly, we conclude our work in Section 5.

2 Approaches

2.1 Autoregressive Translation

Given a source sentence $\mathbf{x}$, an NMT model generates each target word $\mathbf{y}_t$ conditioned on previously generated ones $\mathbf{y}_{<t}$. Accordingly, the probability of generating $\mathbf{y}$ is computed as:

$$p(\mathbf{y}|\mathbf{x}) = \prod_{t=1}^{T} p(\mathbf{y}_t|\mathbf{x}, \mathbf{y}_{<t}; \theta) \qquad (1)$$

*Work was done when Di Wu was visiting at JD.

Proceedings of the 18th International Conference on Spoken Language Translation, pages 182–191
Bangkok, Thailand (Online), August 5–6, 2021.

where T is the length of the target sequence and the parameters θ are trained to maximize the likelihood of a set of training examples according to $\mathcal{L}(\theta) = \arg\max_\theta \log p(\mathbf{y}|\mathbf{x};\theta)$. Typically, we choose Transformer (Vaswani et al., 2017) as its SOTA performance. The training examples can be formally defined as follows:

$$\overrightarrow{\mathrm{B}} = \{(\mathbf{x}_i, \mathbf{y}_i)\}_{i=1}^{N} \quad (2)$$

where N is the total number of sentence pairs in the training data. Note that in standard MT training, the $\mathbf{x}$ is feed to the encoder and $\mathbf{y}_{<t}$ to the decoder to finish the conditional estimation for $\mathbf{y}_t$, thus the utilization of $\overrightarrow{\mathrm{B}}$ is directional, i.e. $\mathbf{x}_i \rightarrow \mathbf{y}_i$. In the preliminary experiments, we utilized autoregressive translation (AT) model for *translation*, *case correction* and *punctuation generation* tasks as its powerful modelling ability and generation accuracy.

2.2 Bidirectional Pretraining

Motivation The motivation is when human learn foreign languages with translation examples, e.g. $\mathbf{x}_i$ and $\mathbf{y}_i$. Both directions of this example, i.e. $\mathbf{x}_i \rightarrow \mathbf{y}_i$ and $\mathbf{y}_i \rightarrow \mathbf{x}_i$, may help human easily master the bilingual knowledge. Motivated by this, Levinboim et al. (2015); Liang et al. (2007) propose to modelling the invertibility between bilingual languages. Cohn et al. (2016) introduce extra bidirectional prior regularization to achieve symmetric training from the point view of training objective. He et al. (2018); Zheng et al. (2019) enhance the coordination of bidirectional corpus with model level modifications. Different from the above methods, we model both directions of a given training example by a simple data manipulation strategy.

Our Implementation Many studies have shown that pretraining could transfer the knowledge and data distribution, hence improving the generalization (Hendrycks et al., 2019; Mathis et al., 2021). Here we want to transfer the bidirectional knowledge among the corpus. Specifically, we propose to first pretrain MT models on bidirectional corpus, which can be defined as follows:

$$\overleftrightarrow{\mathrm{B}} = \{(\mathbf{x}_i, \mathbf{y}_i) \cup (\mathbf{y}_i, \mathbf{x}_i)\}_{i=1}^{N} \quad (3)$$

such that the θ in Equation 1 can be updated by both directions, then the bidirectional pretraining (BiPT) objective can be formulated as:

$$\mathcal{L}_{\mathrm{BiPT}}(\theta) = \overbrace{\arg\max_\theta \log p(\mathbf{y}|\mathbf{x};\theta)}^{\text{Forward:}\overrightarrow{\mathcal{L}_\theta}} \quad (4)$$

$$\underbrace{+ \arg\max_\theta \log p(\mathbf{x}|\mathbf{y};\theta)}_{\text{Backward:}\overleftarrow{\mathcal{L}_\theta}} \quad (5)$$

where the forward $\overrightarrow{\mathcal{L}_\theta}$ and backward $\overleftarrow{\mathcal{L}_\theta}$ are optimized iteratively. From data perspective, we achieve the bidirectional updating as follows: 1) swapping the source and target sentences of a parallel corpus, and 2) appending the swapped version to the original. Then the training data was doubled to make better and full use of the costly bilingual corpus. The pretraining can acquire general knowledge from bidirectional data, which may help *better* and *faster* learning further tasks. Thus, we early stop bidirectional training at 1/3 of the total steps. To ensure the proper training direction, we further train the pretrained model on required direction $\overrightarrow{\mathrm{B}}$ with the rest of 2/3 training steps. Considering the effectiveness of pretraining (Mathis et al., 2021) and clean finetuning (Wu et al., 2019), we introduce a combined pipeline: $\overleftrightarrow{\mathrm{B}} \rightarrow \overrightarrow{\mathrm{B}}$ as out best training strategy.

2.3 Denoising Pretraining

Motivation The motivation is when human learn one language, one of the best practices for language acquisition is to correct the sentence errors, e.g. $noised(\mathbf{x}_i) \rightarrow \mathbf{x}_i$ and $noised(\mathbf{y}_i) \rightarrow \mathbf{y}_i$. Motivated by this, Lewis et al. (2020) propose several noise adding approaches and denoise them with end-to-end pretraining. Liu et al. (2020b) introduce this idea to the multilingual scenarios. Different from above monolinugal denoising pretraining approaches, we proposed a simpler noise function and apply them to each side of the parallel data.

Our Implementation Here we want the model to understand the source- and target-side languages well. For noise function $noised(\cdot)$, we apply the common noise-injection practice, i.e. removing, replacing, or nearby swapping one time for a random word with a uniform distribution in a sentence (Edunov et al., 2018; Ding et al., 2020a). Then the size of the original parallel data doubled as follows:

$$\mathrm{S}_{\mathrm{src}} = \{noised(\mathbf{x}_i), \mathbf{x}_i\}_{i=1}^{N} \quad (6)$$

$$\mathrm{S}_{\mathrm{tgt}} = \{noised(\mathbf{y}_i), \mathbf{y}_i\}_{i=1}^{N} \quad (7)$$

where S_{src} and S_{tgt} can be combined to update the end-to-end model to achieve denoising pretraining. such that the θ in Equation 1 can be updated by denoising both the source and target data, then the denoisig pretraining (DPT) objective can be formulated as:

$$\mathcal{L}_{\text{DPT}}(\theta) = \overbrace{\arg\max_{\theta} \log p(\mathbf{x}|noised(\mathbf{x});\theta)}^{\text{Source Denoising:}\mathcal{L}_\theta^S} \quad (8)$$

$$+ \underbrace{\arg\max_{\theta} \log p(\mathbf{y}|noised(\mathbf{y});\theta)}_{\text{Target Denoising:}\mathcal{L}_\theta^T} \quad (9)$$

where the Source Denoising : $\mathcal{L}_\theta^S$ and Target Denoising : $\mathcal{L}_\theta^T$ are optimized iteratively. The pretraining can store knowledge of the source and target languages into the shared model parameters, which may help *better* and *faster* learning further tasks. Similar to bidirectional pretraining in §2.2, we early stop denoising training at 1/3 of the total steps, and tune the model normally with the rest of 2/3 training steps. This process can be formally denoted as such pipeline: $S_{src} + S_{tgt} \rightarrow \overrightarrow{B}$.

Note that Bidirectional Pretraining (BiPT) and Denoising Pretraining (DPT) can be combined and further enhance the model performance (The effect of their complementary can be found in Table 7). In particular, the combination order of BiPT and DPT are empirically inspired by human learning behavior, where a good interpreter will first master at least one language (usually the mother tongue), and then learn other languages and achieve bilingual translation. Thus, the combined pretraining process follows DPT $\rightarrow$ BiPT. In combined pretraining setting, we will train longer until the model converges completely.

2.4 Nonautoregressive Translation

Different from autoregressive translation (Bahdanau et al., 2015; Vaswani et al., 2017, AT) models that generate each target word conditioned on previously generated ones, non-autoregressive translation (Gu et al., 2018, NAT) models break the autoregressive factorization and produce the target words in parallel. Given a source sentence $\mathbf{x}$, the probability of generating its target sentence $\mathbf{y}$ with length T is defined by NAT as:

$$p(\mathbf{y}|\mathbf{x}) = p_L(T|\mathbf{x};\theta) \prod_{t=1}^{T} p(\mathbf{y}_t|\mathbf{x};\theta) \quad (10)$$

where $p_L(\cdot)$ is a separate conditional distribution to predict the length of target sequence. Typicallly, most NAT models are implemented upon the framewok of Transformer (Vaswani et al., 2017). In the preliminary experiments, we utilized NAT for *translation, case correction* and *punctuation generation* tasks as NAT can well avoid the error accumulation and exposure bias problems during generation. Also, we employ several advanced structure (Gu et al., 2019; Ding et al., 2020b) (*Levenshtein* with source local context modelling) and our proposed training strategies (Ding et al., 2021a,b,c) as default settings.

2.5 Bidirectional Self-Training

Besides improving NMT at model level, many researchers turn to data perspective, including exploiting the parallel and monolingual data. The most representative approaches include: a) Back Translation (**BT**, Sennrich et al. 2016) combines the synthetic data generated with target-side monolingual data and parallel data; b) Knowledge Distillation (**KD**, Kim and Rush 2016) trains the model with sequence-level distilled parallel data; c) data diversification (**DD**, Nguyen et al. 2020) diversifies the data by applying KD and BT on parallel data. Clearly, self-training is at the core of above approaches, that is, they generate the synthetic data either from source to target or reversely, with either monolingual or bilingual data.

To this end, we propose a bidirectional self-training approach for both parallel and monolingual data (including source and target, respectively). Specifically, the base teacher models are trained with original parallel data in the first iteration (Round 1 in Table 6), and based on these forward- and backward-teachers, all available Swahili & English sentences can be used to generate the corresponding synthetic English & Swahili sentences. After balanced-sampling between synthetic and authentic data, the concatenated data can be used to train the second iteration teachers (Round 2 in Table 6).

To reveal why our approach works, we show the results in Table 8 from the point view of data complexity (Zhou et al., 2020). Self-training reduces the data complexity, thus increasing the model deterministic and in turn enhancing the model performance.

	Features
LM Features	BERT LM (Devlin et al., 2019)
	Transformer LM (Bei et al.)
	N-gram LM (Stolcke, 2002)
In-domain features	Moore-Lewis (Moore and Lewis, 2010)
Rule-based features	Illegal characters (Bei et al.)
Count Features	Word count

Table 1: Features for back translation data selection.

2.6 Data Selection Features for Back Translation

Inspired by Ding and Tao (2019), where their cycle-translation strategy (generating high quality in-domain data) for back translation obtain substantial gains, we carefully design criteria for choosing monolingual in-domain corpus. First, we employ rule-based features, language model features. The feature types are described in Table 1. Our BERT language model used here is trained from scratch by the open-source tool[1] with target side data. The Moore-Lewis in-domain scoring strategy (Moore and Lewis, 2010) is used where the language model scores are trained with Transformer (Vaswani et al., 2017). We score all sentences in non-autoregressive fashion[2] to utilize contextualized information.

According to our observations, by using above multiple data selection filters, issues like illegal characters, unfluent and domain unmatched sentences could be significantly reduced. The data statistics for back translation monolingual data can be found in Table 5.

2.7 Tagged Back Translation

Back-translation (Sennrich et al., 2016; Bojar et al., 2018), translating the large scale monolingual corpus to generate synthetic parallel data by Target-to-Source pretrained model, has been widely utilized to improve the translation quality. However, recent studies find that back translation increase the target-original test set performance rather than source-original ones from the perspective of translationese[3] (Zhang and Toral, 2019; Graham et al., 2020). To eliminate such concerns, we leverage tagged back translation (Caswell et al., 2019) to improve the source-original testing performance. The implementation is straightforward, that is, adding a simple tag on the beginning of each source-side synthetic sentence. The detailed reason why this trick works can be found in Marie et al., 2020.

To ensure tagged back translation works well for our task, we carefully selected the target side in-domain monolingual data (§2.6). Final results in Table 7 show the effectiveness of tagged back translation #9 against competitive model #8 (+1.9 BLEU scores).

[1]https://github.com/huggingface/pytorch-pretrained-BERT

[2]https://github.com/alphadl/EasyScore

[3]Source-Original denotes the testing data originating in the source language, while target-original denotes the data translating from the target language.

src	*Msimu uliopita wa Siltala kwenye ligi ilikuwa* **2006-07**
pred	*Siltala's previous season in the league was* **2006 at 07**
+post	*Siltala's previous season in the league was* **2006-07**

Table 2: Example of the effectiveness of post-processing in handling inconsistent number translation.

2.8 Transductive Fine-Tuning

The key idea of transductive finetune is that source input sentences from the validation and test sets are firstly translated to the target language space with the best well-performed NMT model, which results in a pretranslated synthetic dataset. Then models are finetuned on the generated synthetic dataset. We borrow this concept from previous systems (Wu et al., 2020b; Wang et al.). We empirically show that transductive finetune (#10 – 11 in Table 7) indeed improves the official validation performance but harms the performance of our sampled valid& test set that co-distributed with the training set. Note that we randomly sampled 5K/ 5K sentences from the training set as valid and test sets, respectively, to avoid the sub-optimal problem caused by the distribution gap. Experimental details can be found in §3 and 4.

2.9 Reranking N-best Hypotheses

As the NMT decoding being generally from left to right, this leads to label bias problem (Lafferty et al., 2001). To alleviate this problem, besides using NAT (§2.4), we rerank the n-best hypotheses through training a k-best batch MIRA ranker (Cherry and Foster, 2012) with multiple features on validation set. The feature pool we integrated include R2L (right-to-left) translation model, T2S (target-to-source) translation model, language model and IBM model 2 alignment score. After multi-feature reranking, the best hypothesis was retained.

Right-to-Left NMT Model The R2L NMT model using the same training data but with inverted target sentences (*i.e.*, reverse target side characters "a b c d"→"d c b a"). Then, inverting the hypothesis in the n-best list can obtain perplexity score by R2L model.

Target-to-Source NMT Model The T2S model was initially trained for back-translation, we can employ this model to assess the translation adequacy as well by adding the T2S feature to reranking feature pool.

Language Model Besides above features, we employ language models as an auxiliary feature to give the fluent sentences better scores such that the results are easier to understand by human.

2.10 Post Processing

Besides general post-processing (*i.e.*, de-BPE, detokenization and de-truecase [4]), we also used a post-processing algorithm (Wang et al., 2018) for inconsistent number, date translation, for example, "*2006-07*" might be segmented as "*2006 -@@ 07*" by BPE, resulting in the wrong translation "*2006 at 07*". Our post-processing algorithm will search for the best matching number string from the source sentence to replace these types of errors, see Table 2.

3 Data Preparation

For ASR task, we downloaded all available Swahili speech-to-text data[5], such as openslr[6] and IARPA Babel[7] etc., as training corpus and employ all default settings in Kaldi[8] to preprocess and train them. To simplify the ASR task, we lowercased all Swahili sentences and removed punctuation. To rejuvenate these case and punctuation information, we design two pipeline tasks after ASR: *case correction* task and *punctuation generation*. Also, it is worth noting that we design some rules to perform the "voice activity detection" process for the official speech testset. Take a piece of speech in Figure 1 for example, partial of speech in the red box will be keep as the valid input.

Available Parallel Corpus	#Sent.
CCAligned	2,044,993
Tanzil	138,253
ParaCrawl	132,517
WikiMatrix	51,387
GlobalVoices	32,307
TED2020	9,754
Gamayun	5,000
WikiMedia	771
Total	2,414,982

Table 3: Statistics of parallel data.

Sampled Mono. Corpus	#Sent.
commoncrawl English	4,366,344
commoncrawl Swahili	38,928
+ upsampling (14×)	544,992

Table 4: Statistics of monolingual data.

For NMT task, the parallel datasets we utilized are described at Table 3, including CCAligned (El-Kishky et al., 2020), Tanzil (Tiedemann, 2012), ParaCrawl [9], WikiMatrix (Schwenk et al., 2019), GlobalVoices (Tiedemann, 2012), TED2020 (Reimers and Gurevych, 2020), WikiMedia (Tiedemann, 2012) and Gamayun [10]. The monolingual data we utilized are described in Table 4 and Table 5, where the monolingual data in Table 4 are used to train the system $\#1-8$ in Table 7, and data in Table 5 are used to train the system $\#9-11$ in Table 7, respectively. Table 6 denotes how the data used and generated by iterative bidirectional self-training (§2.5). The total data size after two round of bidirectional self-training is 50.4M, and after tagged back translation, the final data volume is 60.4M.

To avoid the sub-optimal problem caused by the distribution gap between official validation and training data, we randomly sampled 5K/ 5K sentences from the training set as valid and test sets, respectively. The randomly sampled valid sentences are used to optimize the hype-parameters.

[4]https://github.com/moses-smt/mosesdecoder/tree/master/scripts

[5]https://iwslt.org/2021/low-resource

[6]https://www.openslr.org/25/

[7]https://catalog.ldc.upenn.edu/LDC2017S05

[8]https://github.com/kaldi-asr/kaldi

[9]https://www.paracrawl.eu/index.php

[10]https://gamayun.translatorswb.org/data/

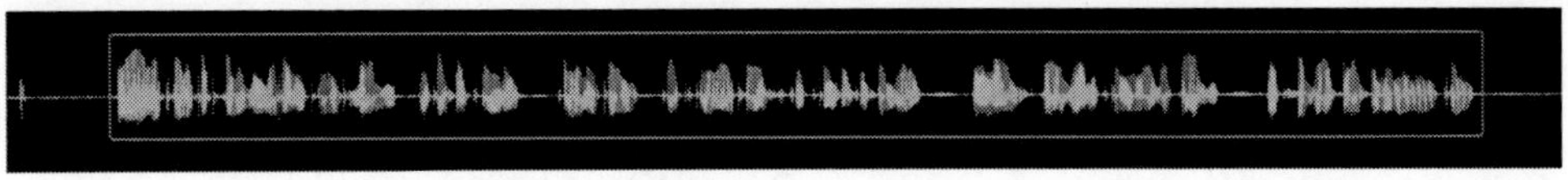

Figure 1: An example of how our rule-based voice activity detection model works on the waveform. Note that only the part in the red box will be retained as a valid fragment.

Mono. Corpus for Tagged BT	#Sent.
Totally collected corpus	
commoncrawl English	30,513,498
Cleaned corpus with criteria in §2.6	
in domain English	10,000,000

Table 5: Statistics of monolingual data for Tagged Back-Translation.

#	Data Statistics	#Sent.
	Preparing for Self-Training	
1	parallel English	2.4M
2	parallel Swahili	2.4M
3	monolingual English	4.4M
4	monolingual Swahili	0.4M
	Self-Training Round 1	
5	synthetic parallel	9.6M
6	authentic parallel	2.4M
7	+ upsampling (4×)	9.6M
8	concat #5 and #7	19.2M
	Self-Training Round 2	
9	refined parallel #8	19.2M
10	concat #8 and #9	38.4M
11	upsampled authentic parallel #6 (5×)	12.0M
12	concat #10 and #11	50.4M

Table 6: Data statistics for bidirectional self-training. Note that #5 "synthetic parall" comes from monolingual English (#3), monolingual Swahili (#4), parallel English (#1), and parallel Swahili (#2). In our preliminary experiments, 4× (#7) and 5× (#11) upsampling strategies perform best in their corresponding settings, thus leaving as the default settings.

4 Experiments

Settings For *case correction* and *punctuation generation* tasks mentioned in §3, we tried Autoregressive Transformer-BASE (AT, §2.1), Non-Autoregressive model (NAT, §2.4) and our previously designed SLOTREFINE (Wu et al., 2020a). In our preliminary experiments, NAT and SlotRefine work better on *case correction* and *punctuation generation* tasks, respectively, thus leaving as the default components in our final speech translation pipeline.

For NMT task, we tried Autoregressive Transformer-BIG (AT, §2.1) and Non-Autoregressive model (NAT, §2.4) in preliminary experiments, and found that AT performs robust on all settings. Thus we employ Transformer-BIG for all MT systems. Inspired by He et al. (2019), we empirically adopt large batch strategy (Edunov et al., 2018) (i.e. 458K tokens/batch) to optimize the performance. The learning rate warms up to 1×10^{-7} for 10K steps, and then decays for 30K (data volumes range from 2M to 10M) / 50K (data volumes large than 10M) steps with the cosine schedule. For regularization, we tune the dropout rate from [0.1, 0.2, 0.3] based on validation performance, and apply weight decay with 0.01 and label smoothing with $\epsilon = 0.1$. We use Adam optimizer (Kingma and Ba, 2015) to train models. We evaluate the performance on an ensemble of last 10 checkpoints to avoid stochasticity.

For fair comparison, the metric we employed is sacreBLEU (Post, 2018). Training set, validation set and test set are processed consistently. Both Swahili and English sentences are performed tokenization and truecasing with Moses scripts (Koehn et al., 2007). In order to limit the size of vocabulary of NMT models, we adopted byte pair encoding (BPE) (Sennrich et al., 2016) with 32k operations. Larger beam size may worsen translation quality (Koehn and Knowles, 2017), thus we set beam_size=10 when performing n-best reranking (§2.9). All models were trained on 4 16GB `NVIDIA V100` GPUs.

Main results Our main experiment is shown in Table 7, our baseline system is developed with the original parallel corpus and last-10 ensemble strategy. Unsurprisingly, the baseline system relatively performs the worst.

The proposed *Bidirectional Pretrain* in §2.2 and *Denoising Pretrain* in §2.3 could consistently and significanly improve the model performance, showing their effectiveness in low resource scenarios (Zhang and Tao, 2020). Clearly, combining *Bidirectional Pretrain* and *Denoising Pretrain*

#	Models	Valid	Test	Δ_{ave}	Off. Valid	Δ
1	**Baseline** (w/ Para. Data)	47.1	48.5	–	31.8	–
2	`+Bidrectional Pretrain`	48.5	49.9			
3	`+Denoising Pretrain`	48.6	49.6			
4	`+Combination of #2 and #3`	48.9	50.1	+1.7		
5	**Bi. Self-Training** (w/ Mono. & Para. Data)	49.4	50.8	+2.3		
6	`+Combination of #2 and #3`	50.1	51.6	+3.1		
7	**Iterative Bi. Self-Training**	49.7	50.9	+2.5		
8	`+Combination of #2 and #3`	50.5	51.8	+3.4	38.2	+6.4
9	**#8 + Tagged Back Translation**	52.4	53.1	+5.0	40.1	+8.3
10	**#9 + Transductive Finetune**	51.8	53.0	+4.6	41.5	+9.7
11	+Iterative `+#10`	51.6	52.8	+4.4	41.9	+10.1
12	**#11 + Reranking**	52.1	53.5	+5.0	42.3	+10.5
13	**#12 + Post Processing**	52.5	54.0	+5.5	42.6	+10.8
	SacreBLEU of Final Submission (#13) on official test set **25.3**					

Table 7: Sacrebleu of Sw→En on our randomly sampled "Valid/ Test" sets and official validation set "Off. Valid", where "Δ" represents the performance gains compared with baseline #1. The submitted system is #13.

Data	Compl.	BLEU
Baseline	7.87	47.1
Bi. Self-Training	5.34	49.4
Iterative Bi. Self-Training	**4.89**	**49.7**

Table 8: Explanation of why Bidirectional Self-Training works. The data complexity "Compl." is measured on their corresponding training sets and alignment information is trained with *fast-align* (Dyer et al., 2013). The BLEU scores are reported on our sampled validation set.

could achieve better results (averaged +1.7 BLEU scores), indicating their complementary.

As shown in #5 and #7, the proposed *Bidirectional Self-Training* and its refined iterative version, could consistently enhance the model. To explore why self-training improves model performance, we discuss it from the point view of data complexity. As shown in Table 8, with the *Bidirectional Self-Training* iteratively progresses, the data complexity becomes lower, leading to the better BLEU scores. Notably, the combination of our proposed two pretraining approaches push the SOTA performance up to higher points. We believe that the effect of our proposed two pretrain strategies are still under-investigated, which will leave as future works. Overall, with strategies #2 – 8, the model performance in terms of official validation test achieves surprisingly **+6.4** BLEU scores.

The *Tagged Back Translation* (§2.7) with in-domain monolingual data significantly improves the performance of both our sampled test set and official valid set by +5.0 and +8.3 against baseline, respectively.

We empirically show that *Transductive FineTune* (§2.8) indeed improves the official validation performance but harms the performance of our sampled valid& test set that co-distributed with the training set. This indicates that tranductive learning is a effective practice to transfer a well-trained model across domains.

And the last two strategies *Reranking* (§2.9) and *Post Processing* (§2.10) could further improve the official validataion BLEU score from 41.9 to 42.6, which substantially outperforms the baseline by +10.8 BLEU score.

5 Conclusion and Future Work

This paper presents the University of Sydney & JD's speech machine translation system for IWSLT2021 Swahili→English task. The whole system is pipelined, containing ASR, case correction, punctuation generation and NMT tasks, and we main focused on NMT task.

We leveraged multi-dimensional strategies and frameworks to improve the translation qualities, which achieves surprisingly **+10.8 BLEU** scores improvement against baseline and ranks the **1st** among all the participants. We find that our proposed BIDIRECTIONAL PRETRAINING (§2.2) and DENOISING PRETRAINING (§2.3) can consistently improves the competitive baselines. Also, we employ BIDIRECTIONAL SELF-TRAINING in §2.5 and TAGGED BT in §2.7 make the most of the existing parallel and monolingual data.

In the future, we would like to polish other components in the pipeline to achieve better performance. Also, it is worthy to try an end-to-end approach with cross-modal structures to incorporate audio and vision knowledge (Xu et al., 2021). For robust model training and data utilization, we would explore better strategies, e.g. adversarial training (Wu et al., 2021) and curriculum learning (Liu et al., 2020a; Zhou et al., 2021).

Acknowledgments

We would thank anonymous reviewers for their considerate proofreading and valuable comments.

References

Dzmitry Bahdanau, KyungHyun Cho, and Yoshua Bengio. 2015. Neural machine translation by jointly learning to align and translate. In *Proceedings of ICLR 2015*.

Chao Bei, Hao Zong, Yiming Wang, Baoyong Fan, Shiqi Li, and Conghu Yuan. An empirical study of machine translation for the shared task of WMT18. In *WMT*.

Ondřej Bojar, Christian Federmann, Mark Fishel, Yvette Graham, Barry Haddow, Philipp Koehn, and Christof Monz. 2018. Findings of the 2018 conference on machine translation (WMT18). In *WMT*.

Isaac Caswell, Ciprian Chelba, and David Grangier. 2019. Tagged back-translation. In *WMT*, Florence, Italy.

Colin Cherry and George Foster. 2012. Batch tuning strategies for statistical machine translation. In *NAACL*.

Trevor Cohn, Cong Duy Vu Hoang, Ekaterina Vymolova, Kaisheng Yao, Chris Dyer, and Gholamreza Haffari. 2016. Incorporating structural alignment biases into an attentional neural translation model. In *NAACL*.

Jacob Devlin, Ming-Wei Chang, Kenton Lee, and Kristina Toutanova. 2019. Bert: Pre-training of deep bidirectional transformers for language understanding. In *NAACL*.

Liang Ding and Dacheng Tao. 2019. The University of Sydney's machine translation system for WMT19. In *WMT*.

Liang Ding, Longyue Wang, Xuebo Liu, Derek F. Wong, Dacheng Tao, and Zhaopeng Tu. 2021a. Progressive multi-granularity training for non-autoregressive translation. In *findings of ACL*.

Liang Ding, Longyue Wang, Xuebo Liu, Derek F. Wong, Dacheng Tao, and Zhaopeng Tu. 2021b. Rejuvenating low-frequency words: Making the most of parallel data in non-autoregressive translation. In *ACL*.

Liang Ding, Longyue Wang, Xuebo Liu, Derek F. Wong, Dacheng Tao, and Zhaopeng Tu. 2021c. Understanding and improving lexical choice in non-autoregressive translation. In *ICLR*.

Liang Ding, Longyue Wang, and Dacheng Tao. 2020a. Self-attention with cross-lingual position representation. In *ACL*.

Liang Ding, Longyue Wang, Di Wu, Dacheng Tao, and Zhaopeng Tu. 2020b. Context-aware cross-attention for non-autoregressive translation. In *COLING*.

Chris Dyer, Victor Chahuneau, and Noah A. Smith. 2013. A simple, fast, and effective reparameterization of IBM model 2. In *NAACL*.

Sergey Edunov, Myle Ott, Michael Auli, and David Grangier. 2018. Understanding back-translation at scale. In *Proceedings of EMNLP 2019*.

Ahmed El-Kishky, Vishrav Chaudhary, Francisco Guzmán, and Philipp Koehn. 2020. CCAligned: A massive collection of cross-lingual web-document pairs. In *EMNLP 2020*.

Yvette Graham, Barry Haddow, and Philipp Koehn. 2020. Statistical power and translationese in machine translation evaluation. In *EMNLP*.

Jiatao Gu, James Bradbury, Caiming Xiong, Victor OK Li, and Richard Socher. 2018. Non-autoregressive neural machine translation. In *ICLR*.

Jiatao Gu, Changhan Wang, and Junbo Zhao. 2019. Levenshtein transformer. In *NeurIPS*.

Fengxiang He, Tongliang Liu, and Dacheng Tao. 2019. Control batch size and learning rate to generalize well: Theoretical and empirical evidence. In *NeurIPS*.

Tianyu He, Xu Tan, Yingce Xia, Di He, Tao Qin, Zhibo Chen, and Tie-Yan Liu. 2018. Layer-wise coordination between encoder and decoder for neural machine translation. In *NeurIPS*.

Dan Hendrycks, Kimin Lee, and Mantas Mazeika. 2019. Using pre-training can improve model robustness and uncertainty. In *ICML*.

Frederick Jelinek. 1997. *Statistical methods for speech recognition*. MIT press.

Yoon Kim and Alexander M. Rush. 2016. Sequence-level knowledge distillation. In *EMNLP*.

Diederik P. Kingma and Jimmy Ba. 2015. Adam: A method for stochastic optimization. In *ICLR*.

Philipp Koehn. 2009. *Statistical machine translation*. Cambridge University Press.

Philipp Koehn, Hieu Hoang, Alexandra Birch, Chris Callison-Burch, Marcello Federico, Nicola Bertoldi, Brooke Cowan, Wade Shen, Christine Moran, Richard Zens, Chris Dyer, Ondrej Bojar, Alexandra Constantin, and Evan Herbst. 2007. Moses: Open source toolkit for statistical machine translation. In *ACL*.

Philipp Koehn and Rebecca Knowles. 2017. Six challenges for neural machine translation. In *WNMT*.

John D. Lafferty, Andrew McCallum, and Fernando C. N. Pereira. 2001. Conditional random fields: Probabilistic models for segmenting and labeling sequence data. In *ICML*.

Tomer Levinboim, Ashish Vaswani, and David Chiang. 2015. Model invertibility regularization: Sequence alignment with or without parallel data. In *NAACL*.

Mike Lewis, Yinhan Liu, Naman Goyal, Marjan Ghazvininejad, Abdelrahman Mohamed, Omer Levy, Veselin Stoyanov, and Luke Zettlemoyer. 2020. Bart: Denoising sequence-to-sequence pretraining for natural language generation, translation, and comprehension. In *ACL*.

P. Liang, D. Klein, and Michael I. Jordan. 2007. Agreement-based learning. In *NeurIPS*.

Xuebo Liu, Houtim Lai, Derek F Wong, and Lidia S Chao. 2020a. Norm-based curriculum learning for neural machine translation. In *ACL*.

Yinhan Liu, Jiatao Gu, Naman Goyal, Xian Li, Sergey Edunov, Marjan Ghazvininejad, Mike Lewis, and Luke Zettlemoyer. 2020b. Multilingual denoising pre-training for neural machine translation. *TACL*.

Benjamin Marie, Raphael Rubino, and Atsushi Fujita. 2020. Tagged back-translation revisited: Why does it really work? In *ACL*.

Alexander Mathis, Thomas Biasi, Steffen Schneider, Mert Yuksekgonul, Byron Rogers, Matthias Bethge, and Mackenzie W Mathis. 2021. Pretraining boosts out-of-domain robustness for pose estimation. In *WACV*.

Robert C. Moore and William Lewis. 2010. Intelligent selection of language model training data. In *ACL*.

Hermann Ney. 1999. Speech translation: Coupling of recognition and translation. In *ICASSP*.

Xuan-Phi Nguyen, Shafiq Joty, Wu Kui, and Ai Ti Aw. 2020. Data diversification: A simple strategy for neural machine translation. In *NeurIPS*.

Matt Post. 2018. A call for clarity in reporting BLEU scores. In *WMT*.

Nils Reimers and Iryna Gurevych. 2020. Making monolingual sentence embeddings multilingual using knowledge distillation. In *EMNLP*.

Holger Schwenk, Vishrav Chaudhary, Shuo Sun, Hongyu Gong, and Francisco Guzmán. 2019. Wikimatrix: Mining 135m parallel sentences in 1620 language pairs from wikipedia. *arXiv*.

Rico Sennrich, Barry Haddow, and Alexandra Birch. 2016. Improving neural machine translation models with monolingual data. In *ACL*, Berlin, Germany.

Andreas Stolcke. 2002. Srilm-an extensible language modeling toolkit. In *IWSLT*.

Jörg Tiedemann. 2012. Parallel data, tools and interfaces in opus. In *LREC*.

Ashish Vaswani, Noam Shazeer, Niki Parmar, Jakob Uszkoreit, Llion Jones, Aidan N Gomez, Lukasz Kaiser, and Illia Polosukhin. 2017. Attention is all you need. In *Proceedings of NIPS 2017*.

Longyue Wang, Zhaopeng Tu, Xing Wang, Li Ding, Liang Ding, and Shuming Shi. Tencent AI lab machine translation systems for WMT20 chat translation task. In *WMT*.

Qiang Wang, Bei Li, Jiqiang Liu, Bojian Jiang, Zheyang Zhang, Yinqiao Li, Ye Lin, Tong Xiao, and Jingbo Zhu. 2018. The NiuTrans machine translation system for WMT18. In *WMT*.

Di Wu, Yiren Chen, Liang Ding, and Dacheng Tao. 2021. Bridging the gap between clean data training and real-world inference for spoken language understanding. *arXiv*.

Di Wu, Liang Ding, Fan Lu, and Jian Xie. 2020a. Slotrefine: A fast non-autoregressive model for joint intent detection and slot filling. In *EMNLP*.

Lijun Wu, Yiren Wang, Yingce Xia, QIN Tao, Jianhuang Lai, and Tie-Yan Liu. 2019. Exploiting monolingual data at scale for neural machine translation. In *EMNLP*.

Shuangzhi Wu, Xing Wang, Longyue Wang, Fangxu Liu, Jun Xie, Zhaopeng Tu, Shuming Shi, and Mu Li. 2020b. Tencent neural machine translation systems for the wmt20 news translation task. In *WMT*.

Yufei Xu, Qiming Zhang, Jing Zhang, and Dacheng Tao. 2021. Vitae: Vision transformer advanced by exploring intrinsic inductive bias. *arXiv*.

Jing Zhang and Dacheng Tao. 2020. Empowering things with intelligence: a survey of the progress, challenges, and opportunities in artificial intelligence of things. *IEEE Internet of Things Journal*.

Mike Zhang and Antonio Toral. 2019. The effect of translationese in machine translation test sets. In *WMT*.

Zaixiang Zheng, Hao Zhou, Shujian Huang, Lei Li, Xin-Yu Dai, and Jiajun Chen. 2019. Mirror-generative neural machine translation. In *ICLR*.

Chunting Zhou, Graham Neubig, and Jiatao Gu. 2020. Understanding knowledge distillation in non-autoregressive machine translation. In *ICLR*.

Lei Zhou, Liang Ding, Kevin Duh, Ryohei Sasano, and Koichi Takeda. 2021. Self-guided curriculum learning for neural machine translation. In *IWSLT*.

mixSeq: A Simple Data Augmentation Method for Neural Machine Translation

Xueqing Wu [1], **Yingce Xia** [2], **Jinhua Zhu** [1], **Lijun Wu** [2], **Shufang Xie** [2], **Tao Qin** [2]
[1] University of Science and Technology of China [2]Microsoft Research Asia
jwuwuwu24@gmail.com, teslazhu@mail.ustc.edu.cn
{yingce.xia,lijuwu,shufxi,taoqin}@microsoft.com

Abstract

Data augmentation, which refers to manipulating the inputs (e.g., adding random noise, masking specific parts) to enlarge the dataset, has been widely adopted in machine learning. Most data augmentation techniques operate on a single input, which limits the diversity of the training corpus. In this paper, we propose a simple yet effective data augmentation technique for neural machine translation, *mixSeq*, which operates on multiple inputs and their corresponding targets. Specifically, we randomly select two input sequences, concatenate them together as a longer input as well as their corresponding target sequences as an enlarged target, and train models on the augmented dataset. Experiments on nine machine translation tasks demonstrate that such a simple method boosts the baselines by a non-trivial margin. Our method can be further combined with single-input based data augmentation methods to obtain further improvements.

1 Introduction

Data augmentation, which enlarges the training corpus by manipulating the inputs through given rules, has been widely used in machine learning tasks. For image classification, there are various data augmentation methods, including cropping, flipping, rotating,cut-out (DeVries and Taylor, 2017), etc. For natural language processing (briefly, NLP), similar data augmentation methods also exist, like randomly swapping words (Lample et al., 2018a), dropping words (Iyyer et al., 2015), and masking specific words (Xie et al., 2017). With data augmentation, the main content of the input is not affected but the noise is introduced so as to increase the diversity of the training set. The effectiveness of above data augmentation methods has been verified by their strong performance improvements in both image processing and NLP tasks. For example, with the combination of data augmentation and meta-learning, state-of-the-art result of image classification is achieved (Cubuk et al., 2019).

Most existing data augmentation methods take one sample from the training set as input, which might limit the scope and diversity of the training corpus. Mixup (Zhang et al., 2018) is a recently proposed data augmentation method, where two samples from the training corpus are leveraged to build a synthetic sample. Specifically, let x_1, x_2 denote two images from the training set, and y_1, y_2 denote their corresponding labels. The synthetic data $(\lambda x_1 + (1-\lambda)x_2, \lambda y_1 + (1-\lambda)y_2)$ is introduced to the augmented dataset, where λ is randomly generated. Such a strategy is further enhanced in follow-up works (Zhang et al., 2019; Berthelot et al., 2019). Pair sampling (Inoue, 2018) is another data augmentation method where the synthetic sample is built as $(0.5x_1 + 0.5x_2, y_1)$. In comparison, according to our knowledge, such ideas are not leveraged in NLP tasks (e.g., machine translation). Therefore, in this work, we explore along this direction to see whether augmenting data through mixing multiple sentences is helpful.

In sequence learning tasks, two inputs x_1 and x_2 might contain different numbers of units (e.g., words or subwords). Besides, for sequence generation tasks, their labels y_1 and y_2 are of different lengths. Therefore, it is not practical to sum them up directly. Instead, we choose to concatenate two inputs and the two labels to get the synthetic data. We find that it is important to use a special token to separate the two sentences in a synthetic data. We name our proposed method as *mixSeq*.

mixSeq is a simple yet very efficient and effective data augmentation method. We conduct experiments on 9 machine translation tasks and find that *mixSeq* can boost the baseline by 0.66 BLEU on average. Specifically, on FLORES Sinhala↔English, our method can improve the baseline by 1.03 points. *mixSeq* can be further combined with data augmen-

Proceedings of the 18th International Conference on Spoken Language Translation, pages 192–197
Bangkok, Thailand (Online), August 5–6, 2021.

tation methods working on a single input, e.g., randomly dropping, swapping or masking words, to further improve the performance (see Table 3).

Normally, *mixSeq* randomly samples the two concatenated sequences. However, if the two concatenated sequences are contextually related, we can enhance our *mixSeq* to a context-aware version: *ctxMixSeq*, which will result in better performance (see Table 4).

2 Our Method

Notations: Let $\mathcal{X}$ and $\mathcal{Y}$ denote two language spaces, which are collections of sentences in the corresponding languages. The target of neural machine translation (briefly, NMT) is to learn a mapping from $\mathcal{X}$ to $\mathcal{Y}$. Let $\mathcal{D} = \{(x_i, y_i)\}_{i=1}^N$ denote the bilingual NMT training corpus, where $x_i \in \mathcal{X}, y_i \in \mathcal{Y}$, and N is the number of training samples. Let $\texttt{concat}(\cdots)$ denote the concatenation operation, where the input sequences are merged into a longer one, and each input is segmented by a space.

Training Algorithm: We propose *mixSeq*, a simple yet effective data augmentation method, which generates new samples by operating on two existing samples. The algorithm is shown in Algorithm 1.

Algorithm 1: *mixSeq*

1 *Input*: $\mathcal{D} = \{(x_i, y_i)\}_{i=1}^N$, augmented size $\hat{N}$; sentence border label `<sep>`;
2 Initialize $\hat{\mathcal{D}} = \{\}$;
3 **for** $k \leftarrow 1$ *to* $\hat{N}$ **do**
4   Sample two indices i and j from `SamplingFunc(N)`;
5     $\tilde{x}_k$ = `concat(`x_i`, <sep>, `x_j`)`;
    $\tilde{y}_k$ = `concat(`y_i`, <sep>, `y_j`)`;
6     $\hat{\mathcal{D}} = \hat{\mathcal{D}} \cup \{(\tilde{x}_k, \tilde{y}_k)\}$;
7 **end**
8 Upsample or downsample $\mathcal{D}$ to size $\hat{N}$ and get a new dataset $\tilde{\mathcal{D}}$; train an NMT model on $\tilde{\mathcal{D}} \cup \hat{\mathcal{D}}$, which is of size $2\hat{N}$.

In *mixSeq*, the most important step is to build an augmented dataset $\hat{\mathcal{D}}$. As shown from line 3 to line 7 in Algorithm 1, we first sample two aligned sequence pairs (x_i, y_i) and (x_j, y_j) (the design of sampling rule `SamplingFunc` is left to the next part). Then we concatenate their source sentences and the target sentences respectively with a special label `<sep>` separating two samples, and get two longer sequences, $\tilde{x}_k$ and $\tilde{y}_k$ (line 5 in Algorithm 1). We eventually obtain the augmented dataset $\hat{\mathcal{D}}$ with size $\hat{N}$. After that, we upsample or downsample $\mathcal{D}$ to the same size as $\hat{N}$ and obtain $\tilde{\mathcal{D}}$. Finally, we train our translation models on $\tilde{\mathcal{D}} \cup \hat{\mathcal{D}}$.

Design of `SamplingFunc`: We have two forms of `SamplingFunc`, which corresponds to two variants of our algorithm:
(1) In general cases, `SamplingFunc` randomly samples i and j from $\{1, 2, \cdots, N\}$. For ease of reference, we still use *mixSeq* to denote this variant.
(2) When contextual information is available, i.e., the parallel data is extracted from a pair of aligned document, `SamplingFunc` only samples consecutive sequences in a given document. Assume x_i/y_i represent the i-th sentence in the document, then `SamplingFunc` only samples $(i, i+1)$ index pairs.We use *ctxMixSeq* to denote this variant. *ctxMixSeq* is related to context-aware machine translation (Tiedemann and Scherrer, 2017). The difference is that, during inference, *ctxMixSeq* uses a single sequence as the input, while Tiedemann and Scherrer (2017) uses multiple sequences including the contextual information.

Discussions: *mixSeq* operates on two sequences, while previous data augmentation methods like randomly dropping, swapping or masking words usually operate on a single sequence. These methods can be combined with *mixSeq* to bring further improvements (see Table 3).

3 Experiments

We conduct experiments on the following machine translation tasks to evaluate our method: IWSLT'14 German↔English and Spanish↔English; FLORES English↔Nepali and English↔Sinhala; and WMT'14 English→German. We abbreviate English, German, Spanish, Nepali and Sinhala as En, De, Es, Ne and Si.

3.1 Setup

Datasets: For IWSLT'14 De↔En, following Edunov et al. (2018), we lowercase all words, tokenize them, and apply BPE with $10k$ merge operations (Sennrich et al., 2016) to obtain of the subword representations[1]. The validation set is split from the training set and the test set is the concatenation of *tst2010, tst2011, tst2012, dev2010*

[1] Preprocessing script: `https://github.com/pytorch/fairseq/blob/master/examples/translation/prepare-iwslt14.sh`.

and *dev2012*. For IWSLT'14 Es↔En, the preprocessing is the same as that for De↔En without lowercasing the words. We use *tst2013* and *tst2014* as the validation and test sets respectively. For FLORES En↔Ne and En↔Si datasets, we used the BPE version of dataset provided by Guzmán et al. (2019). For WMT'14 En→De, we concatenate *newstest2012* and *newstest2013* as the validation set and use *newstest2014* as the test set. The statistics of the datasets are shown in Table 1. On all tasks, the vocabulary is shared between the source language and the target language.

Task	Training	Validation	Test
De↔En	$160k$	$7.3k$	$6.8k$
Es↔En	$184k$	$1.2k$	$1.3k$
En↔Ne	$563k$	$2.6k$	$2.8k$
En↔Si	$405k$	$2.9k$	$2.8k$
WMT	4.5M	$3k$	$3k$

Table 1: The number of sentences in the training, validation and test sets of IWSLT De↔En, Es↔En, FLORES En↔Ne, En↔Si, and WMT datasets.

Models and Training Strategy: For *mixSeq*, we set $\hat{N}$ as $5N$; for *ctxMixSeq*, we set $\hat{N}$ as N. We choose Transformer (Vaswani et al., 2017) as our translation model. For IWSLT tasks, the dimensions of the embedding, feed-forward network and number of layers of the Transformer models are 256, 1024 and 6 respectively. The dropout rate is 0.3. The batch size is 6000 tokens, and we train the models for $300k$ steps. For FLORES tasks, we use exact the same architecture and training strategy as those in (Guzmán et al., 2019) for fair comparison. The model is a 5-layer Transformer with embedding dimension and feed-forward network dimension 512 and 2048. The batch size is $16k$. The baseline model is trained for 100 epochs, while *mixSeq* is trained for 10 epochs considering our enlarged dataset is 10 times larger than the original dataset. For WMT task, the dimensions of the embedding, feed-forward network and number of layers of the Transformer models are 1024, 4096 and 6 respectively. The batch size is 4096 tokens per GPU. We train on eight V100 GPUs and accumulate the gradients for 16 times before updating. For all models, we use Adam with learning rate 5×10^{-4} and the `inverse_sqrt` learning rate scheduler to optimize the models. All models are trained until convergence.

Evaluation: We use beam search with beam width of 5 and length penalty of 1.0 to generate sequences. The generation quality is evaluated by BLEU score.

3.2 Results

The results of standard Transformer and *mixSeq* on small-scale datasets are shown in the first section of Table 2. We adopt another baseline, pair sampling (Inoue, 2018) into NMT for comparison, which can produce a synthetic dataset $\tilde{\mathcal{D}}_{ps}$ made up of pairs $(\texttt{concat}(x_1, \texttt{<sep>}, x_2), y_1)$, $(x_1, y_1) \in \mathcal{D}$, $(x_2, y_2) \in \mathcal{D}$. The results of pair sampling (briefly, PS) are in the third column of Table 2. *mixSeq* generally brings good improvements and significantly outperforms the baseline on all tasks except for two (En→De and En→Si). The pair sampling baseline performs poorly on all tasks. This is because pair sampling requires the translation model to translate the first part of the input (i.e., x_1) while ignoring the second part (i.e., x_2), which is against the goal of NMT. It is also worth noting that the time and number of steps required to converge on the augmented dataset and the original dataset are similar.

Task	Transformer	*mixSeq*	PS
En→De	29.18	29.46	29.09
De→En	34.96	35.78‡	35.22
En→Es	39.61	40.30†	38.95
Es→En	40.94	41.39†	40.80
En→Ne	4.28	5.26‡	4.20
Ne→En	7.68	8.38‡	7.51
En→Si	1.21	1.49	0.88
Si→En	6.68	7.71‡	6.02
WMT	29.15	29.61	-

Table 2: BLEU scores of IWSLT De↔En, Es↔En, FLORES En↔Ne, En↔Si, and WMT En→De. ‡ and † indicate that *mixSeq* outperforms Transformer in the significance test with $p < 0.01$ and $p < 0.05$, respectively.

We also evaluate *mixSeq* on a large-scale dataset, WMT'14 En→De, and the results are shown in the second section of Table 2. Due to resource limitation, we do not try pair sampling. Our method improves the BLEU score by 0.46, which shows that *mixSeq* is a generally effective method for NMT.

We further compare and combine our method with data augmentation methods on one sequence, including randomly dropping, masking and swapping words. We conduct experiments on IWSLT'14 De↔En. As shown in Table 3, our method brings further improvement when combined with existing data augmentation method on a single sequence. The baseline is improved by up to 0.82 BLEU.

Method	De→En	En→ De
Transformer	34.96	29.18
mixSeq	35.78	29.46
Drop	35.30	29.03
Drop + *mixSeq*	36.01	29.22
Swap	34.52	28.73
Swap + *mixSeq*	34.73	28.98
Mask	35.78	29.49
Mask + *mixSeq*	36.63	30.00

Table 3: Comparison and combination with data augmentation on single sequences.

To verify the effectiveness of *ctxMixSeq*, we conduct experiments on IWSLT'14 En↔De, where contextual information is available. As discussed in Section 2, Tiedemann and Scherrer (2017) is similar with *ctxMixSeq*, except that it takes two sequences $\texttt{concat}(x_{t-1}, \texttt{<sep>}, x_t)$ as the input during inference. We denote this inference method as *2in* (two inputs). Another baseline proposed in Tiedemann and Scherrer (2017) is that the NMT model is trained on dataset $\mathcal{D} \cup \tilde{\mathcal{D}}_a$, where $\tilde{\mathcal{D}}_a = \{\texttt{concat}(x_{t-1}, \texttt{<sep>}, x_t), y_t\}_{t=2}^{N}$. This can be seen as a context-aware version of pair sampling and we briefly denote it as *ctxPS*. The results are in Table 4. *ctxMixSeq* outperforms all baselines proposed by Tiedemann and Scherrer (2017). Compared to *mixSeq*, *ctxMixSeq* brings consistent improvements, especially when combined with *mixSeq*.

Method	En→De	De→En
mixSeq	29.46	35.78
ctxMixSeq	29.65	35.96
ctxMixSeq + 2in	29.50	35.79
ctxPS	29.26	35.48
ctxPS + 2in	29.29	35.78
ctxMixSeq + mixSeq	29.74	36.09

Table 4: Results of context-aware versions of *mixSeq* on IWSLT'14 En↔De.

With *mixSeq*, we find that the alignment is enhanced. We visualize the source-target attention maps obtained by our method. Given $(x_i, \texttt{<sep>}, x_j)$ and the corresponding translation $(y_i, \texttt{<sep>}, y_j)$, we find that most attention weight of y_i is assigned to x_i, with little assigned to x_j. Similar phenomena is observed for y_j. In this way, the attention mechanism is enhanced, which might explain the performance improvements.

	En→Es	Es→En	En→Ne	Ne→En
mixSeq	40.3	41.4	5.26	8.28
No <sep>	38.9	41.1	4.83	8.10

Table 5: Result of *mixSeq* with/without <sep>.

3.3 Analysis

In this section, we conduct ablation study on the usage of <sep> and the effect of concatenating more than two sequences.

Ablation Study of the Usage of <sep>

To evaluate the effect of <sep> token, we remove the <sep> from sequences as another baseline. We conduct the experiments on IWSLT En↔Es and FLORES En↔Ne datasets, and report the results in Table 5. We find that our method performs poorly without <sep>, sometimes even worse than the Transformer. Our conjecture is that <sep> helps the model learn to align each part of the input to the corresponding part of the output, which can improve the representation learning.

Concatenating More Sequences

We wonder whether the BLEU scores can be further boosted by concatenating more sequences. We move a step forward by randomly concatenating three sequences, and build a synthetic dataset $\hat{\mathcal{D}}_3$ with $\hat{N}_3$ examples. Experiments are conducted on FLORES En↔{Ne, Si} datasets, and results are shown in Table 6. In the third and fourth rows, $\hat{N} = \hat{N}_3 = 5N$. In the last row, we set $\hat{N} = \hat{N}_3 = 2.5N$ to ensure the number of synthetic data remains the same.

Dataset	En→Ne	Ne→En	En→Si	Si→En
$\mathcal{D}$	4.28	7.68	1.21	6.68
$\mathcal{D} \cup \hat{\mathcal{D}}$	5.26	8.38	1.49	**7.71**
$\mathcal{D} \cup \hat{\mathcal{D}}_3$	5.39	**8.88**	2.08	7.50
$\mathcal{D} \cup \hat{\mathcal{D}} \cup \hat{\mathcal{D}}_3$	**5.43**	8.25	**2.21**	7.47

Table 6: Results of concatenating various numbers of sequences.

The results show that, although both $\mathcal{D} \cup \hat{\mathcal{D}}_3$ and $\mathcal{D} \cup \hat{\mathcal{D}} \cup \hat{\mathcal{D}}_3$ settings can bring some improvements, the improvements are not consistent among different datasets. Further work is needed on how to use more samples for data augmentation.

4 Related Work

Most existing data augmentation methods in NMT operate on one single input. Fadaee et al. (2017) replaced common words with rare words under the guidance of language models to improve the translation of rare words. In unsupervised learning, Lample et al. (2018b) proposed to randomly drop, swap, or mask words. Gao et al. (2019) verifies the effectiveness of such methods in supervised NMT. RAML (Norouzi et al., 2016) randomly inserted, deleted or substituted words in the target sequence with probability exponentially decreasing with the edit distance. SwitchOut (Wang et al., 2018) extended RAML by both manipulating on the source side and the target side. Gao et al. (2019) proposed to "softly replace" words by replacing the one-hot representation of words with a distribution on the vocabulary. A concurrent work similar to ours is (Kondo et al., 2021), where `<sep>` is not leveraged. In other fields, data augmentation methods operating on multiple samples have been proposed. Mixup (Zhang et al., 2018) generated a synthetic sample by averaging two inputs and the two labels. It is further applied to semi-supervised learning to enlarge the dataset (Berthelot et al., 2019). Pair sampling (Inoue, 2018) only averaged the two inputs but not the labels.

5 Conclusion and Future Work

In this work, we proposed a simple yet effective data augmentation method for NMT, which randomly concatenates two training samples to enlarge the datasets. Experiments on nine machine translation tasks demonstrate the effectiveness of our method. For future work, there are a few directions to explore. First, we will apply our method to more NLP tasks. Second, we will theoretically analyze when and why it works. Third, we will study and design more effective data augmentation methods.

References

David Berthelot, Nicholas Carlini, Ian Goodfellow, Nicolas Papernot, Avital Oliver, and Colin A Raffel. 2019. Mixmatch: A holistic approach to semi-supervised learning. In *Advances in Neural Information Processing Systems 32*, pages 5049–5059.

Ekin D Cubuk, Barret Zoph, Dandelion Mane, Vijay Vasudevan, and Quoc V Le. 2019. Autoaugment: Learning augmentation strategies from data. In *Proceedings of the IEEE conference on computer vision and pattern recognition*, pages 113–123.

Terrance DeVries and Graham W Taylor. 2017. Improved regularization of convolutional neural networks with cutout. *arXiv preprint arXiv:1708.04552*.

Sergey Edunov, Myle Ott, Michael Auli, David Grangier, and Marc'Aurelio Ranzato. 2018. Classical structured prediction losses for sequence to sequence learning. In *Proceedings of the 2018 Conference of the North American Chapter of the Association for Computational Linguistics: Human Language Technologies, Volume 1 (Long Papers)*, pages 355–364, New Orleans, Louisiana. Association for Computational Linguistics.

Marzieh Fadaee, Arianna Bisazza, and Christof Monz. 2017. Data augmentation for low-resource neural machine translation. *arXiv preprint arXiv:1705.00440*.

Fei Gao, Jinhua Zhu, Lijun Wu, Yingce Xia, Tao Qin, Xueqi Cheng, Wengang Zhou, and Tie-Yan Liu. 2019. Soft contextual data augmentation for neural machine translation. In *Proceedings of the 57th Annual Meeting of the Association for Computational Linguistics*, pages 5539–5544.

Francisco Guzmán, Peng-Jen Chen, Myle Ott, Juan Pino, Guillaume Lample, Philipp Koehn, Vishrav Chaudhary, and Marc'Aurelio Ranzato. 2019. The flores evaluation datasets for low-resource machine translation: Nepali–english and sinhala–english. In *Proceedings of the 2019 Conference on Empirical Methods in Natural Language Processing and the 9th International Joint Conference on Natural Language Processing (EMNLP-IJCNLP)*, pages 6100–6113.

Hiroshi Inoue. 2018. Data augmentation by pairing samples for images classification. *CoRR*, abs/1801.02929.

Mohit Iyyer, Varun Manjunatha, Jordan Boyd-Graber, and Hal Daumé III. 2015. Deep unordered composition rivals syntactic methods for text classification. In *Proceedings of the 53rd Annual Meeting of the Association for Computational Linguistics and the 7th International Joint Conference on Natural Language Processing (Volume 1: Long Papers)*, pages 1681–1691, Beijing, China. Association for Computational Linguistics.

Seiichiro Kondo, Kengo Hotate, Masahiro Kaneko, and Mamoru Komachi. 2021. Sentence concatenation approach to data augmentation for neural machine translation. *arXiv preprint arXiv:2104.08478*.

Guillaume Lample, Alexis Conneau, Ludovic Denoyer, and Marc'Aurelio Ranzato. 2018a. Unsupervised machine translation using monolingual corpora only. *ICLR*.

Guillaume Lample, Myle Ott, Alexis Conneau, Ludovic Denoyer, and Marc'Aurelio Ranzato. 2018b. Phrase-based & neural unsupervised machine translation. *EMNLP*.

Mohammad Norouzi, Samy Bengio, Navdeep Jaitly, Mike Schuster, Yonghui Wu, Dale Schuurmans, et al. 2016. Reward augmented maximum likelihood for neural structured prediction. In *Advances In Neural Information Processing Systems*, pages 1723–1731.

Rico Sennrich, Barry Haddow, and Alexandra Birch. 2016. Neural machine translation of rare words with subword units. In *Proceedings of the 54th Annual Meeting of the Association for Computational Linguistics (Volume 1: Long Papers)*, pages 1715–1725, Berlin, Germany. Association for Computational Linguistics.

Jörg Tiedemann and Yves Scherrer. 2017. Neural machine translation with extended context. In *Proceedings of the Third Workshop on Discourse in Machine Translation*, pages 82–92, Copenhagen, Denmark. Association for Computational Linguistics.

Ashish Vaswani, Noam Shazeer, Niki Parmar, Jakob Uszkoreit, Llion Jones, Aidan N Gomez, Łukasz Kaiser, and Illia Polosukhin. 2017. Attention is all you need. In *Advances in neural information processing systems*, pages 5998–6008.

Xinyi Wang, Hieu Pham, Zihang Dai, and Graham Neubig. 2018. Switchout: an efficient data augmentation algorithm for neural machine translation. *arXiv preprint arXiv:1808.07512*.

Ziang Xie, Sida I Wang, Jiwei Li, Daniel Lévy, Aiming Nie, Dan Jurafsky, and Andrew Y Ng. 2017. Data noising as smoothing in neural network language models. *ICLR*.

Hongyi Zhang, Moustapha Cisse, Yann N Dauphin, and David Lopez-Paz. 2018. mixup: Beyond empirical risk minimization. *ICLR*.

Hongyi Zhang, Yann N Dauphin, and Tengyu Ma. 2019. Fixup initialization: Residual learning without normalization. *ICLR*.

On Knowledge Distillation for Translating Erroneous Speech Transcriptions

Ryo Fukuda[1], **Katsuhito Sudoh**[1,2], **and Satoshi Nakamura**[1,2]
[1]Nara Institute of Science and Technology, Japan
[2]AIP, RIKEN, Japan
{fukuda.ryo.fo3, sudoh, s-nakamura}@is.naist.jp

Abstract

Recent studies argue that knowledge distillation is promising for speech translation (ST) using end-to-end models. In this work, we investigate the effect of knowledge distillation with a cascade ST using automatic speech recognition (ASR) and machine translation (MT) models. We distill knowledge from a teacher model based on human transcripts to a student model based on erroneous transcriptions. Our experimental results demonstrated that knowledge distillation is beneficial for a cascade ST. Further investigation that combined knowledge distillation and fine-tuning revealed that the combination consistently improved two language pairs: English-Italian and Spanish-English.

1 Introduction

Speech translation (ST) converts utterances in a source language into text in another language. Conventional ST systems called *cascade* or *pipeline* ST consist of two components: automatic speech recognition (ASR) and machine translation (MT). In the cascade ST, the error propagation from ASR to MT seriously degrades the ST performance. On the other hand, a new ST system called *end-to-end* or *direct* ST uses a single model to directly translate the source language speech into target language text (Bérard et al., 2016). Such an end-to-end approach is a new paradigm in ST and is attracting much research attention. However, a naive end-to-end ST without additional training, such as ASR tasks, remains inferior to a cascade ST (Liu et al., 2018; Salesky and Black, 2020). Additionally, it requires parallel data of the source language speech and the target language text, which cannot be obtained easily in practice.

Recent ST studies have incorporated the techniques of cascade ST to end-to-end STs. Multi-task training with an ASR subtask has been used successfully in end-to-end ST (Weiss et al., 2017; Anastasopoulos and Chiang, 2018; Sperber et al., 2019). Initializing an end-to-end ST with a pre-trained ASR or MT has also become a common approach (Bérard et al., 2018; Bansal et al., 2019; Inaguma et al., 2020; Wang et al., 2020; Bahar et al., 2021).

In this work, we focus on the cascade approach due to its performance advantage against end-to-end STs. Another reason is that cascade ST models can be incorporated into end-to-end STs, as shown in previous studies.

During the training of an MT model for a cascade ST, we can use clean human transcripts for the source language speech as input. However, since the MT in a cascade ST always receives ASR output during inferences, ASR errors should be propagated to the MT model to cause translation errors. What if we use erroneous speech transcriptions by ASR for training? That approach means the MT model is trained to translate *erroneous* transcriptions into *correct* text, which would not generally be appropriate. One possible solution is to use both types of input (clean and erroneous transcriptions) for training, not just one. The question is how to use them. What is the proper training strategy for cascade STs? This is what we want to learn.

In this work, we address such problems by applying knowledge distillation to cascade STs. We distill the knowledge of a teacher model based on clean transcriptions to a student model based on erroneous transcriptions. We also investigate the joint use of knowledge distillation and fine-tuning. Experimental results revealed that the knowledge distillation improved the robustness against ASR errors and that the knowledge distillation after the fine-tuning provided more significant improvement.

Proceedings of the 18th International Conference on Spoken Language Translation, pages 198–205
Bangkok, Thailand (Online), August 5–6, 2021. ©2021 Association for Computational Linguistics

2 Related work

Some ST studies have tackled the problem of ASR error propagation. N-best hypotheses (Zhang et al., 2004; Quan et al., 2005), confusion networks (Bertoldi and Federico, 2005; Bertoldi et al., 2007), and lattices (Matusov and Ney, 2010; Sperber et al., 2017a) were used to include ASR ambiguity in the ST process.

Osamura et al. (2018) used the weighted sum of embedding vectors for ASR word hypotheses based on their posterior probabilities. Sperber et al. (2017b) and Xue et al. (2020) showed that translation accuracy against erroneous speech transcriptions can be improved by introducing pseudo ASR errors in the training data of MT.

Knowledge distillation (KD) (Buciluǎ et al., 2006; Hinton et al., 2015) is a method of transferring knowledge from a teacher to a student model. Typically, the student model is trained by minimizing the KL-divergence (Kullback and Leibler, 1951) loss between the output probability distributions of the teacher and student models (word-level KD). Sequence-level knowledge distillation (sequence-level KD) (Kim and Rush, 2016a) targets the token-sequence generated by the teacher model using beam search. In our experiments, sequence-level KD outperformed word-level one, and Kim and Rush (2016b) showed similar trends. Therefore, in our experiments, we call it KD.

The KD technique is prevalent in many applications of machine learning, including MT (non-autoregressive machine translation (Gu et al., 2017), simultaneous translation (Ren et al., 2020), etc.). Typically, it is used to distill knowledge from a larger teacher model to a smaller or faster student model. Recent works (Furlanello et al., 2018; Yang et al., 2018) have shown that the student model's accuracy exceeds that of the teacher model, even if its size is identical as the student model. KD has also been applied to ST. Gaido et al. (2020) applied KD to an end-to-end ST using an MT model based on clean transcriptions as the teacher of the end-to-end ST model. Our work focuses on the application of KD to a cascade ST using a teacher model based on clean transcripts for the student model that takes erroneous inputs.

Dakwale and Monz (2019) proposed distillation as a remedy for the effective use of noisy parallel data for machine translation. They first trained the teacher model only on high-quality, clean data. Then they fed the source-side of the noisy parallel

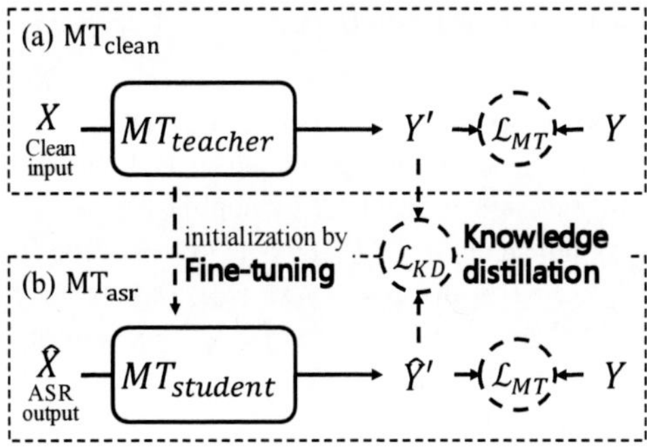

Figure 1: Overview of key concepts of methods

data into the teacher model and trained the student model to translate from the noisy source to the teacher's output. The main difference between their work and ours is that we have loosely equivalent source sentences (clean or erroneous transcription), which can be paired with the same target sentence. Therefore, the student model can be trained with more reliable objectives obtained by feeding clean transcriptions to the teacher model.

3 Cascade ST

Suppose triplet $W = (w_1, ..., w_J)$, $X = (x_1, ..., x_K)$, and $Y = (y_1, ..., y_L)$, where $W(1 \leq j \leq J)$, $X(1 \leq k \leq K)$, and $Y(1 \leq l \leq L)$ are sequences of the speech features in a source language, the corresponding transcribed source language tokens, and translated target language tokens.

In a cascade ST, first the ASR model is trained by the W and X pair. Then the MT model is trained to translate from X to Y. The loss function of MT model $\mathcal{L}_{MT}$ is defined using cross entropy:

$$\mathcal{L}_{MT} = -\sum_{l=1}^{L} \sum_{v \in V}^{|V|} logP(y_l = v), \quad (1)$$

where $P(y_l = v)$ is the posterior probability of candidate v in target language vocabulary V at time l in Y:

$$P(y_l = v) = p(v|X, y_{<l}; \theta). \quad (2)$$

4 Proposed method

When training an MT model, we can also use $\hat{X}$ instead of X, which is the output of the ASR model. We call the model trained with clean input X $\mathrm{MT}_{\mathrm{clean}}$ (Fig. 1(a)) and the one trained with ASR-based input $\hat{X}$ $\mathrm{MT}_{\mathrm{asr}}$ (Fig. 1(b)).

4.1 Joint use of KD and FT

To most effectively exploit both clean input X and ASR-based input $\hat{X}$, we introduce two training techniques: KD and fine-tuning. In KD, the student model is trained using $\hat{X}$ by minimizing loss $\mathcal{L}_{KD}$. As shown in Fig. 1, $\mathcal{L}_{KD}$ is the loss between $Y' = (y_1^{'}, ..., y_M^{'})$ and $\hat{Y} = (\hat{y_1}, ..., \hat{y_N})$, where $Y'(1 \leq m \leq M)$ and $\hat{Y}(1 \leq n \leq N)$ are the outputs of the teacher and student models. We use the sequence-level KD so that $\mathcal{L}_{KD}$ is calculated by replacing L with M and l with m in Eq. 1.

On the other hand, fine-tuning (FT) has been widely used for domain adaptation in MT (Sennrich et al., 2016a). Di Gangi et al. (2019c) showed that a model fine-tuned with ASR-based input becomes robust to erroneous ASR input while maintaining high performance for clean input. Following this finding, we employ FT for MT training. In FT, the student model with $\hat{X}$, which inherits the parameters of the teacher model with X, is trained by minimizing $\mathcal{L}_{MT}$ (Fig. 1).

In addition to the independent use of KD and FT, we examined their possible combinations:

- **FT+KD**. Apply these techniques at the same time. Unlike regular FT, we use loss $\mathcal{L}_{KD}$ instead of $\mathcal{L}_{MT}$.
  Specifically, (1) the teacher model is trained with clean input X and loss $\mathcal{L}_{MT}$. Then (2) the student model is trained with ASR-based input $\hat{X}$ and loss $\mathcal{L}_{KD}$, inheriting the parameters of the teacher model.

- **KD→FT**. Perform additional training with $\mathcal{L}_{MT}$ to the model trained by KD.
  Specifically, (1) the student model is trained with $\hat{X}$ and $\mathcal{L}_{KD}$. Then (2) fine-tune the model with $\hat{X}$ and $\mathcal{L}_{MT}$.

- **FT→KD**. Perform additional training with $\mathcal{L}_{KD}$ to the model trained by FT.
  Specifically, (1) the student model is trained with $\hat{X}$ and $\mathcal{L}_{MT}$, inheriting the parameters of the teacher model. Then (2) fine-tune the model with $\hat{X}$ and $\mathcal{L}_{KD}$.

5 Experiments

5.1 Dataset

We conducted experiments for English to Italian and Spanish to English NMT. For English-Italian, we used MuST-C (Di Gangi et al., 2019a), a multilingual ST corpus built from TED talks. It contains triplets of about 250K segments of English speeches, transcripts, and Italian translations. We used audio and transcript pairs to train the ASR. To train the MT model, we used transcripts as clean input and ASR outputs as noisy input.

For Spanish-English, we used LDC Fisher Spanish speech with new English translations (Post et al., 2013; Salesky et al., 2018). It has the following roughly 140K segments of multi-way parallel data:

1. Spanish disfluent speech
2. Spanish clean transcriptions
3. Spanish erroneous transcriptions (ASR output)
4. English disfluent translations
5. English fluent translations

When we train the MT model, we used (5) as output. For the sake of reproducibility we used (2) or (3) as clean or noisy input included in the dataset.

We preprocessed the text data with Byte Pair Encoding (BPE) (Sennrich et al., 2016b) to split the sentences into subwords. The vocabulary size was set to 8,000 in all the languages. For the English audio, we extracted 80-channel log mel filterbank features (25-ms window size and 10-ms shift) and applied an utterance-level CMVN.

To evaluate the performance, we calculated the case-sensitive BLEU with sacreBLEU.[1] We measured BLEU for both the ASR-based and clean input to evaluate the ASR error robustness and the topline performance in an ideal situation without ASR errors.

5.2 Model

We used the Transformer (Vaswani et al., 2017) implementation of Fairseq[2] to construct both the ASR and the MT. The hyper-parameters of the model generally follow the Transformer Base settings (Vaswani et al., 2017). Each encoder and decoder has 6 sub-layers. We set the word embedding dimensions, the hidden state dimensions, and the feed-forward dimensions to 512, 512, and 2,048. We performed the sub-layer's dropout with a probability of 0.1 and employed 8 attention heads for both the encoder and the decoder. The model is trained using Adam with an initial learning rate

[1] https://github.com/mjpost/sacreBLEU

[2] https://github.com/pytorch/fairseq

ST Type	System	ASR-based input	Clean input
End-to-end	ST + ASR-PT (Di Gangi et al., 2019b)[1]	16.8	
	ST + ASR-PT (*ESPnet*)[2]	21.5	
	ST	17.0	
	ST + ASR-PT	21.4	
Cascade	$\mathrm{MT}_{\mathrm{clean}}$ (Di Gangi et al., 2019b)[1]	18.9	-
	$\mathrm{MT}_{\mathrm{clean}}$	22.4	29.7
	$\mathrm{MT}_{\mathrm{asr}}$	22.1	27.2
	$\mathrm{MT}_{\mathrm{asr}} + \mathrm{FT}$	23.2	29.8
	$\mathrm{MT}_{\mathrm{asr}} + \mathrm{KD}$	22.5	28.2
	$\mathrm{MT}_{\mathrm{asr}} + \mathrm{FT} + \mathrm{KD}$	23.4	29.9
	$\mathrm{MT}_{\mathrm{asr}} + \mathrm{KD} \rightarrow \mathrm{FT}$	23.1	29.3
	$\mathrm{MT}_{\mathrm{asr}} + \mathrm{FT} \rightarrow \mathrm{KD}$	**23.5**	**30.2**

Table 1: ST systems on MuST-C English-Italian. Test BLEU reported. [1]End-to-end (above) or cascade ST (below) systems using Fairseq's Transformer Base model, which resembles our conditions. [2]End-to-end ST system using ESPnet resembles our conditions chosen from a report (https://github.com/espnet/espnet/blob/master/egs/must_c/st1/RESULTS.md).

of 0.0007, $\beta_1 = 0.9$, and $\beta_2 = 0.98$, following Vaswani et al. (2017). We used 4,096 tokens per mini-batch and eight iterations of forward-passes, accumulated gradients, and back-propagated them. Validation was performed every 1,000 updates, and the test checkpoint with the best loss was stored.

For English-Italian, we also built several end-to-end ST variants using Fairseq for comparison with the cascade models. All the settings are identical as in MT: using Transformer described above and trained with label-smoothed cross entropy loss.

6 Results

6.1 English-Italian

Table 1 shows the BLEU results for the English to Italian NMT. In the end-to-end systems, a naive model (ST) without any additional technique, such as an ASR subtask, was significantly lower than the others and was significantly improved by pre-training the ASR encoder (ST + ASR-PT).

The cascade methods worked better than the end-to-end methods. In the cascade ST, the performance of a system trained using only ASR input ($\mathrm{MT}_{\mathrm{asr}}$) was worse (0.3-BLEU drop for the ASR-based test data and 2.5-BLEU drop for the clean test data) than the clean input ($\mathrm{MT}_{\mathrm{clean}}$). The ASR-based training data contained erroneous transcriptions of WER 14.49, leading to degradation. On the other hand, some systems trained using both ASR input and clean input were better than $\mathrm{MT}_{\mathrm{clean}}$ when translating clean input. This indicates that the training with ASR errors may contribute to regularize the model, which yields improvements.

The FT for the ASR-based input ($\mathrm{MT}_{\mathrm{asr}} + \mathrm{FT}$) showed improvements for the ASR-based input (+1.1 BLEU). Compared to FT, KD ($\mathrm{MT}_{\mathrm{asr}} + \mathrm{KD}$) produced a small improvement with the ASR-based input (+0.4 BLEU). In the KD, a teacher model got a BLEU score of 41.6 on the reference for training data.

With respect to the joint use of FT and KD, simultaneously applying these techniques ($\mathrm{MT}_{\mathrm{asr}} + \mathrm{FT} + \mathrm{KD}$) shows only slight improvements (+0.2 BLEU for ASR-based test data and +0.1 BLEU for clean test data), compared to FT only ($\mathrm{MT}_{\mathrm{asr}} + \mathrm{FT}$). Applying FT after KD ($\mathrm{MT}_{\mathrm{asr}} + \mathrm{KD} \rightarrow \mathrm{FT}$) was inferior to the other combinations, especially for clean data, probably because the MT was not trained with clean input. Distilling knowledge after FT ($\mathrm{MT}_{\mathrm{asr}} + \mathrm{FT} \rightarrow \mathrm{KD}$) gave the best score for both the ASR-based and the clean test data. FT enables the student model to learn good parameter values, and KD provides the student model with its upper bounds from the teacher model.

6.2 Spanish-English

Table 2 shows the overall results for the Spanish to English cascade ST. They are similar to those in English-to-Italian; FT and KD improved BLEU, and combining them yielded more significant improvements. However, the gap was larger for the clean test data between systems only trained on the ASR-based input ($\mathrm{MT}_{\mathrm{asr}}$) and only on the clean input ($\mathrm{MT}_{\mathrm{clean}}$). The ASR-based training data contained many erroneous transcriptions of WER 36.5,

System	Fisher/Test 0		Fisher/Test 1	
	ASR-based input	Clean input	ASR-based input	Clean input
$\mathrm{MT}_{\mathrm{clean}}$	17.5	**26.8**	17.0	**26.1**
$\mathrm{MT}_{\mathrm{asr}}$	17.5	17.6	16.9	17.2
$\mathrm{MT}_{\mathrm{asr}} + \mathrm{FT}$	18.3	24.9	17.5	24.5
$\mathrm{MT}_{\mathrm{asr}} + \mathrm{KD}$	18.5	16.5	17.9	16.2
$\mathrm{MT}_{\mathrm{asr}} + \mathrm{FT} + \mathrm{KD}$	18.8	25.2	18.0	24.9
$\mathrm{MT}_{\mathrm{asr}} + \mathrm{KD} \rightarrow \mathrm{FT}$	17.8	15.7	17.1	15.3
$\mathrm{MT}_{\mathrm{asr}} + \mathrm{FT} \rightarrow \mathrm{KD}$	**19.0**	25.2	**18.4**	25.2

Table 2: ST systems on Fisher Spanish-English. Test BLEU for two fluent references reported.

causing more serious degradation. It also differs from the English-to-Italian experiments in that KD ($\mathrm{MT}_{\mathrm{asr}} + \mathrm{KD}$) was superior to FT ($\mathrm{MT}_{\mathrm{asr}} + \mathrm{FT}$) for the ASR-based test data when it was used alone. In KD, BLEU using the teacher model as training data was 48.0, which is higher than 41.6 for English-Italian. One possible reason is that there was a higher upper bound that can be trained by KD. Another difference was a gap between the clean and ASR-based inputs, which have many erroneous transcriptions of WER 36.5. In such a case, parameter initialization by FT may not be very helpful.

In spite of the differences between the two experiments, we achieved consistent improvement by combining FT and KD.

7 Discussion

We analyzed the results with the Spanish to English models to discuss how erroneous transcriptions affect translation results and how KD and FT work.

Erroneous transcription The example below shows the problem of error propagation:

- (Clean input) *uno super, super nuevo que salio*
- (ASR output) *en un* <u>*sur*</u> *super nuevo que salio*
- (Reference) *One super new that came out*
- ($\mathrm{MT}_{\mathrm{asr}}$ with ASR-based input) *In the* <u>*South,*</u> *it came out*
- ($\mathrm{MT}_{\mathrm{asr}} + \mathrm{KD}$ with ASR-based input) *In a super new one that came out.*

Here the Spanish word *super* was misrecognized as *sur* by the ASR. This error was propagated to MT, and $\mathrm{MT}_{\mathrm{asr}}$ translated it as *South*. Although the word's translation itself from *sur* to *South* was not wrong, but it is not what we wanted. The model trained by KD ignored this error and generated a more proper sentence.

We found such ASR error correction phenomena in the results, although KD and FT did not directly address this issue.

Effect of Knowledge Distillation Spoken language parallel data have translations of colloquial spoken utterances. They increase the difficulty of training MT. For instance:

- (Clean input) *le ayuda si si, no es, no es interesante pero entonces, a ba- entonces ya despues cuando eso termino, tiene que escribir varios asi, ensayos, hacer un analisis*
- (Reference) *You have to write some essays like that, to make an analysis*
- (KD teacher) *It helps her yes, it's not interesting but then, when I finish, you have to write several, you have to make an analysis*

A human translator ignored many disfluent utterances from the original text, resulting in low fidelity. Here are some other examples:

- Inconsistent translations: "*De Venezuela*" was translated into "*From Venezuela*" at one time and "*Venezuela?*" at another time.
- All-caps: "*donde hay problemas*" was capitalized and translated into "*WHEN TROUBLE ARISES.*"
- Omission of a part of speech: "*Porque, tengo el, el bodysuit, pero*" was translated into "*I have the bodysuit..*" The conjunction "*pero* (but)" was removed for fluency.

The MT model can be confused by such translations. KD forces the student model to mimic literal teacher translations that may include some errors instead of reproducing translations of colloquial spoken utterances.

Effect of Fine-tuning Sometimes the fine-tuned MT model corrected the ASR errors:

- (Clean input) *Eh, para mi pues, eh, tengo como diez mil canciones en, en el, en la Ipod*
- (ASR output) *eh para mi pues eh tengo como diez mil canciones en en la epod*
- (Reference) *I have ten thousand songs in the Ipod.*
- (MT_{clean} with ASR-based input) *To me, I have about ten thousand songs in the ethics*
- (MT_{asr} + FT with ASR-based input) *I have about ten thousand songs in the Ipod*

The ASR misrecognized "*Ipod*" as "*epod*," and the model before FT, which was only trained with clean inputs, incorrectly translated it as "*ethics*." As a result of the FT with ASR-based inputs, the model successfully translated it as "*Ipod*." The FT for the erroneous ASR outputs may have provided robustness against common errors.

8 Conclusion

We presented and discussed the benefits of using two machine learning techniques in cascade ST: knowledge distillation and fine-tuning. Our experimental results showed the advantages of the proposed method in two different conditions. Our results also suggest that combining knowledge distillation and fine-tuning is more beneficial than using either one because they have different roles.

In future work, we will incorporate our findings into an end-to-end ST to grow speech translation.

Acknowledgements

Part of this work was supported by JSPS KAKENHI Grant Number JP17H06101.

References

Antonios Anastasopoulos and David Chiang. 2018. Tied multitask learning for neural speech translation. In *Proceedings of the 2018 Conference of the North American Chapter of the Association for Computational Linguistics: Human Language Technologies, Volume 1 (Long Papers)*, pages 82–91, New Orleans, Louisiana. Association for Computational Linguistics.

Parnia Bahar, Tobias Bieschke, Ralf Schlüter, and Hermann Ney. 2021. Tight integrated end-to-end training for cascaded speech translation. In *2021 IEEE Spoken Language Technology Workshop (SLT)*, pages 950–957. IEEE.

Sameer Bansal, Herman Kamper, Karen Livescu, Adam Lopez, and Sharon Goldwater. 2019. Pre-training on high-resource speech recognition improves low-resource speech-to-text translation. In *Proceedings of the 2019 Conference of the North American Chapter of the Association for Computational Linguistics: Human Language Technologies, Volume 1 (Long and Short Papers)*, pages 58–68.

Alexandre Bérard, Laurent Besacier, Ali Can Kocabiyikoglu, and Olivier Pietquin. 2018. End-to-end automatic speech translation of audiobooks. In *2018 IEEE International Conference on Acoustics, Speech and Signal Processing (ICASSP)*, pages 6224–6228. IEEE.

Alexandre Bérard, Olivier Pietquin, Christophe Servan, and Laurent Besacier. 2016. Listen and translate: A proof of concept for end-to-end speech-to-text translation. *arXiv preprint arXiv:1612.01744*.

Nicola Bertoldi and Marcello Federico. 2005. A new decoder for spoken language translation based on confusion networks. In *IEEE Workshop on Automatic Speech Recognition and Understanding, 2005.*, pages 86–91. IEEE.

Nicola Bertoldi, Richard Zens, and Marcello Federico. 2007. Speech translation by confusion network decoding. In *2007 IEEE International Conference on Acoustics, Speech and Signal Processing-ICASSP'07*, volume 4, pages IV–1297. IEEE.

Cristian Buciluă, Rich Caruana, and Alexandru Niculescu-Mizil. 2006. Model compression. In *Proceedings of the 12th ACM SIGKDD international conference on Knowledge discovery and data mining*, pages 535–541.

Praveen Dakwale and Christof Monz. 2019. Improving neural machine translation using noisy parallel data through distillation. In *Proceedings of Machine Translation Summit XVII Volume 1: Research Track*, pages 118–127.

Mattia A. Di Gangi, Roldano Cattoni, Luisa Bentivogli, Matteo Negri, and Marco Turchi. 2019a. MuST-C: a Multilingual Speech Translation Corpus. In *Proceedings of the 2019 Conference of the North American Chapter of the Association for Computational Linguistics: Human Language Technologies, Volume 1 (Long and Short Papers)*, pages 2012–2017, Minneapolis, Minnesota. Association for Computational Linguistics.

Mattia A Di Gangi, Matteo Negri, and Marco Turchi. 2019b. Adapting transformer to end-to-end spoken language translation. In *INTERSPEECH 2019*, pages 1133–1137. International Speech Communication Association (ISCA).

Mattia Antonino Di Gangi, Enyedi Robert, Brusadin Alessandra, and Marcello Federico. 2019c. Robust neural machine translation for clean and noisy speech transcripts. In *16th International Workshop on Spoken Language Translation 2019*.

Tommaso Furlanello, Zachary Lipton, Michael Tschannen, Laurent Itti, and Anima Anandkumar. 2018. Born again neural networks. In *International Conference on Machine Learning*, pages 1607–1616. PMLR.

Marco Gaido, Mattia A. Di Gangi, Matteo Negri, and Marco Turchi. 2020. On knowledge distillation for direct speech translation.

Jiatao Gu, James Bradbury, Caiming Xiong, Victor OK Li, and Richard Socher. 2017. Non-autoregressive neural machine translation. *arXiv preprint arXiv:1711.02281*.

Geoffrey Hinton, Oriol Vinyals, and Jeff Dean. 2015. Distilling the knowledge in a neural network. *arXiv preprint arXiv:1503.02531*.

Hirofumi Inaguma, Shun Kiyono, Kevin Duh, Shigeki Karita, Nelson Yalta, Tomoki Hayashi, and Shinji Watanabe. 2020. ESPnet-ST: All-in-one speech translation toolkit. In *Proceedings of the 58th Annual Meeting of the Association for Computational Linguistics: System Demonstrations*, pages 302–311, Online. Association for Computational Linguistics.

Yoon Kim and Alexander M Rush. 2016a. Sequence-level knowledge distillation. *arXiv preprint arXiv:1606.07947*.

Yoon Kim and Alexander M. Rush. 2016b. Sequence-level knowledge distillation. In *Proceedings of the 2016 Conference on Empirical Methods in Natural Language Processing*, pages 1317–1327, Austin, Texas. Association for Computational Linguistics.

Solomon Kullback and Richard A Leibler. 1951. On information and sufficiency. *The annals of mathematical statistics*, 22(1):79–86.

Dan Liu, Junhua Liu, Wu Guo, Shifu Xiong, Zhiqiang Ma, Rui Song, Chongliang Wu, and Quan Liu. 2018. The ustc-nel speech translation system at iwslt 2018. *arXiv e-prints*, pages arXiv–1812.

Evgeny Matusov and Hermann Ney. 2010. Lattice-based asr-mt interface for speech translation. *IEEE transactions on audio, speech, and language processing*, 19(4):721–732.

Kaho Osamura, Takatomo Kano, Sakriani Sakti, Katsuhito Sudoh, and Satoshi Nakamura. 2018. Using spoken word posterior features in neural machine translation. *architecture*, 21:22.

Matt Post, Gaurav Kumar, Adam Lopez, Damianos Karakos, Chris Callison-Burch, and Sanjeev Khudanpur. 2013. Improved speech-to-text translation with the fisher and callhome spanish–english speech translation corpus. In *International Workshop on Spoken Language Translation*.

Vu Hai Quan, Marcello Federico, and Mauro Cettolo. 2005. Integrated n-best re-ranking for spoken language translation. In *Ninth European Conference on Speech Communication and Technology*.

Yi Ren, Jinglin Liu, Xu Tan, Chen Zhang, Tao Qin, Zhou Zhao, and Tie-Yan Liu. 2020. SimulSpeech: End-to-end simultaneous speech to text translation. In *Proceedings of the 58th Annual Meeting of the Association for Computational Linguistics*, pages 3787–3796, Online. Association for Computational Linguistics.

Elizabeth Salesky and Alan W Black. 2020. Phone features improve speech translation. In *Proceedings of the 58th Annual Meeting of the Association for Computational Linguistics*, pages 2388–2397, Online. Association for Computational Linguistics.

Elizabeth Salesky, Susanne Burger, Jan Niehues, and Alex Waibel. 2018. Towards fluent translations from disfluent speech. *2018 IEEE Spoken Language Technology Workshop (SLT)*.

Rico Sennrich, Barry Haddow, and Alexandra Birch. 2016a. Improving neural machine translation models with monolingual data. In *Proceedings of the 54th Annual Meeting of the Association for Computational Linguistics (Volume 1: Long Papers)*, pages 86–96, Berlin, Germany. Association for Computational Linguistics.

Rico Sennrich, Barry Haddow, and Alexandra Birch. 2016b. Neural machine translation of rare words with subword units. In *Proceedings of the 54th Annual Meeting of the Association for Computational Linguistics (Volume 1: Long Papers)*, pages 1715–1725, Berlin, Germany. Association for Computational Linguistics.

Matthias Sperber, Graham Neubig, Jan Niehues, and Alex Waibel. 2017a. Neural lattice-to-sequence models for uncertain inputs. *arXiv preprint arXiv:1704.00559*.

Matthias Sperber, Graham Neubig, Jan Niehues, and Alex Waibel. 2019. Attention-passing models for robust and data-efficient end-to-end speech translation. *Transactions of the Association for Computational Linguistics*, 7:313–325.

Matthias Sperber, Jan Niehues, and Alex Waibel. 2017b. Toward robust neural machine translation for noisy input sequences. In *International Workshop on Spoken Language Translation (IWSLT)*.

Ashish Vaswani, Noam Shazeer, Niki Parmar, Jakob Uszkoreit, Llion Jones, Aidan N Gomez, Łukasz Kaiser, and Illia Polosukhin. 2017. Attention is all you need. In *Advances in neural information processing systems*, pages 5998–6008.

Changhan Wang, Yun Tang, Xutai Ma, Anne Wu, Dmytro Okhonko, and Juan Pino. 2020. Fairseq S2T: Fast speech-to-text modeling with fairseq. In *Proceedings of the 1st Conference of the Asia-Pacific*

Chapter of the Association for Computational Linguistics and the 10th International Joint Conference on Natural Language Processing: System Demonstrations, pages 33–39, Suzhou, China. Association for Computational Linguistics.

Ron J Weiss, Jan Chorowski, Navdeep Jaitly, Yonghui Wu, and Zhifeng Chen. 2017. Sequence-to-sequence models can directly translate foreign speech. *Proc. Interspeech 2017*, pages 2625–2629.

Haiyang Xue, Yang Feng, Shuhao Gu, and Wei Chen. 2020. Robust neural machine translation with asr errors. In *Proceedings of the First Workshop on Automatic Simultaneous Translation*, pages 15–23.

Chenglin Yang, Lingxi Xie, Siyuan Qiao, and Alan Yuille. 2018. Knowledge distillation in generations: More tolerant teachers educate better students. *arXiv preprint arXiv:1805.05551*.

Ruiqiang Zhang, Genichiro Kikui, Hirofumi Yamamoto, Frank K Soong, Taro Watanabe, and Wai-Kit Lo. 2004. A unified approach in speech-to-speech translation: integrating features of speech recognition and machine translation. In *COLING 2004: Proceedings of the 20th International Conference on Computational Linguistics*, pages 1168–1174.

Self-Guided Curriculum Learning for Neural Machine Translation

Lei Zhou*
Nagoya University
zhou.lei@a.mbox.nagoya-u.ac.jp

Liang Ding
The University of Sydney
ldin3097@sydney.edu.au

Kevin Duh
Johns Hopkins University
kevinduh@cs.jhu.edu

Shinji Watanabe
Carnegie Mellon University
shinjiw@ieee.org

Ryohei Sasano
Nagoya University
sasano@i.nagoya-u.ac.jp

Koichi Takeda
Nagoya University
takedasu@i.nagoya-u.ac.jp

Abstract

In supervised learning, a well-trained model should be able to recover ground truth accurately, i.e. the predicted labels are expected to resemble the ground truth labels as much as possible. Inspired by this, we formulate a difficulty criterion based on the recovery degrees of training examples. Motivated by the intuition that after skimming through the training corpus, the neural machine translation (NMT) model "knows" how to schedule a suitable curriculum according to learning difficulty, we propose a self-guided curriculum learning strategy that encourages the NMT model to learn from easy to hard on the basis of recovery degrees. Specifically, we adopt sentence-level BLEU score as the proxy of recovery degree. Experimental results on translation benchmarks including WMT14 English⇒German and WMT17 Chinese⇒English demonstrate that our proposed method considerably improves the recovery degree, thus consistently improving the translation performance.

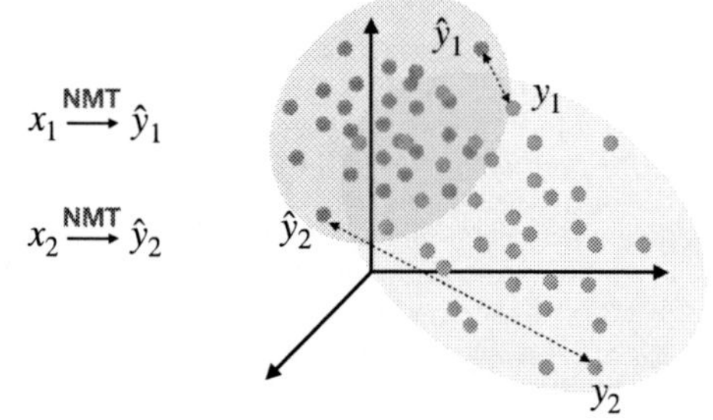

Figure 1: The NMT model is well-trained on parallel corpus $\mathbb{D}$, $\{(x_1, y_1), (x_2, y_2)\} \in \mathbb{D}$. $\hat{y}_i$ is translated from x_i. The distance between the *ground truth* y_i and the *NMT generated hypothesis* $\hat{y}_i$ represents the recovery degree (dashed arrows), which is computed by sentence-level BLEU in our case. Blue- and green-colored examples represent the NMT learned distribution and the empirical distribution, respectively. Taking x_1 and x_2 as the input, the training example (x_1, y_1) shows a better *recovery degree*, which means it's easier to be mastered than (x_2, y_2).

1 Introduction

Inspired by the learning behavior of humans, Curriculum Learning (CL) for neural network training starts from a basic idea of "starting small", namely better to start from easier aspects of a task and then progress towards aspects with increasing level of difficulty (Elman, 1993). Bengio et al. (2009) achieves significant performance boost on several tasks by forcing models to learn training examples following an order from "easy" to "difficult". They further explain CL method with two important constituents: *how to rank training examples* by learning difficulty and *how to schedule the presentation of training examples* based on that rank.

In the field of neural machine translation (NMT), empirical studies have shown that CL strategies contribute to both convergence speed and model performance (Zhang et al., 2018; Platanios et al., 2019; Zhang et al., 2019; Liu et al., 2020; Zhan et al., 2021; Ruiter et al., 2020). These CL strategies vary by difficulty criteria and curriculum schedules. Early difficulty criterion depends on manually crafted features and prior knowledge such as sentence length and word rarity (Kocmi and Bojar, 2017). The drawback lies in the fact that humans understand learning difficulty differently from NMT models. Recent works choose to derive difficulty criteria based on the probability distribution of training examples to approximate the perspective of NMT models. For instance, Platanios et al. (2019) turn discrete numerical difficulty scores into relative probabilities and then construct

*Part of this work was done when the first author visited CLSP, JHU.

Proceedings of the 18th International Conference on Spoken Language Translation, pages 206–214
Bangkok, Thailand (Online), August 5–6, 2021. ©2021 Association for Computational Linguistics

the difficulty criterion, while others derive difficulty criterion from independently trained language model (Zhang et al., 2019; Dou et al., 2020; Liu et al., 2020) and word embedding model (Zhou et al., 2020b). Xu et al. (2020) derive difficulty criterion from the NMT model in the training process. And these difficulty criteria are applied to either fixed curriculum schedule (Cirik et al., 2016) or dynamic one (Platanios et al., 2019; Liu et al., 2020; Xu et al., 2020; Zhou et al., 2020b).

A well-trained NMT model estimates the optimal probability distribution mapping from the source language to the target language, which is assumed to be able to recover the ground truth translations accurately (Liu et al., 2021). However, if we perform inference on the training set, many of the predictions are inconsistent with the references. It reflects the **distribution shift** between the NMT model leaned distribution and the empirical distribution of training corpus, as Figure 1 illustrated. For a training example, a high recovery degree between prediction and ground-truth target sentence means it's easier to be mastered by the NMT model while a lower recovery degree means it's more difficult (Ding and Tao, 2019; Wu et al., 2020b). To this end, we employ this recovery degree as the difficulty criterion, where the recovery degree is computed by the sentence-level BLEU. We put forward an analogy of this method that humans can schedule a personal and effective curriculum after skimming over a textbook, namely *self-guided curriculum*.

In this work, we cast the recovery degree of each training example as its learning difficulty, enforcing the NMT model to learn from examples with higher recovery degrees to those with lower degrees. Also, we implement our proposed recovery-based difficulty criterion with fixed and dynamic curriculum schedules. Experimental results on two machine translation benchmarks, i.e., WMT14 En-De and WMT17 Zh-En, demonstrate that our proposed self-guided CL can alleviate the distribution shift problem in vanilla NMT models, thus consistently boosting the performance.

2 Problem Definition

For a better interpretation of curriculum learning for neural machine translation, we put the discussion of various CL strategies into a probabilistic perspective. Such perspective also motivates us to derive this recovery-based difficulty criterion.

2.1 Neural Machine Translation

Let $\mathcal{S}$ and $\mathcal{T}$ represent the probability distributions over all possible sequences of tokens in source and target languages, respectively. We denote the distribution of a random source sentence $\mathbf{x}$ and $\mathbf{y}$ as $P_{\mathcal{S}}(\mathbf{x})$ and $P_{\mathcal{T}}(\mathbf{y})$. NMT model is to learn a conditional distribution $P_{\mathcal{S},\mathcal{T}}(\mathbf{y}|\mathbf{x})$ with a probabilistic model $P(y|x;\theta)$ parameterized by θ, where θ is estimated by minimizing the objective:

$$J(\theta) = -\mathbb{E}_{x,y\sim P_{\mathcal{S},\mathcal{T}}(\mathbf{x},\mathbf{y})} \log P(y|x;\theta) \qquad (1)$$

2.2 Curriculum Learning for Neural Machine Translation

CL methods decompose the NMT model training into K phases, enforcing the optimization trajectory in parameter space to visit a series of points $\theta^1, \ldots, \theta^K$. Each training phase can be viewed as a sub-optimal process, optimized on a subset $\mathbb{D}_k$ of the training corpus $\mathbb{D}$:

$$J(\theta^k) = -\mathbb{E}_{x,y\sim \hat{P}_{\mathbb{D}_k}} \log P(y|x;\theta^k) \qquad (2)$$

where $\hat{P}_{\mathbb{D}_k}$ is the empirical distribution of $\mathbb{D}_k$. According to the definition of curriculum learning, the optimization difficulty increases from $J(\theta^1)$ to $J(\theta^K)$ (Bengio et al., 2009). In practice, it's achieved by grouping training examples into subsets in ascending order of learning difficulty. The process splitting $\mathbb{D}$ into K subsets can be formulated as follows:

- score $\leftarrow d(z^n)$, $z^n \in \mathbb{D}$, where $d(\cdot)$ is a difficulty criterion
- For $k = 1, \ldots, K$ do; $\mathbb{D}_k \leftarrow \{z^n|\text{Constraint}(d(z^n), k)\}$

z represents examples in $\mathbb{D}$, $\mathbb{D} = \{z^n\}_{n=1}^N$, $z^n = (x^n, y^n)$. Training corpus $\mathbb{D}$ is split into K subsets $\{\mathbb{D}_1, \ldots, \mathbb{D}_K\}$, that $\bigcup_{k\in K} \mathbb{D}_k = \mathbb{D}$.

With these notations, we review the DIFFICULTY CRITERIA in existing CL methods from a probabilistic perspective as these methods generally derive difficulty criteria from a probabilistic distribution. For example:

Explicit Feature $d(x^n) = P_{\mathbb{D}}(\text{Feature}(x^n))$, where $\text{Feature}(\cdot)$ is handcrafted features and linguistic prior knowledge such as sentence length and word rarity. With the cumulative density function (CDF), numerical scores are mapped into a relative probability distribution over all training examples (Platanios et al., 2019). Only features of source sentences are taken into consideration in their practice.

Language Model $d(x^n) = -\frac{1}{I}\log P_{\text{LM}}(w_1^n, \ldots, w_I^n)$, where a language model is adopted to estimate the perplexity of each sentence $x = w_1, \ldots, w_I$. Language models trained on source and target side can be used jointly, e.g., $d(x^n) + d(y^n)$ (Zhou et al., 2020b). In other works (Zhang et al., 2019; Dou et al., 2020), language models in different domains are adopted to compute the cross-entropy difference of each sentence, indicating its difficulty for domain adaptation.

Word Embedding $d(x^n) = \sum_{i=1}^{I} \|\mathbf{w}_i^n\|$, where $\mathbf{w}_1, \ldots, \mathbf{w}_I$ is a distributed representation of source sentence x mapped through a independent word embedding model. In the case of Liu et al. (2020), the norm of word vector on the source side is used as the difficulty criterion. They also use the CDF function to assure the difficulty scores are within $[0, 1]$.

NMT Model $d(z^n; \theta^k) = \frac{l(z^n;\theta^k) - l(z^n;\theta^{k-1})}{l(z^n;\theta^{k-1})}$, $l(z^n; \theta^k) = -\log P(y^n|x^n; \theta^k)$, where θ^k represents the NMT model parameters at the kth training phase. The decline of loss is defined as the difficulty criterion in Xu et al. (2020). Besides, the score of cross-lingual patterns may also be a proper difficulty criterion for NMT (Ding et al., 2020a; Zhou et al., 2020a; Wu et al., 2021), which we leave as the future work.

We now turn to CURRICULUM SCHEDULING. There are two controlling factors, extraction of training set and training phase duration. In other words, how to split training corpus into subsets and when to load them. Given K mutual exclusive subsets $\{\mathbb{D}_1, \ldots, \mathbb{D}_K\} \subseteq \mathbb{D}$, there are two general regimens loading them as training progresses: one pass and baby steps. In *one pass* regimen, k subsets $\mathbb{D}_k$ are loaded as training set one by one, while in *baby steps* regimen, these subsets are merged into the current training set one by one (Cirik et al., 2016). According to Cirik et al. (2016), baby steps outperforms one pass. Later approaches generally take the idea of baby steps in that easy examples are not cast aside while the probability increases for difficulty examples to be batched.

On top of baby steps, we can summarize existing works into two schedule settings: fixed schedule and dynamic schedule. In *fixed schedule*, both training set extraction and training phase duration are fixed (Cirik et al., 2016; Zhang et al., 2019). The size of the training set scales up by a certain proportion of the total training examples, usually $|\mathbb{D}_k| = N/K$ at the beginning of a new training phase. And each training phase spends a fixed number of training steps. In *dynamic schedule*, either training set extraction or training phase duration is dynamic. Depending on which controlling factor is dynamic, we group existing dynamic schedules into two types: the competence type and the self-paced type. Competence-based CL method is proposed by (Platanios et al., 2019). In *competence* type of dynamic schedule, training set extraction is dynamic while the training phase duration is fixed. At the beginning of a training phase, the CL algorithm compute the model competence c at the moment, then extract examples with difficulty scores lower than c as the training set for the current phase, $\{z^n|d(z^n) \leq c, z^n \in \mathbb{D}\}$. For K training phases, the competence-based schedule is to determine $(K-1)$ upper limits with a scale factor within range of $d(z^n)$, which is $[0, 1]$. Platanios et al. (2019) take training steps $1, \ldots, t, \ldots, T$ as the scale factor, thus the general form of competence function is : $c(t) = \min\left(1, \sqrt[p]{t\frac{1-c_0^p}{T} + c_0^p}\right)$. Recent works develop model competence by introducing different scale factors, such as the norm of the source embedding of the NMT model (Liu et al., 2020) and BLEU score on validation set (Xu et al., 2020). Another type of dynamic schedule is the *self-paced* one (Jiang et al., 2015; Zhou et al., 2020b), in which training set extraction is fixed while the training phase duration is dynamic. After a training phase begins, it goes on until convergence or until meeting certain conditions. For example in Zhou et al. (2020b), model training will progress to the next phase if the model uncertainty stops decline.

3 Methodology

As mentioned above, due to the distribution shift problem, predictions made by a well-trained vanilla NMT model can be inconsistent with the references when performing inference on the training set. Training examples with higher recovery degrees are easier to be masted by the NMT model while those with lower recovery degrees are likely to be more difficult. Table 1 shows a comparison of two training examples with distant recovery de-

High Recovery Degree (BLEU 77.01)	
Source	该动议如被通过，提案或修正案中后被核准的各部分应合成整体再付表决。
Reference	If the motion for division is carried, those parts of the proposal or of the amendment which are subsequently approved shall be put to the vote as a whole.
Prediction	If the motion for division is carried , those parts of fm draft resolution or of the amendment that are subsequently approved shall be put to the vote as a whole.
Low Recovery Degree (BLEU 5.19)	
Source	并且慢慢地，非常缓慢地把头抬到它的眼睛正好可以直视哈利的位置便停了下来。它朝哈利使了一下眼色。
Reference	Slowly, very slowly, it raised its head until its eyes were on a level with Harry's. It winked.
Prediction	Slowly and very slowly – thinking his head up, still adding to poster him gladly stare to stopped Harry's face alone, and then blurted it out to Harry like a stop.

Table 1: Examples from WMT17 Chinese⇒English with distant recovery degrees measured by sentence-level BLEU score. We mark prediction errors with red underline.

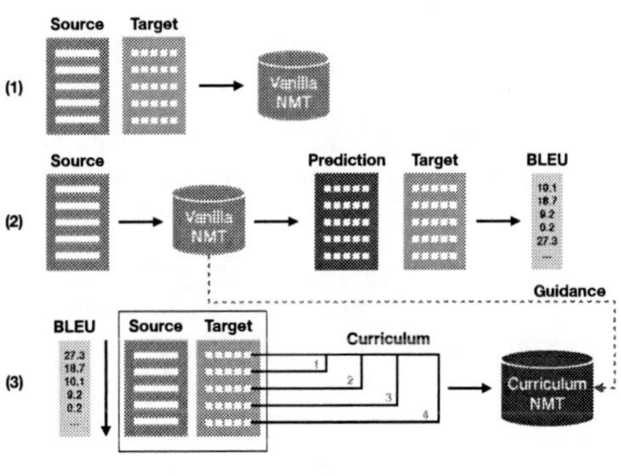

Figure 2: Workflow of self-guided CL strategy

grees.

In this section, we first introduce our recovery-based difficulty criterion and then propose to implement this criterion with fixed and dynamic curriculum schedules. The workflow of our proposed self-guided curriculum learning strategy is illustrated in Figure 2.

3.1 Difficulty Criterion

The objective function of the vanilla model can be written as an average distribution over the training corpus $\mathbb{D}$:

$$J(\varphi) = \mathbb{E}_{x,y \sim \hat{p}_{\mathbb{D}}} L(f(x^n; \varphi), y^n) \quad (3)$$

where $f(x^n; \varphi)$ represents model's prediction and L is the loss function. As noted in Section 2, curriculum learning minimizes the objective $J(\theta)$ with a set of sub-optimal processes from easy to difficult. Examples that better fit into the average distribution learned by the vanilla model with parameter φ get higher recovery degrees. Starting curriculum learning on a set of examples with higher recovery degrees is to start optimizing $J(\theta)$ from a smaller parameter space in the neighborhood of parameter φ. In the machine translation scenario, we care more about model performance in terms of translation quality. So we choose BLEU score, the de facto automatic metric for MT, to measure the recovery degree. The difficulty criterion based on sentence-level BLEU score is as follows:

$$d(z^n) = -\text{BLEU}(f(x^n; \varphi), y^n) \quad (4)$$

Other reference-based automatic metrics for MT are applicable in this difficulty criterion as well.

3.2 Curriculum Scheduling

Following basic operations of the baby steps regimen, we first split training corpus $\mathbb{D}$ into K mutual exclusive subsets $\{\mathbb{D}_1, \ldots, \mathbb{D}_K\}$, corresponding to K training phases. With difficulty criterion $d(\cdot)$, we define the corpus splitting function g:

$$\begin{aligned} g(d(\cdot)) : \mathbb{D} &\longrightarrow \{\mathbb{D}_1, \ldots, \mathbb{D}_K\}, \\ &\mid \forall a \in \mathbb{D}_k, \forall b \in \mathbb{D}_{k+1}, d(a) \leq d(b) \end{aligned} \quad (5)$$

Then we explore both fixed and dynamic schedules:

Fixed In fixed schedule, the training duration of each training phase is predefined. At the beginning

Algorithm 1: Fixed Scheduling

Input: Parallel corpus $\mathbb{D} = \{z^n\}_{n=1}^N$, $z^n = (x^n, y^n)$

Train vanilla model φ on $\mathbb{D}$

Compute difficulty score $d(z^n)$, $z^n \in \mathbb{D}$ with φ by Eq. 4

Split $\mathbb{D}$ into subsets $\{\mathbb{D}_1, \ldots, \mathbb{D}_K\}$ by Eq. 5

$\mathbb{D}_{\text{train}} = \varnothing$

for $k = 1, \ldots, K$ **do**

  $\mathbb{D}_{\text{train}} = \mathbb{D}_{\text{train}} \cup \mathbb{D}_k$

  for *training steps* $t = 1, \ldots, T$ **do**

    Train CL model θ^k on $\mathbb{D}_{\text{train}}$

Output: Trained CL model θ

Algorithm 2: Dynamic Scheduling

Input: Parallel corpus $\mathbb{D} = \{z^n\}_{n=1}^N$, $z^n = (x^n, y^n)$

Train vanilla model φ on $\mathbb{D}$

Compute difficulty score $d(z^n)$, $z^n \in \mathbb{D}$ with φ Eq. 4

Split $\mathbb{D}$ into subsets $\{\mathbb{D}_1, \ldots, \mathbb{D}_K\}$ by Eq. 5

$\mathbb{D}_{\text{train}} = \varnothing$

for $k = 1, \ldots, K$ **do**

  $\mathbb{D}_{\text{train}} = \mathbb{D}_{\text{train}} \cup \mathbb{D}_k$

  for *training steps* $t = 1, \ldots, T$ **do**

    Train CL model θ^k on $\mathbb{D}_{\text{train}}$

    Compute model recovery degree o_c and o_v, Eq.6,7

    if $o_c > o_v$ **then**

      Stop and move to the next phase

Output: Trained CL model θ

of the kth training phase, subset $\mathbb{D}_k$ is merged into the current training set. After finished with T steps, the training progresses to the next phase $k + 1$, see Algorithm 1:

Dynamic We follow the *self-paced* type of dynamic schedule as described in Section 2, in which training duration is dynamic while training set extraction is done before training starts. We define the condition of training phase progressing by the model recovery degree. In training phase k, if the CL model constantly demonstrates recovery degrees higher than the vanilla model on the newly merged subset $\mathbb{D}_k$, the CL model training will advance to the training phase $k + 1$. For easier operation, we randomly sub-sample $\mathbb{D}'_k$ from $\mathbb{D}_k$ for model recovery validation. Based on the performance on $\{x^n, y^n\} \in \mathbb{D}'_k$, which is measured by corpus-level BLEU score, we compute model recovery degree of the CL model at current training phase k by:

$$o_c(k) = \text{BLEU}(f(x^n; \theta^k), y^n) \quad (6)$$

Similarly, with the same additional validation set $\mathbb{D}'_k$, we compute model recovery degree of the vanilla model by:

$$o_v(k) = \text{BLEU}(f(x^n; \varphi), y^n) \quad (7)$$

If $o_c > o_v$, training phase will progress to the next one. Otherwise, the current training phase will go on until it reaches the predefined maximum time steps T, and then moves to the next phase. The training process is as described in Algorithm 2.

4 Experiments

4.1 Datasets

We conduct experiments on two machine translation benchmarks: WMT'14 English⇒German (En-De) and WMT'17 Chinese⇒English (Zh-En). For En-De, the training set consists of 4.5 million sentence pairs. We use newstest2012 as the validation set and report test results on both newstest2014 and newtest2016 for fair comparison with existing approaches. For Zh-En, we follow (Hassan et al., 2018) to extract 20 million sentence pairs as the training set. We use newsdev2017 as the validation set and newstest2017 as the test set. Chinese sentences are segmented with a word segmentation toolkit Jieba[1]. Sentences in other languages are tokenized with Moses[2]. We learn Byte-Pair Encoding(BPE) (Sennrich et al., 2016) with 32k merge operations. And we learn BPE with a shared vocabulary for En-De. We use BLEU (Papineni et al., 2002) as the automatic metrics for computing recovery degree and evaluating model performance with statistical significance test (Collins et al., 2005).

4.2 Model Settings

We perform proposed CL method with the FAIRSEQ[3] (Ott et al., 2019) implementation of the

[1]https://github.com/fxshy/jieba

[2]https://github.com/mosesdecoder

[3]https://github.com/pytorch/fairseq

#	Systems	WMT14 EnDe		WMT16 EnDe		WMT17 ZhEn	
		BLEU	Δ	BLEU	Δ	BLEU	Δ
1	Transformer BASE	27.30	-	32.76‡	-	23.69†	-
2	w/ Competence-based CL	28.19†	-	32.84‡	-	24.30†	-
3	w/ Norm-based CL	28.81†	-	-	-	25.25†	-
4	w/ Uncertainty-aware CL	-	-	33.93‡	-	25.02‡	-
	This work						
5	Transformer BASE	27.63	-	33.03	-	23.78	-
6	w/ SGCL Fixed	28.16$^{\uparrow}$	0.53	33.55$^{\uparrow}$	0.52	24.65$^{\uparrow}$	0.87
7	w/ SGCL Dynamic	**28.62**$^{\Uparrow}$	0.99	**34.07**$^{\Uparrow}$	1.04	**25.34**$^{\Uparrow}$	1.56

Table 2: Experiment results on WMT14 En⇒De with newstest2014 and newstest2016, and WMT17 Zh⇒En. For baseline and existing CL methods, Row 1-4, "†" marks the results from Liu et al. (2020), and "‡" marks the results from Zhou et al. (2020b). Since Platanios et al. (2019) only report their results on En⇒De newstest2016, up to 30.16, which is lower than later implementations, we show the implemented results of the Competence-based CL method from Liu et al. (2020) and Zhou et al. (2020b) instead. For the results of our proposed methods, "$\Uparrow/\uparrow$" indicates significant difference ($p < 0.01/0.05$) from Transformer BASE.

Transformer BASE (Vaswani et al., 2017). For regularization, we use the dropout of 0.3 and 0.1 for En-De and Zh-En respectively, with label smoothing ϵ = 0.1. We train the model with a batch size of approximately 128K tokens. We use Adam (Kingma and Ba, 2015) optimizer. The learning rate warms up to 5×10^{-4} in the first 16K steps and then decays with the inverse square-root schedule. We evaluate the translation performance on an ensemble of the top 5 checkpoints to avoid stochasticity. We use shared embeddings for En-De experiments. All our experiments are conducted with 4 NVIDIA Quadro GV100 GPUs.

4.3 Curriculum Learning Settings

The vanilla model and the CL model share the same Transformer BASE setting. For the recovery degree, we let the trained vanilla model make predictions of source sentences in the training corpus with beam size set to 1 for we only need to reveal the recovery feature at the moment. Then we evaluate the predictions with sentence-level BLEU score. Specifically, we use `fairseq-score` to get sentence-level BLEU score, which implements smoothing method 3, i.e., NIST smoothing method (Chen and Cherry, 2014) by default. According to Zhou et al. (2020b), 4 baby steps is superior to those with larger baby steps, so we choose to decompose the CL training into 4 training phases. Implementing the proposed difficulty criterion, we investigate the performance of two curriculum schedules:

- **SGCL Fixed** represents self-guided curriculum learning with fixed schedule.
- **SGCL Dynamic** represents self-guided curriculum learning with dynamic schedule.

5 Results

Table 2 summarises our experimental results together with existing CL methods. Row 1 shows the results of the standard Transformer BASE on these benchmarks. Row 2-4 demonstrate results from existing curriculum learning approaches. Row 5 shows the results of our Transformer BASE implementation, and row 6-7 are the results of our proposed CL models. For En-De, if existing works report results on one of newstest2014 and newstest2017, then only the reported one is shown. We report results on them both for fair comparison.

We train our implemented baseline of Transformer BASE and proposed CL models for 300k steps. For both SGCL Fixed and SGCL Dynamic methods, we observe superior performances over the strong baseline on all three test sets of two benchmarks, which agree with existing approaches that curriculum learning can facilitate the NMT model. And if we compare the two scheduling methods, SGCL Dynamic outperforms SGCL Fixed. A possible reason is that the dynamic schedule encourages the CL model to spend more steps on the more difficult subset. Encouragingly, we observe considerable gains over other curriculum learning counterparts.

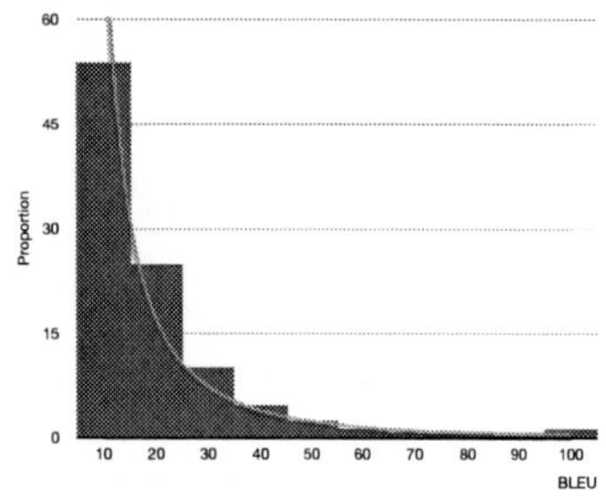

Figure 3: Recovery degree (sentence-level BLEU) distribution of the training set.

Subset	Range	Average
$\mathbb{D}_1$	17.72 - 100.00	35.62
$\mathbb{D}_2$	9.18 - 17.72	12.77
$\mathbb{D}_3$	5.16 - 9.18	6.97
$\mathbb{D}_4$	0.00 - 5.16	3.35

Table 3: Range and average of recovery degree (sentence-level BLEU) in subsets $\{\mathbb{D}_1, \mathbb{D}_2, \mathbb{D}_3, \mathbb{D}_4\}$

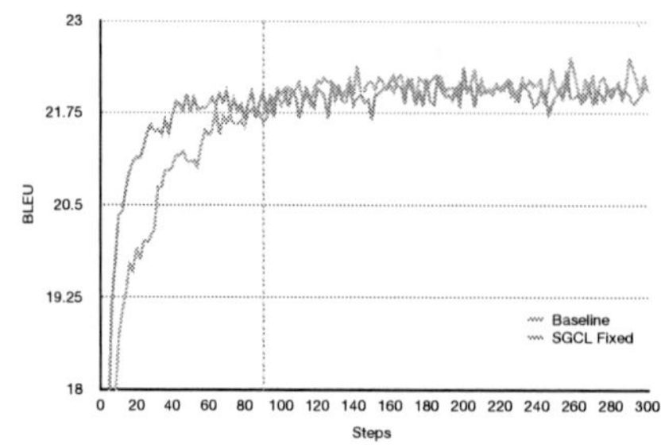

(a) Baseline vs. SGCL Fixed

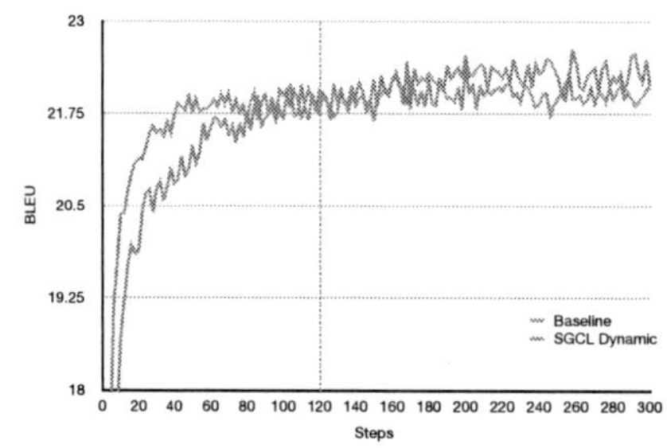

(b) Baseline vs. SGCL Dynamic

Figure 4: Learning curves w.r.t BLEU scores.

6 Analysis

6.1 Recovery Degree

We conduct experiments on En-De for further analysis of the proposed CL methods.

As described in Section 3, we adopt sentence-level BLEU score to measure the recovery degrees of all examples in the training corpus with a vanilla NMT model. When making predictions with the vanilla model, we set the beam size to 1 for simplicity. So the recovery degrees could be lower than test results of a strong baseline. If we look at the distribution in terms of BLEU score on all training examples, as Figure 3 illustrated, the distribution is very dense in the region with lower scores. Specifically, more than 53.9% training examples get a recovery degree lower than 10. It reflects the distribution shift problem of well-trained vanilla NMT mode, that the model learned distribution and empirical distribution on training corpus are inconsistent.

In our case, the training corpus is split into 4 subsets with about equal size, $\{\mathbb{D}_1, \mathbb{D}_2, \mathbb{D}_3, \mathbb{D}_4\}$. Table 3 is the range and average of recovery degrees of each subset, revealing the learning difficulty of each subset merges into training set as training phase progress. We also look at the average lengths of source sentences in these 4 subsets, which are 22.40, 23.84, 25.33, 29.35, reflecting a gentle increase. As a comparison, if we sort the training examples by lengths of source sentences and split them into 4 subsets, the average lengths become 10.96, 18.66, 27.00, 44.30. So we can infer that the recovery degree is related to but not fully depend on sentence length, indicating that shorter sentences are not always easier to be masted by the NMT model.

6.2 Learning Curves

Figure 4 demonstrates the learning curves of baseline vs. SGCL Fixed and baseline vs. SGCL Dynamic. As illustrated, the baseline converges faster at the beginning but stays at a lower level as training progresses, while proposed CL methods show constant improvements and outperform the baseline in the later training process. A possible reason that the CL models don't outperform the baseline at the beginning might be, they boost their performance after all training examples are merged into the training set. After all training examples are included, CL models are able to maintain better growth momentum than the baseline.

We also observe that the SGCL Dynamic gains more significant improvements over the baseline than the SGCL Fixed. Given 300k training steps, different curriculum schedules suggest different

Source	然而，就在大部分互联网医疗企业挣扎在A轮或B轮的融资路上的时候，有几家细分领域领先企业仍能获得资本热捧。
Reference	However, just as the majority of internet medical companies struggle on the way of a round or b round of financing, several segment-leading enterprises can still be favored by investors.
Vanilla (8.61)	However, even as most internet healthcare companies struggle to raise money in a or b rounds, a few of the leading segments still enjoy the capital boom.
SGCL (27.45)	However, even as most internet health companies struggle with a round or b round of financing, several segments leading business still enjoy the capital boom.

Table 4: Predictions made by the Vanilla model and the SGCL Dynamic model with a same input sentence. We mark the errors with red underline. The number in parentheses, e.g. (8.61) are sentence-level BLEU scores.

ways of splitting the training steps. For the SGCL Fixed, we empirically define the training steps spent on phase 1 to phase 4 as 30k, 30k, 30k, 210k. That is to say, after 90k steps, the model is training with all examples in the training corpus. For SGCL Dynamic, as mentioned in Section 3, if the CL model outperforms the vanilla model on the newly merged subset, training progresses to the next phase. In practice, after new examples merge into the training set, we first train for 20k steps and then check the performance of the CL model every 10k steps. As a result, the model starts to train with all training examples after 120k steps and tends to spend more time steps in later training phases, consistent with other existing dynamic scheduling methods.

6.3 Case Study

Figure 4 presents a case study in Zh-En. It indicates that our approach achieves a performance boost because of better lexical choice. To better understand how our approach alleviates the low-recovery problem, we conduct statistic analysis on the sentence-level BLEU scores of predictions made by the vanilla model and the CL model on the test set. It shows that the proportion of predictions with a BLEU score under 10 is 10.0% with the vanilla model and is down to 8.1% with the CL one.

7 Conclusion

In this work, we propose a self-guided CL strategy for neural machine translation. The intuition behind it is that after skimming through all training examples, the NMT model naturally learns how to schedule a curriculum for itself. We discuss existing difficulty criteria for curriculum learning from a probabilistic perspective, which also explains our motivation for deriving a difficulty criterion based on recovery degree. Moreover, we corporate this recovery-based difficulty criterion with both fixed and dynamic curriculum schedules. Empirical results show that with a self-guided CL strategy, the NMT model achieves better performance over the strong baseline on translation benchmarks. In the future, we will corporate recovery-based difficulty criterion with other dynamic scheduling methods. Also, it will be interesting to apply our proposed CL strategy to different scenarios, e.g., non-autoregressive generation (Gu et al., 2018; Wu et al., 2020a; Ding et al., 2020b).

Acknowledgments

Lei Zhou is supported by a project commissioned by the New Energy and Industrial Technology Development Organization (NEDO). The authors wish to thank the anonymous reviewers for their insightful comments and suggestions.

References

Yoshua Bengio, Jérôme Louradour, Ronan Collobert, and Jason Weston. 2009. Curriculum learning. In *ACM*.

Boxing Chen and Colin Cherry. 2014. A systematic comparison of smoothing techniques for sentence-level bleu. In *WMT*.

Volkan Cirik, Eduard Hovy, and Louis-Philippe Morency. 2016. Visualizing and understanding curriculum learning for long short-term memory networks. *CoRR*.

Michael Collins, Philipp Koehn, and Ivona Kučerová. 2005. Clause restructuring for statistical machine translation. In *ACL*.

Liang Ding and Dacheng Tao. 2019. The University of Sydney's machine translation system for WMT19. In *WMT*.

Liang Ding, Longyue Wang, and Dacheng Tao. 2020a. Self-attention with cross-lingual position representation. In *ACL*.

Liang Ding, Longyue Wang, Di Wu, Dacheng Tao, and Zhaopeng Tu. 2020b. Context-aware cross-attention for non-autoregressive translation. In *COLING*.

Zi-Yi Dou, Antonios Anastasopoulos, and Graham Neubig. 2020. Dynamic data selection and weighting for iterative back-translation. In *EMNLP*.

Jeffrey L Elman. 1993. Learning and development in neural networks: The importance of starting small. *Cognition*.

Jiatao Gu, James Bradbury, Caiming Xiong, Victor O. K. Li, and R. Socher. 2018. Non-autoregressive neural machine translation. In *ICLR*.

Hany Hassan, Anthony Aue, Chang Chen, Vishal Chowdhary, Jonathan Clark, Christian Federmann, Xuedong Huang, Marcin Junczys-Dowmunt, William Lewis, Mu Li, et al. 2018. Achieving human parity on automatic chinese to english news translation. *arXiv*.

Lu Jiang, Deyu Meng, Qian Zhao, Shiguang Shan, and Alexander G Hauptmann. 2015. Self-paced curriculum learning. In *AAAI*.

Diederik P. Kingma and Jimmy Ba. 2015. Adam: A method for stochastic optimization. In *ICLR*.

Tom Kocmi and Ondřej Bojar. 2017. Curriculum learning and minibatch bucketing in neural machine translation. In *RANLP*.

Xuebo Liu, Houtim Lai, Derek F. Wong, and Lidia S. Chao. 2020. Norm-based curriculum learning for neural machine translation. In *ACL*.

Xuebo Liu, Longyue Wang, Derek F. Wong, Liang Ding, Lidia S. Chao, and Zhaopeng Tu. 2021. Understanding and improving encoder layer fusion in sequence-to-sequence learning. *ICLR*.

Myle Ott, Sergey Edunov, Alexei Baevski, Angela Fan, Sam Gross, Nathan Ng, David Grangier, and Michael Auli. 2019. fairseq: A fast, extensible toolkit for sequence modeling. In *NAACL-HLT*.

Kishore Papineni, Salim Roukos, Todd Ward, and Wei-Jing Zhu. 2002. Bleu: a method for automatic evaluation of machine translation. In *ACL*.

Emmanouil Antonios Platanios, Otilia Stretcu, Graham Neubig, Barnabas Poczos, and Tom Mitchell. 2019. Competence-based curriculum learning for neural machine translation. In *NAACL-HTL*.

Dana Ruiter, Josef van Genabith, and Cristina España-Bonet. 2020. Self-induced curriculum learning in self-supervised neural machine translation. In *EMNLP*.

Rico Sennrich, Barry Haddow, and Alexandra Birch. 2016. Neural machine translation of rare words with subword units. In *ACL*.

Ashish Vaswani, Noam Shazeer, Niki Parmar, Jakob Uszkoreit, Llion Jones, Aidan N Gomez, Lukasz Kaiser, and Illia Polosukhin. 2017. Attention is all you need. In *Neural IPS*.

Di Wu, Liang Ding, Fan Lu, and Jian Xie. 2020a. SlotRefine: A fast non-autoregressive model for joint intent detection and slot filling. In *EMNLP*.

Di Wu, Liang Ding, Shuo Yang, and Dacheng Tao. 2021. Slua: A super lightweight unsupervised word alignment model via cross-lingual contrastive learning. *ArXiv*.

Shuangzhi Wu, Xing Wang, Longyue Wang, Fangxu Liu, Jun Xie, Zhaopeng Tu, Shuming Shi, and Mu Li. 2020b. Tencent neural machine translation systems for the WMT20 news translation task. In *WMT*.

Chen Xu, Bojie Hu, Yufan Jiang, Kai Feng, Zeyang Wang, Shen Huang, Qi Ju, Tong Xiao, and Jingbo Zhu. 2020. Dynamic curriculum learning for low-resource neural machine translation. In *COLING*.

Runzhe Zhan, Xuebo Liu, Derek F Wong, and Lidia S Chao. 2021. Meta-curriculum learning for domain adaptation in neural machine translation. In *AAAI*.

Xuan Zhang, Gaurav Kumar, Huda Khayrallah, Kenton Murray, Jeremy Gwinnup, Marianna J Martindale, Paul McNamee, Kevin Duh, and Marine Carpuat. 2018. An empirical exploration of curriculum learning for neural machine translation. *arXiv*.

Xuan Zhang, Pamela Shapiro, Gaurav Kumar, Paul McNamee, Marine Carpuat, and Kevin Duh. 2019. Curriculum learning for domain adaptation in neural machine translation. In *NAACL*.

Lei Zhou, Liang Ding, and Koichi Takeda. 2020a. Zero-shot translation quality estimation with explicit cross-lingual patterns. In *WMT*.

Yikai Zhou, Baosong Yang, Derek F. Wong, Yu Wan, and Lidia S. Chao. 2020b. Uncertainty-aware curriculum learning for neural machine translation. In *ACL*.

Between Flexibility and Consistency: Joint Generation of Captions and Subtitles

Alina Karakanta[1,2], **Marco Gaido**[1,2], **Matteo Negri**[1], **Marco Turchi**[1]
[1] Fondazione Bruno Kessler, Via Sommarive 18, Povo, Trento - Italy
[2] University of Trento, Italy
akarakanta,mgaido,negri,turchi}@fbk.eu

Abstract

Speech translation (ST) has lately received growing interest for the generation of subtitles without the need for an intermediate source language transcription and timing (i.e. captions). However, the joint generation of source captions and target subtitles does not only bring potential output quality advantages when the two decoding processes inform each other, but it is also often required in multilingual scenarios. In this work, we focus on ST models which generate consistent captions-subtitles in terms of structure and lexical content. We further introduce new metrics for evaluating subtitling consistency. Our findings show that joint decoding leads to increased performance and consistency between the generated captions and subtitles while still allowing for sufficient flexibility to produce subtitles conforming to language-specific needs and norms.

1 Introduction

New trends in media localisation call for the rapid generation of subtitles for vast amounts of audiovisual content. Speech translation, and especially direct approaches (Bérard et al., 2016; Bahar et al., 2019), have recently shown promising results with high efficiency because they do not require a transcription (manual or automatic) of the source speech but generate the target language subtitles directly from the audio. However, obtaining the intralingual subtitles (hereafter "captions") is necessary for a range of applications, while in some settings captions need to be displayed along with the target language subtitles. Such "bilingual subtitles" are useful in multilingual online meetings, in countries with multiple official languages, or for language learners and audiences with different accessibility needs. In those cases, captions and subtitles should not only be consistent with the visual and acoustic dimension of the audiovisual material but also between each other, for example in the number of blocks (pieces of time-aligned text) they occupy, their length and segmentation. Consistency is vital for user experience, for example in order to elicit the same reaction among multilingual audiences, or to facilitate the quality assurance process in the localisation industry.

Previous work in ST for subtitling has focused on generating interlingual subtitles (Matusov et al., 2019; Karakanta et al., 2020a), a) without considering the necessity of obtaining captions consistent with the target subtitles, and b) without examining whether the joint generation leads to improvements in quality. We hypothesise that knowledge sharing between the tasks of transcription and translation could lead to such improvements. Moreover, joint generation with a single system can avoid the maintenance of two different models, increase efficiency, and in turn speed up the localisation process. Lastly, if joint generation improves consistency, joint models could increase automation in subtitling applications where consistency is a desideratum.

In this work, we address these issues for the first time, by jointly generating both captions and subtitles for the same audio source. We experiment with the following models: 1) **Shared Direct** (Weiss et al., 2017), where the speech encoder is shared between the transcription and the translation decoder, 2) **Two-Stage** (Kano et al., 2017), where the transcript decoder states are passed to the translation decoder, and 3) **Triangle** (Anastasopoulos and Chiang, 2018), which extends the two-stage by adding a second attention mechanism to the translation decoder which attends to encoded speech inputs. We compare these models with the established approaches in ST for subtitling: an independent direct ST model and a cascade (ASR+MT) model. Moreover, we extend the evaluation beyond the usual metrics used to assess transcription and

Proceedings of the 18th International Conference on Spoken Language Translation, pages 215–225
Bangkok, Thailand (Online), August 5–6, 2021. ©2021 Association for Computational Linguistics

translation quality (respectively WER and BLEU), by also evaluating the form and consistency of the generated subtitles.

Sperber et al. (2020) introduced several lexical and surface metrics to measure consistency of ST outputs, but they were only applied to standard, non-subtitle, texts. Subtitles, however, are a particular type of text structured in blocks which accompany the action on screen. Therefore, we propose to measure their consistency by taking advantage of this structure and introduce metrics able to reward subtitles that share similar structure and content.

Our contributions can be summarised as follows:

- We employ ST to directly generate both captions and subtitles without the need for human pre-processing (transcription, segmentation).
- We propose new, task-specific metrics to evaluate subtitling consistency, a challenging and understudied problem in subtitling evaluation.
- We show increased performance and consistency between the generated captions and subtitles compared to independent decoding, while preserving adequate conformity to subtitling constraints.

2 Background

2.1 Bilingual subtitles

New life conditions maximised the time spent in front of screens, transforming today's mediascape in a complex puzzle of new actors, voices and workflows. Face-to-face meetings and conferences moved online, opening up participation for global audiences. In these new settings multilinguality and versatility are dominant, and manifested in business meetings with international partners, conferences with world-wide coverage, multilingual classrooms and audiences with mixed accessibility needs. Given these growing needs for providing inclusive and equal access to audiovisual material for a multifaceted audience spectrum, efficiently obtaining high-quality captions and subtitles is becoming increasingly relevant.

Traditionally, displaying subtitles in two languages in parallel (bilingual or dual subtitles) has been common in countries with more than one official languages, such as Belgium and Finland (Gottlieb, 2004). Recently, however, captions along with subtitles have been employed in other countries to attract wider audiences, e.g. in Mainland China English captions are displayed along with Mandarin subtitles. Interestingly, despite doubling the amount of text that appears on the screen and the high redundancy, it has been shown that bilingual subtitles do not significantly increase users' cognitive load (Liao et al., 2020).

One group which undoubtedly benefits from the parallel presence of captions and subtitles are language learners. Captions have been found to increase learners' L2 vocabulary (Sydorenko, 2010) and improve listening comprehension (Guichon and McLornan, 2008). Subtitles in the learners' native language (L1) are an indispensable tool for comprehension and access to information, especially for beginners. In bilingual subtitles, the captions support learners in understanding the speech and acquiring terminology, while subtitles serve as a dictionary, facilitating bilingual mapping (García, 2017). Consistency is particularly important for bilingual subtitles. Terms should fall in the same block and in similar positions. Moreover, similar length and equal number of lines can prevent long distance saccades, assisting in spotting the necessary information in the two language versions. Several subtitling tools have recently allowed for combining captions and subtitles on the same video (e.g. Dualsub[1]) and bilingual subtitles can be obtained for Youtube videos[2] and TED Talks.[3]

Another aspect where consistency between captions and subtitles is present is in subtitling templates. A subtitling template is a source language/English version of a subtitle file already segmented and containing timestamps, which is used to directly translate the text in target languages while preserving the same structure (Cintas and Remael, 2007; Georgakopoulou, 2019; Netflix, 2021). This process reduces the cost, turn-around times and effort needed to create a separate timed version for each language, and facilitates quality assurance since errors can be spotted across the same blocks (Nikolić, 2015). These benefits motivated our work towards simultaneously generating two language versions with the maximum consistency, where the caption file can further serve as a template for multilingual localisation. This paper is a first step towards maximising automation for the generation of high-quality multiple language/accessibility subtitle versions.

[1] https://www.dualsub.xyz/

[2] https://www.watch-listen-read.com/

[3] https://amara.org/en/teams/ted/

2.2 MT and ST for subtitling

Subtitling has long sparked the interest of the Machine Translation (MT) community as a challenging type of translation. Most works employing MT for subtitling stem from the statistical era (Volk et al., 2010; Etchegoyhen et al., 2014) or even before, with example-based approaches (Melero et al., 2006; Armstrong et al., 2006; Nyberg and Mitamura, 1997; Popowich et al., 2000; Piperidis et al., 2005). With the neural era, the interest in automatic approaches to subtitling revived. Neural Machine Translation (NMT) led to higher performance and efficiency and opened new paths and opportunities. Matusov et al. (2019) customised a cascade of ASR and NMT for subtitling, using domain adaptation with fine-tuning and improving subtitle segmentation with a specific segmentation module. Similarly, using cascades, Koponen et al. (2020) explored sentence- and document-level NMT for subtitling and showed productivity gains for some language pairs. However, bypassing the need to train and maintain separate components for transcription, translation and segmentation, direct end-to-end ST systems are now being considered as a valid and potentially more promising alternative (Karakanta et al., 2020a). Indeed, besides the architectural advantages, they come with the promise to avoid error propagation (a well known issue of cascade solutions), reduce latency, and better exploit speech information (e.g. prosody) without loss of information thanks to a less mediated access to the source utterance. To our knowledge, no previous work has yet explored the effectiveness of joint automatic generation of captions and subtitles.

2.3 Joint generation of transcription and translation

The idea of generating transcript and translation has been previously addressed in (Weiss et al., 2017; Anastasopoulos and Chiang, 2018). These papers presented different solutions (e.g. shared decoder and triangle) with the goal of improving translation performance by leveraging both ASR and ST data in direct ST. Later, Sperber et al. (2020) evaluated these methods with the focus of jointly producing consistent source and target language texts. Their underlying intuition is that, since in cascade solutions the translation is derived from the transcript, cascades should achieve higher consistency than direct solutions. Their results, however, showed that triangle models achieve the highest consistency among the architectures tested (considerably better than that of cascade systems) and have competitive performance in terms of translation quality. Direct independent and shared models, instead, do not achieve the translation quality and consistency of cascades. However, all these previous efforts fall outside the domain of automatic subtitling and ignore the inner structure of the subtitles and their relevance when considering consistency.

3 Methodology

3.1 Models

To study the effectiveness of the different existing ST approaches in the subtitling scenario, we experiment with the following models:

The **Multitask Direct Model (DirMu)** model consists of a single audio encoder and two separate decoders (Weiss et al., 2017): one for generating the source language captions, and the other for the target language subtitles. The weights of the encoder are shared. The model can exploit knowledge sharing between the two tasks, but allows for some degree of flexibility since inference for one task is not directly influenced by the other task.

The **Two-Stage (2ST)** model (Kano et al., 2017) also has two decoders, but the transcription decoder states are passed to the translation decoder. This is the only source of information for the translation decoder as it does not attend to the encoder output.

The **Triangle (Tri)** model (Anastasopoulos and Chiang, 2018) is similar to the two-stage model, but with the addition of an attention mechanism to the translation decoder, which attends to the output embeddings of the encoder. Both `2ST` and `Tri` support coupled inference and joint training.

We compare these models with common solutions for ST. The **Cascade (Cas)** model is a combination of an ASR + NMT components; the ASR transcribes the audio into text in the source language, which is then passed to an NMT system for translation into the target language. The two components are trained separately and can therefore take advantage of richer data for the two tasks. The cascade features full dependence between transcription and translation, which will potentially lead to high consistency.

The **Direct Independent (DirInd)** system consists of two independent direct ST models, one for the transcription (as in the ASR component of the cascade) and one for the translation. It hence lies on the flexibility edge of flexibility-consistency spectrum compared to the models above.

3.2 Evaluation of subtitling consistency

While some metrics for evaluating transcription-translation consistency have been proposed in (Sperber et al., 2020), these do not capture the peculiarities of subtitling. The goal for consistent captions/subtitles is having the same structure (same number of subtitle blocks) and same content (each pair of caption-subtitle blocks has the same lexical content). Consider the following example:

0:00:50,820, 00:00:53,820
To put the assumptions very clearly:
Enonçons clairement nos hypothèses : le capitalisme,

00:00:53,820, 00:00:57,820
capitalism, after 150 years, has become acceptable,
après 150 ans, est devenu acceptable, au même titre

00:00:58,820, 00:01:00,820
and so has democracy.
que la démocratie.

In the example above, three blocks appear sequentially on the screen based on timestamp information, and each of them contains one line of text in English (caption) and French (subtitle). Since the source utterance is split across the same number of blocks (3), the captions and subtitles have the same structure. However, the captions and subtitles do not have the same lexical content. The first block contains the French words *le capitalisme*, which appear in the second block for the English captions. Similarly, *au même titre* corresponds to the third block in relation to the captions. This is problematic because terms do not appear in the same blocks (e.g. capitalism), and also leads to sub-optimal segmentation, since the French subtitles are not complete semantic units (logical completion occurs after *hypothèses* and *acceptable*).

We hence define the consistency between captions and subtitles based on two aspects: the structural and the lexical consistency. Structural consistency refers to the way subtitles are distributed on a video. In order to be structurally consistent, captions and subtitles for each source utterance should be split across the same number of blocks. This is a prerequisite for bilingual subtitles, since each caption-subtitle pair has the same timestamps. In other words, the captions and subtitles should appear and disappear simultaneously. Therefore, we define **structural consistency** as the percentage of utterances having the same number of blocks between captions and subtitles.

The second aspect of subtitling consistency is lexical consistency. Lexical consistency means that each caption-subtitle pair has the same lexical content. It is particularly important for ensuring synchrony between the content displayed in the captions and subtitles. This facilitates language learning, when terms appear in similar positions, and quality assurance, as it is easier to spot errors in parallel text. We define **lexical consistency** as the percentage of words in each caption-subtitle pair that are aligned to words belonging in the same block. In our example, there are six tokens of the subtitles which are not aligned to captions of the same block: *le capitalisme , au même titre*. For obtaining this score, we compute the number of words in each caption aligned to the corresponding subtitle and vice versa. For each caption-subtitle pair, this process results in two lexical consistency scores: $\text{Lex}_{caption \to subtitle}$ and $\text{Lex}_{subtitle \to caption}$, where, in the former, the number of aligned words is normalised by the number of words in the caption, while, in the latter, by the number of words in the subtitle. These two quantities are then averaged into a single value (Lex_{pair}). The corpus-level lexical consistency is obtained by averaging the Lex_{pair} of all caption-subtitle pairs in the test set.

4 Experimental setting

4.1 Data

For our experiments we use MuST-Cinema (Karakanta et al., 2020b), an ST corpus compiled from subtitles of TED talks. For a sound comparison with Karakanta et al. (2020a), we conduct the experiments on 2 language pairs, English→French and English→German. The breaks between subtitles are marked with special symbols, <eob> for breaks between blocks of subtitles and <eol> for new lines inside the same block. The training data contain 408 and 492 hours of pre-segmented audio (229K and 275K sentences) for German and French respectively. For tuning and evaluation we use the official development and test sets. We expect the captions and subtitles of TED Talks to have high consistency, since the captions serve as the basis for translating the speech in target subtitles.

The text data is segmented into sub-words with Sentencepiece (Kudo and Richardson, 2018) with the unigram setting. In line with recent works in ST, we found that a small vocabulary size is beneficial for the performance of ST models. Therefore, we set a shared vocabulary of 1024 for all models except the MT component of the cascade, where vocabulary size is set to 24k. The special symbols <eob> and <eol> are kept as a single token.

For the audio input, we use 40-dimensional log Mel filterbank speech features. The ASR encoder was pretrained on the IWSLT 2020 data, i.e. Europarl-ST (Iranzo-Sánchez et al., 2020), Librispeech (Panayotov et al., 2015), How2 (Sanabria et al., 2018), Mozilla Common-Voice,[4] MuST-C (Cattoni et al., 2020), and the ST TED corpus.[5]

4.2 Model training

The ASR and ST models are trained using the same settings. The architecture used is S-Transformer, (Di Gangi et al., 2019), an ST adaptation of Transformer, which has been shown to achieve high performance on different speech translation benchmarks. Following state-of-the-art systems (Potapczyk and Przybysz, 2020; Gaido et al., 2020), we do not add 2D self-attentions. The size of the encoder is set to 11 layers, and to 4 layers for the decoder. The ASR model used to pretrain the encoder, instead, has 8 encoder and 6 decoder layers. The additional 3 encoder layers are initialised randomly, similarly to the adaptation layer proposed by Bahar et al. (2019). As distance penalty, we choose the logarithmic distance penalty. We optimise using Adam (Kingma and Ba, 2015) (betas 0.9, 0.98), 4000 warm-up steps with initial learning rate of 0.0003, and learning rate decay with the inverse square root of the iteration. We apply label smoothing of 0.1, and dropout (Srivastava et al., 2014) is set to 0.2. We further use SpecAugment (Park et al., 2019), a technique for online data augmentation, with augment rate of 0.5. Training is completed when the validation perplexity does not improve for 3 consecutive epochs.

The MT component is based on the Transformer architecture (big) (Vaswani et al., 2017) with similar settings to the original paper. Since the ASR component outputs punctuation, no other pre-processing (except for BPE) is applied to the training data. In order to ensure a fair comparison with the direct and joint models, the MT component is trained only on MuST-Cinema data.

All experiments are run with the fairseq toolkit (Ott et al., 2019). Training is performed on two K80 GPUs with 11 GB memory and models converged in about five days. Our implementation of the `DirMu`, `Tri` and `2ST` models is publicly available at: `https://github.com/mgaido91/FBK-fairseq-ST/tree/acl_2021`

[4] `https://voice.mozilla.org/`

[5] `http://iwslt.org/doku.php?id=offline_speech_translation`

4.3 Evaluation

We evaluate three aspects of the automatically generated captions and subtitles: 1) quality, 2) form, and 3) consistency. For **quality** of transcription we compute WER on unpunctuated, lowercased output, while for quality of translation we use SacreBLEU (Post, 2018).[6] We report scores computed at the level of utterances, where the output sentences contain subtitle breaks. A break symbol is considered as another token contributing to the score.

For evaluating the **form** of the subtitles, we focus on the conformity to the subtitling constraints of length and reading speed, as well as proper segmentation, as proposed in (Karakanta et al., 2019). We compute the percentage of subtitles conforming to a maximum length of 42 characters/line and a maximum reading speed of 21 characters/second.[7] The plausibility of segmentation is evaluated based on syntactic properties. Subtitle breaks should be placed in such a way that keeps syntactic and semantic units together. For example, an adjective should not be separated from the noun it describes. We consider as plausible only those breaks following punctuation marks or those between a content word (chunk) and a function word (chink). We obtain Universal Dependencies[8] PoS-tags using the Stanza toolkit (Qi et al., 2020) and calculate the percentage of break symbols falling either in the punctuation or the content-function groups as plausible segmentation.

Lastly, we evaluate structural and lexical **consistency** between the generated captions and corresponding subtitles, as described in Section 3.2. Word alignments are obtained using fast_align (Dyer et al., 2013) on the concatenation of MuST-Cinema training data and the system outputs. Text is tokenised using Moses tokeniser and the consistency percentage is computed on tokenised text.

En→Fr	WER	SacreBLEU	Length	Read_speed	Segment.	Struc.	Lex.
Cas	19.69	**26.9**	.94 / .93	.85 / .70	.86 / .82	**.98**	**.99**
DirInd	19.69	24.0	.94 / **.94**	.85 / **.73**	.86 / **.84**	.75	.86
DirMu	**17.73**	25.2	**.95** / .93	.85 / **.73**	**.87** / .80	.77	.87
2ST	19.05	25.6	**.95** / **.94**	.85 / .71	**.87** / .82	.83	.84
Tri	18.93	25.3	.93 / .91	.85 / .72	**.87** / .82	.82	.92
En→De							
Cas	18.52	**19.9**	.94 / .90	.62 / .58	.86 / .76	**.95**	**.96**
DirInd	18.52	18.1	.94 / **.92**	.62 / .59	.86 / **.78**	.73	.86
DirMu	**16.95**	18.7	**.95** / **.92**	.62 / .59	**.87** / .73	.75	.82
2ST	18.93	*19.6*	.94 / **.92**	.62 / **.60**	.86 / .76	.82	.81
Tri	19.10	*19.8*	.93 / **.92**	.62 / **.60**	**.87** / .76	.78	.91

Table 1: Results for quality (WER and BLEU), subtitling conformity (Length, Reading speed and Segmentation), and subtitling consistency (Structural and Lexical) for model outputs for French and German. Conformity scores are reported for captions / subtitles. **Bold** denotes the best score. Results that are not statistically significant – according to pairwise bootstrap resampling (Koehn, 2004), p<0.05 – than the best score are reported in *italics*.

5 Results

5.1 Transcription/Translation quality

We first examine the quality of the systems' outputs. The first two columns of Table 1 show the WER and SacreBLEU score for the examined models.

In terms of **transcription quality**, `DirMu` (Multitask Direct – see Section 3.1) obtains the lowest WER for both languages (17.73 for French and 16.95 for German). As far as the rest of the models are concerned, there is a different tendency for French and German. `Tri` (Triangle) and `2ST` (Two-Stage) perform equally better than the `Cas`/`DirInd` for French, while the `Cas`/`DirInd` have higher transcription quality than `Tri` and `2ST` for German. An explanation for this incongruity is that these two models perform coupled inference, therefore the benefit of the joint decoding for the transcription can be related to similarities in terms of vocabulary between the two languages. Since French has a higher vocabulary similarity to English, with many words in TED Talks being cognates (e.g. specialised terminology), it is possible that joint decoding favours the transcription for French but not for German.

When it comes to **translation quality**, `Cas` outperforms all other models for French with 26.9 BLEU points, while the differences are not statistically significant among `DirMu`, `2ST` and `Tri`. For German, however, `Cas`, `2ST` and `Tri` perform on par. The model obtaining the lowest scores is `DirInd`. This finding confirms our hypothesis that joint decoding, despite being more complex, improves translation quality thanks to the knowledge shared between the two tasks at decoding time.

In comparison to previous works, our transcription results are contrary to Sperber et al. (2020), who obtained the lowest WER with the cascade and direct independent models. However, for translation quality our best models are `Cas`, `2ST` and `Tri`, as in previous work. Moreover, in line with Anastasopoulos and Chiang (2018), the gains for `Tri` are higher for translation than for transcription. Comparing the BLEU score of our `DirInd` models to the models in (Karakanta et al., 2020a), we found that our models achieve higher performance with 20.07 BLEU compared to 18.76 for French and 13.55 compared to 11.92 for German.

All in all, we found that coupled-inference, supported by `Cas`, `2ST` and `Tri`, improves translation but not transcription quality. On the contrary, multitasking as in `DirMu` is beneficial for transcription, possibly because of a reinforcement of the speech encoder. However, could this improvement come at the expense of conformity to the subtitling constraints?

5.2 Subtitling conformity

Columns 3-5 of Table 1 show the percentage of captions/subtitles conforming to the length, reading speed and segmentation constraints discussed in Section 4.3. We observe that joint decoding does not lead to significant losses in conformity. Specifically, the captions generated by `DirMu` have the highest conformity in terms of length (95%), reading speed (85% and 62%) and segmentation quality (87%). Moreover, the high conformity score for

[6] `BLEU+c.mixed+#.1+s.exp+tok.13a+v.1.4.3`

[7] In line with the TED Talk guidelines: `https://www.ted.com/participate/translate/guidelines`

[8] `https://universaldependencies.org/`

DirMu correlates with the low WER, showing that quality goes hand-in-hand with conformity.

For the conformity of the target language subtitles, instead, the picture is different. Even though the differences are not large, Cas has lower conformity to length (93% and 90%) and reading speed (70% and 58%). The segmentation scores show that, despite their high translation quality, the systems featuring coupled inference (Cas, Tri and 2ST) are constrained by the structure of the captions and segment subtitles in positions which are not optimal for the target language norms (82% and 76%). DirInd, on the contrary, has higher conformity compared to the other models (94% and 92% for length, 73% and 59% for reading speed), as well as segmentation quality (84% and 78%). DirInd is left to determine the most plausible segmentation for the target language without being bound by consistency constraints from the source. The lowest segmentation quality of subtitles is achieved by DirMu (80% and 73%).

We can conclude that the quality improvements of coupled inference and multi-tasking come with a slight compromise of subtitling conformity, as a result of loss of flexibility in decoding.

5.3 Subtitling consistency

The last two columns of Table 1 present the results for the subtitling consistency.

In terms of **Structural consistency** (Struc.), the model achieving the highest scores is Cas, with 98% and 95% of the utterances being distributed along the same number of blocks. As expected, the lowest structural consistency is achieved by DirInd (75% and 73%), which determines independently the positions of the block symbols. Among the joint models, Tri outputs captions and subtitles with higher consistency than DirMu, but both are outperformed by 2ST (83% and 82%). Our hypothesis is that by attending only the caption decoder, 2ST behaves similarly to the cascade, and the translation decoder better replicates the block structure. We noted that the reference captions and subtitles have lower consistency (92% both for French and German) than the cascade. This shows that the cascade copies the same <eob> tokens and achieves extreme structural consistency, which is a desideratum for our study case but may be harmful in other scenarios, since it leads to lower conformity (see Section 5.2). Indeed, in scenarios where consistency is not a key, subtitlers should have the flexibility to adjust subtitling segmentation to suit the needs of their target languages (Oziemblewska and Szarkowska, 2020).

The **Lexical consistency** (Lex.) results show that Cas is the model with the highest content overlap in parallel caption-subtitle blocks with 99% and 96% of the words being aligned to the same block. As with the structural consistency, the lexical consistency of the cascade is higher than the references (95% for French, 86% for German). The direct model with the highest lexical consistency is Tri (92% and 91%). Interestingly, despite its high structural consistency, 2ST does not distribute the content consistently in the parallel blocks, achieving the lowest conformity (81%). The DirMu also achieves lower consistency than DirInd for German (82% compared to 86%) but not for French (87% compared to 86%). It is worth noting that lexical consistency is generally lower for German than for French. Indeed, a 100% lexical consistency between subtitles in languages with different word order is not always feasible or even appropriate. For example, the main verb in an English subordinate clause appears in the second position while in German at the end of the sentence. In order to adhere to grammatical rules, words in subtitles of different languages often have inter-block reordering. Therefore, the balance between flexibility and consistency is manifested here as a compromise between grammaticallity and preservation of the same lexical content on each pair of subtitles.

To sum up, the results of structural consistency show that the models are able to preserve the block structure between captions and subtitles in more than 75% of the utterances. In addition, the high lexical consistency shows that the block symbols are not inserted randomly, but placed in a way that preserves the same lexical content in the parallel blocks.

All in all, our results show that the evaluation of captions and subtitles is a multifaceted process that needs to be addressed from multiple aspects: quality, conformity and consistency. Missing one of the three can lead to wrong conclusions. For instance, only considering quality and consistency could lead to disregard the importance of conformity and consider independent solutions an obsolete technology. Secondly, among the Direct architectures, the use of techniques that allow linking the generation process of captions and subtitles helps to achieve overall better quality and consistency than independent decoding, with a slight discount in conformity, especially for the target subtitles. Between the DirMu, 2ST and Tri, there is not a model that outperforms all the others in all the metrics, so the choice mainly depends on the application scenario. Lastly, comparing the Cascade and the Direct, the Cascade seems to be the best choice, but recent advancements in Direct approaches result in competitive solutions with increased efficiency of maintaining one model for both tasks.

6 Analysis

6.1 Evaluation of Lexical Consistency

In this section, we test the reliability of the lexical consistency metric. The metric depends on the successful word alignment, which, especially for low quality text, might be sub-optimal. We therefore manually count the number of words in the subtitles which do not appear in the corresponding captions. The task is performed on the first 347 sentences of the output of DirMu for French and German. We then estimate the mean absolute error between the consistency metric computed using the manual and the automatic alignments. As an additional step, we compute how often the automatic and the manual annotations agree in their judgement of consistent/non-consistent content in each block.

The mean absolute error between the manually and the automatically computed score is .08 for French and .11 for German. The metric may not be able to account for very small score differences between systems, however, when inspecting the differences between manual and automatic annotation we noticed that most errors appear in very low quality outputs or where lexical content was missing, and lead to a misalignment of only a few words. These cases were in fact challenging even for the human annotator. Instead, the agreement in the consistent/not-consistent judgement is high, with .85 for French and .75 for German. Considering the difficulty of aligning sentences belonging to languages with different word ordering, and the lower quality of German outputs, it is not surprising that the word aligner from English to German affects more our metric. However, these results show that the real impact is moderate and the metric is consistent with the human judgements in the majority of cases.

6.2 Does structural consistency extend to line breaks?

But what happens with the line breaks? Does a one-line caption correspond to a one-line subtitle in the output of our models? Having the same number of lines between caption and subtitle blocks is a more challenging scenario, since the subtitles tend to expand because of different length ratios between languages and translation strategies such as explicitation. For instance, for the target languages considered in this work (French and German) the length of the target subtitles when subtitling from English has been reported to be 5%-35% higher.[9] If structural consistency is enforced to line breaks, it may compromise either the quality of the translation or the conformity to the subtitling constraints. In case of a one-liner caption, important information may be not rendered in the corresponding subtitle in order to match a shorter length of the caption, or the length constraint will be violated since the longer subtitle will not be adequately segmented in two lines. In order to ensure that our models do not push the structural consistency to an extreme, we compute the percentage of caption-subtitle blocks having the same number of lines.

	Cas	DirInd	DirMu	2ST	Tri	Ref
Fr	67%	49%	54%	59%	57%	67%
De	66%	47%	55%	53%	51%	66%

Table 2: Percentage of subtitle blocks containing the same number of lines for French and German outputs.

Table 2 confirms that caption and subtitle blocks do not always have the same number of lines, since only 67% and 66% of blocks in the caption/subtitle references have the same number of lines. When it comes to the models, the cascade exactly matches the percentages of the references, while the direct models have even lower percentage of equal number of lines. Among the direct models, again the DirInd shows the lowest similarity. We observed that more line breaks were present in the target subtitles, which ensures length conformity, since the target subtitles expand (source-target character ratio of 0.91 for French and 0.93 for German).

[9] https://www.andiamo.co.uk/resources/expansion-and-contraction-factors/ http://www.aranchodoc.com/wp-content/uploads/2017/07/Text-Expansion-Contraction-Chart3.png https://www.kwintessential.co.uk/resources/expansion-retraction

Therefore, the fact that structural consistency allows for flexibility in relation to the number and position of line breaks is key to achieving high quality and conformity.

7 Conclusions

In this work we explored joint generation of captions and subtitles as a way to increase efficiency and consistency in scenarios where this property is a desideratum. To this aim, we proposed metrics for evaluating subtitling consistency, tailored to the structural peculiarities of this type of translation. We found that coupled inference, either by models supporting end-to-end training (`2ST`, `Tri`) or not (`Cas`), leads to quality and consistency improvements, but with a slight degradation of the conformity to target subtitle constraints. The final architectural choice depends on the flexibility versus conformity requirements of the application scenario.

The findings of this work have provided initial insights related to the joint generation of captions and subtitles. One future research direction is towards improving the quality of generation by using more recent, higher-performing ST architectures. For example, Liu et al. (2020) extended the notion of the dual decoder by adding an interactive attention mechanism which allows the two decoders to exchange information and learn from each other, while synchronously generating transcription and translation. Le et al. (2020) proposed two variants of the dual decoder of Liu et al. (2020), the cross and parallel dual decoder, and experimented with multilingual ST. While neither of these works reported results on consistency, we expect that they are relevant to our scenario and have the potential of jointly generating multiple language/accessibility versions with high consistency. Moving beyond generic architectures, in the future we are planning to experiment with tailored architectures for improving consistency between automatically generated captions and subtitles. One important insight emerging from this work is that different degrees of conformity are required, or even appropriate, depending on the application scenario and languages involved. Given these challenges, we are aiming at developing approaches which allow for tuning the output to the desired degree of conformity, whether lexical, structural or both. We hope that this work will contribute to the line of research efforts towards improving efficiency and quality of automatically generated captions and subtitles.

References

Antonios Anastasopoulos and David Chiang. 2018. Tied multitask learning for neural speech translation. In *Proceedings of the 2018 Conference of the North American Chapter of the Association for Computational Linguistics: Human Language Technologies, Volume 1 (Long Papers)*, pages 82–91, New Orleans, Louisiana. Association for Computational Linguistics.

Stephen Armstrong, Colm Caffrey, and Marian Flanagan. 2006. Translating DVD Subtitles from English-German and English-Japanese Using Example-Based Machine Translation. In *MuTra 2006—Audiovisual Translation Scenarios: Conference Proceedings*.

Parnia Bahar, Tobias Bieschke, and Hermann Ney. 2019. A Comparative Study on End-to-end Speech to Text Translation. In *Proceedings of International Workshop on Automatic Speech Recognition and Understanding (ASRU)*, pages 792–799, Sentosa, Singapore.

Alexandre Bérard, Olivier Pietquin, Christophe Servan, and Laurent Besacier. 2016. Listen and Translate: A Proof of Concept for End-to-End Speech-to-Text Translation. In *NIPS Workshop on end-to-end learning for speech and audio processing*, Barcelona, Spain.

Roldano Cattoni, Mattia A. Di Gangi, Luisa Bentivogli, Matteo Negri, and Marco Turchi. 2020. MuST-C: A Multilingual Corpus for end-to-end Speech Translation. Computer Speech & Language Journal. Doi: https://doi.org/10.1016/j.csl.2020.101155.

Jorge Diaz Cintas and Aline Remael. 2007. *Audiovisual Translation: Subtitling*. Translation practices explained. Routledge.

Mattia Antonino Di Gangi, Matteo Negri, and Marco Turchi. 2019. Adapting Transformer to End-to-end Spoken Language Translation. In *INTERSPEECH*, pages 1133–1137.

Chris Dyer, Victor Chahuneau, and Noah A. Smith. 2013. A simple, fast, and effective reparameterization of IBM model 2. In *Proceedings of the 2013 Conference of the North American Chapter of the Association for Computational Linguistics: Human Language Technologies*, pages 644–648, Atlanta, Georgia. Association for Computational Linguistics.

Thierry Etchegoyhen, Lindsay Bywood, Mark Fishel, Panayota Georgakopoulou, Jie Jiang, Gerard van Loenhout, Arantza del Pozo, Mirjam Sepesy Maučec, Anja Turner, and Martin Volk. 2014. Machine Translation for Subtitling: A Large-Scale

Evaluation. In *Proceedings of the 9th International Conference on Language Resources and Evaluation (LREC)*, pages 46–53.

Marco Gaido, Mattia A. Di Gangi, Matteo Negri, and Marco Turchi. 2020. End-to-end speech-translation with knowledge distillation: FBK@IWSLT2020. In *Proceedings of the 17th International Conference on Spoken Language Translation*, pages 80–88, Online. Association for Computational Linguistics.

Boni García. 2017. Bilingual subtitles for second-language acquisition and application to engineering education as learning pills. *Computer Applications in Engineering Education*, 25(3):468–479.

Panayota Georgakopoulou. 2019. Template files: The Holy Grail of subtitling. *Journal of Audiovisual Translation*, 2(2):137–160.

Henrik Gottlieb. 2004. Subtitles and international anglification. *Nordic Journal of English Studies*, 3:219–230.

Nicolas Guichon and Sinead McLornan. 2008. The effects of multimodality on l2 learners: Implications for call resource design. *System*, pages 85–93.

Javier Iranzo-Sánchez, Joan Albert Silvestre-Cerdà, Javier Jorge, Nahuel Roselló, Giménez. Adrià, Albert Sanchis, Jorge Civera, and Alfons Juan. 2020. Europarl-ST: A Multilingual Corpus For Speech Translation Of Parliamentary Debates. In *Proceedings of 2020 IEEE International Conference on Acoustics, Speech and Signal Processing (ICASSP)*, pages 8229–8233, Barcelona, Spain.

Takatomo Kano, Sakriani Sakti, and Satoshi Nakamura. 2017. Structured-based Curriculum Learning for End-to-end English-Japanese Speech Translation. In *Annual Conference of the International Speech Communication Association (InterSpeech)*, pages 2630–2634.

Alina Karakanta, Matteo Negri, and Marco Turchi. 2019. Are Subtitling Corpora really Subtitle-like? In *Sixth Italian Conference on Computational Linguistics, CLiC-It*.

Alina Karakanta, Matteo Negri, and Marco Turchi. 2020a. Is 42 the answer to everything in subtitling-oriented speech translation? In *Proceedings of the 17th International Conference on Spoken Language Translation*, pages 209–219, Online. Association for Computational Linguistics.

Alina Karakanta, Matteo Negri, and Marco Turchi. 2020b. MuST-cinema: a speech-to-subtitles corpus. In *Proceedings of the 12th Language Resources and Evaluation Conference*, pages 3727–3734, Marseille, France. European Language Resources Association.

Diederik Kingma and Jimmy Ba. 2015. Adam: A method for stochastic optimization. In *3rd International Conference for Learning Representations*.

Philipp Koehn. 2004. Statistical Significance Tests for Machine Translation Evaluation. In *Proceedings of the 2004 Conference on Empirical Methods in Natural Language Processing*, pages 388–395, Barcelona, Spain. Association for Computational Linguistics.

Maarit Koponen, Umut Sulubacak, Kaisa Vitikainen, and Jörg Tiedemann. 2020. MT for subtitling: User evaluation of post-editing productivity. In *Proceedings of the 22nd Annual Conference of the European Association for Machine Translation (EAMT 2020)*, pages 115–124.

Taku Kudo and John Richardson. 2018. SentencePiece: A simple and language independent subword tokenizer and detokenizer for neural text processing. In *Proceedings of the 2018 Conference on Empirical Methods in Natural Language Processing: System Demonstrations*, pages 66–71, Brussels, Belgium. Association for Computational Linguistics.

Hang Le, Juan Pino, Changhan Wang, Jiatao Gu, Didier Schwab, and Laurent Besacier. 2020. Dual-decoder transformer for joint automatic speech recognition and multilingual speech translation. In *Proceedings of the 28th International Conference on Computational Linguistics*, pages 3520–3533, Barcelona, Spain (Online). International Committee on Computational Linguistics.

Sixin Liao, Jan-Louis Kruger, and Stephen Doherty. 2020. The impact of monolingual and bilingual subtitles on visual attention, cognitive load, and comprehension. *The Journal of Specialised Translation*.

Yuchen Liu, Jiajun Zhang, Hao Xiong, Long Zhou, Zhongjun He, Hua Wu, Haifeng Wang, and Chengqing Zong. 2020. Synchronous Speech Recognition and Speech-to-Text Translation with Interactive Decoding. In *The Thirty-Fourth AAAI Conference on Artificial Intelligence (AAAI-20)*. Association for the Advancement of Artificial Intelligence (www.aaai.org).

Evgeny Matusov, Patrick Wilken, and Yota Georgakopoulou. 2019. Customizing neural machine translation for subtitling. In *Proceedings of the Fourth Conference on Machine Translation (Volume 1: Research Papers)*, pages 82–93, Florence, Italy. Association for Computational Linguistics.

Maite Melero, Antoni Oliver, and Toni Badia. 2006. Automatic Multilingual Subtitling in the eTITLE Project. In *Proceedings of ASLIB Translating and the Computer 28*.

Netflix. 2021. Subtitle template timed text style guide. https://partnerhelp.netflixstudios.com/hc/en-us/articles/219375728-English-Template-Timed-Text-Style-Guide. Last accessed: 02/05/2021.

Kristijan Nikolić. 2015. The pros and cons of using templates in subtitling. In Rocío Baños Piñero and Jorge Díaz Cintas, editors, *Audiovisual Translation in a Global Context: Mapping an Ever-changing Landscape*, pages 192–202. Palgrave Macmillan UK, London.

Eric Nyberg and Teruko Mitamura. 1997. A Real-Time MT System for Translating Broadcast Captions. In *Proceedings of the Sixth Machine Translation Summit*, pages 51–57.

Myle Ott, Sergey Edunov, Alexei Baevski, Angela Fan, Sam Gross, Nathan Ng, David Grangier, and Michael Auli. 2019. fairseq: A fast, extensible toolkit for sequence modeling. In *Proceedings of the 2019 Conference of the North American Chapter of the Association for Computational Linguistics (Demonstrations)*, pages 48–53, Minneapolis, Minnesota. Association for Computational Linguistics.

Magdalena Oziemblewska and Agnieszka Szarkowska. 2020. The quality of templates in subtitling. A survey on current market practices and changing subtitler competences. *Perspectives*, 0(0):1–22.

Vassil Panayotov, Guoguo Chen, Daniel Povey, and Sanjeev Khudanpur. 2015. Librispeech: An ASR corpus based on public domain audio books. In *2015 IEEE International Conference on Acoustics, Speech and Signal Processing (ICASSP)*, pages 5206–5210, South Brisbane, Queensland, Australia.

Daniel S. Park, William Chan, Yu Zhang, Chung-Cheng Chiu, Barret Zoph, Ekin D. Cubuk, and Quoc V. Le. 2019. SpecAugment: A Simple Data Augmentation Method for Automatic Speech Recognition. *Interspeech 2019*.

Stelios Piperidis, Iason Demiros, and Prokopis Prokopidis. 2005. Infrastructure for a Multilingual Subtitle Generation System. In *9th International Symposium on Social Communication*, pages 24–28.

Fred Popowich, Paul McFetridge, Davide Turcato, and Janine Toole. 2000. Machine Translation of Closed Captions. *Machine Translation*, pages 311–341.

Matt Post. 2018. A call for clarity in reporting BLEU scores. In *Proceedings of the Third Conference on Machine Translation: Research Papers*, pages 186–191, Brussels, Belgium. Association for Computational Linguistics.

Tomasz Potapczyk and Pawel Przybysz. 2020. SR-POL's system for the IWSLT 2020 end-to-end speech translation task. In *Proceedings of the 17th International Conference on Spoken Language Translation*, pages 89–94, Online. Association for Computational Linguistics.

Peng Qi, Yuhao Zhang, Yuhui Zhang, Jason Bolton, and Christopher D. Manning. 2020. Stanza: A python natural language processing toolkit for many human languages. In *Proceedings of the 58th Annual Meeting of the Association for Computational Linguistics: System Demonstrations*, pages 101–108, Online. Association for Computational Linguistics.

Ramon Sanabria, Ozan Caglayan, Shruti Palaskar, Desmond Elliott, Loïc Barrault, Lucia Specia, and Florian Metze. 2018. How2: A Large-scale Dataset For Multimodal Language Understanding. In *Proceedings of Visually Grounded Interaction and Language (ViGIL)*, Montréal, Canada. Neural Information Processing Society (NeurIPS).

Matthias Sperber, Hendra Setiawan, Christian Gollan, Udhyakumar Nallasamy, and Matthias Paulik. 2020. Consistent transcription and translation of speech. *Transactions of the Association for Computational Linguistics*, 8:695–709.

Nitish Srivastava, Geoffrey E Hinton, Alex Krizhevsky, Ilya Sutskever, and Ruslan Salakhutdinov. 2014. Dropout: a simple way to prevent neural networks from overfitting. *Journal of machine learning research*, 15(1):1929–1958.

Tetyana Sydorenko. 2010. Modality of input and vocabulary acquisition. *Lang Learn Technol*, pages 50–73.

Ashish Vaswani, Noam Shazeer, Niki Parmar, Jakob Uszkoreit, Llion Jones, Aidan N Gomez, Łukasz Kaiser, and Illia Polosukhin. 2017. Attention is all you need. In *Advances in Neural Information Processing Systems*, pages 6000–6010.

Martin Volk, Rico Sennrich, Christian Hardmeier, and Frida Tidström. 2010. Machine Translation of TV Subtitles for Large Scale Production. In *Proceedings of the Second Joint EM+/CNGL Workshop "Bringing MT to the User: Research on Integrating MT in the Translation Industry (JEC'10)*, pages 53–62, Denver, CO.

Ron J. Weiss, Jan Chorowski, Navdeep Jaitly, Yonghui Wu, and Zhifeng Chen. 2017. Sequence-to-Sequence Models Can Directly Translate Foreign Speech. In *Proceedings of Interspeech 2017*, pages 2625–2629, Stockholm, Sweden.

Large-Scale English-Japanese Simultaneous Interpretation Corpus: Construction and Analyses with Sentence-Aligned Data

Kosuke Doi[1] **Katsuhito Sudoh**[1,2] **Satoshi Nakamura**[1,2]
[1]Nara Institute of Science and Technology
[2]AIP, RIKEN
{doi.kosuke.de8, sudoh, s-nakamura}@is.naist.jp

Abstract

This paper describes the construction of a new large-scale English-Japanese Simultaneous Interpretation (SI) corpus and presents the results of its analysis. A portion of the corpus contains SI data from three interpreters with different amounts of experience. Some of the SI data were manually aligned with the source speeches at the sentence level. Their latency, quality, and word order aspects were compared among the SI data themselves as well as against offline translations. The results showed that (1) interpreters with more experience controlled the latency and quality better, and (2) large latency hurt the SI quality.

1 Introduction

Simultaneous interpretation (SI) is a task of translating speech from a source language into a target language in real-time. Unlike consecutive translation, where the translation is done after the speaker pauses, in SI the translation process starts while the speaker is still talking. With recent developments in machine translation and speech processing, various studies have been conducted aiming at automatic speech translation (Pino et al., 2020; Wu et al., 2020; Inaguma et al., 2021; Bahar et al., 2021), including SI (Oda et al., 2014; Zheng et al., 2019; Arivazhagan et al., 2019; Zhang et al., 2020; Nguyen et al., 2021), based on speech corpora.

Existing speech corpora can be classified into *Speech Translation* corpora or *Simultaneous Interpretation* corpora, as defined by Zhang et al. (2021). Table 1 lists publicly-available SI corpora. Although a large number of *Speech Translation* corpora have been published, the number of SI corpora remains very limited. Both types of corpora are comprised of audio data and their corresponding translations, although how the translations are generated is different. For *Speech Translation* corpora, a translation is based on complete audio data or transcripts; for SI corpora, human interpreters actually do SI. SI corpora are useful not only for the construction of automatic SI systems but also for translation studies.

Corpora	Language	Hours
Toyama et al. (2004)	En↔Jp	182
Paulik and Waibel (2009)	En↔Es	217
Shimizu et al. (2014)	En↔Jp	22
Zhang et al. (2021)	Zh→En	68
Ours	En↔Jp	304.5

Table 1: Existing SI corpora and ours

To facilitate research in the field of SI, we are constructing a new large-scale English↔Japanese SI corpus[1]. We recorded the SIs of lectures and press conferences and amassed over 300 hours of such data. Some lectures have SI data generated by three interpreters with different amounts of experience, as in Shimizu et al. (2014), which enables comparisons of SI differences based on experience.

In this paper, we describe the construction of a new corpus and present the results of its analysis. Its design follows the framework of Shimizu et al. (2014). The analysis was conducted on a subset of lectures that have SI data from three interpreters. In some parts of the data, the source speech and the SI data were manually aligned at the sentence level to compare the following properties: latency, quality, and word order, all of which are typically investigated in translation studies. We compared those SI data among them as well as against translations that are generated offline. Importantly, we adopt an automatic metric and a manual analysis to evaluate the SI quality.

[1]A part of the corpus is available at https://dsc-nlp.naist.jp/data/NAIST-SIC/

Proceedings of the 18th International Conference on Spoken Language Translation, pages 226–235
Bangkok, Thailand (Online), August 5–6, 2021.

2 Related Work

2.1 Existing SI Corpora

Despite their usefulness, the number of SI corpora is very limited (Table 1). The Simultaneous Interpretation Database (SIDB) is an English↔Japanese SI corpus, which consists of over 180 hours of recordings, including both monologues (lectures) and dialogues (travel conversations).

Shimizu et al. (2014) also constructed an English↔Japanese SI corpus. It is a relatively small corpus (22 hours), and has the following two notable features: (1) all the speeches have SI data from three interpreters with different amounts of experience; and (2) offline translations are available for some of the speeches. The features allow comparisons among the SI data themselves as well as with the translation data.

In language pairs other than English↔Japanese, Paulik and Waibel (2009) developed an SI system using SI data collected from European Parliament Plenary Sessions (EPPS), which are broadcast live by satellite in the various official languages of the European Union. Zhang et al. (2021) proposed the first large-scale Chinese→English *Speech Translation* and SI corpus.

2.2 Translation Studies

In translation studies, SI characteristics have typically been investigated from the aspects of latency, quality, and word order. For evaluating latency by human interpreters, Ear-Voice Span (EVS) is commonly used as a metric. EVS denotes the lag between the original utterances and the corresponding SIs.

The analysis of quality often relies on a manual evaluation of the corpus data (Fantinuoli and Prandi, 2021). Ino and Kawahara (2008), for example, investigated SI faithfulness based on manual annotation of the data. SI aims to translate a source speech with low latency and high quality, where the two factors are in a trade-off relationship. However, previous studies (*e.g.*, Lee, 2002) argued that a longer latency negatively affects SI quality.

Word order has also been intensively studied in the field. Recent research by Cai et al. (2020) demonstrated a statistical study based on SIDB and compared word order between translation and SI.

3 Corpus Construction

3.1 Material

Our corpus consists of the SIs of four kinds of materials. For the English→Japanese direction, the interpreters interpreted TED talks[2].

TED: TED offers short talks on various topics from science to culture. The videos of the talks are available on its website. More importantly, TED talks have been manually transcribed and translated by volunteers, and Japanese translations (*i.e.*, subtitles) are available for many talks.

For the Japanese→English direction, the interpreters interpret speech from the following materials.

TEDx: TEDx is an event where local speakers present topics to local audiences. The events are held under a license granted by TED, and the talks follow the format of TED talks. The videos are available on YouTube as well as on the TED website.

CSJ: The Corpus of Spontaneous Japanese (Maekawa, 2003) consists of academic lectures and speeches on everyday topics. It contains audio data and their transcripts with linguistic annotations.

JNPC: The Japan National Press Club (JNPC) annually organizes about 200 press conferences involving Japanese and foreign guest speakers from politicians to business representatives. The press conferences are video-recorded and available online[3]. For some of them, transcripts are provided on its website.

3.2 Recording

Professional simultaneous interpreters with different amounts of experience participated in the recordings. Each interpreter was assigned a rank based on length of experience, as in Shimizu et al. (2014) (Table 2). The recordings were made from 2018 to 2020.

Interpreters wore a headset and interpreted speech while watching video on a computer. They only listened to the audio when interpreting the CSJ speech because no videos were available. The interpreters were provided in advance documents related to the speech to improve the SI quality. In

[2]`https://www.ted.com/`
[3]`https://www.jnpc.or.jp/`

Amount of experience	Rank
15 years	S-rank
4 years	A-rank
1 years	B-rank

Table 2: Ranks of simultaneous interpreters

Direction	Source	2018	2019	2020
En→JA	TED	67+12*	50	50
Jp→EN	TEDx	12*	40	0
	CSJ	33	0	0
	JNPC	4	36.5	0
Total		128	126.5	50
Cum.		128	254.5	304.5

Table 3: Recorded hours of our SI corpus. Figures with asterisk (*) indicate parts with SI data generated by three interpreters with different amounts of experience (*i.e.,* 4 hours × 3 interpreters).

fact, related information or materials (*e.g.,* presentation slides) are usually provided to them in their actual work. The following are the details of the documents given in our recording procedures:

- TED, TEDx (2018): Summary of talk; referenceable during SI.
- TED (2019-): English transcripts from TED website; *not* referenceable during SI.
- TEDx (2019-): Japanese subtitles generated by YouTube; *not* referenceable during SI.
- CSJ: 10% summary of Japanese transcripts; referenceable during SI.
- JNPC: No documents provided.

Table 3 shows the details of the recorded hours of our corpus. In spontaneous speech, sentence boundaries are ambiguous, and it is difficult to provide the number of sentences included in our corpus. A total of four hours of TED and TEDx recorded in 2018 were interpreted by interpreters from all three ranks (4 hours × 3 interpreters = 12 hours; marked with asterisk). The other talks were interpreted by either an S-rank or an A-rank interpreter. About half of the recorded SIs have been manually transcribed. The whole corpus consists of SIs of more than 1200 talks. The average talk length by materials is the following: TED 11.20 minutes, TEDx 15.85 minutes, CSJ 13.55 minutes, and JNPC 84.33 minutes.

```
EN_0001 13363 17427 Oliver was an extremely dashing.
EN_0002 17427 22248 handsome, charming and largely unstable male
EN_0003 22248 25433 that I completely lost my heart to.
JA_0001 14860 16416 (F えー)オリバーは<H>
JA_0002 17500 21555 (F えー)(F このー)凄くハンサムで魅力的な
JA_0003 22125 24347 (F えー)そして私が
JA_0004 24945 28556 (F えー)(?)大好きな<H>(F えー)男性です。
```

Figure 1: Example of an SI transcript: Preceding each utterance, IDs and start/end times are annotated. Some discourse tags are used: F: fillers, (?): unintelligible, ⟨H⟩: prolongations.

4 Corpus Analyses

4.1 Data

The English→Japanese SI data from 14 TED talks were analyzed based on three properties: latency, quality, and word order. The talks were a subset of 12 hours of recordings of SI data from interpreters of each rank (see Table 3).

The SI data were aligned to the source speech based on segments. A transcript example is shown in Fig. 1. Each segment is annotated with an ID, start/end times, and discourse tags (*e.g.,* fillers, slips of the tongue, pauses). A segment does not necessarily correspond to a sentence.

In addition to the SI data, offline translation data (*i.e.,* Japanese subtitles) were used to examine the SI quality and word order. Disfluencies in the SI data were removed with the help of discourse tags. Then the SI and translation data were automatically divided into *bunsetsus*[4] using the Juman++ Japanese morphological analyzer[5] (Morita et al., 2015) and the KNP parser (Kawahara and Kurohashi, 2006).

4.2 Sentence Alignment

For subsequent corpus analyses, the SI data of 14 talks were manually aligned at the sentence level with the source speeches by the first author to fairly compare the data of the interpreters of each rank. Since the segments in the SI transcripts were based on the interpreters' utterances, they did not necessarily match among the interpreters. Thus, we gave sentence alignments based on the sentences of the English transcripts segmented using the following rules:

[4] A *bunsetsu* is a basic unit of dependency in Japanese that consists of one or more content words and the following zero or more function words (Kawahara and Kurohashi, 2006).

[5] We used Juman++ ver.1.02 rather than the development version of Juman++ V2 (Tolmachev et al., 2018).

```
EN_0177 469789 471829 I've got two questions for you.
JA_0116 XXXXXX 473315 二つの質問がありますよ。

EN_0178 471829 473469 (Laughter)
JA_0000 XXXXXX XXXXXX __null__

EN_0179 473469 476069 You know what's coming now, right?
JA_0117 474778 476197 質問分かってるんですね。
```

Figure 2: Example of sentence-level alignment

- segments ending with a period (.) or a period + a double quotation mark (.")
- segments ending with a question mark (?) or a question mark + a double quotation mark (?")
- segments ending with a closed parenthesis

Japanese segments were aligned to English sentences by the following rules[6]:

- Words/phrases that are not interpreted: ignored.
- Sentences that are not interpreted: marked as `__drop__` in Japanese segments.
- Sentences that are not interpreted *intentionally*: marked as `__skip__` in Japanese segments. (*e.g.,* Thank you.)
- Sentences that do not need to be interpreted: marked as `__null__` in Japanese segments. (*e.g.,* (Laughter))
- No corresponding English sentence: add `__null__` to English segments.
- Japanese segments that correspond to multiple English sentences: divide where it corresponds to the boundary of English sentences. Mark XXXXX for end/start times of Japanese segments.
- English segments that consist of multiple sentences: divide at sentence boundary. Mark XXXXX for end/start times of segments.

An example of the data aligned at the sentence level is shown in Fig. 2. Each sentence is delimited by one blank line.

4.3 Metrics

Latency: As a latency metric, EVS was calculated for each sentence. Since the start/end times of the transcribed speech segments are available in our data, we separately calculated EVS at the beginning and the end of a sentence[7]:

$$EVS_{start} = start\ time_{JP} - start\ time_{EN}$$
$$EVS_{end} = end\ time_{JP} - end\ time_{EN}.$$

However, we failed to calculate EVS in some sentences because some segments were divided into multiple segments during the sentence-level alignment, and the start/end times were unavailable. Furthermore, EVS at the end of sentences can become negative if the interpreter quit interpreting in the middle of a sentence. These cases were excluded from our analyses.

Quality: To evaluate the SI quality, we calculated two metrics[8].

The first one was BERTScore (Zhang et al., 2019), which is also used to evaluate machine translations (*e.g.,* Edunov et al., 2020). It is based on contextualized subword embeddings and is expected to capture meanings rather than surface forms like BLEU (Papineni et al., 2002). It would be appropriate for evaluating the aspects of SIs used by interpreters, including anticipation, summarization, and generalization. BERTScores were calculated between SIs (candidates) and offline translations (references) for each sentence.

The other quality metric was the *bunsetsu-level semantic preservation score* (BSPS), which evaluated the faithfulness of the SIs against the translations. An example is shown in Fig. 3. Similar to Ino and Kawahara (2008), each *bunsetsu* that appeared in the translation was considered a unit of ideas. Then we counted the number of *bunsetsus* in the SI that conveyed the ideas. If a *bunsetsu* in the SI successfully conveyed its idea in the translation, it got one point. If the *bunsetsu* in the SI partially conveyed an idea, it got half a point. The BSPS for a given sentence was calculated by adding the points and dividing by the number of ideas in the translation.

To calculate BSPS, we manually created *bunsetsu* level alignments for three talks, which were selected based on the following procedures:

- Assign a score of 1-3 to the SI data (14 talks × 3 interpreters) based on the overall quality.

[6]Subjectively judged by the authors, except for the boundaries of the English sentences.

[7]Due to the limitations of our data, we calculated a simplified EVS, which was different from that in previous studies.

[8]We focused on faithfulness in this paper, although other factors may affect SI quality (*e.g.,* grammaticality, delivery).

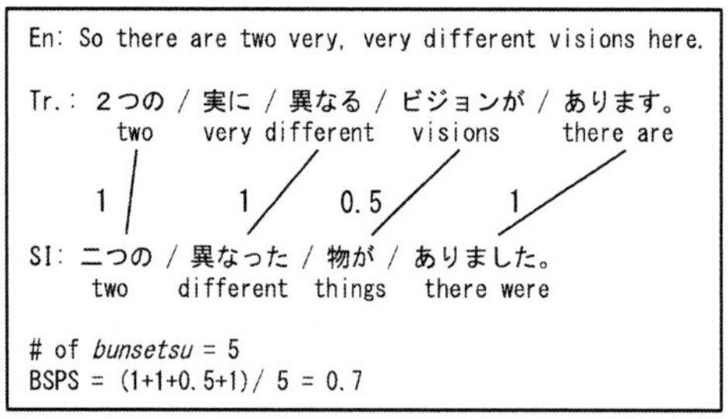

Figure 3: Example of calculating BSPS

- Calculate the average for each talk and assign a label of `high`, `mid`, or `low`.
- Choose one talk from each label.

The talks labeled `high` are those that are easy to interpret, and the talks labeled `low` are difficult. We chose three talks: AlexanderWagner_2016X (`Ale`), NickBostrom_2015 (`Nic`), and LaurelBraitman_2014S (`Lau`), for easy, medium, and difficult levels.

Word Order: To examine the differences in word order between SI and offline translation, we computed Kendall's K distance (Kendall, 1938), ranging [0, 1], and equaling 0 if the two lists are identical and 1 if one list is the reverse of the other. The metric, which captures pairwise disagreements between two lists, can measure the degree of reordering. K was calculated based on the *bunsetsu* level alignment shown in Fig. 3.

4.4 Results

4.4.1 Overall Trend

Table 4 provides basic statistics for the SI data of the 14 TED talks. B-rank interpreters produced the longest SIs (`# Bunsetsu`), but they frequently added something that the original speaker did not say (`en null`). The ratio of `en null` decreased as the amount of experience became longer. In addition, the ratio of `drop` for S-rank interpreters (9.22) was lower than that for the others (A-rank: 21.67, and B-rank: 15.69). These results suggest that the SI generated by higher ranked interpreters tends to have higher overall quality.

At the sentence level, S-rank interpreters produced the most *bunsetsus* (`Bunsetsu. per sent.`). A one-way ANOVA detected significant differences among groups ($F(2, 5818) = 21.881, p < 0.001$), and the following Tukey's test showed that S- and B-rank interpreters produced significantly more *bunsetsus* than A-rank interpreters ($p < 0.001$). Although the difference between S- and B-ranks is not significant, the results suggest that interpreters with more experience also did better at the sentence level. This point is discussed below in Section 4.4.3.

In Table 4, we can also see that higher ranked interpreters tended to have higher `skip` ratios. However, the differences among the groups were not statistically significant based on a one-way ANOVA ($F(2, 39) = 0.5172, p = 0.6002$).

4.4.2 Latency

Table 5 compares the latency measured by EVS. A-rank interpreters had the largest latency both at the beginning and at the end of sentences, followed by B- and S-rank interpreters. The amount of latency ranged from 2 to 4 seconds, which was consistent with the majority of previous studies (see Robbe, 2019).

However, a relatively great number of EVS took large values (> 5 seconds). The relationship between EVS and sentence length in the source language is shown in Fig. 4. As Pearson's correlation coefficient indicates ($r = 0.2584, 0.1206$, respectively), sentence length in the target language did not seem to affect EVS, which did not match the results reported in Lee (2002).

EVS_{start} became large because interpreters sometimes did not interpret the earlier part of the sentence, as in this example:

> (En) A week later, Ping was discovered in the apartment alongside the body of her owner, and the vacuum had been running the entire time.
> (A-rank) そしてずっと掃除機がオンになったまま残されていたんですけれとも、[And the vacuum had been running the entire time.]

The EVS_{end} results suggest that S- and B-rank interpreters might wrap up the sentence to a certain extent when the next sentence started, but A-rank interpreters might cling to the sentence, resulting in larger EVS_{end}. A large EVS_{end} seemed to negatively impact the SI of the subsequent sentence, as reported in Lee (2002). Focusing on the top 10% of sentences whose EVS_{end} was large ($N = 187$), 56.68% of their subsequent sentences were not interpreted at all (*i.e.,* `drop`) by A-rank interpreters.

Interpreter	# Seg.	# Sent.	# Bunsetsu	Bunsetsu. per sent.	Skip (%)	Drop (%)	En null (%)
S-rank	2750	1902	12292	**6.47**	**2.00**	9.36	0.68
A-rank	2609	1948	10414	5.41	1.58	**22.54**	2.50
B-rank	**3077**	**1998**	**12523**	6.27	1.13	16.13	**6.05**
avg.	2812	1949.33	11743.00	6.05	1.57	16.01	3.08

Table 4: Comparison of SI data among interpreters with different amounts of experience

Interpreter	Start	End
S-rank	2.95	2.48
A-rank	**3.57**	**3.89**
B-rank	3.46	2.79

Table 5: Comparison of EVS (seconds) among interpreters with different amounts of experience. Figures are averages of each sentence.

Interpreter	Pre.	Rec.	F1
S-rank	**0.6544**	**0.6396**	**0.6465**
A-rank	0.5374	0.5221	0.5292
B-rank	0.6238	0.6115	0.6171

Table 6: Comparison of BERTScores among interpreters with different amounts of experience. Scores are averages of each sentence, where 0 is assigned to `drop` and `skip`.

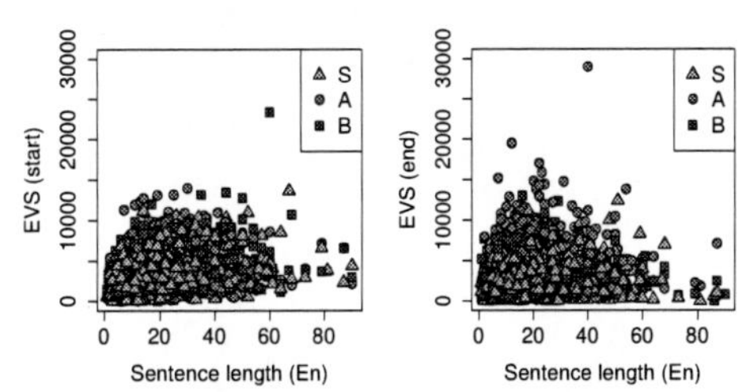

Figure 4: Relationship between EVS and sentence length of original speech

4.4.3 Quality

BERTScore: The quality of the SI data measured by BERTScore is shown in Table 6. Precision was higher than Recall in all three interpreter ranks. The results match our intuition because simultaneous interpreters sometimes summarize or generalize the content of the original speech to handle latency, and not all the content is interpreted. BERTScore captured the quality of SI well in the following example:

> (En) We did this experiment for real.
> (Ref) 実際にこの実験を行ってみました。
> (A-rank) これを実際にしました。 [Did this for real.]

The F1 score of the example was 0.8325. Although the wording that corresponds with "did" is different between the translation (Ref) and the interpretation, BERTScore captured the similarity of the meaning. On the other hand, as shown in the next example, BERTScore did not always do well, especially when interpreters used a strategy:

> (En) We can all think of some examples, right?
> (Ref) 例を挙げる事ができると思います。
> (S-rank) 例えば、 [For example.]

The F1 score of the example was 0.5519. The interpreter adopted a strategy (summarization) and conveyed the core ideas of the original utterance, although BERTScore struggled to capture them.

Comparing the three interpreter ranks, S-rank interpreters achieved the highest scores in Precision, Recall, and F1. A one-way ANOVA detected significant differences among groups ($F(2, 5045) = 65.802, 70.095, 68.386$ for Precision, Recall, and F1, $p < 0.001$), and the following Tukey's test showed that the differences among all the groups were significant ($p < 0.05$). The scores of the A-rank interpreters were probably lower than those of B-rank interpreters because of the high `drop` ratio.

***Bunsetsu-level Semantic Preservation Score*:** BSPS was calculated for the three talks, `Ale` (easy), `Nic` (medium), and `Lau` (difficult). The results in Table 7 indicate that the higher ranked interpreters achieved higher BSPS, except for `Ale`. In fact, the low ratio of `drop` and `en null` (8.33 and 0.00) suggest that the B-rank interpreter did well on `Ale`, which matched the human evaluation results. One of the human evaluators remarked that key words such as proper nouns were well translated or ap-

Talk	Interpreter	BSPS
Ale	S-rank	0.5671
(easy)	A-rank	0.4316
	B-rank	**0.5871**
Nic	S-rank	**0.4471**
(medium)	A-rank	0.3715
	B-rank	0.3411
Lau	S-rank	**0.4130**
(difficult)	A-rank	0.3618
	B-rank	0.3207

Table 7: Comparison of BSPS among three talks and interpreter's rank

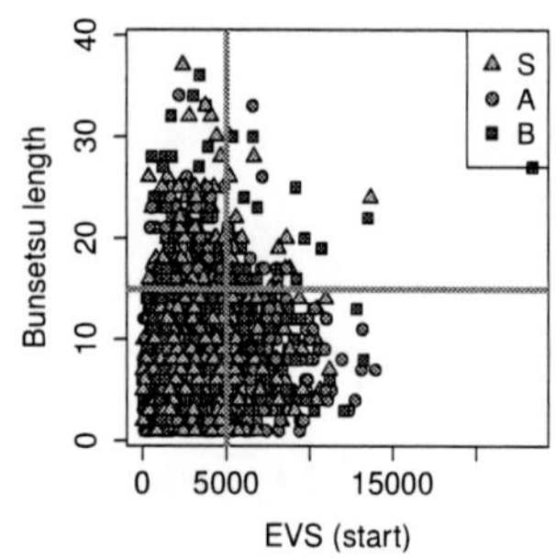

Figure 5: Relationship between EVS_{start} and the number of *bunsetsus* in SIs

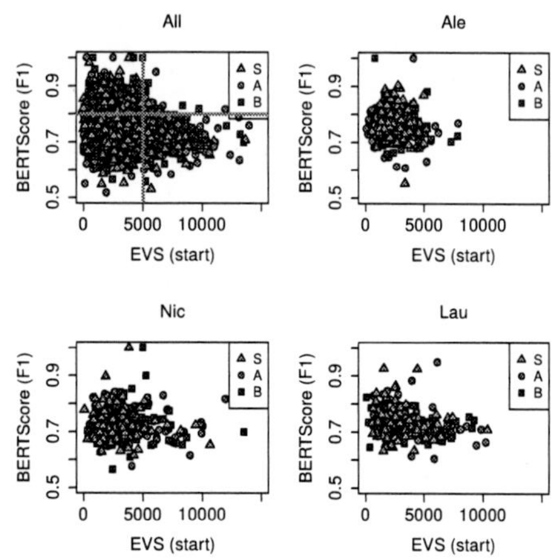

Figure 6: Relationship between EVS_{start} and BERTScore (F1)

propriately rephrased to corresponding Japanese words.

The BSPS results imply that higher ranked interpreters generated better SIs at the sentence level. The metric captured how many ideas, which were presented in the original speech, were actually covered in each sentence of the SIs. S-rank interpreters produced the most *bunsetsus* per sentence (Table 4), probably because they reproduced more of the ideas presented in the original speech.

Relationship between latency and quality: Since previous studies have shown that higher latency damages quality (*e.g.*, Lee, 2002), we investigated the relationship between them based on EVS_{start}. In Section 4.4.2, the negative effect of a large EVS_{end} on the following sentence was discussed; in this section, we examine whether a large EVS_{start} hurts the quality of the sentence being processed.

Fig. 5 shows the relationship between EVS_{start} and the number of *bunsetsus* in SIs. When the latency increased ($>$ 5 seconds), few SIs had large numbers of ($>$ 15) *bunsetsu*. The large EVS_{start} indicated that the original sentence was long, which expected a longer SI. A similar tendency was found for BERTScore and BSPS. From Figs. 6 and 7, SIs with a large EVS_{start} tended to get low scores.

The relationship between EVS_{start} and the quality metrics of `Ale`, `Nic`, and `Lau` is shown in Figs. 6 and 7. When the talk was easy to interpret (`Ale`), the standard deviation was smaller than the other talks (`Ale`= 1.33, `Nic`= 2.25, `Lau`= 2.16). Furthermore, the S-rank interpreters' standard deviation was smaller than that of the others (*e.g.*, S= 1.06, A= 1.68, B= 1.27 for `Ale`).

The above results suggest that a large EVS_{start} negatively affected the quality of the sentence being processed.

4.5 Human Evaluation

The quality of the SI data was further examined through human evaluations. Three professional translators (*i.e.*, *not* interpreters) subjectively evaluated the faithfulness of each sentence on a scale of 1 (incomprehensible), 2 (poor), 3 (minor errors), and 4 (acceptable). Table 8 shows that higher ranked interpreters received higher scores, which matched the BERTScore and BSPS results. The B-rank interpreter interpreted `Ale` well, which was mentioned in the overall comments by the translators. Individual differences of interpreters (*e.g.*, background knowledge) could affect the SI quality because not necessarily the same interpreters interpreted the three talks.

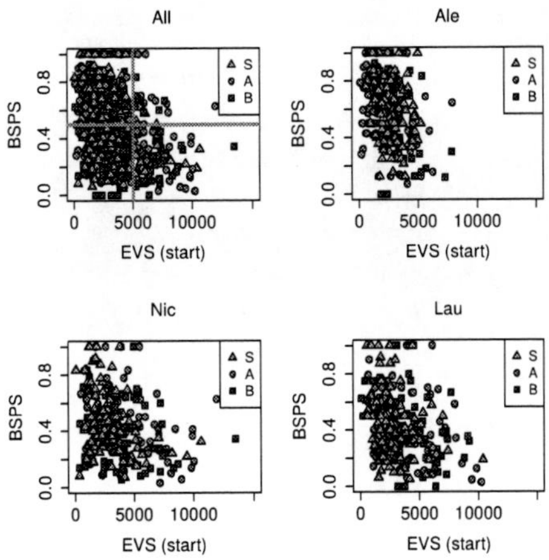

Figure 7: Relationship between EVS_{start} and BSPS

From Table 8, human evaluation scores were low, most often less than 2. One possible reason is that the translators were strict about the sentence structure in the source language, as in this example:

> (En) People are motivated by different values perhaps.
> (A-rank) 人のモチベーションは／違う物によって／起こってきます。 [People's motivation / by different things / is raised.]
> (Human evaluation scores) 1, 3, 2

The verb phrase (are motivated) was interpreted with a noun (motivation) to maintain the word order of the English sentence, while the rater A indicated the disagreement in his overall comment and assigned one point. Future work will involve human evaluation with simultaneous interpreters.

Pearson's correlation coefficient was calculated between the human evaluation scores and the two metrics. BSPS achieved relatively higher correlations with human judgments than BERTScore (Table 9). However, if the correlations were examined talk by talk, BSPS correlated poorly with the human evaluations in `Nic_S` (ranging around $r = 0.3$), and the correlation between BERTScore (F1) and human evaluation was relatively high (ranging around $r = 0.45$). Further research is needed on the behavior of the metrics.

4.5.1 Word Order

The differences in word order between the SI data and the offline translations measured by Kendall's K distance are shown in Table 10. Because of the difference between English (SVO and head-initial) and Japanese (SOV and head-final), the difference between SI and translation (*i.e.,* large K) suggests that the interpreters adopted a strategy of maintaining the word order of the source language. However, differences due to interpreter ranks were not clear, and we observed sentences with relatively large K (> 0.7).

An example is shown in Table 11, whose K was 0.75. In the translation (Ref), the word order was almost reversed from the English sentence, although the simultaneous interpreter successfully interpreted in the first-in-first-out manner. The example matched the word order patterns reported in Cai et al. (2020), who found that simultaneous interpreters often preferred maintaining the word order in the original speech when interpreting nominal modifiers and dependent clauses.

Talk_Rank	Rater A	Rater B	Rater C
Ale_S	1.46	**1.83**	2.52
Ale_A	1.32	1.46	1.94
Ale_B	**2.39**	1.76	**3.08**
Lau_S	**1.23**	**1.61**	2.03
Lau_A	1.17	1.43	**2.47**
Lau_B	0.82	0.84	1.48
Nic_S	**1.53**	**1.45**	1.98
Nic_A	1.38	1.40	**2.40**
Nic_B	1.05	1.14	1.43

Table 8: Comparison of subjective evaluations by three professional translators

Metric	Rater A	Rater B	Rater C
BSPS	0.4724	0.4640	0.4372
BERTScore (P)	0.2696	0.2281	0.2658
BERTScore (R)	0.3326	0.2966	0.3380
BERTScore (F1)	0.3125	0.2728	0.3131

Table 9: Correlation between human evaluations and quality metrics

Interpreter	Ale	Nic	Lau
S-rank	0.1118	0.0987	0.0832
A-rank	0.1467	0.1023	0.0767
B-rank	0.1347	0.0796	0.0985

Table 10: Comparison of Kendall's K distance among three talks and interpreter ranks

Source	Example
En	That's a huge problem if you think about, especially, an economy like Switzerland, which relies so much on the trust put into its financial industry.
Ref	金融業界の/信用に/大きく依存する/スイスのような/経済を/考えると、/これは巨大な問題です。 [put into financial industry / the trust / which relies so much on / like Switzerland / an economy / if you think about / that's a huge problem]
B-rank	これは、大きな問題です。/特に、/スイスの様な/経済を/考えてみると/そうでしょう。/ 金融業界に対する/信頼/によって成り立っている/国だからです。 [that's a huge problem / especially / like Switzerland / an economy / if you think about / it's true / on its financial industry / the trust / based on / it's a country]

Table 11: Example of interpretations with large K

5 Conclusion

We described the construction of a new large-scale English↔Japanese SI corpus that contains SI data generated by simultaneous interpreters with different amounts of experience (S-, A-, and B-ranks) from identical lectures. Focusing on latency, quality, and word order, we compared the SI data among interpreter ranks and against offline translations. The S-rank interpreters controlled latency and quality better than the other two ranks. We strongly believe that our new corpus will be a useful resource for further research in translation studies and for the construction of automatic SI systems.

Acknowledgments

This research was supported by JSPS KAKENHI Grant Number JP17H06101.

References

Naveen Arivazhagan, Colin Cherry, Wolfgang Macherey, Chung-Cheng Chiu, Semih Yavuz, Ruoming Pang, Wei Li, and Colin Raffel. 2019. Monotonic infinite lookback attention for simultaneous machine translation. In *Proceedings of ACL*, pages 1313–1323.

Parnia Bahar, Tobias Bieschke, Ralf Schlüter, and Hermann Ney. 2021. Tight integrated end-to-end training for cascaded speech translation. *arXiv*, arXiv:2011.12167.

Zhongxi Cai, Koichiro Ryu, and Shigeki Matsubara. 2020. What affects the word order of target language in simultaneous interpretation. In *Proceedings of IALP*, pages 135–140.

Sergey Edunov, Myle Ott, Marc'Aurelio Ranzato, and Michael Auli. 2020. On the evaluation of machine translation systems trained with back-translation. In *Proceedings of ACL*, pages 2836–2846.

Claudio Fantinuoli and Bianca Prandi. 2021. Towards the evaluation of simultaneous speech translation from a communicative perspective. *arXiv*, arXiv:2103.08364.

Hirofumi Inaguma, Tatsuya Kawahara, and Shinji Watanabe. 2021. Source and target bidirectional knowledge distillation for end-to-end speech translation. *arXiv*, arXiv:2104.06457.

Kinuyo Ino and Kiyoshi Kawahara. 2008. Comparative analysis of simultaneous mode and prepared mode in broadcast interpreting. *Interpreting and Translation Studies*, 8:37–55. (in Japanese).

Daisuke Kawahara and Sadao Kurohashi. 2006. A fully-lexicalized probabilistic model for japanese syntactic and case structure analysis. In *Proceedings of HLT-NAACL*, pages 176–183.

Maurice Kendall. 1938. A new measure of rank correlation. *Biometrika*, 30(1/2):81–93.

Tae-Hyung Lee. 2002. Ear voice span in english into korean simultaneous interpretation. *Meta*, 47(4):596–606.

Kikuo Maekawa. 2003. Corpus of spontaneous japanese: Its design and evaluation. In *Proceedings of ISCA/IEEE Workshop on Spontaneous Speech*, pages 7–12.

Hajime Morita, Daisuke Kawahara, and Sadao Kurohashi. 2015. Morphological analysis for unsegmented languages using recurrent neural network language model. In *Proceedings of EMNLP*, pages 2292–2297.

Ha Nguyen, Yannick Estève, and Laurent Besacier. 2021. An empirical study of end-to-end simultaneous speech translation decoding strategies. *arXiv*, arXiv:2103.03233.

Yusuke Oda, Graham Neubig, Sakriani Sakti, Tomoki Toda, and Satoshi Nakamura. 2014. Optimizing segmentation strategies for simultaneous speech translation. In *Proceedings of ACL*, pages 551–556.

Kishore Papineni, Salim Roukos, Todd Ward, and Wei-Jing Zhu. 2002. Bleu: a method for automatic evaluation of machine translation. In *Proceedings of ACL*, pages 311–318.

Matthias Paulik and Alex Waibel. 2009. Automatic translation from parallel speech: Simultaneous interpretation as mt training data. In *Proceedings of ASRU*, pages 496–501.

Juan Pino, Qiantong Xu, Xutai Ma, Mohammad Javad Dousti, and Yun Tang. 2020. Self-training for end-to-end speech translation. In *Proceedings of Interspeech*, pages 1476–1480.

Elisa Robbe. 2019. *Ear-voice span in simultaneous conference interpreting en-es and en-nl: A case study*. Doctoral dissertation, Ghent University.

Hiroaki Shimizu, Graham Neubig, Sakriani Sakti, Tomoki Toda, and Satoshi Nakamura. 2014. Collection of a simultaneous translation corpus for comparative analysis. In *Proceedings of LREC*, pages 670–673.

Arseny Tolmachev, Daisuke Kawahara, and Sadao Kurohashi. 2018. Juman++: A morphological analysis toolkit for scriptio continua. In *Proceedings of EMNLP*, pages 54–59.

Hitomi Toyama, Shigeki Matsubara, Koichiro Ryu, Nobuo Kawaguchi, and Yasuyoshi Inagaki. 2004. Ciair simultaneous interpretation corpus. In *Proceedings of Oriental COCOSDA*.

Anne Wu, Changhan Wang, Juan Pino, and Jiatao Gu. 2020. Self-Supervised Representations Improve End-to-End Speech Translation. In *Proc. Interspeech 2020*, pages 1491–1495.

Ruiqing Zhang, Xiyang Wang, Chuanqiang Zhang, Zhongjun He, Hua Wu, Zhi Li, Haifeng Wang, Ying Chen, and Qinfei Li. 2021. Bstc: A large-scale chinese-english speech translation dataset. *arXiv*, arXiv:2104.03575. Version 3.

Ruiqing Zhang, Chuanqiang Zhang, Zhongjun He, Hua Wu, and Haifeng Wang. 2020. Learning adaptive segmentation policy for simultaneous translation. In *Proceedings of EMNLP*, pages 2280–2289.

Tianyi Zhang, Varsha Kishore, Felix Wu, Kilian Q. Weinberger, and Yoav Artzi. 2019. Bertscore: Evaluating text generation with bert. *arXiv*, arXiv:1904.09675. Version 3.

Baigong Zheng, Renjie Zheng, Mingbo Ma, and Liang Huang. 2019. Simultaneous translation with flexible policy via restricted imitation learning. In *Proceedings of ACL*, pages 5816–5822.

Inverted Projection for Robust Speech Translation

Dirk Padfield*
Google Research
padfield@google.com

Colin Cherry*
Google Research
colincherry@google.com

Abstract

Traditional translation systems trained on written documents perform well for text-based translation but not as well for speech-based applications. We aim to adapt translation models to speech by introducing actual lexical errors from ASR and segmentation errors from automatic punctuation into our translation training data. We introduce an inverted projection approach that projects automatically detected system segments onto human transcripts and then re-segments the gold translations to align with the projected human transcripts. We demonstrate that this overcomes the train-test mismatch present in other training approaches. The new projection approach achieves gains of over 1 BLEU point over a baseline that is exposed to the human transcripts and segmentations, and these gains hold for both IWSLT data and YouTube data.

1 Introduction

Speech translation is an important field that becomes more relevant with every improvement to its component technologies of automatic speech recognition (ASR) and machine translation (MT). It enables exciting applications like live machine interpretation (Cho and Esipova, 2016; Ma et al., 2019) and automatic foreign-language subtitling for video content (Karakanta et al., 2020).

However, translation of speech presents unique challenges compared to text translation. Traditional text translation systems are often trained with clean, well-structured text consisting of (source language, target language) sentence pairs gathered from text documents. This works well for translating written text, but for cascaded systems composed of speech → automatic transcription → automatic translation, errors from ASR and automatic punctuation are amplified as they pass through the translation system. Such systems suffer from three issues: 1) spoken language structure is different from written language structure and can include aspects like disfluencies and partial sentences, 2) ASR systems are not perfect and introduce errors in the stage from speech to source transcript, and 3) mistakes from automatic punctuation systems can lead to unnatural sentence segments and boundaries (Makhija et al., 2019; Nguyen et al., 2019; Wang et al., 2019). These problems can lead to poor translations and pose unique challenges for MT that are not readily addressed by current methods. In this work, we set out to make MT robust to the second and third issues in particular.

We have developed an approach to train translation models that are robust to transcription errors and punctuation errors, by introducing errors from actual ASR and automatic punctuation systems into the source side of our MT training data. This is similar in spirit to the method of Li et al. (2021), which introduces artificial sentence boundary errors into the training bitext. However, instead of artificial boundaries, our segmentation approach uses actual boundaries generated by the automatic punctuation system, which required the development of our inverted projection technique, and we also include errors from ASR. For a small subset of our training set, we assume access to long-form source audio documents, their corresponding human transcriptions, and translations of those transcriptions. This makes it possible to compare the performance of a baseline model trained on the human transcription with a model trained on source sentences derived from applying ASR transcription and automatic punctuation to the same audio.

Our primary contributions are first to show how to produce training data that captures the errors from automatic transcription and punctuation, which requires a non-trivial re-segmentation of the reference translation that we call *inverted projec-*

*equal contribution

Proceedings of the 18th International Conference on Spoken Language Translation, pages 236–244
Bangkok, Thailand (Online), August 5–6, 2021.

tion; and second to show experimentally that it is actually more important to expose the MT system to segmentation errors than lexical transcription errors when aiming for speech-robust MT.

2 Background

Compounding errors from ASR are known to cause problems when cascaded into MT (Ruiz et al., 2017). These issues are one of the main motivators for end-to-end modeling of speech translation (Weiss et al., 2017; Bansal et al., 2018; Sperber et al., 2019). However, we consider end-to-end modeling out of scope for this study since we aim to benefit from the modularity that comes with a cascaded speech translation strategy. To improve a cascade's robustness to speech input, one can train the MT system with some combination of artificial errors, actual ASR output, or long-form segmentation errors. We discuss each in turn.

Introducing artificial errors into the training set has the advantage of being efficient, and not necessarily tied to a specific ASR system. One can add Gaussian noise to the source embeddings (Cheng et al., 2018) or induce lexical substitutions that may be informed by phonetics (Li et al., 2018; Liu et al., 2019). Sperber et al. (2017) experiment with a noise model that can perform insertions, deletions and substitutions, but find little value in refining the substitutions to account for word frequency or orthographic similarity.

More related to our efforts are those that use actual ASR output. Early experiments used ASR output to replace the source side of parallel text during training (Post et al., 2013; Sperber et al., 2017). These did not perform well, likely because ASR word error rates (WER) on the Fisher Corpus were more than 40%, resulting in an unreliable training signal. Recently, Cheng et al. (2019) showed that, given ASR training corpora (coupled audio-transcription pairs), one can build a robust MT system by training with the normal MT objective on MT corpora, plus a mixture of: (1) an adversarial objective that tries to bring encoder representations for ASR output close to those of human transcriptions; and (2) a normal MT objective that has ASR output as source and machine translations of human transcripts as target. In an IWSLT TED translation scenario, they showed large improvements (+2.5 BLEU) using the second idea alone, which we take as a strong signal that there is much to be gained by training with ASR output on the source side.

Segment \ Token	Human	System
Human	Baseline	Token Robustness
System	Segment Robustness	System Robustness

Table 1: Combinations of segments and tokens.

We consider a long-form scenario where sentence boundaries for the input audio are not given at test time. As such, the method of Li et al. (2021) to make MT robust to segment boundary errors is very relevant. They introduce artificial sentence boundary errors in their training bitext. They first fragment adjacent source sentences, and then produce analogous fragments in the target according to proportional token lengths. We draw inspiration from their approach when building the target sides of our inverted projections.

3 Methods

Our approach to producing MT systems that are robust to automatic transcription errors is to introduce errors from our ASR system into our MT training data. Throughout the discussion of our methods, we make use of both human (manual) and system (automated) transcriptions of the source audio. When discussing the target-side of our training data, we use instead the term "gold" to indicate a trusted reference translation. Throughout our experiments, the gold standard is a human translation of the human transcript (Post et al., 2013; Sperber et al., 2017), though it could just as easily, and much less expensively, be a machine translation of the human transcript (Cheng et al., 2019).

We divide transcription errors into two categories: token and segment errors. A *token* error is any word that is transcribed incorrectly by ASR, such as a homophone substitution or the omission of a mumbled word. Meanwhile, *segment* errors are introduced by failing to correctly break the recognized text into sentence-like segments. A human transcription is expected to have error-free tokens and segments.

Table 1 presents a baseline and three ways to turn long-form Audio-Transcript-Translation triples into robust training data suitable for fine-tuning an NMT model. Training models with human tokens and segments is the common translation mode, so we mark it here as *Baseline*. Training

Human	I	checked	the	**weather**	–	this	evening	.	It	will	**rain**	tomorrow	.
System	I	checked	the	**whether**	.	This	evening	–	it	will	**rein**	tomorrow	.

Table 2: Our running example of human and system transcriptions, with the system having both lexical and segmentation errors. The Levenshtein alignment is given by column alignment, with – indicating insertion or deletion.

with system tokens and human segments is the approach taken by others such as (Cheng et al., 2019), resulting in *Token Robustness*. In the case of long-form ASR, the human segments can be projected onto the ASR output. This is an effective approach for exposing the training model to token errors from ASR, but it has an important disadvantage, as it results in a train-test mismatch because the human segments seen during training will not be available at inference time. We describe this approach in Section 3.2 to provide a comparison to our approaches using system segments and to introduce some of the concepts and tools used in those approaches.

The two approaches using system segments are the main innovations in this paper. Introducing segment errors alone results in *Segment Robustness* (Section 3.3), while segment and token errors together result in *System Robustness* (Section 3.4); that is, MT that is robust to the complete long-form transcription pipeline. We will show in the following sections how we can project system segments onto the source and target text; we call this an *inverted projection*.

3.1 Levenshtein Projection

A key component to all of the approaches in Table 1 is an alignment between the system (ASR) transcription and a human transcription of the same long-form audio. Inspired by common practice in evaluation for long-form speech translation (Matusov et al., 2005), we employ a token-level, case-insensitive Levenshtein alignment of the two transcripts. The Levenshtein alignment is monotonic, parameter-free, and its dynamic programming algorithm is fast enough to be easily applied to very long sequences. We show an example alignment in Table 2. By tracking the alignment of tokens immediately before segment boundaries (always end-of-sentence periods in our example), we can project segment boundaries from one transcription to another, which allows us to produce the various entries in Table 1, as we describe in more detail in the following subsections.

3.2 Token Robustness Training

The first approach to training on ASR sentences is straightforward and is a variant of a published result by Cheng et al. (2019). We Levenshtein-align the human transcript to the system transcript, and project the human sentence boundaries onto ASR. Since each human transcript is already paired with a gold standard translation, this projection makes it easy to align each projected ASR segment with a gold translation. We then train the model with (projected-ASR-source, gold translation) pairs. The Token Robustness training pair derived from our running example from Table 2 is shown in Table 3. The resulting source sentence, marked with $*$, has ASR token errors but human segment boundaries.

The main advantage of this approach is that it uses the gold translations as written; the model trains on well-formed translations. However, it suffers from a serious disadvantage: the model will only train on human segment boundaries, although at test time we will translate according to system segment boundaries, resulting in a train-test mismatch. Our experiments in Section 5 demonstrate that this is a serious drawback. In fact, when the WER is low, the token errors present in Token Robustness training are ignored by the model since they are overwhelmed by segment errors. In Section 3.3, we introduce an approach to overcome this limitation.

3.3 Segment Robustness Training

To address the segment-boundary train-test mismatch present in Token Robustness training, we can invert the projection and use system segments. That is, we project the system segment boundaries onto the human transcription.

System segments are derived from automatic punctuation and sentence splitting of the system transcription. As with Token Robustness, we Levenshtein-align the human transcript to the system transcript, but this time project the system segmentation onto the human transcript. Unlike the Token Robustness scenario, it is non-trivial to get

	Gold De	Ich habe heute Abend das Wetter überprüft .	Morgen wird es regnen .
	Human En	i checked the **weather** this evening .	it will **rain** tomorrow .
$*$	System En	i checked the **whether** . this evening	it will **rein** tomorrow .

Table 3: Token Robustness ($*$). A Levenshtein alignment projects system tokens onto human segments. We have greyed out punctuation and lowercased to show the actual English text used in training.

	Gold De	Ich habe heute Abend *(I have this evening)*	das Wetter überprüft . Morgen wird es regnen . *(the weather checked . It will rain tomorrow .)*
$+$	Human En	i checked the **weather**	this evening . it will **rain** tomorrow .
$**$	System En	i checked the **whether** .	this evening it will **rein** tomorrow .

Table 4: Segment Robustness ($+$) and System Robustness ($**$). A Levenshtein alignment projects human tokens onto system segments, and then human-transcript-to-translation length ratios are used to align the German tokens to both. We have greyed out punctuation and lowercased to show the actual English text used in training.

corresponding segment boundaries for the gold-standard translations when training for Segment Robustness. We could perform a statistical word alignment between the human transcription and its translation to determine word-level interlingual semantic correspondence, but in similar situations such as prefix training for simultaneous translation (Niehues et al., 2018; Arivazhagan et al., 2020), this has not resulted in improvements over a simple proportional length-based heuristic. Therefore, we use human-transcript-to-translation length ratios (in tokens) to segment the gold translations so that their new segment lengths match the projected human source segment lengths. Finally, we train on (projected-human-source, projected-gold-translation) pairs. This is similar to how artificial target sentences were constructed by Li et al. (2021), but in our case, the boundaries are determined by automatic punctuation on ASR output, rather than from introducing boundary errors at random.

Table 4 shows the resulting human English and gold German segments for our running example; the source row marked with $+$ is used in Segment Robustness training. To illustrate the length-ratio token alignment, we can see that the total token length of the human English is 12, and the gold German is 13. The English is segmented into lengths 4 and 8, meaning the German is segmented to lengths $4/12 \cdot 13 = 4.33 \approx 4$ and $8/12 \cdot 13 = 8.66 \approx 9$. The resulting references will not always semantically match the content in the new source segments. In this example, they do not: an English gloss of the German shows that the semantics have diverged. But they are often close enough, and our hypothesis is that the benefit of exposure to realistic source fragments will outweigh the cost of occasional semantic misalignment. Furthermore, we use this robustness data only to fine-tune a system that has seen many semantically valid pairs.

3.4 System Robustness Training

In Section 3.3, the inverted projection approach was applied to the human transcripts. While this may seem unnatural, it provides a measure of the improvement that can be achieved by just adjusting the training set's source segment boundaries so that they match what the model will see during inference. Next, we build upon this approach by injecting the ASR token errors into the training data as well.

Training a model that sees both system token errors and segment boundary errors involves a slight variation on the setup in Section 3.3. We use the same alignment approach, but here we use it only to get projected gold translations since the system transcripts already have system segment boundaries. We then train the model with (system source, projected-gold-translation) pairs.

The main advantage of this approach is that the source side exactly matches the pipeline, completely bridging the train-test mismatch. The disadvantage, as in Section 3.3, is that the system segments may lead to fragmented or semantically misaligned reference sentences. Table 4 marks the source row used for System Robustness training with a $**$.

4 Experimental Setup

4.1 Data

We experiment on the IWSLT English to German (EnDe) speech translation scenario. We use the

IWSLT 2018 EnDe training data, including both the official training set and the leftover TED talks not included in any other test set, for a total of about 2400 talks and 0.25M sentence pairs. We found it beneficial to also include the 4.6M sentence pairs of the WMT 2018 EnDe corpus (Bojar et al., 2018) during training to increase our feasible MT model size and MT accuracy. For the IWSLT data, we scrape the ground truth transcripts and translations from www.ted.com directly because we found that the official IWSLT datasets omit transcriptions for many sentences. Since we are interested in long-form scenarios, we want to be sure to retain all sentences.

We evaluate our models on past IWSLT spoken language translation test sets. We use IWSLT tst2014 (Cettolo et al., 2014) as a dev set, which consists of 14 TED talks and about 1,200 sentences. We test on IWSLT tst2015 (Cettolo et al., 2015), which consists of 12 TED talks totalling about 1,200 sentences. Punctuated ASR transcriptions are obtained from the publicly available Speech-to-Text Google API[1]; using a separate ASR system in this way disconnects the ASR and NMT models, improving modularity. This achieves a WER of 5.5% on tst2015 ignoring case and punctuation. We run a sentence breaker on the punctuated source to determine the segments to be translated by NMT. Since these segments need not match the reference sentence boundaries, especially when punctuation is derived automatically on ASR output, we use our Levenshtein alignment as described in Section 3 to align our translation output with the gold-standard translation's segments before evaluating quality with case-sensitive BLEU (Matusov et al., 2005). All models are trained and tested on lowercased and unpunctuated versions of the source, as doing so is known to improve robustness to ASR output (Li et al., 2021).

4.2 Baseline

For all our experiments, we use a Transformer model (Vaswani et al., 2017) with a model dimension of 1024, hidden size of 8192, 16 heads for multihead attention, and 6 layers in the encoder and decoder. The models are regularized using a dropout of 0.3 and label smoothing of 0.1 (Szegedy et al., 2015). We use a shared SentencePiece tokenizer (Kudo and Richardson, 2018) with a 32k vocabulary. We decided on these settings through hyper-parameter tuning on the IWSLT dev set.

As a baseline, we train a model that includes a mix of WMT and human-transcribed IWSLT data, but with no ASR-transcribed IWSLT data. During training, for each batch, we sample 90% of data from WMT and 10% from IWSLT. This mixture was chosen based on the best performance of a grid-search of weightings between these two datasets evaluated on the IWSLT dev set. Because this baseline has already seen the human transcripts and translations of the IWSLT data, it has already adapted its domain to both news and TED data. By ensuring that this baseline has already adapted, we are able to isolate the effects of ASR errors and segmentation errors on the fine-tuned models. We train the model using pairs of (source, target) sentences, where target German translations are untouched, retaining case and punctuation.

4.3 Model fine-tuning

Starting from the baseline, we fine-tune the model on data from each scenario, each time starting from the same checkpoint of the baseline. The best-performing checkpoint of each fine-tuning experiment is chosen based on the BLEU score on the dev set, and this checkpoint is used to evaluate on the test set. Fine-tuning is about 35x faster than training from scratch in our configuration and converges after running through less than 5 epochs of the IWSLT data ($\approx$0.25M sentence pairs). We repeat each experiment multiple times to account for any variations in the runs.

4.4 Filtering

All of the processing steps described so far have included all of the ASR sentences, regardless of their quality. However, some ASR sentences have high WER compared with the human transcripts. This happens when, for example, the ASR transcribes a video playing in the background that was not included in the gold transcript. These examples can be so egregious that they can confuse the model. To filter the dataset, we remove only from our *training set* all ASR sentences with WER $\geq$ 50% as compared with the human transcripts; this removes approximately 4% of the training data. The sentences with WER between 0% and 50% are useful because they demonstrate ASR errors relative to human transcripts but not egregious errors. We include results on this filtered set as an additional row in our results tables. Note that the filtering is only applied to the training data and is not applied on

[1] `http://cloud.google.com/speech-to-text`

the test set since we wouldn't have access to WER during inference time. This should not be confused with the average WER measured on each test set, which is 5.5% for IWSLT (see Table 5) and 9.0% for YouTube (see Table 6), which is an indicator of the quality of the NMT model's input source sentences generated by the ASR system.

5 Results

5.1 IWSLT results

Table 5 compares the results of the different combinations of segments and tokens from Table 1. For the test set, automatic punctuation is first applied and used to split the ASR output into sentences, and then it is stripped of case and punctuation. Sentences are translated one at a time with whatever system is under test. The checkpoint is chosen according to the dev set for each scenario, and the resulting BLEU scores on the test set are presented in the "ASR" column. For completeness, we also compute the BLEU score on the IWSLT human transcripts using the same model and checkpoint and report it in the "HT" column. As expected, this "HT" score decreases with increasing adaptation to the system tokens and segments, but this does not affect our results because, during inference, our system will only be applied to ASR sentences with automatic punctuation.

The baseline, trained from scratch using the human tokens and human segments (WMT + IWSLT), achieves a score of 26.5 BLEU points on the ASR set. As described in Section 4.2, this baseline training uses only 10% IWSLT data. Since the fine-tuning experiments use 100% IWSLT data, those models are arguably more adapted to the TED domain, which could contribute to any improvements over the baseline. To control for this, we fine-tuned an additional model on 100% human token, human segment IWSLT data, but this yielded no improvement over the baseline, likely because the baseline has already seen this IWSLT data during training. Thus, we didn't include this experiment in Table 5.

All of the fine-tuning experiments in Table 5 start with the baseline from the first row, which was trained without knowledge of the ASR transcripts. The Token Robustness experiment starts from the baseline and fine-tunes on ASR; it shows no improvement compared to the baseline, which indicates that the ASR errors are sufficiently subtle compared to the segment errors so that the model cannot adapt to them. On the other hand, the last 3

Training condition	HT	ASR
Baseline (human tokens and segments)	33.6	26.5
Token Robustness (ASR source, human segments)	32.7	26.0
Segment Robustness (human source, system segments)	32.1	27.1
System Robustness (ASR source, system segments)	32.1	27.4
System Robustness (ASR source with WER $\leq$ 50%, system segments)	32.3	27.6

Table 5: Results on IWSLT tst2015 data. HT stands for "human transcript". All numbers represent the translation BLEU, and each score is the average across 3 runs. The ASR WER on the test sentences is 5.5%.

rows demonstrate significant gains when the text is projected using the system segments. In particular, the System Robustness experiment shows an improvement over the Segment Robustness, and the best results are achieved with System Robustness when removing ASR transcripts with high WER. This yields a gain of more than 1 BLEU point over the baseline. This indicates that, once the train-test segment mismatch has been corrected for, the model is able to adapt to and correct the subtle ASR errors. These improvements indicate the value of making the segmentation errors visible to NMT training using the two steps of projecting source and re-aligning translation.

The fact that our Token Robustness model does not improve over the baseline is likely because there are very few lexical errors since our ASR model for English is very good, with a mean WER of 5.5%. This is true even when we use the approach from Section 4.4 to remove high WER ASR sentences during training (results not included in Table 5). This is in contrast to the results of Cheng et al. (2019), which demonstrated improvements using ASR with human segments. Those results, however, were achieved with the ASR model provided by IWSLT 2018, which has a much worse WER than the ASR used in our work.[2] We likely could have replicated their result had we used a weaker ASR model.

Our Segment Robustness approach and dataset are similar to the synthetic segment breaks ap-

[2]Zenkel et al. (2018) report that the IWSLT 2018 ASR has a WER of 22.8% on IWSLT tst2014, while the ASR used in our experiments achieves a WER of 8.0% on the same set.

Training condition	HT	ASR
Baseline (human tokens and segments)	30.3	25.4
Token Robustness (ASR source, human segments)	29.8	25.1
Segment Robustness (human source, system segments)	29.3	26.6
System Robustness (ASR source, system segments)	29.3	26.4
System Robustness (ASR source with WER $\leq$ 50%, system segments)	29.4	26.6

Table 6: Results on 88 English videos from YouTube translated into German. No new models were trained in these experiments: the models trained in Table 5 were directly evaluated on these videos. The ASR WER on the test sentences is 9.0%.

proach in (Li et al., 2021). According to Table 5, our results yielded a BLEU score of 27.1, which is similar to the score of 27.0 reported in Table 4 of that paper, which represents their best result from training with synthetic segment breaks.

5.2 YouTube results

To test the generalization of our approach, we applied the models trained on the IWSLT data in Section 5.1 to another dataset consisting of 88 English videos selected from YouTube. The videos are selected to have a single speaker, and are truncated to a length of roughly 1 minute, perhaps interrupting a sentence. Each of the 920 sentences in the human transcription of these videos was professionally translated into German.

No new models were trained in this section; every line in Table 6 is a corresponding system from Table 5. For each of the experiments, we take the corresponding model trained on IWSLT and test it on this new YouTube EnDe test set. This enables us to determine the generalization ability of the approach.

According to Table 6, the model performs remarkably similar on this YouTube dataset. In particular, the improvement over the baseline of the System Robustness in the last row is about 1.2 BLEU points, comparable to the 1.1 BLEU point improvement in Table 5.

Note that, because the models were fine-tuned on the IWSLT ASR dataset starting from a mix of WMT and IWSLT, there is a domain mismatch between this training data and the YouTube testing data. Nevertheless, the System Robustness approach shows a clear improvement. Thus, we expect that if we trained a model directly on YouTube data, we would see even higher BLEU scores. This is a task for future work.

6 Conclusions

To aid text-based translation models to adapt to speech data, we introduced an inverted projection approach that projects automatically detected system segments onto human transcripts and then re-segments the gold translations to align with the projected human transcripts. This approach overcomes the train-test mismatch present in previous attempts to train on long-form ASR output by exposing MT training to both token and segment errors, exactly matching the source transcription pipeline used at test time. The results demonstrate a gain of over 1 BLEU point on both IWSLT data and YouTube data.

For future work, we aim to train models on languages with higher ASR WER since our English WER is very low (5.5%). We also plan to experiment with MT targets during training to address the data bottleneck. And we also plan to investigate whether we can eliminate segmentation altogether with document-level speech translation.

Acknowledgments

We would like to thank Naveen Ari, Te I, and Wolfgang Macherey for their deep discussions about this work and for their helpful suggestions while reviewing our paper.

References

Naveen Arivazhagan, Colin Cherry, Wolfgang Macherey, and George Foster. 2020. Re-translation versus streaming for simultaneous translation. In *Proceedings of the 17th International Conference on Spoken Language Translation*, pages 220–227, Online. Association for Computational Linguistics.

Sameer Bansal, Herman Kamper, Karen Livescu, Adam Lopez, and Sharon Goldwater. 2018. Low-resource speech-to-text translation. In *Proceedings of INTERSPEECH*.

Ondřej Bojar, Christian Federmann, Mark Fishel, Yvette Graham, Barry Haddow, Philipp Koehn, and Christof Monz. 2018. Findings of the 2018 conference on machine translation (WMT18). In *Proceedings of the Third Conference on Machine Translation: Shared Task Papers*, pages 272–303, Belgium, Brussels. Association for Computational Linguistics.

Mauro Cettolo, Jan Niehues, Sebastian Stüker, Luisa Bentivogli, Roldano Cattoni, and Marcello Federico. 2015. The IWSLT 2015 evaluation campaign. In *International Workshop on Spoken Language Translation (IWSLT)*.

Mauro Cettolo, Jan Niehues, Sebastian Stüker, Luisa Bentivogli, and Marcello Federico. 2014. Report on the 11th IWSLT evaluation campaign. In *International Workshop on Spoken Language Translation (IWSLT)*.

Qiao Cheng, Meiyuan Fang, Yaqian Han, Jin Huang, and Yitao Duan. 2019. Breaking the data barrier: Towards robust speech translation via adversarial stability training. In *International Workshop on Spoken Language Translation (IWSLT)*.

Yong Cheng, Zhaopeng Tu, Fandong Meng, Junjie Zhai, and Yang Liu. 2018. Towards robust neural machine translation. In *Proceedings of the 56th Annual Meeting of the Association for Computational Linguistics (Volume 1: Long Papers)*, pages 1756–1766, Melbourne, Australia. Association for Computational Linguistics.

Kyunghyun Cho and Masha Esipova. 2016. Can neural machine translation do simultaneous translation? *CoRR*, abs/1606.02012.

Alina Karakanta, Matteo Negri, and Marco Turchi. 2020. Is 42 the answer to everything in subtitling-oriented speech translation? In *Proceedings of the 17th International Conference on Spoken Language Translation*, pages 209–219, Online. Association for Computational Linguistics.

Taku Kudo and John Richardson. 2018. SentencePiece: A simple and language independent subword tokenizer and detokenizer for neural text processing. In *Proceedings of the 2018 Conference on Empirical Methods in Natural Language Processing: System Demonstrations*, pages 66–71, Brussels, Belgium. Association for Computational Linguistics.

Daniel Li, Te I, Naveen Arivazhagan, Colin Cherry, and Dirk Padfield. 2021. Sentence boundary augmentation for neural machine translation robustness. In *ICASSP 2021 - 2021 IEEE International Conference on Acoustics, Speech and Signal Processing (ICASSP)*, pages 7553–7557.

Xiang Li, Haiyang Xue, Wei Chen, Yang Liu, Yang Feng, and Qun Liu. 2018. Improving the robustness of speech translation. *CoRR*, abs/1811.00728.

Hairong Liu, Mingbo Ma, Liang Huang, Hao Xiong, and Zhongjun He. 2019. Robust neural machine translation with joint textual and phonetic embedding. In *Proceedings of the 57th Annual Meeting of the Association for Computational Linguistics*, pages 3044–3049, Florence, Italy. Association for Computational Linguistics.

Mingbo Ma, Liang Huang, Hao Xiong, Renjie Zheng, Kaibo Liu, Baigong Zheng, Chuanqiang Zhang, Zhongjun He, Hairong Liu, Xing Li, Hua Wu, and Haifeng Wang. 2019. STACL: Simultaneous translation with implicit anticipation and controllable latency using prefix-to-prefix framework. In *Proceedings of the 57th Annual Meeting of the Association for Computational Linguistics*, pages 3025–3036, Florence, Italy. Association for Computational Linguistics.

K. Makhija, T. Ho, and E. Chng. 2019. Transfer learning for punctuation prediction. In *2019 Asia-Pacific Signal and Information Processing Association Annual Summit and Conference (APSIPA ASC)*, pages 268–273.

Evgeny Matusov, Gregor Leusch, Oliver Bender, and Hermann Ney. 2005. Evaluating machine translation output with automatic sentence segmentation. In *International Workshop on Spoken Language Translation (IWSLT)*.

Binh Nguyen, Vu Bao Hung Nguyen, Hien Nguyen, Pham Ngoc Phuong, The-Loc Nguyen, Quoc Truong Do, and Luong Chi Mai. 2019. Fast and accurate capitalization and punctuation for automatic speech recognition using transformer and chunk merging.

Jan Niehues, Ngoc-Quan Pham, Thanh-Le Ha, Matthias Sperber, and Alex Waibel. 2018. Low-latency neural speech translation. In *Proceedings of INTERSPEECH*, pages 1293–1297.

Matt Post, Gaurav Kumar, Adam Lopez, Damianos Karakos, Chris Callison-Burch, and Sanjeev Khudanpur. 2013. Improved speech-to-text translation with the fisher and callhome spanish–english speech translation corpus. In *International Workshop on Spoken Language Translation (IWSLT)*.

Nicholas Ruiz, Mattia Antonino Di Gangi, Nicola Bertoldi, and Marcello Federico. 2017. Assessing the tolerance of neural machine translation systems against speech recognition errors. In *Proc. Interspeech 2017*, pages 2635–2639.

Matthias Sperber, Graham Neubig, Jan Niehues, and Alex Waibel. 2019. Attention-passing models for robust and data-efficient end-to-end speech translation. *Transactions of the Association for Computational Linguistics*, 7:313–325.

Matthias Sperber, Jan Niehues, and Alex Waibel. 2017. Toward robust neural machine translation for noisy input sequences. In *International Workshop on Spoken Language Translation (IWSLT)*.

Christian Szegedy, Vincent Vanhoucke, Sergey Ioffe, Jonathon Shlens, and Zbigniew Wojna. 2015. Rethinking the inception architecture for computer vision. *CoRR*, abs/1512.00567.

Ashish Vaswani, Noam Shazeer, Niki Parmar, Jakob Uszkoreit, Llion Jones, Aidan N. Gomez, Lukasz Kaiser, and Illia Polosukhin. 2017. Attention is all you need. *CoRR*, abs/1706.03762.

Xiaolin Wang, Masao Utiyama, and Eiichiro Sumita. 2019. Online sentence segmentation for simultaneous interpretation using multi-shifted recurrent neural network. In *Proceedings of Machine Translation Summit XVII Volume 1: Research Track*, pages 1–11, Dublin, Ireland. European Association for Machine Translation.

Ron J Weiss, Jan Chorowski, Navdeep Jaitly, Yonghui Wu, and Zhifeng Chen. 2017. Sequence-to-sequence models can directly transcribe foreign speech. In *Proceedings of INTERSPEECH*.

Thomas Zenkel, Matthias Sperber, Jan Niehues, Markus Müller, Ngoc-Quan Pham, Sebastian Stüker, and Alex Waibel. 2018. Open source toolkit for speech to text translation. *Prague Bull. Math. Linguistics*, 111:125–135.

Towards the evaluation of automatic simultaneous speech translation from a communicative perspective

Claudio Fantinuoli
Mainz University/KUDO
fantinuoli@uni-mainz.de

Bianca Prandi
Mainz University
prandi@uni-mainz.de

Abstract

In recent years, automatic speech-to-speech and speech-to-text translation has gained momentum thanks to advances in artificial intelligence, especially in the domains of speech recognition and machine translation. The quality of such applications is commonly tested with automatic metrics, such as BLEU, primarily with the goal of assessing improvements of releases or in the context of evaluation campaigns. However, little is known about how the output of such systems is perceived by end users or how they compare to human performances in similar communicative tasks.

In this paper, we present the results of an experiment aimed at evaluating the quality of a real-time speech translation engine by comparing it to the performance of professional simultaneous interpreters. To do so, we adopt a framework developed for the assessment of human interpreters and use it to perform a manual evaluation on both human and machine performances. In our sample, we found better performance for the human interpreters in terms of intelligibility, while the machine performs slightly better in terms of informativeness. The limitations of the study and the possible enhancements of the chosen framework are discussed. Despite its intrinsic limitations, the use of this framework represents a first step towards a user-centric and communication-oriented methodology for evaluating real-time automatic speech translation.

1 Introduction

Real-time or simultaneous speech translation (ST) aims at translating a continuous speech input from one language to another with the lowest latency[1] and highest quality possible. In recent years, automatic speech translation systems have been developed at scale, and their quality has improved significantly (Sperber and Paulik, 2020). At present, research is increasingly focusing on end-to-end trainable encoder-decoder models, i.e. speech-to-speech (STS) or speech-to-text (STT) translation systems that directly match source and target language (Di Gangi et al., 2018; Jia et al., 2019; Ansari et al., 2020). Nonetheless, the cascading approach is de facto still the mainstream solution for speech translation (ST). The main reason is that this approach benefits from the remarkable improvements in automatic speech recognition (ASR) (Chiu et al., 2018) and machine translation (MT) (Barrault et al., 2020) obtained thanks to the wealth of task-specific data available. In cascading systems, the process of translating from speech to text or from speech to speech is performed by a series of concatenated modules. In most cases, these systems apply ASR to the speech input, and then pass the results on to an MT engine. Since a short latency is an important characteristic of such systems, the translation is rendered while the source is unfolding, on the basis of different approaches ranging from simple time delay to complex agents that establish when the context is sufficient to perform the translation. Several additional components can be integrated into this pipeline, such as text normalization (Fügen, 2008), suppression of speech disfluencies (Fitzgerald et al., 2009), prosody transfer (Kano et al., 2018), and so forth.

Real-time ST systems have the potential to be used in communicative settings, such as institutional events, lectures, conferences, etc. in order to make multilingual content accessible in real-time, thus increasing inclusion and participation when human services for language accessibility are not available, such as live interlingual subtitling (Romero-Fresco and Pöchhacker, 2017) or conference interpreting (Pöchhacker, 2016). So far, the evaluation of ST in general, and real-time ST in par-

[1]In this context, we broadly define latency as the time delay from when an utterance is pronounced in the source language to when it gets translated in the target language.

Proceedings of the 18th International Conference on Spoken Language Translation, pages 245–254
Bangkok, Thailand (Online), August 5–6, 2021.

ticular, has been framed in the domain of computer science (CS). In CS, automatic metrics are applied in order to compare systems and monitor progress over time[2]. However, little is known about how such systems, that for the sake of this paper we will define as machine interpreting (MI) systems[3], perform in real communication settings and whether they are able to meet the needs of end users. To the best of our knowledge, no evaluation framework has been developed and deployed in the past to assess the performance of such systems from a communicative perspective.

To address this shortcoming, in the present contribution we apply a user-centric evaluation framework derived from Interpreting Studies (IS) to the task of assessing an automatic system for ST. Moving towards an evaluation framework that takes into consideration the authentic communicative setting, we compare the performances of the automated system with the performances of professional simultaneous interpreters. We do so in order to assess the level of usability of such framework and to benchmark the performances of the machine, inferring the suitability of the ST system for the proposed communication task from its comparison with the human performance.

The rest of the paper is organised as follows. In Section 2, we present an overview of research areas in the field of automatic speech translation and human interpreting evaluation. In Section 3, we illustrate our research methodology and the experimental design. Section 3.1 describes the dataset created for this task, while Section 3.2 introduces the framework used to evaluate the performance of the machine and of the human interpreters. Section 4 presents the results of the evaluation and Section 5 discusses and puts the results into perspective. Section 6 concludes the paper with final remarks.

2 Related work

The evaluation of simultaneous speech translation, independently of whether the process is performed by a human or a machine, is a topic central both to the domain of Computer Science and of Interpreting Studies.

[2]See for example the methodology used for the shared task of the International Conference on Spoken Language Translation 2021 available at https://iwslt.org/2021/simultaneous

[3]We tentatively define as Machine Interpreting all automatic methods of real-time speech translation, i.e. cascading, end-to-end, into text, into speech, etc. that are used in the context of real-life communication.

In CS, ST is typically evaluated in terms of quality and latency. Similar to MT, the approach used consists in the application of automatic metrics in order to allow for a fast and objective evaluation of the systems (Ma et al., 2020). However, due to its novelty, the ST research community currently lacks a universally adopted evaluation methodology. Quality is generally measured by BLEU (Papineni et al., 2002; Post, 2018), TER (Snover et al., 2006) and METEOR (Banerjee and Lavie, 2005). The approach to compare system outputs against source texts, gold standard translations, and other system outputs represents, despite the limitations of such metrics (Babych, 2014), a widely accepted evaluation methodology. The measurement of latency, which broadly corresponds to the ear-voice span of human interpreting (e.g. Gile, 2009), represents a more challenging task that still lacks sufficient clarity and consistency. In this context, several metrics have been introduced, such as Average Proportion (AP) (Cho and Esipova, 2016), Continues Wait Length (CW) (Gu et al., 2017), Average Lagging (AL) (Ma et al., 2020), Differentiable Average Lagging (DAL) (Cherry and Foster, 2019). Generally speaking, the evaluation approach used in CS is product-oriented. The concept of quality is limited to measuring proximity in the linguistic surface between translation and ground truth. It does not take into consideration the user perception, the pragmatic aspect of communication, and, intrinsically, cannot consider the translation process as embedded in a communicative event (e.g. Angelelli, 2002).

This is different to IS. Since human interpretation always occurs in a specific communicative setting, the need to evaluate it accordingly has always been in focus. Here, the pursuit of conceptual and methodological tools for the empirical study and assessment of quality has a long tradition, particularly in the conference domain and simultaneous modality (e.g. Pöchhacker, 2002; Kalina, 2005; Collados Aís and García Becerra, 2015). Despite the different perspectives that have been adopted to define and evaluate quality, there is considerable agreement among scholars on a number of criteria which are considered fundamental when evaluating human interpretation. Most criteria of quality are associated with the product-oriented perspective and can be subsumed in two main areas, the first one focusing primarily on the interpretation or target-text as "a 'faithful' image" (Gile, 2009) or "exact and faithful reproduction" (Jones, 2002) of the original speech, the second one on the notion of intelligibility, also called clarity, target-text comprehensibility, linguistic acceptability, stylistic correctness, etc. Such evaluation is centred on the view of interpreting as a language processing task. At an even higher level, quality can also be seen under the paradigm of a holistic idea of successful communication. From this perspective, interpreting is assessed on the basis of whether it successfully allows the parties involved in a particular context of interaction to achieve their communicative goal, as judged from the various perspectives in and on the communicative event (Gile, 2009). The focus of this perspective is no longer on the product (the rendition), but rather on the communicative action performed to achieve a certain purpose and effect, and therefore on the holistic function of facilitating communicative interaction (Pöchhacker, 2002).

From a methodological perspective, quality in interpretation has been evaluated through surveys (Feldweg, 1996), measures of performance through experimentation (Shlesinger, 1995), or corpus-based analysis (Bendazzoli, 2018). Different to the CS approach, which is based on automatic metrics, the analysis of data in IS is performed on the basis of a manual evaluation of the corpus data.

While such evaluation frameworks have been designed and used regularly in the domain of machine translation, very few attempts have been made so far to evaluate the performance of automatic speech translation system both in the context of the product-based and of the holistic/communicative approach. A few pilot studies on the usability of ST systems have only been performed in the context of dialogue interpreting (Cürten, 2016; Wonisch, 2017), while only one has been attempted in the area of real-time ST (Müller et al., 2016). We believe that such approaches, if appropriately adapted to the research desideratum at hand, could contribute to a better understanding and evaluation of machine speech translation systems.

3 Data and methodology

As discussed in the previous section, ST systems are typically evaluated by means of automatic metrics using reference datasets. Although such evaluations are useful to compare systems among each other, one of their main limitations is that they do not take into consideration the communicative setting nor the perception of their usefulness by final users. To overcome this limitation, we select and apply to the assessment of ST a user-centric framework commonly used for the evaluation of human interpretation.

In order to understand the potential usefulness of the automatically generated translation, we compare the machine performance with a gold standard: the interpretation delivered by professional human interpreters in the real context of the event. Simultaneous interpretation (SI) is the modality most commonly used to provide multilingual access in real-time[4]. Since we assume that the service provided by professional interpreters allows communication among the parties in the event, we consider it to be our "communicative" ground truth. This gold standard is not an ideal rendition of the original, but it comes with all the benefits and limitations of the real simultaneous translation used at a specific event to overcome language barriers. By means of this comparison we can infer, at least to some extent, the communicative performance of the machine in the context of a real communicative event. The overall question driving our research is therefore "How does the performance of a speech-to-text translation system compare with human SI?".

To answer this question we compile a corpus of speeches in English delivered in real-life contexts and align them with their human interpreted versions into Italian as well as with the output of a simultaneous STT translation system chosen for this task. The dataset is described in Section 3.1. We manually assess the quality of the human and automatic renditions (transcriptions) on the basis of the evaluation framework described in Section 3.2. This evaluation represents an attempt to apply a more user-centric approach to the assessment of the automatic service provided by STT translation systems.

3.1 Dataset

There are several speech translation corpora currently available, such as MuST-C (Di Gangi et al., 2019) and Europarl-ST (Iranzo-Sánchez et al., 2020). They generally contain source speeches in one language and the corresponding written or, in a few cases, spoken translations in the target language(s). While they are useful to explore end-to-end ST, for example to train the language models, they have not been designed with the goal of

[4]The other would be interlingual respeaking for the creation of live subtitling which is, however, still in its infancy.

assessing such systems from a communicative perspective. As a matter of fact, the target language component of the corpus is in most cases an edited translation, therefore a product of mediated, offline, and decontextualized work.

To overcome this limitation, we create a new pilot corpus of speeches (lectures) and of their live translations which would allow us to conduct a better evaluation of the machine output by comparing it with the gold standard produced by humans in a real communicative event (see Section 3).

The main rationale behind the creation of our corpus is the selection of naturally occurring data on which to conduct our observation, both for the original speech and, most importantly, for the gold standard (the basis of the comparison).

The five speeches selected for the corpus are randomly extracted from two series of talks ("Festival dell'economia" and "Meeting di Rimini") that had been originally interpreted simultaneously from English into Italian by five different interpreters. Both the original speeches and their interpretations are publicly available on the web[5]. After choosing the events, 2-minute extracts are randomly selected from each speech. The small size of the corpus does not allow for generalizations, but should provide indications on the suitability of the chosen evaluation framework. With this approach, the ecological validity is maximal, as the research data are drawn from real interpreted events, while the level of control is minimal, making data harder to interpret, especially when it comes to causality (Baekelandt and Defrancq, 2020).

The speeches included in the corpus[6] are summarised in Table 1. While all the speakers had presented in English, three were native speakers (texts 1, 3 and 5) and two were not (texts 2 and 4). As for the source text delivery mode, four speakers presented "impromptu" speeches (texts 1, 2 , 4 and 5) and one a "read-aloud" speech (text 3). The topics included: economy (text 1), bit coin (text 2), artificial intelligence (text 3), green growth (text 4) and medicine (text 5), with different degrees of technicality. The audio quality was good for all speeches. The speed of delivery ranges from 142 to 160 words per minute (wpm) and is in line with typical speech rates at conferences (e.g. Seeber, 2015).

Similar to Batista et al. (2008), the corpus for evaluation is presented in written form. Since the output of the STT is already produced by the engine as written text, only the source speeches and the human interpretations are transcribed by means of an ASR engine and manually corrected. The ST output is included in the corpus without modifications. The five texts are segmented in utterances and aligned with the interpretations. The number of segments for each text ranges from 16 to 20.

Text	Duration	Words	Speed (wpm)
1	2' 10"	347	160
2	2' 02"	288	142
3	2' 00"	320	160
4	2' 01"	304	157
5	2' 07"	320	151

Table 1: Corpus features

For this experiment, we choose the real-time ST service offered by Azure Speech Translation [7]. The main reason for this choice is that the service is available as a commercial API and represents the state-of-the art of cascading systems. Different to human interpreters, who deliver the translation orally, this API translates speech into written text without any form of speech synthesis. In principle, this generates an asymmetry in the evaluation. However, since the selected framework requires the evaluation to be performed on the written transcriptions, this lack of symmetry has been deemed as non central for the purpose of this experiment.

To collect the data of the ST engine, a simple Web application was created by the authors around the API. The application sends the original speech to the API and records the real-time translation returned by the service. Because the evaluation is performed on written transcriptions, in this experiment the latency of the system was not taken into account, and only the final translation hypothesis generated was considered for the evaluation. This is a major limitation of this study that needs to be addressed in future experiments.

3.2 Evaluation framework and procedure

For the investigation and the comparison of the human and the machine output, an evaluation framework derived from the Interpreting Studies

[5] `https://www.festivaleconomia.it/` and `https://www.meetingrimini.org`

[6] The corpus is available at `https://cai.uni-mainz.de/steval`.

[7] `https://azure.microsoft.com/en-en/services/cognitive-services/speech-translation/`

(Tiselius, 2009) is chosen and slightly adapted. The framework is "assumed to account for central aspects of the interpreted event but not for its entirety as a communicative event" (Tiselius, 2009, p. 99). As discussed in Section 1, at this stage we follow a product-based approach to quality assessment in IS, leaving the situated evaluation of the interpreted event for later explorations, for which an extended framework comprising additional communicative perspectives and criteria should be defined. Notwithstanding the limitations of this approach, one of the advantages of Tiselius's framework against automatic metrics lies in its being user-centric and in line with the corpus-based evaluation already established in Interpreting Studies to assess the quality of human interpretation.

Tiselius defines the framework as "an easy-to-use tool that can be implemented by laypeople in order to assess a transcribed version of a simultaneous interpreting performance" (Tiselius, 2009, p. 99). This aspect is particularly important for possible future use of the framework. In order to further streamline it, we slightly simplified the evaluation scale, and adapted its wording in order to make it suitable to express a judgement on both human and automatic speech translation.

The framework aims at assessing the target production on the basis of two dimensions:

- Intelligibility, defined as the evaluation of the target text in terms of fluency, clarity, adequacy etc., performed without a comparison with the source text
- Informativeness, defined as the evaluation of the target text in terms of semantic information content, performed with a comparison with the source text

The two dimensions reflect the main criteria at the core of the product-oriented approach to quality evaluation in IS (Section 2). 6 raters with a background in interpreting and translation are asked to conduct the evaluation of the human interpretation (HI) and the machine output (MI). For each speech, the raters are asked to assess on a six-point Likert scale first the intelligibility of the HI and of the MI output (without a comparison with the source speech nor a comparison between the two outputs), then to evaluate the informativeness of the two renditions (HI and MI) by comparing each one to the source speech.

While this methodology represents a first step towards a more holistic approach to the evaluation of ST, it also presents a series of shortcomings:

- The product-based evaluation of the gold standard, the HI, is conducted on transcriptions and not on the audio output. Not only do prosody, modulation of voice, hesitations, etc. constitute distinctive aspects of spoken (human) language, but they are also actively used by human interpreters to reach several communicative goals. They contribute, for example, to disambiguate oral speech, explicate references, etc. The evaluation on the basis of transcriptions deprives the evaluator of these key features, with obvious negative implications for the quality scores. A viable option could be to perform the evaluation on the basis of an audio corpus, thus retaining all the features of spoken language during the evaluation of the human interpreters. Another promising way to address this shortcoming would be to resort to interlingual respeaking as a gold standard instead of HI. Since the output of respeakers is a written rendition of the original in the target language, it would make the output of human and automatic ST more comparable.
- Notwithstanding the efforts made to keep the framework as simple as possible, the evaluation procedure proves quite time-consuming. Conducting evaluation campaigns on a bigger scale with this framework may be hampered by this aspect.
- The item definitions in the six-point scale are not sufficiently straightforward to guide the rater in taking a decision. Further simplification and rewording are required.
- The assessment does not take into consideration latency, which is important to judge the real-time translation at a communicative level, especially as far as the user experience is concerned. The ST system used in the experiment, for example, performed real-time adaptations on the target language, i.e. modifying the translation hypothesis while receiving increasing context from the source speech. The impact on comprehension and user friendliness of both this aspect and disfluencies in the human rendition should be studied more attentively in future.

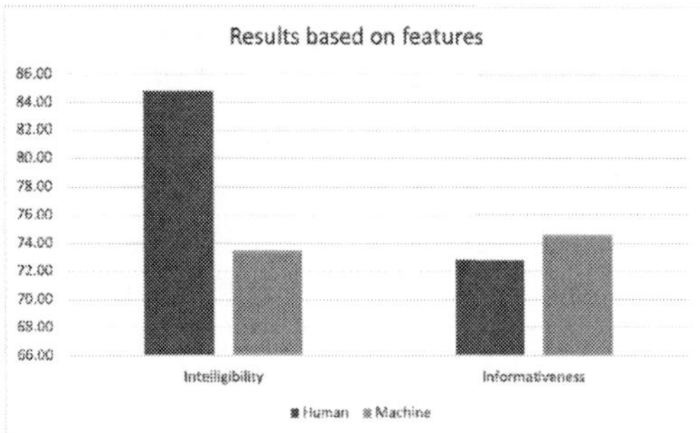

Figure 1: Intelligibility and informativeness scores for the human and the machine output.

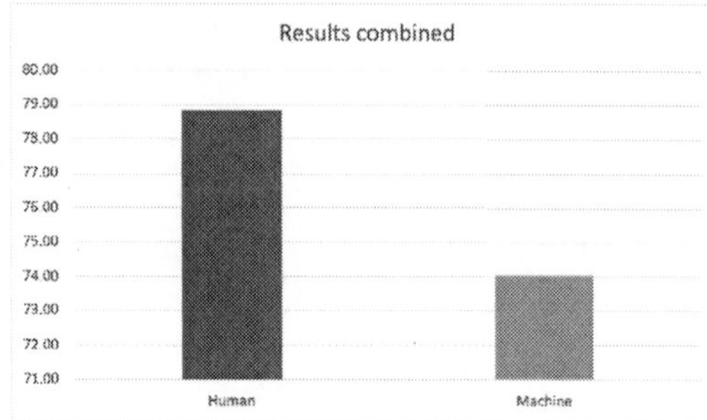

Figure 2: Scores combined for the human and the machine output.

- As will become clear in Section 4, resorting to human interpretation instead of written translation as a gold standard calls for new strategies in the evaluation. Because human interpreters and ST systems perform the task using a different approach (linear for machines, interpretive for humans), the comparison using classical methodologies may be inadequate.

The shortcomings of the evaluation framework should be addressed in a follow-up study.

4 Results

The scores for each of the two parameters (intelligibility and informativeness) are summed for each speech, output and rater and then averaged. The relative percentage score is calculated on the maximum amount of points obtainable for each text. The figures below illustrate the results of data analysis.

As shown by Figure 1, human interpreters obtain better scores for intelligibility (84.84 % to 73.49 %), while the machine output is rated slightly better than the human interpretations in terms of informativeness (74.63 % to 72.82 %).

When combining the scores for the two rating criteria (Figure 2), the human output surpasses machine output by 4.77 percentage points. It can be argued that the two parameters do not have the same weight in terms of their impact on the success of the communicative event. At this stage of evaluation, however, we decide to combine them without any weight and to leave this more in-depth analysis to a later phase of development of our evaluation framework.

Figure 3 illustrates the standard deviation (SD) for the two evaluation parameters for all 5 speeches.

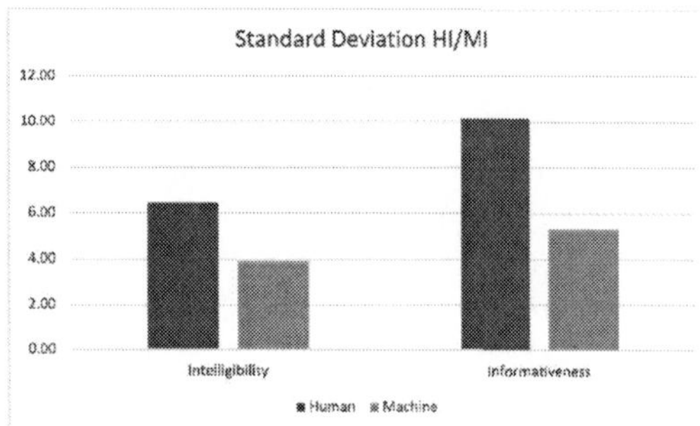

Figure 3: Standard deviation of the intelligibility and informativeness scores (human and machine output).

Both for the criterion intelligibility and for the criterion informativeness, the SD for the human output is larger than for the machine output, for which the scores are very close to each other in our sample.

This result suggests that variables such as topic, density, speed of the original speech, accents, etc. affect less the machine than the human interpreter. On the one hand, this is quite surprising if one considers that aspects such as performance of ASR with foreign accents, to name but one example, are considered detrimental in automatic language processing (Kitashov et al., 2018; Shi et al., 2021). On the other hand, the larger SD for the human output may point to the fact that humans tend to have a high degree of variance in performances due to different background knowledge, skills, etc. Because of the small size of the corpus, the trends observed in the present study cannot be generalized and the analysis should be conducted on a larger sample.

In order to verify the adequacy of the evaluation methodology, and in particular of the rating scales used to assess intelligibility and informativeness achieved by the human and the machine interpretation, Krippendorff's α is calculated for the two evaluation criteria and the two types of output. This measure is chosen as it allows to overcome the problems presented by Fleiss's κ (Hayes and Krippendorff, 2007), another common measure of intercoder reliability used when multiple raters are involved (see Mellinger and Hanson, 2016). The statistic is interpreted like other measures of reliability, with higher scores indicating higher intercoder reliability. Overall, α values are below the lowest value (.667) defined as acceptable by Krippendorff (2013) for tentative conclusions, and well below the recommended value of .800 (ibid.). The α is considerably lower than these values for both intelligibility and informativeness in human interpreting (α = .442 and .607 respectively). The α for MI intelligibility is .658, while the value of interrater reliability for the category of informativeness in MI is barely acceptable (α = .676). Overall, these results suggest that applying the evaluation scale derived from IS *as is* for the comparison of HI and MI output presents limitations that need to be addressed in future work, for instance in terms of the optimisation of the scoring rubric and the inclusion of further dimensions in the evaluation scale.

5 Discussion

The differences in the raters' evaluation of the human and machine output can be better understood by analysing several phenomena retrieved from the corpus. The complexity of the evaluation and, inherently, of the comparison between human and machine interpretation is strictly linked with the pragmatic nature of HI, which often calls for interventions on the part of the interpreter. Such interventions, emerging on the linguistic surface of the interpreted text, may be evidence of underlying strategic behaviour exercised, for instance, to favour comprehension, or may be the result of emergency coping tactics aimed at preventing a disruption of the rendition in adverse conditions, for instance in the case of particularly information-dense or fast speeches. Phenomena such as generalisation, addition and (intentional) omission (see for instance Gile, 2009; Kohn and Kalina, 2002) seem to occur more often in human SI than in written translation, and are entirely absent in the automatic translation of speech. The MT engine lacks any linguistic phenomena that may index intentional interventions, not only because it lacks deliberateness, but also because it has been trained on written (and not interpreted) texts. This fundamental difference may limit the ability of a classic evaluation framework (both manual and automatic) to provide an assessment of quality which reflects the communicative success of an event mediated by human or by machine interpretation. In order to illustrate our argument, we report several example passages from the corpus complete of their rendition by the human interpreters and by the ST engine.

In the following example (Table 2), the human interpreter added a reference to the financial crisis ("momento della crisi finanziaria") implicit in the temporal reference provided by the speaker (2009). At the same time, one unit of information ("where a lot of people were looking for this phrase") was left out by the human interpreter, while it is present in the machine output.

Table 2: Addition

S	*So you have this spike around 2009 where a lot of people were looking for this phrase*
HI	perché nel 2009 abbiamo un picco, momento della crisi finanziaria
MI	quindi avete questo picco intorno al 2009 o molte persone stavano cercando questa frase

In the following example (Table 3), the interpreter opted for a generalisation: "we've not spent enough energy, time, and money" was summed up in "we really have to do more", which conveys the same key message while making explicit what is meant by the original speaker, but is less precise than the automatic rendition, more adherent to the source text.

Table 3: Generalisation

S	*It's clear that we've not spent enough energy, time, and money in protecting our healtcare workers*
HI	Quindi ecco. Dobbiamo veramente fare di più per proteggere i nostri operatori sanitari
MI	È chiaro che non abbiamo speso abbastanza energia, tempo e denaro per proteggere i nostri operatori sanitari

The two examples discussed above illustrate an inherent conundrum in the evaluation, i.e. how to evaluate pragmatic interventions by the interpreter. Whether such interventions should be considered as justifiable or not and which rendition, the human or the machine, is more appreciated by the end-user and more conducive to the same communicative goal pursued by the speaker cannot be reflected in an evaluation framework such as the one chosen for this initial exploration. Furthermore, these phenomena substantiate our argument that a framework for the evaluation of ST in comparison with HI requires a broader perspective.

Another key point of comparison between HI and ST lies in the presence and evaluation of errors. It may be argued that blatant errors are more apparent in ST than in professional HI, as exemplified by the following passage:

Table 4: Blatant error in MI

S	*So 9 billion of dollars have been raised through ICOs*
HI	per cui ci sono adesso 9 miliardi di dollari che sono stati raccolti attraverso queste operazioni di ICO
MI	Quindi 9 miliardi di dollari sono stati raccolti attraverso i devoti ghiacciati

The erroneous translation in the automatic output ("devoti ghiacciati", i.e. iced pious), clearly due to a speech recognition issue (Example 4), is immediately recognisable as such by the (human) end-user. This type of blatant mistake seems to be a distinctive characteristic of MI and is more frequent than in neural machine translation because of the key features of oral speech. It would be interesting to explore the effects of this error type in a real-life communicative event. However, human interpreters may also commit severe mistakes. Let us consider the following case:

Table 5: Blatant error in HI

S	*we have lots of historical examples of overestimating how fast it will kick in*
HI	Ci sono esempi storici in questo senso di sottovalutazione della velocità in cui le cose sono cambiate
MI	abbiamo molti esempi storici di sopravvalutazione della velocità con cui prenderà il via

At first sight, the HI may appear more elegant and fluent than the automatic output (the median intelligibility score for this segment is 5). Thus, the wrong rendition of "overestimating" with "sottovalutazione" (EN: underestimating), due to erroneous anticipation or to having misheard the speaker's words, may go unnoticed without a comparison with the source text.

The examples discussed above emphasise on the one hand that the type of mistakes end-users are confronted with may be of very different nature. The effects of the various types of mistakes on communication and their evaluation by human raters may also vary, and should be explored within a framework that takes into account the communicative perspective. On the other hand, this comparison also stresses the need to compare ST not with the ideal of HI but with the variability of human performances.

6 Conclusion and Future Work

This paper reports on an experiment that compares the output of a real-time speech-to-text translation system with the performance of human interpreters. The main goal was to expand the methodology that is used nowadays to evaluate such systems from the purely computational approach based on automatic metrics to a more user-centric and communication-oriented one. To do so, we apply an evaluation framework derived from Interpreting Studies and let six evaluators assess the performance of humans and machines according to the criteria of intelligibility and informativeness. The results show a better performance by humans in terms of intelligibility and a slightly better performance by the machine in terms of accuracy.

Despite several drawbacks of the framework adopted, the path initiated with this study may bear fruits in terms of better understanding and evaluating the output of speech-to-text and speech-to-speech translation systems in the context of situated multilingual communication and its pragmatic context. The study also highlights several limitations of the approach chosen. They are mainly related to the difficulty of defining objective criteria in the evaluation of quality of interpreted texts, and to the intrinsic shortcomings of evaluating a communicative event only on the basis of the product of the translation process without the contextual embedding of the evaluation in the communicative setting. Such shortcomings need to be addressed in future work.

References

Claudia Angelelli. 2002. Interpretation as a Communicative Event: A Look through Hymes' Lenses. *Meta*, 45(4):580–592.

Ebrahim Ansari, Amittai Axelrod, Nguyen Bach, Ondřej Bojar, Roldano Cattoni, Fahim Dalvi, Nadir Durrani, Marcello Federico, Christian Federmann, Jiatao Gu, Fei Huang, Kevin Knight, Xutai Ma, Ajay Nagesh, Matteo Negri, Jan Niehues, Juan Pino, Elizabeth Salesky, Xing Shi, Sebastian Stüker, Marco Turchi, Alexander Waibel, and Changhan Wang. 2020. FINDINGS OF THE IWSLT 2020 EVALUATION CAMPAIGN. In *Proceedings of the 17th International Conference on Spoken Language Translation*, pages 1–34, Online. Association for Computational Linguistics.

Bogdan Babych. 2014. Automated MT evaluation metrics and their limitations. *Tradumàtica: tecnologies de la traducció*, (12):464.

Annelies Baekelandt and Bart Defrancq. 2020. Elicitation of particular grammatical structures in speeches for interpreting research: enhancing ecological validity of experimental research in interpreting. *Perspectives*, pages 1–18.

Satanjeev Banerjee and Alon Lavie. 2005. METEOR: An Automatic Metric for MT Evaluation with Improved Correlation with Human Judgments. In *Proceedings of the ACL Workshop on Intrinsic and Extrinsic Evaluation Measures for Machine Translation and/or Summarization*, pages 65–72, Ann Arbor, Michigan. Association for Computational Linguistics.

Loïc Barrault, Magdalena Biesialska, Ondřej Bojar, Marta R. Costa-jussà, Christian Federmann, Yvette Graham, Roman Grundkiewicz, Barry Haddow, Matthias Huck, Eric Joanis, Tom Kocmi, Philipp Koehn, Chi-kiu Lo, Nikola Ljubešić, Christof Monz, Makoto Morishita, Masaaki Nagata, Toshiaki Nakazawa, Santanu Pal, Matt Post, and Marcos Zampieri. 2020. Findings of the 2020 Conference on Machine Translation (WMT20). In *Proceedings of the Fifth Conference on Machine Translation*, pages 1–55, Online. Association for Computational Linguistics.

Fernando Batista, Diamantino Caseiro, Nuno Mamede, and Isabel Trancoso. 2008. Recovering capitalization and punctuation marks for automatic speech recognition: Case study for Portuguese broadcast news. *Speech Communication*, 50(10):847–862.

Claudio Bendazzoli. 2018. Corpus-based Interpreting Studies: Past, Present and Future Developments of a (Wired) Cottage Industry. In Mariachiara Russo, Claudio Bendazzoli, and Bart Defrancq, editors, *Making Way in Corpus-based Interpreting Studies*, pages 1–19. Springer Singapore, Singapore. Series Title: New Frontiers in Translation Studies.

Colin Cherry and George Foster. 2019. Thinking Slow about Latency Evaluation for Simultaneous Machine Translation. *arXiv:1906.00048 [cs]*. ArXiv: 1906.00048.

Chung-Cheng Chiu, Tara N. Sainath, Yonghui Wu, Rohit Prabhavalkar, Patrick Nguyen, Zhifeng Chen, Anjuli Kannan, Ron J. Weiss, Kanishka Rao, Ekaterina Gonina, Navdeep Jaitly, Bo Li, Jan Chorowski, and Michiel Bacchiani. 2018. State-of-the-art Speech Recognition With Sequence-to-Sequence Models. *arXiv:1712.01769 [cs, eess, stat]*. ArXiv: 1712.01769.

Kyunghyun Cho and Masha Esipova. 2016. Can neural machine translation do simultaneous translation? *arXiv:1606.02012 [cs]*. ArXiv: 1606.02012.

Ángela Collados Aís and Olalla García Becerra. 2015. Quality. In Holly Mikkelson and Renee Jourdenais, editors, *The Routledge handbook of interpreting*, Routledge Handbooks in Applied Linguistics. Routledge, London ; New York.

Giulia Cürten. 2016. *Maschinelles Dolmetschen mit Google Übersetzer.* Ph.D. thesis, University of Vienna.

Mattia A. Di Gangi, Roldano Cattoni, Luisa Bentivogli, Matteo Negri, and Marco Turchi. 2019. MuST-C: a Multilingual Speech Translation Corpus. In *Proceedings of the 2019 Conference of the North*, pages 2012–2017, Minneapolis, Minnesota. Association for Computational Linguistics.

Mattia Antonino Di Gangi, Roberto Dessì, Roldano Cattoni, Matteo Negri, and Marco Turchi. 2018. Fine-tuning on Clean Data for End-to-End Speech Translation: FBK @ IWSLT 2018. *arXiv:1810.07652 [cs, eess, stat]*. ArXiv: 1810.07652.

Erich Feldweg. 1996. *Der Konferenzdolmetscher im internationalen Kommunikationsprozeß.* Julius Groos, Heidelberg. Bibtex: feldweg_konferenzdolmetscher_1996.

Erin Fitzgerald, Keith Hall, and Frederik Jelinek. 2009. Reconstructing False Start Errors in Spontaneous Speech Text. In *Proceedings of the 12th Conference of the European Chapter of the ACL (EACL 2009)*, pages 255–263. Association for Computational Linguistics.

Christian Fügen. 2008. *A System for Simultaneous Translation of Lectures and Speeches.* Ph.D. thesis, University of Karlsruhe.

Daniel Gile. 2009. *Basic Concepts and Models for Interpreter and Translator Training: Revised edition*, 2nd edition. John Benjamins Publishing Company, Amsterdam.

Jiatao Gu, Graham Neubig, Kyunghyun Cho, and Victor O. K. Li. 2017. Learning to Translate in Real-time with Neural Machine Translation. *arXiv:1610.00388 [cs]*. ArXiv: 1610.00388.

Andrew F. Hayes and Klaus Krippendorff. 2007. Answering the Call for a Standard Reliability Measure for Coding Data. *Communication Methods and Measures*, 1(1):77–89.

Javier Iranzo-Sánchez, Joan Albert Silvestre-Cerdà, Javier Jorge, Nahuel Roselló, Adrià Giménez, Albert Sanchis, Jorge Civera, and Alfons Juan. 2020. Europarl-ST: A Multilingual Corpus For Speech Translation Of Parliamentary Debates. *arXiv:1911.03167 [cs, eess]*. ArXiv: 1911.03167.

Ye Jia, Ron J. Weiss, Fadi Biadsy, Wolfgang Macherey, Melvin Johnson, Zhifeng Chen, and Yonghui Wu. 2019. Direct speech-to-speech translation with a sequence-to-sequence model. *arXiv:1904.06037 [cs, eess]*. ArXiv: 1904.06037.

Roderick Jones. 2002. *Conference Interpreting Explained*. Routledge, Manchaster.

Sylvia Kalina. 2005. Quality Assurance for Interpreting Processes. *Meta: Journal des traducteurs*, 50(2):768.

Takatomo Kano, Shinnosuke Takamichi, Sakriani Sakti, Graham Neubig, Tomoki Toda, and Satoshi Nakamura. 2018. An end-to-end model for cross-lingual transformation of paralinguistic information. *Machine Translation*, 32(4):353–368.

Fedor Kitashov, Elizaveta Svitanko, and Debojyoti Dutta. 2018. Foreign English Accent Adjustment by Learning Phonetic Patterns. *arXiv:1807.03625 [cs, eess, stat]*. ArXiv: 1807.03625.

Kurt Kohn and Sylvia Kalina. 2002. The Strategic Dimension of Interpreting. *Meta*, 41(1):118–138.

Klaus Krippendorff. 2013. *Content analysis: an introduction to its methodology*, 3rd ed edition. SAGE, Los Angeles ; London.

Xutai Ma, Mohammad Javad Dousti, Changhan Wang, Jiatao Gu, and Juan Pino. 2020. SimulEval: An Evaluation Toolkit for Simultaneous Translation. *arXiv:2007.16193 [cs]*. ArXiv: 2007.16193.

Christopher D. Mellinger and Thomas Hanson. 2016. *Quantitative Research Methods in Translation and Interpreting Studies*. Routledge, London.

Markus Müller, Sarah Fünfer, Sebastian Stüker, and Alex Waibel. 2016. Evaluation of the KIT Lecture Translation System. In *Proceedings of the Tenth International Conference on Language Resources and Evaluation LREC 2016, Portorož, Slovenia, May 23-28, 2016*.

Kishore Papineni, Salim Roukos, Todd Ward, and Wei-Jing Zhu. 2002. BLEU: A Method for Automatic Evaluation of Machine Translation. In *Proceedings of the 40th Annual Meeting of the Association for Computational Linguistics (ACL)*, pages 311–318.

Matt Post. 2018. A Call for Clarity in Reporting BLEU Scores. In *Proceedings of the Third Conference on Machine Translation: Research Papers*, pages 186–191, Belgium, Brussels. Association for Computational Linguistics.

Franz Pöchhacker. 2002. Quality Assessment in Conference and Community Interpreting. *Meta*, 46(2):410–425.

Franz Pöchhacker. 2016. *Introducing Interpreting Studies*, 2nd edition. Routledge.

Pablo Romero-Fresco and Franz Pöchhacker. 2017. Quality assessment in interlingual live subtitling: The NTR Model. *Linguistica Antverpiensia, New Series – Themes in Translation Studies*, 16.

Kilian G. Seeber. 2015. Cognitive load in simultaneous interpreting: Measures and methods. In Maureen Ehrensberger-Dow, Susanne Göpferich, and Sharon O'Brien, editors, *Benjamins Current Topics*, volume 72, pages 18–33. John Benjamins Publishing Company, Amsterdam. Bibtex: seeber_cognitive_2015.

Xian Shi, Fan Yu, Yizhou Lu, Yuhao Liang, Qiangze Feng, Daliang Wang, Yanmin Qian, and Lei Xie. 2021. The Accented English Speech Recognition Challenge 2020: Open Datasets, Tracks, Baselines, Results and Methods. *arXiv:2102.10233 [cs, eess]*. ArXiv: 2102.10233.

Miriam Shlesinger. 1995. Stranger in Paradigms: What Lies Ahead for Simultaneous Interpreting Research? *Target*, 7(1):7–28. Bibtex: shlesinger_stranger_1995.

Matthew Snover, Bonnie Dorr, Richard Schwartz, Linnea Micciulla, and John Makhoul. 2006. A study of translation edit rate with targeted human annotation. In *In Proceedings of Association for Machine Translation in the Americas*, pages 223–231.

Matthias Sperber and Matthias Paulik. 2020. Speech Translation and the End-to-End Promise: Taking Stock of Where We Are. *arXiv:2004.06358 [cs]*. ArXiv: 2004.06358.

Elisabet Tiselius. 2009. Revisiting Carroll's scales. In Claudia V. Angelelli and Holly E. Jacobson, editors, *American Translators Association Scholarly Monograph Series*, volume XIV, pages 95–121. John Benjamins Publishing Company, Amsterdam.

Alexander Wonisch. 2017. *Skype Translator: Funktionsweise und Analyse der Dolmetschleistung in der Sprachrichtung Englisch-Deutsch*. Ph.D. thesis, Wonisch, Alexander (2017) Skype Translator: Funktionsweise und Analyse der Dolmetschleistung in der Sprachrichtung Englisch-Deutsch. Masterarbeit, University of Vienna.

Tag Assisted Neural Machine Translation of Film Subtitles

Aren Siekmeier[*], **WonKee Lee**[*], **Hongseok Kwon**[†], and **Jong-Hyeok Lee**[*†]
Pohang University of Science and Technology
[*]Department of Computer Science and Engineering
[†]Graduate School of Artificial Intelligence
{asiekmeier,wklee,hkwon,jhlee}@postech.ac.kr

Abstract

We implemented a neural machine translation system that uses automatic sequence tagging to improve the quality of translation. Instead of operating on unannotated sentence pairs, our system uses pre-trained tagging systems to add linguistic features to source and target sentences. Our proposed neural architecture learns a combined embedding of tokens and tags in the encoder, and simultaneous token and tag prediction in the decoder. Compared to a baseline with unannotated training, this architecture increased the BLEU score of German to English film subtitle translation outputs by 1.61 points using named entity tags; however, the BLEU score decreased by 0.38 points using part-of-speech tags. This demonstrates that certain token-level tag outputs from off-the-shelf tagging systems can improve the output of neural translation systems using our combined embedding and simultaneous decoding extensions.

1 Introduction

Neural machine translation (NMT) uses neural networks to translate unannotated text between a source and target language, but without additional linguistic information certain ambiguous inputs may be translated incorrectly. Consider the following examples:

1) Titanic struggles between good and evil.
   ✓ 선과 악 사이의 엄청난 투쟁.
   big fight between good and evil
   ✗ 타이타닉은 선과 악 사이에서 투쟁 중이다.
   The Titanic is fighting between good and evil

2) Titanic struggles to stay afloat.
   ✓ 타이타닉은 침몰하지 않도록 고군분투 중이다.
   The Titanic is struggling not to sink
   ✗ 침몰하지 않기 위한 엄청난 투쟁.
   big fight not to sink

In (1), "Titanic" is best translated as a common adjective; in (2), it most likely refers to a named entity, the famous ship. In addition to the bare token sequences, part-of-speech or named entity annotation of each token, provided manually or automatically, could provide additional information to improve the quality of translation.

Natural language processing (NLP) tools have benefited from the same explosion in deep learning and neural network developments that has spurred NMT. NLP tools include part-of-speech (POS) taggers, identifying the syntactic function of each input token, and named entity recognition systems. Named entity recognition (NER) identifies which tokens refer to named entities, including proper nouns such as people, place names, organizations, or dates. Recently, automatic named entity recognition (NER) systems have seen much development and refinement with the same deep learning tools used for NMT (Li et al., 2020). Automatic neural NER systems have achieved accuracy exceeding 92% F_1 scores in many languages and domains (Wang et al., 2019; Akbik et al., 2018). NER tags produced by these systems are useful in many other natural language processing contexts, such as coreference resolution, entity linking, or entity extraction (Ferreira Cruz et al., 2020). POS taggers have also achieved very high accuracy exceeding 98% on public treebank datasets (Akbik et al., 2018). We aim to use tags from publicly available pre-trained tagging systems as additional features to improve NMT training and output.

Tag assisted NMT requires modifications to the neural architecture to accommodate a tag at each token position. The encoder must learn an embedding that combines information from each token and its tag, then compute a hidden state from these embeddings. The decoder must learn to predict tokens and their tags simultaneously from the decoder state. Adding tag information to the predic-

Proceedings of the 18th International Conference on Spoken Language Translation, pages 255–262
Bangkok, Thailand (Online), August 5–6, 2021.

tion and corresponding training loss encourages the model to incorporate this information into its latent representations to improve outputs.

Compared to an untagged baseline system on word-tokenized data, our tagged translation system improved the BLEU score by 1.61 points on German to English parallel film subtitles data tagged with publicly available pre-trained named entity recognition systems, while part-of-speech tagging decreased the score by 0.38 BLEU points. Subword tokenization reduced these effects to +0.22 points and –0.22 points respectively. Nonetheless, this demonstrates the feasibility of using certain pre-trained tagging outputs to improve translation quality.

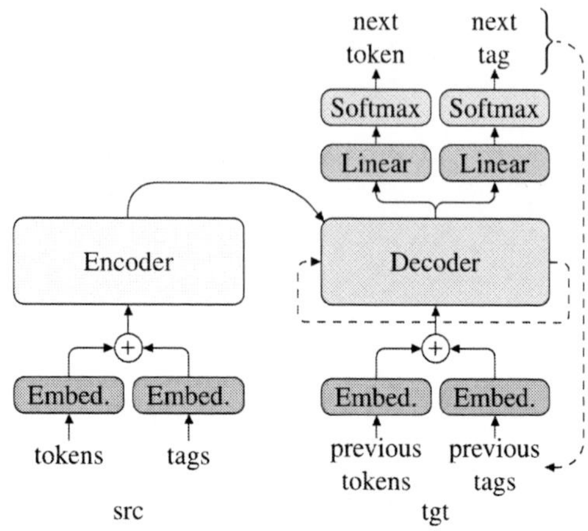

Figure 1: Tagged seq2seq

2 Related Work

Very early work addressed named entity translation by treating automatically identified named entities with a special translation system, usually a transliterator (Babych and Hartley, 2003). This work did not attempt to integrate the translation models for one to benefit from information learned by the other.

Later, especially with neural machine translation (NMT) systems, source-side feature augmentation research studied the inclusion of linguistic feature information into the source-side token embeddings, usually by adding in or concatenating additional learned feature vectors to the token embedding vectors, as we do in this work (Sennrich and Haddow, 2016; Hoang et al., 2016b; Ugawa et al., 2018; Modrzejewski et al., 2020; Modrzejewski, 2020; Armengol-Estapé et al., 2020). This approach can also be adopted on the target-side, as presented here or in (Hoang et al., 2016a, 2018; Nguyen et al., 2018). However, these methods only add linguistic feature information to the input, without encouraging the system to model that information in any particular way.

Factored translation systems, under both statistical and neural machine translation, instead explore the addition of externally supplied linguistic features to the raw text at both input and output. These features include part-of-speech (POS) tags, word lemmatizations, morphological analysis, and semantic analysis (Koehn and Hoang, 2007; Garcia-Martinez et al., 2016, 2017; Tan et al., 2020). Factored translation models map feature-augmented input into feature-augmented output, however outputs include only an underlying lemma together with the predicted features. These systems also use a rule-based morphology toolkit in post-processing to generate the output surface forms from predicted output features, requiring knowledge of appropriate rule systems for the output language. An additional tagged architecture (Nădejde et al., 2017) predicted syntax-tagged surface forms, but did so by appending the tags to the surface form tokens directly, rather than predicting separate factors. In general, the focus of factored models has been to increase vocabulary coverage, for example of highly agglutitanative languages with rich morphologies, rather than our goal of disambiguating polysemous of polysyntactic words or otherwise handling named entities in a more nuanced way.

Finally, one previous work does consider a fully tagged (both source and target) factored neural model predicting tags with surface forms with independent layers in much the same way as presented here (Wagner, 2017). This work showed negative results for various syntactic tag types on IWSLT'14 shared task data (Cettolo et al., 2014), whereas this work presents NER and POS tags on film subtitles data.

3 Tagged seq2seq

We implemented two extensions to the standard seq2seq encoder-decoder architecture for neural machine translation to use token-level tags to improve translation results.[1] By combining token and tag embeddings in the input and simultaneously predicting tokens and tags in the output, the NMT

[1]Code at https://github.com/compwiztobe/tagged-seq2seq

system learned to translate tagged source sentences to tagged target sentences (Figure 1). We used a Transformer encoder and decoder for the base seq2seq model (Vaswani et al., 2017). Tags are added to the data as a preprocessing step.

3.1 Combined embedding

Learning an embedding for every possible token and tag combination would enormously increase the model's learnable parameter count. Furthermore, training data is likely to be sparse in its coverage of all possible pairs, but not in its coverage of the token and tag vocabularies separately. Therefore, we instead learn a separate embedding vector for each possible token and each possible tag, effectively concatenating these two vocabularies (rather than taking the product space). The embedding vectors for the token and tag at each position are then added to combine information from both channels into a single vector, so as not to increase the size of subsequent model layers and the capacity of the model, apart from the additional tag embedding vectors.

3.2 Simultaneous prediction

The decoder state d_i at each step is conditioned on the target prefix and the encoded source sentence (3).

$$d_i = \text{Decoder}(\text{prefix}, \text{src}) \tag{3}$$

This shared decoder state is used to predict both the next token and the next tag, with token and tag feature projections T and $\mathcal{T}$ (4 and 5).

$$P(\text{token } k \mid \text{prefix}; \text{src}) = \text{softmax}_k(T^\top d_i) \tag{4}$$

$$P(\text{tag } k \mid \text{prefix}; \text{src}) = \text{softmax}_k(\mathcal{T}^\top d_i) \tag{5}$$

We model these probabilities independently (6) for the same data sparsity and model size reasons as the embeddings, and we can compute each pair probability and loss accordingly (7).

$$\begin{aligned} &P(\text{token}, \text{tag} \mid \text{prefix}; \text{src}) \\ &\quad = P(\text{token} \mid \text{pre.}; \text{src}) \cdot P(\text{tag} \mid \text{pre.}; \text{src}) \end{aligned} \tag{6}$$

$$\begin{aligned} \mathcal{L} = &-\log P(\text{token} \mid \text{prefix}; \text{src}) \\ &-\log P(\text{tag} \mid \text{prefix}; \text{src}) \end{aligned} \tag{7}$$

This combined loss encourages the shared decoder state d_i to model the correct tag identity so that it can be used by the token prediction layer to improve translation.

4 Data Preparation

4.1 Subtitles corpus

Our experiments focused on film subtitles in German and English. The Opus project provided a parallel German to English subtitles corpus from OpenSubtitles (Tiedemann, 2012; Aulamo et al., 2020). This data was cleaned with some rudimentary sentence length filtering, and randomly divided into a 3 million sentence-pair training split (about 49 million tokens), along with 100,000 pair validation and test splits (about 1.6 million tokens each).

4.2 Tagging "off the shelf"

Flair NLP tools systems have achieved state-of-the-art results on the sequence labeling tasks such as the CoNLL'03 NER dataset and universal part-of-speech tagging from Universal Dependency treebanks (Akbik et al., 2018; Tjong Kim Sang and De Meulder, 2003; Nivre et al., 2020). We used the publicly available pre-trained multilingual NER and universal POS taggers.[2] NER tags followed the `BIOES` system with four entity classes: `PER`, person; `LOC`, location; `ORG`, organization; and `MISC`, miscellaneous. Four classes with four span markers, plus the null span marker `O`, gave the same 17-tag vocabulary for NER on both German and English. Meanwhile, POS tags came from the same 17-tag universal POS tag set for both languages.

Around 3% of words in the OpenSubtitles corpus were tagged as named entities (non `O`). We further divided the test split based on whether any named entities were found in either the source or the target sentence. Out of 100,000 test pairs, 79,201 had no named entities, and 20,799 had some.

4.3 Tokenization

Word tokenization, as used by the tagging systems, is most straightforward for maintaining one-to-one alignments between tokens and their assigned tags. For word tokenization experiments, vocabularies of size 35,012 for German and 17,196 for English were selected, resulting in an unknown word replacement rate of 3%.

This unknown word replacement was considerably higher on rare word categories, for example named entities saw a 25 – 30% rate of unknown words outside the selected word vocabulary. To alleviate this it is also possible to consider subword

[2]Models at `https://huggingface.co/flair/{ner,upos}-multi`

Table 1: BLEU scores on word-tokenized sentences with or without named entities, for models with or without NER tags.

	BLEU (%)		
NER tags	no NEs	some NEs	all
−src, −tgt[3]	34.70	32.43	34.15
+src, −tgt[4]	*34.89*	*32.14*	*34.22*
−src, +tgt[5]	*35.69*	*35.03*	*35.53*
+src, +tgt	**35.84**	**35.50**	**35.76**
improvement	↑ **1.14**	↑ **3.07**	↑ **1.61**

Table 2: BLEU scores for word models with POS tags.

POS tags	BLEU (%)
−src, −tgt	34.15
+src, −tgt	***34.21***
−src, +tgt	*33.70*
+src, +tgt	33.77
improvement	↓ 0.38

tokenization, so additional experiments were conducted with a shared SentencePiece (Kudo, 2018) vocabulary of 32,000 subwords, built from the training split and used to tokenize both languages.

After subword tokenization, the `BIOES` structure of named entity spans was propagated across subword tokens in the natural way to maintain spans. For POS tags, subwords received the same tag as their parent word.

5 Experiments

We used a Transformer encoder and decoder (Vaswani et al., 2017) for the base seq2seq system, each with 6 layers and 8 attention heads, and layer and embedding dimensions 512. Training was done for 40 epochs at half precision with the optimizer known as Adam (Kingma and Ba, 2015) with $\beta = (0.9, 0.98)$ and an inverse square root learning schedule with maximum learning rate 5×10^{-4} after 500 updates and decay 1×10^{-4}. Parameter updates occurred after every 8,192 token-tag pairs at most (rounding off to complete sentences), with 30% dropout and label smoothing of 0.1 on the training loss.

At inference time, a beam of 5 candidates was maintained, and the models were evaluated with their BLEU score on the token sequence only (tagging accuracy was not evaluated due to the difficulty of establishing alignment).

6 Results

BLEU scores from untagged and tagged translation experiments show an improvement from the use of NER tags (Table 1). Adding NER tags, the BLEU score on sentences containing some named entities improved by a larger margin, 3.07 points, presumably due to the tags' assistance with translating those named entities. We also note an improvement in the BLEU score on sentences containing no named entities, which increased by 1.14 points. This suggests that given `O` tag information the model can also treat common words with confidence that they are not named entities and should not be translated as such. These improvements averaged out to a net gain of 1.61 BLEU points on the entire test split.

We also evaluated a model trained with POS tags, but found a decrease in BLEU score (Table 2). Translation scores with POS tags decreased by 0.38 BLEU points. There are two ways to understand this in comparison with NER tags. First, POS tags carry a significant amount of information about the sentence, not only helping to disambiguate between different word senses by part-of-speech, but also assisting the model with encoding the sentence's syntactic structure. Compared to NER tags, this amount of structural information might be difficult to model with the same decoder architecture used for token prediction. Second, POS tags tend to carry the same amount of information for each tag at each position, compared to NER tags only conveying most of their information at the named entity spans which are few and far between. This also lends itself to the idea that POS tags have a higher information content that is less easily modeled by the decoder, leading to worse results than NER tagging.

6.1 Enhanced baselines and ablation study

For both NER and POS tagged results, the baseline was the same Transformer architecture trained only on untagged data (without adding tag embeddings or predicting tags from the decoder). Adding in only source-side tag embeddings could be considered an enhanced baseline, since this kind of

[3]baseline

[4]enhanced baseline / ablation study

[5]ablation study

Table 3: BLEU scores on subword-tokenized sentences with or without named entities, for models with or without NER tags.

	BLEU (%)		
NER tags	no NEs	some NEs	all
−src, −tgt	35.77	36.51	35.96
+src, −tgt	*35.83*	*36.75*	*36.06*
−src, +tgt	*35.88*	*36.82*	*36.12*
+src, +tgt	**35.94**	**36.92**	**36.19**
improvement	↑ **0.17**	↑ **0.41**	↑ **0.22**

Table 4: BLEU scores for subword models with or without POS tags.

POS tags	BLEU (%)
−src, −tgt	35.96
+src, −tgt	***36.20***
−src, +tgt	*35.69*
+src, +tgt	35.74
improvement	↓ 0.22

feature augmentation has already been studied in depth (Sennrich and Haddow, 2016; Hoang et al., 2016b). Our results show that this source-only tagging does not provide significant benefits compared to training on untagged data (Table 1), although for POS tagging this remains the best result.

On the other hand, adding in target-side tags while also predicting them from the decoder, without adding in source-side tag embeddings could be considered an ablation test to isolate the effects of our main contribution: target-side tag decoding. Our results show that this target tagging provides the same benefit as the fully tagged training regime, demonstrating that it is the simultaneous tag decoding that accounts for the entire effect observed. For NER tagging this was an improvement in BLEU scores, but for POS tagging scores decreased when adding target tagging.

Whereas source-side tag information is added into the embeddings without any modification to the training objective, target-side tag predictions are a part of the modified training loss, so that it is the target-side tag prediction that pushes the model to incorporate accurate knowledge of the tags into its learning representations. That NER tag modeling improved results while POS tag modeling did not is consistent with our earlier observation that POS tag modeling seems to be more difficult than NER tag modeling, and is not done effectively by the current architecture.

6.2 Subword tokenization experiments

Experiments with subword tokenized data showed similar effects, but of a significantly reduced size. Adding NER tags improved the results, adding 0.22 points to the BLEU score, with the improvement again coming largely from the target side tagging, and again showing a larger improvement on sentences with named entities than on those without (Table 3). Adding POS tags hurt results, decreasing the score by 0.22, and again we see that source-only tagging is best case for POS tagging (Table 4). However, the reduced magnitude of these deltas to the range of 0.1 – 0.4 BLEU points suggests these are not significant changes to the translation performance, in the subword tokenization case.

It would appear that subword tokenization interferes with the benefits of tagging the data. Since tags are aligned one-to-one with the input words, subword tokenization destroys this alignment, and copying tags across a word's constituent subwords may interfere with the model's ability to make sense the of tag information. In particular for named entities, rare words are likely to tokenized into a larger number of subword tokens, exacerbating this effect. The set of embeddings for the subwords in a word may not be as useful to the model for translating a named entity or other rare category as the single embedding learned specifically for the full word in a word tokenization setting, and further these subword embeddings may be affected by other contexts unrelated to the larger word. Specifically for the named entity case, subword tokenization algorithms might prioritize the atomicity of certain rare words tagged as named entities in order to counteract this.

6.3 Token prediction and tagging loss

Due to the conditional independence assumption, the cross-entropy loss (7) conveniently decomposes into separate terms for tokens and tags (8), allowing us to measure the relative information content of each channel (Table 5).

$$\begin{aligned} \mathcal{L} &= -\log P(\text{token} \mid \text{prefix; src}) \\ &\quad - \log P(\text{tag} \mid \text{prefix; src}) \\ &= \mathcal{L}_{\text{token}} + \mathcal{L}_{\text{tag}} \end{aligned} \tag{8}$$

Table 5: Token prediction and tagging loss.

		↓ cross entropy (bits)		
		$\mathcal{L}_{\text{token}}$	$\mathcal{L}_{\text{tag}}$	$\mathcal{L}$
no tags	−src, −tgt	2.000	—	2.000
NER	+src, −tgt	2.006	—	2.006
	−src, +tgt	2.001	0.183	2.184
	+src, +tgt	**1.985**	0.183	2.168
POS	+src, −tgt	2.007	—	2.007
	−src, +tgt	1.995	*0.697*	2.692
	+src, +tgt	**1.972**	*0.695*	2.673

While adding tag information naturally increases the overall cross-entropy, as there are more possibilities to account for and to be predicted, restricting our attention only to the token loss shows that the token-level cross-entropy is consistently reduced from 2.000 (base-2) to 1.985 with NER tags or 1.972 for POS tags. This shows how both tag types can add disambiguating information to the token prediction process, with POS tags naturally add more of such information, since they carry syntactic information.

Looking only at tag-level cross-entropy, it's interesting to notice that the POS tagging loss is significantly higher than the NER tagging loss. While this could be simply because the lower-bound inherent entropy is higher (POS tags naturally contain more information, being more uniformly distributed than NER tags), this could also be consistent with the idea that POS tag modeling is more difficult, explaining the decreased translation scores observed with POS tag prediction.

7 Model Limitations

It should not go unnoticed that the typical inference algorithms for sequence labeling, particularly the BiLSTM-CRF inference employed by most NER systems, are incompatible with the autoregressive sequence decoding algorithms (greedy decoding and beam search) used for inference by seq2seq models. That the beam decoding algorithm (and autoregressive likelihood model) used here for tags was unable to account for (be conditioned on) the as-yet uncomputed right context was cause for much apprehension before experimental results became available. These positive results notwithstanding, future work could explore how to better incorporate the full tagging context in tag decoding, perhaps, for example, by predicting the sequence more wholistically with non-autoregressive decoding (Gu et al., 2018).

We also imagine that the design of the underlying seq2seq architecture may lend itself to certain types of sequence labeling. For example, the bidirectional context modeled by a BiLSTM-based translation model may be more suitable for certain types of sequence labeling tasks than the Transformer's attentional activations. Because our contributions are agnostic to the type of sequence labeling (NER or part-of-speech tagging or any other kind) as well as to the design of the encoder and decoder, future experiments should also explore these possibilities.

8 Conclusion

We implemented extensions to existing neural machine translation models that allow the use of off-the-shelf token-level tagging systems to improve translation accuracy. Translation inputs and training outputs were tagged with pre-trained sequence labeling systems. A standard encoder-decoder architecture was extended to include tag embeddings and tag prediction at each token position. At model input, token and tag embedding vectors were added to produce a combined embedding. At model output, the final decoder layer used separate softmax layers to predict tokens and tags. During training, a combined loss function encouraged the model to learn token and tag information jointly.

This tag assisted translation system was tested against baseline token-only systems on a German to English film subtitle corpus with both word and subword tokenization. Subword tokenization reduced the size of the effect, suggesting the need for specialized subword tokenization to prioritize the integrity of important word categories. However, on word tokenized data, the 1.61 point increase in BLEU score using named entity tags demonstrates that the proposed architecture is useful for improving translation outputs with automatic named entity recognition, while the 0.38 point decrease using part-of-speech tags indicates more difficulty in utilizing that tag information. Further examination of the cross-entropy showed that adding tags reduced the token cross-entropy thereby improving token modeling. Future experiments can explore the use of other types of tag data as well as other decoding paradigms.

Acknowledgments

Many thanks go to my colleagues Jeesoo Bang, Jaehun Shin, and Baikjin Jung in the Knowledge and Language Engineering Lab (POSTECH) for their many hours generously spent discussing these research topics. These results would not have been possible without their support.

This work was carried out as part of the HPC Support Project supported by the Ministry of Science and ICT (MSIT) and the National IT Industry Promotion Agency (NIPA), and was funded by the Institute of Information & Communications Technology Planning & Evaluation (IITP) supported by the Korean government (MSIT): Grant No. 2019-0-01906, Graduate School of Artificial Intelligence (POSTECH).

References

Alan Akbik, Duncan Blythe, and Roland Vollgraf. 2018. Contextual string embeddings for sequence labeling. In *Proceedings of the 27th International Conference on Computational Linguistics*, pages 1638–1649, Santa Fe, New Mexico, USA. Association for Computational Linguistics.

Jordi Armengol-Estapé, Marta R Costa-jussà, and Carlos Escolano. 2020. Enriching the transformer with linguistic factors for low-resource machine translation. *arXiv preprint arXiv:2004.08053*.

Mikko Aulamo, Umut Sulubacak, Sami Virpioja, and Jörg Tiedemann. 2020. OpusTools and parallel corpus diagnostics. In *Proceedings of the 12th Language Resources and Evaluation Conference*, pages 3782–3789, Marseille, France. European Language Resources Association.

Bogdan Babych and Anthony Hartley. 2003. Improving machine translation quality with automatic named entity recognition. In *Proceedings of the 7th International EAMT workshop on MT and other language technology tools, Improving MT through other language technology tools, Resource and tools for building MT at EACL 2003*.

M. Cettolo, J. Niehues, S. Stüker, L Bentivogli, and Marcello Federico. 2014. Report on the 11th IWSLT evaluation campaign. In *Proceedings of the 11th International Workshop on Spoken Language Translation*, pages 2–16.

André Ferreira Cruz, Gil Rocha, and Henrique Lopes Cardoso. 2020. Coreference resolution: Toward end-to-end and cross-lingual systems. *Information*, 11:74.

Mercedes Garcia-Martinez, Loïc Barrault, and Fethi Bougares. 2016. Factored Neural Machine Translation Architectures. In *International Workshop on Spoken Language Translation (IWSLT'16)*, Seattle, United States.

Mercedes Garcia-Martinez, Loïc Barrault, and Fethi Bougares. 2017. Neural Machine Translation by Generating Multiple Linguistic Factors. In *5th International Conference Statistical Language and Speech Processing SLSP 2017*, Statistical Language and Speech Processing 5th International Conference, SLSP 2017, Le Mans, France, October 23–25, 2017, Proceedings, Le Mans, France. 11 pages, 3 figues, SLSP conference.

Jiatao Gu, James Bradbury, Caiming Xiong, Victor O. K. Li, and Richard Socher. 2018. Non-autoregressive neural machine translation. In *6th International Conference on Learning Representations, ICLR 2018, Conference Track Proceedings*, Vancouver, BC, Canada.

Cong Duy Vu Hoang, Trevor Cohn, and Gholamreza Haffari. 2016a. Incorporating side information into recurrent neural network language models. In *Proceedings of the 2016 Conference of the North American Chapter of the Association for Computational Linguistics: Human Language Technologies*, pages 1250–1255, San Diego, California. Association for Computational Linguistics.

Cong Duy Vu Hoang, Gholamreza Haffari, and Trevor Cohn. 2016b. Improving neural translation models with linguistic factors. In *Proceedings of the Australasian Language Technology Association Workshop 2016*, pages 7–14, Melbourne, Australia.

Cong Duy Vu Hoang, Gholamreza Haffari, and Trevor Cohn. 2018. Improved neural machine translation using side information. In *Proceedings of the Australasian Language Technology Association Workshop 2018*, pages 6–16, Dunedin, New Zealand.

Diederik P. Kingma and Jimmy Ba. 2015. Adam: A method for stochastic optimization. In *3rd International Conference on Learning Representations, ICLR 2015, Conference Track Proceedings*, San Diego, CA, USA.

Philipp Koehn and Hieu Hoang. 2007. Factored translation models. In *Proceedings of the 2007 Joint Conference on Empirical Methods in Natural Language Processing and Computational Natural Language Learning (EMNLP-CoNLL)*, pages 868–876, Prague, Czech Republic. Association for Computational Linguistics.

Taku Kudo. 2018. Subword regularization: Improving neural network translation models with multiple subword candidates. In *Proceedings of the 56th Annual Meeting of the Association for Computational Linguistics (Volume 1: Long Papers)*, pages 66–75, Melbourne, Australia. Association for Computational Linguistics.

J. Li, A. Sun, J. Han, and C. Li. 2020. A survey on deep learning for named entity recognition. In *IEEE*

Transactions on Knowledge and Data Engineering, Los Alamitos, CA, USA. IEEE Computer Society.

Maciej Modrzejewski. 2020. *Improvement of the Translation of Named Entities in Neural Machine Translation*. Ph.D. thesis, Karlsruhe Institute of Technology Department of Informatics Institute for Anthropomatics and Robotics.

Maciej Modrzejewski, Miriam Exel, Bianka Buschbeck, Thanh-Le Ha, and Alexander Waibel. 2020. Incorporating external annotation to improve named entity translation in NMT. In *Proceedings of the 22nd Annual Conference of the European Association for Machine Translation*, pages 45–51, Lisboa, Portugal. European Association for Machine Translation.

Maria Nădejde, Siva Reddy, Rico Sennrich, Tomasz Dwojak, Marcin Junczys-Dowmunt, Philipp Koehn, and Alexandra Birch. 2017. Predicting target language CCG supertags improves neural machine translation. In *Proceedings of the Second Conference on Machine Translation*, pages 68–79, Copenhagen, Denmark. Association for Computational Linguistics.

Quang-Phuoc Nguyen, Joon-Choul Shin, and Cheol-Young Ock. 2018. An evaluation of translation quality by homograph disambiguation in korean-x neural machine translation systems. In *Annual Conference on Human and Language Technology*, pages 504–509. Human and Language Technology.

Joakim Nivre, Marie-Catherine de Marneffe, Filip Ginter, Jan Hajič, Christopher D. Manning, Sampo Pyysalo, Sebastian Schuster, Francis Tyers, and Daniel Zeman. 2020. Universal Dependencies v2: An evergrowing multilingual treebank collection. In *Proceedings of the 12th Language Resources and Evaluation Conference*, pages 4034–4043, Marseille, France. European Language Resources Association.

Rico Sennrich and Barry Haddow. 2016. Linguistic input features improve neural machine translation. In *Proceedings of the First Conference on Machine Translation: Volume 1, Research Papers*, pages 83–91, Berlin, Germany. Association for Computational Linguistics.

Samson Tan, Shafiq Joty, Lav Varshney, and Min-Yen Kan. 2020. Mind your inflections! Improving NLP for non-standard Englishes with Base-Inflection Encoding. In *Proceedings of the 2020 Conference on Empirical Methods in Natural Language Processing (EMNLP)*, pages 5647–5663, Online. Association for Computational Linguistics.

Jörg Tiedemann. 2012. Parallel data, tools and interfaces in OPUS. In *Proceedings of the Eight International Conference on Language Resources and Evaluation*, Istanbul, Turkey. European Language Resources Association.

Erik F. Tjong Kim Sang and Fien De Meulder. 2003. Introduction to the CoNLL-2003 shared task: Language-independent named entity recognition. In *Proceedings of the Seventh Conference on Natural Language Learning at HLT-NAACL 2003 - Volume 4*, CONLL '03, page 142–147, USA. Association for Computational Linguistics.

Arata Ugawa, Akihiro Tamura, Takashi Ninomiya, Hiroya Takamura, and Manabu Okumura. 2018. Neural machine translation incorporating named entity. In *Proceedings of the 27th International Conference on Computational Linguistics*, pages 3240–3250, Santa Fe, New Mexico, USA. Association for Computational Linguistics.

Ashish Vaswani, Noam Shazeer, Niki Parmar, Jakob Uszkoreit, Llion Jones, Aidan N. Gomez, Łukasz Kaiser, and Illia Polosukhin. 2017. Attention is all you need. In *Proceedings of the 31st International Conference on Neural Information Processing Systems*, NIPS'17, pages 6000–6010, Red Hook, NY, USA. Curran Associates Inc.

Martin Wagner. 2017. *Target Factors for Neural Machine Translation*. Ph.D. thesis, Karlsruhe Institute of Technology Department of Informatics Institute for Anthropomatics and Robotics.

Zihan Wang, Jingbo Shang, Liyuan Liu, Lihao Lu, Jiacheng Liu, and Jiawei Han. 2019. CrossWeigh: Training named entity tagger from imperfect annotations. In *Proceedings of the 2019 Conference on Empirical Methods in Natural Language Processing and the 9th International Joint Conference on Natural Language Processing (EMNLP-IJCNLP)*, pages 5154–5163, Hong Kong, China. Association for Computational Linguistics.

A Statistical Extension of Byte-Pair Encoding

David Vilar[*]
Amazon

Marcello Federico
Amazon

Abstract

Sub-word segmentation is currently a standard tool for training neural machine translation (MT) systems and other NLP tasks. The goal is to split words (both in the source and target languages) into smaller units which then constitute the input and output vocabularies of the MT system. The aim of reducing the size of the input and output vocabularies is to increase the generalization capabilities of the translation model, enabling the system to translate and generate infrequent and new (unseen) words at inference time by combining previously seen sub-word units. Ideally, we would expect the created units to have some linguistic meaning, so that words are created in a compositional way. However, the most popular word-splitting method, Byte-Pair Encoding (BPE), which originates from the data compression literature, does not include explicit criteria to favor linguistic splittings, nor to find the optimal sub-word granularity for the given training data. In this paper, we propose a statistically motivated extension of the BPE algorithm and an effective convergence criterion that avoids the costly experimentation cycle needed to select the best sub-word vocabulary size. Experimental results with morphologically rich languages show that our model achieves nearly-optimal BLEU scores and produces morphologically better word segmentations, which allows to outperform BPE's generalization in the translation of sentences containing new words, as shown via human evaluation.

1 Introduction

Sub-word segmentation is currently a standard tool for machine translation systems (see e.g. the systems submitted to WMT and IWSLT evaluations (Barrault et al., 2019; Niehues et al., 2019), as well as systems for a wide variety of NLP tasks (see e.g. Devlin et al. (2018) and derived works). The goal is to split words (both in the source and target language) into smaller units which then constitute the input and output of the machine translation system. The goal is twofold: On the one hand, sub-word splitting reduces the size of the input and output vocabularies. This is specially important when using neural models, as the size of the input layer is fixed and thus the vocabulary size cannot be dynamically adjusted. On the other hand, it tries to increase the generalization capabilities of the translation model, enabling the system to accept and/or generate new words at translation time by combining previously seen units. The most widespread method used for sub-word splitting in neural machine translation is Byte Pair Encoding (BPE), introduced by Sennrich et al. (2016). Since then, BPE has become a default preprocessing step for many NLP tasks.

The BPE extraction algorithm is an adaptation of the algorithm introduced by Gage (1994) for data compression. The main idea of this algorithm is to replace the most frequent pair of bytes found in the input data with a new, unseen byte. The process is repeated until no more byte pairs are repeated or until no free bytes are available. Sennrich et al. (2016) took this algorithm as a starting point, considering characters instead of bytes, and joining them using the same criterion to produce sub-word units (more details can be found in Section 3).

One potential problem with this approach is that the objective of the original BPE algorithm differs from the goals for which it is being used for translation, as detailed above. While it is certainly effective for the first objective (reducing the vocabulary size), it is arguable whether it is appropriate for the goal of generating new words (Ataman et al., 2017; Huck et al., 2017; Banerjee and Bhattacharyya, 2018).

Intuitively, in order to generate new words, we would expect the sub-word units to have some linguistic meaning, so that a new word can be created

[*] Now at Google.

Proceedings of the 18th International Conference on Spoken Language Translation, pages 263–275
Bangkok, Thailand (Online), August 5–6, 2021.

beklagen

↓

bek@@ lagen

bewertungsinstrumente

↓

bewer@@ t@@ ungsin@@ stru@@ mente

Table 1: Examples of unsatisfactory BPE splitting of German words. The two words are segmented by breaking the underlying morphological structure.

in a compositional way. Being purely frequency driven, BPE does not take this intuition into consideration, as illustrated in the two German word examples in Table 1 taken from the WMT'19 training data. For the first word, the split "be@@ klagen" would be more satisfactory as the word is derived from "klagen" (*complain*); the second word is a compound word, with the splits "bewertungs@@ instrumente" (*assessment instruments*), separating the two words, and "bewert@@ ung@@ s@@ instrument@@ e" being morphologically more informed alternatives.

The BPE algorithm also introduces an additional practical problem. The original formulation does not specify a criterion for stopping the creation of new symbols. If the algorithm runs for an unlimited time, it will merge all sub-words into the original input vocabulary, which is clearly undesired. In practice, one specifies a fixed number of merges to be carried out, or a threshold frequency and when the considered symbols fall below this value the algorithm is stopped. It is however not clear how to set these hyperparameters, although they can have a drastic effect on translation quality depending on the translation direction, task and amount of data (Denkowski and Neubig, 2017; Sennrich and Zhang, 2019). Furthermore, these hyperparameters are rarely optimized, as evaluating them constitutes a full training-evaluation cycle, which is notoriously costly.

In this paper we introduce a new criterion for defining sub-word units that tries to address these shortcomings. We introduce a probability distribution over the units which in turn induces a likelihood function over the corpus which we can optimize. We will show how this statistical approach can guide the extraction process towards more linguistically satisfying units, while still remaining a purely data driven approach. Having a well founded optimization criterion also allows us to define a data driven stopping criterion. Our proposed criterion allows to select a nearly optimal number of units using only an intrinsic measure on the training corpus, thus dramatically reducing experimentation costs.

2 Related work

As stated in the introduction, our starting point is the BPE algorithm introduced in (Sennrich et al., 2016). In this work, the authors adapt the data compression algorithm by Gage (1994) to the task of sub-word unit generation.

Some authors have tried to expand the extraction of sub-word units by leveraging linguistic information. Sánchez-Cartagena and Toral (2016) use morphological segmentation for Finnish and compare the effectiveness of these sub-word units for the WMT evaluation. The system using this segmentation approach together with other extensions performed best in human evaluation. Huck et al. (2017) follow a similar approach with the addition of compound splitting for translation into German, achieving improvements of around 0.5 BLEU points on WMT data. Ataman and Federico (2018) propose to replace BPE with unsupervised morphological segmentation which also takes morphological coherence into consideration during prediction of the sub-words. Experiments run under small-data conditions on TED Talks in five directions, all from/to English, show systematic improvements on Arabic, Turkish, Czech, but not on Italian and German. Banerjee and Bhattacharyya (2018) also use unsupervised morphological units generated by Morfessor (Virpioja et al., 2013) as input for a neural machine translation system and report improvements for low-resource conditions. Macháček et al. (2018) follow a similar approach for translation into Czech on WMT data, but were not able to obtains improvements over the standard BPE approach.

An alternative model to BPE which is also widely used was presented by Kudo (2018), which can be considered as an extension of (Schuster and Nakajima, 2012). They show that using a purely statistical approach, they are able to achieve sub-word units that are better linguistically motivated. Similar to our approach, a probability distribution over the sub-word units is defined with the goal of improving the likelihood over the training data. The strategy for defining the sub-word units differ in his approach and ours. While we start with single characters and expand the units, Kudo (2018) starts with a large set of sub-word units and prunes iteratively until reducing the number to a desired quantity. Segmentation probabilities are modeled with a multinomial distribution trained via expectation maximization.

In order to improve generalization of the segmentation model (i.e. performance on new words), different regularization approaches have been proposed. Kudo (2018) applies different segmentations at training time. For each parameter update, segmentations for each word are sampled from a smoothed posterior distribution computed from the multinomial distribution. Along the same line, Provilkov et al. (2019), proposed to generate alternative segmentations directly with BPE, by randomly dropping out merging rules. These approaches, as noted by Kudo (2018), can be seen as variants of the ensemble training principle, where many different models are trained (and finally combined) on different subsets of the training data. Our work differs with respect to (Kudo, 2018) in that we train an observable model in a stepwise fashion, like BPE, by maximizing the likelihood of the training data. Thus, we expect our approach to be more efficient than Kudo (2018). Differently from Kudo (2018) and Provilkov et al. (2019), we do not apply regularization, however nothing prevents from applying the drop out method also to our merging rules, although we expect that our model has already learned more general segmentation rules than BPE.

To the best of our knowledge, there has been little previous work on automatically determining the number of sub-word units to produce by segmentation algorithms. Kreutzer and Sokolov (2018) integrate segmentation into the NMT system and find that the system favors character-based translation over sub-word segmentation. Henderson (2020) pointed out that determining vocabulary sizes for NLP tasks is one of the few aspects that is still done manually, and suggests it as one possible direction for future improvement of NLP models.

3 The Byte Pair Encoding (BPE) algorithm

The BPE training algorithm as presented in (Sennrich et al., 2016) is shown in Algorithm 1. It closely follows the original BPE for data compression algorithm by Gage (1994). The algorithm receives as input a text as a sequence of words, which in turn are represented as sequences of characters. The single characters constitute the initial set of symbols. At each iteration the pair of symbols (occurring inside words) with highest frequency is selected and substituted with a new symbol. This substitution is recorded as a new rule. This merging operation is repeated for a fixed number of steps. The algorithm returns the sorted list of merging rules.

Algorithm 1: BPE training algorithm.

Input: training corpus S of words split into character sequences; number N of rules

Output: list R of N merge rules

1 $R := [\,]$

2 **while** $\text{length}(R) \leq N$ **do**

3 $\quad (x, y) := \underset{(x,y)}{\text{argmax}} \{\text{count}_S(x, y)\}$

4 $\quad rule := \langle (x, y) \rightarrow xy \rangle$

5 $\quad S := \text{apply}(rule, S)$

6 $\quad R := \text{append}(rule, R)$

7 **return** R

Algorithm 2: BPE inference algorithm

Input: list R of merge rules; word w split into characters

Output: segmented word

foreach $rule \in R$ **do**

$\quad$ **if** $\text{matches}(rule, w)$ **then**

$\quad\quad w := \text{apply}(rule, w)$

$\quad\quad$ **continue**

return w

Algorithm 2 shows how to apply the set of rules extracted by Algorithm 1 to a new text. It basically looks up the ordered list of rules and applies as many of them as possible.

4 The statistical BPE (S-BPE) algorithm

We can generalize the criterion for BPE unit selection by adjusting line 3 of Algorithm 1. Specifically, we define a probability distribution over the BPE units and define a maximum likelihood optimization criterion.

Let S be a corpus of words w from a vocabulary V, and let each word be decomposed as a sequence of symbols (initially characters) s from an alphabet Σ. The log-likelihood of S can be written as:

$$L(S, \Sigma) = \sum_{s \in \Sigma} C_{S,\Sigma}(s) \log \Pr(s) \quad (1)$$

where $C_{S,\Sigma}(s)$ is the count of symbol s in corpus S, in which words are segments according to Σ, i.e.:

$$C_{S,\Sigma}(s) = \sum_{w \in V} C_S(w) C_\Sigma(s, w) \quad (2)$$

Algorithm 1 initializes Σ with single characters (Σ_0). Then, at each step n of training, it selects the pair of symbols with the highest frequency or, equivalently, joint probability:

$$(x, y) = \operatorname*{argmax}_{x,y \in \Sigma_{n-1}} p_{n-1}(x, y) \quad (3)$$

thus defining the new alphabet[1]

$$\Sigma_n = \{xy\} \cup \Sigma_{n-1} \quad (4)$$

where the probability distribution p_{n-1} is defined over the elements of the alphabet Σ_{n-1}.

From a statistical modeling perspective, however, we would be more interested in rules for which the training data likelihood increases, i.e.:

$$L(S, \Sigma_n) > L(S, \Sigma_{n-1}) \quad (5)$$

It can be shown (see the Appendix for a derivation) that for any pair of symbols $x, y \in \Sigma_{n-1}$, the following inequality holds, which provides a lower bound for the increase in likelihood:

$$\begin{aligned} L(S, \Sigma_n) >& L(S, \Sigma_{n-1}) \\ &+ C_{S,\Sigma_n}(xy) \log \frac{p_n(xy)}{p_n(x)p_n(y)}, \end{aligned} \quad (6)$$

where as usual Σ_n includes xy as given in Equation 4. Intuitively we can interpret the rightmost term as the likelihood of each word that contains the bigram xy being increased by merging the two symbols[2]. It also provides a good tie-in to our linguistic intuition about sub-word units: if two units appear only in combination with each other, they probably do not have linguistic meaning on their own. Thus the probability mass will shift to the probability of the joint symbol, and the probability of the single elements will be greatly reduced. On the other hand, if x or y do have linguistic meaning, e.g. verb suffixes, they are likely to have a high probability of appearing in the text, and thus the gain from joining them together is not as big.

The above inequality thus suggests the new update rule:

$$\begin{aligned} (x, y) = & \operatorname*{argmax}_{(x,y):\Sigma_n = \{xy\} \cup \Sigma_{n-1}} C_{S,\Sigma_n}(xy) \times \\ & \left[\log p_n(xy) - \log p_n(x) - \log p_n(y) \right]. \end{aligned} \quad (7)$$

Note an important difference between Equations (3) and (7): In (3) we use a bigram probability $p_{n-1}(x, y)$ computed on $\Sigma_{n-1} \times \Sigma_{n-1}$, while in (7) we use a unigram probability $p_n(xy)$ computed on Σ_n. The two probabilities are expected to be close but not the same.

Note that in practice, in the course of the algorithm the count for a unit may drop to 0 (due to all the occurrences being combined with another unit to form a new pair), thus producing a probability of 0. In order to avoid computation of $\log 0$ in Equation (7) we use Laplace smoothing for the computation of all probabilities.

4.1 Stopping criterion

One open question when defining BPE units is how many operations to carry out. As shown in Algorithm 1, this number is a parameter of the extraction algorithm, and there is no defined way to select it. The number of units has an important effect on the quality of the translation system (see Section 5), but selecting the optimal number involves training and testing a translation system for each candidate, at a high computational cost. Thus, normally system builders resort to previous experience and select a number of units that has worked well on previous tasks, although the performance can be very task dependent.

With the statistical formulation of BPE, for each operation we can compute a corresponding (approximate) increase in likelihood on the training corpus through Equation 6. Looking at the evolution of the likelihood, we can define a criterion of when to stop defining new units. Specifically, let us define δ_i as the (approximate) increase in likelihood when defining the i-th BPE unit. We will stop the algorithm, and thus define the number of units N, when $\delta_N \leq k\delta_1$, with $k < 1$. In order to improve the robustness of the criterion, in practice it is better to average each δ_i with the previous M values.

[1] Notice that by implementing Σ_n as an ordered list (stack), we get the list of rules R of Algorithm 1 and Algorithm 2.

[2] This is similar to the pointwise mutual information criterion used to detect collocations (Church and Hanks, 1990).

Language	Sentences	Tokens English	Foreign
German	5.9M	121.0M	114.1M
Romanian	612.4K	15.9M	16.2M
Latvian	4.5M	66.8M	56.3M
Estonian	879.9K	22.7M	17.0M
Turkish	207.7K	5.1M	4.5M
Finnish	2.6M	61.1M	43.9M

Table 2: Training corpora statistics. Tokenization was carried out using the Moses tokenizer.

Of course, one could argue that we just substituted one parameter of the algorithm with another, which also has to be selected externally. However, as we will show in Section 5, the same value obtains nearly optimal results for most language arcs.

Another possibility that could be considered for defining the number of operations is to measure the evolution of the likelihood on an external development corpus, and stop the iterations when the likelihood decreases. We implemented this approach, but found that the likelihood on the development corpus increases monotonically for each new unit extracted (up to the maximum number we allowed for the experiments), and thus it does not provide a useful stopping criterion for the algorithm.

5 Experimental results

We conducted experiments for machine translation in a variety of languages, focusing on morphologically rich ones, using the data available from the latest WMT evaluation campaign where the language pair was used. We include results for Finish (Fi), German (De) [WMT'19], Estonian (Et), Turkish (Tr) [WMT'18], Latvian [WMT'17] and Romanian (Ro) [WMT'16], all paired with English (En) and for both translation directions. We used all available corpora for translation model training, except ParaCrawl. Corpora statistics can be found in Table 2. It can be seen that we experiment with a wide variety of corpus sizes, varying between 200K sentences up to nearly 6 million.

For BPE training, the corpora were subsampled to 1M sentences for BPE training[3], and a common BPE model was trained for the source and target languages (which also share the same embedding matrix). Experiments were carried out using Sockeye (Hieber et al., 2017) using mostly the default settings, except for a transformer architecture consisting of 20 encoder layers and 2 decoder layers (Hieber et al., 2020). The corpora were tokenized using the Moses tokenizer.

5.1 Analysis of BPE segmentation

We will start by focusing on the analysis of the produced sub-word units. Table 3 shows some differences between the statistical approach and the standard approach on words found in the German training data. The first example clearly shows how BPE does not use any linguistic information, even splitting the pair of characters 'ue', which is an alternative form of the letter 'ü'. In contrast, S-BPE produces a much more morphologically motivated split by separating the 's' at the end, which denotes genitive case. In the next two examples, S-BPE splits the words as derived forms of other words ('stehenden' and 'laeufige', respectively). In the last two examples, S-BPE correctly splits compound words into individual components. For none of these cases the standard BPE finds a linguistically satisfying sub-word decomposition. However note that although S-BPE improves over BPE, a more refined morphological splitting would still be possible for the last two examples.

Revisiting the examples of Table 1, we see that "beklagen" is now split into "be@@ kla@@ gen", and "bewertungsinstrumente" into "bewer@@ tungs@@ instrumente", which do not exactly correspond to the splitting points suggested in Section 1, but are more satisfactory than the BPE segmentation.

In order to quantify these improvements we use the data provided by the Morpho Challenge 2010 shared task (Kurimo et al., 2010). As part of the data of this evaluation, a morphological segmentation of words was provided for English, Finnish and Turkish. We applied the BPE and S-BPE models to the development dataset, and computed the F1-score of the produced segmentations, using the morphological segmentation as reference. For BPE segmentation, we selected the optimal segmentation as measured by the BLEU score on the translations of the WMT test data (see also Section 5.3). The results[4] are shown in Table 4. As English is a common language for all investigated language arcs, we provide results for the different language

[3]Experiments with the standard BPE training did not show any difference in performance between using the downsampled corpus or the full corpus.

[4]Note that these scores are for comparison of BPE and S-BPE only, and will be clearly outperformed by dedicated systems for the task.

Word	BPE	S-BPE
ungluecks	unglu@@ ecks	unglueck@@ s
anstehenden	anstehenden	an@@ stehenden
vorlaeufige	vorlaeufi@@ ge	vor@@ laeufige
gefangengenommen	gefan@@ gen@@ genommen	gefangen@@ genommen
finanzdienstleistungen	finanzdienstleistungen	finanz@@ dienstleistungen

Table 3: Segmentation examples of German words: S-BPE produces consistent segmentations of single and compound words, while BPE breaks in some cases the morphological structure of words.

Language	Arc	BPE	S-BPE
English	→ Fi	23.81	**24.68**
	→ De	**25.46**	24.82
	→ Ro	23.07	**26.96**
	→ Lv	20.84	**25.74**
	→ Et	20.83	**23.09**
	→ Tr	22.47	**25.67**
Finnish	→ En	12.14	**14.57**
Turkish	→ En	**23.00**	22.90

Table 4: Morpho Challenge results (F1 score).

pairs. It can be seem that S-BPE produces more linguistically motivated splits of English words in five out of six cases. For Finnish, S-BPE also produces better linguistic units, while for Turkish the F1 score is nearly identical. In light of these results we can affirm that in most cases S-BPE produces more linguistically motivated units than standard BPE.

5.2 Human evaluation

In the previous section we showed how S-BPE produces more linguistically motivated units. Of course, the main question is if these units help the system produce better translations. We hypothesize that S-BPE affects mainly single words, specially unknown words or words rarely seen in training (e.g. morphological variations of known words), and this effect is hardly captured by BLEU. Therefore we focus on human evaluation first and will present results with BLEU in the next section.

We carried out a human evaluation on English-German and English-Turkish (both directions) with a subset of test sentences where at least one unknown word was found. BLEU did not show significant differences between BPE and S-BPE on this subset of sentences. A blind test was carried out with 7 members of our department, all native speakers of Turkish (1) or German (6) and experts in NLP.

The evaluators were shown a source sentence, together with a highlighted word, and the output of the BPE and S-BPE systems. They had to answer two questions: which system produced a better translation of the highlighted word? And, which system produced a better translation of the sentence overall? Table 5 shows examples of the German-to-English test sentences highlighting the translations of the unknown German word inside the translations of the sentence, as produced with BPE and S-BPE. (For completeness we also show the segmentation of the unknown German word.)

The results of the human evaluation are shown on Table 6. It can be seen that when BPE and S-BPE produce different translations for the words being evaluated, in the majority of cases human graders prefer the translations produced with S-BPE. In particular, for language arcs involving German, the percentage of sentences for which translations based on S-BPE are preferred over translations based on BPE is 41.3% vs. 23.3% and 41.5% vs. 29.3%. These results are statistical significant (using a paired proportion test, with $p < 0.01$). It is known that German has a high lexical prolificity, with a high number of morphological variations as well as compound words. In fact, out of 2 000 sentences of the De→En test set 736 (36.8%) contain unknown words. These results confirm the superior generalization of S-BPE over BPE, both at the word and sentence levels.

For Turkish we also observe a preference for the S-BPE translations of unknown words, as well as a general preference for S-BPE sentences for English to Turkish translation, with no clear winner for the reverse direction. The statistical significance of these results is lower than for German, clearly due to the smaller amount of evaluated sentences.

5.3 Translation results

In this section we present global translation results, evaluated using BLEU scores. Table 7 compares

	Segmentation	Sentence
Source		Wegen der Umstellung auf den neuen Abgas- und **Verbrauchsprüfstandard** WLTP gebe es Produktionsausfälle bei Audi, sagte Schot der "Heilbronner Stimme".
Reference		After conversion to the new emissions and **consumption standard** WLTP, there were production losses at Audi, Schot told the 'Heilbronner Stimme'.
BPE	verbrau@@ ch@@ spru@@ ef@@ standard	Due to the changeover to the new exhaust and **exhaust test standard** WLTP there were production downs at Audi, said the "Heilbronner Stimme".
S-BPE	verbrauch@@ spruef@@ standard	Due to the changeover to the new WLTP exhaust and **consumption testing standard**, production was lost at Audi, Schot said "Heilbronner Voice".
Source		Es gibt keine **Abbiegespur** auf den Haaße-Hügel.
Reference		There is no **turning lane** on Haaße Hügel.
BPE	ab@@ bi@@ e@@ ges@@ pur	There is no **bending** on the Haasse Hill.
S-BPE	ab@@ bie@@ ge@@ spur	There is no **turning lane** on the Haasse hill.
Source		In der **Haushaltwarenabteilung** im Obergeschoss kippt der Geflügelte einen mit Espresso zubereiteten Cocktail namens "Golden Eye", passend zum Festival-Award.
Reference		In the **household goods department** on the upper floor, the winged man tips down a cocktail made with espresso called "Golden Eye", which is suited to the festival award.
BPE	haushalt@@ war@@ enab@@ teilung	In the **household section** on the upper floor, the poultry tick a cocktail prepared with espresso called "Golden Eye", in line with the festival award.
S-BPE	haushalt@@ waren@@ abteilung	In the **household goods department** on the upper floor the poultry tilts a cocktail prepared with espresso called "Golden Eye", matching the festival award.
Source		Der 46-jährige Fahrer des **Notarztautos** hatte am Samstagnachmittag mit Blaulicht und Martinshorn eine rote Ampel überfahren.
Reference		The 46 year old driver of the **ambulance** ran a red light on Saturday afternoon with the blue lights flashing and siren sounding.
BPE	not@@ arz@@ tau@@ tos	The 46-year-old driver of the **notary car** had passed a red light on Saturday afternoon with the blue light and Martinshorn.
S-BPE	no@@ tar@@ z@@ t@@ autos	The 46-year-old driver of the **emergency car** had overrun a red traffic light on Saturday afternoon with blue-light and Martinshorn.

Table 5: Translation examples showing the impact of morphologically wrong segmentation by BPE and how statistical BPE avoids such errors. Notice that the words causing the errors were not observed at training time.

	Better word		Better sentence	
Arc	BPE	S-BPE	BPE	S-BPE
En → De	10.0%	21.3%**	23.3%	41.3%**
De → En	17.1%	26.3%**	29.3%	41.5%**
En → Tr	11.8%	23.5%	11.8%	35.3%*
Tr → En	18.9%	39.6%*	30.2%	30.2%

Table 6: Results of the human evaluation. The numbers indicate the proportion of wins by each system (ties are omitted from the table for brevity). Evaluated sentences, in top-down order, were 150, 369, 34, and 53, respectively. Statistical significance, measured with a paired proportion test, is reported for $p < 0.01$ (**) and $p < 0.05$ (*).

the BLEU scores for the different language pairs using BPE for a range of sub-word unit numbers (from 4K to 96K). One first observation is that the number of units has an important effect on translation performance. We can see that the effect can be as much as 2 BLEU points (Et → En). The optimal number of operations also varies greatly between languages, with En → Fi obtaining optimum performance at 96K (although without much variability), while other arcs like e.g. En → Tr having the best performance at just 4K operations. If we conduct a similar grid search for S-BPE, we can draw similar conclusions about the optimal number of operations, noting that the effect of choosing an incorrect number operations is even more important. The full results can be found in the Appendix.

Table 7 also shows the results of using the stopping criterion described in Section 4.1, with stop-

	BPE							
Arc	4K	8K	16K	32K	48K	64K	96K	S-BPE (#ops)
En → Fi	20.79	20.95	20.89	20.92	20.93	20.90	**21.08**	**20.92*** (7 269)
Fi → En	23.33	23.63	**23.71**	22.94	22.95	22.89	23.17	**23.86*** (7 719)
En → De	36.93	37.62	37.60	38.00	**38.38**	38.15	38.17	37.46 (5 864)
De → En	34.43	34.35	35.12	**35.22**	34.71	35.04	34.80	**34.84** (5 704)
En → Ro	23.98	**24.08**	23.78	22.88	22.85	22.88	22.77	**23.92*** (7 169)
Ro → En	33.18	**33.45**	32.63	31.15	31.20	31.08	31.52	32.73 (7 709)
En → Lv	17.27	17.41	**17.72**	17.26	16.86	16.86	17.11	**17.35*** (6 819)
Lv → En	18.26	18.50	**18.59**	18.50	18.32	18.32	18.59	**18.65*** (7 334)
En → Et	**17.28**	16.90	16.83	15.98	15.92	15.71	16.17	**17.18*** (7 039)
Et → En	**22.17**	21.95	21.76	20.90	20.07	20.03	20.51	**22.06*** (7 464)
En → Tr	**13.00**	12.69	12.00	12.02	11.77	11.73	11.47	**12.89*** (8 384)
Tr → En	17.66	**17.85**	17.19	16.80	16.98	17.04	16.60	**17.84*** (9 114)

Table 7: Results for different language pairs. For BPE we use the number of operations given in the head of the table (4K, 8K, etc.), for S-BPE we use early stopping (with $k = 0.002$ and averaging the last 5 iterations). The symbol * marks systems for which S-BPE is not significantly different than the best BPE system. S-BPE results in bold are within ± 0.4 BLEU of the optimal BPE result.

ping parameter set to $k = 0.002$ and averaging over the last 5 iterations. These values were obtained empirically by doing a grid search over a small set of values and languages. It can be seen that the results obtained for most translation directions are in the range of the optimal result obtained by BPE, with many results not being statistical significantly different, as computed with the bootstrap method (Koehn, 2004), with 99% confidence interval. One can also consider that there is additional variability due to random initialization of the NMT optimization algorithm, in our experience in the range of ± 0.4 BLEU. We also marked the systems within this range in the table.[5]

It is also worth noting that for the language arcs where the stopping criterion is outperformed by the optimized baseline BPE extraction, the difference in performance is smaller than the difference due to choosing an incorrect number of operations on the standard BPE approach.

In conclusion, we do not see a clear difference in BLEU scores with S-BPE with respect to the standard BPE approach, using the optimal number of operations. However, as Sections 5.1 and 5.2 show, we obtain focused improvements on single words, which improves the translation quality as perceived by human judges.

6 Conclusions and future work

We introduced a statistical extension of BPE extraction. It introduces a well-founded objective for unit selection, which also allows the definition of a statistically motivated stopping criterion. Using this approach we achieve nearly optimal machine translation performance as measured with BLEU, while at the same time producing more linguistically motivated units. This leads to better translations of single words, which increases the translation quality as perceived by human judges, especially in the case of sentences containing unseen words. Using the stopping criterion we approximate the optimal selection of number of units, without the need to perform the costly optimization required by BPE, involving a full training-evaluation cycle for each tested number of operations.

Regarding future work, we observe that the probability distributions defined for our approach are closely related to those used for n-gram language models. Thus, smoothing methods can be applied, which can enhance the robustness of the method for unseen events, which opens a wide variety of possible extensions of this work.

The code is available from `https://github.com/amazon-research/statistical-byte-pair-encoding`.

[5]We did not do an extensive search for random initializations for this investigations due to the high number of experiments involved.

References

Duygu Ataman and Marcello Federico. 2018. An Evaluation of Two Vocabulary Reduction Methods for Neural Machine Translation. In *Proceedings of the 13th Conference of the Association for Machine Translation in the Americas (Volume 1: Research Papers)*, pages 97–110, Boston, MA. Association for Machine Translation in the Americas.

Duygu Ataman, Matteo Negri, Marco Turchi, and Marcello Federico. 2017. Linguistically motivated vocabulary reduction for neural machine translation from Turkish to English. *The Prague Bulletin of Mathematical Linguistics*, 108(1):331–342.

Tamali Banerjee and Pushpak Bhattacharyya. 2018. Meaningless yet meaningful: Morphology grounded subword-level NMT. In *Proceedings of the Second Workshop on Subword/Character LEvel Models*, pages 55–60, New Orleans. Association for Computational Linguistics.

Loïc Barrault, Ondřej Bojar, Marta R. Costa-jussà, Christian Federmann, Mark Fishel, Yvette Graham, Barry Haddow, Matthias Huck, Philipp Koehn, Shervin Malmasi, Christof Monz, Mathias Müller, Santanu Pal, Matt Post, and Marcos Zampieri. 2019. Findings of the 2019 conference on machine translation (WMT19). In *Proceedings of the Fourth Conference on Machine Translation (Volume 2: Shared Task Papers, Day 1)*, pages 1–61, Florence, Italy. Association for Computational Linguistics.

Kenneth Ward Church and Patrick Hanks. 1990. Word association norms, mutual information, and lexicography. *Computational Linguistics*, 16(1):22–29.

Michael Denkowski and Graham Neubig. 2017. Stronger baselines for trustable results in neural machine translation. In *Proceedings of the First Workshop on Neural Machine Translation*, pages 18–27, Vancouver. Association for Computational Linguistics.

Jacob Devlin, Ming-Wei Chang, Kenton Lee, and Kristina Toutanova. 2018. Bert: Pre-training of deep bidirectional transformers for language understanding.

Philip Gage. 1994. A new algorithm for data compression. *The C Users Journal*, 12(2):23–38.

James Henderson. 2020. The unstoppable rise of computational linguistics in deep learning. *arXiv:2005.06420 [cs]*.

Felix Hieber, Tobias Domhan, Michael Denkowski, and David Vilar. 2020. Sockeye 2: A toolkit for neural machine translation. *Proceedings of EAMT 2020, project track*.

Felix Hieber, Tobias Domhan, Michael Denkowski, David Vilar, Artem Sokolov, Ann Clifton, and Matt Post. 2017. Sockeye: A toolkit for neural machine translation. *ArXiv e-prints*, abs/1712.05690.

Matthias Huck, Simon Riess, and Alexander Fraser. 2017. Target-side word segmentation strategies for neural machine translation. In *Proceedings of the Second Conference on Machine Translation*, pages 56–67, Copenhagen, Denmark. Association for Computational Linguistics.

Philipp Koehn. 2004. Statistical significance tests for machine translation evaluation. In *Proceedings of the 2004 Conference on Empirical Methods in Natural Language Processing*, pages 388–395, Barcelona, Spain. Association for Computational Linguistics.

Julia Kreutzer and Artem Sokolov. 2018. Learning to segment inputs for NMT favors character-level processing. In *Proceedings of the 15th International Workshop on Spoken Language Translation*, pages 166–171, Bruges, Belgium.

Taku Kudo. 2018. Subword regularization: Improving neural network translation models with multiple subword candidates. In *Proceedings of the 56th Annual Meeting of the Association for Computational Linguistics (Volume 1: Long Papers)*, pages 66–75, Melbourne, Australia. Association for Computational Linguistics.

Mikko Kurimo, Sami Virpioja, Ville T Turunen, et al. 2010. Proceedings of the Morpho Challenge 2010 Workshop. In *Morpho Challenge Workshop; 2010; Espoo*. Aalto University School of Science and Technology.

Dominik Macháček, Jonáš Vidra, and Ondřej Bojar. 2018. Morphological and language-agnostic word segmentation for NMT. In *International Conference on Text, Speech, and Dialogue*, pages 277–284. Springer.

J. Niehues, R. Cattoni, S. Stüker, M. Negri, M. Turchi, T. Ha, E. Salesky, R. Sanabria, L. Barrault, L. Specia, and M. Federico. 2019. The IWSLT 2019 Evaluation Campaign. In *Proceedings of the 16th International Workshop on Spoken Language Translation (IWSLT 2019)*, Hong Kong, China.

Ivan Provilkov, Dmitrii Emelianenko, and Elena Voita. 2019. BPE-Dropout: Simple and Effective Subword Regularization. *arXiv:1910.13267 [cs]*.

Víctor M. Sánchez-Cartagena and Antonio Toral. 2016. Abu-MaTran at WMT 2016 translation task: Deep learning, morphological segmentation and tuning on character sequences. In *Proceedings of the First Conference on Machine Translation: Volume 2, Shared Task Papers*, pages 362–370, Berlin, Germany. Association for Computational Linguistics.

Mike Schuster and Kaisuke Nakajima. 2012. Japanese and korean voice search. In *2012 IEEE International Conference on Acoustics, Speech and Signal Processing (ICASSP)*, pages 5149–5152. IEEE.

Rico Sennrich, Barry Haddow, and Alexandra Birch. 2016. Neural Machine Translation of Rare Words with Subword Units. In *Proceedings of the 54th Annual Meeting of the Association for Computational Linguistics (Volume 1: Long Papers)*, pages 1715–1725, Berlin, Germany. Association for Computational Linguistics.

Rico Sennrich and Biao Zhang. 2019. Revisiting low-resource neural machine translation: A case study. In *Proceedings of the 57th Annual Meeting of the Association for Computational Linguistics*, pages 211–221, Florence, Italy. Association for Computational Linguistics.

Sami Virpioja, Peter Smit, Stig-Arne Grönroos, and Mikko Kurimo. 2013. Morfessor 2.0: Python implementation and extensions for morfessor baseline. D4 julkaistu kehittämis- tai tutkimusraportti tai -selvitys.

Appendix

A Full derivation of likelihood increase

Lemma Given a, b, c such that $a > 0$, $b > a$ and $0 < c < b$ we have:

$$\frac{a-c}{b-c} < \frac{a}{b}. \tag{1}$$

Proof. By assumption denominators are positive, hence we can rearrange (1) as: $b(a-c) < a(b-c)$. By assumption, $a(b-c) < ab$ from which we get $b(a-c) < ab$ and $(a-c) < a$ which is true by assumption.□

Define the count of a sub-word unit $s \in \Sigma$ for a corpus S and a sub-word vocabulary Σ as $C_{S,\Sigma}(s)$. The likelihood function is then defined as

$$L(S, \Sigma) = \sum_{s \in \Sigma} C_{S,\Sigma}(s) \log p(s) \tag{2}$$

We are interested in the increase in likelihood at step n

$$\Delta L_n(S) = L(S, \Sigma_n) - L(S, \Sigma_{n-1}). \tag{3}$$

When adding a new rule $\langle (x, y) \rightarrow xy \rangle$ in step n of the algorithm, thus defining Σ_n, we can express the likelihood increase as[1]

$$\begin{aligned}
\Delta L_n(S) = & \sum_{s \in \Sigma_{n-1} \setminus \{x,y\}} \left(C_{S,\Sigma_n}(s) \log p_n(s) - C_{S,\Sigma_{n-1}}(s) \log p_{n-1}(s) \right) \\
& + \sum_{s \in \{x,y\}} \left(C_{S,\Sigma_n}(s) \log p_n(s) - C_{S,\Sigma_{n-1}}(s) \log p_{n-1}(s) \right) \\
& + C_{S,\Sigma_n}(xy) \log p_n(xy)
\end{aligned} \tag{4}$$

We note that for $s \in \Sigma_{n-1} \setminus \{x, y\}$

$$C_{S,\Sigma_n}(s) = C_{S,\Sigma_{n-1}}(s) \quad \text{and} \quad p_n(s) > p_{n-1}(s) \tag{5}$$

as the total number of observations (denominator of p_n) shrinks after combining two symbols. Thus, for the first term in equation 4 we have

$$\sum_{s \in \Sigma_{n-1} \setminus \{x,y\}} \left(C_{S,\Sigma_n}(s) \log p_n(s) - C_{S,\Sigma_{n-1}}(s) \log p_{n-1}(s) \right) > 0. \tag{6}$$

This quantity is expected to be small, specially when the number of produced symbols increases.

Next, let us note that for the counts of the units involved in the new rule, we have

$$\begin{aligned}
C_{S,\Sigma_n}(x) &= C_{S,\Sigma_{n-1}}(x) - C_{\Sigma_n}(xy) \\
C_{S,\Sigma_n}(y) &= C_{S,\Sigma_{n-1}}(y) - C_{\Sigma_n}(xy)
\end{aligned} \tag{7}$$

(the equation holds for both x and y because the $C_{\Sigma_n}(xy)$ is added to the total amount of units).

For the probability of x and y we are reducing the occurrences and the total number of events by the same positive amount, which is lower that the sample size. Hence, by subtracting the same counts from the sample size and from the previous Lemma we can derive:

$$\begin{aligned}
p_n(x) = \frac{C_{S,\Sigma_n}(x)}{C_{S,\Sigma_n}(\cdot)} &= \frac{C_{S,\Sigma_{n-1}}(x) - C_{S,\Sigma_n}(xy)}{C_{S,\Sigma_{n-1}}(\cdot) - C_{S,\Sigma_n}(xy)} \\
&< \frac{C_{S,\Sigma_{n-1}}(x)}{C_{S,\Sigma_{n-1}}(\cdot)} = p_{n-1}(x)
\end{aligned} \tag{8}$$

[1] As some counts may decrease to 0 when defining a new pair, we use the convention $0 \log 0 = 0$.

and similarly for y.

Using (6) and (8) in (4) we obtain

$$\Delta L_n(S) > \sum_{s\in\{x,y\}} \Big(C_{S,\Sigma_n}(s) \log p_n(s) - C_{S,\Sigma_{n-1}}(s) \log p_n(s) \Big) \\ + C_{S,\Sigma_n}(xy) \log p_n(xy) \tag{9}$$

and using the count relations from (7) we arrive at

$$\Delta L_n(S) > C_{S,\Sigma_n}(xy) \left[\log p_n(xy) - \log p_n(x) - \log p_n(y)\right] . \tag{10}$$

B Additional S-BPE results

(a) English-to-German

# ops	BPE	S-BPE
4K	36.93	36.47
8K	37.62	37.11
16K	37.60	37.04
32K	38.00	37.59
48K	**38.38**	36.71
64K	38.15	**37.90**
96K	38.17	37.88

(b) German-to-English

# ops	BPE	S-BPE
4K	34.43	33.78
8K	34.35	34.38
16K	35.12	**35.56**
32K	**35.22**	34.84
48K	34.71	35.18
64K	35.04	35.17
96K	34.80	34.60

(c) English-to-Romanian

# ops	BPE	S-BPE
4K	23.98	24.09
8K	**24.08**	**24.16**
16K	23.78	23.64
32K	22.88	22.14
48K	22.85	19.09
64K	22.88	17.85
96K	22.77	16.85

(d) Romanian-to-English

# ops	BPE	S-BPE
4K	33.18	**32.82**
8K	**33.45**	32.80
16K	32.63	32.70
32K	31.15	29.63
48K	31.20	24.78
64K	31.08	22.80
96K	31.52	21.58

(e) English-to-Latvian

# ops	BPE	S-BPE
4K	17.27	16.86
8K	17.41	17.11
16K	**17.72**	**17.26**
32K	17.26	17.26
48K	16.86	16.86
64K	16.86	16.86
96K	17.11	17.11

(f) Latvian-to-English

# ops	BPE	S-BPE
4K	18.26	18.32
8K	18.50	**18.59**
16K	**18.59**	18.50
32K	18.50	18.33
48K	18.32	18.32
64K	18.32	18.32
96K	18.59	18.59

(g) English-to-Estonian

# ops	BPE	S-BPE
4K	**17.28**	**17.62**
8K	16.90	17.26
16K	16.83	17.07
32K	15.98	15.91
48K	15.92	14.21
64K	15.71	12.32
96K	16.17	11.09

(h) Estonian-to-English

# ops	BPE	S-BPE
4K	**22.17**	**21.91**
8K	21.95	21.79
16K	21.76	21.83
32K	20.90	20.80
48K	20.07	17.95
64K	20.03	15.58
96K	20.51	13.58

(i) English-to-Turkish

# ops	BPE	S-BPE
4K	**13.00**	**13.28**
8K	12.69	12.93
16K	12.00	12.05
32K	12.02	7.62
48K	11.77	6.30
64K	11.73	5.75
96K	11.47	5.25

(j) Turkish-to-English

# ops	BPE	S-BPE
4K	17.66	17.72
8K	**17.85**	**17.87**
16K	17.19	17.25
32K	16.80	11.83
48K	16.98	9.19
64K	17.04	8.24
96K	16.60	7.61

(k) English-to-Finnish

# ops	BPE	S-BPE
4K	20.79	20.60
8K	20.95	**21.03**
16K	20.89	20.82
32K	20.92	20.56
48K	20.93	21.00
64K	20.90	20.13
96K	**21.08**	20.63

(l) Finnish-to-English

# ops	BPE	S-BPE
4K	23.33	23.57
8K	23.63	**23.75**
16K	**23.71**	23.49
32K	22.94	23.05
48K	22.95	22.92
64K	22.89	21.95
96K	23.17	20.21

Table 7: Translation results for different language pairs with BPE and S-BPE, varying the number of operations. In bold, the best result for each language arc.

Integrated Training for Sequence-to-Sequence Models Using Non-Autoregressive Transformer

Evgeniia Tokarchuk[1,2], Jan Rosendahl[2], Weiyue Wang[2], Pavel Petrushkov[1], Tomer Lancewicki[1], Shahram Khadivi[1], and Hermann Ney[2]

[1]eBay Inc., Aachen, Germany
[2]RWTH Aachen University, Aachen, Germany
e.tokarchuk@uva.nl
{ppetrushkov,tlancewicki,skhadivi}@ebay.com
{rosendahl,wwang,ney}@cs.rwth-aachen.de

Abstract

Complex natural language applications such as speech translation or pivot translation traditionally rely on cascaded models. However, cascaded models are known to be prone to error propagation and model discrepancy problems. Furthermore, there is no possibility of using end-to-end training data in conventional cascaded systems, meaning that the training data most suited for the task cannot be used. Previous studies suggested several approaches for integrated end-to-end training to overcome those problems, however they mostly rely on (synthetic or natural) three-way data. We propose a cascaded model based on the non-autoregressive Transformer that enables end-to-end training without the need for an explicit intermediate representation. This new architecture (i) avoids unnecessary early decisions that can cause errors which are then propagated throughout the cascaded models and (ii) utilizes the end-to-end training data directly. We conduct an evaluation on two pivot-based machine translation tasks, namely French→German and German→Czech. Our experimental results show that the proposed architecture yields an improvement of more than 2 BLEU for French→German over the cascaded baseline.

1 Introduction

Many complex natural language applications such as speech translation (Sperber and Paulik, 2020) or pivot translation (Utiyama and Isahara, 2007; De Gispert and Marino, 2006) traditionally rely on cascaded models. The technique of model cascading is commonly used to solve problems that can be divided into a sequence of sub-problems where the solution to the first problem is used as an input to the second and so on. Typically cascaded systems include several consecutive and independently trained models, each of which aims to solve a particular sub-task. For example in a cascaded speech translation system an automatic speech recognition model receives the audio signal as an input and generates a transcription as an output of the first sub-task. This output could be passed to a system that adds punctuation and capitalization to the sequence, before, as a final step, a machine translation system is applied.

Cascaded models are appealing if there is more training data for each of the sub-tasks than for the full task. Examples for such scenarios include automatic speech translation (AST), image captioning in non-English languages, and non-English machine translation. However, cascaded models are prone to error propagation, meaning that decision errors in the first model are forwarded to and possibly amplified by the second model. Usually, there is also a loss of information when passing information between models since the interface between models traditionally requires each model to output a discrete decision. This means that the deeper knowledge that the model may encode in its representation of the output is reduced to a 'surface form' of a particular prediction, which is passed on to the following model. Lastly, in conventional cascaded system there is no possibility to make use of end-to-end training data, meaning that the training data most suited for the task cannot be used.

To tackle these problems, several approaches for integrated end-to-end training of cascaded models have been proposed and applied to different NLP tasks (Bahar et al., 2021; Sperber et al., 2019; Sung et al., 2019). Integrated end-to-end training is usually achieved by merging the consecutive models and fine-tuning the resulting system on the end-to-end training data. Although the idea of this approach is simple, it remains an open challenge how to choose the interface between the models in such a way that they can be trained, e.g. by gradient propagation. Furthermore, most of these approaches rely on synthetic or natural multi-way

Proceedings of the 18th International Conference on Spoken Language Translation, pages 276–286
Bangkok, Thailand (Online), August 5–6, 2021. ©2021 Association for Computational Linguistics

training data, i.e. data that does not only provide an (input, output) pair but also the correct label for all sub-tasks involved. For a detailed discussion of the literature, we refer to Section 2. In this work we focus on the task of pivot-based machine translation, i.e. the translation from a source (src) language via a pivot (piv) language to the desired target (trg) language, as an example for a two-stage task that is traditionally solved by model cascading.

We propose a cascaded model based on the non-autoregressive Transformer (NAT) that enables end-to-end training without the need for an explicit intermediate representation, that is inevitable in autoregressive models. This new architecture (i) avoids unnecessary early decisions that can cause errors which are then propagated throughout the cascaded models (ii) utilizes the src→trg, src→piv and piv→trg training data and (iii) communicates the full information from the src→piv model downstream by providing a natural interface between the src→piv and piv→trg models.

2 Related Work

Several approaches were proposed in recent years to address the weaknesses of the traditional cascaded models. Early works investigated the applications of the N-best list decoding both in speech translation and pivot-based translation (Woszczyna et al., 1993; Lavie et al., 1996; Och and Ney, 2004; Utiyama and Isahara, 2007). The N-best list decoding allows to pass multiple intermediate hypotheses and avoid unnecessary early decisions. An efficient alternative to the n-best list is lattices, which replaced the n-best list for the speech translation models (Zhang et al., 2005; Schultz et al., 2004; Matusov et al., 2008). However, the usage of the discrete decisions does not allow to train cascaded model jointly on src→trg data.

Most recent works are focusing instead on the joint or integrated training for sequence-to-sequence cascaded models. Thus, (Cheng et al., 2017) suggested a joint training approach for the pivot-based neural machine translation. In their work, two attention-based RNN models (Bahdanau et al., 2015) are trained jointly with different connection terms in the objective function and the src→trg as a bridging corpus. Another approach is to apply the transfer-learning technique for pivot-based NMT (Kim et al., 2019), meaning that the direct src→trg model is initialized with the respective weights from the pre-trained models, and fine-tuned on src→trg corpus through the trainable adapter. Pivot-based NMT is typically used in a low-resource src→trg setup, and multilingual NMT systems proved to be successful in this scenario (Johnson et al., 2017; Aharoni et al., 2019; Zhang et al., 2020). To tackle a low-resource NMT problem, (Kim et al., 2019) also explore different ways to extend the back-translation idea (Sennrich et al., 2016a) for src→piv→trg scenarios. However, since this work aims to provide the general framework for the integrated training of cascaded sequence-to-sequence models, we do not aim for comprehensive comparisons with multilingual NMT systems and various data augmentation strategies. We refer to (Kim et al., 2019) for in-depth comparison studies.

In speech translation, the tight model integration for the cascaded models also attracted attention from the community. (Anastasopoulos and Chiang, 2018; Wang et al., 2019; Sperber et al., 2019) discussed either use of attention or hidden state vectors as a connection interface for the tight model integration in cascaded systems. Recently, (Bahar et al., 2021) proposed to use posterior distribution as an input to the encoder of the second model.

3 Background

3.1 Sequence-to-Sequence modeling

The modeling of the sequence-to-sequence problems, namely converting the source sequence f_1^J in one domain to the target sequence e_1^I in another domain, is nowadays usually done using encoder-decoder deep neural networks (Sutskever et al., 2014; Bahdanau et al., 2015; Vaswani et al., 2017). The purpose of the encoder is to map the input sequence f_1^J to a continuous, hidden vector representation h, from which the decoder decodes the target sequence.

In applications such as machine translation, the Transformer (Vaswani et al., 2017), an attention-based sequence-to-sequence model, is considered state of the art (Barrault et al., 2020).

Commonly the probability distribution over the target sequences in sequence-to-sequence models is expressed by a left-to-right factorization:

$$p(e_1^I|f_1^J) = \prod_{i=1}^{I} p(e_i|e_1^{i-1}, f_1^J). \qquad (1)$$

These models are also called *autoregressive*, meaning that each consecutive token in the target sequence depends on the left context of the same sequence.

3.2 Non-Autoregressive NMT

In contrast to the autoregressive modelling approach, the non-autoregressive Transformer (Gu et al., 2018) assumes that all tokens in the target sequence are generated independently of each other. This means in particular that there is no need for a search procedure at inference time since target tokens can be generated and optimized in parallel. However, current approaches also need an explicit length model as additional input to the decoder. Gu et al. (2018) utilize the standard Transformer architecture and provide several modifications in order to obtain a non-autoregessive machine translation system.

Recent works proposed to relax the independence constraints during training and use *iterative decoding* for the NAT, meaning that instead of only one decoding pass, the model relies on the multiple passes, and conditional dependence might be used on the consecutive passes to achieve better performance (Ghazvininejad et al., 2019; Gu et al., 2019; Lee et al., 2018; Stern et al., 2019). Such decoding procedure allows shrinking the gap between the performance of the autoregressive and non-autoregressive models.

3.3 Pivot-based Machine Translation

A cascading system p_{s2t} for pivot-based machine translation consists of a src→piv model p_{s2p} and a piv→trg model p_{p2t}, which typically have a disjoint parameter set. While both models are trained independently, they work in cooperation when producing the translation, i.e., the most likely target sequence $\hat{e}_1^{\hat{I}}$ for the given source sequence f_1^J. The pivot sequence z_1^K can be viewed as a latent variable, and the target sequence probability can be expressed by summing over all pivot sequences:

$$\begin{aligned} p_{\text{s2t}}(e_1^I|f_1^J) &= \sum_{z_1^K} p_{\text{p2t}}(e_1^I|z_1^K, f_1^J)p_{\text{s2p}}(z_1^K|f_1^J) \\ &= \sum_{z_1^K} p_{\text{p2t}}(e_1^I|z_1^K)p_{\text{s2p}}(z_1^K|f_1^J). \end{aligned}$$

Since the sum over all possible pivot hypothesis z_1^K is intractable in practice, instead *two-pass decoding* is used as an approximation to obtain the target hypotheses:

$$\hat{z}_1^{\hat{K}} = \operatorname*{argmax}_{K,z_1^K} \prod_{k=1}^{K} p_{\text{s2p}}(z_k|z_1^{k-1}, f_1^J) \quad (2)$$

$$\hat{e}_1^{\hat{I}} = \operatorname*{argmax}_{I,e_1^I} \prod_{i=1}^{I} p_{\text{p2t}}(e_i|e_1^{i-1}, \hat{z}_1^{\hat{K}}). \quad (3)$$

We investigate the stability and potential for improvement of this interface in the Section 6.1.

4 Model Integration

Starting from the conventional cascaded model, as described in Section 3.3, we propose to connect the two consecutive encoder-decoder models through an end-to-end trainable interface. The src→piv model consists of both Encoder$_{s2p}$ and Decoder$_{s2p}$, similarly the piv→trg model consists of Encoder$_{p2t}$ and Decoder$_{p2t}$. We introduce an interface which connects Decoder$_{s2p}$ to the Encoder$_{p2t}$. The main requirement for this connection interface is to be differentiable to make the gradient propagation possible. In order to fulfill this requirement, we follow the previous work (see more in Section 2) and choose to focus on two possible interfaces:

- **Decoder States Interface**: Pass the final sequence of hidden states vectors of the last src→piv Decoder$_{s2p}$ layer as an input to the Encoder$_{p2t}$. The input embedding layer and positional encoding layer are omitted in the Encoder$_{p2t}$, and the hidden states vector is then used directly as an input to the next self-attention block (see Figure 1a).

- **Decoder Posteriors Interface**: Pass the probability distribution $p_{s2p}(z_1^K|i, f_1^J)$ of the Decoder$_{s2p}$. The embedding matrix E from Encoder$_{p2t}$ is used to calculate a 'soft embedding'

$$\sum_{v \in V} E_v p_{s2p}(z_k = v|f_1^J).$$

  Hence, the Decoder$_{s2p}$ and Encoder$_{p2t}$ are connected through the softmax layer, as shown shown in Figure 1b.

Note that the decoder posteriors interface requires the src→piv and piv→trg model to share a common vocabulary V.

Two autoregressive encoder-decoder models can be connected through these interfaces as shown

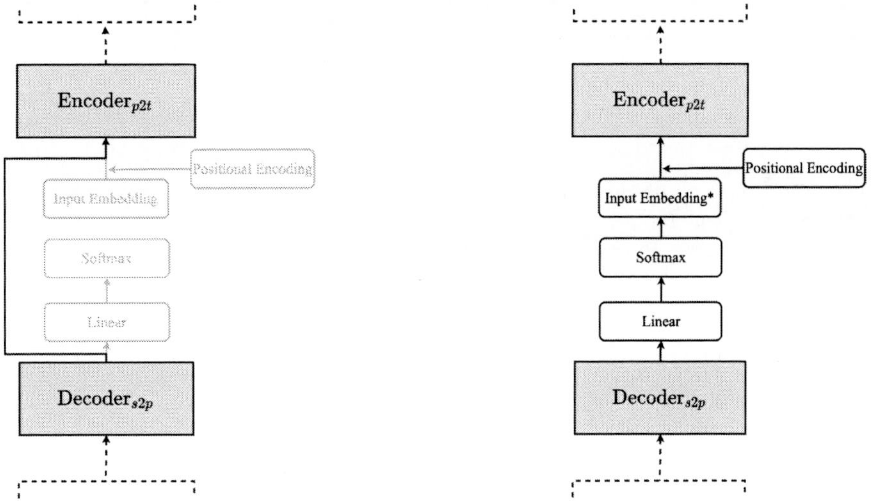

(a) Decoder States Interface. (b) Decoder Posteriors Interface.

Figure 1: Two proposed connection interfaces between src→piv and piv→trg models for integrated training. The blocks in gray represents are omitted layers of the original cascaded Transformer architecture. For simplicity we do not show the Encoder$_{s2p}$ and Decoder$_{p2t}$.
*Note that the input embedding is now a full fledged matrix multiplication, not a multiplication with a one-hot vector which is equivalent to a column selection.

in Figure 2a. However, at training time the Decoder$_{s2p}$ requires a pivot sequence as an input. If there is no access to the three-way src→piv→trg data, the pivot sequence has to be obtained by doing a search in training, which is computationally very prohibitive in a real world task, or via forward or backward translation beforehand (synthetic data). The disadvantage of using synthetic data is that the pivot sequences remain static throughout the training, this means that the cascaded src→piv→trg model is trained on pivot sequences which become less relevant the more training updates the src→piv models receives. To avoid a sub-optimal, discrete intermediate representation while still benefit from the model integration, we propose to replace src→piv autoregressive Transformer with a non-autoregressive one as shown in Figure 2b. The usage of NAT allows to replace the pivot sequence with a sequence of unknowns during the training on src→trg data. Since the decoder states interface do not use the embeddings of the Encoder$_{p2t}$, similar to other works, the Encoder$_{p2t}$ can be safely omitted in the integrated model (Figure 2c).

Training such a cascaded model can be done with the following steps:

- *Pre-training*:
  - Train src→piv model on src→piv corpora
  - Train piv→trg model on piv→trg corpora
- *Concatenation*: Concatenate the models in the cascade through the interface and initialize respective components with the pre-trained weights.
- *Fine-tuning*: fine-tune the resulting integrated model on the src→trg data.

This yields a src→trg architecture in which all parameters are pre-trained and which makes use of all parameters from the pre-trained models, with the exception of one linear layer and an embedding matrix in the decoder states interface. Please note that although we are focusing on pivot-based NMT as our target task, we argue that the proposed integration method can be easily adapted to any Transformer-based cascaded model.

5 Experimental Results

To test and verify the proposed cascaded model, we conduct experiments on French→German and German→Czech data from the WMT 2019 news translation task[1].

[1] `http://www.statmt.org/wmt19/`

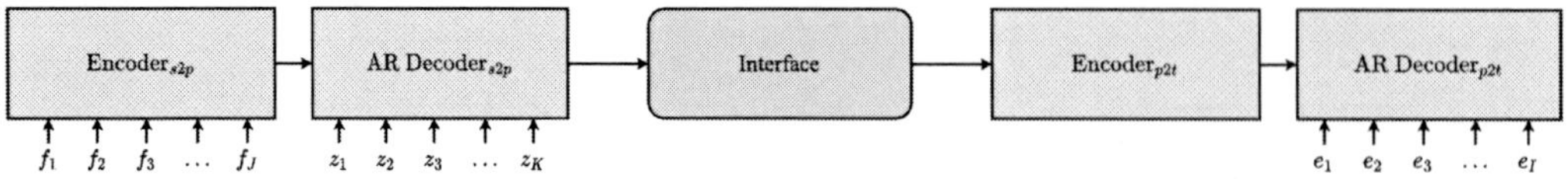

(a) AR-based integrated model.

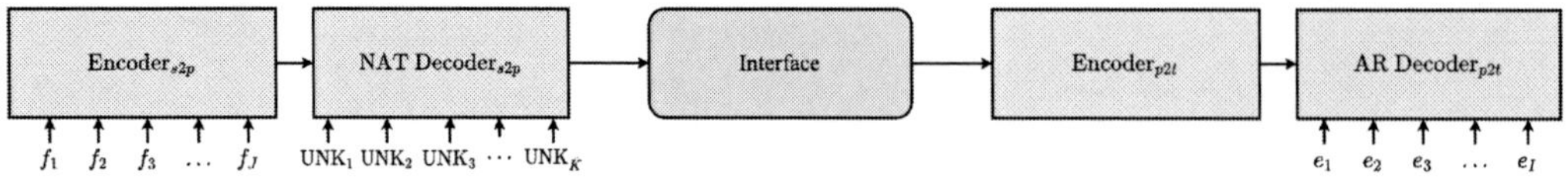

(b) NAT-based integrated model.

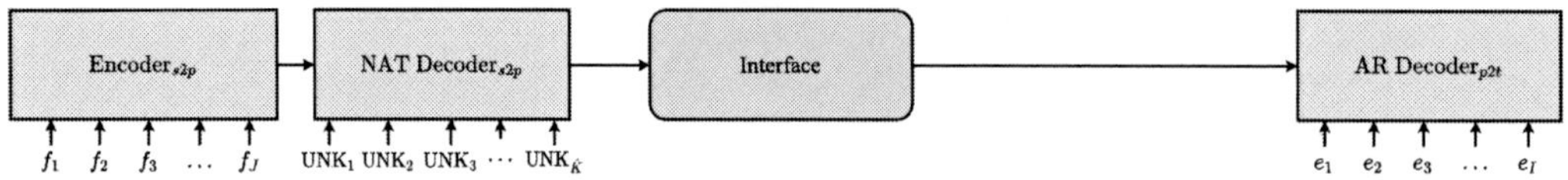

(c) Three-components NAT-based integrated model.

Figure 2: Different variants of the encoder-decoder model integration through the connection interface.

5.1 Data

Training data for French→German includes Europarl corpus version 7 (Koehn, 2005), CommonCrawl[2] corpus and the newstest2008-2010. The total number of parallel sentences is 2.3M.

The original German→Czech task was constrained to unsupervised translation, but we utilized the available parallel data to relax these constraints. The corpus consists of NewsCommentary version 14 (Tiedemann, 2012) and we extended it by including newssyscomb2009[3] and the concatenation of previous years test sets newstest2008-2010 from the news translation task. The total amount of parallel sentences is 230K.

For both tasks we use newstest2011 as the development set and newstest2012 as the test sets. The data statistics, including pre-training data, are collected in Table 1.

		Sentences	Words (target)
direct data	French→German	2.3M	53M
pre-train	French→English	35M	905M
	English→German	9.7M	221M
direct data	German→Czech	230K	4.5M
pre-train	German→English	9.1M	180M
	English→Czech	49M	486M

Table 1: Training data overview.

[2]https://commoncrawl.org/

[3]http://www.statmt.org/wmt09/system-combination-task.html

5.2 Preprocessing

For each parallel corpus, we apply a standard preprocessing procedure: First, we tokenize each corpus using the Moses[4] tokenizer. Then a true-casing model is trained on all training data and applied to both training and test data. In the final step, we train *byte-pair encoding* (BPE) (Sennrich et al., 2016b) with 32000 merge operations. In order to enable model integration, we train BPE jointly on all available data for the respective language.

5.3 Model and Training

We implement the models described in Section 4 using the *fairseq* (Ott et al., 2019) sequence-to-sequence extendable framework. As non-autoregressive src→piv model, we choose the Conditional Masked Language Model (CMLM) (Ghazvininejad et al., 2019) with 6 layers for both encoder and decoder, and a standard 6 layer 'base' Transformer for the piv→trg system (Vaswani et al., 2017). For each interface, the length of the pivot sequence is set to the length of the source sequence by default. More on the length modeling is discussed in the Section 6.4. For the decoder states interface, the last decoder is used for all the experiments.

For model fine-tuning, the Adam optimizer (Kingma and Ba, 2015) with $\beta = \{(0.9, 0.98)\}$ and the learning rate 0.5×10^{-5} is used for all the models. The

[4]http://www.statmt.org/moses/

learning rate is reduced during training based on the inverse square root of the update. Additionally, 10,000 and 4,000 warm-up updates have been used for French→German and German→Czech accordingly. The dropout is set to 0.1 for French→German and 0.3 for German→Czech. We set the effective batch size to 65,536 following the fairseq recommendations for the non-autoregressive models. Although CMLM provides the Mask-Predict decoding algorithm (Ghazvininejad et al., 2019), in our work we only use one iteration and obtain probability distribution and hidden states from the fully masked sequence, which means that each token is only conditioned on the source tokens. Results are reported using the *sacreBLEU*[5] implementation of BLEU (Papineni et al., 2002).

We compare our models against three baselines:

- *direct baseline*: The direct baseline is the Transformer base model, which is trained only on src→trg (direct) parallel data.
- *AR pivot baseline*: A baseline system composed of cascading a src→piv and a piv→trg autoregressive (AR) models. These two models are autoregressive Transformer 'base' models with six layers of encoder and decoder, respectively. The individual models are trained on either src→piv or piv→trg data. There is no fine-tuning on the src→trg data, and results are reported based on the inference only.
- *NA pivot baseline*: Similarly to the AR baseline, we provide the results for the non-autoregressive (NA) pivot baseline. The main difference is that the non-autoregressive CMLM model is selected as the src→piv model. We follow standard training procedure for the CMLM as described in (Ghazvininejad et al., 2019), and as for hyperparameters, we rely on the fairseq guidelines[6]. While pre-training, a random mask is applied to the decoder input, meaning that the number of observed and masked tokens varies for each batch. During decoding, we employ five decoding iterations to achieve better performance on the src→piv model. The Transformer base piv→trg model is trained in the same way as for the AR pivot baseline.

[5] `https://github.com/mjpost/sacrebleu`

[6] `https://github.com/pytorch/fairseq/blob/master/examples/nonautoregressive_translation/scripts.md`

Additionally, we compare our NA integrated model with the AR integrated model (2a) based on the synthetic data generation (Hilmes, 2020). Synthetic data is generated by the forward pass of the src→piv model offline before fine-tuning on the src→trg data, meaning that the pivot hypotheses stay the same during fine-tuning.

We report the best results for the proposed cascaded model with the different interfaces in Table 2. The best checkpoint is selected based on BLEU score of the development set. The results show up to 2.1% BLEU improvements for the decoder states and decoder posteriors interfaces on French→German compare to the pivot baseline. On the other hand, there is a 2.0% BLEU degradation of the performance while using decoder posteriors interface on German→Czech compare to the pivot baseline and up to 2.3% BLEU degradation using decoder states interface. We suppose that such degradation can be based on the training data size since the German→Czech is ten times smaller than French→German. To check on our assumption, we perform additional analysis with the different training data partitions in Section 6.2. Moreover, according to the decoder states interface results, the usage of the additional encoder showed its usefulness compared to the three-components architecture.

6 Analysis

6.1 Error Propagation

Error propagation is a well-known problem of cascaded models. In the following we investigate how significantly errors in one model influence the following models. To this end, we monitor both the individual model performance and the end-to-end cascaded performance by running experiments on a three-way test set that consists of (source, pivot, target) triples. For that purpose, we extract 3000 overlapping sentences from `NewsCommentary v14` for WMT French→English and WMT English→German to create a new test set that is disjoint with the training data. We train a 6-layer 'base' Transformer for French→English (src→piv) and another for English→German (piv→trg). In order to analyse the impact of disturbances and simulate errors in the French→English system, we generate a weaker hypothesis by:

		French→German		German→Czech	
		BLEU[%]		BLEU[%]	
		dev	test	dev	test
AR	direct baseline	20.0	20.4	13.5	14.0
	pivot baseline	19.5	20.7	18.8	18.1
NA Int.	Pivot hypothesis (NA pivot baseline)	17.1	18.1	17.3	16.6
	Decoder States w/o Encoder$_{p2t}$	20.9	21.8	15.5	15.5
	Decoder States w Encoder$_{p2t}$	21.5	22.8	16.5	16.7
	Decoder Posteriors	21.6	22.7	16.8	17.0
AR Int.	Decoder States†	20.6	21.2	16.6	16.8
	Decoder Posteriors†	20.5	21.1	17.9	17.1

Table 2: Results for integrated training with different non-autoregressive (NA) interfaces on src→trg data in comparison to autoregressive (AR) baseline model. All pivot/cascaded models are pre-trained on the respective data. We use `newstest{2011,2012}` as dev and test respectively. Results marked with † are taken from (Hilmes, 2020).

- Applying artificial character-level noise: With a probability of p_{noise} each character in the decoded pivot hypothesis is replaced with a random character from the character set of the sentence
- Using a weaker checkpoint than the baseline
- Reducing the beam size to 1 (greedy search)

By applying these procedures, we control the performance of the src→piv model while maintaining a stable performance for the piv→trg model. As is shown in Figure 3, the errors in the src→piv model are actually deflated by the piv→trg system, since a loss of 1.0 BLEU in the src→piv system results in only a drop of around 0.5 BLEU for the cascaded src→trg system.

Similarly, we conduct experiments in the other direction. By improving the quality of the prediction from the src→piv model, we study the potential gain for the src→trg task. For that purpose, we translate each source sentence to a 10-best list of pivot sentences. Using the pivot reference from the three-way test set we can select the single best hypothesis based on the sentence-level BLEU

The sentence with the best BLEU score among ten candidates is then passed to the piv→trg model. This cheating experiment results in an improvement of 6.2% absolute BLEU on the src→piv model, which in turn however only results in 1.4% absolute BLEU improvement on the cascaded src→trg model. We conclude that (i) the piv→trg models weakens both improvements and errors of

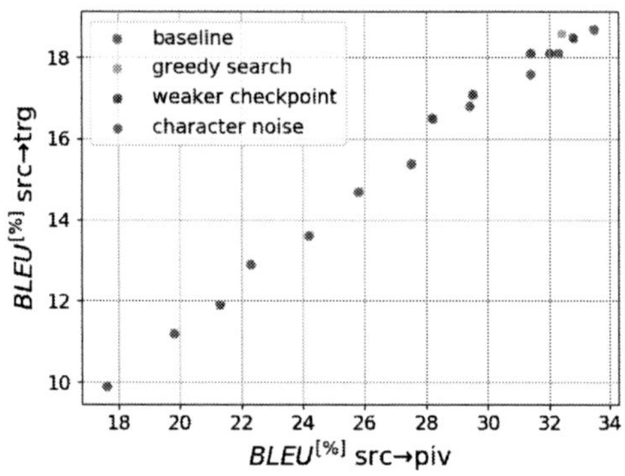

Figure 3: Impact of errors in the src→piv model on the performance of the cascaded src→trg system.

the src→piv model and (ii) the ambiguities in an src→piv 10-best list hold room for an improvement of over 1.0 BLEU.

6.2 Effect of Training Data Size

To investigate how much the NAT-based integrated model quality depends on the training data size, we train our model on randomly sampled 50%, 30%, and 10% selections of the original French→German training corpus. To prevent overfitting on a small corpus, we increase the dropout rate to 0.3 compared to 0.1 on full French→German corpus. The Table 3 shows that when training on 10% of the original data, the discrepancy between the best model performance is around 2.4% BLEU. This setup simulates the data conditions of German→Czech since the total amount of training sentences in German→Czech corpus is around 10% of the French→German corpus. Based on our experimental results, we suppose that the integrated model needs some minimum amount of parallel src→trg data to achieve the acceptable performance.

data percentage	BLEU[%]
100%	21.5
50%	21.0
30%	20.6
10%	19.1

Table 3: French→German dev set results using different training data partitions. The data percentage refers to the relative size of the training corpus comparing to the full French→German training set. All experiments use the decoder states interface for NAT-based integrated training.

6.3 Effect of Model Pre-training

In our experiments for the NAT-based integrated model, we solely rely on the models' pre-training, which means that instead of random initialization for the NAT-based integrated model components, we utilize the weights from the respective pre-trained models. In this section, we study the importance of model pre-training and its impact on the final model performance. For that purpose, we train the NAT-based integrated model with various initialization options.

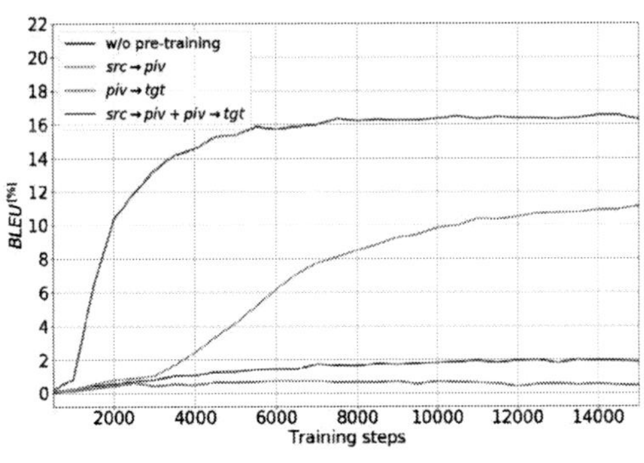

Figure 4: German→Czech dev set results for different parameter pre-training schemes. src→piv indicates that both Encoder$_{s2p}$ and Decoder$_{s2p}$ are pre-trained and all other parameters are randomly initialized. We use a similar notation for the other pre-training schemes. All experiments use the decoder states interface for NAT-based integrated training.

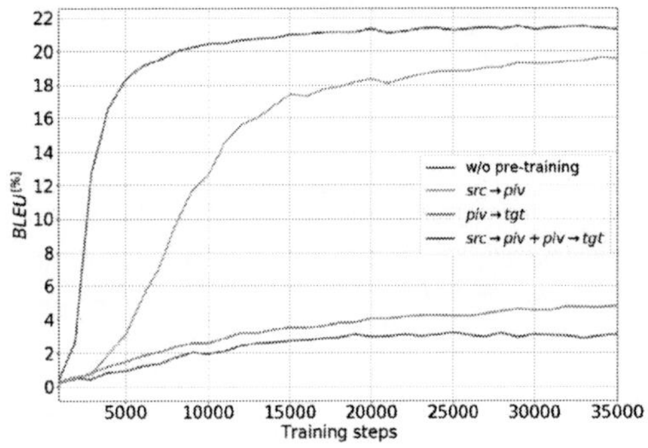

Figure 5: French→German dev set results for different parameter pre-training schemes. All experiments use the decoder states interface for NAT-based integrated training.

Figure 4 and Figure 5 show that initialization of scr→piv encoder and decoder is crucial for the final model performance. Without initialization or with pre-training only piv→trg encoder and decoder, it is impossible to train the end-to-end system. We see a similar trend while using the decoder posteriors interface.

6.4 Length Modeling

Length modeling for the non-autoregressive decoder is one of the bottlenecks for our proposed NAT-based integrated model. The pivot sequence length has to be set in advance, and it can not be refined. In most of our experiments, we set the length of the intermediate sequence to be equal to the source sequence length both in training and test time. As a result, we do not fine-tune the length model using the src→trg data. Moreover, the assumption that source length should match the pivot length does not hold for every language pair. In Table 4 we experiment with using different length estimates and report how it affects the end-to-end translation quality.

The results show that better length modeling can lead to more than 2% BLEU improvements. However, for our experiments, we have not tried any sophisticated length prediction methods. We suppose that further exploration will be beneficial for the integrated model performance.

6.5 Decoder Iterations

The iterative refinement of the hypotheses by a non-autoregressive decoder plays an essential role in achieving better performance (Ghazvininejad et al., 2019; Gu et al., 2019). We observe that, the NA

	French→German	German→Czech
length source	BLEU[%]	BLEU[%]
random	19.2	14.6
source	21.6	16.8
target	18.9	16.5
predicted	21.3	17.2

Table 4: Results for the different pivot length estimates on the dev set. Length source `random` refers to the length choice based on uniform distribution in the interval $[2, 100)$. `predicted` refers to the usage of the CMLM length prediction component for length assignment. `source` and `target` indicate the length choice based on the source sequence or target sequence lengths. All experiments use the decoder posteriors interface for NAT-based integrated training.

baseline with one decoder iteration of the src→piv model results in 8.2 BLEU on the French→German development set, while five iterations of the same decoder yield 17.1 BLEU. However, simply increasing the number of iterations during decoding with the integrated model does not lead to similar improvements. Note that the output of the NA decoder is handed to an encoder, which a) more expressive than a softmax layer and b) is trained on the single-iteration output. This mismatch between training and decoding could be the reason why decoder iterations are not beneficial for the integrated model. Additionally, we experimented with decoder iterations during training of the integrated model, but it breaks the gradient propagation. Although our initial experiments with the iterations have been unsuccessful, we think that they can be applied for training using such approaches as Gumbel-Softmax (Jang et al., 2017).

6.6 Knowledge Distillation

Sequence-level knowledge distillation (KD) (Kim and Rush, 2016) proved to be useful for the training of non-autoregressive models (Zhou et al., 2020). Although it improves the src→piv model performance, our initial experiments show that KD results in a 0.1-0.3 BLEU degradation on the integrated model.

7 Conclusion

In this work, we propose a novel architecture for the integrated training of cascaded models based on a non-autoregressive Transformer. We train the model on src→piv, piv→trg, and src→trg data overcoming a drawback of conventional cascaded models. Moreover, it provides a natural interface between two Transformer-based models and avoids unnecessary early decisions for intermediate representations. Our experimental results on the task of pivot-based machine translations show that the NAT-based integrated model outperforms the pivot baseline by up to 2.1% BLEU on WMT French→German.

We analyze the integrated model and conclude that the src→piv system is crucial for the final translation performance. Further work is required to apply established NAT improvements to this new architecture, such as iterative decoding in the cascaded training and further experiments on knowledge distillation in the src→piv pre-training, both of which show significant improvements in standalone systems (Ghazvininejad et al., 2019; Gu et al., 2018, 2019; Zhou et al., 2020). Additionally, more sophisticated techniques for length modeling, such as an external length model or multiple length candidates, can be applied in the future to improve the quality of the pivot hypotheses.

Even though we test our cascaded architecture on the task for pivot-based machine translation, we can use the architecture in any application, where a combination of sequential models is beneficial.

Acknowledgments

Authors affiliated with RWTH Aachen University have partially received funding from the European Research Council (ERC) (under the European Union's Horizon 2020 research and innovation programme, grant agreement No 694537, project "SEQCLAS") and eBay Inc. The work reflects only the authors' views, and none of the funding agencies is responsible for any use that may be made of the information it contains.

We would like to thank Yunsu Kim and Benedikt Hilmes for providing the autoregressive integrated model results.

References

Roee Aharoni, Melvin Johnson, and Orhan Firat. 2019. Massively multilingual neural machine translation. In *Proceedings of the 2019 Conference of the North American Chapter of the Association for Computational Linguistics: Human Language Technologies, Volume 1 (Long and Short Papers)*, pages 3874–3884, Minneapolis, Minnesota. Association for Computational Linguistics.

Antonios Anastasopoulos and David Chiang. 2018. Tied multitask learning for neural speech translation. In *Proceedings of the 2018 Conference of the North*

American Chapter of the Association for Computational Linguistics: Human Language Technologies, Volume 1 (Long Papers), pages 82–91, New Orleans, Louisiana. Association for Computational Linguistics.

Parnia Bahar, Tobias Bieschke, Ralf Schlueter, and Hermann Ney. 2021. Tight integrated end-to-end training for cascaded speech translation. In *IEEE Spoken Language Technology Workshop*, Shenzhen, China. To appear.

Dzmitry Bahdanau, Kyunghyun Cho, and Yoshua Bengio. 2015. Neural machine translation by jointly learning to align and translate. *ICRL 2015*.

LoÃ¯c Barrault, Magdalena Biesialska, OndÅ™ej Bojar, Marta R. Costa-jussÃ, Christian Federmann, Yvette Graham, Roman Grundkiewicz, Barry Haddow, Matthias Huck, Eric Joanis, Tom Kocmi, Philipp Koehn, Chi-kiu Lo, Nikola LjubeÅ¡iÄ‡, Christof Monz, Makoto Morishita, Masaaki Nagata, Toshiaki Nakazawa, Santanu Pal, Matt Post, and Marcos Zampieri. 2020. Findings of the 2020 conference on machine translation (wmt20). In *Proceedings of the Fifth Conference on Machine Translation*, pages 1–55, Online. Association for Computational Linguistics.

Yong Cheng, Qian Yang, Yang Liu, Maosong Sun, and Wei Xu. 2017. Joint training for pivot-based neural machine translation. In *Proceedings of the Twenty-Sixth International Joint Conference on Artificial Intelligence, IJCAI-17*, pages 3974–3980, Melbourne, Australia.

Adrià De Gispert and Jose B Marino. 2006. Catalan-english statistical machine translation without parallel corpus: bridging through spanish. In *Proc. of 5th International Conference on Language Resources and Evaluation (LREC)*, pages 65–68.

Marjan Ghazvininejad, Omer Levy, Yinhan Liu, and Luke Zettlemoyer. 2019. Mask-predict: Parallel decoding of conditional masked language models. In *Proceedings of the 2019 Conference on Empirical Methods in Natural Language Processing and the 9th International Joint Conference on Natural Language Processing (EMNLP-IJCNLP)*, pages 6112–6121, Hong Kong, China. Association for Computational Linguistics.

Jiatao Gu, James Bradbury, Caiming Xiong, Victor O. K. Li, and Richard Socher. 2018. Non-autoregressive neural machine translation. In *6th International Conference on Learning Representations, ICLR 2018, Vancouver, BC, Canada, April 30 - May 3, 2018, Conference Track Proceedings*. OpenReview.net.

Jiatao Gu, Changhan Wang, and Junbo Zhao. 2019. Levenshtein transformer. In H. Wallach, H. Larochelle, A. Beygelzimer, F. d'Alché-Buc, E. Fox, and R. Garnett, editors, *Advances in Neural Information Processing Systems 32*, pages 11181–11191. Curran Associates, Inc.

Benedikt Hilmes. 2020. Investigation on the model architecture for pivot-based neural machine translation. Bachelor's thesis, Department of Computer Science, RWTH Aachen University, August.

Eric Jang, Shixiang Gu, and Ben Poole. 2017. Categorical reparameterization with gumbel-softmax. In *5th International Conference on Learning Representations, ICLR 2017, Toulon, France, April 24-26, 2017, Conference Track Proceedings*. OpenReview.net.

Melvin Johnson, Mike Schuster, Quoc V. Le, Maxim Krikun, Yonghui Wu, Zhifeng Chen, Nikhil Thorat, Fernanda Viégas, Martin Wattenberg, Greg Corrado, Macduff Hughes, and Jeffrey Dean. 2017. Google's multilingual neural machine translation system: Enabling zero-shot translation. *Transactions of the Association for Computational Linguistics*, 5:339–351.

Yoon Kim and Alexander M. Rush. 2016. Sequence-level knowledge distillation. In *Proceedings of the 2016 Conference on Empirical Methods in Natural Language Processing*, pages 1317–1327, Austin, Texas. Association for Computational Linguistics.

Yunsu Kim, Petre Petrov, Pavel Petrushkov, Shahram Khadivi, and Hermann Ney. 2019. Pivot-based transfer learning for neural machine translation between non-english languages. In *Conference on Empirical Methods in Natural Language Processing*, Hong Kong, China.

Diederik P. Kingma and Jimmy Ba. 2015. Adam: A method for stochastic optimization. In *3rd International Conference on Learning Representations, ICLR 2015, San Diego, CA, USA, May 7-9, 2015, Conference Track Proceedings*.

Philipp Koehn. 2005. Europarl: A parallel corpus for statistical machine translation. In *MT summit*, volume 5, pages 79–86.

Alon Lavie, Donna Gates, Marsal Gavalda, Laura Mayfield, Alex Waibel, and Lori Levin. 1996. Multilingual translation of spontaneously spoken language in a limited domain. In *COLING 1996 Volume 1: The 16th International Conference on Computational Linguistics*.

Jason Lee, Elman Mansimov, and Kyunghyun Cho. 2018. Deterministic non-autoregressive neural sequence modeling by iterative refinement. In *Proceedings of the 2018 Conference on Empirical Methods in Natural Language Processing*, pages 1173–1182, Brussels, Belgium. Association for Computational Linguistics.

Evgeny Matusov, Björn Hoffmeister, and Hermann Ney. 2008. Asr word lattice translation with exhaustive reordering is possible. In *Interspeech*, pages 2342–2345, Brisbane, Australia.

Franz Josef Och and Hermann Ney. 2004. The alignment template approach to statistical machine translation. *Computational Linguistics*, 30(4):417–449.

Myle Ott, Sergey Edunov, Alexei Baevski, Angela Fan, Sam Gross, Nathan Ng, David Grangier, and Michael Auli. 2019. fairseq: A fast, extensible toolkit for sequence modeling. In *Proceedings of NAACL-HLT 2019: Demonstrations*.

Kishore Papineni, Salim Roukos, Todd Ward, and Wei-Jing Zhu. 2002. Bleu: a method for automatic evaluation of machine translation. In *Proceedings of the 40th Annual Meeting of the Association for Computational Linguistics*, pages 311–318, Philadelphia, Pennsylvania, USA. Association for Computational Linguistics.

Tanja Schultz, S. Jou, S. Vogel, and S. Saleem. 2004. Using word latice information for a tighter coupling in speech translation systems. In *INTERSPEECH*.

Rico Sennrich, Barry Haddow, and Alexandra Birch. 2016a. Improving neural machine translation models with monolingual data. In *Proceedings of the 54th Annual Meeting of the Association for Computational Linguistics (Volume 1: Long Papers)*, pages 86–96, Berlin, Germany. Association for Computational Linguistics.

Rico Sennrich, Barry Haddow, and Alexandra Birch. 2016b. Neural machine translation of rare words with subword units. In *Proceedings of the 54th Annual Meeting of the Association for Computational Linguistics (Volume 1: Long Papers)*, pages 1715–1725, Berlin, Germany. Association for Computational Linguistics.

Matthias Sperber, Graham Neubig, Jan Niehues, and Alex Waibel. 2019. Attention-passing models for robust and data-efficient end-to-end speech translation. *Transactions of the Association for Computational Linguistics*, 7:313–325.

Matthias Sperber and Matthias Paulik. 2020. Speech translation and the end-to-end promise: Taking stock of where we are. In *Proceedings of the 58th Annual Meeting of the Association for Computational Linguistics*, pages 7409–7421, Online. Association for Computational Linguistics.

Mitchell Stern, William Chan, Jamie Kiros, and Jakob Uszkoreit. 2019. Insertion transformer: Flexible sequence generation via insertion operations. In *Proceedings of the 36th International Conference on Machine Learning, ICML 2019, 9-15 June 2019, Long Beach, California, USA*, volume 97 of *Proceedings of Machine Learning Research*, pages 5976–5985. PMLR.

T. Sung, J. Liu, H. Lee, and L. Lee. 2019. Towards end-to-end speech-to-text translation with two-pass decoding. In *ICASSP 2019 - 2019 IEEE International Conference on Acoustics, Speech and Signal Processing (ICASSP)*, pages 7175–7179.

Ilya Sutskever, Oriol Vinyals, and Quoc V Le. 2014. Sequence to sequence learning with neural networks. In Z. Ghahramani, M. Welling, C. Cortes, N. D. Lawrence, and K. Q. Weinberger, editors, *Advances in Neural Information Processing Systems 27*, pages 3104–3112. Curran Associates, Inc.

Jörg Tiedemann. 2012. Parallel data, tools and interfaces in opus. In *Proceedings of the Eight International Conference on Language Resources and Evaluation (LREC'12)*, Istanbul, Turkey. European Language Resources Association (ELRA).

Masao Utiyama and Hitoshi Isahara. 2007. A comparison of pivot methods for phrase-based statistical machine translation. In *Human Language Technologies 2007: The Conference of the North American Chapter of the Association for Computational Linguistics; Proceedings of the Main Conference*, pages 484–491, Rochester, New York. Association for Computational Linguistics.

Ashish Vaswani, Noam Shazeer, Niki Parmar, Jakob Uszkoreit, Llion Jones, Aidan N Gomez, Ł ukasz Kaiser, and Illia Polosukhin. 2017. Attention is all you need. In I. Guyon, U. V. Luxburg, S. Bengio, H. Wallach, R. Fergus, S. Vishwanathan, and R. Garnett, editors, *Advances in Neural Information Processing Systems 30*, pages 5998–6008. Curran Associates, Inc.

Dingmin Wang, Meng Fang, Yan Song, and Juntao Li. 2019. Bridging the gap: Improve part-of-speech tagging for Chinese social media texts with foreign words. In *Proceedings of the 5th Workshop on Semantic Deep Learning (SemDeep-5)*, pages 12–20, Macau, China. Association for Computational Linguistics.

M. Woszczyna, N. Coccaro, A. Eisele, A. Lavie, A. McNair, T. Polzin, I. Rogina, C. P. Rose, T. Sloboda, M. Tomita, J. Tsutsumi, N. Aoki-Waibel, A. Waibel, and W. Ward. 1993. Recent advances in janus: A speech translation system. In *Proceedings of the Workshop on Human Language Technology*, HLT '93, page 211–216, USA. Association for Computational Linguistics.

Biao Zhang, Philip Williams, Ivan Titov, and Rico Sennrich. 2020. Improving massively multilingual neural machine translation and zero-shot translation. In *Proceedings of the 58th Annual Meeting of the Association for Computational Linguistics*, pages 1628–1639, Online. Association for Computational Linguistics.

R. Zhang, Gen ichiro Kikui, H. Yamamoto, and W. Lo. 2005. A decoding algorithm for word lattice translation in speech translation. In *IWSLT*, pages 23–29.

Chunting Zhou, Jiatao Gu, and Graham Neubig. 2020. Understanding knowledge distillation in non-autoregressive machine translation. In *8th International Conference on Learning Representations, ICLR 2020, Addis Ababa, Ethiopia, April 26-30, 2020*. OpenReview.net.

Data Augmentation by Concatenation for Low-Resource Translation: A Mystery and a Solution

Toan Q. Nguyen
University of Notre Dame
tnguye28@nd.edu

Kenton Murray
Johns Hopkins University
kenton@jhu.edu

David Chiang
University of Notre Dame
dchiang@nd.edu

Abstract

In this paper, we investigate the driving factors behind concatenation, a simple but effective data augmentation method for low-resource neural machine translation. Our experiments suggest that discourse context is unlikely the cause for concatenation improving BLEU by about +1 across four language pairs. Instead, we demonstrate that the improvement comes from three other factors unrelated to discourse: context diversity, length diversity, and (to a lesser extent) position shifting.

1 Introduction

Many attempts have been made to augment neural machine translation (MT) systems to use discourse context (Junczys-Dowmunt, 2019; Stojanovski and Fraser, 2019; Saunders et al., 2020; Zhang et al., 2018; Sun et al., 2020; Läubli et al., 2018; Kim et al., 2019; Tan et al., 2019; Zheng et al., 2020; Jean et al., 2017). One particularly simple method is to concatenate consecutive pairs of sentence-pairs during training, but not during translation (Agrawal et al., 2018; Tiedemann and Scherrer, 2017; Ngo and Trinh, 2021; Kondo et al., 2021).[1] In this paper, we confirm that this simple method helps, by roughly +1 BLEU across four low-resource language pairs. But we demonstrate that the reason it helps is *not* discourse context, because concatenating *random* pairs of sentence-pairs yields the same improvement.

Instead, we view concatenation as a kind of data augmentation or noising method (one which pleasantly requires no alteration to the text, unlike data augmentation methods that disturb word order (Belinkov and Bisk, 2018; Anastasopoulos et al., 2019) or replace words with automatically-selected words (Gao et al., 2019; Fadaee et al., 2017; Wang et al., 2018)). Concatenating random sentences is easier than concatenating consecutive sentences, because many parallel corpora discard document boundaries, drop sentence-pairs, or even reorder sentence-pairs, so it can be difficult to know which sentence-pairs are truly consecutive.

But the fact that random concatenation helps so much creates a mystery, which is the focus of the paper. If the reason is not discourse context, what is the reason? We consider three new hypotheses:

- Random concatenation creates greater diversity of positions, because it lets the model see sentences shifted by effectively random distances.
- Random concatenation creates greater diversity of contexts, helping the model learn what *not* to attend to.
- Random concatenation creates greater diversity of sentence lengths within a minibatch.

Through a careful ablation study, we demonstrate that all three of these factors more or less contribute to the improvement, and together completely explain the improvement.

2 Concatenation

We first present the concatenation methods and confirm that they improve low-resource translation.

2.1 Methods

Let $D_{\text{orig}} = \{(x_i, y_i) \mid i = 1, \ldots, N\}$ be the original training data. We consider two concatenation strategies:

CONSEC Concatenate consecutive sentence-pairs: $D_{\text{new}} = \{(x_i x_{i+1}, y_i y_{i+1}) \mid i = 1, \ldots, N-1\}$.

[1] As this paper was being finalized, Kondo et al. (2021) published independent work also presenting random concatenation as data augmentation for NMT. They find that concatenation helps the model translate long sentences better, while the focus of the present paper is to explain thoroughly why it helps.

Proceedings of the 18th International Conference on Spoken Language Translation, pages 287–293
Bangkok, Thailand (Online), August 5–6, 2021.

RAND Same as CONSEC, but randomly permute D_{orig} before concatenation.

For example, consider the following en→vi sentence pairs:

And I think back . → *Và tôi nghĩ lại .*

I think back to my father . → *Tôi nghĩ lại về cha tôi .*

With <BOS>/<EOS> markings, the concatenated sentence-pairs would be:

source input: *And I think back . <EOS> I think back to my father . <EOS>*

target input: *<BOS> Và tôi nghĩ lại . <BOS> Tôi nghĩ lại về cha tôi .*

target output: *Và tôi nghĩ lại . <EOS> Tôi nghĩ lại về cha tôi . <EOS>*

Since consecutive training examples often come from the same document, CONSEC lets the model look at some of the discourse context during training. In RAND, however, the concatenated sentences are almost always unrelated. In both cases, we train models on the combined data, $D_{\text{orig}} \cup D_{\text{new}}$.

2.2 Initial experiments

We experiment on four low-resource language pairs: {Galician, Slovak} to English and English to {Hebrew, Vietnamese} (Qi et al., 2018; Luong and Manning, 2015) using Transformer (Vaswani et al., 2017). We use the same setup as Nguyen and Salazar (2019), with PreNorm, FixNorm and ScaleNorm, as it has been shown to perform well on low-resource tasks. Since the data comes pre-tokenized, we only apply BPE. Data statistics and hyper-parameters are summarized in Table 1.

For baseline, the training data is D_{orig}. For concatenation, we first create D_{new}, then combine it with D_{orig} to create the training data. Following Morishita et al. (2017), we randomly shuffle the training data and read it in chunks of 10k examples. Each chunk is sorted by source length before being packed into minibatches of roughly 4096 source/target tokens each.

We calculate tokenized BLEU using `multi-bleu.perl` (Koehn et al., 2007) and measure statistical significance using bootstrap resampling (Koehn, 2004).

As seen in Table 2, concatenation consistently outperforms the baseline across all datasets with significant improvement ($p < 0.01$) on almost every case. We observe that there is generally more improvement with less training data. For example, en→he with more than 200k training examples gets only +0.5 BLEU, but gl→en with only 10k sentences achieves +1.3 BLEU. On average, this method yields +1 BLEU over all four language pairs. We can also see that concatenating consecutive or random sentence pairs results in similar performance. For this reason, all the following ablation studies are conducted with RAND unless noted otherwise.

3 Analysis

Why does a method as simple as concatenation help so much? We reject the initial hypothesis that the model is assisted by discourse context (§3.1) and consider three new hypotheses related to data augmentation (§3.2–§3.4).

3.1 Discourse context

Since consecutive sentences often come from the same document, CONSEC provides the model with more discourse context during training. For RAND, however, the two sentences in a generated example are unlikely to have any relation at all. Despite this difference, we can see from Table 2 that both CONSEC and RAND achieve similar performance.

To better understand whether discourse context plays any role here, we conduct a simple experiment. We perform concatenation just as in CONSEC and RAND, but on the dev set (as well as the training set), and measure BLEU on the concatenated dev set. The new BLEU scores are shown in Table 3, showing that even having discourse context available at translation time does not enable CONSEC to do better than RAND. While we acknowledge that there could be improvement due to discourse context that is not captured by BLEU, we can also say that the gain in BLEU that we do observe with concatenation is independent of the availability of discourse context.

3.2 Position shifting

Since the Transformer uses absolute positional encodings, if a word is observed only a few times, the model may have difficulty generalizing to occurrences in other positions. Moreover, if there are too few long sentences, the model may have difficulty translating words very far from the start of the sentence. In concatenation, the second sentence is shifted by a random distance n with n being the first sentence's length in the sense that its positions

	train/dev/test sents. (x1000)	train steps/epoch	epochs	layers	heads	dropout	BPE ops.
gl→en	10/0.68/1	100	1000	4	4	0.4	3k
sk→en	61/2.27/2.45	600	200	6	8	0.3	8k
en→vi	133/1.55/1.27	1500	200	6	8	0.3	8k
en→he	210/4.52/5.51	2000	200	6	8	0.3	8k

Table 1: Some statistics of the datasets and models used.

	gl→en		sk→en		en→vi		en→he		average			
	dev	test	dev	test	dev	test	dev	test	dev	Δ	test	Δ
baseline	22.9	20.7	29.2	30.3	29.0	32.7	30.3	28.1	27.8		28.0	
CONSEC	24.9	22.9†	30.3	31.5†	29.2	33.5†	30.6	28.6†	28.8	+1.0	29.1	+1.1
RAND	25.3	23.1†	30.3	31.6†	29.2	33.0	30.8	28.5†	28.9	+1.1	29.0	+1.0

Table 2: Consecutive (CONSEC) and random (RAND) concatenation give the same BLEU improvement across our four low-resource language pairs. † = statistically significant improvement on the test set compared to baseline ($p < 0.01$).

	dev BLEU				
	gl→en	sk→en	en→vi	en→he	avg
CONSEC	23.5	29.6	29.7	31.1	28.5
RAND	24.0	29.2	29.4	31.3	28.5

Table 3: Even when we concatenate consecutive sentence-pairs during translation, CONSEC does not outperform RAND. All BLEU scores in this table are computed on concatenated versions of the dev sets, and so are not comparable with the scores in other tables.

Row		gl→en	sk→en	en→vi	en→he	avg	Δ
1	**baseline**	22.9	29.2	29.0	30.3	27.8	
2	**baseline + sim-shift**	22.7	29.8	29.0	30.4	28.0	+0.2
3	**baseline + uniform-shift**	23.8	29.8	29.3	30.5	28.4	+0.6
4	**RAND**	25.3	30.3	29.2	30.8	28.9	+1.1
5	**RAND + uniform-shift**	25.5	30.7	29.14	30.7	29.0	+1.2

Table 4: Position shifting improves accuracy somewhat, but the version of position shifting that mimics that of concatenation (sim-shift) gives less of an improvement than shifting by distances uniformly sampled from [0, 100] (uniform-shift). All BLEU scores are on dev sets.

Row		gl→en	sk→en	en→vi	en→he	avg	Δ
1	**RAND**	25.3	30.3	29.2	30.8	28.9	
2	**RAND + mask**	24.3	30.0	28.9	30.6	28.5	−0.4
3	**RAND + sep-batch**	24.9	30.1	29.1	30.6	28.7	−0.2
4	**RAND + mask + sep-batch**	23.2	29.8	29.3	30.5	28.2	−0.7
5	**RAND + mask + sep-batch + reset-pos**	23.1	29.6	28.9	30.5	28.0	−0.9

Table 5: Masking attention to prevent concatenated sentences from attending to one another (**mask**) reduces accuracy. Forming minibatches so as to prevent concatenation from increasing length diversity (**sep-batch**) also reduces accuracy. When we do both and also remove the effect of position shifting (**reset-pos**), we eliminate essentially all the improvement due to concatenation. All BLEU scores are on dev sets.

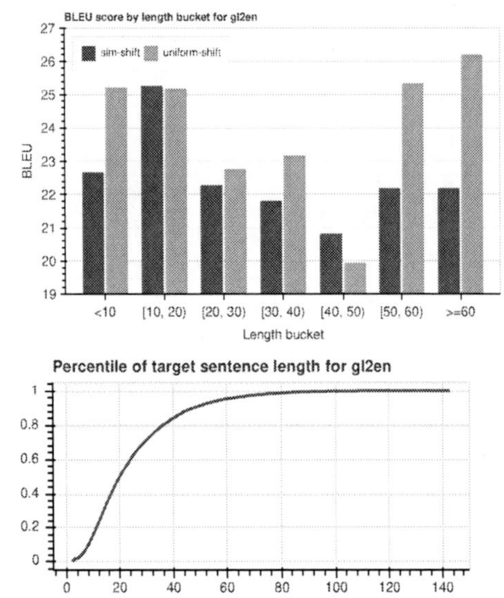

Figure 1: gl2en: dev BLEU scores by length bucket (top) and its train length percentile (bottom).

are indexed from n instead of 0. We hypothesize that this allows the model to see, and thus, to be better-trained on more positions.

If the improvement indeed comes from position shifting, we should be able to reproduce it without concatenation. In concatenation, we train on $D_{\text{orig}} \cup D_{\text{new}}$. While D_{new} has the same number of sentences as D_{orig} (§2.1), each sentence is a concatenation of two sentences in D_{orig}. This means that in total, 1/3 of sentences are shifted. So, we simulate the position-shifting that occurs in concatenation as follows. For each sentence-pair (f_i, e_i) in the training data, with probability 1/3, choose a random training sentence pair (f_j, e_j) and shift f_i by $|f_j|$ and e_i by $|e_j|$. We call this system sim-shift.

We also try a more uniform shifting method, called uniform-shift, in which we sample, with probability 0.1, distances s and t uniformly from [0, 100] and shift f_i by s and shift e_i by t.

Lines 1–3 in Table 4 show that both uniform-shift and sim-shift do help somewhat. Surprisingly, sim-shift is outperformed by uniform-shift, especially for gl→en with a gap of 0.9 BLEU. We attribute this to the fact that uniform-shift tends to shift sentences for longer distances and hence better generalizes to longer sentences. Indeed, as shown in Figure 1 (bottom), most training sentences in gl→en are shorter than 60. In Figure 1 (top), we see that uniform-shift outperforms sim-shift by the largest margin on the longest sentences. Nevertheless, adding uniform-shift on top of RAND (Table 4, row 5) only improves it very slightly.

To conclude, we show that position shifting can have a positive impact on low-resource NMT. However, it seems to contribute only a small part of the improvement due to concatenation, as we will confirm below (§3.5).

3.3 Context diversity

In an attention layer, each query word is free to attend to any key word, and the model must learn to distinguish the keys that are related to a query from those that are not. Let us call the former *positive contexts* and the latter *negative contexts*. While positive contexts are important for determining how to translate a word, it is not trivial to generate more positive contexts, as it requires creating more parallel sentences that actually use the word. By contrast, creating more negative contexts is easy; this is what concatenation does. So one hypothesis is that concatenation helps by creating more negative contexts to improve the model's ability to attend to positive contexts.

To test this, we modify RAND by masking all self-attentions so that, in each concatenated example, each sentence can only attend to itself and not the other sentence. Similarly, in cross-attention, each target sentence can only attend to its corresponding source sentence, not the other one. Table 5, row 2 shows that this masking removes a large part of the improvement due to concatenation, showing that the availability of negative contexts during training does help during translation.

3.4 Length diversity

The last possible effect of concatenation that we consider is also the most subtle. Following previous work (Morishita et al., 2017; Ott et al., 2019), we first sort sentences by length, then splitting into minibatches of a fixed number of tokens. This puts sentences of similar lengths into the same minibatch, which improves computation efficiency as there is less padding. However, as observed by Morishita et al. (2017), short and long sentences are qualitatively different, so creating a minibatch of only short sentences or only long sentences approximates the full gradient less well than a minibatch of random sentences would.

With random concatenation, we again put examples of similar lengths into the same minibatch, but each example may consist of two sentences of very different lengths. Thus, it improves diversity within a minibatch while retaining efficiency. We hypothesize that this greater length diversity is part of the reason concatenation helps.

To evaluate this hypothesis, we try a different batch generation strategy from the one described above in Section 2.2. In this setup, called **sep-batch**, we make two changes. First, the creation of D_{new} comes after sorting by sentence length (but before division into minibatches), so that in D_{new}, each example comes from two similar-length ones. Second, we create batches from D_{orig} and D_{new} separately so there is no mixture of short sentences in D_{orig} and long sentences in D_{new}.

As we can see in Table 5, removing length diversity (**sep-batch**, row 3) causes a small negative impact of −0.2 BLEU. So length diversity may be a contributing factor to concatenation's improvement.

3.5 Feature ablation

We have shown that all three hypotheses (position diversity, context diversity, and length diversity) seem to contribute to the BLEU improvement due to concatenation. To see whether these hypotheses exhaustively explain it, we test all three together. First, we apply **mask** and **sep-batch** together, resulting in a drop of −0.7 BLEU (Table 5, row 4).

Finally, to remove the effect of position shifting, we additionally reset the positions of the second sentence in every concatenated example so they start at 0 again (**reset-pos**). Applying this on top of **mask** and **sep-batch**, it brings about the largest drop of −0.9 BLEU compared to RAND, resulting in a final model that is very close to the baseline (28.0 vs. 27.8 in Table 4, row 4). Indeed, this model is only significantly different from the baseline on sk→en ($p < 0.01$). We conclude that these three hypotheses completely account for the improvement due to concatenation.

4 Conclusion

Random concatenation is a simple and surprisingly effective data augmentation method for low-resource NMT. Although the improvement of +1 BLEU it yields seems mysterious at first, we have shown that it can be explained by the fact that concatenation increases positions, context, and length diversity. Of these three factors, context diversity seems to be the most important.

Acknowledgements

This paper is based upon work supported in part by the Office of the Director of National Intelligence (ODNI), Intelligence Advanced Research Projects Activity (IARPA), via contract #FA8650-17-C-9116. The views and conclusions contained herein are those of the authors and should not be interpreted as necessarily representing the official policies, either expressed or implied, of ODNI, IARPA, or the U.S. Government. The U.S. Government is authorized to reproduce and distribute reprints for governmental purposes notwithstanding any copyright annotation therein.

References

Ruchit Rajeshkumar Agrawal, Marco Turchi, and Matteo Negri. 2018. Contextual handling in neural machine translation: Look behind, ahead and on both sides. In *21st Annual Conference of the European Association for Machine Translation*, pages 11–20.

Antonios Anastasopoulos, Alison Lui, Toan Q. Nguyen, and David Chiang. 2019. Neural machine translation of text from non-native speakers. In *Proceedings of the 2019 Conference of the North American Chapter of the Association for Computational Linguistics: Human Language Technologies, Volume 1 (Long and Short Papers)*, pages 3070–3080, Minneapolis, Minnesota. Association for Computational Linguistics.

Yonatan Belinkov and Yonatan Bisk. 2018. Synthetic and natural noise both break neural machine translation. In *Proceedings of the Sixth International Conference on Learning Representations*.

Marzieh Fadaee, Arianna Bisazza, and Christof Monz. 2017. Data augmentation for low-resource neural machine translation. In *Proceedings of the 55th Annual Meeting of the Association for Computational Linguistics (Volume 2: Short Papers)*, pages 567–573, Vancouver, Canada. Association for Computational Linguistics.

Fei Gao, Jinhua Zhu, Lijun Wu, Yingce Xia, Tao Qin, Xueqi Cheng, Wengang Zhou, and Tie-Yan Liu. 2019. Soft contextual data augmentation for neural machine translation. In *Proceedings of the 57th Annual Meeting of the Association for Computational Linguistics*, pages 5539–5544, Florence, Italy. Association for Computational Linguistics.

Sebastien Jean, Stanislas Lauly, Orhan Firat, and Kyunghyun Cho. 2017. Does neural machine translation benefit from larger context? *arXiv preprint arXiv:1704.05135*.

Marcin Junczys-Dowmunt. 2019. Microsoft translator at WMT 2019: Towards large-scale document-level neural machine translation. In *Proceedings of the Fourth Conference on Machine Translation (Volume 2: Shared Task Papers, Day 1)*, pages 225–233, Florence, Italy. Association for Computational Linguistics.

Yunsu Kim, Duc Thanh Tran, and Hermann Ney. 2019. When and why is document-level context useful in neural machine translation? In *Proceedings of the Fourth Workshop on Discourse in Machine Translation (DiscoMT 2019)*, pages 24–34, Hong Kong, China. Association for Computational Linguistics.

Philipp Koehn. 2004. Statistical significance tests for machine translation evaluation. In *Proceedings of the 2004 Conference on Empirical Methods in Natural Language Processing*, pages 388–395, Barcelona, Spain. Association for Computational Linguistics.

Philipp Koehn, Hieu Hoang, Alexandra Birch, Chris Callison-Burch, Marcello Federico, Nicola Bertoldi, Brooke Cowan, Wade Shen, Christine Moran, Richard Zens, Chris Dyer, Ondřej Bojar, Alexandra Constantin, and Evan Herbst. 2007. Moses: Open source toolkit for statistical machine translation. In *Proceedings of the 45th Annual Meeting of the Association for Computational Linguistics Companion Volume Proceedings of the Demo and Poster Sessions*, pages 177–180, Prague, Czech Republic. Association for Computational Linguistics.

Seiichiro Kondo, Kengo Hotate, Masahiro Kaneko, and Mamoru Komachi. 2021. Sentence concatenation approach to data augmentation for neural machine translation. In *Proc. NAACL Student Research Workshop*. To appear.

Samuel Läubli, Rico Sennrich, and Martin Volk. 2018. Has machine translation achieved human parity? a case for document-level evaluation. In *Proceedings of the 2018 Conference on Empirical Methods in Natural Language Processing*, pages 4791–4796, Brussels, Belgium. Association for Computational Linguistics.

Minh-Thang Luong and Christopher D. Manning. 2015. Stanford neural machine translation systems for spoken language domain. In *International Workshop on Spoken Language Translation*, Da Nang, Vietnam.

Makoto Morishita, Yusuke Oda, Graham Neubig, Koichiro Yoshino, Katsuhito Sudoh, and Satoshi Nakamura. 2017. An empirical study of mini-batch creation strategies for neural machine translation. In *Proceedings of the First Workshop on Neural Machine Translation*, pages 61–68, Vancouver. Association for Computational Linguistics.

Chinh Ngo and Trieu H. Trinh. 2021. Better translation for Vietnamese. `https://blog.vietai.org/sat/`. (Accessed on 04/27/2021).

Toan Q. Nguyen and Julian Salazar. 2019. Transformers without tears: Improving the normalization of self-attention. In *Proc. Workshop on Spoken Language Translation*.

Myle Ott, Sergey Edunov, Alexei Baevski, Angela Fan, Sam Gross, Nathan Ng, David Grangier, and Michael Auli. 2019. fairseq: A fast, extensible toolkit for sequence modeling. In *Proceedings of the 2019 Conference of the North American Chapter of the Association for Computational Linguistics (Demonstrations)*, pages 48–53, Minneapolis, Minnesota. Association for Computational Linguistics.

Ye Qi, Devendra Sachan, Matthieu Felix, Sarguna Padmanabhan, and Graham Neubig. 2018. When and why are pre-trained word embeddings useful for neural machine translation? In *Proceedings of the 2018 Conference of the North American Chapter of the Association for Computational Linguistics: Human Language Technologies, Volume 2 (Short Papers)*, pages 529–535, New Orleans, Louisiana. Association for Computational Linguistics.

Danielle Saunders, Felix Stahlberg, and Bill Byrne. 2020. Using context in neural machine translation training objectives. In *Proceedings of the 58th Annual Meeting of the Association for Computational Linguistics*, pages 7764–7770, Online. Association for Computational Linguistics.

Dario Stojanovski and Alexander Fraser. 2019. Combining local and document-level context: The LMU Munich neural machine translation system at WMT19. In *Proceedings of the Fourth Conference on Machine Translation (Volume 2: Shared Task Papers, Day 1)*, pages 400–406, Florence, Italy. Association for Computational Linguistics.

Zewei Sun, Mingxuan Wang, Hao Zhou, Chengqi Zhao, Shujian Huang, Jiajun Chen, and Lei Li. 2020. Capturing longer context for document-level neural machine translation: A multi-resolutional approach. *arXiv preprint arXiv:2010.08961*.

Xin Tan, Longyin Zhang, Deyi Xiong, and Guodong Zhou. 2019. Hierarchical modeling of global context for document-level neural machine translation. In *Proceedings of the 2019 Conference on Empirical Methods in Natural Language Processing and the 9th International Joint Conference on Natural Language Processing (EMNLP-IJCNLP)*, pages 1576–1585, Hong Kong, China. Association for Computational Linguistics.

Jörg Tiedemann and Yves Scherrer. 2017. Neural machine translation with extended context. In *Proceedings of the Third Workshop on Discourse in Machine Translation*, pages 82–92, Copenhagen, Denmark. Association for Computational Linguistics.

Ashish Vaswani, Noam Shazeer, Niki Parmar, Jakob Uszkoreit, Llion Jones, Aidan N. Gomez, Łukasz Kaiser, and Illia Polosukhin. 2017. Attention is all you need. In *Advances in Neural Information Processing Systems*, volume 30. Curran Associates, Inc.

Xinyi Wang, Hieu Pham, Zihang Dai, and Graham Neubig. 2018. SwitchOut: an efficient data augmentation algorithm for neural machine translation. In *Proceedings of the 2018 Conference on Empirical Methods in Natural Language Processing*, pages 856–861, Brussels, Belgium. Association for Computational Linguistics.

Jiacheng Zhang, Huanbo Luan, Maosong Sun, Feifei Zhai, Jingfang Xu, Min Zhang, and Yang Liu. 2018. Improving the transformer translation model with document-level context. In *Proceedings of the 2018 Conference on Empirical Methods in Natural Language Processing*, pages 533–542, Brussels, Belgium. Association for Computational Linguistics.

Zaixiang Zheng, Xiang Yue, Shujian Huang, Jiajun Chen, and Alexandra Birch. 2020. Towards making the most of context in neural machine translation. In *Proceedings of IJCAI-PRICAI*.

Author Index

Association for Computational Linguistics
209 N. Eighth Street
Stroudsburg, Pennsylvania 18360

ISBN 978-1-7138-3378-9

CURRAN ASSOCIATES INC.
proceedings.com